Lecture Notes in Artificial Intelligence   12413

Subseries of Lecture Notes in Computer Science

Series Editors

Randy Goebel
University of Alberta, Edmonton, Canada
Yuzuru Tanaka
Hokkaido University, Sapporo, Japan
Wolfgang Wahlster
DFKI and Saarland University, Saarbrücken, Germany

Founding Editor

Jörg Siekmann
DFKI and Saarland University, Saarbrücken, Germany

More information about this subseries at http://www.springer.com/series/1244

Vasiliki Vouloutsi · Anna Mura ·
Falk Tauber · Thomas Speck ·
Tony J. Prescott · Paul F. M. J. Verschure (Eds.)

Biomimetic and Biohybrid Systems

9th International Conference, Living Machines 2020
Freiburg, Germany, July 28–30, 2020
Proceedings

 Springer

Editors
Vasiliki Vouloutsi ⓘ
SPECS, Institute for Bioengineering
of Catalonia
Barcelona, Spain

Anna Mura
SPECS, Institute for Bioengineering
of Catalonia
Barcelona, Spain

Falk Tauber ⓘ
University of Freiburg
Freiburg, Germany

Thomas Speck ⓘ
University of Freiburg
Freiburg, Germany

Tony J. Prescott ⓘ
University of Sheffield
Sheffield, UK

Paul F. M. J. Verschure ⓘ
SPECS, Institute for Bioengineering
of Catalonia
Barcelona, Spain

ISSN 0302-9743   ISSN 1611-3349   (electronic)
Lecture Notes in Artificial Intelligence
ISBN 978-3-030-64312-6   ISBN 978-3-030-64313-3   (eBook)
https://doi.org/10.1007/978-3-030-64313-3

LNCS Sublibrary: SL7 – Artificial Intelligence

This Springer imprint is published by the registered company Springer Nature Switzerland AG
The registered company address is: Gewerbestrasse 11, 6330 Cham, Switzerland

Preface

These proceedings contain the papers presented at the 9th International Conference on Biomimetic and Biohybrid Systems (Living Machines 2020), held online during July 28–30, 2020. The international conferences in the Living Machines series are targeted at the intersection of research on novel life-like technologies inspired by the scientific investigation of biological systems, *biomimetics*, and research that seeks to interface biological and artificial systems to create biohybrid systems. The conference aim is to highlight the most exciting international research in both of these fields united by the theme of "Living Machines."

The Living Machines conference series was first organized by the Convergent Science Network (CSN) of biomimetic and biohybrid systems to provide a focal point for the gathering of world-leading researchers and the presentation and discussion of cutting-edge research in this rapidly emerging field. The modern definition of biomimetics is the development of novel technologies through the distillation of principles from the study of biological systems. The investigation of biomimetic systems can serve two complementary goals. First, a suitably designed and configured biomimetic artifact can be used to test theories about the natural system of interest. Second, biomimetic technologies can provide useful, elegant, and efficient solutions to unsolved challenges in science and engineering. Biohybrid systems are formed by combining at least one biological component – an existing living system – and at least one artificial, newly engineered component. Through passing information in one or both directions, such a system forms a new hybrid bio-artificial entity.

The abiding desire to imitate the functionality of living organisms dates back hundreds of years. Early examples of biomimetic artifacts can be found as early as 400BC, by Archytas, an ancient Greek philosopher. He was the creator of "the first autonomous volatile machine of antiquity," namely the Flying Pigeon. This device was one of the first studies on how birds fly. Its structure resembled that of a bird with a pointed front, similar to a bird's beak, and its aerodynamic shape and mechanisms allowed the Pigeon to fly for approximately 200 meters. Centuries later, around the European Renaissance, we observe endeavors that explore the reproduction of aspects of living organisms in machines, while revealing important information regarding their nature. Leonardo da Vinci is a great example of linking human kinesiology and anatomy with his "Knight" in 1495, while his study of birds resulted in numerous sketches of various flying machines.

What initially started as a philosophical idea turned into a mechanical revolution. Already during the 18th century, machines not only imitated the external appearance of an organism but also simulated its functionalities of behaviors. A way to appreciate the early simulation of living beings is the central idea of "moving anatomy" in the creations of Jacques de Vaucanson (1709–1782), a French inventor and artist. His mechanical artifacts (like the "Flute Player" or the "Digesting Duck") intended to approximate the anatomical, physiological, and behavioral characteristics of their biological counterparts. The tendency of this period to use machines that resemble nature climaxed with the creations of Pierre Jaquet-Droz (1721–1790) that later constituted the basis for constructing prosthetic limbs.

Nowadays, the study and modeling of biological systems has led to the acquisition of insights into a plethora of domains ranging from architecture to materials, sensors, and control systems, and even robotics. The Velcro is an example of a fastening system inspired by the tiny hooks found in the surface of burs. The leaves of the lotus plant have inspired the creators of umbrellas and hydrophobic paints and coatings. Hypodermic needles were inspired by observing how snakes deliver poison through their fangs. Japan's bullet trains were remodeled after the Kingfisher's beak to reduce air resistance and boom sounds, while at the same time the trains now travel 10% faster and use 15% less energy. The Eastgate Centre, a shopping mall and office space in Zimbabwe, whose ventilation and cooling system was done entirely by natural means, was inspired by the self-cooling mounds of African termites. These remarkable advances are only some of the many examples that biomimetic approaches have to offer, and several new approaches were presented in the Living Machines conference.

The main conference took the form of a two-day single-track oral and poster presentation program that included four plenary lectures from leading international researchers in biomimetic and biohybrid systems: Auke Ijspeert (Swiss Federal Institute of Technology in Lausanne, Switzerland) on animal locomotion and biorobots; Bas Overvelde (Soft Robotic Matter group, The Netherlands) on adaptive and modular soft robotic systems; Li Zhaoping (Max Planck Institute, Germany) on visual systems in humans, animals, and machines; and Holk Cruse (Bielefeld University, Germany) on insect-inspired hexapod controllers. There were also 12 regular talks and 2 poster spotlights featuring 29 posters. Session themes included: collective and emergent behaviors in animals and robots; biomimetic vision and control; insect-inspired robotic systems; advances in soft robotics; and biomimetic and biohybrid systems.

The conference was complemented by two online workshops. More specifically, the "Growing structures: bioinspired innovation insights for architecture and robotics" workshop was organized by Barbara Mazzolai, Thomas Speck, and Mirko Kovac. Cross-disciplinary talks in this workshop showed current initiatives and major perspectives on the form-structure-function-relationship on various hierarchical levels of biological materials and structural systems; growing and building strategies in plants and animals; plant-inspired technologies for adaptable and growing robots; as well as biomimetic and biorobotics architectural installations and buildings. The "Shared workspace between humans and robots" workshop was organized by Apostolos Axenopoulos, Dimitrios Giakoumis, Eva Salgado, Vicky Vouloutsi, and Anna Mura. The aim of this workshop was to present and discuss together with scientific and industrial stakeholders' novel technological approaches that facilitate the collaboration between robots and humans towards solving challenging tasks in a shared working space without fences.

The Living Machines conference traditionally chooses historical and inspirational venues at the crossroads between life and human sciences. This year the conference was to take place at the Botanical Garden of Freiburg. However, the world is crossing uncharted territory as it faces the COVID-19 pandemic. This outbreak is having a significant impact on our life, health, and economy as more than 20 million people have been affected. COVID-19 also has an impact on how our society communicates, and the scientific communities are also affected by this terrible pandemic. To act in complete observance of safety and ethical practices, and to maintain the scientific research and knowledge exchange with new lockdown-proof methods and technologies, the conference this year was held online. The conference was hosted by the Cluster of Excellence at the University of Freiburg, Germany, and by the "Living, Adaptive and Energy-autonomous Materials Systems (livMatS)" (www.livmats.uni-freiburg.de). The workshops were hosted by the Cluster of Excellence at the University of Freiburg. The great success of the first virtual edition of the conference follows previous successful editions in Nara, Japan in 2019; Paris, France in 2018; Stanford, USA in 2017; Edinburgh, UK in 2016; Barcelona, Spain in 2015; Milan, Italy in 2014; London, UK in 2013; and Barcelona, Spain in 2012.

We would like to thank our hosts for the conference, workshops, and poster sessions held at the Cluster of Excellence at the University of Freiburg and livMatS.

We also wish to thank the many people that were involved in making the 9th edition of Living Machines possible: Thomas Speck and Paul Verschure co-chaired the meeting; Vasiliki Vouloutsi chaired the Program Committee and edited the conference proceedings; Tony Prescott chaired the international Steering Committee; and Anna Mura was the general organization chair and also coordinated the Web and communications. Thomas Speck and his group, including Falk Tauber and Sonja Seidel, provided local organizational support. We are grateful to the SPECS lab at the Institute for Bioengineering of Catalonia (IBEC) in Barcelona for the assistance in the organization and technical support. We would also like to thank the authors and speakers who contributed their work, and the members of the Program Committee for their detailed and considered reviews. We are grateful to the four keynote speakers who shared with us their vision of the future.

Finally, we wish to thank the organizers and sponsors of Living Machines 2020: the SPECS-lab at Institute for Bioengineering of Catalonia IBEC, the Catalan Institution for Research and Advanced Studies (ICREA), and the University of Freiburg. Additional support was also provided by Springer. Living Machines 2020 was also supported by Sensors and the IOP Physics journal *Bioinspiration & Biomimetics*, which will publish a special issue of articles based on the best conference papers. The Biomimetics - Open Access Journal, livMatS, microTEC Südwest, 3D Bio-Net, and GrowBot awarded the first and second best papers and posters.

July 2020

Vasiliki Vouloutsi
Anna Mura
Falk Tauber
Thomas Speck
Tony J. Prescott
Paul F. M. J. Verschure

Organization

Conference Chairs

Thomas Speck — University of Freiburg, Germany
Paul F. M. J. Verschure — SPECS Lab, IBEC, Spain; BIST, Spain; ICREA, Spain

Program Chair

Vasiliki Vouloutsi — SPECS Lab, IBEC, Spain; BIST, Spain

Local Organizers

Thomas Speck — University of Freiburg, Germany
Falk Tauber — University of Freiburg, Germany
Sonja Seidel — University of Freiburg, Germany

Communications

Anna Mura — SPECS Lab, IBEC, Spain; BIST, Spain

Conference Website

Anna Mura — SPECS Lab, IBEC, Spain; BIST, Spain

Workshop Organizers

Falk Tauber — University of Freiburg, Germany
Anna Mura — SPECS Lab, IBEC, Spain; BIST, Spain

International Steering Committee

Minoru Asada — Osaka University, Japan
Joseph Ayers — Northeastern University, USA
Mark Cutkosky — Stanford University, USA
Marc Desmulliez — Heriot-Watt University, UK
José Halloy — Université Paris Diderot, France
Nathan Lepora — University of Bristol, UK
Uriel Martinez-Hernandez — University of Bath, UK
Barbara Mazzolai — Istituto Italiano di Tecnologia, Italy
Anna Mura — SPECS Lab, IBEC, Spain
Tony Prescott — The University of Sheffield, UK
Roger Quinn Case — Western Reserve University, USA

Thomas Speck	University of Freiburg, Germany
Paul F. M. J. Verschure	SPECS Lab, IBEC, BIST, ICREA, Spain
Vasiliki Vouloutsi	SPECS Lab, IBEC, Spain
Stuart Wilson	The University of Sheffield, UK

Program Committee

Jonathan Aitken	The University of Sheffield, UK
Kentaro Arikawa	Sokendai, Japan
Yoseph Bar-Cohen	Jet Propulsion Lab, USA
Glen Berseth	UC Berkeley, USA
Maria Blancas	IBEC, Spain
Frank Bonnet	EPFL Lausanne, Switzerland
Jordan Boyle	University of Leeds, UK
David Buxton	The University of Sheffield, UK
David Cameron	The University of Sheffield, UK
Leo Cazenille	Université Paris Diderot, France
Jorg Conradt	KTH, Sweden
Vassilis Cutsuridis	University of Lincoln, UK
Simon M. Danner	Drexel University, USA
Alex Dewar	University of Sussex, UK
Richard Suphapol Diteesawat	University of Bristol, UK
Julien Dupeyroux	Delft University of Technology, The Netherlands
Volker Dürr	Bielefeld University, Germany
Adrián Fernández Amil	IBEC, Spain
Ismael Tito Freire González	IBEC, Spain
Marco Galli	IBEC, Spain
Benoît Girard	CNRS, Sorbonne Université, France
Philippe Grönquist	ETH Zürich, Switzerland
Oscar Guerrero Rosado	IBEC, Spain
Alfonso Gómez-Espinosa	ITESM, Mexico
Auke Ijspeert	EPFL Lausanne, Switzerland
Akio Ishiguro	Tohoku University, Japan
Alejandro Jimenez Rodriguez	The University of Sheffield, UK
DaeEun Kim	Yonsei University, South Korea
Konstantinos Lagogiannis	King's College London, UK
William Lewinger	University of Dundee, UK
Sock Ching Low	IBEC, Spain
Héctor López Carral	IBEC, Spain
Martina Maier	IBEC, Spain
Michael Mangan	The University of Sheffield, UK
Uriel Martinez-Hernandez	University of Bath, UK
Lin Meng	Tianjin University, China
Zaffar Mubariz	University of Essex, UK

Contents

Improving Recall in an Associative Neural Network Model
of the Hippocampus 1
   Nikolaos Andreakos, Shigang Yue, and Vassilis Cutsuridis

Iterative Learning Control as a Framework for Human-Inspired Control
with Bio-mimetic Actuators 12
   Franco Angelini, Matteo Bianchi, Manolo Garabini, Antonio Bicchi,
   and Cosimo Della Santina

Efficient Fine-Grained Object Detection for Robot-Assisted
WEEE Disassembly. 17
   Ioannis Athanasiadis, Athanasios Psaltis, Apostolos Axenopoulos,
   and Petros Daras

Integrated Topological Planning and Scheduling for Orchestrating Large
Human-Robot Collaborative Teams 23
   Ioannis Chatzikonstantinou, Ioannis Kostavelis, Dimitrios Giakoumis,
   and Dimitrios Tzovaras

Programming Material Intelligence: An Additive Fabrication Strategy
for Self-shaping Biohybrid Components. 36
   Tiffany Cheng, Dylan Wood, Xiang Wang, Philip F. Yuan,
   and Achim Menges

Multi-material 3D-Printer for Rapid Prototyping of Bio-Inspired
Soft Robotic Elements 46
   Stefan Conrad, Thomas Speck, and Falk Tauber

Kinematic and Kinetic Analysis of a Biomechanical Model of Rat Hind
Limb with Biarticular Muscles 55
   Kaiyu Deng, Nicholas S. Szczecinski, Alexander J. Hunt, Hillel J. Chiel,
   and Roger D. Quinn

How to Reduce Computation Time While Sparing Performance During
Robot Navigation? A Neuro-Inspired Architecture for Autonomous Shifting
Between Model-Based and Model-Free Learning 68
   Rémi Dromnelle, Erwan Renaudo, Guillaume Pourcel, Raja Chatila,
   Benoît Girard, and Mehdi Khamassi

An Image-Based Method for the Morphological Analysis of Tendrils
with 2D Piece-Wise Clothoid Approximation Model   80
  Jie Fan, Francesco Visentin, Emanuela Del Dottore,
  and Barbara Mazzolai

Cholinergic Control of Chaos and Evidence Sensitivity in a Neocortical
Model of Perceptual Decision-Making   92
  Adrián F. Amil, Jordi-Ysard Puigbò, and Paul F. M. J. Verschure

Biomechanical Characterization of Hook-Climber Stems for Soft
Robotic Applications   97
  Isabella Fiorello, Alessio Mondini, and Barbara Mazzolai

Robotics Application of a Method for Analytically Computing Infinitesimal
Phase Response Curves   104
  Marshaun N. Fitzpatrick, Yangyang Wang, Peter J. Thomas,
  Roger D. Quinn, and Nicholas S. Szczecinski

Machine Morality: From Harm-Avoidance to Human-Robot Cooperation   116
  Ismael T. Freire, Dina Urikh, Xerxes D. Arsiwalla,
  and Paul F. M. J. Verschure

Haptic Object Identification for Advanced Manipulation Skills   128
  Volker Gabler, Korbinian Maier, Satoshi Endo, and Dirk Wollherr

Response of a Neuromechanical Insect Joint Model to Inhibition
of fCO Sensory Afferents   141
  Clarissa Goldsmith, Nicholas S. Szczecinski, and Roger D. Quinn

Distributed Adaptive Control: An Ideal Cognitive Architecture Candidate
for Managing a Robotic Recycling Plant   153
  Oscar Guerrero Rosado and Paul F. M. J. Verschure

Standing on the Water: Stability Mechanisms of Snakes on Free Surface   165
  Johann Herault, Étienne Clement, Jonathan Brossillon, Seth LaGrange,
  Vincent Lebastard, and Frederic Boyer

From Models of Cognition to Robot Control and Back Using Spiking
Neural Networks   176
  Stefan Iacob, Johan Kwisthout, and Serge Thill

A Framework for Resolving Motivational Conflict via Attractor Dynamics . . .   192
  Alejandro Jimenez-Rodriguez, Tony J. Prescott, Robert Schmidt,
  and Stuart Wilson

Insect Inspired View Based Navigation Exploiting Temporal Information   204
  Efstathios Kagioulis, Andrew Philippides, Paul Graham,
  James C. Knight, and Thomas Nowotny

Split-Belt Adaptation Model of a Decerebrate Cat Using a Quadruped
Robot with Learning   217
    Kodai Kodono and Hiroshi Kimura

A Simple Platform for Reinforcement Learning of Simulated
Flight Behaviors   230
    Simon D. Levy

Biohybrid Wind Energy Generators Based on Living Plants   234
    *Fabian Meder, Marc Thielen, Giovanna Adele Naselli, Silvia Taccola,
    Thomas Speck, and Barbara Mazzolai*

Snapshot Navigation in the Wavelet Domain   245
    *Stefan Meyer, Thomas Nowotny, Paul Graham, Alex Dewar,
    and Andrew Philippides*

Optimization of Artificial Muscle Placements for a Humanoid
Bipedal Robot   257
    Connor Morrow, Benjamin Bolen, and Alexander J. Hunt

Robofish as Social Partner for Live Guppies.   270
    *Lea Musiolek, Verena V. Hafner, Jens Krause, Tim Landgraf,
    and David Bierbach*

Bioinspired Navigation Based on Distributed Sensing in the Leech   275
    *Sebastian T. Nichols, Catherine E. Kehl, Brian K. Taylor,
    and Cynthia Harley*

A Plausible Mechanism for *Drosophila* Larva Intermittent Behavior   288
    Panagiotis Sakagiannis, Miguel Aguilera, and Martin Paul Nawrot

Robophysical Modeling of Bilaterally Activated and Soft
Limbless Locomotors   300
    *Perrin E. Schiebel, Marine C. Maisonneuve, Kelimar Diaz,
    Jennifer M. Rieser, and Daniel I. Goldman*

A Synthetic Nervous System Model of the Insect Optomotor Response   312
    Anna Sedlackova, Nicholas S. Szczecinski, and Roger D. Quinn

Using the Neural Circuit of the Insect Central Complex for Path Integration
on a Micro Aerial Vehicle   325
    Jan Stankiewicz and Barbara Webb

Can Small Scale Search Behaviours Enhance Large-Scale Navigation?   338
    *Fabian Steinbeck, Paul Graham, Thomas Nowotny,
    and Andrew Philippides*

Modeling the Dynamic Sensory Discharges of Insect
Campaniform Sensilla   342
   Nicholas S. Szczecinski, Sasha N. Zill, Chris J. Dallmann,
   and Roger D. Quinn

Evaluation of Possible Flight Strategies for Close Object Evasion
from Bumblebee Experiments   354
   Andreas Thoma, Alex Fisher, Olivier Bertrand, and Carsten Braun

Biomimetic Design of a Soft Robotic Fish for High Speed Locomotion   366
   Sander C. van den Berg, Rob B. N. Scharff, Zoltán Rusák, and Jun Wu

The Use of Social Sensorimotor Contingencies in Humanoid Robots   378
   Vasiliki Vouloutsi, Anna Chesson, Maria Blancas, Oscar Guerrero,
   and Paul F. M. J. Verschure

Fast Reverse Replays of Recent Spatiotemporal Trajectories in a Robotic
Hippocampal Model   390
   Matthew T. Whelan, Tony J. Prescott, and Eleni Vasilaki

Using Animatlab for Neuromechanical Analysis: Linear Hill Parameter
Calculation   402
   Fletcher Young, Alexander J. Hunt, Hillel J. Chiel, and Roger D. Quinn

Spatio-Temporal Memory for Navigation in a Mushroom Body Model   415
   Le Zhu, Michael Mangan, and Barbara Webb

Author Index   427

Improving Recall in an Associative Neural Network Model of the Hippocampus

Nikolaos Andreakos[1], Shigang Yue[1] (ID), and Vassilis Cutsuridis[1,2(✉)] (ID)

[1] School of Computer Science, University of Lincoln, Lincoln, UK
{nandreakos,syue,vcutsuridis}@lincoln.ac.uk
[2] Lincoln Sleep Research Center, University of Lincoln, Lincoln, UK

Abstract. The mammalian hippocampus is involved in auto-association and hetero-association of declarative memories. We employed a bio-inspired neural model of hippocampal CA1 region to systematically evaluate its mean recall quality against different number of stored patterns, overlaps and active cells per pattern. Model consisted of excitatory (pyramidal cells) and four types of inhibitory cells: axo-axonic, basket, bistratified, and oriens lacunosum-moleculare cells. Cells were simplified compartmental models with complex ion channel dynamics. Cells' firing was timed to a theta oscillation paced by two distinct neuronal populations exhibiting highly regular bursting activity, one tightly coupled to the trough and the other to the peak of theta. During recall excitatory input to network excitatory cells provided context and timing information for retrieval of previously stored memory patterns. Dendritic inhibition acted as a non-specific global threshold machine that removed spurious activity during recall. Simulations showed recall quality improved when the network's memory capacity increased as the number of active cells per pattern decreased. Furthermore, increased firing rate of a presynaptic inhibitory threshold machine inhibiting a network of postsynaptic excitatory cells has a better success at removing spurious activity at the network level and improving recall quality than increased synaptic efficacy of the same threshold machine on the same network of excitatory cells, while keeping its firing rate fixed.

Keywords: Associative memories · Brain · Inhibition

1 Introduction

Associative memory (AM) is the ability to learn and remember the relationship between items, events, places and/or objects which may be unrelated [18]. AM is one of the oldest artificial neural networks' paradigms [19, 20]. In these models storing patterns was done via changes in connection strengths between artificial neurons which crudely mimicked biological ones. Old memories were recalled when a noisy, partial or complete version of a previously stored pattern was presented to the network. However, these AM devices were not very flexible. They had to be told when to store a memory pattern and when to recall it.

© Springer Nature Switzerland AG 2020
V. Vouloutsi et al. (Eds.): Living Machines 2020, LNAI 12413, pp. 1–11, 2020.
https://doi.org/10.1007/978-3-030-64313-3_1

In 2010 a much more flexible model was introduced that controlled for itself the storage and recall of patterns of information arriving at unpredictable rates [1]. The model was based upon the many details were then known about the neuronal hippocampal circuit [21, 22]. The model explored the functional roles of somatic, axonic and dendritic inhibition in the encoding and retrieval of memories in region CA1. It showed how theta modulated inhibition separated encoding and retrieval of memories in the hippocampus into two functionally independent processes. It predicted that somatic (basket cell) inhibition allowed generation of dendritic calcium spikes that promoted synaptic long-term plasticity (LTP), while minimizing cell output. Proximal dendritic (bistratified cell (BSC)) inhibition controlled both cell output and suppressed dendritic calcium spikes, thus preventing LTP, whereas distal dendritic (OLM cell) inhibition removed interference from (new and old) memory patterns trying to be encoded during recall. The mean recall quality of the model was tested as function of memory patterns stored. Recall dropped as more patterns were stored due to interference between previously stored memories. Proximal dendritic inhibition was held constant as the number of memory patterns stored was increased.

Here, we more systematically investigated the mechanisms to improve the recall performance of [1]. In particular, we examined how selective modulation of feedforward/feedback excitatory/inhibitory pathways targeting inhibitory and excitatory cells may influence the thresholding ability of dendritic inhibition to remove at the network level spurious activities, which may otherwise impair the recall performance of the network, and improve its mean recall quality as more and more overlapping memories were stored.

2   Materials and Methods

2.1   Neural Network Model

Figure 1 depicts the simulated neural network model of region CA1 of the hippocampus. The model consisted of 100 pyramidal cells (PC), 1 axo-axonic cell (AAC), 2 basket cells (BC), 1 BSC and 1 OLM cell. The neuronal dynamics of the model cells with respect to a theta rhythm is depicted in Fig. 2. Model cells were simplified compartmental models with complex ion channel dynamics. Simplified morphologies including the soma, apical and basal dendrites and a portion of the axon were used for each cell type. The biophysical properties of each cell were adapted from cell types reported in the literature, which were extensively validated against experimental data in [4–7, 13]. In the model, AMPA, NMDA, GABA-A and GABA-B synapses were considered. GABA-A were present in all strata, whereas GABA-B were present in medium and distal SR and SLM dendrites. AMPA synapses were present in SLM (EC connections) and SR (CA3 connections), whereas NMDA were present only in SR (CA3 connections). The complete mathematical formalism of the model has been described elsewhere [1]. Schematic representations of model cells can be found in [12]. The dimensions of the somatic, axonic and dendritic compartments of model cells, the parameters of all passive and active ionic conductances, synaptic waveforms and synaptic conductances can be found in [12]. All simulations were performed using NEURON [8] running on a PC with eight CPUs under Windows 10.

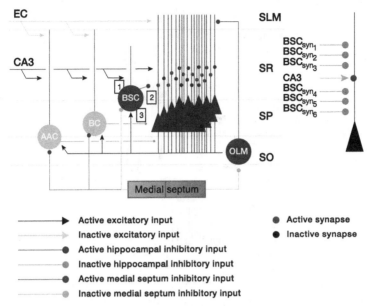

Fig. 1. (*Left*) Associative neural network model of region CA1 of the hippocampus. During retrieval only PC, BSC, and OLM cells are active. AAC and BC are inactive due to strong medial septum inhibition. BSC and PC are driven on their SR dendrites by a strong CA3 excitatory input, which presented the contextual information. Red circles on PC dendrites represent active synapses, whereas black circles on PC dendrites represent inactive synapses. EC: Entorhinal cortical input; CA3: Schaffer collateral input; AAC: Axo-axonic cell; BC: basket cell; BSC: bistratified cell; OLM: oriens lacunosum-moleculare cell; SLM: stratum lacunosum moleculare; SR: stratum radiatum; SP: stratum pyramidale; SO: stratum oriens. (*Right*) Model CA1-PC with excitatory and inhibitory synaptic contacts on its SR dendrites.

2.2 Inputs

Network was driven by a CA3 Schaffer collateral excitatory input and an MS inhibitory input. The CA3 input was modelled as the firing of 20 out of 100 CA3 pyramidal cells at an average gamma frequency of 40 Hz (spike trains only modelled and not the explicit cells). PCs, BCs, AACs, BSCs received CA3 input in their medial SR dendrites. On the other hand, the MS input was modelled with the rhythmic firing of two populations of 10 septal cells each modulated at opposite phases of a theta cycle (180° out of phase) [16]. Septal cell output was modelled as bursts of action potentials using a presynaptic spike generator. Each spike train consisted of bursts of action potentials at a mean frequency of 8 Hz for a half-theta cycle (125 ms) followed by a half-theta cycle of silence (125 ms). Due to 8% noise in the inter-spike intervals, the 10 spike trains in each septal population were asynchronous. MS_2 input provided GABA-A inhibition to BSCs and OLMs during the encoding cycle, whereas MS_1 input provided GABA-A inhibition to AACs and BCs during the retrieval cycle.

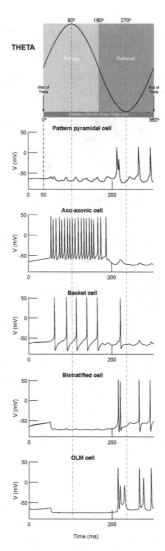

Fig. 2. Voltage traces of model cells with respect to a single theta cycle.

2.3 Network Training and Testing

To test the recall performance of the model the methodology described in [1] was adopted. Briefly, a memory pattern was stored by generating weight matrices based on a clipped Hebbian learning rule; these weight matrices were used to pre-specify the CA3 to CA1 PC connection weights. Without loss of generality, the input (CA3) and output (CA1) patterns were assumed to be the same, with each pattern consisting of N (N = 5 or 10 or 20) randomly chosen PCs (active cells per pattern) out of the population of 100. The 100 by 100 dimensional weight matrix was created by setting matrix entry (i, j), $w_{ij} = 1$ if input PC i and output PC j are both active in the same pattern pair; otherwise weights

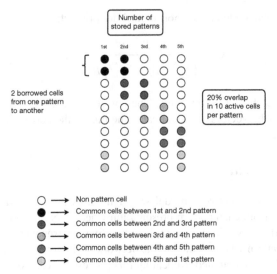

Fig. 3. Set of five memory patterns with 20% overlap between them.

are 0. Any number of pattern pairs could be stored to create this binary weight matrix. The matrix was applied to our network model by connecting a CA3 input to a CA1 PC with a high AMPA conductance ($g_{AMPA} = 1.5$ nS) if their connection weight was 1, or with a low conductance ($g_{AMPA} = 0.5$ nS) if their connection was 0. This approach is in line with experimental evidence that such synapses are 2-state in nature [17].

2.4 Memory Patterns

We created sets of memory patterns at different sizes (1, 5, 10, 20), percent overlaps (0%, 10%, 20%, 40%) and number of active cells per pattern (5, 10, 20). A 0% overlap between 5 patterns in a set meant no overlap between patterns. A 20% overlap between 5 stored patterns meant that 0.2*N cells were shared between patterns 1 and 2, different 0.2*N cells between patterns 2 and 3, and so on (see Fig. 3). For 20 active cells per pattern that meant that a maximum of 5 patterns could be stored by our network of 100 PCs. For 10 active cells per pattern, a maximum of 10 patterns could be stored and for 5 active cells per pattern, a maximum of 20 patterns could be stored. Similar maximum number of patterns could be stored for 10%, 20% and 40% overlap and 5, 10 and 20 active cells per pattern, respectively. In the case of 10% overlap, 5 active cells per pattern, the maximum number of stored patterns was not an integer, so this case was excluded from our simulations.

2.5 Recall Performance Measure

The recall performance metric used for measuring the distance between the recalled output pattern, B, from the required output pattern, B*, was the correlation (i.e., degree of overlap) metric, calculated as the normalized dot product:

$$C - \frac{B \times B^*}{\left(\sum_{i-1}^{N_B} B_i \times \sum_{j-1}^{N_B} B_j^*\right)^{1/2}} \tag{1}$$

where N_B is the number of output units. The correlation takes a value between 0 (no correlation) and 1 (the vectors are identical). The higher the correlation, the better the recall performance.

2.6 Mean Recall Quality

Mean recall quality of a network model was defined as the mean value of all recall qualities estimated from each pattern presentation when an N number of patterns were already stored in the network. For example, when five patterns were initially stored in the network and pattern 1 is presented to the network during recall, then a recall quality value for pattern 1 was calculated. Repeating this process for each of the other patterns (pattern 2, pattern 3, pattern 4, pattern 5), a recall quality value was calculated. The mean recall quality of the network was then the mean value of these individual recall qualities.

2.7 Model Selection

In [1], BSC inhibition to PC dendrites acted as a global non-specific threshold machine capable of removing spurious activity at the network level during recall. In [1] BSC inhibition was held constant as the number of stored patterns to PC dendrites increased. The recall quality of the model in [1] decreased as more and more memories were loaded onto the network (see Figure 14 in [1]). To improve the recall performance of [1] we artificially modulated the synaptic strength of selective excitatory and inhibitory pathways to BSC and PC dendrites as more and more patterns were stored in the network (see Figs. 1 *Left* and 4):

1. Model 1: Increased CA3 feedforward excitation (weight) to BSC (Fig. 4A) increased the frequency of its firing rate. As a result, more IPSPs were generated in the PC dendrites producing a very strong inhibitory environment which eliminated all spurious activity.
2. Model 2: Increased BSC feedforward inhibition (weight) to PC dendrites (Fig. 4B) produced fewer IPSPs, but with greater amplitude, in the PC dendrites.
3. Model 3: Increased PC feedback excitation (weight) to BSC (Fig. 4C) had a similar effect as Model 1, but with less potency.

Comparative analysis of the above three models' recall performance is depicted in Figs. 5 and 6.

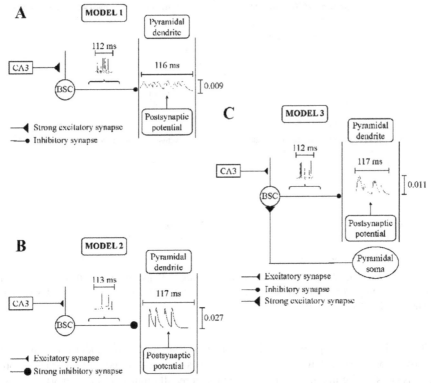

Fig. 4. Schematic drawing of presynaptic BSC firing response and inhibitory postsynaptic potentials (IPSPs) on PC dendrites in (A) 'model 1', (B) 'model 2' and (C) 'model 3'.

3 Results and Discussion

A set of patterns (1, 5, 10, 20) at various percent overlaps (0%, 10%, 20%, 40%) were stored by different number of 'active cells per pattern' (5, 10, 20) without recourse to a learning rule by generating a weight matrix based on a clipped Hebbian learning rule, and using the weight matrix to prespecify the CA3 to CA1 PC connection weights. To test recall of a previously stored memory pattern in the model, the entire associated input pattern was applied as a cue in the form of spiking of active CA3 inputs (those belonging to the pattern) distributed within a gamma frequency time window. The cue pattern was repeated at gamma frequency (40 Hz). During the retrieval only the BSCs and OLM cells were switched on, whereas the AACs and BCs were switched off. The CA3 spiking drove the CA1 PCs plus the BSCs. The EC input (see Fig. 1 *Left*), which excited the apical dendrites of PCs, AACs and BCs, was disconnected during the retrieval.

We can observe from Fig. 5 that the recall performance of 'model 1' is best (C = 1) across all overlaps (0%, 10%, 20%, and 40%). Similarly, the recall performance of 'model 2' is consistently worst when compared to those of 'model 1' and 'model 3' across all overlap conditions even when only 5 patterns were stored. At 0% and 10% overlap, all three models outperformed the Cutsuridis and colleagues 2010 model [1].

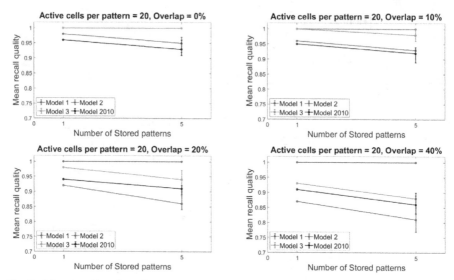

Fig. 5. Mean recall quality of 'model 1', 'model 2', 'model 3' and 'model 2010' as a function of number of stored patterns. Twenty 'active cells per pattern' in a network of 100 PCs for various percentages of overlap (0%, 10%, 20%, 40%).

At 20% and 40% overlap, model 2 did even worse than the '2010 model'. It is clear for large overlaps (20% and 40%) interference effects between stored patterns cause more spurious cells to fire impairing this way the mean recall quality of the network models.

A comparison of the recall performances of models 1, 2, 3, and 2010 for different number of 'active cells per pattern' (cell assembly that code for a particular memory pattern) and number of stored patterns with 40% overlap is evident in Fig. 6. As before, 'model 1' consistently has the best performance (C = 1) for any number of 'active cells per pattern'. As the number of 'active cells per pattern' is decreased, even at 40% overlap between stored patterns, the mean recall quality of all other three models ('Model 2', 'Model 3', 'Model 2010') increases (C ~ 1 for all three models when number of 'active cells per pattern' is 5). This is because as the number of 'active cells per pattern' decrease, the memory capacity of the 100-by-100 dimensional weight matrix between CA3-CA1 increases (i.e. weight matrix has more "0's" and less "1's", so interference effects between stored patterns decrease).

Why was 'model 1' performance so consistently better than 'model 2' and 'model 3' across all conditions? Why the recall quality of 'model 1' was always perfect (C = 1) even when more patterns were stored in the network, more/less 'active cells per pattern' were used to represent a memory and greater percentages of overlap between patterns were used? As we described in section "2.7 – Model selection", 'model 1' was the model where CA3 feedforward excitation to BSC was progressively increased as more and more patterns were stored, while the BSC inhibitory effect (weight) to PC dendrites was held fixed. 'Model 3' was the model where PC feedback excitation to BSC was progressively increased as more and more patterns were stored, while the BSC inhibitory effect to PC dendrites was held fixed. 'Model 2' was the model where the exact opposite took place: the inhibitory effect of BSC to PC dendrites progressively

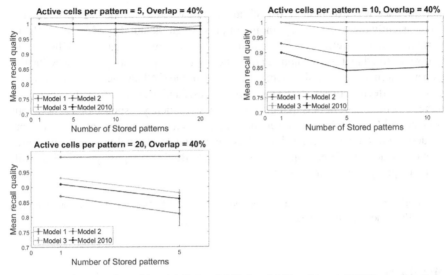

Fig. 6. Mean recall quality of 'model 1', 'model 2', 'model 3' and 'model 2010' as a function of number of stored patterns. Variable number of 'active cells per pattern' (5, 10, 20) in a network of 100 PCs with 40% overlap.

increased as more and more patterns were stored in the network, while keeping the BSC firing rate constant. In all simulations, 'model 1' outperformed 'model 3' across all conditions (overlaps and 'active pattern cells'). This was due to the fact in 'model 1' BSC was excited by 100 CA3-PCs at high frequency (40 Hz), whereas in 'model 3' BSC was excited by 20 CA1-PCs that fired once or twice. Since in 'model 1' the BSC firing frequency response is higher than in 'model 3', then the postsynaptic effect of BSC on the PC dendrites in 'model 1' is higher in frequency and duration (but not in amplitude) than in 'model 3' (see Fig. 4A & C). Thus, 'model 1' has a better success at removing spurious activities and improving recall quality than 'model 3'. Since the BSC frequency response in 'model 2' was fixed, but its postsynaptic effect (weight) on PC dendrites increased, then the amplitude of the inhibitory postsynaptic potentials (IPSPs) on PC dendrites increased (compared to the IPSP amplitudes in models 1 and 3), but their frequency response was low (lower than in models 1 and 3; see Fig. 4B). Each IPSP decayed to almost zero before another IPSP was generated post-synaptically on PC dendrites.

4 Conclusions

A bio-inspired neural model of hippocampal CA1 region [1] was employed to systematically evaluate its mean recall quality against number of stored patterns, percent overlaps and 'active cells per pattern'. Modulation of selective excitatory and inhibitory pathways to BSC and PC dendrites as more and more patterns were stored in the network of 100 CA1-PCs resulted into three models, the performances of which were compared to that of the original 2010 model of Cutsuridis et al. [1]. Of the three models tested, 'Model's

1' performance was excellent across all conditions, whereas 'Model's 2' performance was consistently the worst. A key finding of ours is that the number of 'active cells per pattern' has a massive effect on the recall quality of the network regardless of how many patterns are stored in it. As the number of dedicated cells representing a memory ('active cells per pattern') decrease, the memory capacity of the CA1-PC network increases, so interference effects between stored patterns decrease, and mean recall quality increases. Another key finding of ours is that increased firing frequency response of a presynaptic inhibitory cell (BSC) inhibiting a network of PCs has a better success at removing spurious activity at the network level and thus improving recall quality than an increased synaptic efficacy of a presynaptic inhibitory cell (BSC) on a postsynaptic PC while keeping its presynaptic firing rate fixed.

Acknowledgements. This work was supported in part by EU Horizon 2020 through Project ULTRACEPT under Grant 778062.

References

1. Cutsuridis, V., Cobb, S., Graham, B.P.: Encoding and retrieval in a model of the hippocampal CA1 microcircuit. Hippocampus **20**, 423–446 (2010)
2. Megias, M., Emri, Z.S., Freund, T.F., Gulyas, A.I.: Total number and distribution of inhibitory and excitatory synapses on hippocampal CA1 pyramidal cells. Neuroscience **102**(3), 527–540 (2001)
3. Gulyas, A.I., Megias, M., Emri, Z., Freund, T.F.: Total number and ratio of excitatory and inhibitory synapses converging onto single interneurons of different types in the CA1 areas of the rat hippocampus. J. Neurosci. **19**(22), 10082–10097 (1999)
4. Poirazi, P., Brannon, T., Mel, B.W.: Arithmetic of subthreshold synaptic summation in a model of CA1 pyramidal cell. Neuron **37**, 977–987 (2003)
5. Poirazi, P., Brannon, T., Mel, B.W.: Pyramidal neuron as a 2-layer neural network. Neuron **37**, 989–999 (2003)
6. Santhakumar, V., Aradi, I., Soltetz, I.: Role of mossy fiber sprouting and mossy cell loss in hyperexcitability: a network model of the dentate gyrus incorporating cell types and axonal topography. J. Neurophysiol. **93**, 437–453 (2005)
7. Buhl, E.H., Szilágyi, T., Halasy, K., Somogyi, P.: Physiological properties of anatomically identified basket and bistratified cells in the CA1 area of the rat hippocampus in vitro. Hippocampus **6**(3), 294–305 (1996)
8. Hines, M.L., Carnevale, T.: The NEURON simulation environment. Neural Comput. **9**, 1179–1209 (1997)
9. Amaral, D., Lavenex, P.: Hippocampal neuroanatomy. In: Andersen, P., Morris, R., Amaral, D., Bliss, T., O'Keefe, J. (eds.) The Hippocampus Book, pp. 37–114. Oxford University Press, Oxford (2007)
10. Andersen, P., Morris, R., Amaral, D., Bliss, T., O'Keefe, J.: The Hippocampus Book. Oxford University Press, Oxford (2007)
11. Buhl, E.H., Halasy, K., Somogyi, P.: Diverse sources of hippocampal unitary inhibitory postsynaptic potentials and the number of synaptic release sites. Nature **368**, 823–828 (1994)
12. Cutsuridis, V.: Improving the recall performance of a brain mimetic microcircuit model. Cogn. Comput. **11**, 644–655 (2019). https://doi.org/10.1007/s12559-019-09658-8

13. Buhl, E.H., Han, Z.S., Lorinczi, Z., Stezhka, V.V., Kapnup, S.V., Somogyi, P.: Physiological properties of anatomically identified axo-axonic cells in the rat hippocampus. J. Neurophys. **71**(4), 1289–1307 (1994)

14. Pospischil, M., et al.: Minimal Hodgkin-Huxley type models for different classes of cortical and thalamic neurons. Biol. Cybern. **99**(4–5), 427–441 (2008)

15. Saraga, F., Wu, C.P., Zhang, L., Skinner, F.K.: Active dendrites and spike propagation in multicompartmental models of oriens-lacunosum/moleculare hippocampal interneurons. J. Physiol. **552**, 673–689 (2008)

16. Borhegyi, Z., Varga, V., Szilagyi, N., Fabo, D., Freund, T.F.: Phase segregation of medial septal GABAergic neurons during hippocampal theta activity. J. Neurosci. **24**, 8470–8479 (2004)

17. Petersen, C.C.H., Malenka, R.C., Nicoll, R.A., Hopfield, J.J.: All-or none potentiation at CA3-CA1 synapses. Proc. Natl. Acad. Sci. USA **95**, 4732–4737 (1998)

18. Suzuki, W.A.: Making new memories: the role of the hippocampus in new associative learning. Ann. N. Y. Acad. Sci. **1097**, 1–11 (2007)

19. Steinbuch, K.: Non-digital learning matrices as preceptors. Kybernetik **1**, 117–124 (1961)

20. Willshaw, D., Buneman, O., Longuet-Higgins, H.: Non-holographic associative memory. Nature **222**, 960–962 (1969)

21. Klausberger, T., et al.: Brain-state- and cell-type-specific firing of hippocampal interneurons in vivo. Nature **421**, 844–848 (2003)

22. Klausberger, T., Marton, L.F., Baude, A., Roberts, J.D., Magill, P.J., Somogyi, P.: Spike timing of dendrite-targeting bistratified cells during hippocampal network oscillations in vivo. Nat. Neurosci. **7**, 41–47 (2004)

Iterative Learning Control as a Framework for Human-Inspired Control with Bio-mimetic Actuators

Franco Angelini[1,2]([ID]), Matteo Bianchi[1]([ID]), Manolo Garabini[1]([ID]),
Antonio Bicchi[1,2]([ID]), and Cosimo Della Santina[3,4,5]([ID])

[1] Centro di Ricerca "Enrico Piaggio" and DII, Università di Pisa, Pisa, Italy
frncangelini@gmail.com
[2] Soft Robotics for Human Cooperation and Rehabilitation, IIT, Genova, Italy
[3] Institute of Robotics and Mechatronics, DLR, Oberpfaffenhofen, Weßling, Germany
[4] Department of Informatics, Technical University Munich, Garching, Germany
[5] Cognitive Robotics Department,
Delft University of Technology, Delft, The Netherlands

Abstract. The synergy between musculoskeletal and central nervous systems empowers humans to achieve a high level of motor performance, which is still unmatched in bio-inspired robotic systems. Literature already presents a wide range of robots that mimic the human body. However, under a control point of view, substantial advancements are still needed to fully exploit the new possibilities provided by these systems. In this paper, we test experimentally that an Iterative Learning Control algorithm can be used to reproduce functionalities of the human central nervous system - i.e. learning by repetition, after-effect on known trajectories and anticipatory behavior - while controlling a bio-mimetically actuated robotic arm.

Keywords: Motion and motor control · Natural machine motion · Human-inspired control

1 Introduction

Natural and bio-inspired robot bodies are complex systems, characterized by an unknown nonlinear dynamics and redundancy of degrees of freedom (DoFs). This poses considerable challenges for standard control techniques. For this reason, researchers started taking inspiration from the effective Central Nervous System (CNS), when designing controllers for robots [4,5]. In this work, we test experimentally a model-free controller intended for trajectory tracking with biomimetic robots. We prove that the required tracking performances can be matched, while presenting well-known characteristics of human motor control system, i.e. learning by repetition, mirror-image aftereffect, and anticipatory behavior. We do that by presenting experiments on a robotic arm with two degrees of freedom, each of which is actuated by means of a bio-mimetic mechanism replicating the behavior of a pair of human muscles [7] (Fig. 1(a)).

V. Vouloutsi et al. (Eds.): Living Machines 2020, LNAI 12413, pp. 12–16, 2020.
https://doi.org/10.1007/978-3-030-64313-3_2

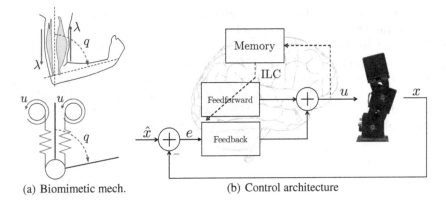

(a) Biomimetic mech.   (b) Control architecture

Fig. 1. The synergy between human musculoskeletal system and the CNS can be imitated by a bio-mimic robot and a proper controller mixing anticipatory (feedforward) and reactive (feedback) actions.

2   From Motor Control to Motion Control

Taking inspiration from the human CNS, we aim at designing a controller able to replicate the characteristics of *paleokinetic level* of Bernstein classification [2]. This provides reflex function and manages muscle tone, i.e. low level feedback and dynamic inversion. We want to do that by reproducing salient features observed in humans.

Learning by repetition [10] (behavior (i)) is the first feature we are interested into. CNS is able to invert an unknown dynamics over a trajectory, just by repeating it several times. This is clear in experiments where an unknown force field is applied to a subject's arm, and she or he is instructed to sequentially reach to track a point in space. In every repetition the tracking is improved until an almost perfect performance is recovered.

Anticipatory behavior [8] (behavior (ii)) is the second characteristic we want to reproduce. The CNS can anticipate the necessary control action relying on motor memory, rather than always reacting to sensory inputs. In control terms this means relying more on feed-forward than on feedback. In humans this characteristic tends to appear more strongly when the motor memory increases.

Finally, humans present aftereffect over a learned trajectory [9] (behavior (iii)). By removing the force field, subjects exhibit deformations of the trajectory specular to the initial deformation due to the force field introduction. This behavior is called mirror-image aftereffect and is the third characteristic we aim at reproducing.

Figure 1(b) shows the control architecture. We suppose no a priori knowledge of system dynamics. We just read the joint evolution and velocity $x \in \mathbb{R}^{2n}$, and we produce a motor action $u \in \mathbb{R}^n$. The purpose of the controller is to perform dynamic inversion of the system, i.e. computing the control action $\hat{u} : [0, t_f) \to \mathbb{R}^m$ able to track a given desired trajectory $\hat{x} : [0, t_f) \to \mathbb{R}^{2n}$. This has to be done by repeating several times the same task and performing it better each time (learning by repetition). To implement this feature, we propose a control law based on Iterative Learning Control (ILC) [3]: $u_{i+1} = u_i + \Gamma_{\mathrm{FFp}}\, e_i(t) + \Gamma_{\mathrm{FFd}}\, \dot{e}_i(t) + \Gamma_{\mathrm{FBp}}\, e_{i+1}(t) + \Gamma_{\mathrm{FBd}}\, \dot{e}_{i+1}(t)$. We call u_i and $e_i \triangleq \hat{x} - x_i$ the control action and the error at the i−th repetition of the task. $\Gamma_{\mathrm{FFp}} \in \mathbb{R}^{m \times 2n}$ and $\Gamma_{\mathrm{FFd}} \in \mathbb{R}^{m \times 2n}$ are the PD control gains of the iterative update while $\Gamma_{\mathrm{FBp}} \in \mathbb{R}^{m \times 2n}$ and $\Gamma_{\mathrm{FBd}} \in \mathbb{R}^{m \times 2n}$ are the PD feedback gains. We analyzed the theoretic control implications of using similar algorithms in [1,6].

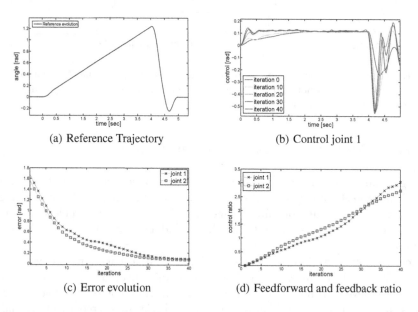

(a) Reference Trajectory

(b) Control joint 1

(c) Error evolution

(d) Feedforward and feedback ratio

Fig. 2. Experimental results. (a) shows the reference trajectory. (b) reports the evolution of control input at joint 1. (c) shows the error over 40 iterations (behavior (i), learning by repetition). (d) depicts the ratio between reactive and anticipatory actions (behavior (ii)).

3   Experimental Results

The goal of the experiments is to prove that the considered ILC-based algorithm can reproduce the discussed human-like behaviors when applied to a biomimetic hardware. The algorithm is applied to a two degrees of freedom planar arm, with bio-mimetic actuation. More specifically, the mechanism mimics a pair of human muscles. The available control input u has been proven to be equivalent to the corresponding signal in λ−model of human muscles [7]. We consider the following gains for the algorithm Γ_{FFp} is blkdiag([1, 0.1],[1.25, 0.0375]), Γ_{FFd} is blkdiag([0.1, 0.001],[0.0375,0.001]), Γ_{FBp} is blkdiag([0.25, 0.025],[0.25, 0.025]), and Γ_{FBd} is blkdiag([0.025, 0.001],[0.025, 0.001]). The desired trajectory (same for both joints) is shown in Fig. 2(a). Note that this is a very challenging reference, having large amplitudes and abrupt changes in velocities. For performance evaluation we use norm 1 of the tracking error. The proposed algorithm learns the task by repeating it 40 times achieving good performance. Figure 2(b) shows the joint 1 control evolution for some meaningful iterations (similar results apply to joint 2). Figure 2(c) proves that the system implements learning by repetition (behavior (i)), reducing the error exponentially to 0 by repeating the same movement. Figure 2(d) depicts the ratio between total feedforward and feedback action, over learning iterations. This shows the predominance of anticipatory action at the growth of sensory--motor memory (behavior (ii)). It is worth to be noticed that feedback it is not completely replaced by feedforward, which is coherent with many physiological evidences (e.g. [10]).

To test the presence of mirror-image aftereffect (behavior (iii)) we introduced an external force field after the above discussed learning process. This field was generated as shown by Fig. 3(a), by two springs connected in parallel to the second joint. Figure 3(b) shows the robot's end effector evolution obtained before (green) and after (red) spring introduction. The algorithm can recover the original performance after few iterations (learning process not shown for the sake of space). Finally the springs are removed, and the end-effector follows a trajectory which is the mirror w.r.t. the nominal one, of the one obtained after field introduction, therefore proving the ability of the proposed algorithm to reproduce mirror-image aftereffect (behavior (iii)).

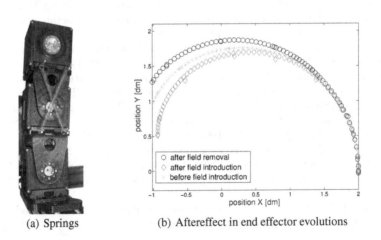

(a) Springs   (b) Aftereffect in end effector evolutions

Fig. 3. The proposed controller presents aftereffect (behavior (iii)). Panel (a) reports the spring interconnection implementing the unknown force field, and Panel (b) end effector evolutions. (Color figure online)

4   Conclusions

In this work we proved experimentally that an ILC-based algorithm can repro- duce - when applied to a biobimetic hardware - several behaviors observed when the central nervous system controls the muscle-skeletal system - namely learning by repetition, experience-driven shift towards anticipatory behavior, and after- effect.

Acknowledgments.. This project has been supported by European Union's Horizon 2020 research and innovation programme under grant agreement 780883 (THING) and 871237 (Sophia), by ERC Synergy Grant 810346 (Natural BionicS) and by the Italian Ministry of Education and Research (MIUR) in the framework of the CrossLab project (Departments of Excellence).

References

1. Angelini, F., et al.: Decentralized trajectory tracking control for soft robots inter- acting with the environment. IEEE Trans. Robot. **34**(4), 924–935 (2018)
2. Bernstein, N.A.: Dexterity and Its Development. Psychology Press (2014)
3. Bristow, D.A., Tharayil, M., Alleyne, A.G.: A survey of iterative learning control. Control Syst. IEEE **26**(3), 96–114 (2006)
4. Cao, J., Liang, W., Zhu, J., Ren, Q.: Control of a muscle-like soft actuator via a bioinspired approach. Bioinspiration Biom. **13**(6), 066005 (2018)
5. Capolei, M.C., Angelidis, E., Falotico, E., Hautop Lund, H., Tolu, S.: A biomimetic control method increases the adaptability of a humanoid robot acting in a dynamic environment. Front. Neurorobot. **13**, 70 (2019)
6. Della Santina, C., et al.: Controlling soft robots: balancing feedback and feedfor- ward elements. IEEE Robot. Autom. Mag. **24**(3), 75–83 (2017)
7. Garabini, M., Santina, C.D., Bianchi, M., Catalano, M., Grioli, G., Bicchi, A.: Soft robots that mimic the neuromusculoskeletal system. In: Ibáñez, J., González- Vargas, J., Azorín, J.M., Akay, M., Pons, J.L. (eds.) Converging Clinical and Engi- neering Research on Neurorehabilitation II. BB, vol. 15, pp. 259–263. Springer, Cham (2017). https://doi.org/10.1007/978-3-319-46669-9_45
8. Hoffmann, J.: Anticipatory behavioral control. In: Butz, M.V., Sigaud, O., Gérard, P. (eds.) Anticipatory Behavior in Adaptive Learning Systems. LNCS (LNAI), vol. 2684, pp. 44–65. Springer, Heidelberg (2003). https://doi.org/10.1007/978-3-540-45002-3_4
9. Lackner, J.R., Dizio, P.: Gravitoinertial force background level affects adaptation to coriolis force perturbations of reaching movements. J. Neurophysiol. **80**(2), 546– 553 (1998)
10. Shadmehr, R., Smith, M.A., Krakauer, J.W.: Error correction, sensory prediction, and adaptation in motor control. Ann. Rev. Neurosci. **33**, 89–108 (2010)

Efficient Fine-Grained Object Detection for Robot-Assisted WEEE Disassembly

Ioannis Athanasiadis[✉], Athanasios Psaltis, Apostolos Axenopoulos, and Petros Daras

Centre for Research and Technology Hellas, Thessaloniki, Greece
johnyath@gmail.com

Abstract. In the current study, a region-based approach for object detection is presented that is suitable for handling very small objects and objects in low-resolution images. To address this challenge, an anchoring mechanism for the region proposal stage of the object detection algorithm is proposed, which boosts the performance in the detection of small objects with an insignificant computational overhead. Our method is applicable to the task of robot-assisted disassembly of Waste Electrical and Electronic devices (WEEE) in an industrial environment. Extensive experiments have been conducted in a newly formed device disassembly segmentation dataset with promising results.

Keywords: Human-robot collaboration · WEEE disassembly · Small object detection

1 Introduction

Human-robot collaboration has been recently introduced in industrial environments, where the fast and precise, but at the same time dangerous, traditional industrial robots have started being replaced with industrial collaborative robots for disassembling of WEEE in WEEE recycling plants [1][1]. The rationale behind the selection of the latter is to combine the endurance and precision of the robot with the dexterity and problem-solving ability of humans. An advantage of industrial collaborative robots (or cobots) is that they can coexist with humans without the need to be kept behind fences. Cobots can be utilised in numerous industrial tasks for automated parts assembling. In the context of the EU-funded project HR-Recycler, industrial collaborative robots are introduced for disassembling of WEEE in WEEE recycling plants. Due to the complexity and high variability of devices, the fully-robotised disassembly is not feasible, thus, a human-robot collaboration scenario is much appreciated. The robot will be able to unscrew, cut or grasp the constituting parts of an electronic device and put them to separate baskets, depending on their type (e.g. capacitors, batteries, PCBs, etc). In this direction, Computer Vision is necessary to assist the robot's

---

[1] https://www.hr-recycler.eu/.

© Springer Nature Switzerland AG 2020
V. Vouloutsi et al. (Eds.): Living Machines 2020, LNAI 12413, pp. 17–22, 2020.
https://doi.org/10.1007/978-3-030-64313-3_3

perception of the surrounding environment. The Deep Learning (DL) era brought great advancements in numerous of Computer vision domains, mainly because DL-based methods are capable of grasping complex relations and handling huge amount of data. Specifically, deep Convolutional Neural Networks (CNNs) have been utilised for the task of object detection. These approaches fall into two categories, namely the two-stage and the one-stage methods. Modern two-stage object detection methods such as Faster R-CNN [9] and Mask R-CNN [3] make use of a trainable network, called Regional Proposal Network (RPN), to propose regions which potentially enclose ground truth objects in. On the other hand, in the one-stage methods, the regions are generated and classified in a single forward pass. The YOLO [8] and the SSD [7] algorithms are the most representative one-stage object detection approaches. In [11] the High Possible Regions Proposal Network is introduced in which a feature map with empowered edge information is formed and passed as an additional feature map in the RPN for more accurate region proposing. Object detection has evolved significantly the latest years, nevertheless, the accuracy in detecting small objects is still limited. To address such limitations, in [10] the use of context information is adapted focusing on detecting small objects. A Generative adversarial networks (GAN) based approach is presented in [4], which generates super resolved representations of small objects, similar to the bigger ones, where the object detection algorithms perform better at detecting. The motivation behind this work is to effectively boost the performance of current two-stage object detection methods in detecting small objects by implementing a more sophisticated anchoring technique. A suitable baseline method is chosen which we gradually enhance by combining cascade architecture and a proposed anchoring mechanism targeted at small-sized objects. Finally in this work, we showcase the ability to amplify DL-based object detection approaches by complementing them with additional handcrafted features, targeted explicitly at compensating for the poor visual representation of the small objects.

2   Methods

State of the art two-stage approaches consist of two discrete modules responsible for region proposing and classifying respectively. At the first stage, a set of *candidate regions* of predefined shape and size, called anchors, is uniformly generated across the image. Thereafter, each anchor is validated on its probability of containing a ground truth object by the RPN. The most confident, in terms of objectness, anchors constitute the *proposed regions* which are then passed to the second stage for further classification.

Baseline: As a baseline approach, Mask R-CNN [3] was chosen for both its state of the art performance and its efficiency in cases where heavy overlapping between the relevant objects occurs. By utilising the Feature Pyramid Network (FPN) approach of [5], Mask R-CNN becomes more appealing to the detection of small objects.

Cascade: The method as described in [2] is applied on the baseline architecture, with the purpose of simultaneously training multiple classifiers optimized at different Interception over Union (IoU) thresholds. Given that each classifier refines the input regions to align better with their corresponding targets, a sequence of cooperative classifiers is deployed to progressively increase their quality as well as the quality of the regions in a single pass.

EA-CNN$_P$: Although the uniform anchoring has proven to be quite effective in most cases, generating anchors in discrete pixel intervals with fixed shape and size often results in misalignment between the anchors and their respective ground truth targets, which can be critical in the case of small objects detection. This can be overcome by generating additional candidate regions through applying the maximally stable extremal regions (MSER) algorithm on an image edge-enhanced by simplified Gabor wavelets (SGWs). From this step, only the small-sized edge information regions, referred to as *edge anchors*, are considered. Finally, all the edge anchors are passed to the second stage classifier along with the regions proposed by the RPN.

EA-CNN$_C$: The integration of the edge anchors into the RPN should retain the scale-specific feature maps of the FPN and the mapping between bounding box regressors and identical-shaped anchors. To this end, the edge anchors are refined to match the closest available shape, size and location configurations, as dictated by the hyper-parameters of ratio, scale, and input image dimension respectively. In order to minimize the refinement, additional enlarged feature maps dedicated to the edge anchors, called *edge maps*, are introduced, which correspond to different scales relevant to small objects. After the modifications described above the RPN is able to evaluate regions given both edge and regular anchors as input. Based on that, MSER is applied to both grayscale input image and its edge-enhanced version resulting in more but less precise edge anchors (Fig. 1).

3   Experiments

Within the context of HR-Recycler project, a new image dataset was created by capturing multiple PC-Tower devices during their disassembly procedure. The dataset was appropriately annotated by manually segmenting its components at various disassembly stages, which was then used for experimental testing.

Implementation Details: The input images are rescaled such as their biggest side is 512 pixels wide, while their aspect ratio is retained; although feeding images of a higher resolution would most likely result in better detection performance, the application's need for real-time operation is limiting. So as to effectively locate small ground truth targets, we use scales of 10, 12, 15 and 20 pixels with the first one corresponding to the uniformly generated anchors and the rest of them to the edge maps. When the cascade method is used, the base classifier is followed by two extra classification heads of 0.55 and 0.60 IoU thresholds. Finally, for the purpose of generating the edge anchors, the regions

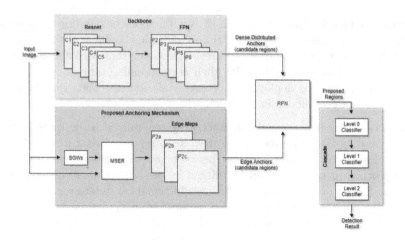

Fig. 1. The architecture combining cascade with EA-CNN$_C$.

produced by the MSER algorithm occupying an area larger than 15^2 pixels or have their aspect ratio falling outside the $[0.5, 2]$ interval, are filtered out.

Results: To evaluate the impact of each method on the detection performance, we report the standard COCO [6] metrics in Table 1. Notably, utilising the cascade approach seems to boost the metrics of the strict IoU threshold. Additionally, improved performance is achieved, in terms of AP_S, when edge anchors are used combined with high-quality cascade classifiers. Moreover, the results shown in Fig. 2, referring to screws, are indicative of the edge anchors' capability to detect significantly small objects.

Table 1. Object detection results on PC-Tower dataset in all classes (all its *components*).

Method	Cascade	$AP_{0.5:0.95}$	$AP_{0.5}$	$AP_{0.75}$	AP_S	$AR_{0.5:0.95}$	AR_S
Baseline	−	40.3	69.8	39.5	23.1	47.3	28.0
	✓	39.5	66.2	40.1	23.6	**48.8**	29.0
EA-CNN$_P$	−	38.7	68.2	38.0	22.9	46.9	28.8
	✓	**40.9**	**70.5**	**42.3**	24.6	48.2	30.1
EA-CNN$_C$	−	39.6	69.5	40.1	**25.5**	47.2	31.4
	✓	40.6	69.5	41.9	25.2	48.4	**32.3**

$AP_{0.5:0.95}$: 29.5 $AP_{0.5:0.95}$: 25.4 $AP_{0.5:0.95}$: 29.1 $AP_{0.5:0.95}$: 37.8
(a)   (b)   (c)   (d)

Fig. 2. Detection performance and AP scores for the class: *screws.* (a) Baseline (b) Cascade (c) EA-CNN$_P$ w/ Cascade (d) EA-CNN$_C$ w/ Cascade

4   Conclusions

In this work an anchoring mechanism utilising heuristic information is proposed; its ability to generate candidate regions that align better with the small-sized ground-truth targets discloses the potential of improving the detection of small objects that current two-stage state-of-the-art algorithms struggle with. The experiments on the PC-Tower disassembly dataset consisted of challenging small-sized components (e.g. screws), exhibit promising results. As future work, integrating the edge anchors into an attention-like mechanism, is considered, while experiments will be further extended using different types of WEEE devices.

Acknowledgments. This work was supported by the European Commission under contract H2020-820742 HR-Recycler.

References

1. Axenopoulos, A., et al.: A hybrid human-robot collaborative environment for recycling electrical and electronic equipment. In: 2019 IEEE SmartWorld, Ubiquitous Intelligence & Computing, Advanced & Trusted Computing, Scalable Computing & Communications, Cloud & Big Data Computing, Internet of People and Smart City Innovation (SmartWorld/SCALCOM/UIC/ATC/CBDCom/IOP/SCI), pp. 1754–1759. IEEE (2019)
2. Cai, Z., Vasconcelos, N.: Cascade R-CNN: high quality object detection and instance segmentation. IEEE Trans. Pattern Analy. Mach. Intell. (2019). https://doi.org/10.1109/tpami.2019.2956516
3. He, K., Gkioxari, G., Dollar, P., Girshick, R.: Mask R-CNN. In: The IEEE International Conference on Computer Vision (ICCV), October 2017
4. Li, J., Liang, X., Wei, Y., Xu, T., Feng, J., Yan, S.: Perceptual generative adversarial networks for small object detection. In: Proceedings of the IEEE Conference on Computer Vision and Pattern Recognition, pp. 1222–1230 (2017)
5. Lin, T.Y., Dollár, P., Girshick, R., He, K., Hariharan, B., Belongie, S.: Feature pyramid networks for object detection. In: Proceedings of the IEEE Conference on Computer Vision and Pattern Recognition, pp. 2117–2125 (2017)
6. Lin, T.-Y., et al.: Microsoft COCO: common objects in context. In: Fleet, D., Pajdla, T., Schiele, B., Tuytelaars, T. (eds.) ECCV 2014. LNCS, vol. 8693, pp. 740–755. Springer, Cham (2014). https://doi.org/10.1007/978-3-319-10602-1_48
7. Liu, W., et al.: SSD: single shot multibox detector. In: Leibe, B., Matas, J., Sebe, N., Welling, M. (eds.) ECCV 2016. LNCS, vol. 9905, pp. 21–37. Springer, Cham (2016). https://doi.org/10.1007/978-3-319-46448-0_2

8. Redmon, J., Divvala, S., Girshick, R., Farhadi, A.: You only look once: unified, real-time object detection. In: Proceedings of the IEEE Conference on Computer Vision and Pattern Recognition, pp. 779–788 (2016)
9. Ren, S., He, K., Girshick, R., Sun, J.: Faster R-CNN: towards real-time object detection with region proposal networks. In: Advances in Neural Information Processing Systems, pp. 91–99 (2015)
10. Ren, Y., Zhu, C., Xiao, S.: Small object detection in optical remote sensing images via modified faster R-CNN. Appl. Sci. 8(5), 813 (2018)
11. Shao, F., Wang, X., Meng, F., Zhu, J., Wang, D., Dai, J.: Improved faster r-cnn traffic sign detection based on a second region of interest and highly possible regions proposal network. Sensors 19(10), 2288 (2019)

Integrated Topological Planning and Scheduling for Orchestrating Large Human-Robot Collaborative Teams

Ioannis Chatzikonstantinou$^{(\boxtimes)}$ (ID), Ioannis Kostavelis (ID), Dimitrios Giakoumis (ID), and Dimitrios Tzovaras (ID)

Centre for Research and Technology Hellas, Information Technologies Institute, 6th km Harilaou - Thermi, 57001 Thessaloniki, Greece
{ihatz,gkostave,dgiakoum,Dimitrios.Tzovaras}@iti.gr
https://www.certh.gr

Abstract. Human-Robot Collaboration (HRC) in industry is a promising research direction that has potential to expand robotics to previously unthinkable application areas. Orchestration of large hybrid human-robot teams carrying out many tasks in parallel within a shop floor faces new challenges due to unique aspects introduced by HRC. This paper presents a new approach to topological and temporal orchestration of hybrid human-robot workforce, considering the capabilities of robot agents as well as the potentially new roles that human operators may acquire in an HRC setting. We propose a two-stage approach to orchestrating large HRC teams: First, an abstract topological and task assignment problem is solved, which does not consider the precise sequence of tasks. Second, the result of the first step is used to initialize a constrained search for an efficient HRC schedule. Initial application of the proposed approach in problems of varying complexity demonstrates encouraging results.

Keywords: Human-robot collaboration · Scheduling · Topology · Optimization · Industry 4.0 · Waste electrical and electronic equipment · Recycling

1 Introduction

Automation of industrial processes through the use of robots is a widely practiced approach in modern industry. As the paradigm in industry shifts to Industry 4.0, new, previously unexplored areas of robotics applications in industry emerge as novel research directions. One such area concerns collaborative work performed in an industrial environment by hybrid human-robot teams. Human-robot collaboration (HRC) is necessary to efficiently address the more challenging tasks

This work has been supported by the European Union Horizon 2020 Research and Innovation program "HR-Recycler" under Grant Agreement no. 820742.

that cannot be adequately tackled through automation of teams of robots alone. Shortcomings in perception, reasoning or actuation of robots, compared to their human counterparts, limit their applicability to tasks requiring high level of corresponding abilities. Combination of robots with humans results in versatile teams and allows achieving the best of both worlds: HRC allows robots to undertake tedious and dangerous tasks from humans [1,2]. At the same time humans assist, supervise and take over tasks that are challenging for robots, or in case of failure.

As an illustrative scenario, the automation of recycling factory floors processing Waste Electrical and Electronic Equipment (WEEE) is mentioned. In such a scenario, a stream of highly heterogeneous end-of-life devices need to be skillfully manipulated in order to extract and sort critical components that are valuable or possess dangerous substances. For a robot, this task presents a significant challenge as it requires increased perception and actuation capabilities. An HRC setup in this case may enable the use of robots in a scenario that would otherwise be exclusive.

In an HRC scenario, one aspect that has vital importance is that of task planning and scheduling. The coordination of single-robot, single-human teams, or HRC teams comprising few robot and human agents has been extensively studied in literature [3–6]. In this scenario, collaboration is on a single main task, e.g. the assembly or disassembly of a single device, and the goal is to assign to agents and sequence operations so as to reach the goal of the task (i.e. satisfy all constraints) while also minimizing a problem-defined objective. There is usually a single workspace that is shared amongst agents, where all tasks are processed.

On the contrary, processes taking place in modern industrial shop floor are on a different scale. The amount of active agents including (including humans and robots) is much larger, and is organized into several smaller teams that process tasks in parallel. Another distinguishing feature is that processes take place in several workstations, which are topologically organized and may be unique in terms of capabilities and tooling. Topology, in fact, is an aspect that is of great importance to achieving a comprehensive orchestration in the large scale, and one that can directly affect efficiency [7,16].

It is evident through the above that the orchestration of HRC teams at the factory scale is a unique problem. Orchestration solutions for large-scale HRC orchestration need to account for the problem's unique properties, such as limitations in robot manipulation abilities, sharing of human resources within the factory floor, non-holonomic constraints in mobile robots etc. This problem is one that has received less attention so far in literature. Nonetheless, efficient orchestration of large scale human-robot collaborative teams is key to achieving factory-wide efficiency [7].

1.1   Contribution

This paper considers the problem of efficiently orchestrating large HRC teams, in industrial settings, to perform tasks that are characterized by collaboration between agents, and between humans and robots in specific. In this context, this paper introduces an HRC orchestration problem definition that considers collaboration features at a large scale. Furthermore, the proposed model considers topological placement of resources in a novel approach that respects factory floor constraints. In addition, we derive an abstract model for accurate approximate evaluation of topological and task assignment scenarios that is simple and fast and as such applicable to stochastic optimization scenarios. Finally, we present the application of the above in a comprehensive optimization workflow for deriving detailed agent assignment and scheduling solutions for large scale HRC.

We emphasize that our work focuses on large-scale distributed collaboration, where it is possible to distribute agents to more than a single workstation as required to improve scheduling. In an HRC setting, for instance, such a scenario may involve robot manipulators in each workstation of a factory floor that perform the bulk of the work, while humans are distributed overseeing workstation clusters, supervising each workstation and performing few tasks that cannot be performed by robots. To the best of the authors' knowledge, there is no other work that addresses this requirement specifically.

This new role of human workers, which leans more towards the supervisory side, has the potential to shift labor conditions in industry, by enabling skilled workers to make use of their skills rather than labor, while at the same time assuming a more responsible role in the production line.

1.2 Paper Outline

The paper is structured as follows: In Sect. 2 a concise review of related work in orchestration of large-scale HRC teams is presented. Section 3 elaborates on the proposed approach, presenting a formal problem definition and a detailed outline of the proposed optimization strategy to address the problem. Section 4 presents a series of preliminary validation experiments. Section 5 provides an overall discussion on derived results. Finally, Sect. 6 concludes the paper.

2 Related Work

2.1 Orchestration of Large HR Teams

Orchestration or robot teams in industry is a distinct research topic that has received significant attention in literature for a long time. This topic considers the scheduling of teams comprising multiple robots to efficiently perform tasks that may be carried out in parallel or that may involve collaboration between individual robots. Orchestration of human-robot teams, on the contrary, has received less attention so far.

In [7], authors propose a multi-stage optimization process for task assignment and scheduling of a multiple robot team factory floor. They propose a series of problem abstractions that are solved with each step incorporating more problem details than the last. Authors report improved results compared to heuristic and pure MILP solutions.

In [8], authors consider the assembly line problem where there is a possibility that human and robots can simultaneously execute tasks at the same workpiece either in parallel or in collaboration. Authors present a MILP problem formulation which concerns both assignment of agents (workers, robots) to workstations, as well as task assignment to each agent. To solve the proposed problem, authors propose a Genetic Algorithm (GA) approach. Even though said work does address assignment of humans and robots to workstation performing collaborative tasks, still there is no consideration of ditributing resources among several workstations, as the present work introduces.

In [9], authors propose an optimization framework that generates task assignments and schedules for a human–robot team with the goal of improving both time and ergonomics. Authors treat the time-ergonomics optimization as a bi-objective problem and perform a real-world task execution comparison between single-worker operation and worker-robot collaborative operation. Subsequently, they use collected data to optimize human and robot task allocation.

In [10], authors consider robot team planning for spatially separated information gathering and situational awareness tasks with the goal of minimizing the expected mission completion time. The proposed planning approach focuses on the handling of contingency tasks, which are unexpected situations that adversely interfere with mission execution. Authors present results from a series of comparisons among different heuristics used to schedule multi-agent robotic tasks.

2.2   The Role of Topological Organization

As it has been previously mentioned, an efficient topological organization within the factory floor, including distributed task assignment, plays an important role in achieving efficiency of the overall factory floor process. There are a series of works that have focused on this issue in literature.

In [11], authors propose a decision making framework for HRC workplace layout generation. Authors distinguish between passive and active resources, passive being resources such as tools and workstations, and active being robots and workers. Evaluation of layout alternatives is based on multiple criteria, namely: Workspace area, reachability and ergonomics, for each of which authors present objective function formulations. Finally, authors present a case study for the proposed approach.

In [12], authors discuss the implementation of an HRC work cell through the use of lean techniques. The paper proposes a hierarchical approach to the design of HRC cells, starting from organization level down to process and detailed design. In addition, authors present a series of commonly occurring lean rules and apply those in deriving a methodology for HRC cell design, and for task assignment and scheduling.

In [13], authors propose a model-based methodology to aid the layout design of a collaborative HRC work cell. Authors consider several aspects in optimizing layout such as geometric properties of the workspace, robot reach, ergonomics etc. Authors make use of inverse kinematics to establish both robot reach but also to evaluate ergonomic conditions for humans. Authors evaluate the proposed approach in an sheet metal fabrication case study.

In [2], authors propose an approach to a collaborative workplace design tool-chain considering different strengths of robot and human. Authors describe an ontology based information model based on the Product-Process-Resource Model (PPR), which accounts for the different active and passive resources taking place in factory process, and addresses topological as well as task assignment concerns. The utility of the model has been validated with process engineers, however currently the proposed approach does not include heuristic capabilities for problem solving.

2.3   Illustrative Example

Hereby the case of device dismantling in a Waste Electrical and Electronic Equipment (WEEE) recycling process taking place in a recycling plant is presented as an illustrative example. In a traditional WEEE recycling process, it is common to have several workstations within the factory floor, where workers use tools to dismantle devices and extract components that contain valuable or hazardous materials. WEEE arrives unsorted in containers, is sorted into types and then distributed to workstations for processing. As part of processing, components of devices that contain valuable or hazardous materials are extracted and sorted. Following device dismantling in workstations, containers with extracted components are moved to other points within the factory floor for further processing. The task of dismantling the device and extracting components is one that is offered for human-robot collaborative processing. This process comprises some steps that may be performed by robot, however others are necessarily performed by humans due to robot perception and manipulation limitations.

In the scenario we envision, human-robot collaboration is performed in two ways: On one hand, at the workstation through the use of a fixed robotic manipulator arm, that undertakes disassembly steps, and on the other hand, in terms of device and component transport, where Autonomous Ground Vehicles (AGVs) are used to autonomously pick devices and components from and to the device and component sorting areas respectively. A diagram of the overall process is shown in Fig. 1.

3   Two-Stage Planning-Scheduling Approach

The simultaneous consideration of topological and temporal properties of HRC orchestration yields a large and complex problem space that is difficult to explore. In order to simplify finding suitable solutions, this paper proposed a two-stage hierarchical approach that comprises stochastic optimization over an abstract problem formulation, followed by a detailed search of a more focused area. Our approach is inspired by previous approaches such as [7], however it is extended to specifically address HRC features.

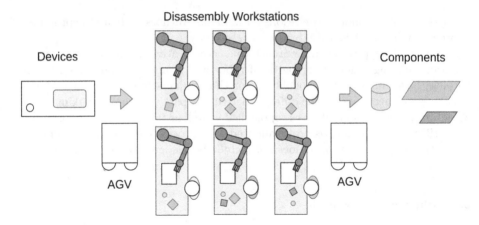

Fig. 1. Illustrative example of device disassembly process flow in a WEEE recycling factory setting.

In the proposed approach, the aim of the first step is to generate a topological and task assignment, without considering detailed scheduling parameters, that optimizes a simplified problem definition that does not consider precise temporal relationships in scheduled tasks. The second step is a detailed search considering full temporal relationships, however it is focused on the area determined from the first step and as such the search space is greatly reduced. An overview of the process is demonstrated in Fig. 2.

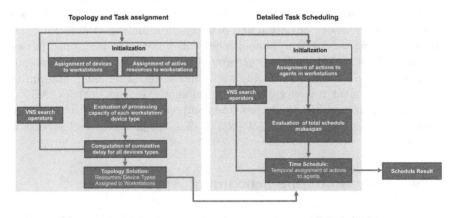

Fig. 2. Overview of the proposed process with the two consecutive steps illustrated.

3.1   Topological and Task Planning

Topological planning is of fundamental significance for the present study. Even though previous studies consider topology, the present one adopts a different approach, namely, we assume a set of pre-determined workstation locations and capabilities, and we aim to select a subset thereof that optimizes some objective function, such as e.g. minimization of travel time. We believe that this approach is more advantageous for application to real-world factory floors, where there are strict constraints that are often tacit in the existing factory floor layout.

In the proposed problem definition, a set of workstations is topologically located within a factory floor. One or more agents (humans, robots) may be assigned to work at one or more workstations. Each agent has unique skills that can be used to carry out tasks. Some of those tasks are localized to workstations, while others require transport of materials or workpieces between workstations and other target locations within the factory. We assume that the factory processes workpieces according to known processes that involve a series of tasks to be performed in sequence. Each workstation is differentiated by assigned agents and assigned workpiece types (and thus process types). A single workpiece is processed in one workstation and no workstation changes are allowed. However, distinct workpieces of the same type may be selected to be processed in more than one workstations, always obeying processing of single workpiece to single station.

For the first step of the process, we consider the following entities:

- Set of workstations W, located within a factory floor with pose defined as $\{x_{w_i}, y_{w_i}, \theta_{w_i}\} \forall w_i \in W$, and each with a set of points of interest (PoI) corresponding to relevant locations in the workstation, such as worker location, robot manipulator base point and AGV dropoff locations.
- Set of processes P that may be carried out by completing specified steps (tasks) for each process.
- Set of tasks T, each of which corresponds to an elementary action that can be performed by an agent and advances the process at hand. $t_i \in p_j, \forall t_i \in T, p_j \in P$
- Set of agents A, each of which corresponds to a worker or robot and is defined by a series of skills.
- Set of skills S indicating the skill of an agent a at task t, where $\forall t_i \in T$ and $a_j \in A \; \exists s_{ij} \in S$
- Set of target locations within the factory L with location $\{x_{l_i}, y_{l_i}\} \forall l_i \in L$
- A set of desired throughput rates per process Q_P, which denote the complete process iterations per process type, per hour, that the factory should achieve.

Given the above entities definition, a solution to the topology and task assignment problem comprises the following elements:

- A matrix S_{aw} of agent-workstation assignments.
- A matrix R_{pw} of process-workstation assignments.

It is noted that even though potential agent to task assignments are computed during the evaluation process, they are not part of the solution, as precise task assignments will be performed as part of the second stage, that is, the detailed process scheduling.

Evaluation of Topological and Task Assignment Solution. To determine whether a solution is feasible and well-performing, a model-based evaluation procedure is followed. The procedure consists of the following steps:

1. For each point of interest at each workstation, find and store shortest path to all targets using A* algorithm.
2. For each agent (worker, robot), find the total workstation assignment count. Total workstation assignment is influential in calculating the performance of each agent.
3. For each task/workstation pair, find the processing time given humans and robots assigned to workstation. Each task is assigned to the assigned agent with the highest relevant skill. Transport task processing times are workstation-dependent.
4. For each process/workstation pair, find the allocation factor B_{pw} i.e. what percentage of the workstation's time is used for this process?
5. For each process, find per workstation processing rate:
   $\tau_{pw} = \sum_{a \in p} \min_a (S_{t,aw}) B_{pw}$
6. For each process, find cumulative processing rate:
   $\tau_p = \sum_{w \in W} \tau_{pw}$
7. For each process and given desired processing rates, find the delay per process:
   $l_p = \tau_p - Q_p \ if \ Q_P < \tau_p, 0 \ otherwise$
8. Find cumulative process delay:
   $l_{tot} = \sum_p l_p$

The primary constraint here is to ensure that the total lag in processing times as resulting from the solution evaluation vs. the desired ones expressed in Q_{tot} is zero, therefore $l_{tot} = 0$.

To optimize the above problem definition, we use Variable Neighborhood Search (VNS) [14]. VNS is a greedy hill descent algorithm that alternates between steps of local search and perturbation (shaking) of solutions to escape local optima. Search strategies (neighborhoods) are exchanged depending on their hill descent performance, which is termed change of neighborhood. As part of this study, we develop a set of search operators that are specific to the problem at hand. The operators are inspired by work on optimizing scheduling problems with VNS [15], and function on problem-specific entities. Specifically, we define neighborhoods with respect to agent-to-workstation assignments, process-to-workstation assignments, and perturbation mechanism based on shuffling of entire workstation assemblies.

3.2 Detailed Task Scheduling

Following derivation of solution to the topological and task assignment problem above, the assignments of agents to workstations, as well as task assignments for each agent are available. These are introduced as constraints to a detailed scheduling problem that takes precise task sequencing into account.

The detailed scheduling problem is formulated as a Mixed-Integer Linear Problem (MILP), which is solved using an available third party solver. The

MILP problem formulation is an extension of our previous work on large scale HRC orchestration [16], that is able to handle variable spatial distances and agent and process assignment constraints to specific workstations. Through this constraints, the search space is limited which results in a faster optimization.

4   Experimental Validation

Initial experimental validation is performed in order to evaluate the precise contribution of the proposed multi-stage optimization approach. We perform a series of evaluations on problems of different size with respect to included agents, workstations and processes. This type of evaluation through the use of synthetic problem definitions is typical in resource allocation and scheduling. In our evaluations, we consider problem instances of up to 10 agents, 10 workstations and three device types with five task for each process. The parameters of each problem are presented in Table 1. In addition, considered worker and robot skills are presented in Table 2.

Table 1. Properties of evaluated problem instances.

Instance	No. device types	No. workers	No. robot arms	No. AGVs	No. pallet trucks
1	3 (3 tasks)	2	2	1	1
2	6 (5 tasks)	3	3	2	2
3	6 (5 tasks)	4	4	2	2
4	9 (5 tasks)	5	6	2	2

Table 2. Agent skills considered in test instances.

Agent	Skills
Worker1	OpenCover: 12 s, ExtractPanel: 20 s, ExtractCapacitor: 18 s, ExtractPCB: 18 s
Worker2	OpenCover: 11 s, ExtractPanel: 20 s, ExtractCapacitor: 20 s, ExtractPCB: 40 s
Worker3	OpenCover: 14 s, ExtractPanel: 18 s, ExtractCapacitor: 20 s, ExtractPCB: 16 s
Worker4	OpenCover: 10 s, ExtractPanel: 16 s, ExtractCapacitor: 25 s
Robot Arm	OpenCover: 32 s, ExtractPanel: 60 s
AGV	Moving speed: 1.0 m/s
Pallet Truck	Moving speed: 0.7 m/s

5 Discussion

Looking at the validation results and with respect to resource allocation and topology, we observed the following:

- We are able to obtain sane resource assignment for teams of human and robot workers that maximizes
- The allocation algorithm "augments" the processing capacity for those device types that are mostly in demand with the aim of reducing the lag in overall device processing capability.
- The augmentation occurs through 1. allocation of additional workstations for the particular device type and 2. allocation of more capable agents to accelerate device processing.
- Human workers are resources that are necessary to perform some disassembly steps. In order to maximize efficiency, the proposed method often resolves to sharing of those resources among more than one workstations. In this sense, even though robots are usually slower in processing than humans, they are allocated to perform tasks in parallel, with humans only intervening for tasks that are absolutely necessary, thus achieving speedup.
- From a topological perspective, the proposed approach generates allocates workstations that minimize the overall transport time, taking into account the fact that the speed of different agents is not the same.
- The above behaviors of the system are emergent and occur as a result of the optimization process.

Table 3, presents results with respect to the number of workstations allocated by the algorithm and the total achieved makespan, i.e. the time needed for all tasks to finish processing. In addition, in Fig. 3 an indicative solution with respect to topology is shown. In this solution instance it may be observed that the algorithm is able to topologically allocate relevant workstations minimizing traveling times, as well as distribute the available resources intelligently in order to maximize throughput.

It is noted that the proposed approach does not require any prior knowledge as to the number, location and type of resources to be assigned. In addition, execution is iterative so that the algorithm can be executed online and accommodate dynamic changes such as desired processing capacity or resource availability.

Table 3. Occupied workstations and makespans for different problem instances

Problem instance	Occupied workstations	Makespan
1	3	696 s
2	4	1326 s
3	5	902 s
4	8	1501 s

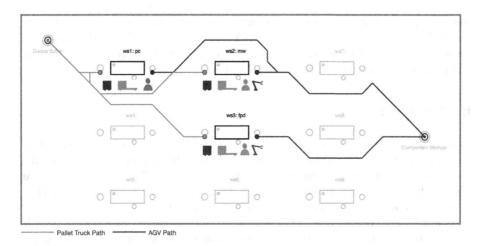

Pallet Truck Path ——— AGV Path

Fig. 3. An instance of topological and task assignment optimization results in a scenario with nine workstations, two workers, two robotic arms, an AGV and an autonomous Pallet Truck. It is noted that no prior constraints are imposed to the system, the assignment is done automatically. Two workstations (ws2, ws3) share a worker and two robots. In another workstation (ws1) another worker carries out tasks. Devices are brought in through the autonomous Pallet Truck, and components are transported using the AGV.

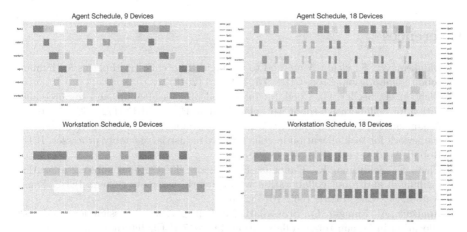

Fig. 4. Two instances of detailed schedule results of different problem sizes: on the left, with 9 devices, on the right with 18 devices. It is seen that workstations are fully utilized all the time.

Specifically with respect to the second part of the proposed method, namely task scheduling, we observed that generated schedules are reasonable and resemble schedules that would be generated by human operators. It was seen that scheduling convergence was faster through the use of the proposed two-step approach, which is an indication that narrowing down the search space through hierarchical consideration of topology and task assignment, and then task scheduling presents a measurable merit. A single instance of a schedule generated through the proposed approach is demonstrated in Fig. 4.

6   Conclusion

This paper presented a new approach for orchestrating large teams of agents consisting of collaborating humans and robots in achieving optimal process efficiency while ensuring that humans are involved in minimally laborious tasks. We specifically focus on the distribution of human agents within factory floors consisting of many workstations, in an efficient manner that promotes supervisory roles in place of copious labor. We propose a multi-stage optimization approach for tackling the large-scale HRC orchestration problem, where the first stage solves an approximate task and topological agent distribution problem, which is introduced as a set of constraints for the second stage of the problem, which solves a fully detailed scheduling problem formulated as MILP. Initial experimental validation yields encouraging results that demonstrate a clear advantage of the proposed approach. The next steps involve further development of heuristics in order to improve efficiency of the scheduling algorithm, as well as further validation in more diverse sets of tasks and topological organizations.

References

1. Blankemeyer, S., et al.: A method to distinguish potential workplaces for human-robot collaboration. Proc. CIRP **76**, 171–176 (2018)
2. Fechter, M., Seeber, C., Chen, S.: Integrated process planning and resource allocation for collaborative robot workplace design. Proc. CIRP **1**(72), 39–44 (2018)
3. Johannsmeier, L., Haddadin, S.: A hierarchical human-robot interaction-planning framework for task allocation in collaborative industrial assembly processes. IEEE Robot. Autom. Lett. **2**(1), 41–48 (2017)
4. Chen, F., Sekiyama, K., Cannella, F., Fukuda, T.: Optimal subtask allocation for human and robot collaboration within hybrid assembly system. IEEE Trans. Autom. Sci. Eng. **11**(4), 1065–1075 (2014)
5. Roncone, A., Mangin, O., Scassellati, B.: Transparent role assignment and task allocation in human robot collaboration. In: 2017 IEEE International Conference on Robotics and Automation (ICRA), pp. 1014–1021. IEEE (2017)
6. Bogner, K., Pferschy, U., Unterberger, R., Zeiner, H.: Optimised scheduling in humanrobot collaboration a use case in the assembly of printed circuit boards. Int. J. Prod. Res. **56**(16), 5522–5540 (2018)
7. Zhang, C., Shah, J.A.: Co-optimizating multi-agent placement with task assignment and scheduling. In: Proceedings of the Twenty-Fifth International Joint Conference on Artificial Intelligence, p. 7 (2016)
8. Weckenborg, C., Kieckhäfer, K., Müller, C., Grunewald, M., Spengler, T.S.: Balancing of assembly lines with collaborative robots. Bus. Res. **13**(1), 93–132 (2019). https://doi.org/10.1007/s40685-019-0101-y

9. Pearce, M., Mutlu, B., Shah, J., Radwin, R.: Optimizing makespan and ergonomics in integrating collaborative robots into manufacturing processes. IEEE Trans. Autom. Sci. Eng. **15**(4), 1772–84 (2018)
10. Shriyam, S., Gupta, S.K.: Incorporation of contingency tasks in task allocation for multirobot teams. IEEE Trans. Autom. Sci. Eng. **17**, 809–822 (2019)
11. Tsarouchi, P., et al.: A decision making framework for human robot collaborative workplace generation. Proc. CIRP **44**, 228–232 (2016)
12. Stadnicka, D., Antonelli, D.: Human-robot collaborative work cell implementation through lean thinking. Int. J. Comput. Integr. Manuf. **32**(6), 580–595 (2019). https://doi.org/10.1080/0951192X.2019.1599437
13. Lietaert, P., Billen, N. and Burggraeve, S.: Model-based multi-attribute collaborative production cell layout optimization. In: 2019 20th International Conference on Research and Education in Mechatronics (REM). IEEE (2019)
14. Mladenovic, N.: Hansen P Variable neighborhood search. Comput. Oper. Res. **24**(11), 1097–1100 (1997)
15. Lei, D., Guo, X.: Variable neighbourhood search for dual-resource constrained flexible job shop scheduling. Int. J. Prod. Res. **52**(9), 2519–2529 (2014)
16. Chatzikonstantinou, I., Giakoumis, D.: A new shopfloor orchestration approach for collaborative human-robot device disassembly. In: 2019 IEEE SmartWorld, Ubiquitous Intelligence & Computing, Advanced & Trusted Computing, Scalable Computing & Communications. Cloud & Big Data Computing, Internet of People and Smart City Innovation (2019)

Programming Material Intelligence: An Additive Fabrication Strategy for Self-shaping Biohybrid Components

Tiffany Cheng[1]([✉]), Dylan Wood[1], Xiang Wang[2], Philip F. Yuan[2], and Achim Menges[1]

[1] Institute for Computational Design and Construction, University of Stuttgart, Stuttgart, Germany
tiffany.cheng@icd.uni-stuttgart.de
[2] College of Architecture and Urban Planning, Tongji University, Shanghai, China

Abstract. This paper presents an integrative approach to adaptive structures, which harnesses the scale and strength of natural material actuators such as wood as well as the functional physical programming of material properties enabled by 3D-printing. Passively actuated adaptive systems represent a growing field within architecture, and wood's innate capacity for hygroscopic responsiveness can be instrumentalized for use as a natural actuator; however, the internal compositions of wood cannot be fully customized. With 3D-printing, it is possible to tailor the internal substructure of physical objects. We introduce a material programming and additive fabrication method for designing macro-scale objects with anisotropic stiffness and elasticity of varying magnitudes using functional patterns, and embedding natural wood actuators into the synthetic 3D-printed structures. In place of electronics and digital control, movement is encoded in the physical material and fabrication logic—demonstrating how self-shaping biohybrid components can emerge from a synergy of natural and synthetic materials.

Keywords: Material programming · Additive manufacturing · Mechanical metamaterials · Bio-based actuation · Autonomous systems

1 Introduction

Passively actuated adaptive systems represent a growing field in architecture and engineering. Many bio-based materials have the capacity to change shape based on external environmental stimuli such as heat or humidity. Wood is a sustainable, readily available, easily machinable, and high-performance construction material with a natural capacity for moisture-induced and direction-dependent swelling and shrinking. By accessing this inherent hygroscopic and orthotropic behavior in a bilayer configuration, wood becomes a natural actuator that can produce shape changes in curvature through bending [12]. This adaptiveness

© Springer Nature Switzerland AG 2020
V. Vouloutsi et al. (Eds.): Living Machines 2020, LNAI 12413, pp. 36–45, 2020.
https://doi.org/10.1007/978-3-030-64313-3_5

alludes to the potential for buildings to be more in tune with the fluctuating climate by automatically self-shading, self-ventilating, and self-stiffening in response to environmental changes [11]. At the same time, when used at increased size and thickness, wood can be employed as a self-shaping mechanism for the manufacture of curved timber components and larger structures [4,6].

The structural properties of wood specific to shrinking and swelling can be adjusted through densification, delignification, or chemical treatment. As a natural material, however, its stark anisotropic behavior within a sheet stock cannot be fully customized [3,5]. Tailoring the direction of hygroscopic actuation can be achieved by combining multiple boards into larger parts, but there are limits due to the existing structure of the material [14,15].

Meanwhile, 3D-printing has enabled the tuning of material properties and functionalities through the manufacture of compliant mechanisms with tailored internal substructures. 3D-printed mechanical metamaterials with a range of functions, from elastic patterns [9] to double curvature [7] to thermally actuated mechanisms [1], have been researched; but existing literature shows that these laboratory prototypes lack the scale, high swelling force, and actuation speed necessary for some building applications.

Macro-Scale Self-shaping Biohybrid Components. We introduce an integrative approach to adaptive structures, which harnesses the scale and actuation strength of wood bilayer actuators as well as the functional programming of varying stiffnesses and elasticities (of defined magnitudes and anisotropies) that extrusion-based 3D-printing enables. Utilizing industrial robotic arms, 3D-printing has already been proven at larger scales [13,16]; it is also possible to 3D-print a working quadcopter drone with an embedded motherboard and other electronic components [8]. But in place of electronics and digital control, we encode movement in the *physical material* and *fabrication logic*.

Through iterative investigations, we assessed the effect of meso-scale [2] functional patterns on macro-scale objects, and explored the tectonic integration between natural and synthetic parts. Finally, we deployed our additive fabrication strategy at full scale, producing meter long components with thicknesses up to 8 cm which are capable of autonomous, shape-changing behaviors.

2   Results

2.1   Functional Patterns for 3D-printing

We formulated a method for producing designed material behaviors within a macro-scale object, in which desired material properties are encoded into the physical matter through meso-scale 3D-printed functional patterns. Using fused filament fabrication (Tec 4 3D-printer, FELIX, Utrecht, Netherlands), we extruded functional patterns at 0.1 mm precision and created a catalogue of functional patterns for stiffness (out-of-plane bending) and elasticity (in-plane

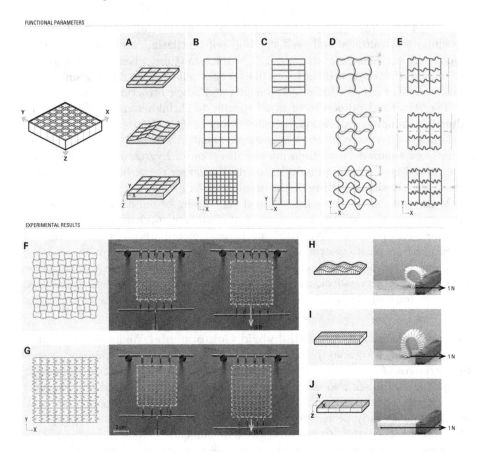

Fig. 1. Functional parameters include (A) pattern height, (B) resolution, (C) grid distribution, (D) amplitude, and (E) frequency. Shown here are the designed behaviors of (F) an isotropic pattern, deforming equally in the X and Y axes, and (G) an anisotropic pattern, deforming only in the Y axis, under a 15 N tension force. Bending bias can be tuned via anisotropy and thickness, as exhibited by testing coupons with one edge on a pin joint and string pulling from the free edge (allowing rotational freedom in the XZ plane): patterns having (H) variable height and anisotropy in the Y direction and (I) anisotropy in the Y direction buckle under a 1 N force, while (J) a pattern with anisotropy in the X direction resists bending of up to 5 N forces.

stretching) with tunable magnitudes and tailored anisotropies. As the baseline, we employed a Cartesian grid that can vary in distribution between the axes; functional patterns were instantiated in a two-dimensional array. Different behaviors were achieved by programming the pattern height (Z thickness), resolution (XY density), grid distribution (anisotropic XY spacing), and the geometry of wavy structures that act as mechanisms for allowing stretching and compression (Fig. 1 A–E). To maintain the best possible mechanical properties, the patterns were translated into a continuous, interwoven, and 3D-printable toolpath.

Materials and Methods for Evaluation. To understand how the functional patterns cause bending and stretching, tests were conducted using thermoplastic copolyester filament (FlexiFil, FormFutura, Nijmegen, Netherlands) with a 0.5 mm extruded width. Physical coupons with dimensions of 50 mm × 50 mm × 5 mm and 50 mm × 25 mm × 5 mm were used to evaluate in-plane stretching and out-of-plane bending, respectively. We quantified the material properties of our physical samples by incrementally applying force with a spring scale (Medio-Line Spring Scale 40025, Pesola, Schindellegi, Switzerland), causing either pulling or deflection.

Analysis of Material Behavior. The amount of in-plane deformation is impacted by the geometry of wave patterns; the frequency and amplitude of the waves affect how much the object can stretch and compress (Fig. 1 F). These parameters can also vary orthogonally to promote anisotropy (Fig. 1 G). Varying the distributions between orthogonal directions will increase bending stiffness in one direction, while promoting flexural compliance and thus out-of-plane bending in the other direction. We found that under the same pulling force, high anisotropy in the direction of loading resists bending (Fig. 1 J) while the opposite anisotropy facilitates bending in the same direction (Fig. 1 I). The thickness of material distributions along each direction additionally tunes the measure of compliance (Fig. 1 H).

2.2 Strategy for Integrating Wood Bilayer Actuators

The biohybrid components gain their self-shaping abilities through natural wood bilayer actuators embedded within the synthetic 3D-printed armature. Although performing discrete functions, each material is programmed to work with the other (Fig. 2 A–C). As a wood bilayer actuator bends in one direction, its 3D-printed armature should be flexible enough to permit unhindered bending in that direction; the neighboring functional patterns should also be aligned to transfer loads in the direction orthogonal to bending. From another perspective, the wood bilayer actuator provides structural integrity in the direction where the 3D-printed armature is weakest, while the surrounding functional patterns enable the wood bilayer actuators to extend its area of influence. To fuse the wood-plastic interface as a holistic entity and prevent damage due to stress concentrations where wood meets plastic, we increase the 3D-printing flow rate of functional patterns surrounding the wood bilayer actuator.

Materials and Methods for Evaluation. We evaluated the integration of the natural and synthetic parts by comparing biohybrid components to a naked wood bilayer actuator. The biohybrid samples (150 mm × 150 mm) were embedded with 150 mm × 30 mm sized wood bilayer actuators. A naked sample with a single wood bilayer actuator of the same size acted as the control for this experiment. The wood bilayer actuators used in these experiments were constructed out of maple veneer and calibrated to be flat at 70% relative humidity (RH).

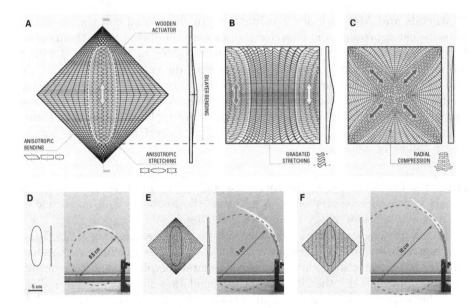

Fig. 2. Integrating natural and synthetic materials necessitates the mediation between discrete parts to work together as one entity. A biohybrid component containing one wood bilayer actuator (A) can display multiple functionalities across areas, transitioning from patterns for anisotropic bending to stretching. Material properties for wood-plastic integration and the interface of their associated patterns can be assigned using a number of strategies; illustrated are designs with (B) two wood actuators of opposing bending orientations and (C) four actuators arranged in radial symmetry. Captured at 40% RH, shown here are (D) the control sample, (E) an integrated sample with strategic patterning, and (F) an integrated sample with non-differentiated patterning.

We compared the shape change of both sample types through image captures, by measuring the bending radii of the wood bilayer actuators at ambient conditions (40% RH).

Analysis of Tectonic Integration. Deviations between the values of the embedded and naked samples were reduced with anisotropic material programming, demonstrating that 3D-printed functional patterns can allow its wood actuator to deform with minimized impediments (Fig. 2 D–F). Biohybrid samples with non-differentiated patterning showed that the 3D-printed armature creates a resistance to the shape change (Fig. 2 F). Anisotropy was used to eliminate (as much as possible) this resistance, and promote flexibility in the direction of bilayer bending; furthermore, programming the 3D-printed armature to stretch and compress (as each side of the bilayer expands and contracts in response to humidity) also aids in the movement (Fig. 2 E).

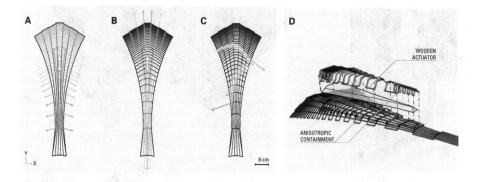

Fig. 3. The additive fabrication strategy was transferred to full scale using robotic extrusion. The production of a biohybrid leg required (A) enough flexibility in the direction of bending, but also (B) high stiffness to transfer loads and support self-weight. Extrusion paths were kept as continuous as possible, (C) following an alternating layer-by-layer logic of diagonal cross-hatching to maximize mechanical performance. The fabrication sequence involved creating containers (D) which indicate the placement of wood actuators as well as provide for them a secure enclosure.

2.3   Multi-material Additive Fabrication and Actuation

To produce the biohybrid components, we devised a fabrication technique for embedding wood bilayer actuators made from maple and spruce within 3D-printed armatures of designed material properties. This requires the synthesizing of multiple materials and processes into one sequence.

Fabrication Logic and Sequence. We equalized the wood moisture content (WMC) of the wood bilayer actuators in a RH controlled box (MiniOne Humidity Generator, Preservatech, Bydgoszcz, Poland) to obtain a flat surface, while also preparing the printing environment with the same RH. Once equalized, the wood bilayer actuators could be laser-cut or milled to tolerance, and then returned to the RH controlled box until starting fabrication. We began the fabrication procedure by 3D-printing the functionally patterned armature until the height of the wood bilayer actuators, leaving voids which indicate their placement. This ensures that the correct locations for each wood bilayer actuator will be easily identified. At this stage, extrusion was paused while the wood bilayer actuators were inserted by hand into their designated voids. Flush with the top of the already 3D-printed parts, the wood bilayer actuators provided a level surface for resuming the 3D-printing. The job was completed by 3D-printing the remaining layers, encasing the wood bilayer actuators and encoding the component with anisotropic stiffnesses, variable thicknesses, and shape-changing behaviors. The completed pieces are then actuated by changing the RH of the surrounding environment, activating the wood bilayer actuators and inducing shape change.

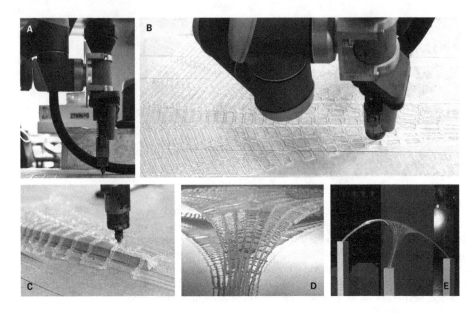

Fig. 4. The biohybrid leg was fabricated with a robotic arm (A) equipped with an end effector for large format extrusion (B). At 10% WMC, the wood bilayer actuator is flat and thus can be embedded (C). Three biohybrid legs were assembled to form a shape-changing tripod (D); exposure to higher humidity environments activates the wood bilayers, shown here curving at 20% WMC and shaping the entire structure (E).

Large-Scale Additive Fabrication. As a proof of concept, we also employed our additive fabrication strategy at full scale using robotic extrusion (Universal Robot UR5 with BAK Extruder Micro) to produce a set of large-scale (100 cm × 50 cm × 8 cm) prototypes. As robot arms afford more freedom in end effectors and motion planning, wood bilayer actuators can be inserted using pick-and-place automation (instead of manual placement) and encased using three-dimensional toolpaths (instead of 2.5D extrusion). Here the focus was on tuning the local bending stiffnesses by mediating between actuator placement and containment, height, and grid distribution of the armature (Fig. 3 A–D). This study demonstrates how these methods for creating self-shaping behaviors are adaptable for larger scale production (Fig. 4 A–E) via a combination of 3D-printed functional patterns and integrated wood bilayer actuators.

3   Conclusion

Through an integrative approach to material programming and additive fabrication, we have demonstrated the ability of macro-scale biohybrid components to intelligently interact with their environments by self-shaping. We encoded climate-responsive movements into a hybrid system of natural and synthetic materials, using 3D-printed functional patterns and integrated wood bilayer actuators. The physical material and fabrication logic, rather than any electronics or digital control, dictate the self-shaping behaviors. We formulated a method for designing and 3D-printing material properties, such as elasticity and compliance of varying magnitudes and anisotropies, using functional patterns. We also detailed the tectonic interface between natural and synthetic parts of the hybrid system. Finally, we established a strategy for producing macro-scale biohybrid components through a sequential process of multi-material additive fabrication.

3.1 Discussion

While our results indicate the potential of leveraging natural wood actuators with 3D-printing, our current approach still has a number of limitations and open questions. The wood bilayer actuators, when embedded in the biohybrid components, must overcome the inherent resistance caused by its 3D-printed armature. This can generally be mitigated by 3D-printing with thermoplastic elastomers. Starting with a lower baseline elastic modulus allows the range of tunable material properties to be expanded, as stiffness is more easily increased through added height and density in the functional patterns. Moreover, thicker wood bilayers could be employed for their higher actuation forces. For further upscaling, it will be important to consider the resultant increase in the structure's self-weight, especially during the self-erecting process. This might be alleviated by the strategic distribution of wood bilayer actuators in the system, coupled with 3D-printed functional patterns that optimize the ratio between strength to weight.

3.2 Outlook and Future Work

Biohybrid parts which move in response to the changing weather without electrical power can potentially serve as a solution to energy-efficient indoor climate control [10]. Although we have shown self-shaping at a range of spatial scales, the adoption of biohybrid components in buildings will require further exploration of the additional functionalities which are enabled by this material programming and additive fabrication approach. For the application of responsive facades that can manage the indoor climate, it will be necessary to overcome the poroelastic time scale. In the case of irreversible self-shaping such as in deployable structures and shells, safety mechanisms for locking the desired shape change will need to be investigated. Beyond the use of wood, other combinations of natural material actuators and synthetic material programming could be particularly interesting for large-scale self-shaping systems.

Acknowledgements. The research was partially supported by the Sino-German Centre for Research Promotion – GZ 1162 – and the German Research Foundation DFG under Germany's Excellence Strategy – EXC 2120/1 – 390831618. Additionally, this work was tested in a workshop setting at the Digital Futures 2018 conference in Shanghai. The authors especially thank Long Nguyen and Ahmad Razavi for their help in developing the system; we would like to also thank the students who participated in our workshop: Chen Cai, Yunyi Chen, Philipp Farana, Osama Hashem, Mu He, Kecheng Huang, Xiaobai Ji, Zhuoqun Jiang, Zeynab Kaseb, Tomas Vivanco Larrain, Siyu Li, Yige Liu, Jiaxin Nie, Yuchi Shen, Zexin Sun, Xuan Tang, Liu Yang, Zhefan Yu, Fei Yue, Tong Zhang, Qingyu Zhu.

References

1. Boley, J.W., et al.: Shape-shifting structured lattices via multimaterial 4D printing. Proc. Natl. Acad. Sci. **116**(42), 20856–20862 (2019). https://doi.org/10.1073/pnas. 1908806116

2. Dow, T.A., Scattergood, R.O.: Mesoscale and microscale manufacturing processes: challenges for materials, fabrication and metrology. In: Proceedings of the ASPE Winter Topical Meeting, vol. 28, pp. 14–19 (2003)

3. Frey, M., Widner, D., Segmehl, J.S., Casdorff, K., Keplinger, T., Burgert, I.: Delignified and densified cellulose bulk materials with excellent tensile properties for sustainable engineering. ACS Appl. Mater. Interfaces **10**(5), 5030–5037 (2018). https://doi.org/10.1021/acsami.7b18646

4. Grönquist, P., Panchadcharam, P., Wood, D., Menges, A., Rüggeberg, M., Wittel, F.K.: Computational analysis of hygromorphic self-shaping wood gridshell structures. Royal Soc. Open Sci. **7**(7), 192210 (2020). https://doi.org/10.1098/rsos. 192210

5. Grönquist, P., et al.: Investigations on densified beech wood for application as a swelling dowel in timber joints. Holzforschung **73**(6), 559–568 (2019). https://doi. org/10.1515/hf-2018-0106

6. Grönquist, P., Wood, D., Hassani, M.M., Wittel, F.K., Menges, A., Rüggeberg, M.: Analysis of hygroscopic self-shaping wood at large scale for curved mass timber structures. Sci. Adv. **5**(9), eaax1311 (2019). https://doi.org/10.1126/sciadv. aax1311

7. La Magna, R., Knippers, J.: Tailoring the bending behaviour of material patterns for the induction of double curvature. In: De Rycke, K., et al. (eds.) Humanizing Digital Reality, pp. 441–452. Springer, Singapore (2018). https://doi.org/10.1007/ 978-981-10-6611-5_38

8. Lewis, J.A., Bell, M.A., Busbee, T.A., Minardi, J.E.: Printed three-dimensional (3D) functional part and method of making (2016)

9. Panetta, J., Zhou, Q., Malomo, L., Pietroni, N., Cignoni, P., Zorin, D.: Elastic textures for additive fabrication. ACM Trans. Graph. **34**(4), 1–12 (2015). https:// doi.org/10.1145/2766937

10. Poppinga, S., et al.: Toward a new generation of smart biomimetic actuators for architecture. Adv. Mater. **30**(19), e1703653 (2018). https://doi.org/10.1002/adma. 201703653

11. Reichert, S., Menges, A., Correa, D.: Meteorosensitive architecture: biomimetic building skins based on materially embedded and hygroscopically enabled responsiveness. Comput.-Aided Des. **60**, 50–69 (2015). https://doi.org/10.1016/j.cad. 2014.02.010

12. Rüggeberg, M., Burgert, I.: Bio-inspired wooden actuators for large scale applications. PLoS One **10**(3), e0120718 (2015). https://doi.org/10.1371/journal.pone. 0120718

13. Soler, V., Retsin, G., Jimenez Garcia, M.: A generalized approach to non-layered fused filament fabrication. In: Nagakura, T., Tibbits, S., Ibañez, M., Mueller, C. (eds.) DISCIPLINES & DISRUPTION, pp. 562–571. Association for Computer Aided Design in Architecture (ACADIA), Cambridge, MA (2017)

14. Wood, D., Vailati, C., Menges, A., Rüggeberg, M.: Hygroscopically actuated wood elements for weather responsive and self-forming building parts - facilitating upscaling and complex shape changes. Constr. Build. Mater. **165**, 782–791 (2018). https://doi.org/10.1016/j.conbuildmat.2017.12.134

15. Wood, D.M., Correa, D., Krieg, O.D., Menges, A.: Material computation–4D timber construction: towards building-scale hygroscopic actuated, self-constructing timber surfaces. Int. J. Archit. Comput. **14**(1), 49–62 (2016). https://doi.org/10.1177/1478077115625522

16. Yuan, P.F., Chen, Z., Zhang, L.: Application of discrete system design in robotic 3-D printed shell structure. In: Proceedings of IASS Annual Symposia, vol. 2018, pp. 1–8 (2018)

Multi-material 3D-Printer for Rapid Prototyping of Bio-Inspired Soft Robotic Elements

Stefan Conrad[1,2(✉)] 📷, Thomas Speck[1,2,3] 📷, and Falk Tauber[1,2] 📷

[1] Plant Biomechanics Group (PBG) Freiburg, Botanic Garden of the University of Freiburg, Freiburg im Breisgau, Germany
stefan.conrad@biologie.uni-freiburg.de

[2] Cluster of Excellence LivMatS @ FIT – Freiburg Center for Interactive Materials and Bioinspired Technologies, University of Freiburg, Freiburg im Breisgau, Germany

[3] Freiburg Center for Interactive Materials and Bioinspired Technologies (FIT), University of Freiburg, Freiburg im Breisgau, Germany

Abstract. A rising trend can be observed in robot development towards the usage of flexible materials, whose properties resemble their biological counterparts. This way of design promises machines that are more adaptive, energy efficient and cost effective. One of the biggest challenges in this growing research field is the fabrication of functional elements, which consist of several embedded materials. The lack of compatible substances and of a proper prototyping technology limits the possible complexity and the degree of automation in prototyping. Furthermore, additive manufacturing techniques are usually designed for predefined purposes and do not have the customizability the research in an innovative field requires. In order to address this problem a novel multi-material 3D-printer with on-demand tool change has been developed. The adaptive locking mechanism in combination with a kinematic coupling allows the device to switch between tools varying in the dispensed material and even work principle. Using specifically developed directly driven filament-print-heads, a series of test specimen has been fabricated. The very reliable and precise extrusion, even of highly flexible material, is demonstrated in form of airtight chambers utilized as pneumatic actuators. In an additional demonstrator the flexible part has been reduced to a single expandable membrane as the active element included in an otherwise stiff housing. A specific design made it possible to embed the membrane in the surrounding, which compensated for the lack of chemical bonding between both substances and created a pneumatic actuator with a much better stability/performance ratio. These demonstrators highlight the great potential to create yet unbuilt biomimetic structures and multi-material systems with this novel multi-material printer.

Keywords: Multi-material 3D-printer · PLA-TPU embedment · Pneumatic actuators · Soft robotics · Biomimetics

© Springer Nature Switzerland AG 2020
V. Vouloutsi et al. (Eds.): Living Machines 2020, LNAI 12413, pp. 46–54, 2020.
https://doi.org/10.1007/978-3-030-64313-3_6

1 Introduction

Soft robots are a key to a safe and natural interaction between machines and humans (Rus and Tolley 2015). The replacement of stiff metal parts by flexible elements with the ability to bend and compress predestines them for applications in a fragile environment and/or for adaptive behavior. In contrast to their traditional relatives using bolts and hinges, soft robotic parts can be designed to better resemble the natural designs of living organisms. Therefore learning from nature and transferring those insights to artificial systems is a useful approach to create lighter and more adaptive mechanisms (Coyle et al. 2018). Like their natural role models such bioinspired or biomimetic systems are usually based on the interaction of different materials integrated in a complex geometry.

Due to its wide range of useable substances and the offered high degree of design freedom there has been a trend towards 3D-printing in the development of soft robots (Gul et al. 2018). Previous studies have shown how different types of additive manufacturing can be used to fabricate solid and flexible structures, soft actuators (Zolfagharian et al. 2016) or soft sensors (Muth et al. 2014). The limiting factor for developing more advanced bioinspired soft robots is still the range of materials that can be used. This is a challenge for both the field of material science and fabrication techniques (Trivedi et al. 2008). So far the PolyJet technology, that applies and cures droplets of varying photopolymer, is mostly used for multi-material prints (Khoo et al. 2015). However, they suffer from high costs and a selection of materials limited to the stock inks distributed by the supplier. On the other hand, more affordable and customizable 3D-printers are usually designed to build visually impressive sculptures for private customers. In product information about these kind of machines the keyword "multi-material" is still used synonymously for "multi-color" (of the same material) and the applied extrusion techniques like mixing and dual extruders have disadvantages for the challenges arising when printing materials of different chemical composition.

In contrast to these systems, this study presents a novel multi-material 3D-printer with on demand tool changing properties. The device is able to process multiple substances within one print by switching between individual tools on runtime. The development included the design of a suitable coupling mechanism, compatible print-heads and the implementation of tool change procedure. The finished device was then used to create several specimens in order to characterize the hardware and to test the reliability of the process.

2 Printer Design

2.1 Printer Geometry and Work Principle

The printer design is based on a commercially available 3-axes system with a carriage moving on the X/Y-plane and an independent Z-axis moving the build platform (Fig. 1A). In contrast to commonly used Y/Z-systems this construction allows it to line up several tools along the X-axis at the printer frame and to reach each of them with the carriage without being affected by the Z-position of the build plate. The tools are safely docked on two pins each with the coupling mechanism oriented towards the coupling of the carriage (Fig. 1E/F). During tool pick up the carriage connects to the interface and pulls it off the pins moving in Y-direction. The individual tool can be freely designed and adapted to the requirements of the component to be produced, provided it is equipped with the coupling interface and docking pinholes and is within the dimensional specifications of the printer. The current setup provides connectors for temperature control and stepper motor drivers for each tool, which could be extended if needed. In contrast to other printers with multiple nozzles on the same tool, this setup avoids any kind of unwanted interaction between the print-heads, since at only one tool is moving above the build platform.

2.2 Coupling Interface

A kinematic coupling is a physical attachment of two separate solid objects with a focus on repeatability and precision. Such a coupling is essential for any kind of tool changing device and has been used on the developed printer. Usually it is realized with a contact surface on the carriage and a corresponding part on the tool it is supposed to pick up. When pressed together both sides form exactly six contact points removing all degrees of freedom and providing a precise and repeatable positioning. There are several designs in existence to achieve this number of contact points but the most popular is the Maxwell design (Slocum 2010), which has been used also in this work. Hereby the "female part" of the coupling consists of three grooves arranged in a triangle (Fig. 1C). Corresponding balls on the counterpart ("male part") only contact the parallel edges of the "groves" at one point each, resulting in the targeted positioning (Fig. 1D). For the implementation in this study, two parallel rods were used providing the same functionality as the grooves.

2.3 Lock Mechanism

To keep the interface physically connected an additional force is needed. Since a directly driven tool for a 3D-printer weighs more than 500 g and is about 100 mm long, a mechanical fixation was chosen, because other mechanisms (e.g. electromagnetic attraction) are too sensitive to the resulting torque. This fixation schematically shown in Fig. 2 is based on a "lock-and-key-principle". A stepper motor with a shortened lead screw moves a rotatable mounted T-shaped key. Driving the motor causes the key to rotate inside the lock (Fig. 2A/B). The lock contains one vertical and one horizontal barrier restraining the keys free rotation to an angle of 90°. When hitting the horizontal barrier the key stops rotating and starts retracting towards the stepper motor (Fig. 2C/D). Thus, it presses the "male" and the "female" side of the kinematic coupling together fastening the connection. To unlock a tool, the motor is driven counterclockwise, releasing the key from the physical connection and rotating it back until the vertical barrier stops it. Once stopped, the key is further extended to ensure no physical connection and safe release from the lock.

Using this approach, the coupling mechanism provides a high tolerance against fabrication deviations of the coupling interface. While being retracted and unretracted, the key crosses a distance of up to 5 mm and is able to pick up a newly assembled tool without any calibration.

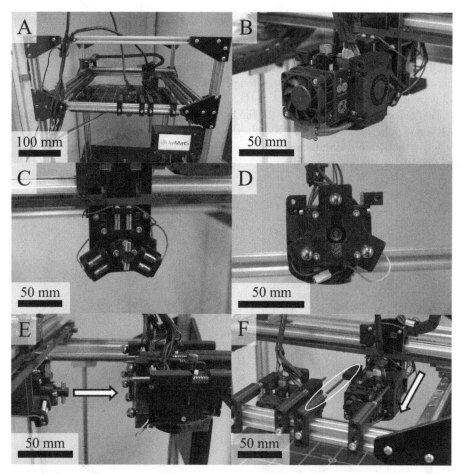

Fig. 1. 3D-printer with on demand tool changing based on a Cartesian geometry. **A:** Printer with one docked tool and one located on the carriage. **B:** Print-head with 3D-printed fan mount. **C:** "Female side" of the kinematic coupling with T-lock in its center (cables soldered to the metal rods to use them as sensor and power supply for a fan on the tool). **D:** "Male side" of the kinematic coupling with keyhole in its center (cables soldered to the metal balls). **E:** Carriage about to pick up a tool from its docking position (side view). **F:** Carriage about to push a tool on the two pins of its docking position (top view).

2.4 Additional Enhancements

During a multi-material print hundreds or even thousands of tool changes can be necessary. Further, the size of the printed object can require fabrication to take hours or even run over night. This extended run time can lead to serious damage if a tool cannot be released properly and then crashes into the next one. Thus, the device needs to recognize the presence of a tool and be able to check if the sensor feedback matches to the actual phase of the tool change process. The most suitable way to realize this is to use the conductive properties of the metal components coupling. By using one of the fixed balls of the tool side to close a circuit between the two rods of the "female side" (Fig. 1C top) the presence or absence of a tool can be detected.

In addition to a fan to cool the hot end, most filaments require a second fan that blows directly onto the extruded filament to accelerate solidification. This fan is located on the print-head as well, but in contrast to its temperature control it is only needed while the tool is in use.

That makes it possible to power the fan by utilizing the other coupling connections as + and − pole (Fig. 1C bottom). By this, the control of the print fan is independent of the active tool, eliminating the need to occupy additional slots on the controller board and simplifying the program code.

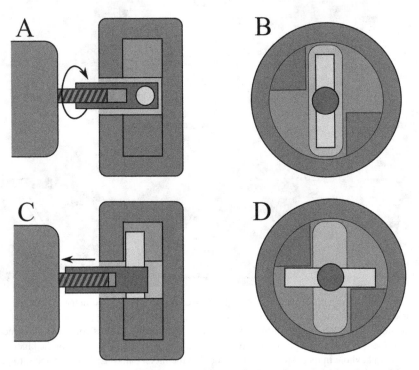

Fig. 2. Schematic illustration of the T-lock principle. **A:** Top view of the key inserted into the lock (unlocked). Driving the stepper motor rotates the key. **B:** Front view of the key inserted into the lock (unlocked), barriers are not touched. **C:** Top view of the locked state. Driving the stepper motor pulls the key and with it the tool towards the connector further fastening the connection and locking the system. **D:** Front view of the locked state. Horizontal barrier stops rotation.

2.5 Print-Heads

The core of each FFF (Fused-filament-fabrication)-print-head is a commercially available extruder-hotend combination driven directly by a stepper motor. In contrast to a Bowden extruder a directly driven one is able not just to handle classic stiff filaments but also very flexible materials, which are essential for the fabrication of soft robots. A constraining guidance of the filament inside the extruder is an additional enhancement to increase the quality of compressible elements. These components were outfitted with cooling fans and connectors for the wiring (Fig. 1B). The backside of the tool forms the "male interface" of the Maxwell coupling (Fig. 1D). Since the nozzle size can be selected specifically for each task, it is possible to tune each print-head for its specific purpose. Small or detailed structures can be printed with a smaller diameter than for example support structures. This saves process time and cost. Like the coupling mechanism, the print-heads do not rely on a precise fabrication. The attached parts and holders are 3D-printed and any resulting deviations can be compensated by defining an individual offset along each axis for the mounted tools.

3   Characterization

In order to characterize the developed device, a series of specimens was designed and fabricated. Hereby the focus was to evaluate the printer's ability to handle a flexible filament precisely and to combine it with traditional stiff materials, since these are the ongoing challenges in soft robotic research. All the specimens were constructed as chambers with an inlet to connect air supply and at least one flexible area that is able to expand under pressure. For the stiff parts polylactid (PLA) was chosen whereas thermoplastic urethane (TPU) served as a flexible material. All specimens were printed with a 0.4 mm nozzle diameter, a layer height of 0.1 mm and a speed of 8 mm/s.

3.1   Pneumatic Actuator

To test the performance of the used extruder, a cuboid actuator was printed with relatively thick and stiff bottom and top of 2.0 mm and thin, expandable sides of 0.8 mm thickness (Fig. 3A). At the bottom a hole was added with a diameter of 3.3 mm, which was slightly smaller than the connector to apply air pressure. The whole object was fabricated in one print process using "Recreus FilaFlex TPU 82A" filament without any support structures. The first layer of the ceiling was printed as hanging bridges from one side to the other. Although flexible filaments are much less convenient to print unsupported structures, the system is able to print them in a high quality. After a few slacking layers, a new stable foundation was formed and the printer continued building a precise and tight top.

Next, the finished chamber was connected to a pneumatic test bench that precisely regulates the applied air pressure. The first load of 1.0 bar confirmed the specimen to be airtight and resilient. During a second test, the pressure was slowly increased and the chamber continued to expand. Once pressure measured 2.5 bar, the connected silicon tube bursted (Fig. 3B).

3.2   Pneumatic Finger

As a second test specimen, a series of the described pneumatic pillows was printed next to each other with a spacing of 1 mm on top of a 7 mm thick backbone underneath, pneumatically connecting the actuators by a groove in the backbone (Fig. 3C). The silicone tube connector for the test bench was located at one of the short sides. The tests showed a significant deformation when pressure was applied. The expanding actuators caused the structure to bend and form a curvature towards the backbone before the connecting silicon tube failed at about 2.5 bar (Fig. 3D).

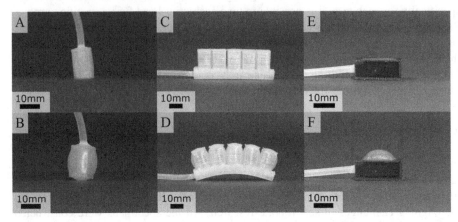

Fig. 3. 3D-printed specimen. **A:** Relaxed pneumatic actuator (0 bar). **B:** Expanded pneumatic actuator (2.5 bar). **C:** Relaxed pneumatic finger (0 bar). **D:** Bended pneumatic finger (2.5 bar). **E:** PLA housing with relaxed flexible membrane (0 bar). **F:** PLA housing with expanded flexible membrane (2.5 bar).

3.3 Stiff Actuator with Flexible Membrane

As L. R. Lopes and A. Silva pointed out (Lopes et al. 2018) the combined print of PLA and TPU necessarily results in material interfaces, which lower the load capacity of the object. Since both substances do not form a strong chemical bond with each other it is not possible to print them like a mono-material object and to expect a reliable and strongly connected result. However, the attachment suffices to print both materials on top of each other and enables a combined handling in additive manufacturing. To compensate for the lack of chemical bonding and form a functional structure, physical restrictions implemented by the design itself are required.

When creating functional pneumatic structures it is usually clearly defined which parts are meant to deform and which are not. Also taking into account the lower costs and better print properties of traditional stiff filaments like PLA it would be desirable to form the functional element solely from TPU, as shown in Fig. 3E. This figure depicts a pneumatic chamber similar to the ones previously described; however this chamber is completely made of PLA except for a flexible membrane in the center of one side. Unlike previous iterations, in the latest version of the demonstrator the flexible elements were printed in direct contact with the print bed. This adjustment enables a much thinner design of the membrane of just 0.3 mm. When pressed onto the built surface, the TPU forms a tight layer and is not restricted in its thickness by the nozzle diameter. The TPU then forms a frame upwards parallel to the stiff surrounding and ends up in a hook embedded in the PLA. Thanks to this design, more than 2.5 bar of pressure can be applied without any leakage at the material interface.

4 Conclusion

In order to address the ongoing challenge to fabricate complex functional parts for the research of soft robots, in particular how to combine different materials in complex geometries, this paper has presented the development of a novel 3D printer with on demand tool change. The developed locking mechanism is adaptive to quite large deviations of the counterpart and requires very little adjustment. In combination with the kinematic coupling, the locking mechanism enables the device to switch rapidly between the prepared tools. The directly driven FFF-print-heads that have been designed for this purpose showed an extrusion precise enough to create airtight chambers, which can be used as pneumatic actuators. The fabrication of cuboid cavities is hampered by hanging bridges in the first layers of the ceiling and therefore limits top layer thinness of a chamber, which is still airtight. Since the expandable sides of the chamber required at least two layers they were limited to 0.8 mm when using a 0.4 mm nozzle. Changing the orientation of the actuating membrane to the bottom side pushed these limits to 0.3 mm. The disadvantage is that all active elements per specimen have to be located there. This problem could be solved by using one print-head to fill cavities and gaps between membranes with soluble support filament. This approach could allow a variable number of thin actuating layers to be printed within one process as long as they are orientated parallel to the X/Y plane. The flexible TPU membrane integrated in a housing of stiff PLA has demonstrated the suitability of the printer for multi-material fabrication. The positively tested concept of embedding a hook-like structure in order to overcome the lack of chemical bonding between PLA and TPU could be modified in many ways and has the potential to lead to an all-in-one print of much more complex functions. Since the coupling mechanism is based on a rudimentary interface, the design of other compatible tools with different work principles is relatively feasible. Some conceivable examples of tools include an inkjet printhead, syringe extruders for high viscous substances or drills.

This novel FFF-multi-material printer and the printed demonstrators highlight the great potential to create yet unbuilt biomimetic structures and multi-material systems.

Acknowledgement. Funded by the Deutsche Forschungsgemeinschaft (DFG, German Research Foundation) under Germany's Excellence Strategy – EXC-2193/1 – 390951807. SC, FE & TS are grateful to the Deutsche Forschungsgemeinschaft for the funding our research.

References

Coyle, S., Majidi, C., LeDuc, P., Hsia, K.J.: Bio-inspired soft robotics: material selection, actuation, and design. Extreme Mech. Lett. **22**, 51–59 (2018). https://doi.org/10.1016/j.eml.2018.05.003

Gul, J.Z., et al.: 3D printing for soft robotics - a review. Sci. Technol. Adv. Mater. **19**(1), 243–262 (2018). https://doi.org/10.1080/14686996.2018.1431862

Khoo, Z.X., et al.: 3D printing of smart materials: a review on recent progresses in 4D printing. Virtual Phys. Prototyp. **10**(3), 103–122 (2015). https://doi.org/10.1080/17452759.2015.1097054

Lopes, L.R., Silva, A.F., Carneiro, O.S.: Multi-material 3D printing: the relevance of materials affinity on the boundary interface performance. Addit. Manuf. **23**, 45–52 (2018). https://doi.org/10.1016/j.addma.2018.06.027

Muth, J.T., et al.: Embedded 3D printing of strain sensors within highly stretchable elastomers. Adv. Mater. (Deerfield Beach Fla.) **26**(36), 6307–6312 (2014). https://doi.org/10.1002/adma.201400334

Rus, D., Tolley, M.T.: Design, fabrication and control of soft robots. Nature **521**(7553), 467–475 (2015). https://doi.org/10.1038/nature14543

Slocum, A.: Kinematic couplings: A review of design principles and applications. Int. J. Mach. Tools Manuf. **50**(4), 310–327 (2015). https://doi.org/10.1016/j.ijmachtools.2009.10.006

Trivedi, D., Rahn, C.D., Kier, W.M., Walker, I.D.: Soft robotics: biological inspiration, state of the art, and future research. Appl. Bion. Biomech. **5**(3), 99–117 (2008). https://doi.org/10.1080/11762320802557865

Zolfagharian, A., Kouzani, A.Z., Khoo, S.Y., Moghadam, A.A.A., Gibson, I., Kaynak, A.: Evolution of 3D printed soft actuators. Sens. Actuat.: Phys. **250**, 258–272 (2016). https://doi.org/10.1016/j.sna.2016.09.028

Kinematic and Kinetic Analysis of a Biomechanical Model of Rat Hind Limb with Biarticular Muscles

Kaiyu Deng[1]([⊠]), Nicholas S. Szczecinski[1], Alexander J. Hunt[2], Hillel J. Chiel[1], and Roger D. Quinn[1]

[1] Case Western Reserve University, Cleveland, OH, USA
kxd194@case.edu
[2] Portland State University, Portland, OR, USA

Abstract. This work presents a biomechanical model of rat hind limbs with biarticular muscles and includes kinematic and kinetic analyses. Our previous model only possessed antagonistic muscle pairs (extensor and flexor) to actuate each joint in the sagittal plane. In this model, we expanded the number of muscles in each limb from 6 to 8, including 3 biarticular muscles: BFP (biceps femoris Posterior), RF (Rectus femoris), and GA (Gastrocnemii). The knee flexor muscle was removed from the previous model. We also developed a new method to calculate the muscle parameter values, including the shape of the length-tension curve, which gives the muscle models more biomimetic response properties. In order to predict muscle stretch and the relationship between passive tension and step-phases during walking, we formulate the inverse kinematics for the limbs and muscles.

Keywords: Rat · Biarticular muscles · Synthetic nervous system · Inverse kinematic analysis

1 Introduction

Roboticists wish to capture the agility of animals in their robots and biologists wish to better understand how animals move. Unlike robot designs, which are usually minimalist, mammalian legged locomotion actuation is often redundant and highly complex. Biologists and roboticists alike often construct extremely simplified biomechanical models that capture only certain components of animal walking. This eases analysis, but makes the model less animal-like. However, a model that replicated all details of animal anatomy may not be appropriate, because it would be too complex to analyze, very difficult to simulate, and there are still many unknowns about how animals control locomotion. Therefore, balancing simplicity and fidelity is the key to designing an informative biomimetic robot or walking simulation model.

Previously, we improved the synthetic nervous system (SNS) of a biomechanical rat hindlimb model by implementing a two-layer neural system with both rhythm generator and pattern formation networks [1]. This model successfully reproduced rat nominal

© Springer Nature Switzerland AG 2020
V. Vouloutsi et al. (Eds.): Living Machines 2020, LNAI 12413, pp. 55–67, 2020.
https://doi.org/10.1007/978-3-030-64413-3_7

walking, hopping, and non-resetting deletions when periodic motions were perturbed. Also, its kinematics more closely matched those of the animal than the kinematics of the former model (Fig. 1). However, the newer model still failed to produce animal-like kinematics. It is possible that one major reason for this shortcoming is that it was actuated by pairs of antagonistic muscles at each joint, unlike the legs of mammals, which are overactuated. This poor kinematic modeling can also be found in other simplified models [2–5].

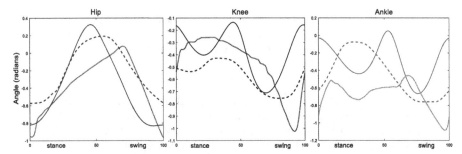

Fig. 1. Comparison of animal joint motion profiles with simulation results. Animal data (solid lines); simulation results from two-layer CPG with the knee–ankle synergy [1] (dashed lines); simulation results from Half-center CPG model [2] (dotted lines) with separate hip, knee and ankle pattern formation circuits. The two-layer CPG model shows closer approximation than the Half-center model in hip and shows better trajectories in knee. However, the phasing of the ankle joint is noticeably different between the animal and the models.

We hypothesized that the model kinematics could more accurately match the animal kinematics if we increased the biological accuracy of the biomechanical model. In rat anatomy [6], there are biarticular (i.e. spanning two leg joints) muscles in the hindlimb which were not taken into consideration in our previous work [1, 2]. Related modeling studies of cat [4, 5] that contain biarticular muscles in their biomechanical model show relatively better simulation results when compared to experimental data. Therefore, we believe biarticular muscles could help solve the issue of matching a rat's joint motion profile.

In this study, we present a new biomechanical model of the rat hind limb with biarticular muscles (BFP, RF, GA). Muscle properties are calculated from published biological data [12, 13]. Additionally, we perform kinematic and kinetic analysis of joint torques and passive muscle forces using the linear Hill muscle model to better understand the dynamics of the new model.

2   Methods

2.1   Biomechanical Modeling

The development of the rat hindlimb model was done in Animatlab [7], a simulation software that enables construction of biomechanical bodies using built-in materials or loading mesh files of skeletons (i.e. individual bones). Animatlab also provides a platform to design a synthetic nervous system (SNS) to actuate muscles and receive proprioceptive feedback. Our model has a simplified skeleton as described previously [1] to reduce simulation time needed to tune the neural parameters. The segments have biologically appropriate dimensional and inertial properties but are implemented with simplified geometrical shapes to speed the simulation. Also, the rat hindlimb model is limited to motion in the sagittal plane. All the muscle properties and insertion points come from the work of Johnson [8] and are transformed from bone centric coordinate systems to Animatlab local coordinate systems to better fit our model [9].

Before this work, there was few biomechanical hindlimb models simulating walking with biarticular muscles, and the neural control strategies used to control them are not fully understood. Therefore, we expanded the musculature from 3 pairs of antagonist muscles which actuate individual joints (Fig. 2A) to the 8 most prominent muscles used in forward locomotion [10], three of which are biarticular. These match similar studies investigating neural control of locomotion in cat [5] and human [11] walking with biarticular muscles (Fig. 2B).

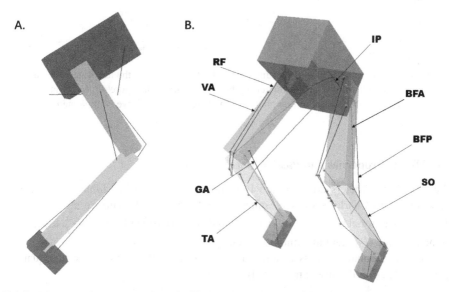

Fig. 2. Biomechanical model of rat hindlimb. (A) Previous model, using antagonist muscles to actuate each joint of the limb. (B) Biarticular model, 8 synergistic muscles cooperate together to actuate the whole limb, 3 of them are biarticular muscles (Red labels). IP: Iliopsoas; BFA: Biceps femoris anterior; BFP: Biceps femoris posterior; SO: Soleus; RF: Rectus femoris; VA: Vastii; GA: Gastrocnemii; TA: Tibialis anterior. (Color figure online)

The new model is composed of 5 monoarticular muscles: Iliopsoas (IP) and biceps femoris anterior (BFA), which actuate the hip joint; Vastii (VA), which actuates the knee joint; and Soleus (SO) and Tibialis Anterior (TA), which actuate the ankle joint. Additionally, there are 3 biarticular muscles: Biceps Femoris Posterior (BFP) and Rectus femoris (RF), which link the hip and knee joint; and Gastrocnemii (GA), which spans the knee and ankle joint.

2.2 Length-Tension Curve

In the previous model, the resting length of each muscle was set to the maximum length the muscle could reach via joint rotation, and thus the muscle always became stronger as the muscle lengthened. This reduced complexity of movement control, but is not biologically accurate. Figure 3 shows how resting length affects the length-tension curve.

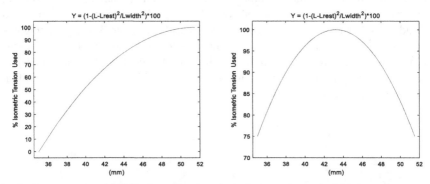

Fig. 3. Same muscle with different resting length. Left figure shows the length-tension curve in the previous model: Muscles get stronger as they lengthen. Right figure shows length-tension curve for the new model: The "falling phase" of the length-tension curve is implemented.

2.3 Muscle Properties and Passive Tension

The muscle parameters are modified from rat muscle data from Johnson's [12] and associated with Charles's work on mice [13]. The rat muscle data we are concerned about are the optimal fiber length (I_0), fiber length to muscle length ratio $\left(\frac{L_f}{L_m}\right)$, maximum isometric force (P_0), and maximum shortening velocity (v_{max}).

We can calculate the passive tension based on the following differential equation (passive force of Hill muscle model [7]):

$$\dot{T} = \frac{K_{SE}}{b}\left(K_{PE}\Delta x + b\dot{x} - \left(1 + \frac{K_{PE}}{K_{SE}}\right)T\right),$$

where Δx is the muscle length minus the resting length (if negative, $\Delta x = 0$), $\dot{x}$ is the muscle contraction velocity, the muscle resting length is defined as the midpoint of the operating range, b is the linear muscle damping, K_{SE} is the series elastic stiffness and K_{PE} is the parallel elastic stiffness.

The linear muscle damping is set to the ratio between maximum isometric force and maximum muscle velocity [14] as follows:

$$b = \frac{1.25P_0}{v_{max}/4}.$$

The series elastic stiffness is defined based on Wilkie's work [15, 16]. When the force is equal to the maximum isometric force, the deflection will be the shortening length of the tendon:

$$K_{se} = \frac{P_o}{I_o \cdot \left(1 - \frac{L_f}{L_m}\right) \cdot f_m},$$

where f_m is the maximum deflection ratio. We chose the value of 4 percent here, as used in Winter's study of Hill-based muscle modeling [17] and the Meijer study of rat medial gastrocnemius muscle [18].

The parallel elastic stiffness is calculated based on the observation that under max load at steady state, the series and parallel elastic components absorb all the force:

$$K_{PE} = \frac{K_{SE} \cdot P_0}{K_{SE} \cdot \left(I_o / \frac{L_f}{L_m}\right) \cdot f_m - P_0}$$

2.4 Inverse Kinematic Analysis

When developing a synthetic neural controller, it is necessary to calculate the desired motoneuron activations [2]. To do this, an inverse kinematic and kinetic analysis was developed to determine muscle attachments points, and therefore the muscle lengths, velocities and forces that lead to desired movements. Inverse kinematics also enables us to convert external forces acting on the feet into joint torques, via the Jacobian.

The analysis is done in Matlab, where the Animatlab model is loaded in and a leg object is automatically constructed [2]. We utilized experimental rat joint profiles from previous work [1] and the following rotational transformation matrix to reproduce rat hind limb walking and track limb segment positions:

$$P(i) = P(i - 1) + C(i - 1) \cdot P_b(i) + C(i - 1) \cdot [I - c(i)] \cdot R(i) \cdot P_j(i)$$

where $P(i)$ is the i th limb segment center of mass position during walking, $P(1)$ is the position of the pelvis, which is [0,0,0]; $P_b(i)$ is the ith limb segment center of mass position relative to the proximal segment of the ith segment; $P_j(i)$ is the ith joint position relative to distal segment of ith joint. I is 3×3 identity matrix and $R(i)$ is the ith segment rotation matrix described below, α, β, γ is a set of Euler angles for the ith segment relative to the proximal segment:

$$R(i) = \begin{bmatrix} 1 & 0 & 0 \\ 0 & cos\alpha_i & -sin\alpha_i \\ 0 & sin\alpha_i & cos\alpha_i \end{bmatrix} \begin{bmatrix} cos\beta_i & 0 & sin\beta_i \\ 0 & 1 & 0 \\ -sin\beta_i & 0 & cos\beta_i \end{bmatrix} \begin{bmatrix} cos\gamma_i & -sin\gamma_i & 0 \\ sin\gamma_i & cos\gamma_i & 0 \\ 0 & 0 & 1 \end{bmatrix}$$

$c(i)$ and $C(i)$ are the joint rotation matrix and accumulative joint rotation matrix based on the ith joint angle (θ_i) during walking:

$$C(i) = C(i - 1) \cdot c(i)$$

$$c(i) = \begin{bmatrix} cos\theta_i + u_x^2(1-cos\theta_i) & u_xu_y(1-cos\theta_i) - u_zsin\theta_i & u_xu_z(1-cos\theta_i) + u_ysin\theta_i \\ u_yu_x(1-cos\theta_i) + u_zsin\theta_i & cos\theta_i + u_y^2(1-cos\theta_i) & u_yu_z(1-cos\theta_i) - u_xsin\theta_i \\ u_zu_x(1-cos\theta_i) - u_ysin\theta_i & u_zu_y(1-cos\theta_i) + u_xsin\theta_i & cos\theta_i + u_z^2(1-cos\theta_i) \end{bmatrix},$$

where u is the joint's axis of rotation vector.

3 Results

3.1 Muscle Parameters

Few researchers have calculated the muscle parameter values (Table 1) according to the method described in the muscle properties section. The ratio of K_{SE} to K_{PE} is approximately 3 to 4 for all of the muscles in our new approach, rather than 1×10^6 as in our previous work [1, 2]. Vivekanandan's study of modeling frog gastrocnemius calf muscle [19] reports a ratio of 2.173; our rat GA ratio is 3.134.

Table 1. Muscle parameters in our model as calculated and based on biological data.

Muscle name	Damping (Ns/m)	K_{SE} (N/m)	K_{PE} (N/m)	$\frac{K_{SE}}{K_{PE}}$	τ (ms)
BFA	24.0387	8549.7733	1973.1775	4.333	2.3
BFP	93.4076	25181.2137	7147.8885	3.523	2.9
VA	196.2	10571.1207	3515.5475	3.007	13.9
GA	224.1208	33823.6592	10792.5989	3.134	5
TA	158.9148	26729.0839	8867.1347	3.014	4.5
SO	79.9129	4274.1887	1421.8812	3.006	14
IP	135.0635	32055.7290	9742.6227	3.290	3.2
RF	381.7271	55397.1043	17294.4563	3.203	5.3

The time constant τ for all the muscles lies within the range of 2 ms to 14 ms. This time constant is the ratio between the damping and total stiffness of the muscle and can be calculated using the equation [14]:

$$\tau = \frac{b}{K_{SE} + K_{PE}}$$

Bawa's study of cat plantaris muscle [20] reports the muscle parameter as $b = 63$ Ns/m, $K_{SE} = 3724$ N/m, and $K_{PE} = 1010$ N/m, where the K_{SE}/K_{PE} ratio is 3.687 and $\tau = 13.3$. These values are similar to the values for our SO muscle, which is an apt comparison because they are both plantarflexion muscles. These similar parameter values support our modeling and tuning approach.

3.2 Muscle Profile During Walking

Since the muscle attachment points (origin, via waypoints, and insertion) are fixed on the limb segment, their motion can be calculated based on the motion of each limb segment. In this way, we calculated muscle length and velocity during leg movements.

Muscle simulated lengths (Fig. 4) are calculated by applying the recorded joint angles from walking live rats [1] (Fig. 1, Solid line) to the model. The lengths of monoarticular flexor muscles (IP, TA) are relatively proportional to joint motion, and the lengths of monoarticular extensor muscles (BFA, SO, VA) are relatively proportional to the negative of the joint motion. For the biarticular muscles, the GA muscle length is affected by both knee flexion and ankle extension, but it appears to depend more on the knee angle than the ankle angle. When compared to the ankle extensor muscle SO, the only similarity is at approximately 50% stride which shortens with relatively the same pace. The length trajectory of the other two biarticular muscles BFP and RF are nearly identical to the pair of monoarticular hip muscles and show no direct dependence on the knee angle. These results show that the knee and the ankle joints are strongly mechanically coupled through the GA muscle, which supports our hypothesis in our previous paper [1] that mechanical entrainment exists and may be important for local stability control.

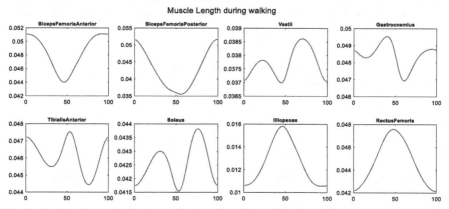

Fig. 4. Simulated muscle length profile during walking. The time frame has been normalized to one step period as in Fig. 1. The y axis is in meters (m). The length of extensor muscles is proportional to the corresponding joint's motion. The length of flexor muscles is negatively proportional to the corresponding joint's motion.

The muscle contraction velocity profiles (Fig. 5) are important for calculating the muscle tension in the next step of the process. Using the muscle length and velocity profile with the Hill muscle equation [7], we obtained the passive tension of each muscle during walking (Fig. 6). The force exerted on Stark's study of rat isolated soleus muscle [21] is 2.09 N and 1.39 N (5.23 and 4.63 N kg^{-1}) for complete isometric contraction when muscle is fixed. Similar values (5.65–6.55 N kg^{-1}) have also been reported by other researchers [22–24]. In our model, the maximum passive tension of SO is 3.118 N which is slightly higher, but considering that our model has fewer muscles than a rat, this higher passive tension is to be expected.

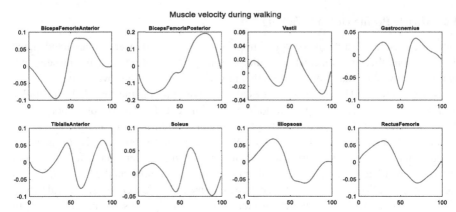

Fig. 5. Simulated muscle length profile during walking. The time frame has been normalized to one step period. The y axis's units are meters per second (m/s).

During walking, the active muscle force generates the desired joint torque and overcomes torques created by the passive muscle forces of the opposing muscle [2]. Thus, the passive tension profile gives us insight into the minimum amount of active tension that needs to be generated. Figure 6 shows that the passive tension from biarticular muscles is substantially higher than monoarticular muscles.

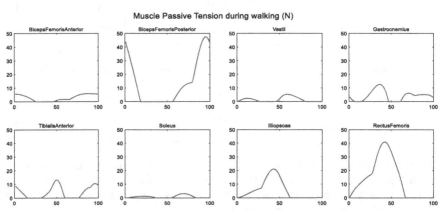

Fig. 6. Simulated muscle passive tension profile during walking. The time frame has been normalized to one step period. The tension magnitudes of biarticular muscles are typically greater than monoarticular muscles. Maximum tension in Soleus is 3.118 N, which is similar to that reported in related studies [21–24].

Figure 7 shows muscle tension trends in different phases of rat walking. During the touch down phase, the hip joint starts to extend. The BFA and BFP muscles are shortening; thus, the passive tension in these muscles is decreasing. The hip flexor muscles RF and IP show opposite trends. The knee joint is already flexed (slightly prior to touch down), causing the tension in affected muscles (BFP and GA) to start to decrease before the touch down phase. During knee extension, the RF and VA show the opposite trend. Passive force on the SO muscle starts to increase during ankle dorsiflexion.

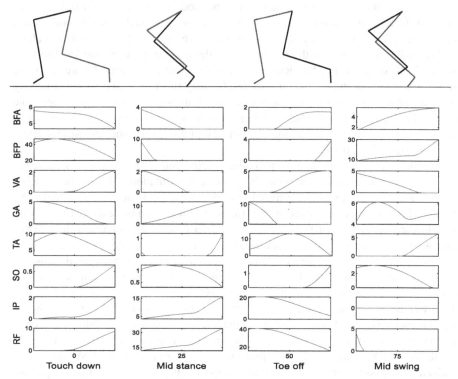

Fig. 7. Cartoon of different phases during simulated rat walking. The y axis is in Newtons and the x axis is normalized to a single stride. Each phase represents 20% of the gait cycle. The muscle passive tension trends are associated with the black color limb for each of four phases. Passive tension on muscles are closely related to joint motion. (Color figure online)

Around mid-stance phase, there is no passive tension in the BFA, BFP, VA and TA muscles since the muscle length is shorter than its resting length. But there is strong active tension acting on these muscles to continue ongoing movement. Passive tension in the antagonistic muscles increases, providing torques that would move the limb back to equilibrium. The exception is the SO muscle because the ankle is already in plantarflexion before the mid-stance phase; thus, its passive tension is decreasing.

The passive tension in the hip joint muscles is reciprocal during toe off and mid-swing phases as compared to the mid stance and touch down phases, since the hip motion is symmetrical between the stance and swing phases. However, the passive tension of muscles that span the knee and ankle joints is mirrored between the stance and swing phases, due to symmetrical kinematics between stance and swing phases. This further indicates that the passive tension in muscles is closely related to joint motion.

4 Discussion

In this manuscript, we present a biomechanical model of a rat hindlimb with biarticular muscles. This model is an expansion of our previous monoarticular model [1]. The largest difference in biomechanics between the new model and the previous one is that the number of muscles was increased from 6 to 8. This causes the forces acting about the knee joint to be substantially different from those in our previous model. The knee is now mostly controlled by biarticular muscles. The other joints' muscles are perturbed by the contraction of the biarticular muscles, but they function largely in the same way as in the previous model (i.e. as antagonistic pairs of muscles). Another difference is the knee and ankle synergies. Rather than producing a synergy by actuating these muscle sets with the same pattern formation network [1], in this model, they are mechanically coupled by the GA muscle.

In order to calculate the desired motoneuron activations, we used several new strategies in the inverse kinematics analysis. With the implementation of biarticular muscles, our previous method to estimate muscle parameter values is no longer suitable. We developed a more biomimetic technique which combines rat muscle data [12, 13] with other researchers' studies on muscle [15–18] to determine those parameter values. When compared with other researchers' reports [19, 20] of muscle parameter values, the similarities support that our approach is a feasible method for modeling biomimetic muscles. Moreover, the new analysis includes the falling phase of the length-tension curve, which models active tension production more accurately. Our previous work obtained the tension from the Hill muscle model, but the force buildup curve was different from that of actual muscle. The fact that our calculated parameters are consistent with experimental reports of the tension of rat soleus [21–24] suggests that our new method of tuning length-tension characteristics is an improvement over our previous method. Also, when analyzing the passive tension in different phases of walking, we found that the passive tension in the muscles is strongly related to joint motion.

Calculating the desired motoneuron activity makes it possible to develop a neural controller that produces that activity. Animatlab natively supports neural control modeling alongside the mechanical modeling, which is the main deference between it and other simulation software like OpenSim. Similar studies on cat [4, 5] and human [11, 25] have proposed control strategies that could help us develop a SNS that does so. The resulting neural controller would expand upon our previous work using a two-level neural system [1]. The increased number and types of muscles in the system would require the Pattern Formation Layer and muscle activation neurons to be expanded.

This hypothetical neural hierarchy (Fig. 8B) is similar to our previous designs (Fig. 8A), but more complex. As was done previously, the new SNS will use separate rhythm generator and pattern formation layers to activate muscles in the leg and generate forward walking. The main difference will be in the pattern formation network: Instead of using two pairs of synergies to control 6 muscles, we will use 3 pairs of synergies to control 8 muscles. These 8 muscles are organized into muscle groups and color coded in the SNS in Fig. 8B. Orange connections represent hip flexion; blue connections represent hip extension; brown connections represent knee extension; black connections represent knee flexion; green connections represent ankle plantarflexion; and the cyan connection represents ankle dorsiflexion. This study will provide fundamental information and insight into how biarticular muscles affect locomotion, and how this new biarticular muscle model reacts to perturbations when compared to our previous model and to animal behavior. Then, findings regarding how to best control biarticular muscles could be applied to our dog robot [3] or other legged robots.

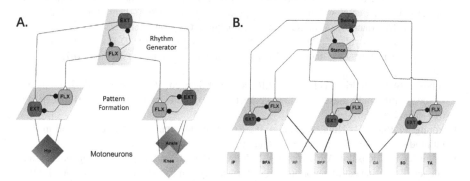

Fig. 8. General hierarchy of synthetic nervous system. (A) Previous model: the knee and ankle joint sharing the same pattern formation network to accomplish muscle synergy. (B) Hypothetical network for new biarticular model: using 3 separate joint pattern formation networks to distribute synergies through motoneuron pools. (Color figure online)

Moreover, as we designed this pipeline of constructing a rat hindlimb walking model by applying kinematic and kinetic analysis to neural control strategies, we could also model other locomotion gaits such as running, and explore the role of the hindlimbs in rearing and climbing. Other gaits will have significant influence on the movements and forces of the leg musculature and knee joint, which could be extended to legged robots.

Acknowledgements. This work was supported by grants from the US-German CRCNS program including NSF IIS160811.

Appendix

Copies of the Matlab code, Animatlab simulation files, raw data, and relevant figures and gifs can be found on-line at: https://github.com/vipamol/Rat-Waking.

References

1. Deng, K., et al.: Neuromechanical model of rat hindlimb walking with two-layer CPGs. Biomimetics **4**, 21 (2019)
2. Hunt, A.J., Szczecinski, N.S., Andrada, E., Fischer, M., Quinn, R.D.: Using animal data and neural dynamics to reverse engineer a neuromechanical rat model. Lect. Notes Comput. Sci. **9222**, 211–222 (2015)

3. Hunt, A., Szczecinski, N., Quinn, R.: Development and training of a neural controller for hind leg walking in a dog robot. Front. Neurorobot. **11**, 1–16 (2017)

4. Ivashko, D.G., Prilutsky, B.I., Markin, S.N., Chapin, J.K., Rybak, I.A.: Modeling the spinal cord neural circuitry controlling cat hindlimb movement during locomotion. Neurocomputing **52–54**, 621–629 (2003)

5. Markin, S.N., et al.: A neuromechanical model of spinal control of locomotion. In: Prilutsky, B.I., Edwards, D.H. (eds.) Neuromechanical Modeling of Posture and Locomotion. SSCN, pp. 21–65. Springer, New York (2016). https://doi.org/10.1007/978-1-4939-3267-2_2

6. Greene, E.C.: Anatomy of the Rat. Hafner Publishing Co., New York, NY, USA (1955)

7. Cofer, D., Cymbalyuk, G., Reid, J., Zhu, Y., Heitler, W.J., Edwards, D.H.: AnimatLab: a 3D graphics environment for neuromechanical simulations. J. Neurosci. Methods **187**, 280–288 (2010)

8. Johnson, W.L., Jindrich, D.L., Roy, R.R., Reggie Edgerton, V.: A three-dimensional model of the rat hindlimb: musculoskeletal geometry and muscle moment arms. J. Biomech. **41**, 610–619 (2008)

9. Young, F., Rode, C., Hunt, A., Quinn, R.: Analyzing moment arm profiles in a full-muscle rat hindlimb model. Biomimetics **4**, 10 (2019)

10. Prilutsky, B.I., Klishko, A.N., Weber, D.J., Lemay, M.A.: Computing motion dependent afferent activity during cat locomotion using a forward dynamics musculoskeletal model. In: Prilutsky, B.I., Edwards, D.H. (eds.) Neuromechanical Modeling of Posture and Locomotion. SSCN, pp. 273–307. Springer, New York (2016). https://doi.org/10.1007/978-1-4939-3267-2_10

11. Aoi, S., et al.: Neuromusculoskeletal model that walks and runs across a speed range with a few motor control parameter changes based on the muscle synergy hypothesis. Sci. Rep. **9**(1), 369 (2019)

12. Johnson, W.L., Jindrich, D.L., Zhong, H., Roy, R.R., Edgerton, V.R.: Application of a rat hindlimb model: a prediction of force spaces reachable through stimulation of nerve fascicles. IEEE Trans. Biomed. Eng. **58**(12), 3328–3338 (2011)

13. Charles, J.P., Cappellari, O., Hutchinson, J.R.: A dynamic simulation of musculoskeletal function in the mouse hindlimb during trotting locomotion. Front. Bioeng. Biotechnol. **6**, 61 (2018)

14. Freivalds, A.: Biomechanics of the Upper Limbs: Mechanics Modeling and Musculoskeletal Injuries. CRC Press, Boca Raton (2011)

15. Wilkie, D.R.: The relation between force and velocity in human muscle. J. Physiol. **110**(3-4), 249–280 (1949)

16. Wilkie, D.R.: The mechanical properties of muscle. Br. Med. Bull. **12**(3), 177–182 (1956)

17. Winters, J.M.: Hill-based muscle models: a systems engineering perspective. In: Winters, J.M., Woo, S.L.Y. (eds.) Multiple Muscle Systems. Springer, New York (1990)

18. Meijer, K., et al.: A Hill type model of rat medial gastrocnemius muscle that accounts for shortening history effects. J. Biomech. **31**(6), 555–563 (1998)

19. Vivekanandan, S., Emmanuel, D.S., Saluja, R.S.: Modelling of gastrocnemius muscle using Hill's equation in COMSOL Multiphysics 4.0 a. Int. J. Comput. Sci. Issues (IJCSI) **9**(3), 396 (2012)

20. Bawa, P., Mannard, A., Stein, R.B.: Predictions and experimental tests of a visco-elastic muscle model using elastic and inertial loads. Biol. Cybern. **22**, 139–145 (1976)

21. Stark, H., Nadja, S.: "F". J. Biomech. **43**(15), 2897–2903 (2010)

22. Close, R.l., Hoh, J.F.Y.: The after-effects of repetitive stimulation on the isometric twitch contraction of rat fast skeletal muscle. J. Physiol. **197**(2), 461–477 (1968)

23. Asmussen, G., Maréchal, G.: Maximal shortening velocities, isomyosins and fibre types in soleus muscle of mice, rats and guinea-pigs. J. Physiol. **416**, 245–254 (1989)

24. Monti, R.J., et al.: Mechanical properties of rat soleus aponeurosis and tendon during variable recruitment in situ. J. Exp. Biol. **206**(19), 3437–3445 (2003)
25. Rueckert, E., d'Avella, A.: Learned parametrized dynamic movement primitives with shared synergies for controlling robotic and musculoskeletal systems. Front. Comput. Neurosci. **7**, 138 (2013)

How to Reduce Computation Time While Sparing Performance During Robot Navigation? A Neuro-Inspired Architecture for Autonomous Shifting Between Model-Based and Model-Free Learning

Rémi Dromnelle[1]([✉]) [iD], Erwan Renaudo[2] [iD], Guillaume Pourcel[1] [iD],
Raja Chatila[1] [iD], Benoît Girard[1] [iD], and Mehdi Khamassi[1] [iD]

[1] Institut des Systèmes Intelligents et de Robotique (ISIR), Sorbonne Universités,
CNRS, 75005 Paris, France
remi.dromnelle@gmail.com
[2] Intelligent and Interactive Systems Lab (IIS), Universität Innsbruck,
6010 Innsbruck, Austria

Abstract. Taking inspiration from how the brain coordinates multiple learning systems is an appealing strategy to endow robots with more flexibility. One of the expected advantages would be for robots to autonomously switch to the least costly system when its performance is satisfying. However, to our knowledge no study on a real robot has yet shown that the measured computational cost is reduced while performance is maintained with such brain-inspired algorithms. We present navigation experiments involving paths of different lengths to the goal, dead-end, and non-stationarity (i.e., change in goal location and apparition of obstacles). We present a novel arbitration mechanism between learning systems that explicitly measures performance and cost. We find that the robot can adapt to environment changes by switching between learning systems so as to maintain a high performance. Moreover, when the task is stable, the robot also autonomously shifts to the least costly system, which leads to a drastic reduction in computation cost while keeping a high performance. Overall, these results illustrates the interest of using multiple learning systems.

1 Introduction

The idea of taking inspiration from how the brain coordinates multiple learning systems to enable more flexibility in robots is getting more and more attention in the robotics community [1–6]. One of the expected advantages of such a strategy would be for robots to autonomously learn which system is the most appropriate for each encountered task or situation. For instance, a robot can learn that different systems are efficient in different subparts of the environment

© Springer Nature Switzerland AG 2020
V. Vouloutsi et al. (Eds.): Living Machines 2020, LNAI 12413, pp. 68–79, 2020.
https://doi.org/10.1007/978-3-030-64313-3_8

[3]. Another expected advantage for a robot is to detect when it can avoid the computation time associated to a costly planning process and rely on cheaper systems if they enable to reach the same level of performance.

In computational neuroscience, reinforcement learning (RL) algorithms have been proposed to account for how animals initially solve a new task through planning within a model-based (MB) system, and progressively shift to model-free (MF) control when learning has converged [7,8]. MF learning is proposed to represent habit learning because it takes a long time to converge, but permits fast and efficient decisions after learning. Moreover, its slowness in learning makes it inflexible in response to task changes, requiring that the brain switches back to a control level similar to MB.

We have previously proposed a way to implement these principles within a classical three-layered robot cognitive architecture, to facilitate integration with other sensing and control components, as well as permit future transfer to different robotic platforms [9]. Here, and after evaluating several arbitration mechanisms between MB and MF learning systems in a previous study [10], we present a novel one which dynamically deals between the quality of learning and the computation cost. We test the new algorithm during simulated and real robot navigation in a task involving paths of different lengths to the goal, dead-ends, and non-stationarity. We find that the algorithm flexibly and consistently switches to MB control after environmental changes, and to MF control when the task is stationary. Overall, the robot achieves the same performance as optimal MB control in the task, while dividing computation time by more than two.

In summary, we propose a MB/MF algorithm using an arbitration mechanism that coordinates the learning systems and efficiently reduces computation cost while maintaining performance. We evaluate the algorithm both on simulated and real robots.

2   Materials and Methods

2.1   A Robotic Architecture with a Dual Decision-Making System

The present work implements a classical three-layer robot cognitive architecture [11,12] composed of a decision, an executive and a functional layer. The decision layer of the proposed architecture (Fig. 1) is composed by two competing experts which generate action propositions, each with its own method and with its own advantages and disadvantages. These two experts are directly inspired by the currently conventional distinction in computational neuroscience models between goal-directed and habitual strategies [8]. The two experts run three processes in a row: learning, inference and decision. This layer is also provided with a meta-controller (MC) in charge of arbitrating between experts. The MC determines which expert's proposed action will be executed in the current state, according to an arbitration criterion.

After that, the decision layer sends the chosen action to the executive layer, who ensures its accomplishment by recruiting robot's skills from the functional layer. The latter consists of a set of reactive sensorimotor loops that control

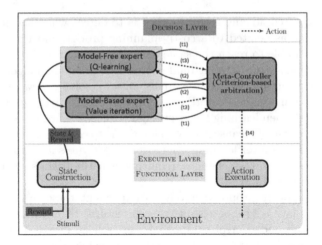

Fig. 1. The generic version of the architecture. Two experts having different properties are computing the next action to do in the current state s. They each send monitoring data to the meta-controller (MC) about their learning status and inference process (t1). The MC designate the winning expert according to a criterion that uses these data and authorizes it to carry out its inference and decision processes (t2). After making a decision, the winning expert sends its proposition to the MC (t3), which sends the action to the Executive Layer (t4). The effect of the executed action generates a new perception, transformed into an abstract Markovian state, and eventually a non null reward r, that are sent to the experts. Each expert learns according to the action chosen by the MC, the new state reached and the reward.

actuators during interaction with the environment. The robot reaches a new state and obtains or not a reward. The two experts use the new state and the reward information to update their knowledge about the executed action. This allows MB and MF experts to cooperate by learning from each others' decision.

Compared to our previous architecture [10], several changes have been made: The overall organization of the decision-making layer and the prioritization of communication between modules have been changed. The MF expert is no longer built as a neural network but as a tabular algorithm. The MC chooses which expert is the most suitable at a given time and in a given state, and no longer simply at a given time. And above all, we have defined a novel arbitration criterion that allows to reduce computational cost while maintaining performance.

2.2   The Decision Layer

Model-Based Expert. The MB expert learns a transition model T and a reward model R of the problem, and uses them to compute the values of actions in each state. These models allow to simulate over several steps the consequences of following a given behavior and to look for desirable states to reach. Consequently, when the robot realizes that the task has changed, it can use this knowledge of the world to instantly find the new relevant behavior. However, this search process is costly in terms of computation time as it needs to simulate several value iterations [13] in each state to find the correct solution.

Learning Process. The learning process of the MB consists in updating the reward and the transition models by interacting with the world. The transition model T is learnt by counting occurrences of transitions (s, a, s'). We build it using the number of visits $V_N(s, a)$ of state s and action a. $V_N(s, a)$ has a maximum value of N and $V_N(s, a, s')$ is the number of visits of the transition (s, a, s') in the last N visits of (s, a). The transition probability $T(s, a, s')$ is defined in (1). This leads to an estimation of the probability to the closest multiple of $1/N$.

$$T(s, a, s') = \frac{V_N(s, a, s')}{V_N(s, a)} \tag{1}$$

The reward model R stores the most recent reward value r_t received for performing action a in state s and reaching the current state s', multiplied by the probability of the transition (s, a, s').

Inference Process. Performing the process of inference consists in planning using a tabular Value Iteration algorithm [13]:

$$Q(s, a) \leftarrow \sum_{s'} T(s, a, s') \left[R(s, a) + \gamma max_{a'} Q(s', a') \right] \tag{2}$$

$Q(s, a)$ is the action-value estimated by the agent for performing the action a in the state s, $R(s, a)$ the probabilistic reward of the reward model R associated with the transition (s, a) and γ the decay rate of future rewards.

Decision Process. Performing the decision process consists in converting the estimation of action-values into a distribution of action probabilities using a softmax function, and drawing the action proposal from this distribution:

$$P(a|s) = \frac{\exp(Q(s, a)/\tau)}{\sum_{b \in \mathcal{A}} \exp(Q(s, b)/\tau)} \tag{3}$$

where τ is the exploration/exploitation trade-off parameter.

Model-Free Expert. The MF algorithm does not use models of the problem to decide which action to do in each state, but directly learns the state-action associations by caching in each state the earned rewards in the value of each action (action-values). Because updating the action-values is local to the visited state, the process is slow and the robot cannot learn the topological relationships between states. Consequently, when the task changes, the robot takes many actions to adopt the new relevant behavior. On the other hand, this method is less expensive in terms of inference duration.

Learning Process. Performing the learning process consists in estimating the action-value $Q(s, a)$ using a tabular Q-learning algorithm:

$$Q(s, a) = Q(s, a) + \alpha \left[R(s) + \gamma max_{a'} Q(s', a') - Q(s, a) \right] \tag{4}$$

$R(s)$ is the instant reward received for reaching the state s and γ the decay rate of future rewards and the s' the state reached after executing a.

Inference Process. Since the MF expert does not use planning, its inference process consists only in reading from the table that contains all the action-values the one that corresponds to performing the action a in the state s.

Decision Process. The decision process is the same as for the MB expert (3).

Meta-controller and Arbitration Method. The MC is in charge of selecting which expert will generate the behavior using a novel arbitration criterion which is a trade-off between the quality of learning and the cost of inference.

Quality of Learning. At each time step t, if the expert E is selected to lead the decision, its action selection probabilities (3) are filtered using a low-pass filter and stored by the system :

$$f(P(a|s, E, t)) = (1.0 - \alpha) * f(P(a|s, E, t - 1)) + \alpha * P(a|s, E, t) \qquad (5)$$

Else, no low-pass filter is applied:

$$f(P(a|s, E, t)) = f(P(a|s, E, t - 1))$$

Using the filtered action probability distribution $f(P(a|s, E, t))$, the MC can compute the entropy $H(s, E, t)$ of each expert, which has previously been found to reflect the quality of learning in humans [14]:

$$H(s, E, t) = -\sum_{a=0}^{|\mathcal{A}|} f(P(a|s, E, t)) \cdot log_2(f(P(a|s, E, t))) \qquad (6)$$

Cost of Inference. At each time step t and for each state s, the duration $T(s, E, t)$ of the inference process of each expert is recorded and filtered in the same way as the action selection probabilities (5).

Arbitration Criterion. Using the quality of learning and the cost of inference, the MC computes one expert-value $Q(s, E, t)$ for each expert:

$$Q(s, E, t) = -(H(s, E, t) + \kappa T(s, E, t)) \qquad (7)$$

where $\kappa = e^{-\eta H(s, MF, t)}$ allows to weight the impact of time in the criterion: The lower the entropy of the distribution of MF action probabilities, the more weight the time taken to perform the inference process has in the equation. η is a constant parameter ($\eta = 7$) weighting the entropy term and set according to a Pareto front analysis [15] (not shown here). We were looking for a κ that minimizes the cost of inference, while maximizing the agent's ability to accumulate reward over time.

Finally, the MC converts the estimation of expert-values $Q(s, E, t)$ into a distribution of expert probabilities using a softmax function (3), and draws the expert proposal from this distribution. The inference process of the unchosen expert is inhibited, which thus allows the system to save computation time.

General Information. Similarly to the Rmax algorithm [13], we initialized the action-values to a value of 1 so to help exploration of non-previously selected actions, since the action-values are updated according to the previous ones.

For the MF expert, we conducted a grid search to find the best parameter-set, i.e. parameters maximizing the total accumulated reward over a fixed duration of 1600 timesteps. We experimentally found that the duration of 1600 actions is a good trade-off between the time needed by the MF to start learning and a reasonable experiment time (1600 actions correspond to about 5 hours of real experiment). We found $\alpha = 0.6$, $\gamma = 0.9$ and $\tau = 0.02$. For the MB expert, we chose $\gamma = 0.95$ and $N = 6$. For the MB expert and the MC, we chose the same value of τ as the MF expert.

2.3 The Experimental Task

We evaluated our cognitive architecture in a navigation task. Since running 1600 actions on the robot takes about six hours, we have created a simulation of the task where the probabilities of transitions are derived from a 13 h exploration of the real arena (without the reward). This simulation allowed us to quickly test multiple coordination criteria and parameterizations, before evaluating them on a real robot.

We used 2.6 m 9.5 m arena containing obstacles (Fig. 2), and a turtlebot. The computer uses ROS [16] to process the signals from its sensors, controls the mobile base and interfaces with our architecture. A Kinect-1 sensor returns an estimate of distance to obstacles in its field of view, completed by contact sensors at the front and sides of the mobile base. The robot localizes itself using the gmapping Simultaneous Location and Mapping Algorithm (SLAM, [17]). During a preliminary environmental exploration phase, the robot incrementally builds a topological map by adding evenly spaced centers, and thus autonomously creating new Markovian states (Fig. 2. A). The current state (of the corresponding MDP) is the closest center from the robot when its previous action is completed and it evaluates the consequences. We chose to build this map beforehand and to reuse it for each of the learning experiments, so as to reduce the sources of behavioral variability. However, note that with the present method the system could start with an empty map and build it incrementally, and that a new map could be used for each experiment.

In this experiment, the robot must learn to reach a specific state of the environment (state 18 – see Fig. 2. B). When it succeeds, it receives a unitary reward and is randomly returned to one of the two initial positions, located in the extremities of the arena (states 0 and 32), to start over. The goal of the robot is first to reach state 18. The experiment involves a stable period where the environment and reward do not change (i.e., until action 1600), followed by a task change where the reward is moved from state 18 to state 34. We also made a second series of experiments where the reward is fixed but obstacles are introduced in the environment. As the state space, the action space is a discrete space. Here, performing an action consists of going forward along 8 equally distributed allocentric directions (Fig. 2. A). As long as the robot has not

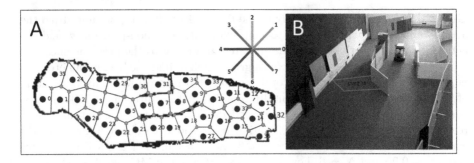

Fig. 2. A. Map of the arena's states. The eight-pointed star indicates the direction (in the map) of each robot actions. **B.** Photo of the arena and a turtlebot heading into the middle corridor. The state 18 (initial reward location) is represented in red. (Color figure online)

changed state, the action is not considered as completed. However, if while the robot moves forward, its contact sensors are activated (it bumps into a wall), then it will move back 0.15 meters and the action is considered as completed. Finally, according to the exact position in which the agent is located within a state, the arrival state will not necessarily be identical for the same action performed. The environment is therefore probabilistic, which multiplies the possibilities for the agent. For the MB expert, this specificity implies that the transitions $T(s, a, s')$ and the rewards $R(s, a)$ are stored respectively in the model of transition T and the model of reward R as probability distributions.

3   Results

We first present the results obtained when a virtual agent performs the task in a simulated environment, and then, the replication of these results in the real environment with a Turtlebot.

3.1   Simulated Task

To evaluate the performance of the virtual agent, we studied four combinations of experts: (1) a MF only agent using only the MF expert to decide, (2) an MB only agent using only the MB expert to decide, (3) a random coordination agent (MC-Rnd) which coordinates the two experts randomly and (4) an Entropy and Cost agent (MC-EC) which coordinates the two experts using the model of arbitration presented in 2.2. We also compare our agent to an agent using a reference learning algorithm in the literature, a DQN [18]. We evaluated iteratively several networks with various number of layers and size of layers, and selected the set of parameters that achieved the best performance. The neural network composed of two hidden layers of 76 neurons which takes as input a vector of size 38 (corresponding to the activity of the states, with 1 if the state is active, and 0 if

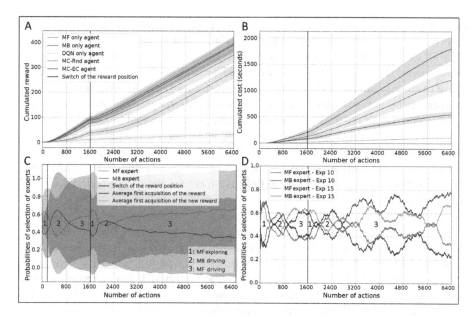

Fig. 3. A. Mean performance for 100 simulated runs of the task. The performance is measured as the cumulative reward obtained over the duration of the experiment. The duration is represented as the number of actions performed by the agent. We use standard deviation as dispersion indicator. At the 1600th action, the reward switches from the state 18 to the state 34. **B**. Mean computational cost for 100 simulated runs of the task. The computational cost is measured as the cumulative time of the inference process over the duration of the experiment in seconds. **C**. Mean probabilities of selection of experts by the MC using the Entropy and Cost criterion for 100 simulated runs of the task. These probabilities are defined by the softmax function of each expert. **D**. Probabilities of selection of experts by the MC using the Entropy and Cost criterion for 2 simulated runs of the task. (Color figure online)

not), returns a vector of size 8 (corresponding to the 8 action-values of the active state) and uses experience replay. Its parameters are $\alpha = 0.1$ $\gamma = 0.95$ and $\tau = 0.05$.

We define the "optimal behaviour" as the behaviour that allows the agent to accumulate the most reward over time (Fig. 3. A). As expected, the MF only agent (red) takes longer to reach the optimal behaviour. On the other hand, the MB only agent (blue) has the best performance. The MC-EC agent (purple) has a non-significantly different performance from the MB only agent, showing that our coordination method does not penalize the agent in terms of cumulated reward. In addition to that, it performs better than the MC-Rnd agent (green) suggesting that our coordination method is more effective than chance to accumulate reward over time. At the 1600th action, the environment is modified (change of reward state). The MF only agent takes longer to recover from environmental change than the other agents. Indeed, the MF expert does not use planning method and only updates its action-values locally: a method that takes longer to be effective. Finally, we can observe that the DQN agent learns and adapts less well than all other agents. As it is a model-free algorithm, it is not surprising that agents using the MB expert are more efficient and adaptive. The DQN is also worse than our tabular MF because it has much more memorized values (i.e. the weights of the network) to adapt before being able to provide correct outputs: the training of deep neural networks generally require several hundred thousand iterations. Such number are much too large, when targeting applications to real robot experiments, where learning on-the-fly is required. Replay mechanisms, or training in simulation, could be used to speed-up learning of the DQN, but these additional computations would clearly increase the computational cost of the resulting system.

Unsurprisingly, the MF only agent has a very low computational cumulated cost (Fig. 3. B) since its inference process simply consists in reading from the table that contains all the actions-values, while the MB only agent has a high computational cost, because its inference process is a planning method. The MC-EC agent, which exhibits a performance similar to the MB, has a computational cost three times smaller: the average cumulative time at the end of the experiment spent by the MB only agent on its inference process is1750 s versus 500s for the MC-EC agent at action 6400. It is to be noted that the meta-controller has in any case a very low cost, similar to the MF expert, of 10^{-5} seconds per iteration on average. In this system, only the MB expert is expensive, with an average cost of 10^{-2} seconds per iteration. The cost of using a meta-controller is therefore negligible compared to what it brings in terms of overall savings.

The dynamics of the selection of the experts by the MC, expressed in terms of selection probabilities (Fig. 3. C), displays three different phases:

The MF Exploring Phase (1 on Fig. 3. C). Before the discovery of the position of the reward, the agent uses mainly the MF expert. This is due to the difference in the method for updating action-values between the two experts. With the same initial values and the set of parameters we have defined, the action-values of the MF expert decrease slightly more than those of the MB expert, which drives a more pronounced decrease of the entropy of the action probability distribution. In addition, since we do not have an expert specialized in exploration, it makes sense to use the cheapest expert until the position of the reward has been discovered. About exploration, other studies propose to deal between three experts: a MB expert, a MF expert and an expert specialized in the exploration of the environment [3].

The MB Driving Phase (2 on Fig. 3. C). After finding the first reward the MB expert progressively takes the lead on the decision because its process of inference needs only to find the reward once to spread action-values into its transition model. It finds the reward more easily than the MF expert, and so, its performance increases.

The MF Driving Phase (3 on Fig. 3. C). The MF expert learns by demonstration from the MB expert, and thus spreads action-values from state to state and eventually, towards the 800th action, it reaches the performance of the MB expert. Because the MF expert is less expensive, the model of arbitration gives it the lead on the decision.

A MF exploring phase starts again at the 1600th action when the rewarded state moves from state 18 to 34. Then, the MB driving and the MF driving phases repeat.

The large standard deviation is explained by the fact that for each experiment, the agent's strategy and behaviour can be very different, notably due to the large number of states and possible actions, but also to the probabilistic nature of the environment. As a result, the time of the switches from one phase to another varied a lot from one individual to another. Nevertheless the individual behavior of each run is consistent with the average behavior presented here (Fig. 3. D).

3.2   Real Task

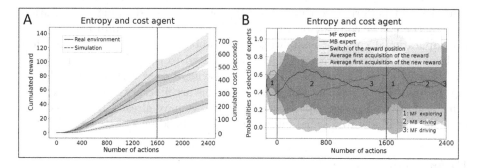

Fig. 4. A. Mean performance (brown) and cost (cyan) for 100 simulated runs (dashed curves) and 10 real runs (solid curves) of the navigation task for the MC-EC agent. **B**. Mean probabilities of selection of experts by the MC using the Entropy and Cost criterion for 10 real runs of the task. (Color figure online)

We evaluated our model of coordination on a real robot to verify that these results cross the reality-gap. Figure 4. A compares the performance and the cost of the MC-EC agent and the real robot (both use the same model of arbitration). The reality gap is visible, with a drop in performance and a cost increase for the real robot compared to the simulation. However, the model still allows the real robot to learn and accumulate reward over time in the same way, and the economy of cost remains advantageous.

Figure 4. B shows the dynamics of selection of the experts by the MC, for the experiments in real environment with the real robot. Again, the three-phases pattern is present, with only a 300 actions mean delay at the beginning of the third phase.

We obtained similar strategy alternations with the environment change consisting of obstacles introduction without moving the reward. We also observed that geographical patterns of coordination of experts emerged over time. These results won't be presented in details here because of space limitations.

4   Discussion

We analyzed the behavior of a three-layered robotic architecture integrating neuro-inspired mechanisms for the coordination of MB and MF reinforcement learning. The novelty relies in the explicit online measure of performance and cost of each system, so as to give control to the system with best current trade-off between the two. We presented real and simulated navigation results in a complex, non-stationary indoor environment. The arbitration criterion proposed in this work allowed the robot to autonomously determine when to shift between systems during learning, generating a coherent temporal decision-making pattern that alternates between strategies over time. This promoted more flexibility than pure MF control in response to task changes, and permitted to reach the same level of performance than pure MB control, while dividing computation time by three. The comparison with DQN showed that using end-to-end RL has a computational cost not compatible with robotic constraints, and that thus building and using a data representation adapted to the task at hand reduces the burden on the RL part of the system, allowing for low-cost on-the-fly learning. In future work, we plan to test whether this architecture is generalizable to other scenarios and larger spaces states, which we have already begun to do by applying our model to a social interaction task defined by 112 states [19].

References

1. Meyer, J.-A., Guillot, A.: Biologically-inspired robots. In: Handbook of Robotics (B. Siciliano and O. Khatib, eds.), pp. 1395–1422. Springer, Berlin (2008). https://doi.org/10.1007/978-3-540-30301-5_61
2. Dollé, L., Khamassi, M., Girard, B., Guillot, A., Chavarriaga, R.: Analyzing interactions between navigation strategies using a computational model of action selection. In: International Conference on Spatial Cognition, pp. 71–86 (2008)
3. Caluwaerts, K., et al.: A biologically inspired meta-control navigation system for the Psikharpax rat robot. Bioinspiration Biomimetics **7**, 025009 (2012)
4. Zambelli, M., Demiris, Y.: Online multimodal ensemble learning using self-learned sensorimotor representations. IEEE Trans. Cogn. Dev. Syst. **9**(2), 113–126 (2016)
5. Banquet, J.-P., Hanoune, S., Gaussier, P., Quoy, M.: From cognitive to habit behavior during navigation, through cortical-basal ganglia loops. In: Villa, A.E.P., Masulli, P., Pons Rivero, A.J. (eds.) ICANN 2016. LNCS, vol. 9886, pp. 238–247. Springer, Cham (2016). https://doi.org/10.1007/978-3-319-44778-0_28
6. Lowrey, K., Rajeswaran, A., Kakade, S., Todorov, E., Mordatch, I.: Plan online, learn offline: efficient learning and exploration via model-based control. In: International Conference on Learning Representations (2019)

7. Daw, N., Niv, Y., Dayan, P.: Uncertainty-based competition between prefrontal and dorsolateral striatal systems for behavioral control. Nat. Neurosci. **8**(12), 1704–1711 (2005)
8. Khamassi, M., Humphries, M.: Integrating cortico-limbic-basal ganglia architectures for learning model-based and model-free navigation strategies. Front. Behav. Neurosci. **6**, 79 (2012)
9. Renaudo, E., Girard, B., Chatila, R., Khamassi, M.: Respective advantages and disadvantages of model-based and model-free reinforcement learning in a robotics neuro-inspired cognitive architecture. In: Biologically Inspired Cognitive Architectures BICA 2015, (Lyon, France), pp. 178–184 (2015)
10. Renaudo, E., Girard, B., Chatila, R., Khamassi, M.: Which criteria for autonomously shifting between goal-directed and habitual behaviors in robots? In: 5th International Conference on Development and Learning and on Epigenetic Robotics (ICDL-EPIROB), pp. 254–260. (Providence, RI, USA) (2015)
11. Gat, E.: On three-layer architectures. In: Artificial Intelligence and Mobile Robots. MIT Press (1998)
12. Alami, R., Chatila, R., Fleury, S., Ghallab, M., Ingrand, F.: An architecture for autonomy. IJRR J. **17**, 315–337 (1998)
13. Sutton, R.S., Barto, A.G.: Introduction to Reinforcement Learning, 1st edn. MIT Press, Cambridge (1998)
14. Viejo, G., Khamassi, M., Brovelli, A., Girard, B.: Modelling choice and reaction time during arbitrary visuomotor learning through the coordination of adaptive working memory and reinforcement learning. Front. Behav. Neurosci. **9**(225) (2015)
15. Powell, T., Sammut-Bonnici, T.: Pareto Analysis (2015)
16. Quigley, M., et al.: ROS: an open-source robot operating system. In: ICRA Workshop on Open Source Software (2009)
17. Grisetti, G., Stachniss, C., Burgard, W.: Improved techniques for grid mapping with Rao-blackwellized particle filters. Trans. Rob. **23**, 34–46 (2007)
18. Mnih, V., et al.: Human-level control through deep reinforcement learning. Nature **518**, 529–533 (2015)
19. Dromnelle, R., Girard, B., Renaudo, E., Chatila, R., Khamassi, M.: Coping with the variability in humans reward during simulated human-robot interactions through the coordination of multiple learning strategies. In: The 29th IEEE International Conference on Robot & Human Interactive Communication (2020)

An Image-Based Method
for the Morphological Analysis of Tendrils
with 2D Piece-Wise Clothoid
Approximation Model

Jie Fan[1,2(✉)], Francesco Visentin[2], Emanuela Del Dottore[2],
and Barbara Mazzolai[2(✉)]

[1] The BioRobotics Institute, Scuola Superiore Sant'Anna, Pontedera, Italy
jie.fan@santannapisa.it
[2] Center for Micro-BioRobotics@SSSA, Istituto Italiano di Tecnologia,
Viale Rinaldo Piaggio, 34, 56025 Pontedera, Italy
{jie.fan,francesco.visentin,emanueladel.dottore,barbara.mazzolai}@iit.it

Abstract. In this work, we present an image-based method based on 2D piece-wise clothoid for curvature approximation, that is used to analyse the morphology of natural tendrils. Starting from our previous work, here we present an advancement of the sorting skeletonization algorithm which now can handle abrupt changes in the direction of the extracted points. Furthermore, we present an automatic method to identify the minimum number of 2D piece-wise clothoid spirals needed to represent a given tendril. In our tests, we found that a range of 4–6 segments were enough to correctly represent curling shapes with high accuracy ($R^2 > 0.9$). The approach can be adopted for the morphological analysis of continuum growing structures, to gain new insights for designing and developing new intelligent robotic systems, such as controllable tendril-like soft robot for exploration of complex environments.

Keywords: Bio-inspiration · Morphological analysis · Soft robotics · 2D piece-wise clothoid · Tendril-like structure · Dynamic programming.

1 Introduction

Bio-inspiration has been guiding and pushing the development of new robotic artefacts. Starting from animals inspiring design and behavior of soft robots, e.g., octopus [1,2], elephant trunk [3], and other animals [4,5], now also plants are the source for new paradigms in robotics [6] and are contributing to the development of innovative technologies [7]. Among many, climbing plants have peculiar

This work has received funding from the European Union's Horizon 2020 Research and Innovation Program under Grant Agreement No. 824074 (GrowBot).

© Springer Nature Switzerland AG 2020
V. Vouloutsi et al. (Eds.): Living Machines 2020, LNAI 12413, pp. 80–91, 2020.
https://doi.org/10.1007/978-3-030-64313-3_9

features which are worth studying [8] to further push technological advancements. They possess specific climbing mechanisms, like stem twining or specialized organs such as tendrils [9], that can be used for designing robotic artefacts with peculiar morphological compliance and integrated intelligent behaviour to negotiate with the complicated surrounding.

Tendrils are specialized, long, filiform, and sensitive organs derived from reproductive structures. Mechanical stimuli trigger in the plant to curl around a supporting structure and direct its growth in an anti-gravity fashion to search for light [10].

According to Darwin [11], tendrils move following three key phases: *circumnutation* in which they search and approach a support, *contact coiling* where they touch to confirm the ideal support and start coiling around it, and *free-coiling* in which they drag themselves towards the support by tightening the coil. The dynamic process of morphological changes reflects tendrils' sensing and decision-making capacity [12] during each perversion growth stage as a function of the external environmental stimuli. Noticeably, many botanists investigated the related morphology of tendrils focusing on their origin and development [9], developmental molecular genetics [13], flexibility property [14], and attachment adaptation [15].

Tendrils have inspired the development of several technologies, like artificial springs [16], safety crutches [17], and robots for space [18] and environmental [19] exploration. Recently, Must et al. [20] proposed a new tendril-like soft robot with reversible actuation based on the plant cell water-balance mechanism.

Even though, experimental and theoretical analysis have been already conducted to describe and understand the mechanisms behind the morphing of tendrils [21], the current challenge in plant-inspired soft robotics remains the correct description of the shape evolution in such natural structures and the relationship between this evolution and the environmental triggering.

We previously approached this issue starting from the morphological analysis, by proposing and applying a piece-wise 2D clothoid spiral-based method that uses a semi-automatic image processing to extract and to represent tendril-like curling structures [22]. However, our approach was highly dependent on human tuned parameters and thus we did not achieve a full automatic optimal selection of segments.

In this paper, we extend our image-based methodology by approximating curling structures with Euler spirals (or clothoids) model in Fresnel Integral with rational approximated form, to limit the number of free parameters and the computational complexity. Euler spirals are already known to well suit for resembling natural curling shapes having linear relations between the curvature and the arc length [23,24], but their application for the morphological modeling of real structures is very limited [25]. Here, we intend to apply such strategy and extend our previous work [22] to achieve the full automatic selection of the optimal number of segments and properly represent different configurations of natural tendrils. Automatizing this phase would allow fastening and make repeatable the process of long sequences analysis, during morphological studies of continuum growing structures.

In addition, we improved our sorting algorithm [22] for ordering 2D unarranged points in the skeleton, by introducing a weight-point association to prevent misleading ordering choices in the presence of sharp curvature change.

The results show that the automatic morphology reconstructing method is reliable and allows to properly describe the morphological evolution of a tendril after mechanical stimulation.

In the following Sect. 2, we present in details each of the steps involved in the proposed image-based morphology reconstruction method. Section 3 provides the analysis and results. And we conclude in Sect. 4 with discussions and future work.

2   Method

The image-based method we propose for the morphological analysis of tendrils and tendril-like structures is composed of five key macro steps, as shown in Fig. 1.

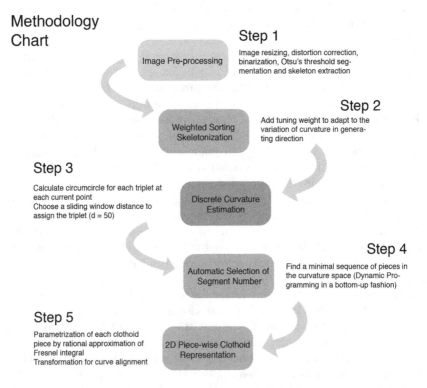

Fig. 1. The complete flowchart of the proposed method. To perform the morphological analysis, we start by pre-processing the acquired images and by performing the skeletonization to extract the points within the region of interest. Then, we estimate the curvature/arclength relationship for each point which is used to compute the minimum number of segments required to represent the tendril. Finally, for each segment we fit a 2D clothoid to obtain the full structure of the tendril.

The first step consists of a pre-processing stage, that includes the image resizing (300×380 pixels), distortion correction and binarization. Then, we apply a classic segmentation method (Otsu's thresholding) to identify the tendril part, and we fill the holes to find the largest region of interest (ROI). We can now extract the skeleton while preserving the topology structure in the ROI.

The points extracted from the skeleton cannot be directly used for the curvature fitting due to the possible presence of branches, holes, unordered regions and sharp corners, which prevent from understanding the correct sorting direction. We already proposed a sorting skeletonization algorithm to address most of the mentioned issues [22]. Here we address the specific issue introduced by the presence of sharp corners. An example of this condition is shown in Fig. 2a and Fig. 2b.

In the following sections, we describe in details each of the successive steps, starting from the weighted sorting algorithm, then we explain how to realize the discrete curvature estimation, the automatic selection of segments, and the shape fitting using the clothoid spirals.

2.1 Weighted Sorting Skeletonization

To define the shape direction from the unordered skeleton points obtained from the pre-processing phase, in [22] we proposed the CollectNeighboringPoints algorithm based on the Moving Least Squares Method (MLSM). The algorithm starts from a randomly chosen starting point (p_s, yellow circled point in Fig. 2c) in the skeleton and it first orders the points in one direction (red arrow), then in the other one (blue arrow). For each point of the skeleton (as in the case of p_t shown in Fig. 2c), it fits a line $L : y = ax + b$ (blue solid line in Fig. 2d) over the N neighboring points $p_i = (x_i, y_i), i \in [1, N]$ collected within a local circular area of radius R.

The sorting direction is determined based on a two-object classifier, where each class represents one of the two possible directions. The classification is achieved by performing the cross product of the vectors of the neighboring points over the direction vector of the fitting line L. This operation is iterated until reaching both ends of the skeleton with all points sorted and collected.

Figure 2d shows the classification of the points into two regions (cyan and magenta areas in figure) separated by a yellow dash-dotted line. The results (Fig. 2e) show that without using weights, a portion of the points in the skeleton remains uncollected (white line above the critical point p_t, Fig. 2e top view). This is because the classifier identifies all the candidate points p_i as belonging to the same class of the current point p_t. As a consequence, we cannot determine the next point to be sorted, p_t is treated as an end-point of the skeleton, and then the sorting loop ends.

To solve the problem, we introduced tuning weights, w_i, for each neighbouring point, p_i, within the radius, R, assigned according to the ratio of the Euclidean distance, $r = ||p_i - p_t||^2$, as follows:

$$w_i = e^{-r^2/R^2}. \tag{1}$$

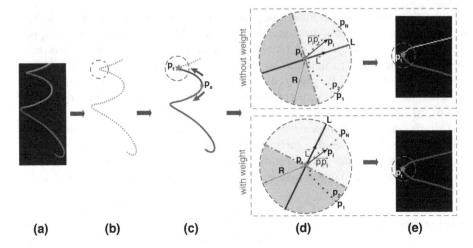

Fig. 2. Previous [22] and current skeleton sorting algorithm procedures. (a) A *passion-flower* tendril with complex morphology. (b) The unordered skeleton points extracted from the pre-processing step. The dashed circle highlights the case of sharp curvature. (c) An evolution of the sorting algorithm starting from point p_s. The following sequence shows how the case is approached by the previous (without weights, top row) and the current (with weights, bottom row) algorithm. (d) The neighbours of p_t are collected within a local circular area of radius R. The blue solid line denotes the fitting line, and the yellow dash-dotted line defines two classes. (e) The sorting results. In the case without weights, the points remain unordered (white line), while when weights are used, all the points of the skeleton are collected and ordered (blue line). (Color figure online)

In this way, we can ensure to strengthen the importance of closest points around the target sorting point, p_t. The fitting then provides a nonlinear diminishing fitting weights for each p_i by minimizing the function:

$$\mathcal{E}_{p_t}(p_1, p_2, \cdots, p_N) = \min_{a,b} \sum_{i=1}^{N} (ax_i + b - y_i)^2 \, w_i. \tag{2}$$

The classifier in the weighted sorting algorithm is now able to separate the points into two classes and all the points of the skeleton are included and sorted (blue line, Fig. 2e bottom view). The sorted points set is denoted as P_{srt} in the following.

2.2 Discrete Curvature Estimation

We now calculate the discrete curvature for the sorted skeleton. Discrete curvature for planar curve can be estimated by computing circumcircle for every triplet (p_{i-1}, p_i, p_{i+1}) at point p_i (Fig. 3b). We assigned a sliding window distance $(d = 50)$ to choose neighbouring points p_{i-d} and p_{i+d} along the skeleton.

Then, we obtained the circumcenter, the correspondent radius, R_i, from each triplet, and the corresponding curvature, k_i, defined as:

$$k_i = \frac{1}{R_i}, \quad \text{where } R_i = R_{circle}(p_{i-d}, p_i, p_{i+d}). \tag{3}$$

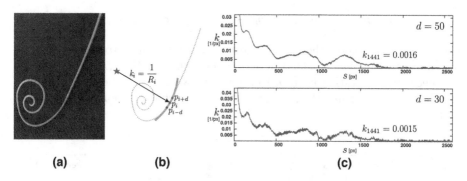

Fig. 3. (a) Displays a natural *passionflower* tendril. (b) Shows the sorted skeleton in yellow points, and the green colored arc shows the fitting circumcircle at point p_i for the triplet (p_{i-d}, p_i, p_{i+d}) with the given curvature $k_i = 1/R_i$. (c) Demonstrates the planar curvature estimation from discrete skeleton points using $d = 50$ (top) and $d = 30$ (bottom). An example of the curvature at point p_{1441} is given as a red dot. (Color figure online)

Then, each point with its own curvature is mapped from pixel-value space to arclength-curvature $(s - k)$ space. In this paper, we compute the arclength for each point, s_i, by integration of the Euclidean distance over each two adjacent points:

$$s_i = \sum_{j=1}^{i} ||p_j - p_{j+1}||_2. \tag{4}$$

The sliding window distance should be defined on the base of the image resolution. This ensures that the curvature is a constant among the triplet points. Also, the choice of the sliding window distance affects the whole curvature smoothness. For example, the case of $d = 30$ presents more noises with respect to a window of $d = 50$ (Fig. 3c).

2.3 Automatic Selection of Segment Number

Our goal is to define an optimal number of piece-wise clothoid curves to describe natural tendril and tendril-like structures and thus analyse their morphologies. An essential step is to define a method that automatically split the curve into the minimal sequence of pieces of linearly varying curvature. To solve the problem, we use dynamic programming[1] with an up-sweep approach. This allows to transfer the optimization of the whole shape into a series of optimal sub-problems. The problem is formalized as finding the minimum path (minimum number of segments) from a certain point, p_i, up to an ending point, p_j (with $i < j$), both selected from the set of sorted list of skeleton points $P_{srt} = \{p_1, p_2, \cdots, p_M\}$, having the minimum fitting error defined as:

$$\mathcal{J}(p_i, p_j) = \min_{i<k<j} \{\mathcal{J}(p_i, p_k) + \mathcal{J}(p_k, p_j), \; \epsilon + \mathcal{E}_{fit}(p_i, p_j)\}, \tag{5}$$

where $\mathcal{J}(p_i, p_j)$ denotes the $M \times M$ cost matrix of fitting errors over the connected piece-wise segments. On the right hand of the equation, $\mathcal{J}(p_i, p_k)$ denotes the specific configuration from p_i to a point p_k which lies in between the start and the end point. Similarly, $\mathcal{J}(p_k, p_j)$ denotes the configuration from p_k to the endpoint p_j.

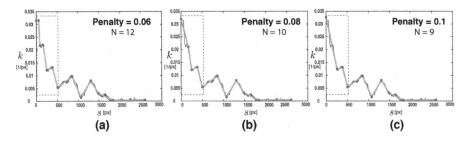

Fig. 4. Results for the automatic selection of segment number with different penalties. The larger the value we choose, the less segments we have (yellow lines), and more error is introduced. The green dashed boxes show the segmentation differences. (Color figure online)

The constant ϵ assigns a penalty factor to the path from p_i to p_j treated as a single segment. Figure 4 shows the fitting obtained with three penalties. The lower the value of ϵ, the higher the number of segments, thus the higher the accuracy. In this paper, we assigned $\epsilon = 0.03$.

The second error factor, $\mathcal{E}_{fit}(p_i, p_j)$, describes the minimal sum of the fitting errors caused by using linear regression on the segment from point p_i to p_j. It is defined as:

$$\mathcal{E}_{fit}(p_i, p_j) = \min_{a_{ij}, b_{ij}} \left(\sum_{t=i}^{j} |a_{ij} \cdot s_t + b_{ij} - \kappa_t|^2 \right), \tag{6}$$

where a_{ij} and b_{ij} are the slope and intercept of the least-square fitting line for all the points p_t between p_i and p_j, s_t and κ_t are calculated by Eq. 4 and Eq. 3 respectively.

---

[1] Bellman k-segmentation algorithm: https://justinwillmert.com/articles/2014/bellman-k-segmentation-algorithm/ .

We apply the dynamic programming method to update the matrix $\mathcal{J}$ by traversing all pairs of (p_i, p_j). Then, from the optimized cost, we select n elements, p_{s_i} with $i = 1, \ldots, n$, that identify the junction points of the piece-wise segments.

2.4 2D Piece-Wise Clothoid Representation

Once the number of segments is selected, the algorithm proceeds with the fitting with the 2D piece-wise clothoid spirals. The Cartesian coordinates of a 2D clothoid spiral can be parameterized by Fresnel integrals form defined as $\pi B \begin{pmatrix} \mathcal{C}(l) \\ \mathcal{S}(l) \end{pmatrix}$. For the purpose of computational efficiency, here we choose a rational approximation with 1.7×10^{-3} error [26], obtained by evaluating the error of polynomial approximation of the equations:

$$
\mathcal{C}(l) = \int_0^l \cos \frac{\pi}{2} \tau^2 \, d\tau \approx \frac{1}{2} - R(l) \sin \left(\frac{1}{2}\pi \left(A(l) - l^2 \right) \right),
$$

$$
\mathcal{S}(l) = \int_0^l \sin \frac{\pi}{2} \tau^2 \, d\tau \approx \frac{1}{2} + R(l) \cos \left(\frac{1}{2}\pi \left(A(l) - l^2 \right) \right),
$$

(7)

having:

$$
R(l) = \frac{0.506l + 1}{1.79l^2 + 2.054l + \sqrt{2}},
$$

(8)

$$
A(l) = \frac{1}{0.803l^3 + 1.886l^2 + 2.524l + 2},
$$

where l denotes the arclength along the clothoid from its initial position.

From normalization based on integration by substitution, we have each clothoid point as:

$$
x = \pi B \cdot \mathcal{C}(l') = \frac{\pi B}{\alpha} \int_0^{l'} \cos \tau^2 \, d\tau,
$$

$$
y = \pi B \cdot \mathcal{S}(l') = \frac{\pi B}{\alpha} \int_0^{l'} \sin \tau^2 \, d\tau,
$$

(9)

where $l' = \alpha l$ with $\alpha = \sqrt{\frac{\pi}{2}}$ is the normalized arclength, and $\frac{\pi B}{\alpha}$ is the scaling factor of the clothoid segment which is a non-negative parameter that defines the degree of linear curvature variation. We can then deduce:

$$
\kappa = \frac{2\alpha^2 l}{\pi B} = \frac{l}{B},
$$

$$
s = \frac{\pi B}{\alpha} l' = \pi B l.
$$

(10)

For each defined segment (from p_{s_i} to p_{s_j}, with $i < j$) we can calculate the segment arclength by:

$$s(p_{s_j}) - s(p_{s_i}) = \pi B \left| l(p_{s_j}) - l(p_{s_i}) \right| = \pi B^2 \left| \kappa(p_{s_j}) - \kappa(p_{s_i}) \right|, \qquad (11)$$

and extract the scaling factor:

$$B = \sqrt{\frac{s(p_{s_j}) - s(p_{s_i})}{\pi \left| \kappa(p_{s_j}) - \kappa(p_{s_i}) \right|}} > 0. \qquad (12)$$

The clothoid approximation of the shape is then obtained by interpolating with the points of each obtained segment by Eq. 9, with successive rotation and translation to extract the final clothoid points approximating the curling shape.

3   Results and Analysis

We evaluate the accuracy and performance of the proposed method by analysing a set of configurations of a natural tendril captured in 2D RGB images (digital camera Canon EOS 550D with Lens Canon EF-S 18–55 mm f/3.5–5.6 IS II) extracted from the Supplementary Video[2] which records the changes in the morphology of a *passionflower* tendril, taken place in about 4 min, after being stimulated with a wooden stick for about 1 min.

From the whole frames sequence, we choose four representative images and we analyzed the morphologies. Figure 5 shows the arclength-curvature relation established for each point of the skeleton (second row) and the minimum segments (third row) obtained by our program.

We adopt R^2 to quantify the curve fitting error, with $R^2 = 1$ expressing the best fitting. Our approach demonstrated to be highly accurate for the analysis of curling shape morphologies, all the results show $R^2 > 0.994$, even with the minimum retrieved number of $N = 4$ segments.

Our approach can then be purposely adopted to analyze the changes over time in the morphology of continuum adaptive structures, like living growing tendrils. Figure 6 shows an example of such analysis for the morphological evolution of our *passionflower* tendril after the induced stimulation. It can be noted there is a portion of the tendril that does not change curvature in time, even though previously stimulated (see Supplementary Video(see footnote 2)), while the most apical region is more dynamic in curvature variation. This result might suggest a well-localized zone for coil actuation, independent from the region of stimulation. However, deeper and focused analysis is worth to establish the relation between the provided stimulus and connected behaviour.

4   Discussion and Future Works

In this work, we present an image-based reconstruction method based on 2D piece-wise clothoid model. We used this method to describe and analyse the different morphologies assumed by a natural tendril after mechanical stimuli.

---

[2] Video link: https://youtu.be/DmbInPlpT1U .

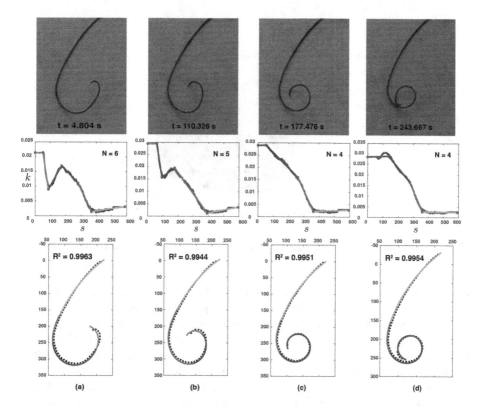

Fig. 5. Results of our methodology for natural tendril morphology analysis. In the first row, four images extracted from a video (see footnote 2) of *passionflower* tendril changing its morphology in time after being rubbed. The second row provides the relationship between the arclength S and the curvature k. The third row shows the morphological representation with the corresponding piece-wise clothoid spiral. The black dashed lines denote the extracted skeleton, coloured solid lines denote each piece of the clothoid curve. Corresponding segments have same colors in second and third row. (Color figure online)

Starting from our previous work [22], we further propose an improvement of the sorting skeletonization algorithm with tuning weights, which is able to solve the situation where the direction vector is misled by the occurrence of sharp corners. Based on this, we present an automatic quantity selection method by dynamic programming to identify the optimal segment number of the 2D piece-wise clothoid. Our method is quantitatively verified by a set of representative images extracted from a video(see footnote 2) showing the shape variation in a *passionflower* tendril. We find that from 4 to 6 segments were enough to describe with high accuracy ($R^2 > 0.9$) the tendril shape across different stages of curling evolution.

In this paper, we analyzed only 2D pictures of tendrils having relatively limited complexity. We in fact neglected strongly self-occluded tendrils, a condition

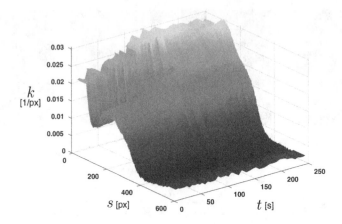

Fig. 6. Arclength and curvature evolution over time of the tendril after stimulation.

that can easily occur in nature but that can be better analyzed in a 3D extension of the present work, which is left for future implementations.

Further steps will also include an analysis of the morphological evolution of natural tendrils during support grasping. This analysis can facilitate the localization of sensory points, structural properties in terms of dimension, elasticity, stiffness, and the relation between the occurring deformation and the area of stimulus contact, time, and delays of deformation, for gaining new knowledge and guide the development of design and behaviour in filiform, continuum bio-inspired robots.

References

1. Laschi, C., Mazzolai, B., Mattoli, V., Cianchetti, M., Dario, P.: Design of a biomimetic robotic octopus arm. Bioinspiration Biomimetics **3**, 015006 (2009)
2. Mazzolai, B., et al.: Octopus-inspired soft arm with suction cups for enhanced grasping tasks in confined environments. In: Advanced Intelligent Systems (2019)
3. Hannan,M.W., Walker, I.: Analysis and initial experiments for a novel elephant's trunk robot. In: International Conference on Intelligent Robots and Systems, vol. 10 (2000)
4. Liljebäck, P., Pettersen, K.Y., Stavdahl, Ø., Gravdahl, J.T.: A review on modelling, implementation, and control of snake robots. Robot. Auton. Syst. **60**, 29–40 (2012)
5. Seok, S., Onal, C.D., Cho, K.-J., Wood, R.J., Rus, D., Kim, S.: Meshworm: a peristaltic soft robot with antagonistic nickel titanium coil actuators. IEEE/ASME Trans. Mechatron. **18**(5), 1485–1497 (2012)
6. Laschi, C., Mazzolai, B., Cianchetti, M.: Soft robotics: technologies and systems pushing the boundaries of robot abilities. Sci. Robot **1**(1), eaah3690 (2016)
7. Mazzolai, B., Mondini, A., Del Dottore, E., Sadeghi, A.: Self-growing adaptable soft robots. In: Mechanically Responsive Materials for Soft Robotics, pp. 363–394 (2020)

8. Burris, J.N., Lenaghan, S.C., Stewart, C.N.: Climbing plants: attachment adaptations and bioinspired innovations. Plant Cell Rep. **37**(4), 565–574 (2017). https://doi.org/10.1007/s00299-017-2240-y
9. Sousa-Baena, M.S., Lohmann, L.G., Hernandes-Lopes, J., Sinha, N.R.: The molecular control of tendril development in angiosperms. New Phytol. **218**(3), 944–958 (2018)
10. Gianoli, E.: The behavioural ecology of climbing plants. AoB Plants **7** (2015)
11. Darwin, C.: The Movements and Habits of Climbing Plants. John Murray, London (1875)
12. Peressotti, A., et al.: Flexible control of movement in plants. Sci. Rep. **218** (2019)
13. Sousa-Baena, M., Lohmann, L., Hernandes-Lopes, J., Sinha, N.: The molecular control of tendril development in angiosperms. New Phytol. **218**, 03 (2018)
14. Vidoni, R., Mimmo, T., Pandolfi, C.: Tendril-based climbing plants to model, simulate and create bio-inspired robotic systems. J. Bionic Eng. **12**, 04 (2015)
15. Burris, J.N., Lenaghan, S.C., Stewart, C.N.: Climbing plants: attachment adaptations and bioinspired innovations. Plant Cell Rep. **37**(4), 565–574 (2017). https://doi.org/10.1007/s00299-017-2240-y
16. Gerbode, S.J., Puzey, J.R., McCormick, A.G., Mahadevan, L.: How the cucumber tendril coils and overwinds. Science **337**(6098), 1087–1091 (2012)
17. Singh, G., Xiao, C., Hsiao-Wecksler, E., Krishnan, G.: Design and analysis of coiled fiber reinforced soft pneumatic actuator. Bioinspiration Biomimetics **13**, 02 (2018)
18. Mehling, J.S., Diftler, M.A., Chu, M., Valvo, M.: A minimally invasive tendril robot for in-space inspection. In: The First IEEE/RAS-EMBS International Conference on Biomedical Robotics and Biomechatronics, 2006. BioRob 2006, February 2006
19. Wooten, M.B., Walker, I.D.: Vine-inspired continuum tendril robots and circumnutations. Robotics **7**, 58 (2018)
20. Must, I., Sinibaldi, E., Mazzolai, B.: A variable-stiffness tendril-like soft robot based on reversible osmotic actuation. Nat. Commun. **10**(1), 1–18 (2019)
21. Feng, J., Zhang, W., Liu, C., Guo, M., Zhang, C.: Homoclinic and heteroclinic orbits in climbing cucumber tendrils. Sci. Rep. **9**, 03 (2019)
22. Fan, J., Dottore, E.D., Visentin, F., Mazzolai, B.: Image-based approach to reconstruct curling in continuum structures. In: 2020 3rd IEEE International Conference on Soft Robotics (RoboSoft), pp. 544–549 (2020)
23. Pickover, C.A.: Mathematics and beauty: a sampling of spirals and 'strange' spirals in science, nature and art. Leonardo **21**(2), 173–181 (1988)
24. Rafsanjani, A., Brulé, V., Western, T.L., Pasini, D.: Hydro-responsive curling of the resurrection plant selaginella lepidophylla. Sci. Rep. **5**, 8064 (2015)
25. Gonthina, P.S., Kapadia, A.D., Godage, I.S., Walker, I.D.: Modeling variable curvature parallel continuum robots using Euler curves. In: 2019 International Conference on Robotics and Automation (ICRA), vol. 05 (2019)
26. Heald, M.A.: Rational approximations for the fresnel integrals (1985)

Cholinergic Control of Chaos and Evidence Sensitivity in a Neocortical Model of Perceptual Decision-Making

Adrián F. Amil[1,2], Jordi-Ysard Puigbò[1,5(✉)], and Paul F. M. J. Verschure[1,3,4]

[1] Institute for Bioengineering of Catalonia (IBEC), Barcelona, Spain
pverschure@ibecbarcelona.eu
[2] Pompeu Fabra University (UPF), Barcelona, Spain
[3] Barcelona Institute of Science and Technology (BIST), Barcelona, Spain
[4] Catalan Institution for Research and Advanced Studies (ICREA), Barcelona, Spain
[5] BitMetrics, Barcelona, Spain

Abstract. Perceptual decision-making in the brain is commonly modeled as a competition among tuned cortical populations receiving stimulation according to their perceptual evidence. However, the contribution of evidence on the decision-making process changes through time. In this regard, the mechanisms controlling the sensitivity to perceptual evidence remain unknown. Here we explore this issue by using a biologically constrained model of the neocortex performing a dual-choice perceptual discrimination task. We combine mutual and global GABAergic inhibition, which are differentially regulated by acetylcholine (ACh), a neuromodulator linked to enhanced stimulus discriminability. We find that, while mutual inhibition determines the phase-space separation between two stable attractors representing each stimulus, global inhibition controls the formation of a chaotic attractor in-between the two, effectively protecting the weakest stimulus. Hence, under low ACh levels, where global inhibition dominates, the decision-making process is chaotic and less determined by the difference between perceptual evidences. On the contrary, under high ACh levels, where mutual inhibition dominates, the network becomes very sensitive to small differences between stimuli. Our results are in line with the putative role of ACh in enhanced stimulus discriminability and suggest that ACh levels control the sensitivity to sensory inputs by regulating the amount of chaos.

Keywords: Acetylcholine · Cortical model · Decision-making · Chaos

The current work has received funding from H2020-EU project VirtualBrainCloud, ID:826421. In addition, Adrián F. Amil is supported by a FI-AGAUR2020 scholarship from the Generalitat de Catalunya.

© Springer Nature Switzerland AG 2020
V. Vouloutsi et al. (Eds.): Living Machines 2020, LNAI 12413, pp. 92–96, 2020.
https://doi.org/10.1007/978-3-030-64413-3_10

Cortical models have been widely used to study how the brain makes decisions about incoming perceptual evidence (e.g., discrimination between two similar stimuli). In particular, it is assumed that competing populations of pyramidal cells tuned to certain stimuli generate attractor dynamics that drive the network into a perceptual decision. However, the contribution of perceptual evidence during the decision process is not uniform and changes through time [1]. Hence, a basic question that remains unanswered is how the sensitivity to perceptual evidence can be modulated in neocortical circuits during perceptual decision-making. To clarify this issue, we developed a spiking neural network (Fig. 1; based on [2]) under cholinergic modulation. Two populations of excitatory neurons with sparse recurrent connections were stimulated following a Gaussian distribution, with the mean representing the amount of perceptual evidence. The competition between the two populations was implemented as mutual inhibition (Parvalbumin-positive interneurons) and global inhibition (Somatostatin-positive interneurons). Neurons were modeled as leaky integrate-and-fire units, with the parameters being grounded in physiology [3]. Excitatory and inhibitory synapses were modeled as single decaying exponentials, with the time constants reproducing slow NMDA and fast GABAergic kinematics, respectively. The differential effect of ACh on the subtypes of GABAergic interneurons [4] was modeled so that high ACh decreased the synaptic efficacies of global inhibition and increased the synaptic efficacies of mutual inhibition and recurrent excitation (Fig. 1). Two task conditions were studied: one in which both stimuli had equal evidence strengths, and another in which one stimulus had stronger evidence. For both conditions, the network dynamics were compared between low and high ACh levels. The state of the network was defined by the combined compound potentials of both excitatory populations. Pseudo phase space trajectories of independent 2-second trials were then plotted, along with their corresponding convergent points. Based on the convergence, thresholds determined by a simple clustering algorithm classified the trials to extract the decision statistics. Additionally, attractor dynamics were studied, and chaos was detected by computing the Lyapunov exponents [5]. The phase trajectories and the corresponding convergent points (Fig. 2A, B) showed the stable formation of two limit-cycle attractors corresponding to one of the populations winning over the other. We observed that the attractors' center of mass was pushed to the extremes of the phase space in the high ACh condition, suggesting a deepening of the attractors. Interestingly, only in the low ACh condition we saw the emergence of a chaotic attractor (Lyapunov exponent of 0.358) in-between the phase space of the two stable attractors. Moreover, decision statistics (Fig. 2C) clearly showed that convergence into the weakest attractor was more preserved under low ACh, hence mitigating the effects of the biased evidence towards one of the stimuli. Contrarily, the network was more likely to converge into the strongest attractor under high ACh, despite the high levels of noise and stimulation overlap. Our results are in line with previous proposals suggesting that chaos is part of a default state of cortical circuits [6] caused by a particular balance between excitation and inhibition [7]. Moreover, it complements previous studies that show how the error landscape can be chaotically bootstrapped across trials to improve the learning performance [8]. In this regard, high ACh levels would (1) disinhibit the circuits, thus reducing chaos at the single-trial level during decisions and enhancing stimulus discriminability; and (2) enhance synaptic plasticity, thus increasing chaos across trials during learning and facilitating the rapid acquisition of priors over stimuli. Finally, our model naturally accounts for the role of ACh in uncertainty estimation [9] by considering that high ACh levels were needed to reduce the chaotic dynamics and correctly classify a stimulus under high levels of noise or variability.

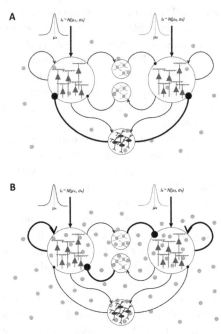

Fig. 1. Neocortical model of perceptual decision-making under cholinergic control. (A) Low ACh levels where global inhibition dominates the dynamics. (B) High ACh levels where recurrent excitation and mutual inhibition dominates. Each pyramidal population receives external stochastic stimulation (perceptual evidence). Excitatory neurons are represented by blue triangular cells. PV+ interneurons are represented by red circular cells. SOM+ interneurons are represented by green elliptical cells. ACh levels are represented by the number of blue circles. Standard arrows correspond to excitatory synapses and circular arrows to inhibitory ones. (Color figure online)

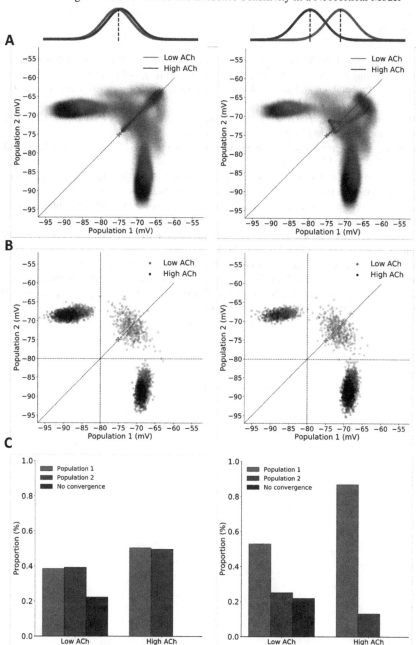

Fig. 2. Network dynamics for "equal" (left column) and "biased" (right column) task conditions. (A) Pseudo phase space showing 2000 trajectories for low and high ACh levels. (B) Points of convergence of the trajectories. The green dashed lines represent the thresholds for decision classification. (C) Decision statistics reflect the network's convergence shown in B. (Color figure online)

References

1. Keung, W., Hagen, T.A., Wilson, R.C.: A divisive model of evidence accumulation explains uneven weighting of evidence over time. Nat. Commun. **11**(1), 1–9 (2020)
2. Wang, X.-J.: Probabilistic decision making by slow reverberation in cortical circuits. Neuron **36**(5), 955–968 (2002)
3. Teeter, C., et al.: Generalized leaky integrate-and-fire models classify multiple neuron types. Nat. Commun. **9**(1), 1–15 (2018)
4. Kawaguchi, Y.: Selective cholinergic modulation of cortical GABAergic cell subtypes. J. Neurophysiol. **78**(3), 1743–1747 (1997)
5. Rosenstein, M.T., Collins, J.J., De Luca, C.J.: A practical method for calculating largest Lyapunov exponents from small data sets. Physica D **65**(1–2), 117–134 (1993)
6. Skarda, C.A., Freeman, W.J.: How brains make chaos in order to make sense of the world. Behav. Brain Sci. **10**(2), 161–195 (1987)
7. van Vreeswijk, C., Sompolinsky, H.: Chaos in neuronal networks with balanced excitatory and inhibitory activity. Science **274**(5293), 1724–1726 (1996)
8. Verschure, P.F.M.J.: Chaos-based learning. Complex Syst. **5**, 359–370 (1991)
9. Puigbò, J.-Y., Arsiwalla, X.D., González-Ballester, M.A., Verschure, P.F.M.J.: Switching operation modes in the neocortex via cholinergic neuromodulation. Mol. Neurobiol. **57**(1), 139–149 (2019). https://doi.org/10.1007/s12035-019-01764-w

Biomechanical Characterization
of Hook-Climber Stems for Soft Robotic
Applications

Isabella Fiorello[1,2]($\boxtimes$), Alessio Mondini[1,2], and Barbara Mazzolai[1]($\boxtimes$)

[1] Center for Micro-BioRobotics@SSSA, Istituto Italiano di Tecnologia, Pontedera, Italy
{isabella.fiorello,barbara.mazzolai}@iit.it
[2] The BioRobotics Institute, Scuola Superiore Sant'Anna, Pontedera, Italy

Abstract. Plants are getting increasing interest from scientists for the development of novel biomimetic products. Especially, the stems of climbing plants possess impressively high-adaptable materials, which can be relevant in robotics for the development of new machines able to work in unpredictable environments. In this work, we present a study on the mechanical properties of the stem of the hook-climber *Galium aparine*. Three different stem regions (basal, middle and apical parts) were analyzed in order to investigate how the mechanical properties vary along the stem. Tensile tests were performed on the different stem parts. Results demonstrated a significant decrease of Young's modulus, the breaking strain and the tensile strength values from the basal to the upper parts. In contrast, we observed a decrease only in the tensile strength between the middle and apical parts. The collected data on the mechanical response of natural plant stems will be used as benchmarks for the design of novel soft robots that can act and move in real unstructured scenarios for exploration and monitoring tasks.

Keywords: Stem materials · Mechanical properties · Tensile tests · Climbing plant-inspired soft robots

1 Introduction

The development of novel systems with compliant smart materials able to adapt to unpredictable environments is fundamental for robotic and engineering applications [1]. Mimicking the biological features of natural materials can offer new solutions to address these issues [2]. Among living organisms, climbing plants show interesting features, especially regarding attachment (i.e., hooks, spines, roots, adhesive pads etc.) and material properties (i.e., high adaptability, flexibility and resistance to mechanical stresses), which are fundamental for the development of new self-adaptable growing machines [3–5]. To this aim, we select the hook-climber *Galium aparine* L., which is a semi-self-supporting fast-growing herbaceous plant able to attach to several host plant species mainly using its leaves, endowed with a ratchet-like climbing mechanism based on micro-hooks for mechanical interlocking [6]. Indeed, *G. aparine* has peculiar stem mechanical properties and impressively high extensibility up to $\approx 29\%$ before failure

© Springer Nature Switzerland AG 2020
V. Vouloutsi et al. (Eds.): Living Machines 2020, LNAI 12413, pp. 97–103, 2020.
https://doi.org/10.1007/978-3-030-64313-3_11

in the basal region [7]. This value is common for aquatic plants [8], but it has never been reported for terrestrial species, and the mechanism behind such high breaking strain is still unclear (i.e., the reorientation of microfibrils seems to be not responsible) [7]. Furthermore, observations of *G. aparine* in the field suggested marked differences between the lower and upper parts of the stem [7], even if the variations of mechanical properties along stem parts have not yet quantified. In this paper, we present a preliminary study on the mechanical properties of *G. aparine* stems at the level of basal, middle and apical regions, based on tensile tests.

2 Materials and Methods

2.1 Biological Materials

G. aparine plants were purchased from a nursery and moved into a growth chamber (temperature 25 °C, 60% humidity, 16 h–8 h light-dark cycle). Pictures of the natural stem sections were obtained with a Hirox KH-7700 digital microscope.

2.2 Tensile Tests

We carried out tensile tests on the different samples (4 cm) collected from the basal, middle and apical parts of the *G. aparine* stems. The basal part was defined as the region closed 0–2 cm to the base, while the middle and the apical parts were defined as the regions closed 4–6 cm and 0–3 cm to the apex, respectively (Fig. 2a). Tensile tests were performed using a UTM (Universal Testing Machine, Zwick/Roell Z005). Both ends of the stem parts were clamped in the jaws of the UTM and stretched at 10 mm/min until the breakage of the stem occurred. We analyzed only samples where the breakage occurred far from the gripping parts. The distance between the clamps was 2 cm. To prevent surface slipping, a sandwich of neoprene rubber and a piece of sandpaper were used, similarly to [7]. During tests, the force (F [N]) *vs.* displacement (D [mm]) curve was recorded using TestXpert II software. To extract the mechanical properties, stress (σ [N/mm^2]) and strain (ε) where computed by:

$$\varepsilon = D/L \quad [9, 10]$$

$$\sigma = F/A \quad [9, 10]$$

where L [mm] is the original length and A [mm^2] is the cross-sectional area.

The cross-sectional areas were calculated by image analysis subdividing them into polygons. The main mechanical parameters were extracted from the resulting stress-strain curve (see Fig. 2a). Particularly, Young's modulus (E), or stiffness of the stem material, was calculated as the fitted-slope of the initial linear elastic part of the curve [9, 10]. Furthermore, the breaking strain (ε_{max}) and the tensile strength (σ_{max}) were also calculated from the curve as the maximum strain and the maximum stress, respectively [9, 10].

2.3 Statistics

We compared tensile test results on the different stem segments with one-way analysis of variance (ANOVA) followed from Tukey's post hoc tests. In all, 19 stem segments were tested. Error bars in bar graphs reported the standard deviation.

3 Main Results

3.1 Variation of Structural and Mechanical Properties Along the Stem

The morphology and anatomy of *G. aparine* stem are summarized in Fig. 1. The lower (i.e., basal) and upper (i.e., middle and apical) parts of the stem are analyzed (see Fig. 1A). Anatomical observations of the lower and upper parts of *G. aparine* stem are reported in [7]. There are evident structural differences between the lower and the upper parts: the lower part is formed from "cable-like" arrangement with a central core of lignified vascular tissue (see Fig. 1B), while the upper part is formed from a "four pointed star-like" arrangement with mechanical tissue and not lignified sclerenchyma in the angles (see Fig. 1C) [7]. The cross-sectional area of the basal parts are ≈ 0.43 mm^2, while the cross-sectional area of the middle and apical parts are ≈ 1.44 mm^2.

Tensile tests highlighted significant differences between the three stem parts (Fig. 2).

An example of a stress-strain plot from which we extracted the main mechanical parameters is reported in Fig. 2A. As expected, the basal part is much more extensible than the middle and apical parts, with significant differences in the breaking strain values ($p < 0.01$); in contrast, the comparison between the measurements on the middle and the apical part have shown no significant differences ($p > 0.01$). Particularly, the ε_{max} ranged from $29 \pm 8\%$ in the basal part to $8 \pm 2\%$ in the middle part and $9 \pm 2\%$ in the apical part (Fig. 2B). Similarly, the stiffness of the stem significantly decreases from basal ($E = 112 \pm 23$ MPa) to upper parts ($p < 0.01$), but there are no significant differences between the middle ($E = 42 \pm 19$ MPa) and apical parts ($E = 33 \pm 14$ MPa) ($p > 0.01$) (Fig. 2C). In contrast, the tensile strength decrease between all three parts (σ_{max} from 8 ± 2 MPa to 1.4 ± 0.4 MPa; $p < 0.01$ between BP and MP, and BP and AP; $p < 0.1$ between MP and AP) (Fig. 2D).

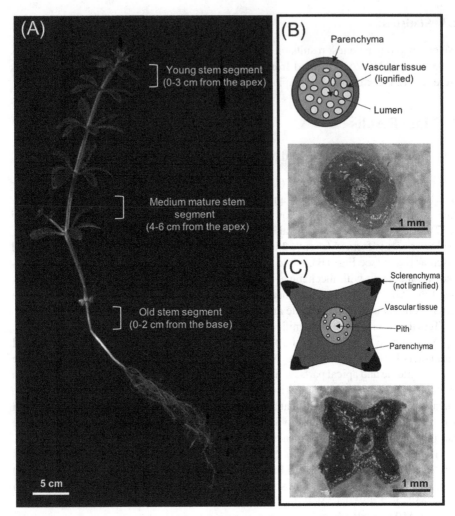

Fig. 1. Morphology and anatomy of the hook-climber *G. aparine* L. (A) Three stem segments were sampled from the basal to the apical stem parts. (B-C) Schematic drawing (upper side) and microscope images (lower side) of the transverse sections of (B) the old stem or (C) the mature-young stem segments.

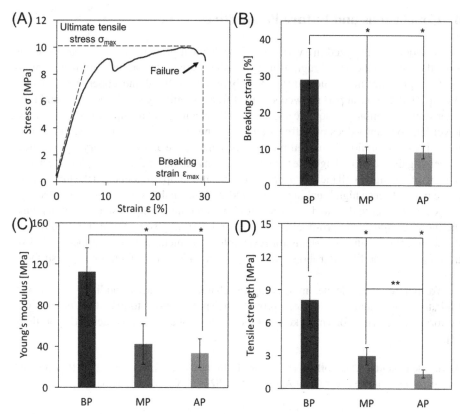

Fig. 2. Tension tests results of different segments of *G. aparine* stems. (A) Example of stress-strain curve for the basal segment of a *G. aparine* stem. The breakage parameters are indicated in the plot. (B-D) Analysis of the mechanical properties (i.e., (B) breaking strain, (C) Young's modulus and (D) breaking stress) of the different stem segments, including the basal part (BP), the middle part (MP) and the apical part (AP). The asterisks indicate statistical significance with $P < 0.01$ (*) or $P < 0.1$ (**) (analysis of variance with ANOVA followed from post-hoc Tukey's test).

4 Conclusions and Future Perspectives

In this work, we analyzed the variation of mechanical properties on *G. aparine* stems from the basal to the apical regions using tensile testing. Our preliminary results highlighted significant mechanical differences between the basal and upper stem regions. As expected, the basal part showed strong stiffness (similarly to climbers [4]) and high extensibility (similarly to aquatic species [7, 8]), in contrast to the upper parts which had lower but constant values of stiffness and breaking strains. These findings, in addition to the presence of directional leaf micro-hooks, may have an evolutionary significance, preventing the stem breakage due to tugs (i.e., from animals or wind) [6, 7]. Future development of this study will include *ad hoc* experimental setup to understand the mechanism at the basis of these high breaking strains and a whole analysis of the stem architecture, in order to deeper understand the structure-function relationship in stem materials. Furthermore, *G. aparine* micro-hooks represent an interesting source of inspiration for the development of artificial systems for reversible attachment on rough surfaces [11–13], useful also for facilitating robots climbing over a wide range of supports and surfaces [13].

We believe these deeper morphological characterizations, in addition to our preliminary biomechanical study, will provide the specifications to prototype novel high-performing materials for vine-like soft robots able to operate in unstructured conditions [3].

Acknowledgments. This work was funded by the European Union's Horizon 2020 Research and Innovation Programme under Grant Agreement No 824074 (GrowBot Project).

References

1. Laschi, C., Mazzolai, B., Cianchetti, M.: Soft robotics: technologies and systems pushing the boundaries of robot abilities. Sci. Robot. **1**, eaah3690 (2016)
2. Schmitt, O.H.: Some interesting and useful biomimetic transforms. In: Third Int. Biophysics Congress, p. 197 (1969)
3. Fiorello, I., Del Dottore, E., Tramacere, F., Mazzolai, B.: Taking inspiration from climbing plants: methodologies and benchmarks–A review. Bioinspiration Biomimetics **15**(3), 031001 (2020)
4. Rowe, N.P., Speck, T.: Stem biomechanics, strength of attachment, and developmental plasticity of vines and lianas. Ecology of Lianas, pp. 323–341 (2014)
5. Speck, T., Burgert, I.: Plant stems: functional design and mechanics. Annu. Rev. Mater. Res. **41**, 169–193 (2011)
6. Bauer, G., Klein, M.C., Gorb, S.N., Speck, T., Voigt, D., Gallenmüller, F.: Always on the bright side: the climbing mechanism of Galium aparine. Proc Biol. Sci. **278**, 2233–2239 (2011)
7. Goodman, A.M.: Mechanical adaptations of cleavers (Galium aparine). Ann. Bot. **95**, 475–480 (2004)
8. Usherwood, J., Ennos, A., Ball, D.: Mechanical and anatomical adaptations in terrestrial and aquatic buttercups to their respective environments. J. Exp. Bot. **48**, 1469–1475 (1997)
9. Niklas, K.J., Spatz, H.-C.: Plant physics. University of Chicago Press (2012)

10. Niklas, K.: Plant biomechanics University of Chicago Press Chicago. London (1992)
11. Fiorello, I., Tricinci, O., Mishra, A.K., Tramacere, F., Filippeschi, C., Mazzolai, B.: Artificial system inspired by climbing mechanism of galium aparine fabricated via 3D laser lithography. In: Conference on Biomimetic and Biohybrid Systems, pp. 168–178 (2018)
12. Andrews, H.G., Badyal, J.P.S.: Bioinspired hook surfaces based upon a ubiquitous weed (Galium aparine) for dry adhesion. J. Adhes. Sci. Technol. **28**, 1243–1255 (2014)
13. Fiorello, I., et al.: Climbing plant-inspired micropatterned devices for reversible attachment. Adv. Funct. Mater. **30**(38), 2003380 (2020)

Robotics Application of a Method for Analytically Computing Infinitesimal Phase Response Curves

Marshaun N. Fitzpatrick[1]($\boxtimes$) (iD), Yangyang Wang[2] (iD), Peter J. Thomas[1] (iD),
Roger D. Quinn[1] (iD), and Nicholas S. Szczecinski[1] (iD)

[1] Case Western Reserve University, Cleveland, OH 44106, USA
marshuan.fitzpatrick@case.edu
[2] The University of Iowa, Iowa City, IA 52242, USA

Abstract. This work explores a method for analytically computing the infinitesimal phase response curves (iPRCs) of a synthetic nervous system (SNS) for a hybrid exoskeleton. Phase changes, in response to perturbations, revealed by the iPRCs, could assist in tuning the strength and locations of sensory pathways. We model the SNS exoskeleton controller in a reduced form using a state-space representation that interfaces neural and motor dynamics. The neural dynamics are modeled after non-spiking neurons configured as a central pattern generator (CPG), while the motor dynamics model a power unit for the hip joint of the exoskeleton. Within the dynamics are piecewise functions and hard boundaries (i.e. "sliding conditions"), which cause discontinuities in the vector field at their boundaries. The analytical methods for computing the iPRCs used in this work apply the adjoint equation method with jump conditions that are able to account for these discontinuities. To show the accuracy and speed provided by these methods, we compare the analytical and brute-force solutions.

Keywords: Infinitesimal phase response curve · Synthetic nervous system · Hybrid exoskeleton

1 Introduction

Research and development of exoskeleton devices to mimic or assist walking have been ongoing since the 1960s [1]. The mechanical design and control strategies for these exoskeletons can vary widely. A collaborative team at Case Western Reserve University and the Cleveland Stokes Veteran's Affairs (VA) hospital is currently developing a hybrid exoskeleton [2]. The exoskeleton is considered a hybrid because it combines functional electrical stimulation (FES) [3] of the user's muscles with the bracing and power assistance of an exoskeleton [4]. Such an exoskeleton will enable patients to regain mobility and act as a form of physical therapy due to the physiological benefits of FES [5]. Specifically, paraplegic patients benefit from the exoskeleton's powered joints that compensate for inadequate muscle activation when using FES.

© Springer Nature Switzerland AG 2020
V. Vouloutsi et al. (Eds.): Living Machines 2020, LNAI 12413, pp. 104–115, 2020.
https://doi.org/10.1007/978-3-030-64313-3_12

Despite the progress of exoskeletons and biped robots to date, their movements remain in general less robust and adaptive compared to those of humans. The robustness and adaptation of human walking is due to the structure and function of the neural control networks within the nervous system. Decades of study in neuroscience and biology have begun to uncover how these controllers operate [6]. Controlling our exoskeleton with a computational model of these networks, which we call a "Synthetic Nervous System" (SNS) [7], may endow it with more robust and adaptive locomotion.

Our ultimate goal is to control our exoskeleton and FES with an SNS model that incorporates sensory feedback to coordinate the motion of different limb segments in a flexible framework that can be altered by descending influences in a task-dependent way. These two features have been shown to underlie periodic motor output in animals [8–10]. Neural models of animal locomotion in [11–13] can serve as a basis for the organization of our SNS model moving forward. However, with the actuators of the exoskeleton more closely resembling servomotors than antagonistic pairs of muscles, design of joint movement controls will be more in line with the design process outlined in [14]. Interjoint coordination will be relying on sensory feedback signals from the positions of other joints and forces on the leg [11, 15].

An expected hurdle to developing and tuning this SNS will be in the coordination of the multiple rhythmic systems, i.e. the oscillation of each joint. Inter-joint coordination arises from sensory pathways between leg joints adjusting the oscillatory phase of the other joints. For example, loading information from the foot adjusts the phase of the hip's control network to generate propulsion [11]. But how should the strength of such pathways be tuned? One tool that quantifies how periodic trajectories are altered by perturbations is the infinitesimal phase response curve, or iPRC. An iPRC reveals how the cycle's phase changes in response to perturbations applied to each of its state variables at different phases throughout its limit cycle. By locating the areas of higher and lower sensitivity, we may be able to design sensory pathways that exploit the oscillators' phase-dependent sensitivity to inputs. In addition, understanding how sensory information alters the relative phase of the joints, we may be able to determine the stability of periodic trajectories (i.e. how the exoskeleton walks) and its robustness to system parameters.

Despite the potential benefits these iPRCs could provide, the process of finding the iPRCs via brute force guess-and-check can require long computation times, especially as the dimensionality of the SNS model grows. Analytical methods for generating iPRCs exist, which should be faster and computationally less expensive than brute force methods. However, such methods mostly consider smooth systems and tend to break down in non-smooth systems due to the Jacobian matrices of the system's vector fields not being well defined [16]. Our model joint model system contains piecewise functions and certain hard boundaries (i.e. "sliding conditions") that make it non-smooth. However, more recently developed analytical methods for finding iPRCs can treat systems whose dynamics contain piecewise functions and sliding conditions [16, 17]. In this work, we will apply these newer methods with a reduced model of our SNS exoskeleton controller to compute its iPRC numerically. We compare this iPRC to one generated via brute force (i.e. repeated perturbed simulation). We then discuss future applications for this work.

2 Methods

This work establishes a system wherein the direction, timing, and speed of the hip joint of a powered exoskeleton is controlled by simple neural network consisting of a central pattern generator (CPG), modeled using two non-spiking leaky neurons. The hip joint is powered by a DC motor with a gearbox, and the rotation of the joint provides feedback to the CPG.

2.1 Motor Dynamics

The hip power unit is the actuator driving the movement. It is composed of a DC motor paired with a transmission to produce a larger torque, while still being capable of out-putting the needed speeds of the hip during walking locomotion. The power unit can be modeled as a motor.

Kirchhoff's Current Law. To model the electrical properties of the motor we use Kirchhoff's Current Law,

$$L \cdot \dot{I} = V_{in} - K_v \cdot \dot{\theta} - R_m \cdot I \tag{1}$$

Where L is the motor armature inductance, V_{in} is the motor voltage input, K_v is the motor speed constant, $\dot{\theta}$ is the angular velocity, R_m is the motor terminal resistance, and I is the motor current. Equation 1 makes up the basis of our motor current state. Due to limitations of the motor controller and transmission inside the power unit, only a certain amount of current can be sourced at once. This restriction introduces a sliding condition to the state equation for current, where it can only reach a set maximum amount of current.

Newton's Law of Motion. To model the mechanical properties of the motor we use Newton's Law of Motion resulting in

$$J \cdot \ddot{\theta} = K_t \cdot I - B \cdot \dot{\theta} - sign(\theta) \cdot \tau_{ext} \tag{2}$$

where the J is the motor mass moment of inertia, K_t is the motor torque constant, B is the motor viscous friction, and τ_{ext} is the external torque, which is used to account for the static friction. Equation 2 makes up the basis of the angular velocity state of the motor.

Angular Position. To describe the dynamics in a state-space representation, we add a differential equation modeling the angular position of the motor,

$$\dot{\theta} = \frac{d\theta}{dt} \tag{3}$$

2.2 Neural Dynamics

The neural dynamics contribute four state variables to the system. These variables model the activation level of the two neurons in our CPG, as well as those neurons' persistent sodium channel inactivation.

Non-spiking Leaky Neuron Model. The neurons are modeled as non-spiking Hodgkin-Huxley compartments with the substitution $U = V - E_r$, as used in [7, 14] to simplify analysis, where E_r is the resting potential, V is the neuron voltage, and U is the activation level above the resting voltage. This gives us

$$C_m \cdot \dot{U} = -G_m \cdot U + G_{syn}(U) \cdot (\Delta E_{syn} - U) + G_{Na} \cdot m_\infty(U) \cdot h \cdot (\Delta E_{Na} - U)$$
$$+ I_{app} + I_{pert} + G_{fb} \cdot (\Delta E_{fb} - U) \tag{4}$$

where C_m is the membrane capacitance, G_m is the membrane conductance, G_{syn} is the instantaneous synaptic conductance, ΔE_{syn} is the synaptic reversal potential, G_{Na} is the sodium conductance, m_∞ is a sigmoid for the persistent sodium channel activation, h is the persistent sodium channel inactivation, ΔE_{Na} is the sodium channel reversal potential, I_{app} is the membrane applied current, and I_{pert} is a small current pulse that is only applied to one of the neurons at the beginning to create an offset to begin oscillation of the CPG. The terms G_{fb} and ΔE_{fb} are feedback terms used to interface feedback pathways with the motor. G_{fb} is the feedback synapse conductance and ΔE_{fb} is the feedback reversal potential.

Central Pattern Generator. The central pattern generator is formed by mutual inhibition between two neurons with persistent sodium channels [14]. The synaptic conductance, G_{syn}, of the inhibitory synaptic connections between the two neurons is described by the piecewise-linear function

$$G_{syn}(U) = \begin{cases} 0, & \text{if } U \leq 0 \\ g_{syn} \cdot \frac{U}{R}, & \text{if } 0 < U < R \\ g_{syn}, & \text{if } U \geq R \end{cases} \tag{5}$$

where R is the expected range of voltage output from the neuron and g_{syn} is the maximum synaptic conductance. To have our network oscillate between the voltage range of 0 to R at steady state when one neuron is inhibited and the other is uninhibited, G_{Na} is found using

$$G_{Na} = \frac{G_m \cdot R}{m_\infty(R) \cdot h_\infty(R) \cdot (\Delta E_{Na} - R)}. \tag{6}$$

The maximum synaptic conductance, g_{syn}, is found using

$$g_{syn} = \frac{-\delta - G_{Na} \cdot m_\infty(\delta) \cdot h_\infty(\delta) \cdot (\delta - \Delta E_{Na})}{\delta - \Delta E_{syn}}. \tag{7}$$

Here, δ is a bifurcation parameter that represents the strength of the synaptic inhibition as the difference between the inhibited neuron's resting potential and the lower threshold of the synapse [14]. The term h_∞ is another sigmoid, similar to m_∞, but for the sodium inactivation channel. The sigmoids are defined as

$$m_\infty(V) = \frac{1}{1 + \exp(S \cdot (R - V))} \tag{8}$$

$$h_\infty(V) = \frac{1}{1 + 0.5 \cdot \exp(S \cdot V)} \tag{9}$$

where S is the maximum slope of the sigmoid.

Sodium Channel Inactivation. The differential equation that governs the sodium channel inactivation term, h, found in Eq. 4 is

$$\dot{h} = \frac{h_\infty(U) - h}{\tau_h(U)} \tag{10}$$

where τ_h is the sodium inactivation time constant found using

$$\tau_h(V) = \tau_{h,max} \cdot h_\infty(V) \cdot \sqrt{0.5 \cdot \exp(S \cdot V)} \tag{11}$$

2.3 Interfacing the Dynamics

With the motor and neural dynamics laid out in the sections above, we must establish coupling terms between them. Our goal is to use the neural states to specify position and velocity commands for the motor. For the CPG to be able to control the movement of the motor, the states of the neural dynamics are integrated in to the motor dynamics as inputs as well as having certain states from the motor dynamics used in new feedback pathways for the neurons.

Neuron Activation as Inputs to the Motor. To have the CPG specify the velocity of the motor, the motor voltage input, V_{in}, becomes a piecewise-linear function of the neuron activation states.

$$V_{in}(U_1, U_2) = P \cdot \min(\max(U_1, 0), R) - \min(\max(U_2, 0), R) \tag{12}$$

where U_1 and U_2 represent the activation states of neurons 1 and 2, respectively. The term P is a gain term represented as

$$P = \frac{4 \cdot K_v}{1000 \cdot R} \tag{13}$$

that limits the maximum commanded speed to 4 rads/s, since this is the approximate speed of the hip joint during walking locomotion found in [18].

Angular Position as Feedback for the Neurons. The feedback synapse conductance, G_{fb}, is set as a function of position θ. If neuron 1 (U_1) was active when θ reaches a certain threshold, the feedback synapse conductance activates to allow a strong inhibitory current to inhibit U_1. With U_1 now inhibited, U_2 is allowed to escape and become the active neuron in the CPG. This causes the angular velocity to switch signs due to Eq. 12, leading to a change in direction. G_{fb} for neurons 1 and 2 are represented by the following piecewise functions

$$G_{fb,1}(\theta) = \begin{cases} 0, & \theta < \theta_{FLX} \\ g_{FB}, & \theta \geq \theta_{FLX} \end{cases} \tag{14}$$

$$G_{fb,2}(\theta) = \begin{cases} 0, & \theta > \theta_{EXT} \\ g_{FB}, & \theta \leq \theta_{EXT} \end{cases} \tag{15}$$

Where g_{FB} is the maximum feedback conductance, θ_{FLX} is the flexion position trigger and θ_{EXT} is the extension position trigger. The current model sets $\theta_{FLX} = 30$ degrees and $\theta_{EXT} = -10$ degrees based on hip angle ranges during locomotion found in [18]. For completeness, all state equations are listed in Table 1 and all variable values and units are shown in Table 2.

Table 1. State equations of the system

Variable name	State equation
Current	$L \cdot \dot{I} = V_{in} - K_v \cdot \dot{\theta} - R_m \cdot I$
Angular position	$\dot{\theta} = \frac{d\theta}{dt}$
Angular velocity	$J \cdot \ddot{\theta} = K_t \cdot I - B \cdot \dot{\theta} - sign(\theta) \cdot \tau_{ext}$
Neuron 1 activation	$C_m \cdot \dot{U}_1 = -G_m \cdot U_1 + G_{syn}(U_2) \cdot (\Delta E_{syn} - U_1) + G_{Na}$ $\cdot m_\infty(U_1) \cdot h_1 \cdot (\Delta E_{Na} - U_1) + I_{app}$ $+ I_{pert} + G_{fb,1}(\theta) \cdot (\Delta E_{fb} - U_1)$
Neuron 2 activation	$C_m \cdot \dot{U}_2 = -G_m \cdot U_2 + G_{syn}(U_1) \cdot (\Delta E_{syn} - U_2) + G_{Na}$ $\cdot m_\infty(U_2) \cdot h_2 \cdot (\Delta E_{Na} - U_2) + I_{app}$ $+ G_{fb,2}(\theta) \cdot (\Delta E_{fb} - U_2)$
Neuron 1 Sdium Channel inactivation	$\dot{h}_1 = \frac{h_\infty(U_1) - h_1}{\tau_h(U_1)}$
Neuron 2 Sodium Channel inactivation	$\dot{h}_2 = \frac{h_\infty(U_2) - h_2}{\tau_h(U_2)}$

Table 2. Parameter values and units.

Variables	Parameter	Base value/Units
V_{in}	Motor Voltage Input	V
K_v	Motor Speed Constant	$5.7886 \frac{V}{rad/s}$
R_m	Motor Armature Resistance	$0.608\,\Omega$
L	Motor Armature Inductance	$0.000463\,H$
K_t	Motor Torque Constant	$4.11\,Nm/A$
B	Motor Viscous Friction	$0.859 \frac{Nm}{rad/s}$
τ_{ext}	External Torque	$2.38\,Nm$
J	Motor Mass Moment of Inertia	$0.444\,kg \cdot m^2$
G_m	Membrane Conductance	$1\,\mu S$
g_{syn}	Max Synaptic Conductance	$0.2819\,\mu S$
ΔE_{syn}	Synaptic Reversal Potential	$-100\,mV$
G_{Na}	Sodium Conductance	$3.1455\,\mu S$
ΔE_{Na}	Sodium Channel Reversal Potential	$50\,mV$
I_{app}	Membrane Applied Current	$0\,nA$
I_{pert}	Membrane Perturbation Current	$1\,nA$
C_m	Membrane Capacitance	$5\,nF$
τ_h	Sodium Inactivation Time Constant	ms
$\tau_{h,max}$	Sodium Inactivation Time Constant Max	$300\,ms$
δ	Bifurcation Parameter	0.1
R	Voltage Range	20
S	Slope of sigmoid	0.05
θ_{FLX}	Hip Flexion Angle	$30°$
θ_{EXT}	Hip Extension Angle	$-10°$

2.4 Deriving/Generating Analytically the Infinitesimal Phase Response Curves (IPRCs)

The system, governed by the state equations shown above in Table 1, exhibits a limit cycle with both piecewise functions and hard boundaries acting as sliding conditions. Deriving iPRCs for piecewise-linear and limit cycles with sliding conditions (LCSCs) have been treated in detail in [16, 17]. However, we will briefly summarize the process.

Finding the Infinitesimal Phase Response Curve via Brute Force. To generate the iPRC of a system via brute force, the unperturbed system is simulated for at least one period. After obtaining this unperturbed limit cycle, the system is integrated up to given phases. Once reaching the given phase, the solution is halted, perturbed in the direction of a basis vector at a sufficiently small magnitude (1E-2–1E-4 are common values [17]) and re-initialized. The system is then integrated after this perturbation for a sufficiently long time (typically 10 times the period). The value of the iPRC for the phase at which the perturbation is applied is calculated as the difference between the duration of the unperturbed and perturbed limit cycles, divided by the magnitude of the perturbation.

Analytically Finding the Infinitesimal Phase Response Curve. For a general smooth nonlinear system which produces a limit cycle, the iPRC can be found using an adjoint equation method [19]. The adjoint equation is

$$\dot{z} = -(DF(\gamma))^T \cdot z, \tag{16}$$

where z is the iPRC and $DF(\gamma)$ is the Jacobian matrix evaluated on the limit cycle γ. Usually, the adjoint equation cannot be used on nonsmooth systems due to the discontinuities present at the boundaries of piecewise functions or sliding conditions. However, [16, 17] introduce methods to account for these discontinuities.

To account for the discontinuities at the boundaries, jump matrices are calculated at each boundary crossing. These jump matrices capture the abrupt changes that happen to the vector field of the system at the boundaries. To use the jump matrices to properly calculate the iPRC, one evaluates the adjoint equation backwards in time. The adjoint equation is calculated backwards in time because the jump matrix at the liftoff point for sliding conditions would not be well defined otherwise, as detailed in Remark 3.9 and Theorem 3.7 in [16]. When a boundary is encountered, the iPRC just before (in forwards time) the boundary is calculated by

$$z^- = \mathcal{J}z^+, \tag{17}$$

where z^- is the iPRC just before the boundary, z^+ is the iPRC just after the boundary and $\mathcal{J}$ is the jump matrix. How to calculate the jump matrix is detailed in Theorem 2.2 for piecewise smooth limit cycles in [17] and Remark 3.10 for LCSCs in [16]. Once z^- is found, one re-initializes the adjoint equation using z^- and continues to evaluate the adjoint equation backwards in time.

3 Results

3.1 Simulation of the Full System

The state equations shown in Table 1 were simulated in MATLAB (The Mathworks, Natick, MA) using its ODE15s solver with relative and absolute tolerances set at 1×10^{-10}, for 5000 ms to produce Fig. 1. Figure 1 shows that the system is rhythmically oscillating. The flattening of the peaks in plot (c) in Fig. 1 verifies and displays the locations of the system's sliding conditions, where the motor's current draw is limited. Because the motor's current draw is a dynamical state variable, this limitation represents a sliding condition, not a discontinuity. The period of the system was calculated as $T \approx 545$ms.

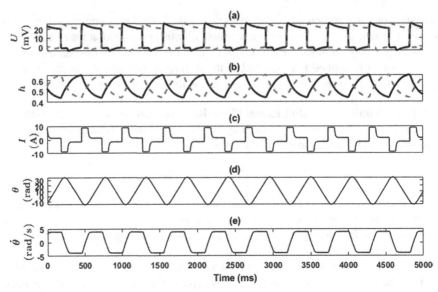

Fig. 1. Simulation results of the SNS controlled hip power unit model. (a): Plot of neuron 1 (U_1) and neuron 2 activation (U_2) represented by black lines and dashed gray lines, respectively. (b): Plot of neuron 1 (h_1) and neuron 2 sodium channel inactivation (h_2) represented by black lines and dashed gray lines, respectively. (c): Plot of the motor current. Sliding conditions take place at the maximum and minimum allowable currents of magnitude $8.76A$. (d): Plot of the angular position of the motor in degrees. (e): Plot of the angular velocity of the motor in radians per second.

3.2 Infinitesimal Phase Response Curve

The brute force and analytical iPRCs of the limit cycle are displayed together in Fig. 2. The perturbation magnitude used for the brute force iPRC was calculated as 10^{-2} times the average absolute value of each state over one period. Two hundred fifty equally spaced given phase positions were used to generate the brute force iPRC. The Jacobian matrix DF used in the adjoint equation for the analytically obtained iPRC was calculated numerically by finite difference. Figure 2 shows good agreement between the brute force and analytical iPRCs. The runtime for the analytical solution was 28.65 s versus more than 5 h for the brute force solution, representing a massive speedup.

4 Discussion

In this work, we present a model wherein the direction, timing, and speed of the hip joint of a powered exoskeleton are controlled by simple neural network consisting of a central pattern generator (CPG), modeled using two non-spiking leaky neurons. The model identifies the CPG, the plant, and the coupling between them in a control architecture directly reflecting the structure of biological motor systems [20]. For this system, we show that the analytical methods in [16, 17] for generating iPRCs of limit cycles containing piecewise-linear functions and sliding conditions agree with the iPRCs calculated for our system via brute force. This method will enable us to precisely tune the interjoint coordinating influences in our exoskeleton control model.

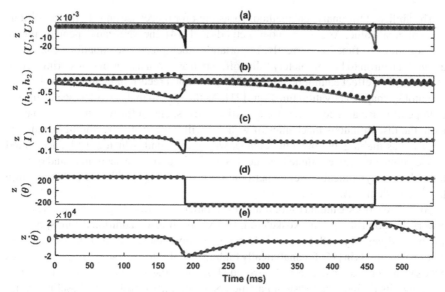

Fig. 2. The brute force (dots) and analytical (lines) iPRCs of the SNS controlled hip power unit model. (a): iPRC of U_1 and U_2 with the brute force iPRC represented by blue and green dots respectively, and the analytical iPRC represented by black and gray lines, respectively. (b): iPRC of h_1 and h_2 with the brute force iPRC represented by blue and green dots respectively, and the analytical iPRC represented by black and gray lines, respectively. (c): iPRC of the motor current. (d): iPRC of the angular position. (e): iPRC of the angular velocity. (Color figure online)

The analytical method for generating iPRCs will enable us to more rapidly tune the parameters of our system. One of our intended uses for the iPRCs is to find and evaluate ideal parameter values for interjoint coordinating influences in our networks. Proper walking emerges from sensory feedback pathways that synapse onto the CPGs to change their oscillation phases [8]. However, it is not clear which states should alter CPG phase, or how strong those influences should be. We can use iPRCs to determine at what phases a network is most sensitive to inputs, and exploit this knowledge to design locomotion-stabilizing coordination pathways. Even though this could be accomplished by generating iPRCs via simulation and brute force [14], the analytical iPRC method is faster and computationally less expensive, allowing quicker evaluation of possible changes to the system.

This analytical method for generating iPRCs will also enable us to determine synaptic sites for descending influences that alter locomotion. Descending influences from the brain are known to be critical for directing (but not necessarily generating) ongoing periodic motor output in all types of animals [9, 10]. However, it is not always clear what parts of the network descending commands modify to alter locomotion, or how strong those influences are. With the ability to rapidly generate iPRCs, we can identify how the parameters of a joint controller change its response to descending signals, and how the form and strength of those signals affect locomotion.

The ability of the analytical methods to account for piecewise and sliding conditions is also of great value. As shown in our methods and [14], the SNS can depend on piecewise equations to function correctly. Importantly, such piecewise equations enable the output of a neuron to be completely "shut off," such as when a neuron stops firing action potentials. This effect cannot be produced by traditional recurrent neural networks with continuous synaptic activation functions [21]. As the system in this work is scaled up and developed for use as a controller for an assistive exoskeleton for walking gait rehabilitation, the discontinuous mechanics of walking will introduce more sliding conditions [22], such as making and breaking contact with the ground, which must be accounted for. We believe we can continue to scale this method up to more accurately and quickly predict how a dynamical system's periodic orbit may be altered by perturbations in a phase-dependent way.

For future work we intend to continue development towards a larger and more realistic network for controlling our exoskeleton, that would include additional joints, as well as expanded sensory pathways and descending commands. We also plan to explore additional methods in [16] for analytically finding the infinitesimal shape response curves (iSRCs) for our systems. The iSRC would show how the values of each state change throughout its period when system parameters are perturbed from their baseline values for the duration of the limit cycle. Understanding how these lasting perturbations alter the periodic trajectory of the system will assist tuning of parameter values. Essentially, by perturbing one or more parameters for the full period of the limit cycle, their effects on the state values can be determined at each instance of the period. With this information, the proper parameter values needed for the trajectory to exhibit key features (i.e. level body height during the stance phase) can be found. We expect this analytical method to again be faster and computationally less expensive than solving the iSRC via brute force, allowing tuning to be done more quickly and efficiently.

References

1. Yan, T., Cempini, M., Oddo, C.M., Vitiello, N.: Review of assistive strategies in powered lower-limb orthoses and exoskeletons. Robot. Auton. Syst. **64**, 120–136 (2015)
2. Chang, S.R., et al.: A muscle-driven approach to restore stepping with an exoskeleton for individuals with para-plegia. J. NeuroEng. Rehabil. **14**, 48 (2017)
3. Lee, B.Y., Ostrander, L.E.: The spinal cord injured patient. Demos (2002)
4. del-Ama, A.J., Koutsou, A.D., Moreno, J.C., de-los-Reyes, A., Gil-Agudo, Á., Pons, J.L.: Review of hybrid exoskeletons to restore gait following spinal cord injury. J, Rehabil. Res. Dev. **49**, 497–514 (2012)
5. Kobetic, R., et al.: Implanted Functional Electrical Stimulation System for Mobility in Paraplegia: A Follow-Up Case Report (1999)
6. Buschmann, T., Ewald, A., von Twickel, A., Büschges, A.: Controlling legs for locomotion—insights from robotics and neurobiology. Bioinspiration Bio-mimetics **10**, 041001 (2015)
7. Szczecinski, N.S., Hunt, A.J., Quinn, R.D.: A functional subnetwork approach to designing synthetic nervous systems that control legged robot locomotion. Front. Neurorobot. **11**, 37 (2017)
8. Rossignol, S., Dubuc, R., Gossard, J.P.: Dynamic sensorimotor interactions in locomotion (2006)

9. Martin, J.P., Guo, P., Mu, L., Harley, C.M., Ritzmann, R.E.: Central-complex control of movement in the freely walking cockroach. Curr. Biol. **25**, 2795–2803 (2015)
10. Chiel, H.J., Beer, R.D.: The brain has a body: adaptive behavior emerges from interactions of nervous system, body and environment (1997)
11. Hunt, A., Schmidt, M., Fischer, M., Quinn, R.: A biologically based neural sys-tem coordinates the joints and legs of a tetrapod. Bioinspiration Biomimet-ics **10**, 055004 (2015)
12. Li, W., Szczecinski, N.S., Quinn, R.D.: A neural network with central pattern genera-tors entrained by sensory feedback controls walking of a bipedal mod-el. Bioinspiration Biomimetics **12**, 065002 (2017)
13. Szczecinski, N.S., et al.: Introducing MantisBot: hexapod robot controlled by a high-fidelity, real-time neural simulation. In: IEEE International Conference on Intelligent Robots and Systems, pp. 3875–3881. Institute of Electrical and Electronics Engineers Inc. (2015)
14. Szczecinski, N.S., Hunt, A.J., Quinn, R.D.: Design process and tools for dy-namic neurome-chanical models and robot controllers. Biol. Cybern. **111**, 105–127 (2017)
15. Klein, T., Lewis, M.A.: A neurorobotic model of bipedal locomotion based on principles of human neuromuscular architecture. In: Proceedings - IEEE In-ternational Conference on Robotics and Automation, pp. 1450–1455. Institute of Electrical and Electronics Engineers Inc. (2012)
16. Wang, Y., Gill, J.P., Chiel, H.J., Thomas, P.J.: Shape versus timing: linear responses of a limit cycle with hard boundaries under instantaneous and static perturbation. https://arxiv.org/abs/1906.04387. Accessed 29 Apr 2020
17. Park, Y., Shaw, K.M., Chiel, H.J., Thomas, P.J.: The infinitesimal phase response curves of oscillators in piecewise smooth dynamical systems. Eur. J. Appl. Math. **29**, 905–940 (2018)
18. Winter, D.A.: Biomechanics and Motor Control of Human Movement. Wiley (2009)
19. Izhikevich, E., Ermentrout, B.: Phase model. Scholarpedia **3**, 1487 (2008)
20. Lyttle, D.N., Gill, J.P., Shaw, K.M., Thomas, P.J., Chiel, H.J.: Robustness, flexibility, and sensitivity in a multifunctional motor control model. Biol. Cybern. **111**, 25–47 (2017)
21. Gabbiani, F., Cox, S.J.: Mathematics for Neuroscientists. 2nd edn. Elsevier Inc. (2017)
22. Branicky, M.S.: Multiple Lyapunov functions and other analysis tools for switched and hybrid systems. IEEE Trans. Autom. Control **43**, 475–482 (1998)

Machine Morality: From Harm-Avoidance to Human-Robot Cooperation

Ismael T. Freire[1,2,3(✉)], Dina Urikh[1,2,3], Xerxes D. Arsiwalla[1,2,3],
and Paul F. M. J. Verschure[1,3,4]

[1] Institute for BioEngineering of Catalonia (IBEC), Barcelona, Spain
ismaeltito.freire@gmail.com
[2] Universitat Pompeu Fabra (UPF), Barcelona, Spain
[3] Barcelona Institue of Science and Technology (BIST), Barcelona, Spain
[4] Catalan Institute for Research and Advanced Studies (ICREA), Barcelona, Spain

Abstract. We present a new computational framework for modeling moral decision-making in artificial agents based on the notion of 'Machine Morality as Cooperation'. This framework integrates recent advances from cross-disciplinary moral decision-making literature into a single architecture. We build upon previous work outlining cognitive elements that an artificial agent would need for exhibiting latent morality, and we extend it by providing a computational realization of the cognitive architecture of such an agent. Our work has implications for cognitive and social robotics. Recent studies in human neuroimaging have pointed to three different decision-making processes, Pavlovian, model-free and model-based, that are defined by distinct neural substrates in the brain. Here, we describe how computational models of these three cognitive processes can be implemented in a single cognitive architecture by using the distributed and hierarchical organization proposed by the DAC theoretical framework. Moreover, we propose that a pro-social drive to cooperate exists at the Pavlovian level that can also bias the rest of the decision system, thus extending current state-of-the-art descriptive models based on harm-aversion.

Keywords: Morality · Moral decision-making · Computational models · Cognitive architectures · Cognitive robotics · Human-robot interaction

1 Introduction

Ever since the ancient Greeks, thinkers across the world have struggled to identify fundamental features that let human beings create complex social structures within and between groups. Today theories coming from a wide range of fields (from evolutionary anthropology to social cognitive neuroscience) are aiming to explain social cooperation that leads to emergence of such phenomena as altruism or moral conduct.

© Springer Nature Switzerland AG 2020
V. Vouloutsi et al. (Eds.): Living Machines 2020, LNAI 12413, pp. 116–127, 2020.
https://doi.org/10.1007/978-3-030-64313-3_13

Although theoretical accounts in this field, as with the majority of eternal questions, tend to fall in the nature-nurture debate, a synthetic approach states that moral reasoning arises from complex social decision-making and involves both unconscious and deliberate processes [1,12,20,37,46].

But what are the mechanisms behind our impressive moral capacities? Is it our ability to make decisions taking others into account? Or is it our ability to predict internal states of others? Can we obtain a better understanding of this phenomenon to contribute to building more cooperative and caring societies? Can we design living machines that can differentiate between what is right and what is wrong? What are the computational mechanisms behind our sense of morality and can it be reproduced in artificial systems? We will try to address those questions through the cross-field integration of insights from philosophy, social cognitive neuroscience, evolutionary anthropology, artificial intelligence and robotics.

In the philosophical tradition, there are two main standpoints that propose different principles behind our moral decision-making. Utilitarianism assumes that morality implies maximizing the total amount of "utility" (a measure of happiness) in the world [27]. Since utilitarians evaluate actions based on their outcomes, their views are called "consequentialist". Deontology, on the other hand, evaluates the actions themselves as being morally justified or not, regardless of their consequences [24]. In the field of artificial intelligence (AI) there have been attempts to implement both of those normative views on morality in artificial systems [43]. The implementations of moral agents are employing two broad approaches: the top-down application of ethical theories, and the bottom-up construction of systems that aim at specified goals or standards which may or may not be specified in explicit theoretical terms [44,45].

A bottom-up approach to ethics in AI addresses norms as being an integral part of the activity of agents rather than explicitly formulated in terms of a general theory [42]. Complex bottom-up architectures excel in their ability to dynamically integrate input from various sources, as demonstrated in their successful application for sensorimotor control in robotics. The reverse side of this coin is usually seen in failures to understand which goals have to be used to assess choices and actions in dynamically changing conditions. Bottom-up agents are most efficient when they are aimed at fulfilling one distinct objective. With multiple goals or confusing sources of information, shaping a clear scenario becomes a challenging task for bottom-up systems [28].

A top-down approach, on the other hand, utilizes the explicitly specified ethical theory and analyzes the resulting computational requirements in order to develop algorithms and agents capable of implementing that theory. These systems can provide clear solutions to moral dilemmas by directly applying the norms specified in their implementation. However, problems intrinsic to consequentalist and deontological approaches will manifest in terms of computational resources. In the case of consequentalist approaches, utility calculations of possible outcomes can scale dramatically, and deontological assessment of the universal validity of a course of action can also lead to increased demands on computational power [42].

It seems that any of the above reviewed strategies that try to implement a normative moral system in an artificial agent will face not only the intrinsic problems specific to that moral school, but also the intrinsic problems of the top-down and bottom-up approaches to building artificial intelligence.

Given the current limitations of both theoretical and implementational accounts, it seems that the old Aristotle's 'golden mean' is still valid, in a sense that a successful artificial system would build upon the advantages of both bottom-up and top-down realizations, as well as consequentialist and deontological perspectives. But if our goal is to achieve functional morality that allows artificial agents to take moral decisions and interact with us in our daily lives, we might also consider a more descriptive (epistemic) perspective that rather deals with morality as a set of socio-cultural norms [2]. As we will see in the next sections, this is consistent with data from cognitive neuroscience literature: moral decision-making in humans combines bottom-up mechanisms sculptured by evolution and learning with top-down mechanisms capable of theory-driven reasoning (Fig. 1).

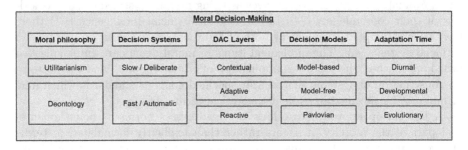

Fig. 1. Relationship between the different dimensions taken into account into the DAC-based computational model of moral decision-making.

2   The Utilitarian and the Deontological Brain

If in the previous section we discussed the ideal and prescriptive nature of moral philosophy, here we review the latest experimental findings in moral-decision making – that is how these moral principles are instantiated in the brain and what computational models are used to explain the observed phenomena. Studies have demonstrated that experimental manipulations can make subjects' decisions lean toward either consequentialism or deontology, suggesting that the two perspectives engage separate neural systems [21]. Consequentalist moral evaluation has been linked to increased activity in lateral frontoparietal regions, whereas deontological processes seem to be more related to the activity of medial prefrontal areas [25]. There is a substantial amount of literature in the field of reinforcement learning that links these cognitive networks associated with consequentialism and deontology with two different computational learning systems, namely model-free and model-based reinforcement learning [10].

A model-based computational system selects actions based on their presumed outcomes while a model-free system chooses actions based on their reinforcement history. Moreover, these computational models have clear functional mapping to the philosophical views of deontology (model-free) and consequentialism (model-based). As for the cognitive networks, the model-free system in the brain uses automatic, fast and reflexive mechanisms that we are believed to be sharing with other species. Model-based system, on the other hand, employs acquired, controlled and reflective mechanisms that are only observed in human adults [1].

Apart from these two cognitive systems, literature suggests existence of another distinct decision-making mechanism that we share with other animals, the one in charge of automatic reflexive approach and withdrawal reactions to appetitive and aversive stimuli, respectively: a so-called Pavlovian system [14]. But what role would Pavlovian system play in moral decision-making? The possible answer could be found in the changing nature of environmental conditions: multiple decision-making modules can provide different benefits in certain contexts. Model-based control works well for simple decisions, but when the decision tree search is computationally costly, model-free and Pavlovian systems can be utilized to guide the search.

One promising attempt to explain the functional utility of the Pavlovian system [10] builds upon puzzling experimental results obtained in two versions of a classic moral dilemma (the so-called 'push-trapdoor divergence'). In this study, a traditional trolley problem (where one was offered to pull a lever to guide a trolley towards a single man in order to save lives of five workers) was modified to substitute the action of pulling the lever for a physical push of the victim. Surprisingly, this change lead to a significant difference in outcomes: subjects were more likely to pull the lever rather than physically push a person towards the track. The role of Pavlovian system here is suggested to be comprised of behavioral suppression aimed at preventing aversive outcome. Such capacity could be used, for instance, for the suppression of trains of thought or behavioral sequences that result in aversive states, or in other words, for a pruning of the decision tree [23]. In the context of the modified trolley setup, a physical push of the victim would be considered a less desirable outcome based on aversive bias induced by the Pavlovian system.

3   Computational Models of Moral Decision-Making

Recent advances coming from the Reinforcement Learning (RL) literature have proposed several ways to combine model-free with model-based learning. Among them, Episodic-RL and Meta-RL are the most relevant ones due to their success in matching human data from several experimental benchmarks and improvements in learning speeds, bringing the sample-inefficiency problem of Deep RL a bit closer to human learning timescales [8].

However, what is still missing in the field of AI is a solid solution that would integrate the three decision-making systems identified by cognitive neuroscience into one single architecture. If we aspire to model human moral decision-making with its complex nuances arising from the interplay between the three processes, as well as to implement them in a robotic system, we have to use a theoretical framework that is able to accommodate them into a single cognitive architecture.

To address that issue, we draw upon the Distributed Adaptive Control theory of mind and brain that proposes that cognition is based on four control layers operating at different levels of abstraction [38–40]. The first level, the Soma layer, contains the whole body of the agent with all the sensors and actuators and represents the interface between the agent and its environment. The Reactive layer integrates the Pavlovian decision-making system that regulates the fast and unconditioned reactions to favorable and averse stimuli, implemented as self-regulated sensorimotor control loops. These reactive interactions with the environment bootstrap the learning of model-free relationships in the Adaptive layer allowing the acquisition of a state-action space of the agent-environment interaction. The Contextual layer acquires temporally extended model-based policies that contribute to the acquisition of more abstract cognitive abilities such as goal selection, memory and planning. These higher-level representations, in turn, affect the behavior of lower layers in a top-down fashion. Control in this architecture is therefore distributed between all layers through interactions in both directions, top-down and bottom-up, as well as laterally within each layer.

The three layers of the Distributed Adaptive Control architecture can be mapped to biological systems as different learning processes operating at different timescales, as recently proposed in [8]. The reactive layer implementing the Pavlovian decision-making system would correspond to adaptation to the environment through slow evolutionary processes. The adaptive layer would then comprise learned behaviors of the model-free decision system, acquired through development. Finally, model-based learning in the contextual layer would happen at the diurnal timescale.

Shaping of cognition through the lens of evolution, development and learning brings us to an apparent contradiction. Paradoxically, the control processes subject to the fastest timescales of adaptation and learning (contextual, model-based) are the ones responsible for providing slow and deliberate decisions. Conversely, the more primitive control mechanisms subject to the slowest forms of adaptation (reactive, Pavlovian) are the ones responsible for producing fast and robust decisions. From a control perspective, however, this observation makes a lot of sense. One the one hand, a reactive system that provides robust and reliable responses when its needed will be intrinsically slow in adapting (robustness), but extremely useful if it is fast in delivering responses towards the most dangerous or vital things of the environment. On the other hand, a system that provides flexible responses to the ever-changing details of the its surroundings might give an organism the necessary advantage against its competitors. Of course, such attention to the details implies a lot of information to take into account, therefore its flexibility comes at a cost in response or processing time.

This robustness/flexibility trade-off [7] points out one important observation: natural selection might not have selected for a general-purpose control system, but for a combination of several specialised systems that cooperating together might overcome their intrinsic individual limitations.

4 Aversive and Appetitive Foundations of Moral Decision-Making

Recent studies diving into the computational and neural substrates of moral decision-making experience the influence of neuroeconomics in their experimental design and therefore, in the models that are developed. For instance, in a series of experimental setups, a group of researchers has tried to investigate assignment of value to certain properties of a moral decision, such as inflicting harm to oneself or to others, through offering economic rewards in exchange for varying levels of electrical shocks [11,47]. Behavioral and neuroimaging results showed that subjects were preferring to harm themselves over others for profit and this moral preference was associated with diminished neural responses in value-sensitive regions to profit accrued from harming others [11]. Computational utilitarian models developed to explain these results build upon the notion of harm aversion. According to this view, harm aversion bias represents our intrinsic avoidance of harming others and affects the way the internal utility computations are integrated into moral decision-making. The notion of harm aversion can also help to explain the puzzling results of the push–trapdoor divergence mentioned before, and it might be an important ingredient of our moral cognition.

However, a computational model and a theoretical view on morality built upon a negative proposition (harm avoidance/inhibitory behavior) would hardly provide a comprehensive picture. In the end, if some part of our moral behavior can indeed be based on a Pavlovian aversive reaction mechanism, other aspects of morality could as well be grounded in an intrinsic preference for appetitive stimuli. Such hypothesis would be backed up by substantial evidence obtained from one-shot prisoner's dilemma experiments where human subjects tend to strive for cooperation as a default intuitive option [9,32–34].

In fact, anthropological accounts of the origins of morality do indeed provide us with a view on morality that stems from a positive proposition: cooperation. Cooperation in large groups of unrelated individuals is believed to be an evolutionary developed human feature [37]. In other words, it is evolutionary beneficial for humans to genuinely prefer moral outcomes because it facilitates cooperation [46]. Among recent theoretical proposals attempting to explain morality, one in particular might seem promising as it integrates conceptual diversity of previous literature into one single theoretical framework capable of making testable predictions: Morality-as-Cooperation (MAC) [12]. MAC defines morality as a collection of biological and cultural solutions to the problems of cooperation and conflict recurrent in human social life. Grounded in the mathematical theory of cooperation (the theory of nonzero-sum games), MAC creates a principled taxonomy of moral values, each of which is expressed as a solution to a distinct cooperation game. In a recent study this taxonomy has been empirically validated through finding instances of these seven moral principles across 60 cultures [13].

5   Machine-Morality-as-Cooperation Through Distributed Adaptive Control

Morality-as-Cooperation seems to be a promising framework for future human studies, but is there any similar synthetic approach addressing moral problems in robotics? From our literature review it seems that the widely accepted angle so far has been the one mirroring the harm aversion perspective in human morality studies, namely harm avoidance: a machine that is moral is defined as the one that does no harm to humans. While acknowledging its utility, we could argue that harm avoidance is a condition necessary but not sufficient to call a machine moral, and our cross-disciplinary review has justified the proposal of a new perspective that could be fruitful in the development of Human-Robot Interaction scenarios: Machine-Morality-as-Cooperation.

Machine-Morality-as-Cooperation (MMAC) is a synthetic and functional approach to modelling machine morality as it incorporates the previous principles adopted in the field -harm avoidance- while also adding a novel dimension grounded in human morality studies: promote cooperation. At the core of this approach lies the implementation of a reactive control system that, inspired by the Pavlovian appetitive and aversive reactive drives, will apply specific rules to ensure both harm avoidance and prosocial cooperative behaviors. Moreover, in order to support both deontological and consequentalist computations, this artificial system should incorporate both model-free and model-based forms of learning. Computational single-architecture integration of the three cognitive networks aimed at implementing Machine-Morality-as-Cooperation uses the Distributed Adaptive Control (DAC) design principles. Several realisations of the DAC architecture have been previously successfully applied and validated on different robotic platforms [26,29,40], and therefore DAC can be a good candidate to instantiate Machine-Morality-as-Cooperation requirements in an autonomous agent.

6   Machine-Morality-as-Cooperation: Prescriptive and Functional Implementations

As with the study of morality, we can discuss the application of Machine-Morality-as-Cooperation from a prescriptive, high-level standpoint, or choose a more grounded and functional way. Both cases deserve attention due to their theoretical and practical implications. In order to realise an ideal implementation of MMAC's cognitive architecture in an artificial autonomous agent, the agent will first have to pass through three specific developmental stages -according to the requirements of each layer- in order to reach its full capacity.

First, the agent will need to acquire its Pavlovian component by engaging in an evolutionary process that will generate a reactive control system adapted to the specific contingencies of the world it will live in [3–5]. This process will be necessary for the agent to develop a basic set of appetitive and aversive behaviors that allow the agent to survive and fulfill its basics needs. A shortcut for this process will be, naturally, either explicit or implicit integration of a fixed set of behaviors (implementing a form of "architectural bias").

Secondly, to train the model-free learning module, the agent will have to learn the valence of its actions through trial and error during the course of its development. This process can occur as learning of weights in a neural network, or as ascribing values to state-action couplets in reinforcement learning algorithms. It will be the equivalent of the pruning process occurring in the human brain during the early stages of development. When it reaches 'maturity' -by completing this developmental stage, it will be ready to build a model of the world [17]. It is important to note that if we aim to develop a competent moral agent able to deal with the complexities of the social world we want it to navigate, it will be necessary to expose this agent to certain degrees of social interaction since the very beginning. This could be done gradually, starting from dyadic interactions in its early stages and scaling to group level scenarios later in its development.

Thirdly, after the second training stage is complete, the agent will be ready to create internal models of the world. In this final stage of training, inspired by the social nature of morality, the model-based learning module will need to make a reliable model not only of its environment, but also of the other agents, with whom it interacts [16,18,19]. Ideally, this model-based mechanism should be able to generate internal models of other agents as well as of higher-order entities such as a group or a population of agents. Recent work has proven computational feasibility of such group-theory-of-mind [36].

Although the training stage of such agent might be complex, the experimental tools required for an attempt to shape such architecture already exist. For each of these three different stages, there are specific benchmarks that we could pursue, each of them coming from a different sub-field of AI and robotics. On the evolutionary stage, the benchmarks can be drawn from artificial life and evolutionary robotics literature [15]. On the developmental stage, several types of dyadic game-theoretical scenarios could be used as training examples of different types of social interactions to test and train the agent [16,17]. For the last stage of learning, benchmarks from the multi-agent reinforcement learning literature, since they deal with massive multi-agent scenarios [30] in which certain norms need to be learned to successfully complete the task [31]. Lastly, the natural target benchmark for this proposed artificial moral agent would be to fit the human behavioral results of the two classical versions of the Trolley Problem, the so-called 'push-trapdoor divergence' [22].

In order to instantiate this approach in a concrete scenario we implemented it in a functional industrial plant arm robot within the framework of HR-Recycler project [6]. The autonomy and interaction capabilities of the industrial arm robot itself are quite limited as it operates with a human worker through assembling/disassembling components in a tabletop setting. It is also important to mention that model-free learning is not a part of this implementation, since the requirements of learning time and context demanded a more robust solution. Therefore, our moral cognitive architecture will operate using only the Reactive and Contextual layers. However, Machine-Morality-as-Cooperation approach promises functional benefits even with these limitations, as it aims at promoting cooperation through putting human worker always first. Promoting cooperation is achieved through optimizing different pre-determined parameters at the reactive level, such as, for instance, speed of operation, distance to human worker and number of tasks allocated to the robot. The target values of those parameters are mapped to actual human preferences obtained from a worker model built in the contextual layer of the architecture. Thanks to this feature, each human worker is seen as a unique context. Contextual layer also comprises information regarding tool use and specifics of each ongoing mechanical task performed. Thus the reactive control systems in charge of harm avoidance is also contextually aware through the regulation of situational parameters such as safe distance, affordances of the object that might pose risks, etc. This dynamic contextual modulation of the target values of each reactive control system is also known as "allostatic control", and has been shown to produce adaptive behavior in both living [35] and artificial [41] systems.

7   Discussion

In this paper, we present a novel computational framework for modeling moral decision-making in artificial agents (Machine-Morality-as-Cooperation) that integrates recent advances from the cross-disciplinary moral decision-making literature into a single architecture. We build upon previous work outlining the cognitive elements that an artificial agent would need for exhibiting latent morality [2], and we extend it by providing a first computational description of the cognitive architecture of such agent.

Recent evidence from the field of cognitive neuroscience describes the key roles of three different decision-making processes (Pavlovian, model-free, model-based) that are defined by distinct neural substrates in the human brain. We have shown how computational models of these three cognitive processes can be implemented in a single cognitive architecture by using the distributed and hierarchical organization proposed by the DAC theoretical framework. Moreover, we propose that a pro-social drive to cooperate exists at the Pavlovian level that can also bias the rest of the decision systems, thus extending current state-of-the-art descriptive models based on harm-aversion.

We believe that the key to advancing our understanding of human morality lies in comprehensive theoretical synthesis across multiple fields that study this phenomenon. The pursuit of implementing morality in living machines will not only affect how we perceive and interact with future autonomous agents: it will help us get a more profound vision of the human cognition. In this view, the question should be not (only) if we can engineer agents capable of moral behavior, but whether we could evolve them, nurture them, and teach them so they "become" moral living machines.

Acknowledgments. This research received funding from H2020-EU, ID: 820742.

References

1. Adolphs, R.: Cognitive neuroscience of human social behaviour. Nat. Rev. Neurosci. **4**(3), 165–178 (2003)
2. Arsiwalla, X.D., Freire, I.T., Vouloutsi, V., Verschure, P.: Latent morality in algorithms and machines. In: Martinez-Hernandez, U., Vouloutsi, V., Mura, A., Mangan, M., Asada, M., Prescott, T.J., Verschure, P.F.M.J. (eds.) Living Machines 2019. LNCS (LNAI), vol. 11556, pp. 309–315. Springer, Cham (2019). https://doi.org/10.1007/978-3-030-24741-6_27
3. Arsiwalla, X.D., Herreros, I., Moulin-Frier, C., Sanchez-Fibla, M., Verschure, P.: Is consciousness a control process? In: Artificial Intelligence Research and Development: Proceedings of the 19th International Conference of the Catalan Association for Artificial Intelligence, Barcelona, Catalonia, Spain, 19–21 October 2016, p. 233. IOS Press (2016)
4. Arsiwalla, X.D., Herreros, I., Moulin-Frier, C., Verschure, P.: Consciousness as an evolutionary game-theoretic strategy. In: Mangan, M., Cutkosky, M., Mura, A., Verschure, P.F.M.J., Prescott, T., Lepora, N. (eds.) Living Machines 2017. LNCS (LNAI), vol. 10384, pp. 509–514. Springer, Cham (2017). https://doi.org/10.1007/978-3-319-63537-8_43
5. Arsiwalla, X.D., Sole, R., Moulin-Frier, C., Herreros, I., Sanchez-Fibla, M., Verschure, P.F.: The morphospace of consciousness. arXiv preprint arXiv:1705.11190 (2017)
6. Axenopoulos, A., et al.: A hybrid human-robot collaborative environment for recycling electrical and electronic equipment. In: 2019 IEEE SmartWorld, Ubiquitous Intelligence & Computing, Advanced & Trusted Computing, Scalable Computing & Communications, Cloud & Big Data Computing, Internet of People and Smart City Innovation (SmartWorld/SCALCOM/UIC/ATC/CBDCom/IOP/SCI), pp. 1754–1759. IEEE (2019)
7. Balas, G.J., Doyle, J.C.: Robustness and performance trade-offs in control design for flexible structures. IEEE Trans. Control Syst. Technol. **2**(4), 352–361 (1994)
8. Botvinick, M., Ritter, S., Wang, J.X., Kurth-Nelson, Z., Blundell, C., Hassabis, D.: Reinforcement learning, fast and slow. Trends Cogn. Sci. **23**(5), 408–422 (2019)
9. Camerer, C.F.: Behavioral Game Theory: Experiments in Strategic Interaction. Princeton University Press, Princeton (2011)
10. Crockett, M.J.: Models of morality. Trends Cogn. Sci. **17**(8), 363–366 (2013). https://doi.org/10.1016/j.tics.2013.06.005
11. Crockett, M.J., Siegel, J.Z., Kurth-Nelson, Z., Dayan, P., Dolan, R.J.: Moral transgressions corrupt neural representations of value. Nat. Neurosci. **20**(6), 879–885 (2017). https://doi.org/10.1038/nn.4557
12. Curry, O.S.: Morality as cooperation: a problem-centred approach. In: Shackelford, T.K., Hansen, R.D. (eds.) The Evolution of Morality. EP, pp. 27–51. Springer, Cham (2016). https://doi.org/10.1007/978-3-319-19671-8_2

13. Curry, O.S., Mullins, D.A., Whitehouse, H.: Is it good to cooperate. Curr. Anthropol. **60**(1), 47–69 (2019)
14. Dayan, P.: How to set the switches on this thing. Curr. Opin. Neurobiol. **22**(6), 1068–1074 (2012)
15. Floreano, D., Keller, L.: Evolution of adaptive behaviour in robots by means of Darwinian selection. PLoS Biol. **8**(1), e1000292 (2010)
16. Freire, I.T., Arsiwalla, X.D., Puigbò, J.Y., Verschure, P.: Modeling theory of mind in multi-agent games using adaptive feedback control. arXiv preprint arXiv:1905.13225 (2019)
17. Freire, I.T., Moulin-Frier, C., Sanchez-Fibla, M., Arsiwalla, X.D., Verschure, P.F.: Modeling the formation of social conventions from embodied real-time interactions. PLoS ONE **15**(6), e0234434 (2020)
18. Freire, I.T., Puigbò, J.Y., Arsiwalla, X.D., Verschure, P.F.: Limits of multi-agent predictive models in the formation of social conventions. Artif. Intell. Res. Dev.: Curr. Chall. New Trends Appl. **308**, 297 (2018)
19. Freire, I.T., Puigbò, J.-Y., Arsiwalla, X.D., Verschure, P.F.M.J.: Modeling the opponent's action using control-based reinforcement learning. In: Vouloutsi, V., Halloy, J., Mura, A., Mangan, M., Lepora, N., Prescott, T.J., Verschure, P.F.M.J. (eds.) Living Machines 2018. LNCS (LNAI), vol. 10928, pp. 179–186. Springer, Cham (2018). https://doi.org/10.1007/978-3-319-95972-6_19
20. Greene, J.D.: The cognitive neuroscience of moral judgment. Cogn. Neurosci. **4**, 1–48 (2009)
21. Greene, J.D., Nystrom, L.E., Engell, A.D., Darley, J.M., Cohen, J.D.: The neural bases of cognitive conflict and control in moral judgment. Neuron **44**(2), 389–400 (2004)
22. Greene, J.: Solving the trolley problem. A companion to experimental philosophy, pp. 175–178 (2016)
23. Huys, Q.J., Eshel, N., O'Nions, E., Sheridan, L., Dayan, P., Roiser, J.P.: Bonsai trees in your head: how the pavlovian system sculpts goal-directed choices by pruning decision trees. PLoS Comput. Biol. **8**(3), e1002410 (2012)
24. Kant, I.: Groundwork of the metaphysic of morals. Trans. HJ Paton. 3rd edn. Harper Torchbooks, New York (1785)
25. Lieberman, M.D.: Social cognitive neuroscience: a review of core processes. Annu. Rev. Psychol. **58**(1), 259–289 (2007). https://doi.org/10.1146/annurev.psych.58.110405.085654
26. Maffei, G., Santos-Pata, D., Marcos, E., Sánchez-Fibla, M., Verschure, P.F.: An embodied biologically constrained model of foraging: from classical and operant conditioning to adaptive real-world behavior in DAC-X. Neural Netw. **72**, 88–108 (2015). https://doi.org/10.1016/j.neunet.2015.10.004
27. Mill, J.S.: Utilitarianism. Longmans, Green and Company (1895)
28. Moulin-Frier, C., Arsiwalla, X.D., Puigbò, J.Y., Sanchez-Fibla, M., Duff, A., Verschure, P.F.: Top-down and bottom-up interactions between low-level reactive control and symbolic rule learning in embodied agents. In: CoCo@ NIPS (2016)
29. Moulin-Frier, C., et al.: DAC-h3: a proactive robot cognitive architecture to acquire and express knowledge about the world and the self. IEEE Trans. Cogn. Dev. Syst. **10**(4), 1005–1022 (2017)
30. Perolat, J., Leibo, J.Z., Zambaldi, V., Beattie, C., Tuyls, K., Graepel, T.: A multi-agent reinforcement learning model of common-pool resource appropriation. In: Advances in Neural Information Processing Systems, pp. 3643–3652 (2017)
31. Peysakhovich, A., Lerer, A.: Consequentialist conditional cooperation in social dilemmas with imperfect information. arXiv preprint arXiv:1710.06975 (2017)

32. Rand, D.G., Greene, J.D., Nowak, M.A.: Spontaneous giving and calculated greed. Nature **489**(7416), 427–430 (2012)
33. Rand, D.G., Nowak, M.A.: Human cooperation. Trends Cogn. Sci. **17**(8), 413–425 (2013)
34. Rand, D.G., et al.: Intuitive cooperation and the social heuristics hypothesis: evidence from 15 time constraint studies. In: Available at ssrn.com/abstract, vol. 2222683 (2013)
35. Sanchez-Fibla, M., et al.: Allostatic control for robot behavior regulation: a comparative rodent-robot study. Adv. Complex Syst. **13**(03), 377–403 (2010)
36. Shum, M., Kleiman-Weiner, M., Littman, M.L., Tenenbaum, J.B.: Theory of minds: understanding behavior in groups through inverse planning. arXiv preprint arXiv:1901.06085 (2019)
37. Tomasello, M., Vaish, A.: Origins of human cooperation and morality. Annu. Rev. Psychol. **64**, 231–255 (2013)
38. Verschure, P.F.: Synthetic consciousness: the distributed adaptive control perspective. Philosophical Trans. R. Soc. B: Biol. Sci. **371**(1701), 20150448 (2016)
39. Verschure, P.F., Pennartz, C.M., Pezzulo, G.: The why, what, where, when and how of goal-directed choice: neuronal and computational principles. Philos. Trans. R. Soc. B: Biol. Sci. **369**(1655), 20130483 (2014)
40. Verschure, P.F., Voegtlin, T., Douglas, R.J.: Environmentally mediated synergy between perception and behaviour in mobile robots. Nature **425**(6958), 620–624 (2003)
41. Vouloutsi, V., Lallée, S., Verschure, P.F.M.J.: Modulating behaviors using allostatic control. In: Lepora, N.F., Mura, A., Krapp, H.G., Verschure, P.F.M.J., Prescott, T.J. (eds.) Living Machines 2013. LNCS (LNAI), vol. 8064, pp. 287–298. Springer, Heidelberg (2013). https://doi.org/10.1007/978-3-642-39802-5_25
42. Wallach, W., Allen, C.: Bottom-up and top-down approaches for modeling human moral faculties. In: Proceedings of the 2005 CogSci Workshop, pp. 149–159 (2005)
43. Wallach, W., Allen, C.: Moral Machines: Teaching Robots Right From Wrong. Oxford University Press, Oxford (2008)
44. Wallach, W., Allen, C., Franklin, S.: Consciousness and ethics: artificially conscious moral agents. Int. J. Mach. Conscious. **3**(01), 177–192 (2011)
45. Wallach, W., Allen, C., Smit, I.: Machine morality: bottom-up and top-down approaches for modelling human moral faculties. AI Soc. **22**(4), 565–582 (2008)
46. Yoder, K.J., Decety, J.: The neuroscience of morality and social decision-making. Psychol. Crime Law **24**(3), 279–295 (2018). https://doi.org/10.1080/1068316X.2017.1414817, https://www.ncbi.nlm.nih.gov/pmc/articles/PMC6372234/pdf/nihms-1500620.pdf
47. Yu, H., Siegel, J.Z., Crockett, M.J.: Modeling morality in 3-D: decision-making, judgment, and inference. Top. Cogn. Sci. **11**(2), 409–432 (2019). https://doi.org/10.1111/tops.12382

Haptic Object Identification for Advanced Manipulation Skills

Volker Gabler[1]([✉])[ID], Korbinian Maier[1][ID], Satoshi Endo[2][ID],
and Dirk Wollherr[1][ID]

[1] Chair of Automatic Control Engineering, Munich, Germany
{v.gabler,korbinian.maier,dw}@tum.de
[2] Chair of Information Oriented Control, Department of Electrical and Computer
Engineering, Technical University of Munich, Munich, Germany
s.endo@tum.de

Abstract. In order to identify the characteristics of unknown objects, humans - in contrast to robotic systems - are experts in exploiting their sensory and motoric abilities to refine visual information via haptic perception. While recent research has focused on either estimating the geometry or material properties, this work strives to combine these aspects by outlining a probabilistic framework that efficiently refines initial knowledge from visual sensors by generating a belief state over the object shape while simultaneously learn material parameters. Specifically, we present a grid-based and a shape-based exploration strategy, that both apply the concepts of Bayesian-Filter theory in order to decrease the uncertainty. Furthermore, the presented framework is able to learn about the geometry as well as to distinguish areas of different material types by applying unsupervised machine learning methods. The experimental results from a virtual exploration task highlight the potential of the presented methods towards enabling robots to autonomously explore unknown objects, yielding information about shape and structure of the underlying object and thus, opening doors to robotic applications where environmental knowledge is limited.

Keywords: Haptic identification · Object classification · Autonomous agents

In order to allow robots to manipulate arbitrary objects, such as electronic waste components for automated disassembly, object identification and knowledge acquisition is crucial. While a rough estimation of the shape of an object can be obtained from visual data, the exact material decomposition remains in general unknown. Nonetheless, these material properties have a distinct effect on the selection of the subsequent manipulation tasks, e.g. the choice of material-dependent cutting tools. In order to allow robots to autonomously identify these object characteristics, one approach is to mimic human behavior in applying haptic data acquisition methods, i.e. actively interacting with the unknown object.

© Springer Nature Switzerland AG 2020
V. Vouloutsi et al. (Eds.): Living Machines 2020, LNAI 12413, pp. 128–140, 2020.
https://doi.org/10.1007/978-3-030-64313-3_14

This approach, known as tactile and haptic exploration, enables robots to significantly increase and extend the results of visual object identification methods. In contrast to recent research in haptics, this work presents an online inference algorithm which is capable of acquiring information not only about the geometry but also about the material parameters of an unknown object.

The remainder of this work is structured as follows: the next section outlines the mathematical problem tackled in this work, followed by an outline on how this work is positioned compared to related work in Sect. 2. The concepts of the proposed grid-based and the shape-based exploration strategies are sketched in Sect. 3. The idea of classifying individual components by their material types is shown in Sect. 4, whereas Sect. 5 outlines the evaluation of the proposed methods in a simulated environment. The summary in Sect. 6 concludes this work.

1   Problem Statement

The task of haptic object identification consists of two main challenges. First, the geometric shape of an object, denoted as M in the context of this work, is in general unknown. Second, the object is characterized by an undefined parameterization Θ, that describes the material properties of an object, e.g. a material classificator that maps each component of M to a finite set of materials. Given the state, control inputs and measurements of a robot as $x_{1..t} = \{x_1, \ldots, x_t\}$, $u = \{u_1 \ldots u_t\}$ and $r_{1..t} = \{r_1, \ldots, r_t\}$ from time-step 0 to the current time step t, the problem is given by finding proper mapping functions

$$M \leftarrow \mathcal{F}_m(x_{1..t}, u_{1..t}, r_{1..t}, \Theta), \tag{1}$$

$$\Theta \leftarrow \mathcal{F}_p(x_{1..t}, u_{1..t}, r_{1..t}, M). \tag{2}$$

Finding proper mappings $\mathcal{F}_m$ and $\mathcal{F}_p$ is non-trivial as they are in general dependent on each other. Nonetheless, when analyzing the problem individually, one can relax these problems and focus on finding these mappings for a fixed Θ or M. As a variety of promising methods on solving these problems individually in literature exists, we continue with an overview of related work.

2   Related Work

Although vision has been established as the backbone of robotic perception, haptic information acquisition has been used to understand or recognize shapes of objects for years [1]. Navarro et al. [16] present an approach for haptic object recognition based on extracting key features of tactile and kinesthetic data using a clustering algorithm, where a tactile sensor performs haptic sensation tasks using different robotic hands. Behbahani et al. [3] have introduced haptic Simultaneous Localisation and Mapping (SLAM) into the field of haptic exploration, which is inspired by visual SLAM techniques [6] and occupancy grid methods [7]. Through adaption of the FastSLAM [15] algorithm, a novel method is proposed to iteratively learn the shape of the surface of objects. The same approach is

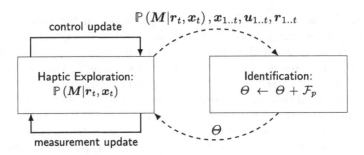

Fig. 1. Proposed framework components. The haptic exploration iteratively decreases model uncertainty, while the identification allows to batch-process a collection of data measurements in order to refine the object parameters Θ.

used to mimic haptic perceptual algorithms from neuroscience in [2]. Another method using haptic SLAM is presented by Schaeffer *et al.* [18], although their algorithms require knowledge about the underlying object shape in advance. Further on, there are methods to detect objects and especially edges of geometries through clever exploration strategies. Pezzementi *et al.* [17] extract features based on data from a tactile sensor array using methods inspired by computer vision techniques. This concept is extended in [14] by actively following contours based on tactile sensor data. Nonetheless, this approach heavily relies on distinct edges and sharp angles in the contour of the object. Another approach is represented in [11], where range data and 2D images are combined to a generic object recognition algorithm. These techniques succeed in solving the geometric shape estimation task, but fail in providing any further information about the underlying material decomposition.

The problem of finding a dedicated choice of control actions that can help to maximize the accuracy of the available information is tackled by Bourgault *et al.* [4], who use an information-theoretic approach to select actions with a high information gain. Similarly Julian *et al.* [12] use sequential Bayesian filters to increase the information gain for a joint state exploration task with multiple robotic agents.

Regarding the aspect of identifying material parameters based on haptic cues promising results have been found in literature. Luo *et al.* [13] provide a detailed review of tactile perception using surface and texture-based information to find material properties and types. Friedl *et al.* [10] identify textures using recurrent spiking neural networks. Decherchi *et al.* [5] classify material types using methods from computational intelligence from contact forces. Xu *et al.* [22] propose a classification algorithm based on texture and propose a Bayesian exploration algorithm which seeks to minimize the uncertainty in the underlying belief [9]. These methods allow to distinguish between different material properties, but fail to simultaneously refine shape estimation and material classification.

2.1   Contribution

In contrast to the stated work, this work outlines a haptic object identification framework that allows to simultaneously refine the shape estimation and regress the underlying material parameters as visualized in Fig. 1. In order to obtain $\mathcal{F}_m$, we incorporate findings from Haptic SLAM [3]. This encourages to maximize the information gain at every step by applying concepts of Bayesian Filter theory [19] in an iterative cycle of control and measurement updates. In order to decouple the simultaneous parameter estimation problem, Θ is assumed to be fixed for K_e steps and only updated once collective data batches of update steps have been obtained. In contrast to the cyclic nature of Bayesian Filters, this module has access to a collection of data measures and can thus run nonlinear regression techniques to regress the material parameters Θ. In the remainder of this work, Θ describes the boundaries of a classifier that maps individual components of an object to a set of available material types. Given this, $\mathcal{F}_p$ is realized by applying unsupervised clustering and model-fitting techniques.[1]

3   Haptic Exploration

Before being able to extract information about the objects in the workspace, the robot has to collect data through exploration. In order to gather this sensor data in an efficient manner, we design a control flow for exploring our environment based on a grid-based and a shape-based representation. Given initial data from e.g. computer vision, an initial belief can be obtained, that can be iteratively updated.

3.1   Grid-Based Exploration

We incorporate the findings from [3], where the belief of the geometry is stored in an occupancy grid consisting of individual cells $c \in \mathcal{C}$. We extend this to

$$\mathcal{M}_t = \{\boldsymbol{M}_t^0, \boldsymbol{M}_t^1, \ldots, \boldsymbol{M}_t^{K_m}\},$$

as an inference grid consisting of binary classifier layers $\boldsymbol{M}_t^k$ for K_m material types, and an occupancy grid for $k = 0$, where each grid $\boldsymbol{M}_t^k$ assigns a class-membership probability to each cell c. However, in contrast to storing actual probability values in the grid as in [7], we use the log-odds-notation $\mathbb{P}(c|\boldsymbol{r}, \boldsymbol{x}) = \frac{\exp \boldsymbol{M}_t^k(c)}{1+\exp \boldsymbol{M}_t^k(c)}$ from [2] to store the current belief of each cell and layer. With all layers being binary classifiers both measurements and states can only take values in $\mathcal{X} = \{0, 1\}$. As the haptic exploration seeks to maximize the expected information gain, a utility metric needs to be defined that encourages to maximize information gain upon choosing the next cell to explore. We incorporate findings from [12], that map the prior belief of a cell to all possible

---

[1] The framework outlined in this work is not restricted to the presented identification method. Nonetheless, this specific example serves as a proof of concept.

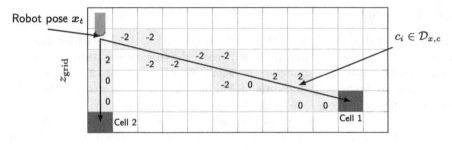

Fig. 2. Basis for utility and accessibility calculations in a 2D grid for two different goal cells, shown in blue. The black arrows show the direct connection from x_t to the goal cells, while the light blue cells indicate $\mathcal{D}_{x,c}$. The gray numbers in the cells show the values of the occupancy layer M_t^0.

measurements. Neglecting the time index by denoting $+ = {t+1}$, the utility of a cell c results in

$$U(c) = \frac{1}{K_m} \sum_{i=1}^{K_m} \sum_{r \in \mathcal{X}} \sum_{\xi^i \in \mathcal{X}} \mathbb{P}\left[r_+ = r | \xi^i\right] \mathbb{P}\left[\xi^i\right] \ln \left(\frac{\mathbb{P}\left[\xi^i | r_+ = r\right]}{\mathbb{P}\left[\xi^i\right]} \right), \qquad (3)$$

where r stands for the possible results of the measurement, which are again given as binary mapping $\mathcal{X}$ for all layers for a given cell in the inference grid, and ξ^i iterates over the possible state of cell c in the dedicated layer of the inference grid. In order to evaluate the uncertainty over all classes, we finally average over all classes K_m and obtain a utility score for each cell in the inference grid. Given the prior belief $\mathbb{P}[\xi]$ and the sensor model $\mathbb{P}[r|\xi]$, the probability $\mathbb{P}[\xi|r]$ can be directly inferred by Bayes' law. However, there are cells with a high utility which may be unreachable for the robot in realistic scenarios, e.g. the inside of rigid bodies or geometries with cavities. Hence, we introduce an accessibility metric evaluating how well cell c is accessible from the current pose of the robot x_t, given a cell-trajectory as visualized in Fig. 2. Denoting the cell-trajectory as a finite set $\mathcal{D}_{x,c} = \{c_1, c_2, \ldots, c_D\}$ of length D, we exploit the log-odds-notation by accumulation of signs of the occupancy layer for each cell:

$$\alpha(\mathcal{D}_{x,c}) = \begin{cases} \frac{1}{D} & \text{if } M_t^0(c_i) = 0 \ \forall c_i \in \mathcal{D}_{x,c}, \\ \left| \frac{1}{D} \sum_{c_i \in \mathcal{D}_{x,c}} -\text{sign}(M_t^0(c_i)) \right| & \text{otherwise}, \end{cases} \qquad (4)$$

where the upper case simply avoids a reachability of 0 for all cells, if the occupancy grid is empty for all cells evaluated. Hence, the final rank and thus the criteria for selecting the next exploration cell is obtained as

$$c^g \leftarrow \underset{c \in \mathcal{C}}{\arg \max}\{\alpha(\mathcal{D}_{x,c})U(c)\}. \qquad (5)$$

A single exploration step is thus given by selecting cell c^g, approaching this cell, starting a measurement by e.g. applying a force upon the object and updating the inference grid based on the new measurement.

3.2   Shape-Based Exploration

A major drawback of the grid-based framework is that the resolution of the grid inevitably leads to uncertainties due to the discretization of the grid. Therefore, we propose a second exploration approach which uses analytic shape representations of geometric primitives, namely spheres, cylinders, boxes and planes. Provided initial data points from e.g. computer vision, we fit initial models that generate a hypothesis for each model shape. As each model-fit is conditionally independent from the others, each hypothesis forms a shape-particle S^i. All shape-particles denoted as $\mathcal{S}_{t=0}$ form a Particle-Filter, where each particle is associated with a belief, initialized by a uniform distribution over all particles.

In order to explore the environment efficiently, a utility metric is needed that minimizes the uncertainty at each step, i.e. to distinguish between various shape candidates. This selection boils down to finding the optimal contact point from a set of candidates $\mathcal{P} = \{p_1, p_2, \dots\}$ representing possible contact points on a surface of a shape-particle. Similar to (3), the utility metric is based on [12] and the concept of mutual information [8]. We further assume a multivariate normal-distributed sensor-model with covariance Σ, such that the utility results in

$$U(\mathcal{P}, \mathcal{S}_t) = \sum_{S^j \in \mathcal{S}_t} \sum_{p_i \in \mathcal{P}} \mathcal{N}(p_i | \mu_j, \Sigma) \mathbb{P}\left[S^j | x_t, r_t\right] \ln \left(\frac{\mathcal{N}(p_i | \mu_j, \Sigma)}{\mathbb{P}\left[S^j | x_t, r_t\right]} \right), \qquad (6)$$

where $\mathbb{P}\left[S^j | x_t, r_t\right]$ is the prior belief of shape S^j within the current particle filter, and μ_j denotes the expected contact point for shape S^j on the particular axis. This utility combines the knowledge of the prior belief with the influence of expected measurements, and therefore allows to estimate the expected impact of these measurements. The utility only depends on prior belief of the shapes and the set of possible contact points $\mathcal{P}$. The selection of an optimal contact point forms the initiation of a single exploration step of the shape-based strategy and is visualized in Fig. 3 with three shape particles. In order to obtain contact points and simultaneously explore the workspace, a set of K_x intermediate positions $\tilde{x}$ are sampled in the near vicinity of the robot x_t. Each of these points is evaluated in parallel by drawing a line to the closest point to each shape. Given these lines, the intersection points of the remaining shapes and the connection lines as well as the closest point define the set $\mathcal{P}$, e.g. $\{c_{2,3}, p_{2,3,2}, p_{2,3,1}\}$ in Fig. 3, from which the utility of testing the selected shape hypothesis, given the sampled starting position, can be obtained. The algorithm then chooses the intermediate starting position that returns the optimal expected utility. In contrast to the grid-based strategy, not only a fixed goal point is chosen, but instead all possible contact points along the selected line are sequentially checked until a measurement can be obtained or a constraint is violated. The exploration step ends with updating the particle beliefs that have been tested with a predefined update weight.

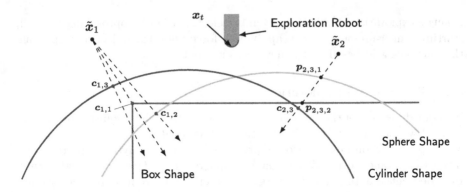

Fig. 3. Choice of next action with 3 shapes shown in 2D. The points $\tilde{x}_1$ and $\tilde{x}_2$ are randomly sampled, each $c_{i,j}$ depicts the possible contact points. On $\tilde{x}_1$, the closest contact points $c_{1,j}$ with each shape are displayed through the dashed lines. For $\tilde{x}_2$ on the right, the contact $c_{2,3}$ with the cylinder shape is shown exemplarily with the respective $p_{2,3,k}$. The points $c_{2,3}$, $p_{2,3,1}$ and $p_{2,3,2}$ are used to calculate the utility for the exploration axis $\tilde{x}_2 \rightarrow c_{2,3}$.

4   Object Identification

As outlined in Sect. 2.1, the task of the object identification is given by applying unsupervised machine-learning methods to generate object classification thresholds or fit the dedicated model parameters given the collected data measurements.

Regarding the grid-based strategy, clustering algorithms such as K-Means and Density-Based-Spatial-Clustering for Applications with Noise (DBSCAN) are suitable methods as the structure of the inference grid is also bound to K classes. Thus, the identification process can be used to update the decision boundaries for each inference layer. Furthermore, the belief of the inference grid layers can be corrected using the collected measurement- and state history.

The shape-based strategy is not solely limited to clustering the collected data but further requires to reject and resample new particles to the filter. For this purpose, the estimation error

$$\epsilon^i = \frac{1}{T} \sum_{t=0}^{T} \left\| \, r_t - \mathbb{E} \left[\, r_t | S^i, x_t, u_t \, \right] \, \right\|_2 \qquad (7)$$

for each particle S^i is obtained in order to determine which particles have a great discrepancy between measured values r_t and the corresponding expected values. Given the recorded data, the least performant K_w particles are removed from the filter. After deleting the inaccurate particles, new shape parametrizations are sampled. In order to obtain proper samples, it is favorable to partition the provided sensor data. Again unsupervised clustering algorithms are a suitable choice here because no further properties about the underlying data is required and the number of current geometric primitives is finite. This results in a deterministic classification, meaning that each measurement is assigned with a class label. Having obtained these individual components, additional model-fits per cluster result in new geometric primitive samples. By finally combining these geometric primitives into a compositioned object a new particle is added to the filter.

5   Evaluation

The outlined algorithm is evaluated with an artificial robot explorer using a simulated environment using the Multi-Joint Dynamics with Contact (MuJoCo) physics engine. The robot is equipped with a force-torque sensor that allows to measure the impact during collision. In order to focus on the exploration process, we directly explore and control in Cartesian space. Thus, the pose of the robot x is controlled via a Cartesian impedance controller:

$$\tau_c = K_s \left(x_d - x\right) - K_d \dot{x} + \tau_{ext}, \tag{8}$$

where τ_c is the applied wrench command, x_d is the desired pose, $\dot{x}$ the velocity, K_s and K_d describe the stiffness and damping matrices, and τ_{ext} describes an additional feed-forward wrench command.

In order to test our methods against the challenges stated in Sect. 1, the robot is faced with a set of unknown objects, which are composed of sub-components of different materials, which differ in their stiffness values. MuJoCo [21] handles all contacts between objects as soft constraints in the dynamic system, which can be seen as a spring-damper system, where one can set the stiffness k_m and damping b_m. These stiffness-damping values are artificial contact values used for simulation dynamics rather than physically realistic values,[2] such as Young's modulus, that a robot can regress by obtaining measurements $r_t = (*)x_t, F_t, \Delta l_t$, i.e. the magnitudes of force and displacement during contact at x_t. In order to assess the relationship between stiffness parameter k_m of a MuJoCo object model and the physical stiffness value $k = \frac{F}{\Delta l}$, we fixed the damping values to $b_m = 1$ for all simulations and performed several experiments with increasing parameter k_m and compared the resulting estimations with the numeric stiffness value $k = \frac{F_{max}}{\Delta l_{max}}$. Applying linear regression, the material stiffness is obtained as

$$k = f_k(k_m) = \gamma k_m + \delta \approx (0.13 \ k_m + 152) \ \text{N/m}. \tag{9}$$

Even though the data is just an approximation of the actual material data, it is sufficient to evaluate the capability of our methods to differentiate between materials and thus to identify the decomposition of an object. The unknown exemplary objects are given as a composition of two boxes for object A and a composition of two cylinders for object B, such that $K_m = 2$. Their shape is visualized as a ground-truth in Fig. 4, where the material classes are visualized

---

[2] We refer to [20] for detailed information.

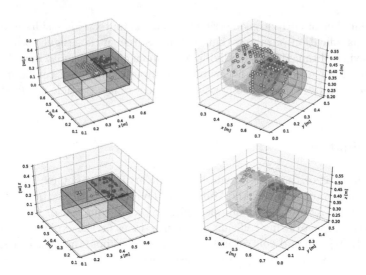

Fig. 4. Classification of data measurements for the grid-based approach in the upper row after $K_E = 12$ (object A) and $K_E = 20$ (object B) and for the shape-based approach in the bottom row after $K_E = 4$. (Color figure online)

in green and yellow. The dedicated material parameters values according to (9) are listed in Table 1. With constant exploration samples K_e of 10 for the grid-based approach and 16 for the shape-based approach, data is iteratively collected and classified according to Fig. 1, leading to the collected samples and estimated materials after K_E episodes shown in Fig. 4.

5.1   Grid-Based Exploration

We employ a grid of 25 cells per dimension with a resolution of 2 cm for each cell. The grid-based algorithm is provided an initial surface estimation, that assigns initial values to M_0^0. However, the initial data only provides a belief for the first layer regarding the occupancy of the grid, so all remaining layers are initialized without any prior knowledge. The clustering in the top row of Fig. 4 shows the material association of the collected data samples after K_E consecutive episodes. While the data for object A reaches a F1-score of 0.966 for yellow and 0.962 for green and is thus clustered into two clearly distinguishable classes, object B reaches a F1-score of only 0.834 for yellow and 0.667 for green, thus fails to assign samples to the correct material type. A major reason for these false classifications lies in distorted measurements, which are likely to occur when the contact angle between robot and surface is very small such that the applied force is nearly parallel to the object surface. A major downside of the current grid-based approach is not having access to the normal vector of the underlying geometry, thus approaching an object at an inapt angle is more likely. Especially if the object is specifically curved, such as object B.

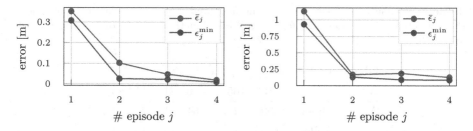

Fig. 5. Evolution of the error metrics of the particle filter over episodes j and their corresponding values for object A on the left and object B on the right.

5.2 Shape-Based Identification

An initial particle set is drawn from 10 data points. The results for object A and B are shown in the bottom row in Fig. 4, after K_E episodes. While the F1-score for object A is slightly less for yellow (0.952) compared to the grid-based approach, it is significantly larger for green (0.987) and for object B for both yellow (0.963) and green (0.987).

In contrast to the grid-based approach, which has been shown to be efficient for spatial object refinement in previous work, the aspect of geometric shape refinement process is further evaluated. Thus, we evaluate the evolution of the mean error $\bar{\epsilon}_j$ over all particles and the minimum error $\epsilon_j^{\min}$ of all particle errors according to (7) as shown in Fig. 5. The fact that the gap between the average estimation error and the best estimate is reducing over time highlights the effect of rejecting false hypothesis candidates at every iteration. Nonetheless, a slight increase is noticeable from episode 2 to episode 3 for object B, that shows the possibility of drawing false candidates in the resampling process. Overall, the evaluation of the error shows the potential of the shape-based algorithm on iteratively improving the shape estimation.

While both methods successfully classify the objects in three out of four test-cases, we close with evaluating the ability of directly estimating the material parameter, i.e. stiffness k in here. The results, obtained as the centers for each cluster, are summarized in Table 1 for both objects and approaches. It has to be noted that the data was evaluated as collected without any outlier removal, which is especially crucial for the stiffness estimation using the grid-based method on object B.

For all components, the stiffness-estimation underestimates the actual values. Again, the small forces upon small contact angles deteriorate these measurements. Besides this, empirical tests have shown that the simulation yields inconsistent measurements if a contact is measured directly on the edge of a geometry. As measurements at the edges are encouraged by the utility metrics in (3) and (6), we leave the investigations of this effect on future work, that will include hardware applications.

Table 1. Estimated stiffness for both methods and objects. The last columns show the estimated stiffness values $\hat{k}_g$ for the grid-based method and $\hat{k}_s$ for the shape-based approach.

Object	Class	k_m	k [N/m]	$\hat{k}_g$ [N/m]	$\hat{k}_s$ [N/m]
A	Yellow	100	165	107.81	113.85
A	Green	10000	1452	615.11	717.02
B	Yellow	1000	282	164.75	104.54
B	Green	8000	1192	397.34	947.15

6   Conclusion

This work presents two main methods that improve the capability of robots on identifying and understanding unknown objects via haptic data acquisition. The first method extends findings in the field of haptic SLAM by extending the basic method based on occupancy grids to inference grids, that further allow to estimate the material type of the individual components. The second method exploits the concept of particle filter and the assumption that arbitrary objects can be represented as a composition of geometric primitives, by iteratively rejecting and resampling new geometric primitive-decompositions as particles. Both these algorithms are further extended by unsupervised machine-learning methods that allow them to refine decision boundaries for individual class memberships. For the shape-based strategy it is also outlined how explicit model fitting can be used to obtain reasonable particle samples.

The final framework is evaluated in a virtual environment, where unknown objects of different material stiffness have to be explored. Both algorithms are evaluated against their classification accuracy, where the grid-based algorithm is significantly outperformed by the shape-based method. The presented results highlight that the methods outlined in this work are a helpful step towards enabling robots in coping with unknown objects and thus increasing their field of applications in the future. For future work, we plan to combine these methods into a hybrid object exploration framework that will be further evaluated on a robot platform and real-world objects.

Acknowledgement. The research leading to these results has received funding from the Horizon 2020 research and innovation programme under grant agreement №820742 of the project "HR-Recycler - Hybrid Human-Robot RECYcling plant for electriCal and eLEctRonic equipment".

References

1. Allen, P., Roberts, K.: Haptic object recognition using a multi-fingered dextrous hand. In: Proceedings of the 1989 IEEE International Conference on Robotics and Automation, pp. 342–347. IEEE Computer Society Press (1989)
2. Behbahani, F.: Reverse-Engineering The Visual and Haptic Perceptual Algorithms in The Brain. Doctor of philosophy, Imperial College London (2016)
3. Behbahani, F., Taunton, R., Thomik, A., Faisal, A.: Haptic SLAM for context-aware robotic hand prosthetics - simultaneous inference of hand pose and object shape using particle filters. In: International IEEE/EMBS Conference on Neural Engineering, NER, vol. 1229297, 719–722 (2015)
4. Bourgault, F., Makarenko, A., Williams, S., Grocholsky, B., Durrant-Whyte, H.: Information based adaptive robotic exploration. In: IEEE/RSJ International Conference on Intelligent Robots and Systems, October 2002, pp. 540–545 (2002)
5. Decherchi, S., Gastaldo, P., Dahiya, R., Valle, M., Zunino, R.: Tactile-data classification of contact materials using computational intelligence. IEEE Trans. Rob. **3**, 635–639 (2011)
6. Durrant-Whyte, H., Bailey, T.: Simultaneous localization and mapping: Part I. IEEE Robot. Autom. Mag. **13**(2), 99–108 (2006)
7. Elfes, A.: Using occupancy grids for mobile robot perception and navigation. Computer **22**(6), 46–57 (1989)
8. Elfes, A.: Robot navigation: integrating perception, environmental constraints and task execution within a probabilistic framework. In: Dorst, L., van Lambalgen, M., Voorbraak, F. (eds.) RUR 1995. LNCS, vol. 1093, pp. 91–130. Springer, Heidelberg (1996). https://doi.org/10.1007/BFb0013955
9. Fishel, J., Loeb, G.: Bayesian exploration for intelligent identification of textures. Front. Neurorobot. **1–20**, (2012)
10. Friedl, K.E., Voelker, A.R., Peer, A., Eliasmith, C.: Human-inspired neurorobotic system for classifying surface textures by touch. IEEE Robot. Autom. Lett. **1**, 516–523 (2016)
11. Hegazy, D., Denzler, J.: Combining appearance and range based information for multi-class generic object recognition. In: Bayro-Corrochano, E., Eklundh, J.-O. (eds.) CIARP 2009. LNCS, vol. 5856, pp. 741–748. Springer, Heidelberg (2009). https://doi.org/10.1007/978-3-642-10268-4_87
12. Julian, B., Angermann, M., Schwager, M., Rus, D.: Distributed robotic sensor networks: an information-theoretic approach. Int. J. Robot. Res. **10**, 1134–1154 (2012)
13. Luo, S., Bimbo, J., Dahiya, R., Liu, H.: Robotic tactile perception of object properties: a review. Mechatronics **18**, 54–67 (2017)
14. Martinez-Hernandez, U., Metta, G., Dodd, T., Prescott, T., Natale, L., Lepora, N.: Active contour following to explore object shape with robot touch. In: 2013 World Haptics Conference, WHC 2013, pp. 341–346 (2013)
15. Montemerlo, M., Thrun, S., Koller, D., Webreit, B.: FastSLAM: a factored solution to the simultaneous localization and mapping problem. In: AAAI/IAAI, pp. 593–598 (2002)
16. Navarro, S., Gorges, N., Wörn, H., Schill, J., Asfour, T., Dillmann, R.: Haptic object recognition for multi-fingered robot hands. In: 2012 IEEE Haptics Symposium, HAPTICS 2012, pp. 497–502. IEEE (2012)
17. Pezzementi, Z., Plaku, E., Reyda, C., Hager, G.: Tactile-object recognition from appearance information. IEEE Trans. Rob. **3**, 473–487 (2011)

18. Schaeffer, M., Okamura, A.: Methods for intelligent localization and mapping during haptic exploration. In: Proceedings of the IEEE International Conference on Systems, Man and Cybernetics, pp. 3438–3445. IEEE (2003)
19. Thrun, S., Burgard, W., Fox, D.: Probabilistic Robotics. MIT Press, Cambridge (2005)
20. Todorov, E.: MuJoCo: Modeling, Simulation and Visualization of Multi-Joint Dynamics with Contact (2018). http://www.mujoco.org/book/index.html
21. Todorov, E., Erez, T., Tassa, Y.: MuJoCo: a physics engine for model-based control. In: IROS, pp. 5026–5033. IEEE (2012)
22. Xu, D., Loeb, G., Fishel, J.: Tactile identification of objects using Bayesian exploration. In: Proceedings of the 2013 IEEE International Conference on Robotics and Automation, pp. 3056–3061 (2013)

Response of a Neuromechanical Insect Joint Model to Inhibition of fCO Sensory Afferents

Clarissa Goldsmith[✉], Nicholas S. Szczecinski, and Roger D. Quinn

Department of Mechanical and Aerospace Engineering,
Case Western Reserve University, Cleveland, OH 44106, USA
cag111@case.edu

Abstract. This work details the development of a neuromechanical model of the stick insect femur-tibia joint control network in order to replicate and explore the "reflex reversal" phenomenon in insect limbs. We believe that understanding this phenomenon will lead to improved robotic joint control. We describe the development of this model using data taken from the extensor half of the network in the insect. To build a plausible model of the complete joint control network, we additionally mirrored the connectivity of the extensor control networks for the flexor. We present the results of experiments performed on the network by selectively inhibiting the system's sensory afferents in an asymmetrical manner and observing the behavior of the simulated joint in open and closed loop scenarios. By inhibiting the network's flexion position and velocity afferents, we are able to demonstrate changeover in the joint from a resistance reflex (RR) to an active reaction (AR) in response to joint flexion. We discuss why the nervous system might modulate joint behavior in this manner, as well as how to apply these findings to improve robotic control.

Keywords: Synthetic nervous system · Drosophibot · Neuromechanical model · Reflex reversal

1 Introduction

Insect legged locomotion has been an area of interest in biologically inspired robotics for many decades. Insects are able to move robustly with relatively simple nervous systems, providing an approachable template for similar motion in robots by mimicking their mechanics, neural processes, and behaviors. Furthermore, robots with enough biological fidelity can serve as testbeds for biological hypotheses, improving understanding in both fields. To this end, we have previously developed Drosophibot, a robot modeled after adult *Drosophila melanogaster* including close attention to low level features found in a variety

Supported by the National Science Foundation (Grant Number: 1704436).

V. Vouloutsi et al. (Eds.): Living Machines 2020, LNAI 12413, pp. 141–152, 2020.
https://doi.org/10.1007/978-3-030-64313-3_15

of insects [8]. Drosophibot serves as a testbed for replicating neuromechanical behaviors on a mechatronic platform, which we believe will eventually lead to robust, adaptive locomotion.

One feature of the nervous system that makes animals so adaptable is their ability to process sensory information in a task- or context-dependent way. One thoroughly studied example of this processing in the control of posture and locomotion is the apparent "reflex reversal" of insect joint control reflexes [5]. Briefly summarizing this behavior, stretching of the femoral chordotonal organ (fCO) (signifying joint flexion) in a standing insect's femur-tibia (FTi) joint will result in a resistance reflex (RR) that attempts to halt the joint motion. However, in an actively walking insect the same stimulus will cause an active reaction (AR) where the muscles allow the flexion to proceed [3,9]. The exact mechanisms in the nervous system that cause this reflex reversal are currently unknown; however, several studies have hypothesized the importance of the groups of non spiking interneurons (NSI) between the sensory neurons receiving stimuli from the fCO and the slow extensor tibiae motorneuron (SETi) [12,13]. In particular, Sauer et al. in ref. [11] found that blocking Chlorine ions (i.e. inhibition) in the fCO sensory cells leads to changes in the NSI activities and eventually the MNs in response to fCO stretching. They suggest that the nervous system may switch between the RR in the resting state and the AR in the active state by selectively inhibiting or disinhibiting fCO afferent cells. Driesang et al. in ref. [7] similarly found that the NSI properties appear unchanged between these two contexts but NSI activity changes, implying that their inputs are changing.

Traditional electrophysiological experimentation methods lack the precision to definitively pinpoint the role of these sensory afferents in reflex reversal [11]. However, by using a neuromechanical model we can selectively inhibit or disinhibit position- or velocity-sensitive afferents with arbitrary precision, theoretically changing NSI activity as observed in the animal and transitioning our joint controller function from the RR to the AR. Bässler et. al. have previously attempted to functionally model reflex reversal in ref. [1] and used the model for simulated joint control. However, as the morphology of the NSI sub-networks had not been characterized at the time of the model's development, the system lacks morphological accuracy. Sauer et. al. later recorded the connectivity of the NSI in ref. [13] and developed a model of the sub-system based on their data, but did not use the model to control a limb or modify it to observe the response. To our knowledge, no dynamic neuromechanical models of this particular sub-network currently exist from which to observe the closed loop joint behavior.

To better understand the reflex reversal mechanism and how it could be applied to robotics, we constructed a neuromechanical model of this reflex loop and explored how its parameter values give rise to these distinct behaviors. In this manuscript, we present the development of our simulation based on previous mappings of the connections to the SETi in stick insects. We validate the model's ability to replicate known biological behavior, then use the model to selectively inhibit groups of position and velocity sensory neurons and observe changes to the joint's reflex in open and closed loop cases. Interestingly, when in the AR configuration, the model does assist imposed flexion motions, but still resists imposed extension motions, suggesting that the AR is demarcating which joint motions are allowable in a context-dependent way. Finally, we discuss the implications of our findings on how the animal nervous system may bring about reflex reversal, as well as how these findings could be applied to robotic joint control.

2   Methods

A simplification of our network structure is shown in Fig. 1. We constructed our simulation in Animatlab 2 [6] based on the network layout for extension presented in Fig. 1 of ref. [13]. In this layout, the E and I type non-spiking interneurons (NSI) receive excitatory stimulus from six position sensory neurons (purple) and ten velocity neurons (orange), as well as delayed inhibitory input from the velocity neurons mediated by a set of six spiking interneurons (yellow). Of these neurons, half respond to fCO elongation (flexion) and half to fCO relaxation (extension). As such, the sensory neurons can be split into four major groupings: Flexion position, flexion velocity, extension position, and extension velocity (Fig. 1). Each sensory neuron includes an arbitrary tonic noise of 0.01 mV to create slight variance in the input signals of each grouping to the NSI. To simplify our network construction, we elected to only model the slow fibers of each muscle, and assumed each muscle would be activated by one slow motorneuron (MN). The outputs from the NSI then synapse onto our slow MNs (red) via graded neurotransmitter release.

The NSI were modeled as non-spiking leaky integrators [6]. As such, the membrane voltage, V, of each NSI varies according to the differential equation:

$$C_m \frac{dV}{dt} = I_{leak} + I_{syn} + I_{app} \tag{1}$$

where

$$I_{leak} = G_m \cdot (E_r - V), \tag{2}$$

$$I_{syn} = \sum_{i=1}^{n} G(s,i) \cdot (E_{s,i} - V), \tag{3}$$

and I_{app} is an optional externally applied stimulus. Equations (2) and (3) define the leak and synaptic currents, respectively. In these equations, V is the current membrane voltage, G_m is the conductance of the cell membrane, C_m is the membrane capacitance, and E_r is the resting potential of the neuron. The instantaneous conductance of the ith synapse models the graded release of neurotransmitter in nonspiking synapses, and is a piecewise-linear function of the presynaptic neuron's instantaneous membrane voltage, V_{pre}:

$$G_{s,i} = G_{max,i} \cdot \begin{cases} 1, & \text{if } V_{pre} > E_{hi} \\ \frac{V_{pre} - E_{lo}}{E_{hi} - E_{lo}}, & \text{if } E_{lo} \leq V_{pre} \leq E_{hi} \\ 0, & \text{if } V_{pre} < E_{lo} \end{cases} \tag{4}$$

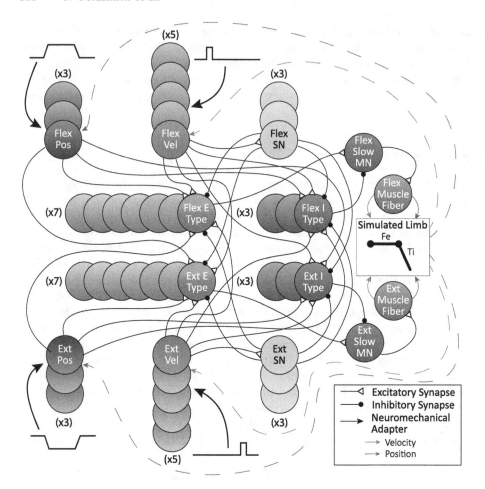

Fig. 1. A simplified view of the simulation network. E and I type non-spiking interneurons (NSI) receive excitatory stimulus from position (purple) and velocity (orange) sensory neurons, as well as delayed inhibitory input from the velocity neurons transmitted through spiking interneurons (yellow). The outputs from the NSI synapse onto the slow MNs (red) to control a mechanically simulated joint via non-spiking slow muscle fibers neurons. In the closed loop case, the position and velocity of the limb provide feedback to the sensory neurons (dashed lines). Otherwise, these connections are omitted and the bolded input signals are used instead. (Color figure online)

where $G_{max,i}$ is the maximum conductance of the synapse, E_{lo} is the synaptic threshold, and E_{hi} is the synaptic saturation. The synapse also has a reversal potential $E_{s,i}$, which varies depending on which neurotransmitter the synapse releases. For more details regarding the tuning of these parameter values, please see [14].

The sensory neurons and motorneurons utilize the integrate-and-fire model for spiking neurons [4]. These neurons exhibit leaky integrator behavior similar to non-spiking neurons up until a threshold value, θ. Their membrane voltages evolve according to Eq. 1, with the added condition that:

$$\text{if } V = \theta, \text{then } V(t) \longleftarrow E_r. \tag{5}$$

When a presynaptic neuron spikes, for each of its synapses, G_s is set to G_{max}, then decays according to the differential equation:

$$\tau_s \frac{dG_s}{dt} = -G_s \tag{6}$$

where τ_s is the time constant of the synapse.

To directly control a simulated limb, we added an additional non-spiking neuron after the slow MNs as an analog for the insect's muscle fibers. We set the time constant of these slow muscle fiber neurons to 2000 ms so the neuron acts as a leaky integrator of synaptic inputs similar to a muscle [15]. The neuron's voltage is then used to command the position and velocity of a simulated, Drosophibot-sized limb through a pair of neuromechanical adapters. The limb's mechanics are governed by the equation of motion:

$$J \cdot \ddot{\theta} = \tau_{ext} + \tau_{flex} - k_{spring} \cdot \theta \tag{7}$$

where J is the moment of inertia of the limb, k_{spring} is the stiffness of the limb's parallel elastic elements and $\tau_{ext,flex}$ are the torques determined by the software to drive the joint at the speeds and to the positions indicated by the adapters. The precise tuning of these adapters can be found in ref. [8].

We defined the synapse conductance strengths in the network according to the relative values given in Fig. 11 of ref. [13] with some additional tuning to more closely match the recorded response of each NSI to stimuli presented in Fig. 2 of ref. [13]. Figure 2 compares the responses of the interneurons in model to those in the animal. As the exact conversion between fCO stretch and injected current has not been characterized, we arbitrarily chose a stimulus strength of 5 nA applied to the sensory neurons over 3.25 s. The stimulus ramps up to and down from the hold current over a period of 0.25 s. Because Drosophibot is about 5 times larger than the stick insect, the length of the stimulus was made about 5 times longer [10].

After validating the behavior of the connections for extension, we expanded the network to include flexion. Control of the full leg's motion was necessary to simulate full joint behavior and observe the effects of modulating the NSI. However, innervation of the flexor muscle is believed to be more complicated than that of the extensor, and the network connections for the flexor slow MN have not been mapped in the insect. In regards to the functional responses of the joint, Bässler et al. recorded the forces of the extensor and flexor tibiae muscles in the stick insect for sinusoidal stimulus of the fCO and found that the forces varied in nearly equal and opposite ways (Fig. 3 in ref. [2]). These results seem to imply that the flexor networks may resemble or mirror those for extension. As such, we elected to mirror the connections from the extensor network onto a series of flexor NSIs, as well as adding a flexor slow MN and slow muscle

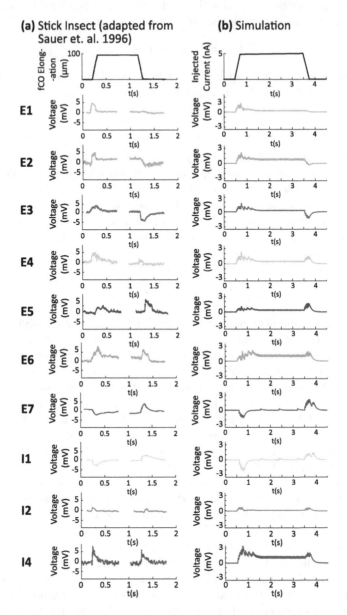

Fig. 2. Each NSI's response to a ramp and hold stimulus in the insect (a) and in our simulation (b). The interneurons are only modulated by active motion of the limb, rather than sustained position. The exact nature of the modulation (excitation, inhibition, or neither) varies depending on the category of interneuron. Our simulated NSI exhibit similar trends to the biological system with similar stimuli, showing that our model adequately simulates known biological behaviors.

fiber. This complete network produced similar behavior to that found by ref. [2] in that the responses of the extensor and flexor slow muscle fibers mirror each other while the fCO is stretched and relaxed in a sinusoidal fashion (Fig. 3).

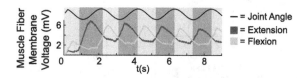

Fig. 3. The response of the flexion and extension muscle fibers in our simulation to a sinusoidal stimulus. The membrane voltages of each neuron exhibit similar levels of excitation during the joint's corresponding motion (e.g. the extension fiber during extension). During the opposite motion, the voltages return to a similar rest value. This behavior aligns with the recorded behavior in ref. [2]

After adding in a plausible stand-in for the flexor sub-network, we performed experiments on the full network to observe the open and closed loop behavior of the joints, then tested the effects of inhibiting sensory afferents as described in Sauer et al. in ref. [11] on the open-loop model. To model such inhibition in our simulation, we increased the time constants of each group of sensory neurons. This has the effect of decreasing the firing frequency in response to the same motion, which is functionally identical to changing the gain of the sensory neurons by altering their conductance [13].

We chose to test the system at time constants of 200 ms (normal value), 2000 ms, and 20,000 ms. A logarithmic range of inhibition helped to ensure distinctive changes between each case. Additionally, while inhibiting one "polarity" of position or velocity neurons (e.g. flexion), we kept the other polarity (e.g. extension) at their normal reactivity. As such, we considered nine types of test cases: One control case, four in which we inhibited a single polarity of either data type, and four in which we inhibited one position group of either polarity and one velocity group. This resulted in 25 total test cases.

For the sensory inhibition tests, we stimulated the sensory neurons directly with the same stimuli used in the NSI validation tests previously. For the open and closed loop tests, the network was instead given less idealized stimuli driven by an "input joint" actually completing the desired flexion. The position and velocity of this motion was then passed to the sensory afferents via additional neuromechanical adapters. This enabled us to easily observe the differences between the input and output motions in the open loop case by changing to which joint the slow muscle fibers connected; in the open loop case, they connected to the original "output" joint, and for closed loop, the connections were changed to connect to the "input" joint.

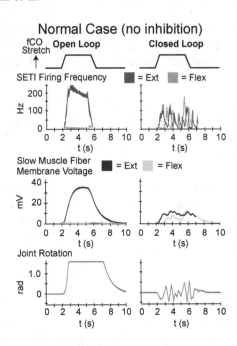

Fig. 4. The response of the slow MNs, muscle fibers, and joint in our simulation to a ramp stimulus corresponding to joint flexion (stretching of the fCO). With no sensory feedback from the joint (open loop), only the extension MN excites and the joint extends to its limit. However, with sensory feedback added (closed loop), the extension and flexion motor neurons fire similarly and the joint attempts to stay roughly at its neutral position. These results support the idea that the joint is attempting to resist flexion in the baseline case.

3   Results

3.1   Normal Case Open and Closed Loop Behavior

Figure 4a shows the slow MN and muscle fiber activity with joint motion at baseline synaptic and membrane conductances in open loop and closed loop configurations. In the open loop case, the limb rapidly extends when it receives stimulus corresponding to fCO elongation (flexion). Once this stimulus abates, the limb returns to its equilibrium position due to the slow decay of the muscle fiber voltage. This MN firing trend resembles that observed in the SETi in Fig. 8 of ref. [13]. Additionally, the corresponding motion from this firing pattern makes logical sense as part of the RR observed in insects; as the limb is receiving feedback for undesired flexion, it attempts to continually extend and counteract the motion. This behavior is further supported by the data from the closed loop case (b). With sensory feedback implemented, the limb oscillates between small angles of flexion and extension throughout the applied stimulus, due to the similar voltages of the extension and flexion muscle fibers. The MNs in the network additionally appear to fire at similar frequencies throughout their corresponding

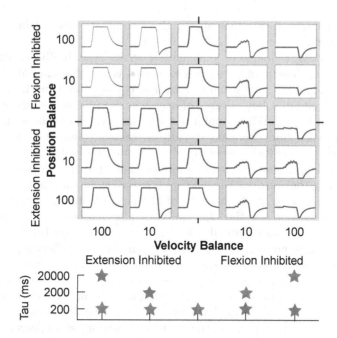

Fig. 5. The joint response of the open loop configuration of the simulation for increased time constants (corresponding to neuron inhibition) of the position and velocity sensory neurons (modalities). The vertical axis corresponds to the velocity balance, while the horizontal to the position balance. In quadrant I (blue), the flexion position and flexion velocity groups are inhibited; for quadrant II (purple), flexion position and extension velocity; quadrant III (green), extension position and extension velocity; and quadrant IV (red), extension position and flexion velocity. The bottom graph shows the specific time constants used for each polarity when changing one of the modalities. (Color figure online)

motion, providing further support for our assumptions of the extension network connections. Overall, in the intact case the limb appears to exhibit behavior consistent with the RR.

3.2 Effect of Sensory Neurons on Motion

Figure 5 shows the open loop joint motion of the system for different combinations of inhibited sensory neurons. The baseline case is included in the center of the figure axes for comparison. Beginning with the velocity axes of the graph, inhibiting either of the velocity neuron groups does not have a large effect on the overall motion of the limb on its own (y-axis). When combined with inhibition of the extension position neurons (red and green quadrants), however, the joint's return speed following stimulus release increases, resulting in a degree of overshoot of the equilibrium position. The extent of this overshoot then decreases as the inhibition of the extension position neurons increases. All of these motions still resemble the resistance reflex from our earlier tests of open and closed loop behavior. Therefore, it does not appear that combinations involving inhibiting the extension neurons result in reflex reversal.

The most drastic change to joint motion occurs when inhibiting the flexion position neurons. The joint's resulting extension is less than half of that of the normal case, while the post-stimulus return to equilibrium is much more rapid. This speed results in a large degree of overshoot into flexion, which is in some cases briefly sustained. When combined with some degree of velocity inhibition, the effect becomes more pronounced, with the cases involving high inhibition of flexion position and velocity resulting in no reaction to joint flexion.

This open loop response resembles motion characterizing the active reaction (AR), allowing the joint to flex and even assisting in the motion. Figure 6a provides a closer look at the activity of the network during these responses. Even in the closed loop case the joint exhibits similar AR behavior, as the sensory inputs to the NSI - and eventually the MNs - are greatly inhibited throughout flexion. This data supports the conclusion that inhibiting the flexion position and velocity sensory neurons is what causes reflex reversal [7]. It is also interesting to note that the system still produces a resistance reflex against unintended joint extension (Fig. 6b). This seems to suggest that sensory afferents does not simply reverse a reflex; instead, it fundamentally changes the operation of the joint, allowing and assisting motions in the intended direction, while preventing those in the unintended direction.

4   Discussion

In this manuscript, we presented a simulated neuromechanical model of an insect FTi joint based on previously observed extension networks in the animal. We performed experiments on the network by selectively inhibiting groups of sensory neurons and observing the joint's response. Our findings suggest that by inhibiting the flexion position sensory neurons, we can cause a transition from a resistance reflex (RR) to an active reaction (AR) response to fCO elongation. Simultaneously inhibiting the flexion velocity neurons then works to amplify this effect, in many cases preventing the flexion neurons from firing during flexion.

Our findings in the inhibited case support the hypothesis that the nervous system may actively modulate the lowest level sensory afferents in order to alter motion and control [7,11]. Such an approach seems counter intuitive from a robotics perspective, since inhibiting sensors means depriving the entire control system of that information. An engineer might attempt to implement this reflex reversal by collecting the same sensory information no matter the context and formulating context-dependent motor commands in response. This way, no sensory information is "lost." Why, then, would the animal nervous system utilize the strategy it does? The distributed nature of the nervous system may necessitate it, as the primary role of the sensory information encoded by the afferents is to execute reflexes for the single joint. Such distributed processing may then be necessary for fast response times and producing capable locomotion.

Additionally, our findings from the inhibited joint's response to extension poses questions about the manner in which the nervous system dictates joint

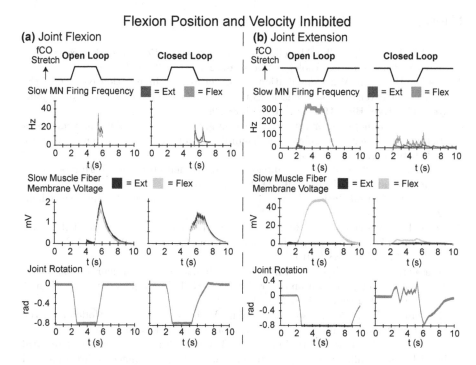

Fig. 6. The response of the flexion and extension SETi and slow muscle fibers in our simulation to two different ramp stimulus while the flexion position and velocity neuron groups have been inhibited by increasing their time constants from 200 ms to 20000 ms. (a) Response to stimulus corresponding to joint flexion (fCO elongation) (b) Response to stimulus corresponding to joint extension (fCO relaxation).

position at this lowest level. Rather than simply defining intended motion or active forces in the joint, the system also seems to use the sensory afferents to define constraint forces. These constraints allow the joint to resist undesired movements from external forces while allowing assistive external forces to move the joint. In the future, we plan to use this concept as the basis for a robotic posture control system in which the nervous system specifies allowable motions, which may be driven either by actuator or external forces.

Both of these hypothetical nervous system functions are starkly different from common robotic methods, and so could provide guidance for improving robotic control. On our robot, Drosophibot, we believe we could achieve similar results by changing the low level characteristics of the Dynamixel AX-12 servomotors actuating the limbs (Robotis, Seoul, South Korea). Additionally, the extensive distribution of the nervous system emphasized in these experiments further motivates distributing computation on the robot. One method of achieving this would be implementing multiple processors (e.g., one per leg) that only communicate occasionally, rather than a central processor receiving sensory information from every leg segment and joint. We will explore these avenues in our future work.

References

1. Bässler, U., Koch, U.T.: Modelling of the active reaction of stick insects by a network of neuromimes. Biolog. Cybern. **62**(2), 141–150 (1989)
2. Bässler, U., Stein, W.: Contributions of structure and innervation pattern of the stick insect extensor tibiae muscle to the filter characteristics of the muscle-joint system. J. Exp. Biol. **199**(10), 2185–2198 (1996)
3. Bässler, U.: Functional principles of pattern generation for walking movements of stick insect forelegs: the role of the femoral chordotonal organ afferences. J. Exp. Biol. **136**(1), 125–147 (1988)
4. Burkitt, A.N.: A review of the integrate-and-fire neuron model: I. Homogeneous synaptic input. Biol. Cybern. **95**(1), 1–19 (2006)
5. Bässler, U.: Neural Basis of Elementary Behavior in Stick Insects. Springer, Cham (2012)
6. Cofer, D., Cymbalyuk, G., Reid, J., Zhu, Y., Heitler, W.J., Edwards, D.H.: AnimatLab: a 3D graphics environment for neuromechanical simulations. J. Neurosci. Meth. **187**(2), 280–288 (2010)
7. Driesang, R.B., Büschges, A.: Physiological changes in central neuronal pathways contributing to the generation of a reflex reversal. J. Comp. Physiol. Sens. Neural. Behav. Physiol. **179**(1), 45–57 (1996)
8. Goldsmith, C.A., Szczecinski, N.S., Quinn, R.D.: Neurodynamic Modeling of the Fruit Fly Drosophila melanogaster. Bioinspiration and Biomimetics
9. Hellekes, K., Blincow, E., Hoffmann, J., Büschges, A.: Control of reflex reversal in stick insect walking: effects of intersegmental signals, changes in direction, and optomotor-induced turning. J. Neurophysiol. **107**(1), 239–249 (2012)
10. Jayaram, K., Mongeau, J.M., Mohapatra, A., Birkmeyer, P., Fearing, R.S., Full, R.J.: Transition by head-on collision: mechanically mediated manoeuvres in cockroaches and small robots. J. R. Soc. Interface **15**(139), 20170664 (2018)
11. Sauer, A.E., Büschges, A., Stein, W.: Role of presynaptic inputs to proprioceptive afferents in tuning sensorimotor pathways of an insect joint control network. J. Neurobiol. **32**(4), 359–376 (1997)
12. Sauer, A.E., Driesang, R.B., Büschges, A., Bässler, U.: Information processing in the femur-tibia control loop of stick insects - 1. The response characteristics of two nonspiking interneurons result from parallel excitatory and inhibitory inputs. J. Compar. Physiol. A **177**(2), 145–158 (1995)
13. Sauer, A.E., Driesang, R.B., Büschges, A., Bässler, U.: Distributed processing on the basis of parallel and antagonistic pathways simulation of the femur-tibia control system in the stick insect. J. Comput. Neurosci. **3**(3), 179–198 (1995)
14. Szczecinski, N.S., Hunt, A.J., Quinn, R.D.: A functional subnetwork approach to designing synthetic nervous systems that control legged robot locomotion. Front. Neurorob. **11**, (37) (2017)
15. Wolf, H.: Inhibitory motoneurons in arthropod motor control: organisation, function, evolution. J. Comp. Physiol. A **200**(8), 693–710 (2014)

Distributed Adaptive Control: An Ideal Cognitive Architecture Candidate for Managing a Robotic Recycling Plant

Oscar Guerrero Rosado[1,2(✉)] and Paul F. M. J. Verschure[1,2,3]

[1] Laboratory of Synthetic Perceptive, Emotive and Cognitive Systems (SPECS),
Institute for Bioengineering of Catalonia (IBEC), Barcelona, Spain
oguerreros@ibecbarcelona.eu
[2] Barcelona Institute of Science and Technology (BIST), Barcelona, Spain
[3] Catalan Institution for Research and Advanced Studies (ICREA), Barcelona, Spain

Abstract. In the past decade, society has experienced notable growth in a variety of technological areas. However, the Fourth Industrial Revolution has not been embraced yet. Industry 4.0 imposes several challenges which include the necessity of new architectural models to tackle the uncertainty that open environments represent to cyber-physical systems (CPS). Waste Electrical and Electronic Equipment (WEEE) recycling plants stand for one of such open environments. Here, CPSs must work harmoniously in a changing environment, interacting with similar and not so similar CPSs, and adaptively collaborating with human workers. In this paper, we support the Distributed Adaptive Control (DAC) theory as a suitable Cognitive Architecture for managing a recycling plant. Specifically, a recursive implementation of DAC (between both single-agent and large-scale levels) is proposed to meet the expected demands of the European Project HR-Recycler. Additionally, with the aim of having a realistic benchmark for future implementations of the recursive DAC, a micro-recycling plant prototype is presented.

Keywords: Cognitive architecture · Distributed Adaptive Control · Recycling plant · Navigation · Motor control · Human-Robot Interaction

1 Introduction

Designing a cutting-edge industrial plant in 2020 is a great challenge. Despite the notable growth in a variety of technological areas in the past decade, including Cyber-Physical Systems (CPS), Internet of Things (IoT), cloud computing, embedded systems, Industrial Integration and Industrial Information Integration, the Fourth Industrial Revolution has not been embraced yet.

Strategic initiatives such as Industrie 4.0 (Germany, 2013) and Made-in-China 2025 (China, 2015) represents firm steps toward such a revolution that aims to go further in automation, focusing on end-to-end digitisation and integration of digital industrial ecosystems [1]. Industry 4.0, which is broadly seen as quasi-synonym of Fourth Industrial Revolution, seeks the combination of the following emerging technologies: a) CPS,

© Springer Nature Switzerland AG 2020
V. Vouloutsi et al. (Eds.): Living Machines 2020, LNAI 12413, pp. 153–164, 2020.
https://doi.org/10.1007/978-3-030-64313-3_16

representing the natural evolution of embedded systems, going from centralised control systems to autonomous machines capable of communicating with each other [2]; b) Cloud computing, that not only provide Industry 4.0 with high-performance computing and low-cost storage but also allow system orchestration by modularisation and sharing resources in a highly distributed way; c) IoT, working as a global network infrastructure that fully integrates identities, attributes and personalities of physical and virtual "Things", thanks to radio-frequency identification and wireless sensor networks [3].

A predecessor of IoT in a country scale industrial context, the Cybersyn Project, can serve us as an example of how important is taking into account the contemporary challenges. This project aimed to collect and transmit economic-related data in real-time to aid Chile's governmental body to make informed decisions in a more democratic manner [4]. Cybersyn began in 1971, however, due to technical, financial and political circumstances met its end in 1973 with Pinochet's dictatorship [5]. To avoid similar failures, any project aiming to get into the Fourth Industrial Revolution must consider contemporary challenges such as: improvement of Information and Communication Technology infrastructures, solving the scalability problem, development of data science and data analytics techniques as well as heterogeneous IoT-related networks. In this work, we address one specific barrier that may hinder progress: the necessity for new architectural models. CPS (e.g. robots) must lead with uncertainty when interacting with the natural world (e.g. industry plant). This uncertainty is due to the changing conditions, the variety of possibilities and the complexity that open environments offer. To tackle this problem, an architecture approach is essential since allows the CPS to be dexterous in different competencies while ensuring safety, security, scalability, and reliability [6]. However, current architectures are not capable of fulfilling all Industry 4.0 requirements. In this paper, a new version of the Distributed Adaptive Control (DAC) architecture is proposed as an ideal candidate to control an industrial plant in a recursive fashion.

Artificial Intelligence approaches have shown promising results when it comes to agents performing simple tasks in dynamic but constrained environments. For example, logarithmic AI solutions have demonstrated successful results (even exceeding human performance levels) in limited domains such as Atari videogames or Go, but its implementation to solve the simplest navigation task is far to be possible. Furthermore, they require a large amount of training in comparison to human learning [7]. In contrast to board games, industrial plants are highly complex and heterogeneous. Robots operating within such a plant need to be equipped with a wide range of capabilities (i.e. navigation, motor control, human-robot interaction, etc.). Due to the complex behaviour required to these robots, an architectural strategy fits better with the necessities. With an appropriately designed architecture able to organise the different plant-specialised modules and information flow, the system should acquire robustness while performing various tasks. Indeed, the challenge of creating such an architecture opens the question of what design principles must be followed. Although control architectures can accomplish the tasks for which they have been designed, in many cases their success is constrained to a predictable environment, and their performance is far from the human-level efficiency [8]. In contrast, cognitive architectures aim to build human-level artificial intelligence by modelling the human mind. Thus, systems driven by a cognitive architecture could reason about problems across different domains, develop insights, adapt to new situations and reflect on themselves [9].

Taking advantage from such cognitive architecture working in a recursive fashion, we propose the creation of a factory operating as a synthetic agent. The term recursive refers to the double-scale functionality of the system: various individual agents that are specialised in different tasks and that are controlled by a higher-level entity, the factory itself. Envisioning a recycling plant with a recursive architecture resonates with the metaphor "Der Mensch als Industriepalast" (Man as an industrial palace) that was proposed by Fritz Kahn. Analogous to a recycling plant, the ingestion of food in Fritz's illustration implies a procedure of treatment, disassembling and classification of the material into different nutrients. For a seamless usage of this disassembled material, the control centre (in the representation of the brain) works on top of the other related systems such as metabolism, blood circulation or respiration.

However, Fritz's illustration depicts a linear process where individual agents are not required to perform dynamically and are hence not involved in the implementation of a cognitive architecture. In contrast, the recycling plant presented here requires a cognitive architecture at both single-agent and large-scale levels, since robots performing tasks of navigation, disassembling, classification, etc. need to work autonomously in a parallel and context-adaptative fashion. The synergic operation of the whole plant depends on the agents' behaviours, which are monitored, controlled and influenced by the large-scale level.

In the following sections, we propose the Distributed Adaptive Control theory of mind and brain (DAC) as a candidate to control a hybrid human-robot recycling plant of Waste Electrical and Electronic Equipment (WEEE) management. Previous work on DAC will elucidate how this architecture supports essential robots' abilities at both single-agent and large-scale levels. Finally, we present a micro-recycling plant as a functional prototype and a benchmark for the implementation of DAC.

2 WEEE Recycling Plant

Recycling awareness is gaining importance, especially since recycling plants have to deal with a significant amount of waste per year. The European Union by 2017 recycled and composted 94 Mt (35.2%) of its municipal solid waste [10]. For this reason, and as in many other industries, recycling plants have incorporated a variety of machinery which processes paper, glass, plastics and other materials on a large scale.

However, society is consuming a growing number of electrical and electronic devices that, after a few years, become into e-waste. This e-waste, namely Waste Electrical and Electronic Equipment (WEEE), cannot be processed by the machinery designed to handle the raw materials mentioned previously. The challenge in WEEE management does not only lie in the correct classification of a device but also its disassembly. Each device (such as a TV screen) has a variety of models, and not all models include the same disassembly procedure, or each procedure may be executed in a different order. Additionally, the handling of sensitive or hazardous material (like mercury lamps) adds an extra level of difficulty in the automation of the processing of e-waste. So far, humans seem to be more skilled in performing device disassembly, as their robotic counterparts can only perform partial disassembly that is not generalised to all types of devices. Nonetheless, this partial performance still represents a relief in the arduous task of component disassembling and material. A solution to expedite this work is the development of hybrid human-robot recycling plants where experienced workers would cooperate with specialised robots. This solution implies splitting the disassembling process into subtasks according to the skills of both humans and robots.

A clear example of this new paradigm is the European Project HR-Recycler, where robotic grippers and mobile robots assist in the recycling process of WEEE. Here, robots not only perform repetitive and automated tasks, but they are endowed with autonomous behaviour adaptive to a changing context. Thus, HR-Recycler represents a step towards Industry 4.0 and an ideal framework to introduce new architecture models able to perform the disassembly task even under conditions of uncertainty (like a dynamic, open space in a hybrid human-robot recycling plant). We propose an enhanced plant where we apply the DAC architecture at both single-agent (robots) and large-scale (plant) levels, shaping a multi-scale recursive architecture.

3   Distributed Adaptive Control

The Distributed Adaptive Control (DAC) [11] is a theory of the principles underlying Mind, Brain and Body Nexus. It is expressed as a robot-based neural architecture that accounts for the stability maintained by the brain between an embodied agent and its environment through action. DAC assumes that any agent, to act, must continuously solve four fundamental questions, the so-called H4W problem [12]: "Why", reflects the motivation in terms of needs, drives and goals; "What", accounts for the objects in the world that actions pertain to; "Where", represents the location of the object and the self; and "When", serves as a temporal reference of the actions. Additionally, a fifth question (Who) was added, referring to the agency [13].

DAC organises the generation of behaviour horizontally across four layers of control. The Somatic Layer defines the fundamental interface between the embodied agent and its environment, including the needs that must be fulfilled to ensure survival. In a robotic system, this layer accounts for its sensors and actuators and sets its predefined needs. The Reactive Layer provides a set of unconditioned responses working as reflexes for given unconditioned stimuli. This layer represents the first stage of the generation of goals since the behaviours produced follow homeostatic and allostatic principles. The Reactive Layer works on top of the Somatic Layer, gathering sensory data and providing reflex responses through the actuators. A clear example of these reflexes is the "stop signal" triggered when a human gets close to the robot trajectory. The Adaptive Layer frees the system from the restricted reflexive system by perceptual and behavioural learning. It follows classical conditioning principles since the value of the sensory input is shaped by experience, and its outputs could result in anticipation response. Thanks to this layer, the robot can adapt its behaviour according to relevant stimuli (i.e. adjusting its security distance depending on the current scenario). Finally, the Contextual Layer allows the generation of behavioural plans or policies based on sequential memory systems. Sequential representations of states of the environment and the sensory-motor contingencies acquired by the agent are stored in the memory systems, allowing behavioural plan recalling by sensory matching and internal chaining. Thus, the Contextual Layer shows action-dependent learning as observed in operant conditioning, allowing abilities such as allocentric-based trajectory planning, crucial for the mobile robot's navigation. In addition to this layered horizontal organisation, the architecture is also vertically distributed across three columns: states of the world obtained by exosensing, states of the self obtained by endosensing and their interaction through action.

The DAC architecture fulfils both the theoretical and practical criteria that must be considered when designing a proper cognitive architecture. On the one hand, at the theoretical level, DAC applies: a) biologically-inspired learning rules such as Hebbian learning, Oja learning rule or associative competition for different purposes, b) provides a solution to the fundamental Symbol Grounding Problem by acquiring the state space of the agent, based on its interaction with the environment, c) escapes from the now by generating behavioural plans or policies based on sensory matching with representations of environment and action states (stored in memory systems), and d) reverse the Referential Indeterminacy Problem, in which the agent has to extract the external concept that was referred, by endowing the system with proactivity to acquire knowledge. On the other hand, DAC has been validated in both single-agent (i.e. robots) and large-scale levels [14–17]. These implementations have supported the adequacy of DAC, from a pragmatic point of view, to perform a diverse set of tasks including foraging, object manipulation or Human-Robot Interaction (HRI).

4   DAC at the Single-Agent Level

Within the recycling context, we propose two types of robots working as single agents that allow for the transportation, disassembling and classification of the different WEEE components. The two robot categories are robotic grippers and mobile robots. We propose that the implementation of DAC does not differ between robots. However, it needs to be adapted for the different tasks these robots perform, based on the data provided by the different sensors, the needs and goals, and the robots' actuators.

In mobile robots, the needs range in different dimensions depending on their related aCell. Based on the project, we define as aCell the workbench related to a specific worker equipped with a robotic arm where different WEEE is disassembled. Mobile robots aim to transport WEEE in an adaptative way; for instance, taking into consideration the disposal of materials or the specific disassembled and classified components. Here, the Reactive Layer is responsible for driving the needs of the robots towards different navigation patterns as well as pick up and place behaviours, that are carried out by the actuators (i.e. motors of the wheels and the lifting platforms). Sensors such as wheels' encoders, proximity sensors and RGB cameras provide the Reactive Layer with the information needed to trigger reflexive behaviours, and the Adaptive Layer with the information required to learn associations, which in turn, assist in the behavioural policies formation by the Contextual Layer.

In the robotic grippers, the needs change from navigation-oriented to motor control-oriented goals, since its porpoise is assist in the disassembling procedure itself. Here, the Reactive Layer processes information regarding pressure, proximity and torque sensors, along with data provided by a camera and triggers reflexive behaviours (like a stop signal for safety). This sensory information forms progressively sensory representations by associative learning at the Adaptive Layer and these associations will then be stored in Contextual Layer modules if the associated behaviours allow reaching goal states. Thus, robotic grippers are not just able to perform reflexive actions such as unscrewing. When endowed with adaptive and contextual capabilities, they could, for example, correctly locate the bolt, apply the appropriate velocity and pressure, and predict when the bolt is going to be unscrewed.

At single-agent level, we consider three essential areas for the successful implementation of a recycling plant where robots work alongside humans for e-waste disassembly: Navigation, HRI and Motor Control. DAC has been tested in these areas supporting its implementation in both mobile and humanoid robots.

4.1 Previous Implementations of DAC: Navigation

Robotic navigation has already been achieved without requiring a cognitive architecture. However, the characteristic of the Industry 4.0 context demands goal-oriented navigation, which adapts to changing environments, needs to be aware of the material transported and the state of the aCell, and ensures the safety of other robots and humans along the trajectory. Due to the complexity of navigation in this context, an architectural approach is more suitable, and the DAC architecture has largely demonstrated its strengths performing foraging tasks with mobile robots.

Aiming to prove that the different computational models proposed by DAC account for functional mapping of specific brain areas and work complementing each other when the system operates as a whole, Maffei et al. [15] embed the version DAC-X in a mobile robot performing a foraging task. In this study, the Somatic Layer computed input signals from the robot's sensors, while the output was calculated as the total motor signal provided by the architecture. Finally, the actions were constrained by the robot's body morphology. The Reactive Layer reflexively mapped sensory states into actions by using feedback controllers that approximated the role of the Brainstem nuclei. Reflexive object avoidance, visual target orientation and computation of bodily states such as needs and drives were obtained by computational models, mimicking the Trigeminal Nucleus, Superior Colliculus and Hypothalamus functions respectively. In the Adaptive Layer, a model of the cerebellar microcircuit allowed associative learning by coupling neutral sensory cues with adaptive responses. The motivation for action arose by modelling the Ventral Tegmental Area for the computation of low-level internal states, and action-selection for behavioural plans was achieved by modelling the Basal Ganglia. Finally, the memory systems of the Contextual Layer comprised a biologically constrained model of the Hippocampus by which the agent acquired an internal representation of the environment; and a model of the Prefrontal Cortex that included mechanisms for storing decision-making and goal-dependent information.

Analysis that discretised the behavioural performance into three phases (early, middle and late trials) showed that at the beginning, the naive agent relies on its reflexes to explore the arena and seek for resources. This initial navigation emerges primarily from the work of the Reactive Layer, resulting in a stochastic trajectory pattern that covered a large part of the arena and had a low item collection rate. After a few trials, the Adaptive Layer took advantage of the local visual landmarks deployed in the floor, thus complementing the primary reactive navigation with adaptive responses. Using the internal representation of space fostered by the Reactive Layer in the explorative trials, the Adaptive Layer allowed goal-directed navigation reducing occupancy of the arena and the mean trajectory length and increasing the collection rate. Finally, at the late trials, the agent ended up displaying a mostly linear trajectory from the home location to the target and back. This linear pattern was achieved thanks to the involvement of the Contextual Layer since it combined a robust representation of the environment and made available the goal locations stored in the long-term memory. These achievements in a hoarding task, by implementing DAC in a mobile robot, support a similar implementation in the context of Industry 4.0.

4.2 Previous Implementations of DAC: Human-Robot Interaction

In the context of a recycling plant, social skills such as empathy, natural language, or social bond formation do not precisely fit the context of collaboration between humans and robots in an industrial plant. However, the human workers will interact with the robots, especially the robotic grippers, as they both will be required to perform tasks with the common goal of disassembling a device. These robots will also consider that workers may show different skills, preferences, and even trust in robots. Perceived safety, collaboration, adaptation to each worker and the completion of a task are critical points for successful Human-Robot Interaction.

An example of a successful collaboration that ensures safety has been shown by [18]. Here, the authors presented a collaborative human-robot assembling task. However, the task was restricted to the assembling of a single component, always following the same steps, and no tool manipulation was required. In contrast, the disassembling process requires tool manipulation and includes a variety of devices, where the disassembly steps may differ. Thus, a more adaptive solution is needed to disassemble different WEEEs while collaborating with the human partner successfully.

Numerous contributions to the field of HRI have been provided by DAC through its implementation in humanoid robots. However, focusing on relevant problems for recycling plants, addressing the anchoring problem is essential. The anchoring problem refers to the process of creating and maintaining the link between raw data provided by the sensors and symbolic representation processed and stored by the system. [16] tackled this problem by defining a representation of knowledge based on the so-called H5W problem. Thus, several entities connected by semantic links (who, how, what, where and when) full describe the situation. In other words, the Somatic Layer is taking the sensory input data (i.e. spatial properties of objects and agents). Subsequently, the Adaptive Layer will translate this data into instances (i.e. unsafe situation) by providing solutions to the H5W problem. Finally, these solutions will be compared with those stored in the Long-Term Memory of the Contextual Layer (that previously showed good results), so the best one will be selected.

In the context of a recycling plant, considering the limited social skills of a robotic gripper, and at the same time that interaction with the worker is needed, we propose two channels of communication. As most plants are considered noisy, and workers wear protection gear, verbal communication is not preferable. For this reason, we will employ a predefined gesture-based communication of a set of fundamental requests to the robot, such as start, stop, take rest position, etc., by providing the workbench with a computer vision system able to solve the anchoring problem. Gestures, combined with a multitouch interactive tablet, will provide more complex interaction scenarios.

4.3 Previous Implementations of DAC: Motor Control

Simple behaviours such as grabbing a tool, unscrewing a bolt or extracting and placing a component during the disassembling task are complex movements that require lengthy training sessions until a robotic gripper can adequately perform such actions.

Although a complete version of DAC has not been applied to control the specific behaviours of a robotic gripper, previous studies have validated the implementation of the DAC architecture for motor control. More specifically, motor control was achieved with the acquisition of affordances, namely the categorisation of goal-relevant properties of objects [19]. Within the context of DAC, Sanchez-Fibla, Duff & Verschure [20] proposed the notion of affordance gradients: object-centred representations that describe the consequences that an action may have on this particular object. Through object-centred force fields, the agent was not just able to predict the outcomes of an action, but also to generalise predictions to actions that the agent has not previously perform. These affordance gradients were acquired through learning in Adaptive Layer, allowing to a mobile robot to push an object from the right side and place it in a target position and orientation. These affordance gradients were recently extended to the acquisition of bimanual affordances in Sanchez-Fibla et al. [21].

5   DAC at the Large-Scale Level

Interestingly, DAC has also shown its capabilities to control an entertainment space. Ada [17] was a large-scale intelligent and interactive environment that was able not just to learn information from its visitors, but also to modify its behaviour guiding their steps toward a given direction. Ada achieved interaction with its visitors by expressing its internal states through global lighting and background sound. Information processing through DAC allowed leveraging multi-modal data from Ada's sensors (cameras, microphones and pressure-sensitive floor) to learn the best way to interact with its visitors following paradigms of classical and operant condition, demonstrating that DAC is not constrained to conventional robots.

6   Multi-scale DAC: A Micro-Recycling Plant

For a recursive multi-scale implementation of DAC architecture, a central system is endowed with DAC operating on a large-scale level, and so controlling the synergic functioning of the single-agent level (Fig. 1). DAC at this large-scale level is implemented more abstractly, since it leverages sensors and effectors of the single-agent level, leading to an intertwined recursive multi-scale architecture. The fact that this central system integrates information from all single agents allows new perceptions such as the amount of aCell that are free or taken, space occupied by mobile robots or mean amount of WEEE disassembled.

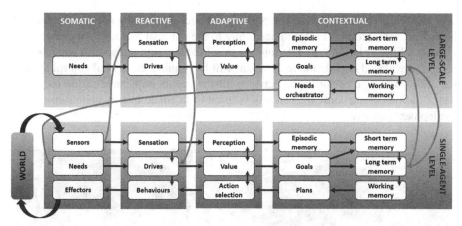

Fig. 1. Recursive DAC. Arrows represent information flow. Blue arrows indicate a connection between modules and layers of the same entity; Yellow arrows represent information sent from single-agent level to large-scale level; Orange arrows represent information sent from a large-scale level to single-agent level. (Color figure online)

By using a wireless connection, the large-scale level creates a network with each single-agent, consisting of three loops. A sensory loop integrates data from the different robots' sensors at the large-scale level, allowing overall interpretation of the context and therefore triggering reflexive signals to every robot (e.g. stopping signals in case of general danger situation). Based on the needs of the large-scale level and the current state of the plant, an orchestrator loop is in charge of modulating the needs of every single agent. This second loop allows the robot to behave in an allostatic way between worker-based and plant-based needs. A third loop is in charge of interconnecting Long-Term Memory modules across the entire plant. By connecting the LTM module of the large-scale level to those LTM modules embedded in each robot, learning generalisation and information sharing occur across single agents. Thus, workers could find the a Cell adapted to their needs even if they change from one workbench to another, or mobile robots could plan their trajectories based on the location and trajectories of others.

To evaluate the candidature of DAC as a perfect candidate architecture to control an industrial plant within the context of Industry 4.0, we are developing a prototype of a micro-recycling plant.

6.1   Micro-Plant Design

To build the closest setup to the HR-Recycler project, our design for a robotic micro-plant includes both mobile robots and robotic arms (Fig. 2). These robots also embed those sensors used in the project (cameras RBG, proximity and pressure sensors, wheels' encoders, etc.). In this prototype, workers are represented by balancing robots that, by using a visual cue, are related to a specific workbench and embed different worker's characteristics. However, unlike HR-Recycler, these robotics workers will no assist in the disassembling process. The robotics arms will be in charge of full disassemble simple devices composed of four parts representing different materials (plastic, metal, paper and risky material). To classify these components, robotics arms also will place the parts of the components into bins coloured according to the material that must be collected in it. Using a lifting platform, mobile robots can lift the bins and transport it when is full. A computer placed outside the micro-plant will be running the central control system that allows synergic performance between all the agents implicated in the recycling plant. Additionally, a conveyor belt will be used to facilitate intermediate steps in the development process.

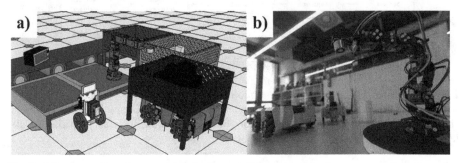

Fig. 2. Micro-recycling plant model and robots. a) 3D sketch of single-agents working synergistically to disassemble WEEE. Mobile robots can lift and transport coloured bins. These bins are coloured according to the material that must be classified in it. Robotics arms adapt its performance based on the presence of a worker represented by balancing robots moving around the plant. b) Functional robots to be implemented in the micro-plant. (Color figure online)

6.2   Future Benchmarks and Expected Results

After testing DAC architecture runs correctly in each of the agents individually, we propose two benchmarks in order to assess the success of the recursive architecture proposed. First, we will evaluate the implemented multi-agent navigation systematically deploying two or more mobile robots that will operate under two conditions: autonomously with the large-scale influence of the plant, and autonomously but without this influence. When the central control system is not enabled, we expect to see navigation adaptative to the contextual characteristics of the environment and goal-oriented behaviour related to the transportation of material from or towards the workbenches. However, coordination between the agents will be not found, unless the central control is enabled, leading to convergence of trajectories and no distribution of spaces, workbenches and materials. Second, we will evaluate the generalisation of worker characteristics by deploying two different robotics arms performing in an adaptive way to the worker situated in its related workbench. With the central control system not enabled, we expect to find adaptive behaviours of both robotics grippers toward their related worker (i.e. distance to the worker based on its trust in robots). However, if the workers are exchanged of the workbench, the adaptative behaviour to the specific worker performer by the previous gripper will not be found in the new place, unless the central control system is enabled.

7 Discussion

In this article, we proposed the Distributed Adaptive Control (DAC) cognitive architecture as a candidate for robot and plant control within the context of Industry 4.0. The implementation of this architecture has been supported by previous works on different robotic areas such as Navigation, Human-Robot Interaction and Motor Control. However, the following issues have not been discussed yet.

The implementation of DAC has been addressed within the context of a hybrid human-robot recycling plant. This kind industrial plant can be perceived as a simplified instance since in comparison with the overall idea of Industry 4.0 it less dependent on other technologies such as IoT or cloud computing. However, although we are convinced that our recursive implementation of DAC could take great advantage of such technology, the Fourth Industrial Revolution will be achieved thanks to discreet but firm steps.

How much must be learned and how much must be prewired by the agents is another important question to solve, in order to maintain both adaptability and efficiency. We propose that basic abilities such as grabbing a tool or creating and navigating a map of the environment are preferably achieved in previous training sessions, so the agent can adapt a behaviour already learned. Hence, the robots just should adapt these abilities already learned to the position of the tool or the trajectory of other mobile robots. Other significant information such as the referred to the worker's abilities and preferences could be integrated directly in the central control system by using questionnaires.

Acknowledgements. This material is based upon work funded by the European Commission's Horizon 2020 HR-Recycler project (HR-Recycler-820742H2020-NMBP-FOF-2018).

References

1. Zhong, R.Y., Xu, X., Klotz, E., Newman, S.T.: Intelligent manufacturing in the context of industry 4.0: a review. Engineering **3**(5), 616–630 (2017)
2. Tan, Y., Goddard, S., Pérez, L.C.: A prototype architecture for cyber-physical systems. ACM SIGBED Rev. **5**(1), 1–2 (2008)
3. Van Kranenburg, R.: The Internet of Things: a critique of ambient technology and the all-seeing network of RFID. Institute of Network Cultures (2008)
4. Beer, S.: Brain of the Firm: The Managerial Cybernetics of Organisation. Wiley (1972)
5. Medina, E.: Cybernetic Revolutionaries: Technology and Politics in Allende's Chile. MIT Press (2011)
6. NSF: Cyber-physical Systems (CPS) (2017)
7. Botvinick, M., Ritter, S., Wang, J.X., Kurth-Nelson, Z., Blundell, C., Hassabis, D.: Reinforcement learning, fast and slow. Trends Cogn. Sci. **23**(5), 408–422 (2019)
8. Vahrenkamp, N., Wächter, M., Kröhnert, M., Kaiser, P., Welke, K., Asfour, T.: High-level robot control with ArmarX. Informatik 2014 (2014)
9. Kotseruba, I., Tsotsos, J.K.: 40 years of cognitive architectures: core cognitive abilities and practical applications. Artif. Intell. Rev. **53**(1), 17–94 (2018). https://doi.org/10.1007/s10462-018-9646-y
10. EPA. https://www.epa.gov/facts-and-figures-about-materials-waste-and-recycling/national-overview-facts-and-figures-materials

11. Verschure, P.F., Kröse, B.J., Pfeifer, R.: Distributed adaptive control: The self-organisation of structured behavior. Robot. Auton. Syst. **9**(3), 181–196 (1992)
12. Verschure, P.F.: Distributed adaptive control: a theory of the mind, brain, body nexus. Biol. Inspired Cogn. Archit. **1**, 55–72 (2012)
13. Lallee, S., Verschure, P.F.: How? Why? What? Where? When? Who? Grounding ontology in the actions of a situated social agent. Robotics **4**(2), 169–193 (2015)
14. Verschure, P.F., Voegtlin, T., Douglas, R.J.: Environmentally mediated synergy between perception and behaviour in mobile robots. Nature **425**(6958), 620–624 (2003)
15. Maffei, G., Santos-Pata, D., Marcos, E., Sánchez-Fibla, M., Verschure, P.F.: An embodied biologically constrained model of foraging: from classical and operant conditioning to adaptive real-world behavior in DAC-X. Neural Netw. **72**, 88–108 (2015)
16. Lallée, S., et al.: Towards the synthetic self: making others perceive me as an other. Paladyn J. Behav. Robot. **1**(open-issue) (2015)
17. Eng, K., Douglas, R.J., Verschure, P.F.: An interactive space that learns to influence human behavior. IEEE Trans. Syst. Man. Cybern.-Part A: Syst. Hum. **35**(1), 66–77 (2004)
18. Cherubini, A., Passama, R., Crosnier, A., Lasnier, A., Fraisse, P.: Collaborative manufacturing with physical human–robot interaction. Robot. Comput.-Integr. Manuf. **40**, 1–13 (2016)
19. Gibson, J.: The Ecological Approach to Visual Perception. Lawrence Erlbaum, Mahwah (1986)
20. Sánchez-Fibla, M., Duff, A., Verschure, P. F.: The acquisition of intentionally indexed and object centered affordance gradients: a biomimetic controller and mobile robotics benchmark. In: 2011 IEEE/RSJ International Conference on Intelligent Robots and Systems, pp. 1115–1121. IEEE (2011)
21. Sánchez-Fibla, M., Forestier, S., Moulin-Frier, C., Puigbò, J.Y., Verschure, P.F.: From motor to visually guided bimanual affordance learning. Adapt. Behav. **28**(2), 63–78 (2020)

Standing on the Water: Stability Mechanisms of Snakes on Free Surface

Johann Herault[1]([⊠])(iD), Étienne Clement[1], Jonathan Brossillon[1],
Seth LaGrange[2], Vincent Lebastard[1](iD), and Frederic Boyer[1]

[1] IMT Atlantique, LS2N, 4 Rue Alfred Kastler, 44300 Nantes, France
johann.herault@imt-atlantique.fr
[2] University of Illinois/INHS, Champaign-Urbana, IL, USA

Abstract. We report an investigation aiming to understand the stability mechanisms of semi-aquatic snakes (like Cottonmouth viper or grass snakes) on a free water surface. To address this complex problem, we start by reviewing the specific morphological features of these snakes. Then, we analyse the poses of a semi-aquatic snake in its natural environment. We show that surface stability is achieved by complex combinations of all three rotational degrees of freedom of each vertebra. Based on a new theoretical model, a control law is developed to seek the finite body deformation from the strain (torsion and bending) to maintain an equilibrium stance (position and orientation). Our conclusions lead us to consider a new actuation mechanism based on a controlled rolling motion for each body segment in order to achieve static and dynamic positioning. During the conference, we will present our new swimming snake-like robot, named NATRIX, that can achieve static and dynamic positioning on a free water surface.

Keywords: Semi-aquatic snake · Bio-inspired robotic · Geometrically exact approach

1 Introduction

Since the 2000s, a new generation of marine robots inspired by eels and aquatic snakes has emerged in academic contexts [1–3]. Still under development for industrial underwater applications [3], these hyper-redundant (HR) serial robots are more compact, manoeuvrable and energy efficient [4] than autonomous surface vehicles (except for passive autonomous marine vehicles). Despite the high potential of these bio-inspired robots, these applications on surface are still inaccessible. Indeed, the snake-like robots suffer from a too precarious surface stability at low speed, or in extreme physical conditions (swell, wind, current). Their morphology, which is the main asset of their announced performance, then becomes a handicap. The net torque of the buoyancy forces associated with certain poses of the robot can destabilize it, and might overturn it. This weakness comes from

---

The title refers to a Richie Havens' song.

© Springer Nature Switzerland AG 2020
V. Vouloutsi et al. (Eds.): Living Machines 2020, LNAI 12413, pp. 165–175, 2020.
https://doi.org/10.1007/978-3-030-64313-3_17

their slender morphology, which makes them particularly sensitive to rolling motions (solid rotation about the longitudinal axis) due to their low axial inertia and their generally highly located centre of mass relative to the buoyancy center (the geometric center of the immersed surface). Rolling motion is considered to be the most harmful degree of freedom, since it produces the highest angular accelerations. To mitigate these effects, current robots are therefore equipped with floats [2], thus increasing their volume and added mass. The empirical adjustment of robot buoyancy is performed *a posteriori*, after the robot design, thus demonstrating the lack of technological solutions dedicated to this problem. Other stabilizers commonly used in marine engineering (roll dampers, fins, etc.) would have an equally detrimental impact (or even worse) on manoeuvrability, since they would considerably increase turbulent drag. Semi-aquatic snakes living near rivers, which can be considered to be true equilibrists "levitating" on the surface, such as the grass snake (Natrix natrix), have developed extraordinary stabilization capacities at the surface. Indeed, the overall stability of the snake is ensured by the cumulative effect of imbalances and balances of each cross-section of the snake. Going into further details, a section may be locally in a stable equilibrium configuration or be unstable due to morphological (muscular deformation of its rib cage) or kinematic (vertebral torsion and bending) deformations or by buoyancy adjustment (lungs). By analogy, one can consider the body of the snake as a continuous chain of torsion pendulums (some of which can be reversed) remaining globally stable thanks to the active control of the distribution of local inclinations. Thus, the snake can play on stabilizing or destabilizing local effects, in order to quickly readjust its position, and counterbalance external disturbances (swell, wind, current).

The present study aims to investigate some aspects of the stability mechanisms of semi-aquatic snakes thanks to biological observations, a theoretical approach, and numerical simulations. More precisely, we address the following questions:

- What are the features of a (semi-)aquatic snake that could explain its stability? (Sect. 2)
- How to model the stability of a floating body undergoing large 3D deformations? (Sect. 3)
- How can the snake stabilize its head while deforming its body? (Sect. 4)
- How can these features be embodied into a bioinspired robot? (conclusion).

2   Morphology, Physiology and Ethology of Aquatic Snakes

To structure our bio-inspired approach, we review for the first time the documented morphological features of partially or fully aquatic snakes that are determinant for static equilibrium on water surface.

Morphology. The morphology of snakes evolving in aquatic environment is determined by a compromise between maritime and terrestrial locomotion.

Brischoux and Shine [5] report a statistic correlation between the medium of locomotion and the aspect ratio of the snake cross-section defined by the ratio of the height over the width (h/w). Fully aquatic snakes have generally an asymmetric cross-section with $h/w = 1.56 \pm 0.5$ (averaged along the body, without the tail), that allows for a more efficient thrust against the water. Terrestrial snakes have a rounder body with $h/w \simeq 1$. For amphibious snakes, the aspect ratio is intermediate with $h/w = 1.2 \pm 0.2$ [5], corresponding to a slightly elliptically deformed body section. The geometry of the cross section is very important for static stability since the immersed surface and the center of buoyancy depend on it (see Sect. 3). The number of vertebra in the vertebral column may vary from 130 to 300 [8]. The interval between two consecutive vertebra allows lateral bending (around $10°$ and $20°$), dorso-ventral bending (few degrees), torsion (very small) and longitudinal displacement (traction-compression) [8]. The major longitudinal muscles are multi-articular and are attached to the vertebral column thanks to multiples tendons spanning large intervals varying between 9 and 33 vertebra [7,8]. As we will see in the next section, the large number of degrees of freedom is a decisive advantage for stabilizing a body on a free surface. Lungs play also a crucial role in the buoyancy control. The lungs of the snakes are long and narrow, and the left lung is generally atrophied or lost for non fully aquatic snakes. For fully aquatic snakes, the lungs can reach 100% of the body length, while for semi-aquatic snake, like the *Nerodia Pictiventris*, the lungs end at 53% of the body length [7]. Note that this snake species experiences a heaving instability at low speed [7], suggesting a correlation between lungs length and swimming stability. Graham [6] showed that the *Pelamis Pletarus* (spending 87% of its time submerged) can vary the volume of its lungs to adjust buoyancy. During surface resting, the average mass density of this snake is particularly small with $\rho = 555$ kg/m^3, and then goes to 770kg/m^3 when it dives. Thus, the respiratory system is involved in postural equilibrium and locomotion of aquatic snakes.

The synergies between the actuation of a large number of degrees of freedom, the ability of controlling its buoyancy and the remarkable perception of its environment could be at the origin of its spectacular sense of balance on water.

In Situ Observations. In our scientific consortium, we have the exceptional opportunity to collaborate with a field biologist, Seth LaGrange, who has observed semi-aquatic snakes exhibiting spectacular poses on water surface. Some of them are reported in Fig. 1. These snakes are adult Cottonmouths (*Agkistrodon piscivorus*) living in close proximity to water and are the most aquatic species in the genus Agkistrodon. Cottonmouths are large, heavy bodies pitvipers reaching lengths of 122 cm. They have large, angular heads with facial pits used for detecting infrared radiation of prey and predators.

The pictures were all taken in southern Illinois on a river called Clear Creek. The snakes are usually using the water to travel. They also exploit water to hunt, look for, returning to a basking site, or escaping predators. Their head is kept inclined and significantly above the water surface. This behaviour can be motivated by a better used of their infrared sense. We may speculate that

Fig. 1. Pictures of cottonmouth on free water surface.

the advantages of their stability and manoeuvrability on the water allows them to either escape or defend themselves from predators. The picture of the snake coiled up on the water is a good example of this (Fig. 1(d)). The cottonmouth only coiled up once it is approached. In this pose, the snake can perform its characteristic gaping of the mouth (Fig. 1(c)) and then be in a position to strike if need be. A geometrical analysis of these poses is performed in the next section.

3   Large Deformation Approach to Investigate Body Poses

To model the behaviour of aquatic snakes, we need a geometrical description of the body that takes into account all the features of the semi-aquatic snake: a large number of body sections, each one having three rotational degrees of freedom and large body deformations. Therefore, we use the geometrically exact approach for slender continuous body [9,10], a framework described briefly in the next section.

The Geometrically Exact Approach. The slender body of the snake is modelled by a continuous inextensible shear-less beam of unitary length with elliptical cross sections (Fig. 2). A Galilean reference frame $\mathcal{F}_G = (0, \mathbf{e}_x, \mathbf{e}_y, \mathbf{e}_z)$ is pinned to the water interface so that the surface corresponds to the altitude $z = 0$. The centerline of the spine of the snake is defined by the set of points located by the position vectors $\mathbf{p}(s) = (x(s), y(s), z(s))$ expressed in $\mathcal{F}_G$, as a function of the curvilinear variable $s \in I = [0, 1]$. The so-called Cosserat beam is made of a continuous stack of elliptical rigid sections of infinitesimal thickness ds (Fig. 2).

We introduce a mobile head frame referenced by $\mathcal{F}_0$ attached to the head with position vector $\mathbf{p}_0$, and an orientation given by the vector set $\{(\mathbf{t}_i)_0\}$. From this vector set, we introduce the rotation matrix $R_0 = ((\mathbf{t}_1)_0|(\mathbf{t}_2)_0|(\mathbf{t}_3)_0)$ allowing for mapping elements from the head frame $\mathcal{F}_0$ to the surface frame $\mathcal{F}_G$. The position $\mathbf{p}(s)$ of the center of each section in $\mathcal{F}_s$ are now expressed from the head position $\mathbf{p}_0$ thanks to the relative position $^0\mathbf{p}(s)$ with $\mathbf{p}(s) = \mathbf{p}_0 + {}^0\mathbf{p}(s)$. The orientations of all the body sections relative to the head frame $\mathcal{F}_0$ are defined by the set of material frames $({}^0\mathbf{t}_1(s), {}^0\mathbf{t}_2(s), {}^0\mathbf{t}_3(s))$. The orthonormal vectors set $\{{}^0\mathbf{t}_i\}_{i=1,2,3}(s)$ expressed in $\mathcal{F}_0$ is composed of the vector $^0\mathbf{t}_1$, which is orthogonal to the local section and tangent to the centerline, and the vectors $^0\mathbf{t}_2$ and $^0\mathbf{t}_3$ that are aligned with the semi-axes of the elliptical section. These vectors define the rotation matrix ^0R_s so that the rotation matrix R_s of the section frame in $\mathcal{F}_G$ is given by the non-commutative matrix product $R_s = R_0{}^0R_s$. Thanks to this parametrization of the head configuration relative to the surface and the body configuration relative to the head frame, one can study independently the influence of the head configuration and the body shape onto the equilibrium of the snake.

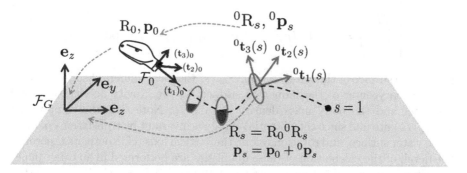

Fig. 2. Geometrically exact representation of the body of the snake in the surface frame

The deformation of the vectors set $\{{}^0\mathbf{t}_i\}(s)$ is parametrized by the field of twist curvature vector $\boldsymbol{\kappa}(s) = (\kappa_1, \kappa_2, \kappa_3)$ defining respectively the torsion, the dorso-ventral bending, and the lateral bending. These fields are assumed to be small to remain in the small strain limit, while the deformation of the body could be large due to the cumulative effect of the strain. They also define the infinitesimal rotations of the vertebra around the axis $\{{}^0\mathbf{t}_i\}(s)$ in the local material vertebra frame $\mathcal{F}_s$

$$\boldsymbol{\kappa}(s) = \sum_i \kappa_i(s)\,{}^0\mathbf{t}_i(s). \tag{1}$$

The evolution equation of the vectors and rotation matrices ^0R_s are given by

$$\frac{d^0\mathbf{t}_i(s)}{ds} = \boldsymbol{\kappa}(s) \times {}^0\mathbf{t}_i(s) \qquad \Longleftrightarrow \qquad \frac{d}{ds}{}^0R_s = {}^0R_s\widehat{\kappa} \tag{2}$$

with $\widehat{\kappa}$ the matrix form of the cross product $\kappa \times (\cdot)$. Therefore, we distinguish the body shape characterized by the fields $(^0R_s, {}^0p_s)$, which is fully determined by the strain $\kappa(s)$, from the head configuration (R_0, p_0), which results from an equilibrium between buoyancy forces and gravity force.

In our model, the strain fields κ is expressed using the Chebychev series expansion at order N as

$$\kappa(s) = \sum_{k=0}^{N-1} \widetilde{\kappa}_k T_k(s) \tag{3}$$

with $\kappa_k \in \mathbb{R}^3$ the component associated with the Chebychev polynomial $T_k(s)$. This decomposition allows us to solve the evolution Eq. 2 with a spectral collocation method exhibiting a fast convergence to the solution [11].

Thanks to the exact configuration (R_s, p_s) of each section in the surface frame $\mathcal{F}_G$, we can compute exactly the wrench exerted by the buoyancy forces and gravity force $(F_z, \Gamma_x, \Gamma_y)$ (heave, roll, pitch)

$$\begin{cases} F_z = a_g \left(\int_0^1 (\rho_w S_{im} - \rho_b S_b) \, ds \right) e_z \\ \\ \begin{pmatrix} \Gamma_x \\ \Gamma_y \\ 0 \end{pmatrix} = a_g \left[\int_0^1 (\rho_w S_{im}) Rq_B + (\rho_w S_{im} - \rho_b S_b) p \, ds \right] \times e_3 \end{cases} \tag{4}$$

with S_b the surface of the cross-section, $S_{im}(s)$ the local immersed surface, $q_B(s)$ the local barycenter of the immersed surface, a_g the gravity acceleration, and the water and the body mass density ρ_w and ρ_b. Note that the components (F_x, F_y, Γ_z) are null since the potential energy is invariant by translations parallel to the water surface, and rotations along the vertical axis (cf. Noether's theorem). The detail of the calculation of these quantities are performed in an other paper [11]. Finally, we are able to compute the net wrench $W^T = (F_z, \Gamma_x, \Gamma_y)$ exerted on the body as a function of the head configuration g_0 defined by its orientation R_0 and its position p_0, and the body shape defined by the fields of strain $\kappa(s)$.

Analysis of the Poses. This tool allows for an analysis of the snakes poses in terms of torsion and bending. All the pictures reported in Fig. 1 support the fact that the body undergoes strong deformations that are combinations of bending and torsion. The pictures (a) and (b) clearly show that sinusoidal bending and body twisting are coupled. The pose reported in pictures (d) shows a positive lateral flexion and torsion producing a helical shape. However, it is difficult to quantify the relative contribution of the lateral or dorso-ventral flexion and the torsion from these single pictures. The dorso-ventral flexion seems to be only localized at the beginning of the rostro-caudal axis to maintain the head like a periscope, while lateral flexion and torsion are required to achieve static stability as suggested by Fig. 1(a) and (b). However, when the body deformation is only composed of torsion κ_1 and lateral flexion κ_3, the body displays clearly a 3D shape in Fig. 3 (A) distinct from the body shape reported in Fig. 1(a) To maintain a vertebral column in a 2D or a quasi-2D plane, the dorso-ventral flexion has to compensate the vertical component of the lateral flexion. In Fig. 3(B), we show how a combination of all three rotational degrees of freedom could maintain a body in a 2D plane. To maintain the vertebral column in a plane, one can show that the lateral flexion $\kappa_3(s)$ and the dorso-ventral flexion $\kappa_2(s)$ have to satisfy the following relations

$$\kappa_2 = \kappa_\perp(s)\sin\left(\int_0^s \kappa_1(x)\mathrm{d}x\right), \qquad \kappa_3 = \kappa_\perp(s)\cos\left(\int_0^s \kappa_1(x)\mathrm{d}x\right) \qquad (5)$$

with $\kappa_\perp(s) = \sqrt{\kappa_2^2(s) + \kappa_3^2(s)}$ the net local flexion, κ_1 the torsion field, and s (or x) the curvilinear variable parametrizing the vertebral column. The amplitude of the fields κ_i are reported on Fig. 3(C).

This is a clear evidence that the snake uses both flexions when the body is locally twisted in order to keep its vertebral column in a quasi 2D shape. Therefore, balance on a water surface is achieved thanks to all three rotational degrees of freedom.

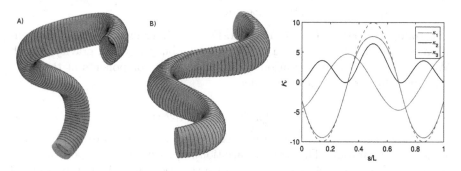

Fig. 3. The figure (A) corresponds to a body shape with only torsion (κ_1, red curve in the right figure) and lateral flexion (κ_3, dashed blue curve in the right figure). The figure (B) corresponds to the same torsion κ_1 (red curve) but with lateral flexion (κ_3, thick blue curve) and dorso-ventral flexion (κ_2, thick black curve) that maintain the central line in a plane. The norm of $\kappa_\perp(s) = \sqrt{\kappa_2^2(s) + \kappa_3^2(s)}$ is kept constant in both examples. (Color figure online)

4 How to Stabilize the Head Configuration

Direct and Inverse Problems. We distinguish two kinds of problems. The direct problem consists in finding the stable head configuration g_0 for a given body shape defined by the strain $\kappa(s)$. This problem is solved by finding the minimum of potential energy (gravity+buoyancy) of the system. In practice, a body will find this equilibrium by a relaxation to the nearest equilibrium. It is well-posed since a countable number of solutions or minima exists for a given body shape, each one depending on the initial conditions. The inverse problem consists in finding the body shape defined by the field $\kappa(s)$ that provides a given stable head configuration g_0. This problem is solved by the snake, when it needs to maintain its head facing a predator while modifying its body shape to prepare an attack or an escaping manoeuvre. Unlike the direct problem, this problem is ill-posed since it exists an infinite number of body strain field $\kappa(s)$ for the same head configuration. The purpose of this section is to illustrate this feature.

In details, we seek a control law that allows us to vary the body shape while keeping the head configuration constant. As an initial approach, the motion will be seen as a succession of equilibrium configurations according to the equilibrium point hypothesis [12]. Hence, we neglect all the inertia effects by computing a quasi-static motion. Then, we consider that body deformations are global rather than local, even if the snake could also strongly bend its body locally (see Fig. 1C and D). Indeed, the complex musculo-tendinous architecture of the snake [7] distributes the stress along its body so producing global body deformations. Moreover, the couplings between peripheral and central motor control generate stereotyped motor behaviour that also produces also global body deformations. Finally, our Chebyshev modal approach will be used to generate these global deformations, so that the body shape is parametrized by the Chebyshev component $\tilde{\kappa}_k$ of the body strain (Eq. 3).

Stabilizing the Head Configuration. From an initially stable head configuration, we are able to compute a variation of the buoyancy and gravity wrench $\delta \mathbf{W}$ as a function of the variation of the Chebyshev components of the body strain $\delta \tilde{\kappa}$, which gives at leading order

$$\delta \mathbf{W} = (\mathcal{D}_{\tilde{\kappa}} \mathbf{W}_N) \, \delta \tilde{\kappa} + o(|\delta \tilde{\kappa}|) \tag{6}$$

with $(\mathcal{D}_{\tilde{\kappa}} \mathbf{W}_N)$ a $3 \times 3N$ Jacobian matrix depending on the body strain κ and the head configuration. The wrench variation is produced by a modification of the immersed part of each body section when the body shape is slightly changed for a constant head configuration. The jacobian matrix is obtained by applying a variation in Eq. 4 in the framework of the geometrically exact approach, and then by integrating exactly each polynomial given by Eq. 3. This process is performed analytically, and implemented in MATLAB. Since $(\mathcal{D}_{\tilde{\kappa}} \mathbf{W}_N)$ is a rectangular matrix, the dimension of its Kernel is larger or equal to $3(N-1)$ with N the order of the Chebyshev truncation (Eq. 3). For an exact representation of the function $\kappa(.)$ belonging to a Hilbert space (with $N \to \infty$), it exists an infinite set of body strain variations that produce no wrench at leading order, and thus no head motion. This is of great interest because it opens the possibility to control independently the stability and the locomotion. Therefore, for an initially stable head configuration g_0 and a given body strain κ, one may decompose any body strain variation $\delta \tilde{\kappa}$ as

$$\delta \tilde{\kappa} = \mathrm{P}_{\parallel} \delta(\tilde{\kappa})_{\parallel} + \mathrm{P}_{\perp} (\delta \tilde{\kappa})_{\perp} \tag{7}$$

with $\mathrm{P}_{\parallel}$ a $3N \times 3(N-1)$ projection matrix to the null space of $(\mathcal{D}_{\tilde{\kappa}} \mathbf{W}_N)$, $\mathrm{P}_{\perp}$ a $3N \times 3$ projection matrix with the three vectors producing a variation of the wrench. The matrices $\mathrm{P}_{\parallel}$ and $\mathrm{P}_{\perp}$ are given by a singular value decomposition of $(\mathcal{D}_{\tilde{\kappa}} \mathbf{W}_N)$. To maintain the head configuration in equilibrium, the wrench must cancel for each strain increment $\delta\tilde{\kappa}$. However, Eq. 6 is a linear approximation of the wrench, and the equilibrium is only satisfied at order $|\delta\kappa|$. Any deformation $\delta\tilde{\kappa}_{\|}$ produces a residual wrench (even small) that must be corrected to avoid a departure from the equilibrium. Hence, we use the component $(\delta\tilde{\kappa})_{\perp}$ to compensate the residual wrench in order to cancel out the net wrench. The ratio $|\delta\kappa_{\perp}|/|\delta\kappa_{\|}|$ is typically of order 10^{-4} so that the body shape variation is essentially controlled by the component $\delta\kappa_{\|}$. The second right-hand side term in Eq. 7 is thus used as a corrector.

Illustration. To illustrate this process, we will uncoil a slender body mimicking a snake. The process consists in decreasing progressively the torsion κ_1 and the bending κ_3 while remaining stable at each time step, to satisfy the equilibrium point hypothesis. At each step, the spectral strain variation $\tilde{\kappa}_i$ at the iteration "i" is proportional to the current strain $\tilde{\kappa}_i$ so that $\delta\tilde{\kappa}_i(s) = -\epsilon\tilde{\kappa}_i$ with $\epsilon = 2 \times 10^{-3}$. The density of the body is fixed to $d = 0.25$ (much lighter than a snake) for a body of unitary length and radius $a = 0.04L$. This geometry corresponds to a 3D printed helical body (left Fig. 4) that has been used to benchmark the code. The code gives a stable head configuration with only 3% of error relative to the observed one (this method and the computation of the error are reported in [11]). This process has required 6000 iterations to reduce the norm of κ by 3. Every 300 iterations, the head configuration is recomputed thanks to the optimization method in order to check the equilibrium head configuration.

The configurations of the central line in the Cartesian space are reported in Fig. 5. The black curve corresponds to the initial state. Some of the iterations are illustrated by a color code so that the body color varies from blue (first iteration) to red (last iteration). The head is marked by the red circle, and we observe that the head orientation is kept constant during the process. At every step, the decrease of the bending κ_3 and the torsion κ_1 is compensated by an increase of κ_2. The oscillatory bending produces ripples along the rods to maintain some sections fully immersed and other fully dry. The final state (right Fig. 4) of the central line is similar to a transversally curved bow with the tail and the center immersed. Note that the initial and final states look similar to the poses of the snakes, which are respectively represented by Fig. 1(d) and Fig. 1(a).

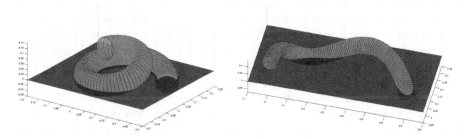

Fig. 4. Inital (left) and final (right) body configurations relative to the water surface

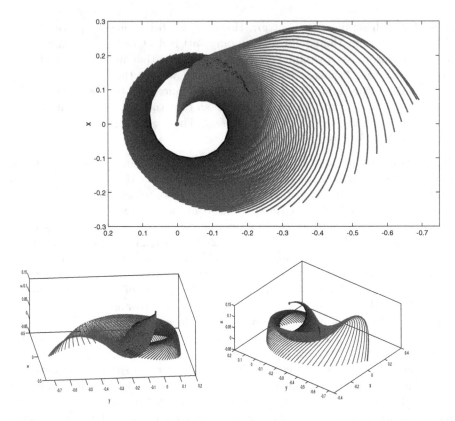

Fig. 5. Top: top view of the superimposition (from blue to red) of the iterative body deformations. Bottom: side views. (Color figure online)

5 Conclusion

In our study, we have demonstrated that snakes use complex combinations of all three rotational degrees of freedom of each vertebra, quantified by the strain κ, to maintain their body in an equilibrium configuration. This is of great interest for biologists since the motor control of the stability should activate complex combinations of muscles to produce these body shapes. We have developed theoretical and numerical tools to quantify and reproduce the performance of these semi-aquatic snakes for a quasi-static motion. We have shown that the head can be maintained in an equilibrium configuration thanks to a control law based on the decomposition of the strain field determined by the Jacobian of the wrench. We have demonstrated that the snakes can reach two equilibria connected by a succession of equilibria. Moreover, many ways exist to connect both equilibria. It will be interesting to investigating the metrics (elastic energy, motor control, time) used by the snake to connect them.

The next step consists in embodying these concepts and laws into a robot. Motivated by our observations, we are currently designing a planar robot that could manoeuvre on the water surface. Each body section is linked by actuated angular joints producing a lateral flexion wave. To provide stability, each body section can rotate while preserving the orientation of the flexion joint. This is analogue to the model reported in Eq. 5, where the robot remains planar while each section can rotate. Each section can adjust its immersed surface thanks to this independent rolling motion, and thus modify the local buoyancy force. The so-called NATRIX robot is illustrated in Fig. 6.

Fig. 6. Illustration of the robot NATRIX.

References

1. Hirose, S., Yamada, H.: Snake-like robots [tutorial]. IEEE Robot. **16**(11), 88–98 (2009)
2. Ijspeert, A.J., Crespi, A., Ryczko, D., Cabelguen, J.-M.: From swimming to walking with a salamander robot driven by a spinal cord model. Science **315**(5817), 1416–1420 (2007)
3. Liljebäck, P., Mill, R.: Eelume: a flexible and subsea resident IMR vehicle. In: OCEANS 2017-Aberdeen. IEEE (2017)
4. Wiens, A.J., Nahon, M.: Optimally efficient swimming in hyper-redundant mechanisms: control, design, and energy recovery. Bioinspir. Biomimet. **7**(4), 046016 (2012)
5. Brischoux, F., Shine, R.: Morphological adaptations to marine life in snakes. J. Morphol. **272**(5), 566–572 (2011)
6. Graham, J.B., Gee, J.H., Robison, F.S.: Hydrostatic and gas exchange functions of the lung of the sea snake Pelamis platurus. Comp. Biochem. Physiol. A Physiol. **50**(3), 477–482 (1975)
7. Jayne, B.C.: Swimming in constricting (Elaphe g. guttata) and nonconstricting (Nerodia fasciata pictiventris) colubrid snakes. Copeia 195–208 (1985)
8. Bauchot, R., et al.: Serpent, artemis editions (2016). ISBN 978-2-8160-1027-5
9. Simo, J.C.: A finite strain beam formulation. The threedimensional dynamic problem. Part I. Comput. Methods Appl. Mech. Eng. **49**(1), 55–70 (1985)
10. Boyer, F., Ali, S., Porez, M.: Macrocontinuous dynamics for hyperredundant robots: application to kinematic locomotion bioinspired by elongated body animals. IEEE Trans. Rob. **28**(2), 303317 (2011)
11. Herault, J.: A geometrically exact approach for floating slender bodies with finite deformations. Appl. Res. Ocean **101**, 102220 (2020)
12. Bernstein, N.: The Coordination and Regulation of Movements (1967)

From Models of Cognition to Robot Control and Back Using Spiking Neural Networks

Stefan Iacob, Johan Kwisthout, and Serge Thill

Donders Institute for Brain, Cognition and Behaviour,
Radboud University Nijmegen, 6525 Nijmegen, HR, The Netherlands
s.iacob@student.ru.nl, {j.kwisthout,s.thill}@donders.ru.nl

Abstract. With the recent advent of neuromorphic hardware there has been a corresponding rise in interest in spiking neural network models for the control of real-world artificial agents such as robots. Although models of cognitive mechanisms instantiated in spiking neural networks are nothing new, very few of them are translated onto real robot platforms. In this paper, we attempt such a translation: we implement an existing, biologically plausible model of reaching (the REACH model) demonstrated in 2D simulation on a UR5e robot arm. We are interested in particular in how well such a translation works since this has implications for similar exercises with a vast library of existing models of cognition. In this particular case, after extensions to operations in 3D and for the particular hardware used, we do find that the model is able to learn on the real platform as it did in the original simulation, albeit without reaching the same levels of performance.

Keywords: Spiking neural networks · Robot control · Bio-plausible models

1 Introduction

1.1 Biologically Inspired Artificial Cognition and Spiking Neurons

Although artificial cognitive systems and, more specifically, robotics can be seen as engineering disciplines, there has traditionally been a strong interest in biological approaches to designing such systems [28]. Work has, over the past decades, spanned simple demonstrations (in terms of robot agent and environment; often virtual) that were based on hypothesised biological mechanisms (see for example early implementations of internal simulation mechanisms [19,31] based on Hesslow's simulation hypothesis [15,16]) to biologically inspired control for autonomous vehicles [8].

A long-going debate in this context concerns the appropriate level at which to base such biological inspiration, with options ranging from the purely behavioural to the physiologically detailed. Several factors can play a role in

© Springer Nature Switzerland AG 2020
V. Vouloutsi et al. (Eds.): Living Machines 2020, LNAI 12413, pp. 176–191, 2020.
https://doi.org/10.1007/978-3-030-64313-3_18

this decision; for example whether the prime purpose of the agent is to be an explanatory model of biological cognition or whether it takes biological inspiration merely to be successful at some task [25], or to what degree physiological details are essential to cognition, as opposed to mere constraints by biology [24].

In this context, spiking neural networks (SNNs) have recently attracted interest in biologically inspired robotics. In part, this is driven by the recent advent of neuromorphic hardware platforms that promise to be able to run relatively large networks in real time (a fundamental requirement for any model operating on a real robotic platform) and, for example, the potential energy efficiency such models may provide [6]. From a more cognitive perspective, however, it is possible that SNNs are a suitable level of abstraction to adequately model natural cognition. This is, for example, the assumption in the so-called neuroengineering framework [13] underlying the semantic pointer architecture [12], a biologically inspired cognitive architecture instantiated entirely in – and constrained by properties of – spiking neurons.

From the perspective of artificial cognitive systems, these two aspects are very compelling: on the one hand, it is increasingly possible to run even large SNNs on state-of-the-art hardware and on the other, there is a large selection of models of cognitive mechanisms in the cognitive sciences literature that are instantiated in SNNs, from simple motor control [10] to higher cognition [14].

While there therefore is a large potential for bringing both strands together in near-future artificial cognitive systems, some caveats remain. Here, we are primarily interested in those arising from the fact that models of interesting cognitive phenomena, by present-day necessity, are rarely instantiated on a physical agent; rather they are demonstrated in simulations that contain the necessary but also sufficient detail to highlight the model's functionality. We therefore explore how the porting of such a model onto a physical platform would work. We start from the aforementioned model of motor control [10], which was demonstrated using a simulated robot arm with two degrees of freedom (DOF) and operating in two dimensions and implement it on a physical robot arm (an UR5e), adapting it for operation in three dimensions. We report on the process as well as on performance comparisons. We chose this model because it captures an essential aspect of sensorimotor cognition that may, at least according to embodied theories of cognition, serve as a fundamental aspect of all cognition [28]; it is therefore likely that most if not all cognitively interesting models on real robots will need to implement similar aspects.

Since spiking neural networks in artificial cognitive systems is a nascent field, this kind of exploration helps adjust expectations and gauge the possibilities and limitations. In addition to illustrating the details of this particular implementation of a (in cognitive terms) fundamental system on a real platform, the paper thus highlights the need for more explorations in this direction so that the potential of taking existing cognitive models onto a real machine operating in the real world can be fully exploited in the future.

In the remainder of the paper, we first present a brief background on some of the particular challenges that SNNs entail for robots and existing SNN models of reaching task. We then present our implementation and reflect on the possibilities and limitations this demonstrates.

2 Background

2.1 Challenges with Robotic Implementations of Spiking Neural Networks

Spiking neural networks (SNNs) have traditionally received less attention over rate-based models. This preference can be explained by the fact that rate-based artificial neural networks (ANNs) are currently easier to model. Their training procedure using error backpropagation with gradient descent is straightforward, as it can be applied to any labeled dataset. On the other hand, SNNs currently do not have convergent and generally applicable learning procedures [5]. Different global and local learning rules have been explored in recent years [11,29,30], but there is still a need for streamlining the learning process. In [4], a more biologically plausible version of backpropagation through time is achieved in spiking recurrent neural networks, by applying eligibility traces. Surrogate Gradients [21] is another strategy for coping with the non-differentiable spike signals, by instead using surrogate derivatives, which are approximations of spikes through differentiable functions.

ANNs are based on the assumption that relevant features of the data can be encoded in neuron spiking frequency. This results in a smoothly varying differentiable signal, with lower temporal resolution compared to SNNs. However, rate-based neurons are easy to model and simulate, as they rely on simple activation functions. SNNs trade model simplicity for temporal resolution and biological plausibility. Because of the temporal nature of spikes, SNNs have the advantage of being able to learn the encoding of signal variations in time as features. The ability to learn temporal patterns is of great use for robots, as embodied agents live in a temporal world. Behaviour is always sequential in nature, which requires the ability to learn how the timing of different motor commands depend on sensory input. Contrary to SNNs, ANNs do not inherently include the time domain in their encoding. Hence, to include temporal information, ANNs require time to be explicitly modelled in the network architecture [17].

Modelling individual spike times requires more complex neuron models, which are computationally harder to simulate on traditional Von Neuman hardware compared to rate-based neurons. However, in recent years we have seen the rise of highly parallel neuromorphic hardware. Already the benefits of SNNs simulated on neuromorphic hardware over non-neuromorphic models have been demonstrated in some proof-of-concept applications [6].

Even with increased simulation speed and energy efficiency, using SNNs effectively in robots remains more complex than training ANNs. Autonomous adaptive robots should ideally be able to learn nonlinear relations between motor commands and environmental effects in a relatively unsupervised manner, such that reward maximizing behaviour can be selected. In order to increase generalisability, and avoid implementations that are too task-specific, this learning should ideally start from minimal pre-defined behaviour. Pairing the biologically plausible SNNs with biologically plausible learning rules to achieve such generalisability has been proven to be a challenging task. Several first steps have been made towards a design pattern for SNN learning [11,20]. However, no straightforward and stable design-pattern exists yet, which is especially true for deep-learning SNNs. To train deep neural networks, we mostly rely on gradient descent learning rules which require differentiable neuron activity. This property is present in rate-based neurons, but not in most spiking neurons. On the other hand, many nonlinearities in robotics applications can be learned without needing multiple layers in the architecture. For example, using the prescribed error sensitivity (PES) learning rule allows a spiking neural network to learn operations such as XOR without multiple layers of neurons [3,29].

This PES learning rule is used, in particular in the adaptive reaching model [10] the present work is based on. In particular, the model uses the learning rule to allow the model to compensate regular perturbations such as force fields or changes in arm weight (while the actual reaching is carried out without learning but merely through computing the necessary joint torque to minimize the distance of the hand to the target). Comparisons with reported performance by human participants in similar force field perturbations [22] shows that the model performs more efficiently than humans. In this paper, as explained abvoe, we aim to move REACH from a purely experimental and simulated setting, to a real world embodied robot arm. We present an extended 3D implementation of REACH, working with a physical robot arm (the UR5e [27]), in a range of target positions.

2.2 SNN Models of Reaching

Most models that compute transformations of basic motor commands to desired end-effector movement can be evaluated in terms of (neuro-) plasticity. On the lower end of the neuroplasticity spectrum, these transformations are specified in the model design, and during run-time are left unchanged, hence no (on-line) learning occurs. On the other end of the spectrum, we have models that start from random synaptic weights and no previous knowledge of the kinematic transformations. These models attempt to learn these transformations through proprioceptive feedback. Here we discuss two papers, each representing one extreme of the plasticity spectrum.

Tieck et al. [26] present an SNN robot arm controller simulated using Nengo – the framework for developing models based on the previously mentioned NEF [3], also used for the REACH model and in our work. The model is based on motor primitives, which in this context refers to a combination of joint angles necessary to achieve a desired Tool Centre Point (TCP) position. The mapping from motor primitives to basic joint commands is trained offline. This means that Nengo estimates the synaptic weights necessary to approximate the desired mappings during build time. Hence, no on-line learning occurs. This is of no concern if the robot arm parameters (e.g. weight and size), remains exactly constant, which is usually the case for reaching tasks. However, from a biological perspective, dealing with changing body parameters (e.g. growth) is an important skill.

Bouganis and Shanahan present a SNN model that can be trained to control a 4 DoF ICub arm [7]. The training procedure makes use of 'motor babbling'

[9], and the learning mechanism used is Spike Timing-Dependent Plasticity. The SNN model is built with Izhikevich neurons [18], and consists of 7 input populations and 4 output populations. The input populations encode proprioceptive feedback (i.e. joint position) and desired cartesian coordinates (i.e. TCP position), whereas the output populations encode the desired motor commands. The input and output populations are connected in an all-to-all manner with STDP synapses. During the motor-babbling phase (i.e. the training phase), the output population activates according to randomly generated motor commands, whereas the input layer activates according to the corresponding desired TCP position, which is computed using forward kinematics equations. By updating the synapse weights according to the STDP learning rule, this model can autonomously learn the inverse kinematics transformations. On the other hand, using a predefined forward kinematics equation to compute goal states corresponding to the generated movements means that this model is also not able to adapt to changes in arm parameters after the training phase. Although the motor babbling learning phase can be viewed as on-line learning, the learning process is stopped in the following 'performance phase', where desired TCP position is fed through the network and the motor commands are given as output.

REACH sits somewhere in between the above mentioned models in terms of plasticity. It is a SNN designed for target reaching with a 2D arm simulation. Most motor equations are pre-defined and estimated during build-time of the network by Nengo, similar to the model by Tieck et al. However, REACH includes an adaptive component: the cerebellum (CB). Similar to its biological counterpart, the REACH CB compensates perturbations and errors in the arm movements. This error compensation is learned on-line with the PES learning rule, using an efferent copy of the torque signal as error signal. REACH was shown to perform well in the 8-reach task, shows human-like reaching movements, and is able learn long-term adaptations to force field perturbations faster than humans. In our view, REACH makes good use of pre-programmed domain knowledge of kinematics, as well as an adaptive component that learns on-line.

3   Methods

Our modified implementation of REACH is based on the original movement equation [10].

$$\mathbf{u} = \hat{\mathbf{J}}^T \mathbf{M_x} \mathbf{u_x} - K_v \mathbf{M} \dot{\mathbf{q}} + \mathbf{u}_{\text{adapt}} \qquad (1)$$

Here, $\mathbf{u}$ is the resulting joint torque output, $\mathbf{u_x}$ is the desired force in hand space, $\hat{\mathbf{J}}$ is the Jacobian, indicating how change in joint angles affects hand position, $\mathbf{M_x}$ the inertia matrix in hand space, the term $K_v \mathbf{M} \dot{\mathbf{q}}$ accounts for the arm's current velocity ($\mathbf{M}$: inertia matrix in joint space, K_v: constant, and $\dot{q}$: joint velocity), and $\mathbf{u}_{\text{adapt}}$ represents the adaptive compensation learned by the cerebellum (CB) network.

In essence, Eq. 1 remains the same, since it does not depend on the number of joint dimenensions and cartesian dimensions. However, the individual components are changed to account for the higher dimensionality and different rotational axes. First of all, $\mathbf{u}$, $\mathbf{u_x}$, $\mathbf{u}_{\text{adapt}}$, and $\dot{\mathbf{q}}$ all need to be changed from 2D to 3D, either due to the increase in number of joints, or increase in number of cartesian dimensions.

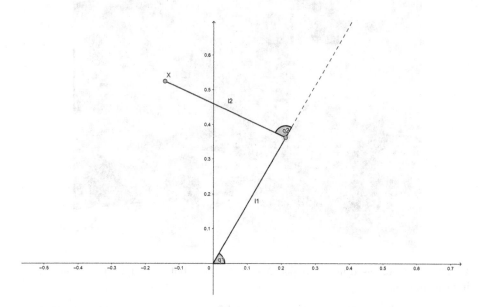

Fig. 1. 2D Arm representation. l_1 and l_2 indicate the segment lengths, and q_1 and q_2 indicate joint angles. $\mathbf{x}$ is the position in Cartesian coordinates of the end-effector.

To explain the remaining differences, we look at how each component is computed in the 2D and 3D REACH implementation respectively.

Jacobian. Consider the 2D, 2-joint arm simulation represented in Fig. 1. The Jacobian $\mathbf{J}$ is defined as the matrix of partial derivatives $\frac{\partial \mathbf{x}}{\partial \mathbf{q}}$, with the following matrix entries:

$$\mathbf{J}_{1,1} = \frac{\partial x_1}{\partial q_1} = -l_1 \sin(q_1) - l_2 \sin(q_1 + q_2) \tag{2}$$

$$\mathbf{J}_{1,2} = \frac{\partial x_1}{\partial q_2} = -l_2 \sin(q_1 + q_2) \tag{3}$$

$$\mathbf{J}_{2,1} = \frac{\partial x_2}{\partial q_1} = l_1 \cos(q_1) + l_2 \cos(q_1 + q_2) \tag{4}$$

$$\mathbf{J}_{2,2} = \frac{\partial x_2}{\partial q_2} = l_2 \cos(q_1 + q_2) \tag{5}$$

We extended this 2D arm model to a 3-joint 3D arm model operating on a physical robot (see Fig. 2, making use of the shoulder pan joint, shoulder lift joint, and elbow joint, where the shoulder pan joint has a rotational axis that

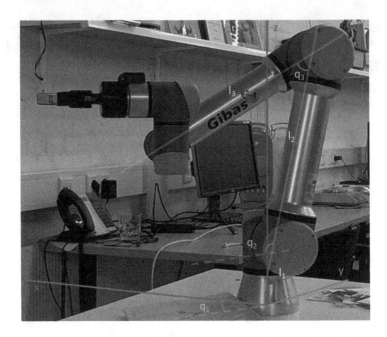

Fig. 2. The UR5e used in this paper. Note that the robot is used a 3-joint arm in this implementation.

is perpendicular on those of the shoulder lift joint and the elbow joint. In this case, the Jacobian has the dimensions of 3 by 3 (3 cartesian dimensions and 3 joint dimensions), with the following matrix entries:

$$\mathbf{J}_{1,1} = \frac{\partial x_1}{\partial q_1} = -l_2 \sin(q_1) \cos(q_2) - l_3 \sin(q_1) \cos(q_2 + q_3) \tag{6}$$

$$\mathbf{J}_{1,2} = \frac{\partial x_1}{\partial q_2} = -l_2 \cos(q_1) \sin(q_2) - l_3 \cos(q_1) \sin(q_2 + q_3) \tag{7}$$

$$\mathbf{J}_{1,3} = \frac{\partial x_1}{\partial q_3} = -l_3 \cos(q_1) \sin(q_2 + q_3) \tag{8}$$

$$\mathbf{J}_{2,1} = \frac{\partial x_2}{\partial q_1} = l_2 \cos(q_1) \cos(q_2) + l_3 \cos(q_1) \cos(q_2 + q_3) \tag{9}$$

$$\mathbf{J}_{2,2} = \frac{\partial x_2}{\partial q_2} = -l_2 \sin(q_1) \sin(q_2) - l_3 \sin(q_1) \sin(q_2 + q_3) \tag{10}$$

$$\mathbf{J}_{2,3} = \frac{\partial x_2}{\partial q_3} = -l_3 \sin(q_1) \sin(q_2 + q_3) \tag{11}$$

$$\mathbf{J}_{3,1} = \frac{\partial x_3}{\partial q_1} = 0 \tag{12}$$

$$\mathbf{J}_{3,2} = \frac{\partial x_3}{\partial q_2} = l_2 \cos(q_2) + l_3 \cos(q_2 + q_3) \tag{13}$$

$$\mathbf{J}_{3,3} = \frac{\partial x_3}{\partial q_3} = l_3 \cos(q_2 + q_3) \tag{14}$$

Inertia Matrix. Secondly we go through the process of creating the inertia matrix in hand-space (i.e. cartesian space) $\mathbf{M_x}$, which is used for compensation of the movement-generated inertia. This compensation is achieved by multiplying the Jacobian with the inertia matrix $\mathbf{M_x}$.

To compute $\mathbf{M_x}$, the first step consists of defining the moments of inertia matrix for each link, which, for a rigid body, is usually expressed by a *moment of inertia tensor*:

$$\mathbf{I} = \begin{bmatrix} I_{xx} & I_{xy} & I_{xz} \\ I_{yx} & I_{yy} & I_{yz} \\ I_{zx} & I_{zy} & I_{zz} \end{bmatrix} \tag{15}$$

However, in 2D REACH both links can only rotate along the z axis (in Fig. 1, only the x and y axis are visible), hence each link only has an I_{zz} moment of inertia, with all other entries set to zero. In the 3D, 3-joint adaptation, we have two different rotational axes, namely one joint that rotates along the z-axis, and two that rotate along the y-axis. Therefore, in the adapted model we use I_{yy} and I_{zz}. Using the moments of inertia, link masses, and Jacobians from the centre of mass of each links, the estimated inertia matrix $\mathbf{M}$ in joint space is computed, from which the hand-space inertia matrix $\mathbf{M_x}$ is estimated. Both are used in Eq. 1.

3.1   Program Design

To control the UR5e we made use of the UR ROS driver, developed by Andersen et al. [1], offering several ROS topics where the robot posts messages about the joint state, and others where the user can post messages about joint commands. We implemented ROS nodes that read from and post on these topics.

With the communication established between the controller and the arm, one communication issue remains: direct torque control is not possible with the UR5e robot. It is however possible to specify goal joint angles and movement duration.

Therefore, the goal is to estimate the angular acceleration and velocity for each joint, given the applied torque over a fixed time period, and then compute the new joint position based on the equation of angular accelerated motion. When assuming the torque constant over the considered time interval, then the motion will be uniformly accelerated, and the new joint position will be given by $q_{new} = q_{old} + \dot{q}t + \frac{\ddot{q}t^2}{2}$. Here, q_{new} and q_{old} refer respectively to the joint angles at the new and the old simulation step. The angular acceleration can be estimated based on the robot arm dynamics equation $\ddot{q} = \mathbf{M}^{-1}(\mathbf{q})(\tau - \mathbf{C}(\mathbf{q}, \dot{\mathbf{q}}))$, where $\mathbf{M}(\mathbf{q})$ is the inertia matrix dependent on the current joint configuration $\mathbf{q}$, and $\mathbf{C}$ is the Coriolis and centripetal term. However, to facilitate this complex torque control and avoid re-computing the inertia matrix every iteration, we chose to drastically simplify the torque control in the UR5e. This can be done without damaging the theoretical implications of this work, as the adaptive CB component of REACH is hypothesized to compensate any mismatch between the control signal and actual performance. Another approximation that was

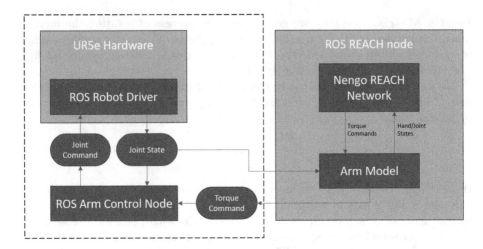

Fig. 3. Functional Diagram of the resulting arm controller. The rectangles indicate components of the program, whereas the ovals represent the ROS topics on which messages are published. The main function of the *ROS Arm Control Node* is to transform the incoming torque messages into publishable joint position messages, since the UR5e hardware is not capable of receiving torque commands. Due to this program structure based on functionality, the components within the dashed rectangle can be used separately from the *ROS REACH node* in combination with other cognitive architectures

necessary for this implementation resulted from the impossibility to estimate velocity over the short time intervals of the torque update. Therefore, we make used of Eq. 16, to update the new position for each simulation step.

$$\theta_{new} = \theta_{old} + \frac{\tau t^2}{2\mathbf{m}} \tag{16}$$

where θ_{old} is a vector containing the current joint angles, τ is a vector with the torques applied on each joint, and $\mathbf{m}$ contains the masses of the arm portion that each joint has to move. The second term in this equation is obtained by integrating the angular acceleration $\ddot{q} = \frac{\tau}{I}$, where for the moment of inertia I we ignore the length of the lengths of the links and instead only use the mass. The time t is the duration that the torque is applied, which we fix to one second. In reality, a torque applied for a much shorter period due to constantly updating the torque, and consequently the goal position each iteration step. Hence, relatively smooth movement is achieved without the use of direct torque. The resulting program structure can be seen in Fig. 3.

REACH Extension. To adapt the Nengo component to the 3D arm model, we first used the unaltered REACH model to control just two joints, thus making sure that the communication between Nengo and ROS works correctly. Next we extended REACH to 3D and 3 joints following the steps described at the beginning of this section.

3.2 Hardware

To allow for 3D movement, the arm needs at least two different rotational axes. Furthermore, REACH outputs joint torque values, so ideally, the arm should be controllable through torque commands. Lastly, to compute these torque commands, REACH necessitates the current joint angles and angular velocities. It should at least be possible to read out the joint angles from the arm. Preferably, angular velocities should be directly readable as well, although these can also be estimated within the model implementation.

We make use of Universal Robot's UR5e, which satisfies most requirements, except for torque control. Instead, the joints can be moved to a specified position, or with a specified angular velocity. Torque control can be approximated by continuously estimating the goal joint angles that would result from the torque command.

3.3 Experiment Design

So far, we have covered the process of transforming 2D simulated REACH into a real 3-joint robot arm controller moving in 3D. From directly observing the behaviour, the arm controller appears to work in a similar fashion to REACH, and succeeds in reaching the given targets. In this subsection we describe what experiments where used to compare the extension of REACH to the original version. In the next section, we discuss the results to these experiments.

To compare our REACH implementation with the results of DeWolf et al. [10], we use an adapted version of the experiment setup that was used in their paper, namely, the 8-reach task. In this task, the robot arm reaches for eight targets, evenly spaced on a circle. After each target, the arm moves back to the centre position before reaching for the next target. Our adaptation to the experiment is as follows: to account for a higher dimensionality, we distributed the targets across a sphere by spacing them according to three equal horizontal

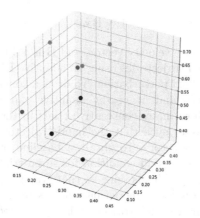

Fig. 4. 9-reach experiment target configuration.

angles and three equal vertical angles, resulting in nine targets, hence we refer to the '9-reach task'. The target orientation is shown in Fig. 4.

The experiment trials are performed by outputting the coordinates of a target from the PMC component for a fixed period, followed by the centre coordinates. This is then repeated for the next targets, until all targets have been presented. The hand position coordinates at each simulation step are saved as a time series, which represent a hand trajectory. It was not yet possible to validate these trajectories as such, as this would require a comparison with human hand trajectories in a similar 3D setting. Obtaining this data was not in the scope of this project.

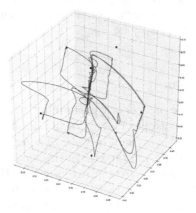

Fig. 5. REACH hand trajectory in without force field perturbations after four trials.

We want to find out whether the adaptive component of the CB is capable of learning to compensate a perturbation force field. We apply a force field to the torque output in a similar fashion as DeWolf et al., based on the human trials by Shadmehr et al. [22]. The perturbation forces are computed as follows:

$$\mathbf{f} = \mathbf{B}\dot{\mathbf{x}} \tag{17}$$

where $\dot{\mathbf{x}}$ is a 3D hand space velocity vector, and $\mathbf{B}$ is a 3 by 3 force-field matrix.

We measure the hand trajectories using an adaptive REACH controller both with and without force field perturbation. To draw a conclusion about the force field learning capabilities and hence the adaptive capabilities of 3-joint, 3D REACH, we measure how many consecutive trials in the force field condition (condition 1) are necessary such that the hand trajectories have a correlation of 0.9 with a baseline trajectory. To obtain a baseline trajectory, we first run the REACH model in the second condition for seven trials, and use the eighth trial as baseline trajectory. This is done so that REACH learns to compensate any inaccuracies in internal arm model parameters (e.g. wrong link weights or moments of inertia). The baseline trajectory is represented in Fig. 5.

To compute the correlation between two trajectories, we use the method described by Shadmehr et al. [22]. First, the hand position trajectories are transformed into hand velocity trajectories. The correlation between trajectory $\mathbf{X}$ and trajectory $\mathbf{Y}$ is obtained through the following equations:

$$\rho(\mathbf{X}, \mathbf{Y}) = \frac{\mathrm{Cov}(\mathbf{X}, \mathbf{Y})}{\sigma(\mathbf{X})\sigma(\mathbf{Y})} \tag{18}$$

$$\mathrm{Cov}(\mathbf{X}, \mathbf{Y}) = E[\mathbf{XY}] - E[\mathbf{X}] - E[\mathbf{Y}] \tag{19}$$

$$\sigma(\mathbf{X}) = \sqrt{E[(\mathbf{X}_i - E[\mathbf{X}])^2])} \tag{20}$$

However, because these are not time series of scalars but rather 3D vectors, the multiplications in the equations above should be seen as inner products, resulting in scalar values.

We measured three runs in the experimental condition (i.e. with force field). Each of these runs consisted of five consecutive trials, in which all nine targets were presented for two seconds each, with the centre target presented between two consecutive targets. For each of the three experiment runs we measured the correlation between the trial trajectories and baseline trajectory.

4 Results

The results can be seen in Fig. 6. The maximum achieved correlation across all the trials is 0.64. Although we see that none of the experiment runs achieve a correlation of 0.9 such as seen in DeWolf et al. [10], we do see that the correlation increases across the trials, indicating that trajectories get closer to the baseline. We also see that the mean absolute error decreases across trial. To verify, we compute a linear fit for each of the experimental runs and test for significant effect of the resulting linear regression with trial number as the predictor (see Table 1). We find statistically significant improvements in correlation with baseline in two of the three experimental runs. Similarly, we find that the hand space error decreases significantly in two of three runs, as does the path length in one run. These findings suggest that the adaptive CB component indeed improves the reaching performance over multiple trials, showing that it is able to compensate the imperfect knowledge about arm parameters, and the inaccurate forward dynamics. That said, given that the ranges in which these values increase or decrease are relatively small (as is the number of total experimental runs), these results should not be over-interpreted but be understood as a demonstration of the concept.

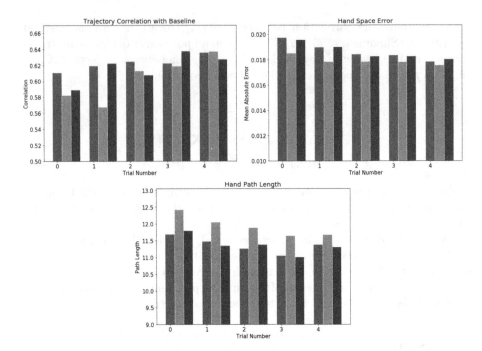

Fig. 6. Top left: correlation between REACH trajectories in a baseline condition (without force field) and trajectories of the force field condition, plotted against trial number. Top right: mean absolute error measured as euclidean distance between hand position and target position, plotted against trial number. Bottom: total path length plotted against trial number. Each colour represents a different experimental run. (Color figure online)

Table 1. Details of the linear fits to individual experimental run shown in Fig. 6. Statistically significant slopes are indicated in bold and with an asterisk (*)

	Correlation with Baseline				
	Slope	Intercept	R^2	Std Err	p
Trial 1	5.32e−03	6.07e−01	8.62e−01	1.23e−03	**2.28e−02** *
Trial 2	1.61e−02	5.56e−01	8.08e−01	4.52e−03	**3.79e−02** *
Trial 3	9.28e−03	5.89e−01	5.95e−01	4.42e−03	1.27e−01
	Mean absolute error				
	Slope	Intercept	R^2	Std Err	p
Trial 1	−4.37e−04	2.00e−02	9.40e−01	6.39e−05	**6.40e−03** *
Trial 2	−1.95e−04	1.85e−02	7.44e−01	6.60e−05	5.97e−02
Trial 3	−3.73e−04	1.98e−02	8.81e−01	7.89e−05	**1.80e−02** *
	Path length				
	Slope	Intercept	R^2	Std Err	p
Trial 1	−1.04e−01	1.17e+01	4.84e−01	6.20e−02	1.92e−01
Trial 2	−1.90e−01	1.25e+01	8.83e−01	4.00e−02	**1.77e−02** *
Trial 3	−1.30e−01	1.18e+01	5.44e−01	6.87e−02	1.55e−01

5   Discussion and Conclusions

In this paper, we have adapted a biologically plausible adaptive spiking neural network model of reaching [10] from a 2D, 2DOF simulated environment onto a physical UR5e operating in 3D, albeit limited to 3DOF for this initial implementation. A major limitation is that we did not evaluate this implementation extensively, in part because we did not implement the model on neuromorphic hardware and used a standard computer instead, which incurs a time penalty. It is therefore likely that future work could find stronger performance than we did in this initial implementation. Nonetheless, we found that the model was able to adapt to force field perturbations on the physical platform as one would expect from the simulated results from the model itself, even when adapted to 3D operation. In that sense, the initial results are encouraging for future implementations of models of cognitive mechanisms on physical platforms.

While the present model is arguably rather limited in any cognitively interesting sense since it merely reaches towards target positions, it does capture a necessary part of sensorimotor cognition and as such forms a basis on which to build more cognitively interesting agents. Grounding of cognitive processes in sensorimotor interaction underlies both general models of cognition [2,12] and specific robotic implementations of, for example, concept grounding [23]. In a larger context, endowing machines such as robots with artificial cognition instantiated in SNNs will require the entire model to be captured by these spiking neurons, including the sensorimotor interactions. This is an aspect that is often abstracted away or simplified in a model that only focusses on a specific mechanism (such as concept grounding, see e.g.. [23]). If the aim is however to achieve a complete robotic cognitive agent, then all these aspects need to be captured in a manner that likely incorporates models such as the REACH model [10]. While framweorks such as the NEF/SPA [12] provide the theory of how this might be achieved, many challenges remain to be resolved in practice, as demonstrated, for instance, by the present implementation of merely porting REACH onto a physical platform operating in three dimensions.

Overall, we have therefore presented an initial implementation of a model that can underlie much cognitive behaviour on a commonly used robotic platform, noting in particular the necessary changes and adapations that were required for this. While our current results are modest at best in terms of performance, we demonstrate the potential that exists as well as details of using a UR5e specifically in this context.

References

1. Andersen, T.T., Rasmussen, S., Exner, F., Steffen, L., Schnell, T.: Universal_robots_ros_driver (2020). https://github.com/UniversalRobots/Universal_Robots_ROS_Driver
2. Barsalou, L.W.: Perceptual symbol systems. Behav. Brain Sci. **22**(4), 577–660 (1999)

3. Bekolay, T., et al.: Nengo: a python tool for building large-scale functional brain models. Front. Neuroinform. **7**(48) (2014). https://doi.org/10.3389/fninf.2013.00048. http://www.frontiersin.org/neuroinformatics/10.3389/fninf.2013.00048/abstract
4. Bellec, G., Scherr, F., Hajek, E., Salaj, D., Legenstein, R., Maass, W.: Biologically inspired alternatives to backpropagation through time for learning in recurrent neural nets (2019)
5. Bing, Z., Meschede, C., Röhrbein, F., Huang, K., Knoll, A.C.: A survey of robotics control based on learning-inspired spiking neural networks. Front. Neurorobot. **12**, 35 (2018). https://doi.org/10.3389/fnbot.2018.00035. https://www.frontiersin.org/article/10.3389/fnbot.2018.00035
6. Blouw, P., Choo, X., Hunsberger, E., Eliasmith, C.: Benchmarking keyword spotting efficiency on neuromorphic hardware. In: Proceedings of the 7th Annual Neuro-inspired Computational Elements Workshop, pp. 1–8 (2019)
7. Bouganis, A., Shanahan, M.: Training a spiking neural network to control a 4-dof robotic arm based on spike timing-dependent plasticity. In: The 2010 International Joint Conference on Neural Networks (IJCNN), pp. 1–8 (2010)
8. da Lio, M., et al.: Exploiting dream-like simulation mechanisms to develop safer agents for automated driving the "Dreams4Cars" EU research and innovation action. In: Proceedings of the 20th IEEE International Conference on Intelligent Transportation Systems (2017). https://doi.org/10.1109/ITSC.2017.8317649
9. Demiris, Y., Dearden, A.: From motor babbling to hierarchical learning by imitation: a robot developmental pathway (2005)
10. DeWolf, T., Stewart, T.C., Slotine, J.J., Eliasmith, C.: A spiking neural model of adaptive arm control. Proc. R. Soc. B: Biol. Sci. **283**(1843), 20162134 (2016)
11. Diehl, P., Cook, M.: Unsupervised learning of digit recognition using spike-timing-dependent plasticity. Front. Comput. Neurosci. **9**, 99 (2015). https://doi.org/10.3389/fncom.2015.00099. https://www.frontiersin.org/article/10.3389/fncom.2015.00099
12. Eliasmith, C.: How to Build a Brain: A Neural Architecture for Biological Cognition. Oxford University Press, Oxford (2013)
13. Eliasmith, C., Anderson, C.H.: Neural Engineering: Computation, Representation, and Dynamics in Neurobiological Systems. MIT Press, Cambridge (2002)
14. Eliasmith, C., et al.: A large-scale model of the functioning brain. Science **338**(6111), 1202–1205 (2012)
15. Hesslow, G.: Conscious thought as simulation of behaviour and perception. Trends Cogn. Sci. **6**(6), 242–247 (2002). https://doi.org/10.1016/S1364-6613(02)01913-7
16. Hesslow, G.: The current status of the simulation theory of cognition. Brain Res. **1428**, 71–79 (2012). https://doi.org/10.1016/j.brainres.2011.06.026
17. Hochreiter, S., Schmidhuber, J.: Long short-term memory. Neural Comput. **9**(8), 1735–1780 (1997). https://doi.org/10.1162/neco.1997.9.8.1735
18. Izhikevich, E.M.: Simple model of spiking neurons. IEEE Trans. Neural Netw. **14**(6), 1569–1572 (2003)
19. Jirenhed, D.A., Hesslow, G., Ziemke, T.: Exploring internal simulation of perception in mobile robots, vol. 86, pp. 107–113. Lund University Cognitive Studies (2001)
20. Kheradpisheh, S.R., Ganjtabesh, M., Thorpe, S.J., Masquelier, T.: STDP-based spiking deep convolutional neural networks for object recognition. Neural Netw. **99**, 56–67 (2018)
21. Neftci, E.O., Mostafa, H., Zenke, F.: Surrogate gradient learning in spiking neural networks. IEEE Signal Process. Mag. **36**, 61–63 (2019)

22. Shadmehr, R., Mussa-Ivaldi, F.A.: Adaptive representation of dynamics during learning of a motor task. J. Neurosci. **14**(5), 3208–3224 (1994)
23. Stramandinoli, F., Marocco, D., Cangelosi, A.: The grounding of higher order concepts in action and language: a cognitive robotics model. Neural Netw. **32**, 165–173 (2012). https://doi.org/10.1016/j.neunet.2012.02.012. Selected Papers from IJCNN 2011
24. Thill, S.: Considerations for a neuroscience-inspired approach to the design of artificial intelligent systems. In: Schmidhuber, J., Thórisson, K.R., Looks, M. (eds.) AGI 2011. LNCS (LNAI), vol. 6830, pp. 247–254. Springer, Heidelberg (2011). https://doi.org/10.1007/978-3-642-22887-2_26
25. Thill, S., Vernon, D.: How to design emergent models of cognition for application-driven artificial agents. In: Twomey, K., Westermann, G., Monaghan, P., Smith, A. (eds.) Neurocomputational Models of Cognitive Development and Processing: Proceedings of the 14th Neural Computation and Psychology Workshop, pp. 115–129. World Scientific Publishing, Singapore (2016). https://doi.org/10.1142/9789814699341_0008
26. Tieck, J.C.V., Steffen, L., Kaiser, J., Roennau, A., Dillmann, R.: Controlling a robot arm for target reaching without planning using spiking neurons. In: 2018 IEEE 17th International Conference on Cognitive Informatics Cognitive Computing (ICCI*CC), pp. 111–116 (2018)
27. Universal Robots: Ur5e (2019). https://www.universal-robots.com/products/ur5-robot/
28. Vernon, D.: Artificial Cognitive Systems: A primer. MIT Press, Cambridge (2014)
29. Voelker, A.R.: A solution to the dynamics of the prescribed error sensitivity learning rule. Centre for Theoretical N Euro-Science, Waterloo (2015)
30. Wu, Y., Deng, L., Li, G., Zhu, J., Shi, L.: Spatio-temporal backpropagation for training high-performance spiking neural networks. Front. Neurosci. **12**, 331 (2018). https://doi.org/10.3389/fnins.2018.00331. https://www.frontiersin.org/article/10.3389/fnins.2018.00331
31. Ziemke, T., Jirenhed, D.A., Hesslow, G.: Internal simulation of perception: a minimal neuro-robotic model. Neurocomputing **68**, 85–104 (2005). https://doi.org/10.1016/j.neucom.2004.12.005

A Framework for Resolving Motivational Conflict via Attractor Dynamics

Alejandro Jimenez-Rodriguez$^{(\boxtimes)}$, Tony J. Prescott , Robert Schmidt ,
and Stuart Wilson

The University of Sheffield, Sheffield, UK
{a.jimenez-rodriguez,t.j.prescott,
robert.schmidt,s.p.wilson}@sheffield.ac.uk

Abstract. Motivation modulates behaviour depending upon contextual
and internal cues. Like animals, successful artificial agents must implement different behavioural strategies in order to satisfy dynamical needs.
Such causal factors emerge from internal homeostatic or allostatic processes, as well as from external stimuli or threats. However, when two or
more needs coalesce, a situation of motivational conflict ensues. In this
work we present a four-stage dynamical framework for the resolution of
motivational conflict based upon principles from dynamical systems and
statistical mechanics. As a central mechanism for the resolution of conflict we propose the use of potentials with multiple wells or minima. This
model leads to behavioural switching either by means of a bifurcation
or by the stochastic escape from one of the wells. We present analytical
and simulation results that reproduce known motivational conflict phenomena observed in the study of animal behaviour, in the case of two
conflicting motivations.

Keywords: Motivation · Motivational conflict · Dynamical systems ·
Behavioural switching · Attractor dynamics

1 Introduction

Dealing with motivational conflict is an important aspect of animal behaviour
[19]. Consider, for example, the conflicting need to eat or drink as studied in
[15,16], or the conflict between aggression and mating as exemplified by the
response of male stickleback fish to territory invasion by a female conspecific [1].
The former conflict is driven by opposing intrinsic needs or *deficits*, the latter is
driven by extrinsic factors, and in both cases conflict resolution requires multiple
needs to be satisfied.

Different types of conflict yield different behavioural patterns. Conflict may
be resolved via time budgeting, modulated by biological rhythms that occur on
different time scales [2]. Or it may be resolved by switching between alternative
behaviour systems that may be inhibited or disinhibited by the current behaviour.
New patterns of behaviour may emerge (ambivalence), and these may be related
(redirection) or unrelated (displacement) to the causes of either motivation [2].

V. Vouloutsi et al. (Eds.): Living Machines 2020, LNAI 12413, pp. 192–203, 2020.
https://doi.org/10.1007/978-3-030-64313-3_19

An influential conceptual model of motivation was introduced by Lorenz [10]. Accordingly, independent reservoirs are filled by 'energies' that are action-specific, and when a corresponding energy threshold is exceeded a valve opens to release the corresponding behavioral pattern. Theoretical investigations of motivational conflict often extend this idea to additionally consider direct interactions between motivations via cross-inhibition [12]. Most early investigations incorporated analogies from control theory [18], and in particular used feedback loops to implement Lorenzian energy build-up with competition between motivations driven by internal deficits. Deficits usually inhibit one another directly [11] or bias a decision switch based on 'tendencies' derived from internal state [7]. Such models can be shown to reproduce a wide range of motivational phenomena, but they have been difficult to map directly onto neural systems.

Here we develop a model of how multiple conflicting motivations, each formulated in homeostatic terms, may be resolved to generate appropriate animal (or robot) behaviour. The model is considered first in theoretical terms, and then in terms of simulated robot behaviour.

2   Behaviour Under Motivational Conflict

The proposed model has four stages: Internal physiological state, motivational dynamical system, behavioural selection and pattern expression.

Internal Physiological State

We describe the internal physiological state of the agent as a dynamical system. What are referred to in the literature as deficits, are encoded in the state vector $x \in \mathbb{R}^n$. For some motivational systems, e.g., thirst or thermoregulation, the state vector can be associated with a physical quantity such as the amount of water or body heat. For others, such as aggression, it can be related to the accumulation of an action-specific 'energy', in the Lorenzian sense [1]. The internal state vector evolves according to the following dynamical law,

$$\dot{x}(t) = -f(x(t)) + g(u(t)) + h(a(t)). \tag{1}$$

The first term on the right, $-f(x)$, represents the decay of the energy, corresponding to the Lorenzian model, with the function f specifying the nature of the decay (e.g., zero-order, first-order etc.) as well as potential interactions between homeostatic systems. The second term represents an external input $u(t)$, with the function g allowing for a linear or nonlinear transformation of that input (i.e., to represent absorption or thermal conductivity dynamics etc.). The final term represents an autonomic homeostatic process, $a(t)$, with h similarly enabling linear or nonlinear transformations.

The physiological processes we consider are assumed to evolve on slower timescales than that which characterises the behavioural responses, in a close submanifold of $\mathbb{R}^n$, given the existence of physiological limits for all processes, i.e., concentrations can not be negative. To illustrate, consider the following examples.

Simple Reservoir. The simplest model is a constant rate of decay of e.g., energy, that can be used to represent *deficits* such as of water or food [7]. Accordingly, the physiological state evolves by $\dot{x}(t) = -\alpha T + u(t)$, where α is the decay rate, T represents some internal autonomic response such as heat generation, and $u(t)$ represents environmental input, e.g., ambient temperature (note that here $f \equiv 0$, $g(u) = u$ and $h(T) = \alpha T$).

Thermoregulation. Consider a recent model of thermoregulatory behaviour proposed by [6], according to which agents are exposed to an ambient temperature x_a and exchange heat upon contact with other agents, $x_c(t)$, resulting in a body temperature, $x(t)$, that evolves according to $\dot{x}(t) = -[k_1 A + k_2(1 - A)]x(t) + [k_1 A x_a(t) + k_2(1 - A)x_c(t)] + G(t)$. Here, k_1 and k_2 are thermal conductivity constants for the exposed area, A, and the non-exposed area of the body, and $G(t)$ is an autonomic heat generation mechanism that encapsulates different physiological heat sources. Again, the three terms in the right hand side correspond to those of the general model.

Additionally, we propose that at the interface between body and brain i) the state vector first has to be compared to some desired state (or set point) to configure deficits or excesses and respond accordingly. Note that the set point can be variable (allostatic) ii) the corresponding quantities must be normalized and expressed in a *common currency* in order to drive behaviour, and iii) responses to states representing physiological extremes should be differentially weighted to avoid fatal consequences (see [13, 18]). The output of these three transformations is what we call a *drive*, and the component transformations can be expressed as

$$x_d = D(x - x_p), \tag{2}$$

where D is a non-linear map defined as $D = (U \circ N)$, that is, $D(x) = U(N(x))$. The component functions correspond to *normalization*, N, and *urgency*, U. Normalization should limit values to the interval $[0, 1]$, and may be linear (compression of the original domain) or non-linear (e.g., a sigmoidal relationship between physiological state and motivation). Urgency expressions should ensure that extreme values of the physiological range give rise to higher drives than those closer to the set points.

Motivational Dynamical System

The motivational state of the agent is modelled as a classical particle undergoing random fluctuations, influenced by the potential $V(x)$. The particle can be thought of as existing in a one-dimensional domain of the *generalized motivational space*, $\mathcal{P}$, which we assume here is equivalent to the real line.

We consider distinct motivations to correspond with specific locations of the phase space $\mathcal{P}$ (Fig. 1). The energy landscape provided by the *motivational potential* specifies regions of minimal energy that trap the particle for a period in its evolution, with unstable regions serving as barriers. This energy landscape is changed dynamically as a function of the motivational factors, i.e., the drives.

More precisely, if $\rho(t)$ represents the position of the particle in the motivational coordinate, its time evolution is given by

$$\dot{\rho} = -\frac{1}{\tau}\frac{\partial V}{\partial \rho} + \sigma dW(t). \tag{3}$$

The first term in the right, $V(\rho, a_m)$, is a potential field that depends upon the drives, and other motivational factors described shortly, and τ is the time constant for the evolution. We formalize the concept of a motivation by restricting $V : \mathcal{P} \times \mathbb{R}^n \to \mathbb{R}$ to be a motivational potential if and only if there exist elements $\bar{\rho}_1, \bar{\rho}_2, \ldots, \bar{\rho}_k$, $k > 0$ such that $\frac{\partial V}{\partial \rho}(\rho_k, a_1, \ldots, a_k) = 0$ when $a_m = 0$ for all $m = 1, \ldots, k$. This characterizes the initial, undisturbed shape with k motivations. The second term to the right in Eq. 3 is a noise term with variance, σ^2. We refer to the variance of the fluctuations, analogous to the influence of heat on Brownian motion, as *arousal*. Note that when $\sigma = 0$, $\frac{dV}{dt} = \frac{\partial V}{\partial \rho}\frac{d\rho}{dt} = -\left[\frac{\partial V}{\partial \rho}\right]^2 < 0$. Therefore the dynamics will always tend to select one motivation. Accordingly, the motivational conflict problem is recast in terms of the *escape* or *Kramers* problems that are familiar in classical statistical mechanics [5]. For fixed drives the motivational state, once trapped at point (a) in Fig. 1, will eventually escape with a probability determined by the height of the barrier at point (b). The higher the drive, the less likely escape it to occur.

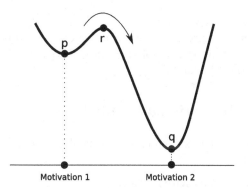

Fig. 1. Concept of motivational potential

Behavioral Selection

We conceptualize each motivation as a state. Different readouts of such states produce *tendencies* towards different actions, which we relate, conceptually, to motivation and behavior via *motivational tendency kernels*. Given a motivation $\bar{\rho}_i$ in the generalized motivational space, a tendency kernel is a function $\xi : \mathcal{P} \to [0, 1]$ with finite support, such that $\xi(\bar{\rho}_i) = 1$.

Using, as an example, a *Gaussian tendency kernel*, $\xi(\phi) = G(\rho|\bar{\rho}_i, \sigma^2)$ with a certain width σ (unrelated to the arousal), the incentive will decay with the distance of the system from a given motivation in the phase space. As a second example, for a *step tendency kernel* the incentive will be maximal within a region $a \leq \bar{\rho}_i \leq b$ around the given motivation (Fig. 2).

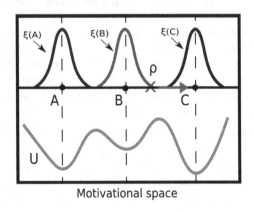

Motivational space

Fig. 2. Illustration of the tendency kernels (top), and the potential U (bottom).

Behavioral Pattern Expression
The tendencies from the previous section are used to modulate behaviours by biasing action selection and/or unfolding Fixed Action Patterns (FAPs), or by modulating Taxes (i.e. chemotaxis).

3   Recasting Motivational Conflict

Here we recast some concepts from classic ideas about motivation in the light of the model outlined.

Switching Between Two Motivations
Some of the early research in motivational conflict was related to the switching between two motivated behaviours (i.e. eating and drinking)[7,14,16,17]. The switching from eating to drinking can be thought of as the escape of the particle from the well corresponding to (p) to that corresponding to (q) in Fig. 1, effectively jumping the barrier (r). As such, the expected escape time will be the latency of the motivation 2 given that the agent is in p, and the bout duration is the time spent in each well.

For the following analyses we make the simplifying assumption that the drives change on a time scale much slower than that governing the motivational particle ρ, that motivations are read out in terms of non-overlapping step tendency kernels, and that the most salient action will always be performed.

Stationary Distribution. It is well know from the theory of Stochastic processes that the dynamics of ρ satisfies the Fokker-Plank equation [5]

$$\frac{\partial p(\rho, t)}{\partial t} = \frac{\partial}{\partial \rho}\left[V'(\rho)p(\rho, t)\right] + \sigma^2 \frac{\partial^2 p(\rho, t)}{\partial \rho^2}, \tag{4}$$

where $V' = dV/dx$, and $p(\rho, t)$ is the probability of finding the particle at position ρ at time t. For long enough times, and slowly varying drives (and, therefore, a fixed potential shape), such a probability distribution will reach a stationary value given by

$$p_\infty(\rho) = K \exp\left(-V(\rho)/\sigma^2\right). \tag{5}$$

This captures the intuition that an agent should spend more time in the deepest well. Note that for very small arousal (σ), the agent will remain trapped in that motivation for as long as the shape of the potential is unchanged.

Motivational Transition. By analogy with the analysis of Kramers for chemical reaction systems [9], the expected exit time of the agent from motivation 1 (p) to motivation 2 (q in Fig. 1) is given by

$$T(p \to q) = \pi \left[|V''(q)|V''(p)|\right]^{1/2} \exp\left\{[V(q) - V(p)]/\sigma^2\right\}. \tag{6}$$

In the absence of arousal, the exit time will be infinity, and two forms of motivational switching emerge. When $\sigma^2 \to 0$, escape becomes improbable and transitions occurs by *competition* [8], defined here as the transition from motivation 1 due to changes in the *causal factors* of motivation 2 (i.e., equivalent to drives). Such a transition occurs when one of the minima is lost due to the increase in the drives for the second motivation. To illustrate, we need to study a specific form of the potential V that is differentiable, for which we choose

$$V(\rho, a, b) = (\bar{\rho}_1 - \rho)^2(\bar{\rho}_2 - \rho)^2 + a(\bar{\rho}_1 - \rho)^2 + b(\bar{\rho}_2 - \rho)^2, \tag{7}$$

where a and b are the corresponding drives for motivation 1 and 2 respectively. For this potential, it can be shown by differentiation that in order for the minima to exist, the following *well relation* must be satisfied:

$$-(\bar{\rho}_1 - \rho)(\bar{\rho}_2 - \rho)\left(\frac{\bar{\rho}_1 + \bar{\rho}_2}{2} - \rho\right) = -\frac{a+b}{2}\rho + \frac{a\bar{\rho}_1 + b\bar{\rho}_2}{2}. \tag{8}$$

As such, wells will exist as long as the line specified by the right hand side intersects with the third-degree polynomial specified on the left hand side (see Fig. 3). If we increase the drive (b), the well in the vicinity of the first motivation disappears and the system will tend inexorably to $\bar{\rho}_2$. In the case when drive a is zero and drive b increases, the corresponding minimum will reach the height of the barrier exactly when $b = \frac{1}{2}\left(\frac{\bar{\rho}_1 - \bar{\rho}_2}{2}\right)^2$. In the well relationship, this change is equivalent to changing the slope and intercept of the line (Fig. 3).

Note that for $a = b \gg 0$, two wells can merge into one. Indeed, whenever $a = b = \frac{\bar{\rho}_1 + \bar{\rho}_2}{2} - \bar{\rho}_1\bar{\rho}_2$, the two wells will converge at the mid-way point, leaving

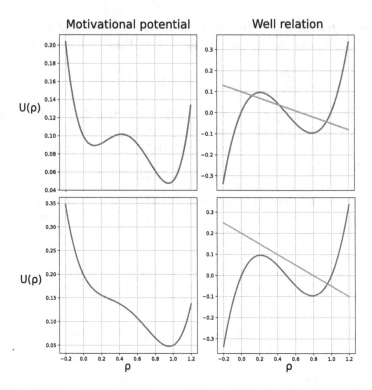

Fig. 3. Top. Existence two wells for $a = 0.05$, $b = 0.1$, $\bar{\rho}_1 = 0$ and $\bar{\rho}_2 = 1$. Bottom. The potential loses one of its minima when the difference between the drives is high enough. The number of minima, and therefore the shape, of the motivational potential is illustrated by the number of points in which the orange line crosses the blue cubic curve.

only one stable state. In this case the two motivations will have equal tendencies, depending on the form of the tendency kernels, and as such the agent would end up dithering.

4   Simulation Results

Time-Sharing

When the "arousal" term in Eq. 6 is non-zero, there is a chance of random transitions between motivations without a corresponding change in the drives. In terms of the motivational literature, these changes can be thought of as time-sharing, where two motivations are observed to switch in bouts of a consistent (average) duration [8], independently from the underlying causal factors.

This can be observed in terms of the potential (Eq. 7), when the two wells have the same depth. Figure 4, left, shows that the stationary distribution predicts an equal time spent by the agent in the two motivational states. The corresponding motivational dynamics display the expected switching that occurs

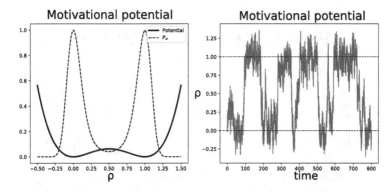

Fig. 4. Time sharing phenomena in the model, $\sigma = 0.12$. Left. The motivational potential (solid) and stationary distribution (dotted) from Eq. (5). Right. Simulation of the behaviour of the motivational particle switching between the two motivations.

more or less frequently depending on the level of arousal, σ. When the heights of the two wells are different, the escape time (and thus the motivational switch) will differ (Eq. 6). In Fig. 5 a simulated experiment for the transition between two motivations shows how the latency and bout duration change as a function of the shape of the potential. A simulated agent starts in the first well corresponding to e.g., hunger, the escape time for the well marks the switch to e.g., thirst, and the bout duration is the time taken to return to hunger. It can be seen from the simulation that the escape time decreases as the relative height of the two wells increases (as the agent becomes thirsty), as predicted by Eq. 6. On the other hand, as the drinking well becomes deeper, it takes a longer time to return to the former motivation. This corresponds to similar phenomena reported in the animal behaviour literature [16].

Thermoregulation Versus Feeding

Here we consider a simulated agent in a two-dimensional (x,y) environment with a chemical (odour) gradient radiating from a food source with a two-dimensional Gaussian profile, and a temperature gradient that is linear in the x coordinate (Fig. 6). The physiological state of the agent consists of two homeostatic variables, energy and temperature, that evolve according to the laws presented in Sect. 2. The normalization and urgency maps in Eq. 2 are given by sigmoidal and cubic functions. The motivational state is given by the potential in Eq. 7 and the parameters a and b are the absolute value of the drives. Motivational kernels for behavioural selection are Gaussian.

We implement two taxis behaviours (and no fixed action patterns) and consider the agent to receive a 'shot' of energy when it enters the vicinity of the food source. The agent is modelled as a Braitenberg vehicle [3] with bilateral sensors for the chemical and temperature signals.

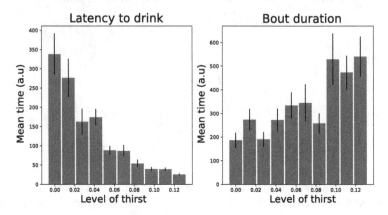

Fig. 5. Left. Latency to motivational switch. Right. Bout duration. $\bar{\rho}_1 = 0$, $\bar{\rho}_2 = 1$, $a = 0$. The value of the drive b assumes values in the interval $[0, 1/8]$, where the upper bound is the theoretical limit at which the first well completely disappears. The escape time is defines as the first time point such $\rho > 0.5$. The bout is assumed to properly start when $\rho > 0.7$. The bout duration is the time it takes to return to $\rho < 0.5$ after the bout has started.

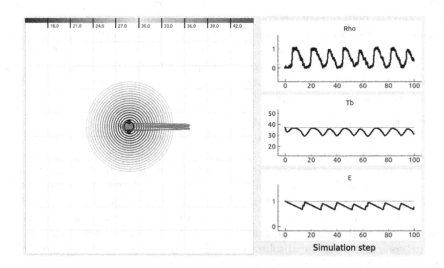

Fig. 6. Simulation environment for the motivated agent. The square to the left represents the 2D arena with a temperature (colored bar at the top) and a chemical (concentric circles in the middle) gradient. The panels to the right display the time course of the motivational dynamical variable ρ (top) and the two homeostatic variables (bottom). The agent moves autonomously back and forth the food source and its preferred spot in the thermal gradient.

The agent and its environment are shown in Fig. 6. Initially, the agent is driven towards a region in which its body temperature is maintained in the thermoneutral zone, which creates a conflict because the food is located in a colder region. Two phenomena are observed. First, the agent hesitates to approach the food, and returns multiple times, illustrating a trade-off between the *cost* of obtaining the food and the level of hunger; only when it is hungry enough is the excursion for the food complete. Secondly, between 40 ms and 60 ms the two minima of the motivational potential merge, and the agent is in an *ambiguous* motivational state (comparable with animal behaviour, see [1]).

Spontaneous transitions are observed when the level of arousal is increased (Fig. 7 at 20 ms), with the motivational state changing in the absence of a corresponding behavioural output. This is comparable with *displacement* phenomena observed in animals, whereby an external cue is shown to drive a novel behaviour that is otherwise unrelated to the current behaviour.

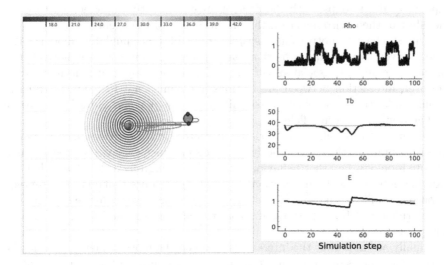

Fig. 7. An increase in arousal increases the rates of spontaneous switching without behavioural output

5   Discussion

We developed a four-stage dynamical model to study how behaviours are affected by motivational conflict. The first stage keeps track of the internal state of the agent, the second represents the motivational state, the third contains multiple readouts or measurements in the motivational phase space that give rise to tendencies for certain behaviours, and the fourth stage controls behaviour expression.

A theoretical analysis revealed how the motivational state of the agent can depend on its internal state, allowing us to recast some motivational phenomena described in the animal behaviour literature. For example, we showed how the fixed points of the motivational dynamical system can disappear, appear, or merge, as a function of internal state. We showed how merging of the fixed points can generate the kinds of ambiguous motivational states that have been observed in some animals [1]. And by incorporating stochasticity, we showed how the model can account for phenomena such as time-sharing [7,14] in terms of spontaneous transitions and disinhibition [15].

Our model resembles several classical approaches [19] to this problem. For example, the changes in the underlying physiological dynamics that are described correspond to Lorenzian energy accumulation, but with the valve that releases behaviour recast as a bistability in the motivational state space. However, early models of motivational conflict typically involve positive feedback loops according to a control theory framework [7,17,18], and our model does not include explicit feedback loops, with the control instead directly implemented through the effect of the environment on the internal state of the agent.

The stochastic motivational system resembles accumulator models [12]. Indeed, given two stochastic motivations, v_1 and v_2, as in [12], the motivational particle, ρ, could be associated with the difference $v_1 - v_2$ of such accumulators. However, interaction between motivations is assumed not to happen explicitly in our model (i.e. no explicit cross-inhibition), but it is instead assumed to be mediated via an external field.

Our decision to embed motivational attractors in a metric space corresponds to an assumption that the underlying space in which behaviours reside has a definite topology, i.e., that behaviours can be meaningfully ordered and that the ordering determines the interactions between behaviours that may be observed in various conflict scenarios. As such, it should be possible to devise experiments to determine a definite pattern of *displacement* phenomena for a given animal (or species).

Finally, we note that the interaction between the motivational state and the readouts resembles observations of the interactions between the lateral hypothalamus and the ventral tegmental area of the mammalian brain, and that the *tendency* readout could be potentially associated with the dopamine signals that relate to value in these areas [4]. Further connections with the neurobiology of decision-making in animal brains, with a focus on possible relationships with reinforcers and reward, will be explored in future work.

Simulation code is available at https://github.com/ABRG-Models/MammalBot/.

Acknowledgments. This work was supported by the EU H2020 Programme as part of the Human Brain Project (HBP-SGA2, 785907).

References

1. Barnard, C.J.: Animal Behaviour: Mechanism, Development, Function and Evolution. Pearson Education, London (2004)
2. Bolhuis, J.J., Giraldeau, L.A.E.: The Behavior of Animals: Mechanisms, Function, and Evolution. Blackwell Publishing, Hoboken (2005)
3. Braitenberg, V.: Vehicles: Experiments in Synthetic Psychology. MIT Press, Cambridge (1986)
4. Dabney, W., et al.: A distributional code for value in dopamine-based reinforcement learning. Nature **577**, 1–5 (2020)
5. Gardiner, C.W.: Handbook of Stochastic Methods: For Physics, Chemistry and the Natural Sciences. Springer, Heidelberg (2004)
6. Glancy, J., Groß, R., Stone, J.V., Wilson, S.P.: A self-organising model of thermoregulatory huddling. PLoS Comput. Biol. **11**(9), e1004283 (2015)
7. Houston, A., Sumida, B.: A positive feedback model for switching between two activities. Anim. Behav. **33**(1), 315–325 (1985)
8. Houston, A.I.: Transitions and time-sharing. Anim. Behav. **30**(2), 615–625 (1982)
9. Kramers, H.A.: Brownian motion in a field of force and the diffusion model of chemical reactions. Physica **7**(4), 284–304 (1940)
10. Lorenz, K.Z.: The comparative method in studying innate behavior patterns. (1950)
11. Ludlow, A.: Towards a theory of thresholds. Anim. Behav. **30**(1), 253–267 (1982)
12. Marshall, J.A., Favreau-Peigne, A., Fromhage, L., Mcnamara, J.M., Meah, L.F., Houston, A.I.: Cross inhibition improves activity selection when switching incurs time costs. Curr. Zool. **61**(2), 242–250 (2015)
13. McFarland, D., Bösser, T., Bosser, T.: Intelligent Behavior in Animals and Robots. MIT Press, Cambridge (1993)
14. McFarland, D.: Mechanisms of behavioural disinhibition. Anim. Behav. **17**, 238–242 (1969)
15. McFarland, D., McFarland, F.: Dynamic analysis of an avian drinking response. Medi. Biol. Eng. **6**(6), 659–668 (1968). https://doi.org/10.1007/BF02474728
16. Roper, T., Crossland, G.: Mechanisms underlying eating-drinking transitions in rats. Anim. Behav. **30**(2), 602–614 (1982)
17. Slater, P.: A simple model for competition between behaviour patterns. Behaviour **67**, 236–258 (1978)
18. Toates, F., Archer, J.: A comparative review of motivational systems using classical control theory. Anim. Behav. **26**, 368–380 (1978)
19. Toates, F., Jensen, P.: Ethological and psychological models of motivation-towards a synthesis. In: Proceedings of the First International Conference on Simulation of Adaptive Behavior on From Animals to Animats, pp. 194–205 (1991)

Insect Inspired View Based Navigation Exploiting Temporal Information

Efstathios Kagioulis$^{(\boxtimes)}$ ⓘ, Andrew Philippides ⓘ, Paul Graham ⓘ,
James C. Knight ⓘ, and Thomas Nowotny ⓘ

Centre for Computational Neuroscience and Robotics, University of Sussex,
Brighton BN1 9QJ, UK
e.kagioulis@sussex.ac.uk

Abstract. Visual navigation is a key capability for robots. There is a
family of insect-inspired algorithms that use panoramic images encountered during a training route to derive directional information from
regions around the training route and thus subsequently visually navigate. As these algorithms do not incorporate information about the
temporal order of training images, we describe one way this could be
done to highlight this information's utility. We benchmark our algorithms
in a simulation of a real world environment and show that incorporating temporal information improves performance and reduces algorithmic
complexity.

Keywords: Visual navigation · Visual homing · Bio-inspired robotics

1 Introduction

Foraging ants have impressive visual navigation capabilities [26]. They can use
celestial visual information as a compass for Path Integration (PI) [19] and use
learnt visual memories to guide complex routes [15] between their nest and a
food source. The ability to travel long routes, guided by stored visual scenes,
prompts the question of how the visual memories are organised in the small
brains of insects [2].

We and others have developed a series of algorithms mimicking ant route
navigation in which ants use a set of views or *snapshots* experienced during a first
(PI-mediated) training route to later navigate by rotating and comparing the
rotated current view with the stored training route views [2,13,22]. Because the
route memories are stored when travelling facing forwards, adopting a heading
which is familiar to them implicitly means that the agent is likely near the
route and facing in a similar direction as when last near that location. In this
way, finding familiar views means recovering the correct direction to move in and
thus routes can be successfully navigated. While these algorithms vary in the way

This work was supported by EPSRC grants EP/P006094/1 and EP/S030964/1 and a
University of Sussex doctoral scholarship.

© Springer Nature Switzerland AG 2020
V. Vouloutsi et al. (Eds.): Living Machines 2020, LNAI 12413, pp. 204–216, 2020.
https://doi.org/10.1007/978-3-030-64313-3_20

that the route memories are stored, being either used to train an artificial neural network (ANN) to learn a compact encoding of the route information [18,22], or instead storing all memories exactly as experienced, (the so-called perfect memory, henceforth, PM, algorithm [3]) what they have in common is that all views are used for the comparison and the sequence they are encountered in is disregarded. For instance, in PM at each step, agents compare the current views to *all* stored snapshots without any consideration of their order.

This means that, while they can quite robustly navigate a variety of environments, they can fail in places where images are very similar (e.g. where a route crosses itself or is very tortuous with different movement directions in close proximity [12]). In such cases it is not obvious which part of the stored route should be used to provide the correct movement direction. In addition, throwing away sequence information and storing/using all the memories to generate a heading is highly inefficient. For instance, for PM, both memory and computation scale linearly with route length, leading to it being deemed computationally impractical and biologically implausible [3] despite generally having the most accurate performance [2].

Given these limitations, it is reasonable to think of alternative ways that stored views could be organised. One possibility is that views could be stored as a sequence, and whilst this could be problematic [21,25], sequence information has been shown to be useful in engineering approaches to navigation [5,17]. Sequence has also been considered as a solution to image distortion due to camera/head tilt [1]. Furthermore, there are some suggestions that ants also use some notion of sequence when recapitulating a route using visual memories [8,23].

In this paper we thus investigate how incorporating the temporal sequence in which snapshots are experienced can improve both run-time and accuracy of the aforementioned route navigation algorithms. To enable us to clearly assess the benefits and weaknesses of this approach, we use temporal information in a purposefully simple way to augment the PM algorithm so that the agent considers only a small sub-sequence of the route memories to extract direction, rather than all of them.

2   Methods

To evaluate the efficacy of our algorithm, we use a virtual environment modelled on the environment of desert ants [13] (Fig. 1 a, b for top down views). We recover panoramic views from a perspective similar to that of an ant (Fig. 2 for example views). As our algorithm relies on comparing stored snapshots and current views, we first describe the image comparison functions, before outlining our new Sequential Memory Window (SMW) algorithm and describing the image pre-processing used. All code was written in python 3.5 using NumPy [20] OpenCV [4] and pandas [16] libraries.

Image Comparison Functions: We use two methods for quantifying the difference between a current view and a stored snapshot. First, we use the Root Mean Squared Error image difference function (IDF) [28]:

$$IDF(C(\boldsymbol{x},\theta),S((\boldsymbol{y},\phi)) = \sqrt{\frac{\sum_{i=1}^{M}\sum_{j=1}^{N}(C_{ij}(\boldsymbol{x},\theta) - S_{ij}(\boldsymbol{y},\phi))^2}{M \times N}} \qquad (1)$$

where $C(\boldsymbol{x},\theta)$ is an $M \times N$ panoramic view from position $\boldsymbol{x}$ at an orientation θ with pixel greyscale values C_{ij} at row i and column j and $S(\boldsymbol{y},\phi)$ is a view stored from position $\boldsymbol{y}$ at orientation ϕ with pixel values S_{ij}.

The second method uses the correlation coefficient (CC) to derive the similarity between images [24] via:

$$CC(C(\boldsymbol{x},\theta),S((\boldsymbol{y},\phi)) = \frac{\sum_{i=1}^{M}\sum_{j=1}^{N}(C_{ij} - \bar{C})(S_{ij} - \bar{S})}{\sqrt{\sum_{i=1}^{M}\sum_{j=1}^{N}(C_{ij} - \bar{C})^2}\sqrt{\sum_{i=1}^{M}\sum_{j=1}^{N}(S_{ij} - \bar{S})^2}} \qquad (2)$$

where $\bar{C}$ and $\bar{S}$ are the mean pixel values of $C(\boldsymbol{x},\theta)$ and $S(\boldsymbol{y},\phi)$ respectively.

To derive a heading from comparing $C(\boldsymbol{x},\theta)$ and $S(\boldsymbol{y},\phi)$, we 'rotate' the current view by varying θ through 360° (in steps of one degree) and use either the IDF or CC to determine the orientation $\hat{\theta}$ at which C best matches S. For the IDF a smaller value indicates a higher similarity while for CC it is the highest value. In both cases the agent will move in the direction that is most familiar thus *pairing visual similarity to action*.

Route Navigation Using a Sequential Memory Window: In our route navigation algorithms, the agent first traverses a predefined route (e.g. blue line in Fig. 1 (A)) during which it periodically stores views, or snapshots. In the experiments in this paper, snapshots are stored every 1 cm and the facing direction of each snapshot is set as the direction to the next snapshot (or the direction of the penultimate snapshot in the case of the last snapshot in the sequence). Unlike our previous work (e.g. [3]), the sequence of the snapshots during the training route is retained, although the distance between them (and as a corollary, the fact that they are regularly sampled) is not important. The agent subsequently navigates by 'rotating' on the spot and comparing rotated versions of the current view individually to a subset of the stored snapshots using either the IDF or CC as described in the previous section. The direction which results in the lowest minimum for the IDF/highest maximum for the CC across the subset of snapshots is selected as the movement direction.

In contrast to the standard PM model [3] which compares the current view to all snapshots, the sequential memory window model compares the current view only to a subset of n consecutive images of the image memory. The best match is used to determine both current movement direction and the start position of the memory window for the next comparison. While other options are possible for initialising the next window, this is reasonable under the assumption that the agent moves fairly directly from start to end and that test points are well-spaced. For the first window, as the test positions are near the start of the route, we use the first snapshot (see Discussion for alternatives).

Pre-processing: All panoramic images are rendered at an original resolution of $[720 \times 150 \times 3]$ in RGB. We typically transform the image to a $[360 \times 75]$ greyscale image using openCV's resize function using bilinear interpolation. As it has been shown that resolution of the images can influence homing accuracy [17, 27] and we know that ants have low resolution vision >1 degree per pixel and use light intensity rather than colour to navigate [9] we transform the image to greyscale and resize it to what, for an ant, would be high-resolution $[360 \times 75]$ (1 degree per pixel), medium resolution $[180 \times 50]$ (2 degree per pixel) and low resolution $[90 \times 25]$ (4 degree per pixel). For pre-processing we compared edge detection and blurring. For blurring, we use a 5×5 Gaussian kernel (low pass filter) with mean 0 and standard deviation 1 in order to remove high-frequency noise and smooth out the image. As the kernel is always the same number of pixels, when we resize the image we effectively scale the amount of smoothing. Fig. 1 c) shows a panoramic image from AntWorld after resizing and blurring. There is some experimental evidence [7] that some ants navigate using simple cues on the horizon as a well defined boundary to derive directional information. As edge detection can separate sky, tussocks and ground, we also test Canny edge detection with a lower bound of 180 and upper bound of 200 (pixel values scale $[0–255]$) [10].

3   Results

To test the algorithms, we derive headings from a grid of test positions spaced in 10cm increments around example routes. All variants are tested against 10 different routes and errors are calculated as the absolute difference between the derived heading and the heading of the nearest snapshot.

Temporal Windows Improve Visual Aliasing Problems: To illustrate the benefits of our sequence based algorithm, we first compare results on a route with a loop in it. The agent is given a training route (blue lines in Fig. 1) and we derive the headings that the agent would follow by each algorithm for all points within 10 cm of the route. The derived headings are indicated in Fig. 1 by blue arrows for the ones that are close to correct and by red arrows for large errors ($>40°$). We highlight errors $>40°$ only to demonstrate the behaviour of SMW against standard PM for a given loop section of a route. In many robotics tasks this error is not acceptable but here we are most concerned with showcasing the difference between algorithms and so highlight large deviations from the route headings.

Errors in orientation when using PM occur because of visual aliasing where a view will match with a route memory that was stored in a completely different location [12]. In other words the current view matches with a memory that looks familiar but is spatially different thus sending the agent in the wrong direction. There are multiple interlinked reasons for such aliasing. It could be that the view from two route locations is very similar. To illustrate the problem we look at a route with a loop.

A   B

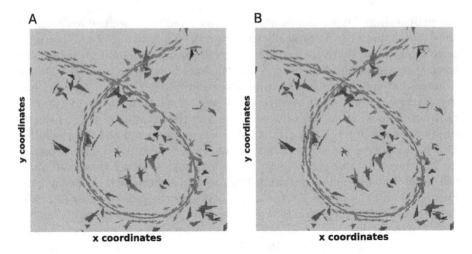

Fig. 1. Two traversals of the same testing route (blue solid line) that contains a loop. Red arrows are errors above a threshold of 40°. **A** Traversal using the standard algorithm. **B** Traversal using sequential perfect memory. (Color figure online)

The first point where we see differences in performance is near the loop intersection Fig. 1. Errors near the loop intersection are due to aliasing where perfect memory matches current views to memory views that are captured either at a different point in the route or near the route intersection in the opposite direction. When the agent is at the intersection, there are two 'correct' directions: either continuing along the route or to omit traversing the loop and turn at the loop intersection. In the PM version we see that the agent chooses which direction based on proximity to the respective part of the route, assuming that no occlusions are affecting the matching. In contrast, because the sequence only searches the images close to the previous match, it gets the correct direction by entering the loop without considering the memories from the perpendicular direction. The same goes for the case of exiting the loop. Of course this is a trivial example, if insects had looped routes, they could deploy other measures, (by reducing the search angle for example to ±90°) although it highlights the key point that temporal information can be useful.

However, if there is partial occlusion from dense vegetation or other obstacles, the sequence can resolve the problem. In these cases, the occluded part of the view often matches noisily while the clear view part can match with partial features from other points in the route. Due to the smaller number of features, there are more aliased points than there would be normally. In this scenario, the window means that the agent is constrained to match the current view with a memory that is spatially nearby and free from occlusions. This means that the partial features it *does* match are likely to be the correct ones, thus keeping the agent on track without generating a lot of angular error. Fig. 2 demonstrates how an occluded window image Fig. 2(B) can disrupt image matching with a

Fig. 2. A situation in which the SMW can be beneficial. In this case the closest image to the test image (**A**) in space was **B** (window image 47) but, because of occlusion the images do not match. However, because of the SMW, the algorithm matched with **C** (window image 39) 8 index places behind even though it also did not match particularly well, instead of matching with an almost random match from the entire route. As a result the agent typically will make less severe errors due to occlusion and/or aliasing.

non-occluded current view Fig. 2(A). However, because stored memories within the window Fig. 2(C) that are free from occlusion provide reasonably similar features they can provide a match that is more likely to keep the agent in the correct direction than images further afar on the route might.

Window Size: The size of the window appears to have a large effect on the degree of error. For very small window sizes, the algorithm produces significant angular error which can be attributed to the window falling behind the actual position of the agent. A smaller window also provides less chances for the agent to match a clear route image when the window contains occluded images. For example, if the window at a given point is part of a route section where views are occluded the matching is going to be false (both in term of the image memory and orientation). On the other hand, if the window is larger, the agent has more chances to match with a memory that is further ahead and not occluded – thus producing a good match.

The error decreases as the window size increases and becomes stable at an average of 7.1° for window sizes between 13 and 16 images (Fig. 3). The error then increases again and, for window sizes greater than 18, it is comparable to Full Perfect Memory at a average of 12.8°. Full perfect memory (PM) can also

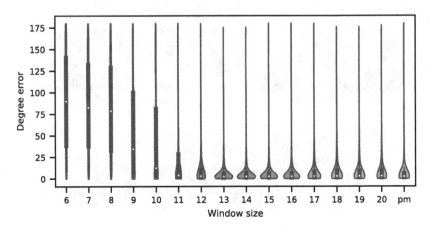

Fig. 3. Average error along routes for different window sizes. Images are compared using IDF matching and the lowest resolution (4° per pixel).

be thought of as an SMW with a window the size of the entire memory. Within the appropriate range of window sizes, SMW produces half the mean error and a flatter distribution of error than PM. The lower mean error can be attributed to correlation coefficient being able to deal with occlusions and generate a smoother familiarity gradient compared to IDF.

Image Matching: Correlation coefficient matching is superior to IDF matching. For smaller window sizes, both methods produce large errors for the reasons mentioned in the previous section. When pre-processing with blur, the IDF requires a larger window size to converge to the same low level of error as CC. After window size 13, the error resulting from both approaches is equivalent. Combining IDF with edge pre-processing yields high error signals even when the window size is large which we believe is due to occlusion having more drastic effects on edges than it does on pixels. Our analysis showed that, when the memory window contains an almost fully occluded image, test images tend to strongly match with it. This is because when there are very few edges, the IDF is small even if the edges do not match at all. The match is so strong that the window stays trapped in that area of the memory for the remainder of the route. As the data show (Fig. 4) the IDF performs relatively well with edge pre-processing, this issue can potentially be avoided by increasing the window size.

In contrast, correlation matching performs better when combined with edge detection than it does with blur. This is because a lot of noise is removed by the edge detector. In addition, the correlation is normalised by the standard deviation of the images, so that it measures better how edges match regardless of how many edges there are. This avoids the false matches with occluded (edge-poor) views we discussed above for the case of the IDF (Fig. 4).

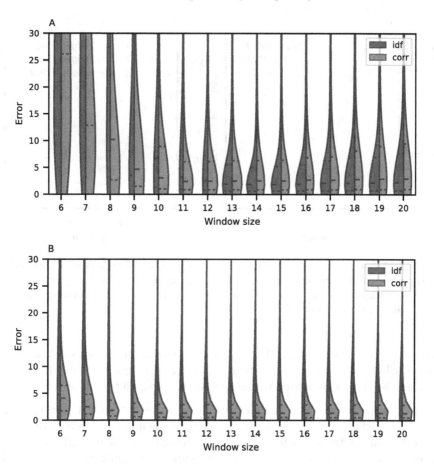

Fig. 4. Split violin plot showing the error distribution for correlation and IDF matching with different window sizes. **A** With blurred images, correlation matching converges to a minimum faster than IDF matching but window sizes 13 to 17 both exhibit similar behaviour. **B** With edge detection pre-processing, the IDF never converges to acceptable error levels while correlation matching converges from window size 10 onwards.

Pre-processing: Pre-processing with blur and correlation matching combined with window sizes between 11 and 15 produce very similar errors independent of the resolution, allowing us to use lower resolution and reduce computation (Fig. 5a). The distributions of observed errors when using high resolution edges and CC matching is lower than the best observed error for blur pre-processing (Fig. 5b). The errors are smaller in this condition but also, for window sizes between 10 and 20, the error distribution does not appear to change, being consistently lower than the best blur based scores. In this case high-res edges consistently outperform low and mid-res edges. This could be accredited to edge detection removing a lot of noise from the images and additionally high-res

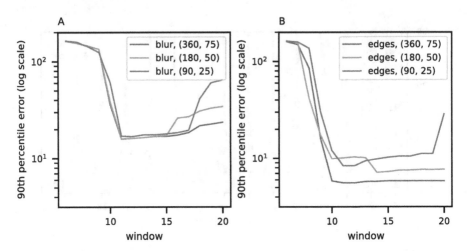

Fig. 5. Each line represents the 90th percentile of the error distribution for correlation matching with various resolutions for small to large window sizes. a) Images are blurred and down-sampled to high, low and medium resolution. b) Edge detection applied paired with high, low and medium resolution.

edges are more detailed thus allowing for more precise matching. Occlusions do not contribute as much to the matching as their edges generate less differences between the images compared to the sum of the pixels in the fill of the objects.

Time Complexity: Time complexity between the full perfect memory and sequential perfect memory is significant. Perfect memory compares every test image with all route images for all angles (assuming a 0 to 360 scan). Sequential perfect memory compares each test image to images within a window – a small fraction of the route memory. For all 10 routes tested, there a little over 800 route images and the best performing window size is 17 images long. Therefore, the perfect memory time complexity is $O(N * R * \theta)$ where N is the number of test images, R the number of route images and θ the degrees of search (360). For the sequential perfect memory, the time complexity is $O(N * W * \theta)$ where N and θ are the same as above and W is the width of the window which can range between sizes 10 and 20 and, by definition, is much smaller than the entire route memory (Fig. 6). It is worth mentioning that the runtime of the full perfect memory is bound to grow with the size of the route while the sequential version is affected only by the size of the window (This is true ONLY for the static database tests as in a real world scenario we would have to consider the speed of the agent as well. But then again with respect to each test position sequential perfect memory would be faster).

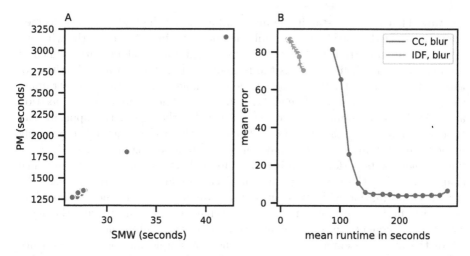

Fig. 6. a) Runtime for PM (y axis) versus SMW (x axis). For the timing we used medium resolution (180, 50) and blur, IDF and the window size 17. SMW is about 10 times faster than PM. b) Runtime and mean error for SMW using IDF or CC. Point represents data for window sizes from 6 through to 20. IDF is much faster but generates larger errors. For CC there is an optimal compromise for the error versus runtime trade-off at window size around 10.

4 Discussion

In this paper we have shown that we can both increase the accuracy of navigation, and reduce the computational cost, by including temporal sequence information in the stored route from training. By focusing on the areas where the algorithm fails which are typically caused by partial occlusion due to vegetation, we showed that performance could be further improved by using correlation-based image comparisons as well as edge enhancement. While changing resolution had a relatively minor effect in terms of improving the best combination of window length and processing parameters, it is clear that there will be an optimal resolution for a given environment, at the cost of increased algorithmic complexity. Likewise, finding the optimal window size is likely to be environment specific and, given that in some situations, accuracy gains are marginal, it might be that the choice is determined by computing time.

For sequence based navigation models, the length of the comparison window is important and not all memory window lengths work. Indeed, we saw that windows that are too small can fail fairly spectacularly. Examining this issue reveals the weakness of this method. If the algorithm gets 'lost' due to an erroneous match, the window can get stuck at that point and never find the correct matching point for subsequent test points. The smaller the window size and the more cluttered the environment, then the higher chance of the window getting 'stuck' and sending the agent in the wrong direction. This is linked to the issue of at what point to start the algorithm and both points could be solved in a similar way. That is, if the starting point is unknown, or the best match is deemed poor, the algorithm needs to run a full memory scan in order to set the window. However, this uncertainty of "where in the world am I?" along with "which of my memories are useful now?" is the fundamental problem of any algorithm of this nature, as by restricting matches one is, amongst other things, constraining the information available to the algorithm. Thus, while a good starting position and initial match could result in a good run for the agent, the opposite can be true. Another limitation is in nest search, where the agent must precisely home from all locations, rather than general route following. To ensure they can find the nest, ants perform learning walks immediately after leaving it, in which snapshots facing the nest from multiple locations are stored. In this case the sequence information will not be important/useful as these memories should all be used to find the nest. At that point a mechanism is required where the agent switches off sequence information and compares across all memories.

In the work presented here, we have used a simple way of using sequence information, aimed at showing the utility of incorporating temporal information in a route navigation algorithm. Other methods of using sequence information may ameliorate the aforementioned issues. We could for instance, update the window such that the best previous match is at the middle or implement a dynamic window length which would grow if matches were deemed poor [11]. However, it is perhaps more profitable to consider complex matching processes and ways of incorporating temporal information. For instance SeqSLAM [17] compares multiple memories within a window to multiple current views and can thus be robust to some bad matches. Another option would be to use artificial neural networks that encode temporal information [6,14] and use these to learn a combined representation of sequence, or indeed position, and route snapshots as in [22]. It is unclear how one would implement a neural network to encode both image snapshots as well as sequence information, but incorporating PI information might be possible, and is the subject of future work.

Our priorities in developing these models is to push the algorithms for use in closed-loop, real world, natural environments as experienced by ants. Assessing how temporal information is useful in such environments, and comparing it to what we know about how temporal information is used by insects, could allow us to not only improve robotic navigation but also illuminate insect neurobiology.

References

1. Ardin, P., Mangan, M., Wystrach, A., Webb, B.: How variation in head pitch could affect image matching algorithms for ant navigation. J. Comp. Physiol. A. **201**(6), 585–597 (2015). https://doi.org/10.1007/s00359-015-1005-8
2. Ardin, P., Peng, F., Mangan, M., Lagogiannis, K., Webb, B.: Using an insect mushroom body circuit to encode route memory in complex natural environments. PLoS Comput. Biol. **12**(2), e1004683 (2016)
3. Baddeley, B., Graham, P., Husbands, P., Philippides, A.: A model of ant route navigation driven by scene familiarity. PLoS Comput. Biol. **8**(1), e1002336 (2012)
4. Bradski, G.: The OpenCV library. Dr. Dobb's J. Softw. Tools (2000)

5. Chancán, M., Hernandez-Nunez, L., Narendra, A., Barron, A.B., Milford, M.: A hybrid compact neural architecture for visual place recognition. IEEE Robot. Autom. Lett. **5**(2), 993–1000 (2020)
6. Funahashi, K., Nakamura, Y.: Approximation of dynamical systems by continuous time recurrent neural networks. Neural Netw. **6**(6), 801–806 (1993)
7. Graham, P., Cheng, K.: Ants use the panoramic skyline as a visual cue during navigation. Curr. Biol. **19**(20), R935–R937 (2009)
8. Graham, P., Mangan, M.: Insect navigation: do ants live in the now? J. Exp. Biol. **218**(6), 819–823 (2015)
9. Graham, P., Philippides, A.: Vision for navigation: what can we learn from ants? Arthropod Struct. Dev. **46**(5), 718–722 (2017)
10. Green, B.: Canny edge detection tutorial (2002). Accessed 6 Mar 2005
11. Hausler, S., Jacobson, A., Milford, M.: Multi-process fusion: visual place recognition using multiple image processing methods. IEEE Robot. Autom. Lett. **4**(2), 1924–1931 (2019)
12. Knight, J.C., et al.: Insect-inspired visual navigation on-board an autonomous robot: real-world routes encoded in a single layer network. In: The 2018 Conference on Artificial Life: A Hybrid of the European Conference on Artificial Life (ECAL) and the International Conference on the Synthesis and Simulation of Living Systems (ALIFE), pp. 60–67. MIT Press (2019)
13. Kodzhabashev, A., Mangan, M.: Route following without scanning. In: Wilson, S.P., Verschure, P.F.M.J., Mura, A., Prescott, T.J. (eds.) LIVINGMACHINES 2015. LNCS (LNAI), vol. 9222, pp. 199–210. Springer, Cham (2015). https://doi.org/10.1007/978-3-319-22979-9_20
14. Lin, T., Horne, B.G., Tino, P., Giles, C.L.: Learning long-term dependencies in NARX recurrent neural networks. IEEE Trans. Neural Netw. **7**(6), 1329–1338 (1996)
15. Mangan, M., Webb, B.: Spontaneous formation of multiple routes in individual desert ants (cataglyphis velox). Behav. Ecol. **23**(5), 944–954 (2012)
16. McKinney, W.: Data structures for statistical computing in python. In: van der Walt, S., Millman, J. (eds.) Proceedings of the 9th Python in Science Conference, pp. 56–61 (2010). https://doi.org/10.25080/Majora-92bf1922-00a
17. Milford, M.J., Wyeth, G.F.: SeqSLAM: visual route-based navigation for sunny summer days and stormy winter nights. In: 2012 IEEE International Conference on Robotics and Automation, pp. 1643–1649. IEEE (2012)
18. Müller, J., Nawrot, M., Menzel, R., Landgraf, T.: A neural network model for familiarity and context learning during honeybee foraging flights. Biol. Cybern. **112**(1), 113–126 (2017). https://doi.org/10.1007/s00422-017-0732-z
19. Müller, M., Wehner, R.: Path integration provides a scaffold for landmark learning in desert ants. Curr. Biol. **20**(15), 1368–1371 (2010)
20. Oliphant, T.: NumPy: A guide to NumPy. Trelgol Publishing, USA (2006). http://www.numpy.org/
21. Philippides, A., Baddeley, B., Cheng, K., Graham, P.: How might ants use panoramic views for route navigation? J. Exp. Biol. **214**(3), 445–451 (2011)
22. Philippides, A., Graham, P., Baddeley, B., Husbands, P.: Using neural networks to understand the information that guides behavior: a case study in visual navigation. In: Cartwright, H. (ed.) Artificial Neural Networks. MMB, vol. 1260, pp. 227–244. Springer, New York (2015). https://doi.org/10.1007/978-1-4939-2239-0_14
23. Schwarz, S., Mangan, M., Webb, B., Wystrach, A.: Route-following ants respond to alterations of the view sequence. J. Exp. Biol. (2020)

24. Sedgwick, P.: Pearson's correlation coefficient. BMJ **345**, e4483 (2012)
25. Smith, L., Philippides, A., Graham, P., Baddeley, B., Husbands, P.: Linked local navigation for visual route guidance. Adapt. Behav. **15**(3), 257–271 (2007)
26. Wehner, R., Boyer, M., Loertscher, F., Sommer, S., Menzi, U.: Ant navigation: one-way routes rather than maps. Curr. Biol. **16**(1), 75–79 (2006)
27. Wystrach, A., Dewar, A., Philippides, A., Graham, P.: How do field of view and resolution affect the information content of panoramic scenes for visual navigation? A computational investigation. J. Comp. Physiol. A. **202**(2), 87–95 (2016). https://doi.org/10.1007/s00359-015-1052-1
28. Zeil, J., Hofmann, M.I., Chahl, J.S.: Catchment areas of panoramic snapshots in outdoor scenes. JOSA A **20**(3), 450–469 (2003)

Split-Belt Adaptation Model of a Decerebrate Cat Using a Quadruped Robot with Learning

Kodai Kodono[✉] and Hiroshi Kimura

Kyoto Institute of Technology, Sakyo-ku Matssugasaki, Kyoto 606-8585, Japan
m9623107@edu.kit.ac.jp, kimura61@kit.ac.jp
http://www.robotlocomotion.kit.ac.jp/kotetsu/

Abstract. We propose a model connecting body dynamics and sensor feedback to investigate gait adaptation mechanisms of decerebrate cats in split-belt waking. In our previous studies, we proposed a leg controller using leg loading/unloading for the leg phase transition of a quadruped robot: "Kotetsu." The purpose of this study is to make a model of split-belt gait adaptation in spinal cats and decerebrate cats to refer to biological knowledge and to evaluate the validity of those models using Kotetsu. We construct the spinal cat model integrating our leg controller with Frigon's spinal cord model. Also, we employ motor learning in the cerebellum by long-term depression for the decerebrate cat model. As the results of experiments, we show that early adaptation in the split-belt walking is obtained by the stance-to-swing leg phase transition mechanism in the spinal cat model. We also show that late adaptation in split-belt walking is obtained by motor learning as the step distance adjustment in the decerebrate cat model. The validity of those models is evaluated by comparing durations of forelegs bi-support phases and duty ratios in the transition from tied-belt to split-belt walking between decerebrate cats and Kotetsu with the decerebrate cat model.

Keywords: Split-belt walk · Decerebrate cat model · Quadruped robot

1 Introduction

1.1 Walking of a Decerebrate Cat on a Split-Belt Treadmill

Animals and humans change the gait and adapt to perturbations while walking. In spite of such evidence, detailed mechanisms of such gait adaptation have not yet been clarified. To investigate such adaptation mechanisms, experiments to make animals [1–4] and humans walk on split-belt[1] treadmills were much

---

[1] The situation of different belt speed in left and right is named split-belt; that of the same belt speed is named tied-belt. A leg on the fast belt or the slow belt is named fast-leg or slow-leg (normal-leg), respectively.

© Springer Nature Switzerland AG 2020
V. Vouloutsi et al. (Eds.): Living Machines 2020, LNAI 12413, pp. 217–229, 2020.
https://doi.org/10.1007/978-3-030-64313-3_21

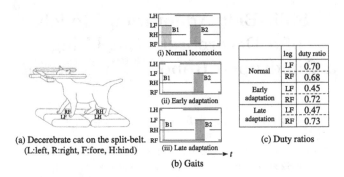

Fig. 1. (a) A decerebrate cat in split-belt walking, which was revised by authors from [3]. (b) gait diagrams and (c) duty ratios of a decerebrate cat on tied-belt: (i) and on split-belt:(ii), (iii). The x-axis of the gait diagram means time t. The gait diagrams were revised by authors from [1,5]. The values of duty ratio were measured based on those gait diagrams dividing the stance phase by the total phase by authors.

conducted. Especially, to investigate the role of the cerebellum in gait adaptation of quadrupedal animals, Yanagihara et al. [1–3] conducted experiments where decerebrate cats walked on split-belt treadmills and proposed a motor learning paradigm such that the cerebellum induces adaptive coordination among limbs in case of the perturbation to one forelimb. In the experiment [1], decerebrate (thalamic) cats[2] walked on a split-belt treadmill shown in Fig. 1-(a) where the LF belt speed was 61 [cm/s] and the other belt speed was 36 [cm/s]. As a result, the gait was changed and became stable according to the time course.

Usually, such experiments are explained using three stages. The first stage corresponds to walking on the tied-belt treadmill initially, and it is also called "normal locomotion." The second stage corresponds to the time course for a while after the change to walking on the split-belt treadmill (perturbation). And the change of the gait induced in this stage is named "early adaptation." The third stage corresponds to the time course sufficient for stabilizing the gait after the perturbation, and the change of the gait induced in this stage is named "late adaptation" [6]. In Fig. 1-(b) & (c), the gait and duty ratios in each stage are shown. Exchanging leg loading between forelegs is performed in bisupport phases, of which sufficient duration is important for the smooth exchange of leg loading [3]. We call the bisupport phase starting on touch down (TD) of RF and terminating on lift off (LO) of LF as "B1," and the bisupport phase starting on TD of LF and terminating on LO of RF as "B2." In Fig. 1-(b), the difference between durations of B1 and B2 is obvious in split-belt walking (ii&iii). In Fig. 1-(c), the duty ratio of each leg changes in each stage. The duration of the stance phase, the swing phase and the step cycle of LF and RF in each stage [1] are shown in Fig. 2.

---

[2] A cat disconnected from upper central nerves with remaining locomotor regions at the sub-thalamic (SLR), cerebellum (CLR) and mesencephalic (MLR) is called a "thalamic cat." On the other hand, a cat disconnected from upper central nerves, including the cerebellum and brain stem, is called a "spinal cat.".

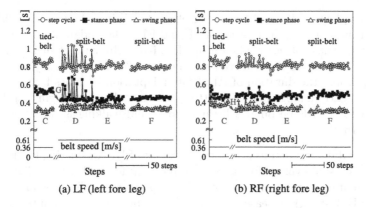

(a) LF (left fore leg)   (b) RF (right fore leg)

Fig. 2. The duration of the stance phase, the swing phase and the step cycle of LF and RF in walking of a decerebrate cat (revised by authors from [1]). In both diagrams, (C) a cat walked on a tied-belt. (D) & (E) a cat walked on split-belt in the first trial. (F) a cat walked on split-belt in the third trial. At the beginning of split-belt walking, durations of the stance phase of LF and the swing phase of RF quickly decreased (G) and (H), respectively. Fluctuations of durations were very large in (D), still not small in (E) and small in (F). The gaps in steps meant standing for approx. 20[min].

The characteristics of each stage are summarized as follows.

(i) normal locomotion
   The duration of B1 and B2 in Fig. 1-(b) and step cycle durations of LF and RF in Fig. 2-(C) are almost equal.
(ii) early adaptation
   As shown in Fig. 2-(G) & (H), durations of the stance phase of LF and the swing phase of RF clearly decrease immediately after the perturbation, respectively. For approx. 50[steps] after the perturbation in (D), fluctuations of those durations and the duration of the step cycle of both legs are very large. As a result, fluctuations of bisupport phase durations (B1 and B2) increases[3] [3]. For the next approx. 50[steps] in (E), such early adaptation that all indexes converge into approx. constant values appear. Although fluctuations of all indexes are still not small, the duty ratio of fast-leg (LF) much decreases, and the duty ratio of slow-leg (RF) increases a little in Fig. 1-(c). While comparing durations of B1 and B2 in the second stage with those in the first stage in Fig. 1-(b), the duration of B2 is approx. equal, but the duration of B1 in early adaptation is extremely short. This extremely short duration of B1 means that exchanging leg loading from LF to RF is not sufficient, and walking is unstable.
(iii) late adaptation
   As shown in Fig. 2-(F), fluctuations of all indexes become small as a result of late adaptation after the sufficient time course. Although durations of the

---

[3] The range of bisupport phase after the perturbation is more than five times it in normal locomotion.

stance phase of LF and the swing phase of RF in (F) are a little different from those in (E), duty ratios of LF and RF at late adaptation are approx. equal to those at early adaptation (Fig. 1-(c)). In spite of such equality of duty ratios, since the relative phase between LF and RF is adjusted in late adaptation, the duration of B1 at late adaptation becomes larger than the one at early adaptation (Fig. 1-(b)). It means that exchanging leg loading from LF to RF becomes a little smooth, and walking is stable under the perturbation.

Let us describe more details about the duration of B1 considering the leg phase duration, the step cycle, and the relative phase in forelimbs. Immediately after the perturbation at the beginning of early adaptation, the duration of the stance phase of LF (fast-leg) decreases due to the direct perturbation from the fast-belt. Besides, the duration of the swing phase of RF (slow-leg) also decreases in spite of no direct perturbation from the fast-belt. As a result, although there exit large fluctuations immediately after the perturbation, the step cycle difference between LF and RF become small (Fig. 2-(E)), and the duration of B1 is not sufficient but at least kept. This adaptation enables split-belt walking to continue even though it is unstable. In addition, in the second half of early adaptation, fluctuations become less. This means that the quick contralateral coordination mechanism between left and right legs does exist in early adaptation.

In late adaptation, since durations of the stance phase and the swing phase of LF and RF are a little adjusted from those in early adaptation, the step cycle difference between LF and RF becomes approx. zero (Fig. 2-(F)). Also, the relative phase between LF and RF is adjusted properly, and the duration of B1 is sufficiently kept. This adaptation enables stable split-belt walking to continue. This means that the delayed learning mechanism does exist in late adaptation [1]. In the case of split-belt walking of a decerebrate cat with long-term depression in the cerebellum being inhibited chemically, early adaptation appears with many large fluctuations, but late adaptation does not appear. This means that the cerebellum plays a key role in such learning functions [3]. Given that the dynamics of walking, these adaptations are specific to quadrupedal walking.

1.2   Proposal of the Gait Adaptation Model of a Decerebrate Cat

In this study, we aim at the constructive model[4] of gait adaptation in split-belt walking of a decerebrate cat. The constructive model can explain the mechanism of gait generation and adaptation as the physical phenomenon while connecting the embodiment and sensor feedback. As one of such constructive models for gait generation and adaptation of a quadruped, we proposed the method [7] using leg loading and unloading for the swing-to-stance and stance-to-swing leg

---

[4] In the constructive model, the dynamics of a single element and dynamics between elements are defined. As a result of simulations or experiments of the interaction between those elements and the environment, we might be able to understand the underlying mechanisms of the non-linear dynamic system constructively.

phase transitions, respectively. On the other hand, Frigon et al. [4] carried split-belt walking experiments with hind legs of a spinal cat and proposed the leg phase transitions model at the spinal cord. In this paper, we employ Frigon's model into our method and construct the spinal cat model for early adaptation. In addition, to show that motor learning is necessary to adapt to split-belt in quadruped walking, we employ the learning function at the cerebellum into the spinal cat model and construct the decerebrate cat model for late adaptation.

As one of the related studies, Fujiki and Aoi et al. [6] proposed such learning model at the cerebellum as adjusting the amount of the phase resetting on TD of each leg, and realized gait adaptation in split-belt walking of a biped robot in simulations and experiments. The target of this study is the pattern adaptation in the non-linear dynamic system, and it is the constructive model with the embodiment in the sense that is mathematically dealing with dynamics of the relative phase between legs. Therefore, it is "the robot controlling model described as the non-linear dynamic system."

On the other hand, we explicitly describe the leg phase transition based on sensor information. Therefore, it is "the model much close to robotics described as the sensory-motor system" in the sense that dynamics of the relative phases among legs emerges through the interaction between the body and environment [7,8]. While using such a model, we aim at constructively clarifying the relation among the embodiment, sensor feedback and motor learning in split-belt walking of a decerebrate cat.

1.3   Indexes and Values of Parameters

Indexes and abbreviations and values of parameters in experiments are shown in Table 1 and 2, respectively. The leg index i is often eliminated if it is obvious. The hat ˆ, the bar ¯ and the tilde ˜ symbols are respectively used to represent the nominal, the measured and the reference values of a single variable.

Table 1. Indexes and abbreviations in this paper.

$L*, R*$	Left, right
$*F, *H$	Fore, hind
i	Leg index $\in \{LF, RF, LH, RH\}$
sw, st	Swing, stance
lp	Leg phase index $\in \{sw, st\}$
$cntr$	Contralateral
LO, TD	Lift off, touch down
$STPD$	Step distance

Table 2. Values of parameters used in experiments ($\hat{\phi}_{PEP} = 2\pi (= 0)$, $\hat{\phi}_{AEP} = 2\pi(1 - \hat{\beta})$, $\hat{\phi} = 2\pi(1 - \hat{\beta})/\hat{T}_{sw}$).

$\hat{T}_{sw}$ [s] 0.20	$\hat{D}$ [m] 0.03	$\hat{\chi}_{TD}$ [N] 1.9
$\hat{\beta}$ 0.7	$\hat{H}$ [m] 0.22	$\hat{\chi}_{LO}$ [N] 8
τ 0.4	ε_D [m] 0.008	

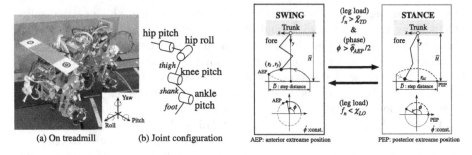

(a) On treadmill   (b) Joint configuration

AEP: anterior extreame position   PEP: posterior extreame position

Fig. 3. A quadruped robot: Kotetsu   **Fig. 4.** Leg controller (LC)

2   Leg Controller (LC)

It is known for the stance-to-swing leg phase transition in decerebrate cats that the transition is initiated by the hip extension, and also that the stance phase is indeterminately prolonged as long as leg loading is over a given threshold. The well-known half-center model of the stance-to-swing leg phase transition at the spinal cord was proposed [9] according to such knowledge. Besides, it was shown using a computer simulation that alternative stepping of the contralateral hind legs can be generated when phase modulations based on leg unloading are used [10]. Being motivated by those half-center and sensory feedback studies, we showed in simulations [7] and experiments [8] using a quadruped (Fig. 3) that rhythmic motion of each leg (gait) is achieved as a result of the phase modulations based on leg loading and that coordinations among legs emerge allowing dynamic walking in the low- to medium- speed range. This leg controller (LC) was a simple model of the central pattern generator (CPG).

Each leg is actuated by the LC [7] shown in Fig. 4. Each LC has two leg phases, swing (sw) and stance (st), and the transfer of activity between them is regulated using sensory information related to the load supported by the leg, or leg loading. Each LC is associated with a simple oscillator with a variable phase ϕ^i of constant angular velocity $\dot{\phi}^i$, where i is the leg index. The positions of the foot at the swing-to-stance and stance-to-swing transition are named as AEP (anterior extreme position) and PEP (posterior extreme position).

Resetting of ϕ^i is employed so that $\phi^i = \hat{\phi}_{AEP}$ and $\phi^i = \hat{\phi}_{PEP}$ at the onset of stance and swing phases, respectively [6]. The leg phase transition is initiated by using the measured normal ground reaction force: f_n^i (leg loading [10]) and the force thresholds: $\hat{\chi}_{TD}$ for TD and χ_{LO}^i for LO. Those are Eq. (1) for the swing-to-stance transition, and Eq. (2) for the stance-to-swing transition.

$$f_n^i > \hat{\chi}_{TD} \ \& \ \phi^i > \hat{\phi}_{AEP}/2 \tag{1}$$

$$f_n^i < \chi_{LO}^i \tag{2}$$

3 Spinal Cat Model for the Leg Phase Transition

3.1 Frigon's Model

While referring to the half-center model of the stance-to-swing leg phase transition [9], Frigon proposed the CPG model for leg phase transitions (Fig. 5). This conceptual model involves sensor inputs such as not only the hip extension and leg loading, but also the hip flexion. Also, this model has mutual inhibition between left and right FHCs as the CIM (contralateral inhibition mechanism). Since our LC described in Sect. 2 uses leg loading/unloading as a sensor input for leg phase transitions, it is easy to construct the model integrating our LC with Frigon's spinal cord model[5]. To sum up, we call the model made up of Kotetsu and LC integrating Frigon's spinal cord model "the spinal cat model".

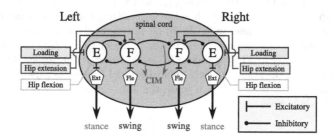

Fig. 5. Frigon's leg phase transitions model at the spinal cord (revised by authors from [4]). Each CPG on left or right is represented by the extensor half-center: EHC (E) and the flexor half-center: FHC (F). The EHC projects to the extensor motor neuron (Ext) while the FHC projects to the flexor motor neuron (Fle). Those motor neurons produce the stance phase and the swing phase, respectively. Leg loading, the hip extension and the hip flexion are feed back to the EHC and the FHC. Left and right FHCs are mutually inhibited by each other as the CIM.

3.2 Employing Frigon's Model into the LC

While referring to Frigon's model, we define χ_{LO}^i in Eq. (2),

$$\chi_{LO}^i = \begin{cases} \hat{\chi}_{LO} \cdot (r_{xc} - \bar{r}_x^i)/(\hat{D}/2) & \text{(if } lp^{cntr} = st) \\ -5 & \text{(otherwise)} \end{cases} \tag{3}$$

where $\hat{\chi}_{LO}$ and $\hat{D}$ are the nominal leg loading threshold for the stance-to-swing transition and the nominal step distance in Fig. 4, respectively. On the other hand, r_x is the x-pos. of the leg tip in the hip pitch joint coordinate (Fig. 4), $\bar{r}_x^i$ is the measured x-pos. while walking, and $r_{xc}(= 0)$ is the x-pos. right under the hip pitch joint of the leg.

---

[5] Frigon proposed the model from the hindlimb adaptation of spinal cats. In this study, we discuss a mechanism considering the dynamics of quadrupedal (not hindquarters) walking. For simplicity, we apply Frigon's model to the fore and hind LCs.

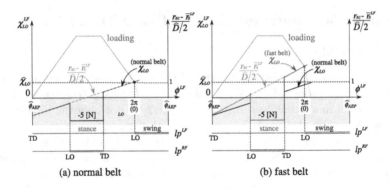

(a) normal belt   (b) fast belt

Fig. 6. The mechanism of the stance-to-swing transition of LF, according to Eq. (2) & (3). RF is the contralateral leg. Black solid lines in (a) & (b) mean χ_{LO}^{LF} on the normal-belt. Red solid line in (b) means χ_{LO}^{LF} on the fast-belt. Brown broken lines in (a) & (b) mean $(r_{xc} - \bar{r}_x^i)/(\hat{D}/2)$, which is the normalizing coefficient of the right hand term in Eq. (3). Green solid lines in (a) & (b) mean expected and simplified leg loading of LF. The horizontal axis means the oscillator phase of LF: ϕ^{LF}. The origin of this axis is not zero, but $\hat{\phi}_{AEP}$. The leg phase: lp^i is the swing or the stance. In gray zone, since χ_{LO}^{LF} is negative, the stance-to-swing transition of LF never occurs. For simplicity, this figure is made with $\phi^{LF} - \phi^{RF} = \pi$ [rad], the duty ratio: $\hat{\beta} = 0.75$ and $\hat{\phi}_{AEP} = \pi/2$ [rad]. (Color figure online)

In Eq. (3), if the leg phase: lp^{cntr} of the contralateral leg for the i-th leg is stance, $\hat{\chi}_{LO}$ is modulated using the coefficient: $r_{xc} - \bar{r}_x^i$ normalized by $\hat{D}/2$. This modulation corresponds with sensor inputs such as the hip extension and flexion in Frigon's model. On the other hand, while $lp^{cntr} = sw$, χ_{LO}^i is negative, and the stance-to-swing transition is prohibited as the CIM. While combining Eq. (3) with Eq. (2), we can integrate sensory inputs (leg loading, the hip extension and the hip flexion) in Frigon's model into the simple equations.

By using Fig. 6-(a), we explain how χ_{LO}^{LF} changes during the stance phase of LF in tied-belt walking while considering the leg phase of the contralateral leg: RF. Due to $r_{xc} < \bar{r}_x^{LF}$ in the 1st half of the stance phase, the coefficient: $(r_{xc} - \bar{r}_x^{LF})/(\hat{D}/2)$ (brown broken line) is negative. However, the coefficient in the 2nd half of the stance phase increases according to backward motion. Although χ_{LO}^{LF} (black solid line) is negative while $lp^{RF} = sw$, it becomes positive after TD of RF and gets close to leg loading (green solid line). After a short while, Eq. (2) gets satisfied, and the leg phase transits from the swing to the stance. Besides, in Fig. 6-(b), while assuming no slip between the belt and the leg tip, since $\bar{r}_x^{LF}$ on the fast belt moves backwards faster than that on the normal belt, χ_{LO}^{LF} draws the red line in Fig. 6-(b), and the stance-to-swing phase transition of LF is advanced in split-belt walking. As a result, the duration of the stance phase and the duty ratio decrease. Since the spinal cat model using the LCs with Eq. (3) involves the leg phase transition mechanism similar to the one of Frigon's model, and can deal with the advanced stance-to-swing phase transition of fast-leg, we consider this spinal cat model is most appropriate as the constructive model for early adaptation in split-belt walking of a decerebrate cat.

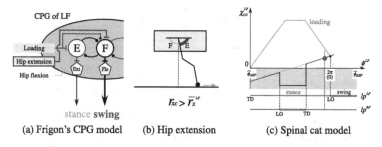

(a) Frigon's CPG model   (b) Hip extension   (c) Spinal cat model

Fig. 7. This figure shows the corresponding at the last stage in the stance phase of LF among (left): the Frigon's model, (middle): the leg tip position with the states of flexor and extensor muscles of the hip joint, and (right): the relationship between the oscillator phase of the LC: ϕ^{LF} (the horizontal axis) and the leg loading threshold: χ_{LO}^{LF} (the vertical axis) in the spinal cat model. The bold line in (left) means that the sensor input is active. The bold line in (middle) means that the muscle (extensor: E) is contracted. The • in (right) means that the value of χ_{LO}^{LF} at the current oscillator phase.

By using the last stage in the stance phase of LF in Fig. 7, we describe the relation between Frigon's model at the spinal cord and our spinal cat model more in details. Since leg loading is low, the depression to the FHC decreases. In addition, since the hip extension of LF is high, the excitation to the FHC increases. Therefore, the activity of the FHC increases, and the activity of the EHC decreases. That is, the flexor and extensor motor neurons are activated and inactivated, respectively. This leads to the stance-to-swing transition. Since the CIM never works due to $lp^{RF} = st$ in Eq. (3), χ_{LO}^{LF} increases according to the decrease of $\bar{r}_x^{LF}$ by backward motion of LF. In addition, leg loading of LF decreases due to the leg load transition from left to right due to rolling motion. Therefore, Eq. (2) for the stance-to-swing transition gets satisfied. Consequently, the stance-to-swing transition is induced in both models after a short while.

3.3 Split-Belt Walking with the Spinal Cat Model

In all experiments of this study shown in Fig. 8-(a), we start from tied-belt (speed: 13.2 [cm/s]), and then change to split-belt (speed of LF belt: 21.6 [cm/s], and speed of other belts not changed). Since the speed of LF belt is changed manually, the controller never detects the exact time of change. Therefore, the vision system over the treadmill is tracking two marks on Kotetsu while walking, detects the approx. time of change by human's hiding a mark and records it. Also, the front of the body of Kotetsu on the treadmill is constrained by two strings to use the similar constraint with a decerebrate cat as shown in Fig. 1-(a). However, the influence of the constraint by strings to rolling motion is little and Kotetsu can exchange leg loading between LF and RF smoothly.

Results of split-belt walking using the spinal cat model are shown in Fig. 8-(b). In tied-belt walking, the stable walk gait appears at [D]. However, just after a change to split-belt walking, the walking gait is much unstable at [E]. Let us consider this unstable walk gait of the spinal cat model in Sect. 4.2.

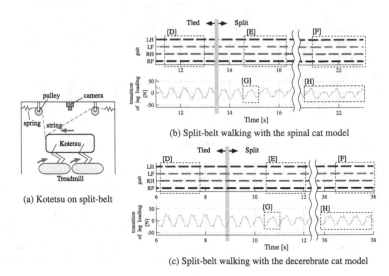

(a) Kotetsu on split-belt

(b) Split-belt walking with the spinal cat model

(c) Split-belt walking with the decerebrate cat model

Fig. 8. Experimental setup: (a). Results of split-belt walking experiments with the spinal cat model: (b) and with the decerebrate cat model: (c). Bottom: the transition of leg loading between LF and RF calculated by $\bar{f}_n^{RF} - \bar{f}_n^{LF}$. Gait on tied-belt: [D]. Gait after the switchover from tied to split (early adaptation): [E]. Gait on split-belt (late adaptation): [F]. Transition of leg loading after the switchover from tied to split: [G]. Transition of leg loading on split-belt: [H].

4   Decerebrate Cat Model with Learning for Late Adaptation

4.1   Employing Step Distance Adjustment into the Spinal Cat Model

Yanagihara et al. showed that nitric oxide (NO) in the cerebellum plays a key role in motor learning, and that late adaptation in split-belt walking of decerebrate cats is the result of long-term depression in cerebellar Purkinje cells [3]. When a decerebrate cat receives the perturbation in split-belt walking, it is observed that the probability of occurrence of climbing fiber responses during such perturbed locomotion is higher than that during unperturbed locomotion, especially much higher in the second half of the swing phase [2].

In this study, we consider the step distance (STPD) as an adjustable motion parameter in the swing phase and propose the decerebrate cat model. We employ the STPD adjustment: Eq. (4) for the leg: i, and use the leg loading threshold: Eq. (5) for the stance-to-swing phase transition rather than Eq. (3). This means that we add the motion learning function for late adaptation in split-belt walking into the spinal cat model described in Sect. 3. We call this "the decerebrate cat model."

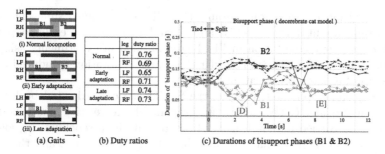

Fig. 9. (a) Gaits of Kotetsu on tied-belt: (i) and on split-belt: (ii) and (iii) with the decerebrate cat model. (b) Duty ratios corresponding with (a). (c) The durations of bisupport phase B1 and B2 in 5 times experiments of split-belt walking of Kotetsu with the decerebrate cat model. [D]: Early adaptation. [E]: Late adaptation.

$$\tilde{D} = \begin{cases} \tau \bar{D}^i - (1-\tau)\tilde{D}^i[n-1] \ (\text{if } |\bar{D}^i - (1-\tau)\tilde{D}^i[n-1]| > \varepsilon_D) \\ \tilde{D}^i[n-1] \qquad\qquad (\text{otherwise}) \end{cases} \quad (4)$$

$$\chi_{LO}^i = \begin{cases} \hat{\chi}_{LO} \cdot (r_{xc} - \bar{r}_x^i)/(\tilde{D}/2) \ (\text{if } lp^{cntr} = st) \\ -5 \qquad\qquad\qquad (\text{otherwise}) \end{cases} \quad (5)$$

In Eq. (4) and Eq. (5), $\tilde{D}^i[n]$ means the reference value of the STPD at the swing and stance phases of the n-th step ($\tilde{D}^i[1] = \hat{D}$). On the other hand, $\bar{D}^i$ means the measured value of the STPD at the stance phase of the $(n-1)$-th step. When the absolute subtraction between measured and reference values is larger than the threshold: ε_D, the calculation for adjustment is done. The constant value: τ for adjusting the learning speed is set as a little bit small ($\tau = 0.4$), but the learning speed is much faster than the one in case of decerebrate cats.

4.2 Split-Belt Walking with the Decerebrate Cat Model

The results of experiments of split-belt walking of Kotetsu using the decerebrate cat model are shown in Fig. 8-(c) and Fig. 9.

Since we are using the very simple decerebrate cat model, its behavior should be very similar to that of the spinal cat model until motor learning functions start to work. When we compare Fig. 8-(b) & (c) just after the change to split-belt walking, the transition of leg loading between LF and RF is perturbed at [G], gait gets unstable at [E] in both cases. Such behavior corresponds to early adaptation in decerebrate cats shown in Fig. 9. In the early adaptation of the decerebrate cat model, the duration of B1 is short at (ii) in Fig. 9-(a) and at [D] in Fig. 9-(c). Let us consider what is happening using Fig. 8-(c). About gaits shown at [E], the duration of the stance phase of LF: T_{st}^{LF} quickly decreases due to the early stance-to-swing transition of LF while being pulled backwards by fast-belt as described in Sect. 3.2. Simultaneously, the duration of the swing phase of RF: T_{sw}^{RF} quickly decreases. As a result, the duty ratio of RF quickly increases a little in Fig. 9-(b), and the duration B1 still remains and contributes to the transition of leg loading from LF to RF even not so sufficient. Since similar results about durations of B1 and B2 and duty ratios at early adaptation with those at early adaptation in Fig. 1 are obtained in experiments using the decerebrate cat model, we can consider that early adaptation is induced at the spinal cord of a decerebrate cat [6].

While keeping split-belt walking, the STPD of LF is adjusted by learning functions in Eq. (4). Consequently, adjustment of the relative phase between LF and RF is carried out by learning functions at the cerebellum, leg loading between LF and RF is exchanged smoothly at [H] in Fig. 8-(c), and the stable gait in split-belt walking different from the gait in tied-belt walking is induced as a result of late adaptation at [F] in Fig. 8-(c). In the late adaptation of the decerebrate cat model, the duration of B1 is prolonged at (iii) in Fig. 9-(a) and at [E] in Fig. 9-(c). But the duration of B2 is also prolonged at (iii) in Fig. 9-(a). Such difference from the result of a decerebrate cat, including the duration of the swing/stance phases should be fixed in our next study.

5   Conclusion

We constructed the spinal cat model integrating our previous leg controller with Frigon's spinal cord model, and the decerebrate cat model adding motor learning function at the cerebellum. We showed by experiments that early adaptation was obtained in the spinal cat model, and late adaptation was obtained by motor learning as the step distance adjustment in the decerebrate cat model. The validity of those models was evaluated by comparing durations of forelegs bisupport phases and duty ratios between decerebrate cats and a quadruped robot with the decerebrate cat model. It does not necessarily mean that this is how the control in the biological system works, but we confirmed that the basis of proposal model concepts could explain the adaptation of split-belt walking.

References

1. Yanagihara, D., Udo, M., Kondo, I., Yoshida, T.: A new learning paradigm: adaptive changes in interlimb coordination during perturbed locomotion in decerebrate cats. Neurosci. Res. **18**, 241–244 (1993)
2. Yanagihara, D., et al.: Climbing fiber responses in cerebellar vermal Purkinje cells during perturbed locomotion in decerebrate cats. Neurosci. Res. **19**, 245–248 (1994)
3. Yanagihara, D., Kondo, I.: Nitric oxide plays a key role in adaptive control of locomotion in cat. Natl. Acad. Sci. **93**, 13292–13297 (1996)
4. Frigon, A., et al.: Left-right coordination from simple to extreme conditions during split-belt locomotion in the chronic spinal adult cat. J. Physiol. **595**(1), 341–361 (2017)
5. Ito, S., Yuasa, H., Luo, Z., Ito, M., Yanagihara, D.: A mathematical model of adaptive behavior in quadruped locomotion. Biol. Cybern. **78**, 337–347 (1998)
6. Fujiki, S., et al.: Adaptation mechanism of interlimb coordination in human split-belt treadmill walking through learning of foot contact timing: a robotics study. J. Roy. Soc. Interface **12**(110), 20150542 (2015). https://doi.org/10.1098/rsif.2015.0542

7. Maufroy, C., Kimura, H., Takase, K.: Integration of posture and rhythmic motion controls in quadrupedal dynamic walking using phase modulations based on leg loading/unloading. Auton. Robot. **28**, 331–353 (2010)
8. Maufroy, C., Kimura, H., Nishikawa, T.: Stable dynamic walking of the quadruped "Kotetsu" using phase modulations based on leg loading/unloading against lateral perturbations. In: Proceedings of ICRA, pp. 1883–1888. IEEE, Saint Paul (2012)
9. Pearson, K.G.: Role of sensory feedback in the control of stance duration in walking cats. Brain Res. **57**(1), 222–227 (2008)
10. Ekeberg, O., Pearson, K.G.: Computer simulation of stepping in the hind legs of the cat: an examination of mechanisms regulating the stance-to-swing transition. J. Neurophysiol. **94**(6), 4256–4268 (2005)

A Simple Platform for Reinforcement Learning of Simulated Flight Behaviors

Simon D. Levy[✉]

Computer Science Department, Washington and Lee University,
Lexington, VA 24450, USA
simon.d.levy@gmail.com

Abstract. We present work-in-progress on a novel, open-source software platform supporting Deep Reinforcement Learning (DRL) of flight behaviors for Miniature Aerial Vehicles (MAVs). By using a physically realistic model of flight dynamics and a simple simulator for high-frequency visual events, our platform avoids some of the shortcomings associated with traditional MAV simulators. Implemented as an OpenAI Gym environment, our simulator makes it easy to investigate the use of DRL for acquiring common behaviors like hovering and predation. We present preliminary experimental results on two such tasks, and discuss our current research directions. Our code, available as a public github repository, enables replication of our results on ordinary computer hardware.

Keywords: Deep reinforcement learning · Flight simulation · Dynamic vision sensing

1 Motivation

Miniature Aerial Vehicles (MAVs, a.k.a. drones) are increasingly popular as a model for the behavior of insects and other flying animals [3]. The cost and risks associated with building and flying MAVs can however make such models inaccessible to many researchers. Even when such platforms are available, the number of experiments that must be run to collect sufficient data for paradigms like Deep Reinforcement Learning (DRL) makes simulation an attractive option.

Popular MAV simulators like Microsoft AirSim [10], as well as our own simulator [7], are built on top of video game engines like Unity or UnrealEngine4. Although they can provide a convincingly realistic flying experience and have been successfully applied to research in computer vision and reinforcement learning, the volume and complexity of the code behind such systems can make it challenging to modify and extend them for biologically realistic simulation.

The author gratefully acknowledges support from the Lenfest Summer Grant program at Washington and Lee University, and the helpful comments of two anonymous reviewers.

© Springer Nature Switzerland AG 2020
V. Vouloutsi et al. (Eds.): Living Machines 2020, LNAI 12413, pp. 230–233, 2020.
https://doi.org/10.1007/978-3-030-64313-3_22

For use in biologically realistic flight modeling, however, simulators like these, suffer from two important limitations. First, video game engines are designed to run in real time for human interaction, making them orders of magnitude too slow to collect sufficient samples for most reinforcement learning algorithms. Second, the use of photo-realistic data rendered at a standard video game frame rate (60–120 fps) makes them suitable for modeling data acquisition by actual video cameras, but unsuitable for the low-resolution, fast/asynchronous visual sensing typical of insects and other organisms [8].

2   OpenAI Gym Environment

OpenAI Gym [2] is a toolkit for developing and comparing reinforcement learning algorithms. In addition to providing a variety of reinforcement learning environments (tasks) like Atari games, it defines a simple Application Programming Interface (API) for developing new environments. Our simulator implements this API as follows:

- reset() Initializes the vehicle's state vector (position and velocity) to zero.
- step() Updates the state using the dynamics equations in [1].
- render() Shows the vehicle state using a Heads-Up-Display (HUD) or third-person view.

In the remainder of this extended abstract, we discuss related projects based on OpenAI Gym and provide a brief overview of work-in-progress on a new simulator designed to address these issues in that framework.

3   Related Work

Ours is one of a very small number of published, open-source projects using OpenAI Gym to learn flight-control mechanisms. Two others of note are (1) Gym-FC, which uses OpenAI Gym and DRL to tune attitude controllers for actual vehicles [6], and (2) Gym-Quad, which has been successfully used to learn landing behaviors with spiking neural nets using a single degree of freedom of control [4]. Because we wished to explore behaviors beyond attitude-control and landing, we found it more straightforward to build our own Gym environment, rather than attempting to modify these already substantial projects.

4   Results to Date

Speedup
Without calling OpenAI Gym's optional render() function, we are able to achieve update rates of around 28 kHz on an ordinary desktop computer – an order of magnitude faster than the 1 kHz rate reported for AirSim [10], and approximately three times fast as the rate we observed with our own UnrealEngine-based simulator.

Learning

As a simple test of applying our platform to a reinforcement-learning task, we used a Proximal Policy Optimization (PPO) agent [9] to learn a challenging behavior, using a dynamics model approximating the popular DJI Phantom quadcopter.

In this behavior, *Lander2D*, the agent was given the vehicle's horizontal and vertical coordinates, their first derivatives, and the vehicle's roll and its first derivative (six degrees of freedom). The control signal consisted of roll and thrust commands (two degrees of freedom). As with the popular Lunar Lander game, the goal was to land the vehicle between two flags in the center of the landscape, with a large penalty (−100 points) for flying outside the landscape, a large bonus (+100 points) for landing between the two flags, and a small penalty for distance from the mid-point, to provide a gradient. (See Fig. 1(a) for an illustration.)

Our preliminary results were encouraging. In the *Lander2D* behavior, the PPO agent learned to land the vehicle in under 9,000 training episodes (around 17 min on a Dell Optiplex 7040 eight-core desktop computer with 3.4 GHz processors). The best score achieved by the agent was competitive with the score obtainable through a heuristic (PID control) approach, around 205 points.

Our current work involves three directions: (1) replacing the PPO agent with a more biologically realistic spiking neural network (SNN); (2) extending our results to a full three-dimensional simulation, as shown in Fig. 1(b); and (3) adding a simulated vision system.

For the third direction – adding visual observation – DRL algorithms have traditionally used convolutional neural network (CNN) layers to enable the network to learn the critical features of the environment from image pixels. CNNs have however come under criticism for lacking biological plausibility and requiring very large amounts of computation time to learn the relationship between the pixels and the world state [5].

To address these issues in a biologically plausible way, we are developing a simple simulation of an event-based vision sensing [8] to incorporate into our platform. Instead of generating simulated events by sampling of an ordinary camera image, our event simulator uses a rudimentary perspective model to generate pseudo-events based on the vehicle state and the position of a simulated target object, represented as a sphere. We plan to use this simulator to model visually-guided predation with SNNs, extending the SNN landing-behavior work presented in [4].

5   Code

Our code, with instructions for reproducing our results, is available at https:// github.com/simondlevy/gym-copter.

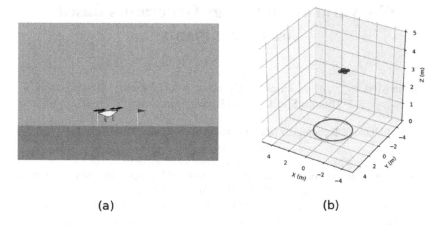

(a)   (b)

Fig. 1. 2D (a) and 3D (b) environments for the Lander task.

References

1. Bouabdallah, S., Murrieri, P., Siegwart, R.: Design and control of an indoor micro quadrotor. In: 2004 Proceedings of the IEEE International Conference on Robotics and Automation, ICRA 2004, vol. 5, pp. 4393–4398 (2004)
2. Brockman, G., et al.: Openai gym. CoRR abs/1606.01540 (2016). http://arxiv.org/abs/1606.01540
3. Cope, A.J., Ahmed, A., Isa, F., Marshall, J.A.R.: MiniBee: a minature MAV for the biomimetic embodiment of insect brain models. In: Martinez-Hernandez, U., et al. (eds.) Living Machines 2019. LNCS (LNAI), vol. 11556, pp. 76–87. Springer, Cham (2019). https://doi.org/10.1007/978-3-030-24741-6_7
4. Hagenaars, J.J., Paredes-Vallés, F., Bohté, S.M., de Croon, G.C.H.E.: Evolved neuromorphic control for high speed divergence-based landings of MAVs (2020)
5. Hinton, G.: What is wrong with convolutional neural nets? MIT Brain and Cognitive Sciences Fall Colloquium Series, 4 December 2014
6. Koch, W., Mancuso, R., West, R., Bestavros, A.: Reinforcement learning for UAV attitude control. ACM Trans. Cyber-Phys. Syst. **3**(2), 22 (2019)
7. Levy, S.D.: Robustness through simplicity: a minimalist gateway to neurorobotic flight. Front. Neurorobot. **14**, 16 (2020). https://doi.org/10.3389/fnbot.2020.00016
8. Posch, C., Serrano-Gotarredona, T., Linares-Barranco, B., Delbruck, T.: Retinomorphic event-based vision sensors: bioinspired cameras with spiking output. Proc. IEEE **102**(10), 1470–1484 (2014)
9. Schulman, J., Wolski, F., Dhariwal, P., Radford, A., Klimov, O.: Proximal policy optimization algorithms (2017). https://arxiv.org/abs/1705.05065
10. Shah, S., Dey, D., Lovett, C., Kapoor, A.: AirSim: high-fidelity visual and physical simulation for autonomous vehicles. In: Field and Service Robotics (2017). https://arxiv.org/abs/1705.05065

Biohybrid Wind Energy Generators Based on Living Plants

Fabian Meder[1]([✉]), Marc Thielen[2], Giovanna Adele Naselli[1], Silvia Taccola[1], Thomas Speck[2,3], and Barbara Mazzolai[1]([✉])

[1] Istituto Italiano di Tecnologia, Center for Micro-BioRobotics, Viale Rinaldo Piaggio 34, 56025 Pontedera, Italy
{fabian.meder,barbara.mazzolai}@iit.it

[2] Plant Biomechanics Group, Botanic Garden, Faculty of Biology, University of Freiburg, Schänzlestraße 1, 79104 Freiburg, Germany

[3] Cluster of Excellence livMatS @ FIT–Freiburg Center for Interactive Materials and Bioinspired Technologies, University of Freiburg, Georges-Köhler-Allee 105, 79110 Freiburg, Germany

Abstract. Biohybrid approaches harnessing living systems and biological tissue to accumulate electrical energy have potential to contribute green and autonomous power sources. We recently discovered that the cuticle-cellular tissue bilayer in higher plant leaves functions as an integrated triboelectric generator that is capable of converting mechanical stimuli into electricity. In this manner, living plants can be used to transduce mechanical energy such as wind energy into electricity. Here, we report on two essential components of the plant-biohybrid energy harvesting prototypes studied in *Ficus microcarpa* and *Rhododendron yakushimanum*, which are 1) the electrodes at the plant tissue that are used to harvest the electrical signals and 2) the wind-induced mechanical interactions between plants and an artificial leaf based on a silicone rubber/indium tin oxide/polyethylene terephthalate multilayer that is installed at the plant's leaf to enhance the power output. We show moreover that in the same manner a *Nerium oleander* plant can directly power 50 LEDs and a digital thermometer under wind excitation. The results reveal design strategies for biohybrid energy harvesters on the basis of living plants that could become autonomous energy sources for sensor networks and environmental monitoring.

Keywords: Biohybrid energy sources · *In vivo* energy sources · Plants · Triboelectric generators · Green energy

1 Introduction

The quest for green, emission-free, resource-saving, and autonomous energy sources requires considering radically new approaches. Among them are biohybrid devices based on natural components and living organisms combined with tailored artificial components making use of nature's fascinating properties. Plant-hybrid technologies

© Springer Nature Switzerland AG 2020
V. Vouloutsi et al. (Eds.): Living Machines 2020, LNAI 12413, pp. 234–244, 2020.
https://doi.org/10.1007/978-3-030-64413-3_23

take advantage of specific material/tissue properties and functionalities of living plants with applications ranging from energy harvesting to sensing [1–8].

Several ways enable producing electricity with living plants such as plant microbial fuel cells [9–15] and glucose biofuel cells [16, 17]. In the latter examples, the conversion from organic matter into electricity is done by an artificial fuel cell that uses organic molecules provided by the plant. However, we recently reported, that plants can directly convert mechanical energy such as from wind into electricity [18, 19]. Plant leaves are covered with a dielectric material, a thin polymer layer named cuticle [20]. This surface accumulates charges upon contact with another material through contact electrification and materials like PTFE and silicone rubber were shown to lead to significant charging of the cuticle [18, 21]. The charges created on the cuticle are electrostatically induced into the ion-conductive cellular tissue leading to a current that can be harvested by an electrode at the plant tissue. In this manner, living plants constitute a triboelectric generator (TENG) with a comparable power output to similarly operated artificial TENGs as tested in our previous study [18]. TENGs are not only considered a possible energy source for the internet of things and sensor networks but are also being discussed for application in larger scale energy harvesting farms with reported power densities of up to several hundred watts per square meter of active surface area [22–24]. Using living plants as opposed to generators based on only artificial materials has several added benefits. Most materials and the structure are provided by the plant, moreover plant's dynamic self-repair and CO_2 compensation through ongoing growth would be extremely difficult to realize in artificial generators. This offers a great opportunity to convert plants into power sources. Yet, it still needs to be understood how to best construct and optimize plant biohybrid systems in order to exploit environmental mechanical energy such as wind.

Here, we report on essential components and behaviours of the plant-biohybrid energy harvesting prototypes by investigating which electrode types at the plant tissue are most efficient in terms of energy harvesting and the mechanism of charge transport in the plant. In addition, we analyse how wind-induced voltages depend on mechanical oscillations and contact of the plant leaves with the artificial components at different wind speeds. Thus, we show how plant movements induced by wind influence charge generation. Moreover, we demonstrate that plant biohybrid generators are capable of directly powering several LEDs and a digital thermometer from wind energy.

2 Materials and Methods

2.1 Plant Species

Ficus microcarpa was purchased at a local plant nursery. *Rhododendron yakushimanum* was provided by the Botanic Garden, University of Freiburg, Germany. *Nerium oleander* was picked outdoor in the region of Tuscany, Italy.

2.2 Assembly of Plant-Biohybrid Energy Harvesters

To manufacture the 'artificial leaves' to be attached to the plants, transparent indium tin oxide (ITO)-coated PET films (thickness 200 μm, nominal sheet resistance 350–500 Ω per square, Thorlabs Inc., USA) were coated with a thin layer of silicone rubber adhesive (Sil-Poxy^{TM}, Smooth-On Inc., USA) applied on the ITO-layer by a doctor blade. Immediately after, a layer of translucent silicone rubber was added (thickness 500 μm, obtained from Modulor GmbH, Germany, previously washed with isopropyl alcohol and dry wiped using dust-free tissue) and dried for a minimum of 24 h. The multilayer sheets were cut into the desired shapes using a laser cutter (VersaLaser VLS3.60, Universal Laser Systems Inc., USA). Self-adhesive Velcro® strips were glued onto the artificial leaf as an attachment system to fix the artificial leaves to the plant leaf's petioles. In addition, to connect the ITO electrode, the silicone film was carefully lifted from the ITO electrode in one corner and a piece of copper tape with conductive glue was attached to the ITO layer. Then the cable was soldered onto the copper tape and the silicone layer was brought back and fixed using the silicone adhesive. All cutting edges were sealed with silicone. The leaves were fixed at the petioles of the natural leaves to obtain biohybrid plant energy harvesters.

2.3 Data Acquisition and Analysis

Voltages were measured with an oscilloscope using a 100 MOhm probe (MSO7014A, Agilent Technologies, USA). Short circuit currents were measured using a high input impedance electrometer (6517B, Keithley, USA). Experiments with different electrodes (further described in the main text) have been conducted in a Faraday cage and, to generate charges in a controlled manner, an artificial leaf segment (25 mm^2) was mechanically actuated to create contact with the leaf of *F. microcarpa* at a frequency of 5 Hz producing an impact force of 0.5 N (the experimental setup was described in detail previously) [18]. Plant hybrid generators were exposed to wind of controllable speed in a specialized phytochamber (height: 2.13 m, depth: 2.75 m, width: 2.5 m) equipped with an active climate control system and a wind source consisting of 96 individually adjustable nozzles that were all oriented towards the plant which was placed in a distance of ~50 cm from the nozzles. A ventilation system (MUB 042-500DV-A2, Systemair, Skinnskatteberg, Sweden, max speed: 1330 rpm) in combination with a frequency converter (VLT® HVAC Drive FC 102, Danfoss, Nordborg, Denmark) allowed controlling the wind speed. Wind speed at the leaf was measured at a distance of ~3 cm in front of the leaf using a hot wire anemometer (405i, Testo SE & Co. KGaA, Germany). During all measurements, illumination was kept constant and the temperature was kept at 22 ± 1 °C. The relative humidity (RH) was typically 50 ± 3%. Videos of leaf oscillations have been recorded with a GoPro Hero7 camera at 240 fps and they were analyzed by automatic and manual positional tracking of plant and artificial leaf tips using the software Tracker, Version 5.1.3. Local derivatives of the vibrational profiles were obtained using Matlab, Version R2019b. The thermometer powered by the plants was a DST-50 Digital Thermometer (Elitech, UK) from which solar cell and battery have been removed before connecting it to the described circuit. The green LEDs were NSPG500DS (Nichia Corp., Japan).

3 Results and Discussion

3.1 Concept and Components of the Plant Biohybrid Wind Energy Harvesters

Figure 1 shows the concept and components of the plant biohybrid wind energy harvester. The plants are equipped with the "artificial leaves" which consist of a triple layer of a 200 μm PET base sheet, coated with a ~50 nm ITO electrode, coated with a 500 μm silicone rubber layer (see illustration in Fig. 1, right). These materials were selected based on our previous studies in which we compared possible dielectric/electrode combinations in more detail [18, 19]. In addition, a Velcro®-based system is used to fix the artificial leaf to the petiole of the plant leaf so that the silicone rubber surface is oriented towards the upper (adaxial) leaf surface. The photograph in Fig. 1 shows a typical assembly. In addition, a cable connects the ITO electrode of the artificial leaf to the harvesting circuit. The second main part of the generator is the plant itself taking advantage of wind-induced leaf motions. When the plant and the artificial leaves move in the wind, the surfaces of both structures come into transient contact leading to the contact electrification of the leaf and the silicone rubber. Thereby opposite charges are created on both surfaces. When the wind-induced leaf oscillations then force the two surfaces to separate, these charges do not longer compensate each other and hence are electrostatically induced into the ion-conductive plant tissue. The lower right illustration in Fig. 1 depicts the expected charge distribution as well as a simple circuit used to measure the generated signals. The plant-converted electricity can be harvested by an electrode in contact with the plant tissue. In similar manner, the charges generated on the artificial leaf are induced into the ITO electrode. The biohybrid device forms a triboelectric generator that uses the plant structure to transduce mechanical into electrical energy and is driven by wind-induced leaf motions.

3.2 Energy Harvesting Electrode at the Plant Tissue

A crucial component of the device is the electrode that connects the plant tissue to the energy harvesting and signal acquisition circuit, respectively. Figure 2 shows voltage and current measurements using four different electrode types placed in or on the stem of a *F. microcarpa* at a distance of 120 mm from the leaf that is converting mechanical excitation into electrical signals. The species was chosen as it was small enough to be analyzed in our Faraday cage and stimulated in a controlled manner by our test apparatus for controlling stimulus and environmental noise as good as possible. Electrodes used (Fig. 2a) were (1) a gold coated pin electrode (0.5 mm diameter 10 mm length) pen-etrating the stem's inner tissue through the bark; (2) a thin-temporary tattoo electrode based on conductive polymer poly(3,4-ethylenedioxythiophene) polystyrene sulfonate PEDOT:PSS as reported in Ref. [25] that was conformally transferred onto the bark surface; (3) an AgCl coated Ag wire that contacts with a KCl gel solution on the bark prepared as reported in Ref. [26]; and (4) a copper film (1.4 mm) attached onto the bark. The measurements were performed while the *F. microcarpa* leaf was exposed to a contact and release excitation at a constant force of 0.5 N and applied by a 25 mm² squared piece of the artificial leaf using an actuator operating at a frequency of 5 Hz. This generated electrical signals of constant magnitude in all tests and allowed to compare the role of

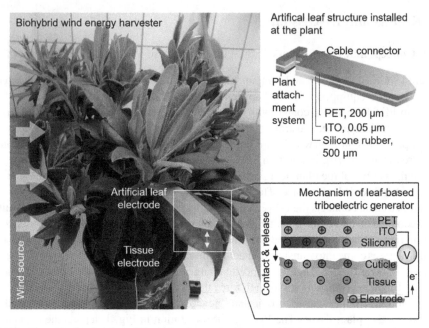

Fig. 1. Photograph of a plant (*Rhododendron yakushimanum*) biohybrid wind energy harvester, illustration of the structure of the artificial leaf and mechanism of energy conversion.

the electrodes. The experimental setup was placed inside a Faraday cage. Figure 2 shows measured voltage V_m and short circuit current measurements I_{SC}. The electrode penetrating the inner tissue gathers the highest voltages and currents. The different electrodes (2–4) operating mainly on the plant surface show significantly lower efficiency in harvesting the charges generated indicating that a connection to the inner tissue is crucial. This confirms that the charges generated at the leaf surfaces are indeed electrostatically induced into the inner tissue and do not significantly conduct *via* the plant surface e.g., by adsorbed water films. The relative humidity during the experiments was ~60%. The tattoo electrode (about 1 μm thick) and the gel electrolyte of the Ag/AgCl electrode are likely capable of connecting partially through openings and pores in the bark to the inner tissue leading to similar voltages as observed at the tissue pin electrode, however, significantly reduced currents were obtained due to the expectedly higher resistance at the given positions. The copper film electrode (4) instead only connects the bark where the generated charges cannot be harvested. The results thus confirm that connecting the inner tissue is essential for harvesting the plant generated charges.

3.3   Wind-Induced Electrical Signals and Mechanical Behavior of the Plant Biohybrid Energy Harvester

Next, the details of wind-induced vibrations of the plant leaf and the artificial leaf are essential for contact electrification of the plant and biohybrid wind energy conversion. Our previous study confirmed that the energy harvesting capability exists in this manner

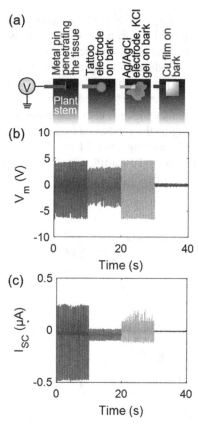

Fig. 2. Efficiency of different electrodes applied as illustrated in (a) and further detailed in the main text for harvesting the plant generated electricity. Voltage V_m (b) and short circuit current I_{SC} (c) as function of electrode type employed at the plant stem to harvest electrical signals. The signals were generated by mechanically stimulating a *F. microcarpa* leaf using a 25 mm^2 segment of the artificial leaf actuated at an impact force of 0.5 N and a frequency of 5 Hz which resulted in signals of constant magnitude allowing to compare the role of the electrodes. The results clearly indicate the metal pin electrode penetrating the inner cellular tissue results in highest accumulated voltages and currents.

theoretically in all land plants bearing a polymeric cuticle with adjacent conductive cellular tissue and we confirmed the effect in eight different species showing different efficiencies [18]. One of the best performing species in this study was *Rhododendron* and *N. oleander* (see below) and we selected, *R. yakushimanum* for further tests also due to its mechanically robust, larger leaf and plant size compared to *F. microcarpa*. We modified the *R. yakushimanum* with an artificial leaf as shown in Fig. 1 and exposed the plant to different air flows of controlled speed. The air was blown from 96 nozzles (~30 mm diameter) towards the plant in a specialized phytochamber. Figure 3 shows the voltage signals V_m that were measured at a pin electrode in the plant tissue at three different wind speeds, 1.4, 3.1, and 4.8 m/s, respectively. In addition, the related cumulative sum of the energy $E_{V_m} = \frac{V_m^2 t}{R_i}$ over the measurement period is shown with t being the data acquisition period and R_i being the inner resistance of the plant-hybrid generator with a value of 70 MΩ as determined earlier [19]. V_m's amplitude and E increase with the wind speed indicating a more efficient charge generation at higher wind speed. A positive voltage peak is obtained as soon as the leaf and the artificial leaf surfaces separate after prior contact. The 'bar codes' under the voltage plots indicate the frequency of the positive maxima which is also increasing with the wind speed with a rate of ~0.74 per 1 m/s as changing the windspeed from 1.4 to 3.1 m/s leads to an increase of the frequency by 1.24 and changing from 3.1 to 4.8 m/s to a frequency increase of 1.27. Next, the motion of the leaf and the artificial leaf was tracked using video analysis of high-speed video recordings of the hybrid plant under wind excitation.

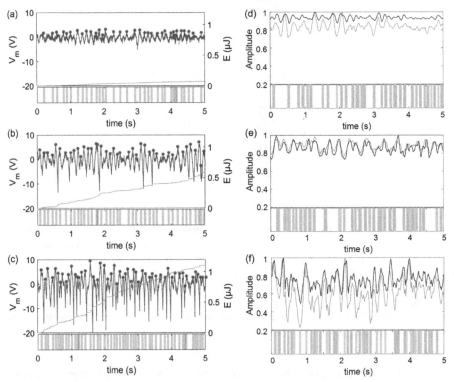

Fig. 3. Voltage V_m measured at the tissue electrode generated by a *R. yakushimanum* modified with one artificial leaf as function of wind speed (a) 1.4 m/s, (b) 3.1 m/s, and (c) 4.8 m/s, respectively. The red stars highlight the positive peaks which occur when the plant leaf and the artificial leaf separate after prior wind-induced contact. The green line shows the related cumulative sum energy as function of time. The grey bars in the lower panel also mark these events illustrating that the frequency increases with wind speed. (e), (f) and (g) show the oscillations of the plant leaf (green) and the artificial leaf (blue) at wind speeds, 1.4 m/s, 3.1 m/s, and 4.8 m/s, respectively. The grey bars in the lower panel indicate the events in the vibrational profiles when the plant leaf travels upwards and the artificial leaf moves simultaneously downwards leading to contact and subsequent separation of both surfaces (Color figure online).

Figure 3 eg. shows the individual oscillations of the plant (green) and the artificial leaf (blue). The phase and frequency of both leaf oscillations describe very similar curves and the amplitude of both increases with increasing wind speed. The bar codes in the graphs indicate the events in the vibrational profiles when the plant leaf moves upwards and the artificial leaf moves simultaneously downwards that were found by analyzing the local derivatives of the vibrational profiles. Such events lead expectedly to contact followed by separation and this is required for effective contact electrification. It can be seen that the frequency of these events increases with the wind speeds similar to that previously observed for the voltage peaks.

Figure 4 directly illustrates the correlation between frequency of voltage peaks and these of the oscillations leading to contact, even though the voltage signals and vibrational profiles have not been recorded simultaneously (however, all parameters wind speed, plant position, etc. were kept constant). The results clearly show that higher wind speed leads to higher vibrational amplitudes and higher contact-separation frequencies, which correspondingly creates higher voltage signals. This confirms that the biohybrid mechanical system that can be explained by two oscillators that are constrained at one point - leaf and artificial leaf fixed at the petiole, is essential for the energy generation, next to materials, electrodes etc. It must be furthermore considered that not only leaf but also the branch movements as well as the turbulent air flows around the plant leaves and the branches are a key driving force influencing this system. This indicates that optimizing the artificial component such as by tailoring its natural frequency can be an option to further elevate the power generation, which will be part of our future investigations including detailed elaborations of the power spectrum and events such as frequency coupling. Moreover, the correlation suggests the opportunity to predict power outputs by observing leaf oscillations for example as function of the wind speed in a location of interest before installing the entire system.

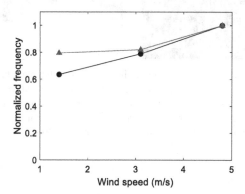

Fig. 4. Comparison and correlation of frequency of positive voltage peaks (black circles) and contact events (red triangles) in the vibrational profiles of the leaves as function of wind speed. (Color figure online)

3.4   Powering LEDs and a Thermal Sensor Under Wind Excitation

The biohybrid wind energy harvesters are capable of directly powering electronic devices from wind energy like LEDs and a digital thermometer as shown in Fig. 5. Therefore, a *N. oleander* plant was modified with four artificial leaves. Both, plant and artificial leaf, were connected to a diode bridge and 50 LEDs or a 50 μF capacitor respectively and exposed to an airflow of ~3 m/s. The LEDs light up discontinuously at each contact and release event between artificial leaf and plant leaf when the power output peaks. The capacitor charges to 1.5 V in only ~15 min providing enough energy for driving the sensing circuit of the digital thermometer including the display showing the reading. This indicates the capability for accumulating sufficient energy for sensing tasks using a plant under wind excitation modified with few artificial leaves pointing towards a perspective power source for sensor networks and environmental monitoring.

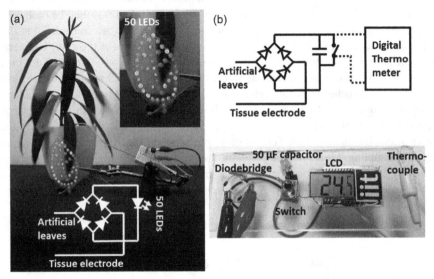

Fig. 5. Powering (a) 50 LEDs and (b) a digital thermometer with a plant biohybrid wind energy harvester using the indicated circuits. A *N. oleander* plant was equipped with four artificial leaves and exposed to wind of ~3 m/s. The LEDs light up instantaneously at each contact between leaf and artificial leaf and the 50 μF capacitor powering the digital thermometer was charged to 1.5 V in about 15 min sufficient to power the sensing circuit for about 20 s.

4   Conclusions

Biohybrid wind energy generators based on living plants provide the opportunity to harvest energy from plant leaf motions as they establish a triboelectric generator. We performed energy harvesting experiments with three different plant species confirming that an electrode at the stem penetrating the bark towards the inner plant tissues is most efficient for harvesting the plant-generated electricity. A biohybrid wind generator was assembled of an artificial leaf consisting of a PET/ITO/silicone rubber that vibrates in the wind together with a plant leaf and the wind induced voltage signals reflect the mechanical interplay of the artificial and the natural leaf. Increasing the wind speed leads to higher energy, amplitude and frequency of both, voltage signal and vibrational profiles. This confirms that the energy generated by the plant correlates with the wind-induced leaf motions indicating a perspective for tailoring the power output by tailoring the mechanical behavior of the system. A single biohybrid plant wind generator is capable of providing sufficient energy to directly power 50 LEDs and a digital thermometer sensing circuit and display. The results demonstrate that living plant-based wind generators are potential autonomous power sources, e.g., for sensor networks and environmental monitoring.

Acknowledgments. This work was funded by GrowBot, the European Union's Horizon 2020 Research and Innovation Programme under Grant Agreement No 824074. TS acknowledges additional funding by the German Research Foundation (DFG) under Germany's Excellence Strategy - EXC-2193/ 1-390951807.

References

1. Giraldo, J.P., Wu, H., Newkirk, G.M., Kruss, S.: Nanobiotechnology approaches for engineering smart plant sensors. Nat. Nanotechnol. **14**, 541–553 (2019). https://doi.org/10.1038/s41565-019-0470-6
2. Wong, M.H., et al.: Nitroaromatic detection and infrared communication from wild-type plants using plant nanobionics. Nat. Mater. **16**, 264–272 (2017). https://doi.org/10.1038/nmat4771
3. Kwak, S.-Y., et al.: A nanobionic light-emitting plant. Nano Lett. **17**, 7951–7961 (2017). https://doi.org/10.1021/acs.nanolett.7b04369
4. Di Giacomo, R., Daraio, C., Maresca, B.: Plant nanobionic materials with a giant temperature response mediated by pectin-Ca^{2+}. Proc. Natl. Acad. Sci. **112**, 4541–4545 (2015). https://doi.org/10.1073/pnas.1421020112
5. Kim, J.J., Allison, L.K., Andrew, T.L.: Vapor-printed polymer electrodes for long-term, on-demand health monitoring. Sci. Adv. **5**, eaaw0463 (2019). https://doi.org/10.1126/sciadv.aaw0463
6. Stavrinidou, E., et al.: Electronic plants. Sci. Adv. **1**, e1501136 (2015). https://doi.org/10.1126/sciadv.1501136
7. Stavrinidou, E., et al.: In vivo polymerization and manufacturing of wires and supercapacitors in plants. Proc. Natl. Acad. Sci. **114**, 2807–2812 (2017). https://doi.org/10.1073/pnas.1616456114
8. Thomas, T., Lew, S., Koman, V.B., Gordiichuk, P., Park, M., Strano, M.S.: The emergence of plant nanobionics and living plants as technology. Adv. Mater. Technol. **1900657**, 1–12 (2019). https://doi.org/10.1002/admt.201900657
9. Nitisoravut, R., Regmi, R.: Plant microbial fuel cells: a promising biosystems engineering. Renew. Sustain. Energy Rev. **76**, 81–89 (2017). https://doi.org/10.1016/j.rser.2017.03.064
10. Strik, D.P., Timmers, R.A., Helder, M., Steinbusch, K.J., Hamelers, H.V., Buisman, C.J.: Microbial solar cells: applying photosynthetic and electrochemically active organisms. Trends Biotechnol. **29**, 41–49 (2011). https://doi.org/10.1016/j.tibtech.2010.10.001

11. Strik, D.P.B.T.B., Bert, H.V.M.H., Snel, J.F.H., Buisman, C.J.N.: Green electricity production with living plants and bacteria in a fuel cell. Int. J. Energy Res. **32**, 870–876 (2008). https://doi.org/10.1002/er.1397

12. Deng, H., Chen, Z., Zhao, F.: Energy from plants and microorganisms: progress in plant - microbial fuel cells. Chemsuschem **5**, 1006–1011 (2012). https://doi.org/10.1002/cssc.201 100257

13. McCormick, A.J., Bombelli, P., Bradley, R.W., Thorne, R., Wenzele, T., Howe, C.J.: Biophotovoltaics: oxygenic photosynthetic organisms in the world of bioelectrochemical systems. Energy Environ. Sci. **8**, 1092–1109 (2015). https://doi.org/10.1039/C4EE03875D

14. Mershin, A., et al.: Self-assembled photosystem-I biophotovoltaics on nanostructured TiO 2 and ZnO. Sci. Rep. **2**, 234 (2012). https://doi.org/10.1038/srep00234

15. Tschörtner, J., Lai, B., Krömer, J.O.: Biophotovoltaics: green power generation from sunlight and water. Front. Microbiol. **10**, 866 (2019). https://doi.org/10.3389/fmicb.2019.00866

16. Flexer, V., Mano, N.: From dynamic measurements of photosynthesis in a living plant to sunlight transformation into electricity. Anal. Chem. **82**, 1444–1449 (2010). https://doi.org/10.1021/ac902537h

17. Miyake, T., et al.: Enzymatic biofuel cells designed for direct power generation from biofluids in living organisms. Energy Environ. Sci. **4**, 5008–5012 (2011). https://doi.org/10.1039/c1e e02200h

18. Meder, F., et al.: Energy conversion at the cuticle of living plants. Adv. Funct. Mater. **28**, 1806689 (2018). https://doi.org/10.1002/adfm.201806689

19. Meder, F., Thielen, M., Mondini, A., Speck, T., Mazzolai, B.: Living plant-hybrid generators for multidirectional wind energy conversion. Energy Technol. **8**, 2000236 (2020). https://doi.org/10.1002/ente.202000236

20. Riederer, M., Müller, C. (eds.) Biology of the Plant Cuticle. Annual Plant Reviews, vol. 23. Blackwell Publishing, Oxford (2006).

21. Kim, D.W., Kim, S., Jeong, U.: Lipids: source of static electricity of regenerative natural substances and nondestructive energy harvesting. Adv. Mater. **30**, 1804949 (2018). https://doi.org/10.1002/adma.201804949

22. Wu, C., Wang, A.C., Ding, W., Guo, H., Wang, Z.L.: Triboelectric nanogenerator: a foundation of the energy for the new era. Adv. Energy Mater. **9**, 1802906 (2019). https://doi.org/10.1002/aenm.201802906

23. Wang, Z.L.: Triboelectric nanogenerators as new energy technology for self-powered chemical sensors. ACS Energy Lett. **7**, 9533–9557 (2013). https://doi.org/10.1021/nn404614z

24. Wang, Z.L., Chen, J., Lin, L.: Progress in triboelectric nanogenertors as new energy technology and self-powered sensors. Energy Environ. Sci. **8**, 2250–2282 (2015). https://doi.org/10.1039/x0xx00000x

25. Ferrari, L.M., et al.: Ultraconformable Temporary Tattoo Electrodes for Electrophysiology. Adv. Sci. **5**, 1–11 (2018). https://doi.org/10.1002/advs.201700771

26. Mousavi, S.A.R., Nguyen, C.T., Farmer, E.E., Kellenberger, S.: Measuring surface potential changes on leaves. Nat. Protoc. **9**, 1997–2004 (2014). https://doi.org/10.1038/nprot.2014.136

Snapshot Navigation in the Wavelet Domain

Stefan Meyer[(⊠)] [iD], Thomas Nowotny[iD], Paul Graham[iD], Alex Dewar[iD], and Andrew Philippides[iD]

University of Sussex, Falmer, Brighton BN1 9RH, UK
s.meyer@sussex.ac.uk

Abstract. Many animals rely on robust visual navigation which can be explained by snapshot models, where an agent is assumed to store egocentric panoramic images and subsequently use them to recover a heading by comparing current views to the stored snapshots. Long-range route navigation can also be explained by such models, by storing multiple snapshots along a training route and comparing the current image to these. For such models, memory capacity and comparison time increase dramatically with route length, rendering them unfeasible for small-brained insects and low-power robots where computation and storage are limited. One way to reduce the requirements is to use a compressed image representation. Inspired by the filter bank-like arrangement of the visual system, we here investigate how a frequency-based image representation influences the performance of a typical snapshot model. By decomposing views into wavelet coefficients at different levels and orientations, we achieve a compressed visual representation that remains robust when used for navigation. Our results indicate that route following based on wavelet coefficients is not only possible but gives increased performance over a range of other models.

Keywords: Insect navigation · Visual homing · Wavelet

1 Introduction

Many insects use view-based route following as part of their navigational toolkit [11,13,35] and it is remarkable that with small brains and low resolution vision their visual route navigation is so efficient and robust [5]. The first computational model of insect visual navigation is the *snapshot model* [4]. This has inspired a series of view-based models. For example [2,3] have modelled how ants might store a set of views to guide them on long routes. Here, it is assumed that the ant stores snapshots experienced during route traversal. When lost, the ant recovers the right orientation by comparing rotated versions of its current view with all

This work was funded by the EPSRC (grant EP/P006094/1) and a University of Sussex scholarship.

V. Vouloutsi et al. (Eds.): Living Machines 2020, LNAI 12413, pp. 245–256, 2020.
https://doi.org/10.1007/978-3-030-64313-3_24

views in memory. The rotation that minimises the difference, or is the most familiar, yields the direction in which the ant should move [2,3,36].

Animals or robots implementing view-based homing face challenges in the memory capacity needed to store views, as well as the computational power to quickly compare them. For snapshot type models, the required memory increases with route length and so does comparison time [1]. Attempts to mitigate this effect have been made, by using different architectures of neural networks. One example would be the use of an infomax model [2,15] to learn a familiarity function for each route. Instead of storing all views this model was trained with route views, such that it can output a familiarity value for any view, and use this for orientation recovery. Storing route views implicitly in an adjustable network like this allows for fixed memory size and comparison time up to a maximum of route length.

Another way of decreasing memory requirements is changing the representation of visual scenes. Many view-based models operate on pixel space [8,32,36]. However, due to its anatomy the insect visual system is highly unlikely to store and compare images in this way. Experimental evidence instead suggests that it implements a system of visual filters [24,25,30], which process views to compressed representations formed by the filter outputs. Image differences can then be calculated in the co-domain of this new mapping. Typical examples of such a visual mapping include frequency based approaches like Fourier [6], Zernike [12] and Wavelet [16] transforms.

Fourier encoded views have been used in robotics in the context of place recognition in the past (e.g. [18]) and adapted for visual homing [27,31]. Extending on these findings, Zernike moments have been found to change between two locations in a way that allows to derive a homing direction [29,33] and similar results have been reported for homing based on a subset of Haar wavelet responses [14].

Fourier transforms provide information about which frequencies occur in a signal, but do not convey any localisation of these frequencies (note, "localisation" here is used in accordance with the signal processing literature to denote the occurrence of a frequency in sample space and not the position of an agent). By contrast, the wavelet transform enables one to localise frequencies. This is done by convolving the input signal with discretely shifted and scaled versions of piecewise continuous functions called wavelets [16]. This property allows one to create a series of filters in a sub-band coding scheme [34], where each filter response yields a coefficient magnitude representing the occurrence of a certain frequency at a given location. Retaining the location of visual information is useful for navigation models (e.g. [23]).

To investigate frequency based image representations for route navigation, we trial a sparse wavelet based representation of views for route following. We chose filters corresponding to 'Haar' wavelets [10] which are plausible approximations to filters that are implemented in the visual system of an insect. Furthermore, they are well localised in space which for spatial tasks may be more important than precise information in the frequency domain. We compare the performance of wavelets, for both single and multi-snapshot navigation, to a series of pixel-based approaches including low-resolution features and skyline representations. We show that wavelets improve navigational performance suggesting promise for future, computationally efficient, navigation models.

2   Methods

In order to investigate frequency based navigation, we utilised seven models of snapshot based route navigation, each of which operated on a different representation of images. The first stage of navigation is for the agent to traverse a pre-defined route (in ants this would be guided by path integration) during which the information needed for later visual navigation is stored. Here we collect images periodically along the route, and use these, after image processing, which is the key part of the investigation, as the stored snapshots.

Models: In order to retrieve a movement direction on a memorized route, a model M maps an image I_Y to T_Y under different rotations r, compares it to a stored snapshot T_X, and returns the rotation $\hat{r}$ that minimises the Rotational Image Difference Function (RIDF) ξ (similar to [36]). In this way a snapshot can be used to recall the direction the agent was facing when the snapshot was stored, also known as a visual compass. We measure performance by calculating the absolute angular error $|\hat{r} - r^*|$ between the angle $\hat{r}$ that minimises the RIDF and the true bearing r^*, which is known for each location. Small values correspond to small errors and can be interpreted as robust orientation recovery.

The most simple model M_{px} is directly operating in pixel space [2]. Comparison and storage are both realised in pixel space, such that the resulting RIDF is given by

$$\xi_{px}(I_X, I_Y, r) = \frac{1}{H * W} \sum_{h}^{H} \sum_{w}^{W} (I_X[w, h] - I_Y^r[w, h])^2 \tag{1}$$

where $I_x[w, h]$ is a pixel value at width w and height h of the snapshot image, $I_y^r[w, h]$ is the pixel value of the current view rotated by r, H is the number of rows and W is the number of columns.

Next, we used three wavelet based models in order to analyse whether and how spatial localization of frequencies can be useful for orientation recovery. Specifically, we used the discrete wavelet transform (DWT) [26]. In order to perform a DWT on an image, it is treated as a 2D signal, where rows and columns are processed separately. Hence, high-pass filter responses at different orientations represent horizontal, vertical and diagonal details (edges), while the low-pass response remains an image approximation (blurred version of the original image). This approximation can be used as input for the next level of filter banks. Each of our three wavelet based models $M_{wv}^{L^*}$ extracts detail coefficients for each orientation (vertical, horizontal, diagonal) for a single level of interest L^* by performing a Haar [10] wavelet based DWT on the image I up to level L^*. It then omits all coefficients for which $L < L^*$ and sets the approximation matrix $c_a(L^*)$ to 0. The remaining coefficients are then shaped into a representation matrix C of size $P \times K$ where $P = \frac{H}{2^{L-1}}$ and $k = \frac{W}{2^{L-1}}$, consisting of 4 coefficient block matrices 0, $c_v(L^*)$, $c_h(L^*)$, $c_d(L^*)$ of size $\frac{P}{2} \times \frac{K}{2}$ representing the orientational coefficients.

$$C(L^*) = \begin{bmatrix} 0 & c_v(L^*) \\ c_h(L^*) & c_d(L^*) \end{bmatrix} \tag{2}$$

For each block matrix, the 1% largest absolute coefficients are determined and the magnitude of the lowest of these is selected as a threshold: Every coefficient in the block that has smaller absolute value is set to zero. The resulting RIDF for any L^* is then given as:

$$\xi_{wv}(C_X, C_Y, r) = \frac{1}{P * K} \sum_p^P \sum_k^K (C_X[p, k] - C_Y^r[p, k]) \tag{3}$$

where C_X and C_Y^r are the coefficient matrices for the view at the origin and the view at the displaced location with orientation r, respectively. It is worth mentioning that rotation is applied to the image before coefficient extraction. It can also easily be seen that ξ_{wv} can be applied in an analogous way to each coefficient block matrix in an isolated fashion, which allows one to analyse the RIDF of each set of coefficients separately. In our experiments we used models with $L=1$, $L=2$ and $L=3$ (filter width 2, 4 and 8 pixel respectively) as models with higher values for L performed poorly in pilot studies. The DWT is performed with MatLab's Wavelet Toolbox.

In order to get an understanding of how much accuracy is lost when discarding the approximation matrix, we additionally used a model M_{gauss} that would use a Gaussian filter on an image with a filter width of $\sigma = 5$ (determined experimentally), limiting the input signal to its lower frequency band. In addition, we compare our results to models which use the height of the skyline, a feature ants can use to navigate [9,21], and which can be viewed as a low spatial frequency signal composed of oriented UV-contrast edges, which the ant visual system is tuned to [7,19,20,22,27,28]. Our final two models, therefore, consist of two approaches for extracting the skyline height in our virtual environment. M_{st} scans an image columnwise from the top until it encounters a pixel that is not sky coloured. The skyline value $S[w]$ at a specific image column w is then given by the difference between height H and the index h of the encountered non-sky pixel. Repeating this procedure for each column of the image will result in a vector S of size $1 \times W$. In an analogous way, M_{sb} scans an image columnwise from the bottom up, until it encounters a pixel that is sky coloured. The resulting RIDF $\xi_s(S_X, S_Y)$ is given as the mean squared error between S_X and S_Y.

Simulated Environment: AntWorld. Experiments are conducted in a virtual environment (AntWorld, Fig. 1), which was reconstructed from an ant field-site in Spain [17]. Lacking major landmarks, the world contains open areas filled with

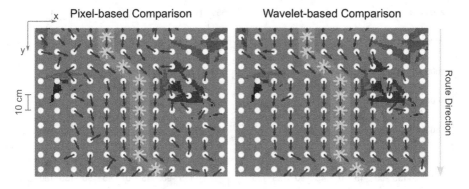

Fig. 1. Example route segments in the AntWorld. White dots show locations on the grid and turquoise dots are points on the route, in this case Route 2 (turquoise corridor). Each position in the vicinity of the route has a red arrow which shows the heading taken by an agent navigating by minimising the RIDF, using the respective view at the turquoise location as training data, with either unprocessed views (Pixel-based Comparison, left panel) or views encoded using wavelets (Wavelet-based Comparison, right panel). Green patches indicate vegetation from the AntWorld simulation. (Color figure online)

occasional and clumped grass tussocks (green patches in Fig. 1). To compare different algorithm variants quickly and objectively, we use views that would be perceived by an agent from 10 cm grid of positions (dots in Fig. 1) for training and testing the navigation algorithms. These views are 360° panoramic greyscale images with a resolution of 720×150 pixels. For testing the algorithms, we generated 4 experimental routes consisting of a series of adjacent points on the grid (turquoise dots in Fig. 1) with the bearing of the agent r^* at each position defined as the direction from the current route point to the next one (red arrows in Fig. 1). To test the algorithms, we used 8 laterally displaced copies of the route (each displaced by 10 cm, up 40 cm in both lateral directions, white dots in Fig. 1) with the "true" bearing of these points set to the bearing of the nearest route point.

3   Results

RIDF: We first investigated how a wavelet based representation of visual input influences navigation in the AntWorld, starting by investigating the shape of the RIDFs when using a single snapshot. To do this we used a view at a typical location and calculated the RIDF ξ_{px} and ξ_{wv} with nearby views. We then compared the heading recovered from the RIDF (i.e. the angle at which the minimum of the RIDFs occurred), $\hat{r}$, with the known target heading r^*. While the direction $\hat{r}_{px}$ for the pixel based RIDF ξ_{px} diverges from the true bearing with increasing distance (Fig. 2.a), the wavelet based RIDF ξ_{wv} maintains a pronounced minimum close to r^* (Fig. 2.b) even when distant from the snapshot location.

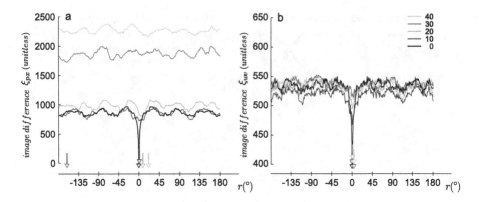

Fig. 2. Rotational Image Difference Functions for pixelwise and wavelet matching. RIDF ξ for 0 cm (black), 10 cm (brown), 20 cm (turquoise), 30 cm (purple) and 40 cm (yellow) displacement from the route, for M_{px} (a) and M_{wv}^1 (b). Coloured arrows indicate the direction r^* that minimises the respective RIDF. (Color figure online)

Furthermore, we observed ξ_{px} to be smoother than any $\xi_{wv(L^*)}$. The calculation of the RIDF in pixel-space involves division by the number of pixels, therefore differences produced by displaced edges do not affect the overall shape much because large homogeneously coloured surfaces of objects raise no difference. On the other hand, wavelet coefficients of level 1 represent the fine details results in large coefficients at edges of objects and not on smooth surfaces. Hence in a rotational movement, every edge contributes considerably to the RIDF, which leads to a more jagged appearance (Fig. 2.b).

Finally, we note that ξ_{px} saturates for bigger displacements, which likely is a property of our routes and environment. Routes are generated such that they remain in the open and do not cross patches of tussocks. Displacements however lead to views at locations that are close to tussocks. These tussocks occlude large amounts of sky, which increases the value of RIDFs.

In an attempt to further understand why we observe higher accuracy for M_{wv}^1, we selected multiple locations, where the model outperformed M_{px} in terms of angular error. Since the ξ_{wv} is determined by the sum of the orientation specific filter responses, we focused on these first. In order to do so, we split ξ_{wv} (shown in Fig. 3.b) into one RIDF for each orientational filter response $c_v(L^*)$ (vertical), $c_h(L^*)$ (horizontal) and $c_d(L^*)$ (diagonal). In the following paragraph we will describe our results using a representative example location (view shown in Fig. 4) in order to visualise our findings in an instructive way.

We observed that the magnitude of the RIDF for each component differs (see Fig. 3.a).

While the vertical coefficients have the highest magnitude, the shape of the overall RIDF showed a pronounced minimum at the correct rotation (Fig. 3.a, red). Vertical coefficients correspond to vertical edges, which in the environment are related to borders of objects, which in the end determine the visual experience of any agent. Aligning vertical edges is hence similar to aligning objects, which is the underlying principle of visual navigation via landmarks. However, when using wavelet based RIDF it is not necessary to actually detect landmarks in two different views, match them and find the best alignment. Thus we assume that the existence of pronounced objects (like certain patches of tussocks) is the most relevant aspect of the environment determining the shape of the RIDF.

For horizontal features we observe multiple pronounced minima, one of which often occurs close to the true direction. However, the global minimum can often lead to erroneous orientation recovery (as seen in the example Fig. 3.a, blue), when not paired with vertical components. Furthermore, we noticed that the difference between the rotation of the global minimum and the rotation of the next lowest local minimum is smaller for vertical than for horizontal features. In our environment, horizontal features correspond to the horizon line, and horizontal edges stemming from objects touching the ground. Hence the main factor that determines the shape of the RIDF is the distance of an object and the visibility of its base, as well as the visibility of the horizon in general.

Lastly, diagonal features produce a flat and noisy RIDF, that did not contribute to the location of the global minimum in a meaningful way (Fig. 3.a, black).

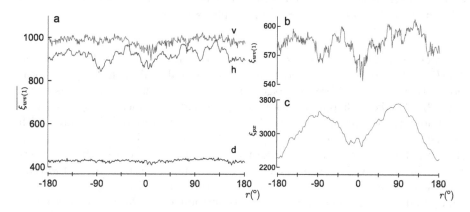

Fig. 3. Decomposed RIDF for separate wavelet components. (a) RIDF for vertical (red, 'v'), horizontal (blue, 'h') and diagonal (black,'d') for separate M_{wv}^1 components at an example position with 0 being the correct orientation. (b) combined RIDF M_{wv}^1 at the same position. (c) RIDF for pixel based model M_{px}. (Color figure online)

After investigating how ξ_{wv} is shaped by its separate components, we next investigated how edge alignment yields more robust orientation recovery. Given our previous results, we focused on the vertical RIDF. We selected points on routes for which $\hat{r}_{px}$ has been erroneous (absolute angular error bigger than 22.5) with regards to lateral displacement, but $\hat{r}_{wv}$ is not. In our experiments, we observed that these positions correspond to locations where displaced positions

Fig. 4. Analysis of recovered headings for wavelet and pixelwise RIDFs. (a.I) snapshot at route location processed by M_{px}. (a.II) View at displaced position (30 cm) in direction r^*, i.e. the correct direction (a.III) View at displaced position in direction $\hat{r}$, set by RIDF minimum with pixelwise matching (a.IV) Difference image between snapshot (a.I) and view with r^* bearing (red colour = larger values in snapshot; blue colour = larger values in view). (a.V) Difference image between snapshot and view with $\hat{r}_{px}$ bearing. (b.I–b.IV) Analogous to (a) but processed by M_{wv}^1.

are in close proximity to tussocks that start to dominate the view (Fig. 4.a.I and 4.a.II). If the object is not as prominent in the visual field at the snapshot location (Fig. 4.a.I), the difference image (Fig. 4.a.IV) -and thus the RIDF- is dominated the pixel difference introduced by the surface of such an object. Hence, $\hat{r}_{px}$ under these circumstances is the heading that overlaps this object with another "dense" and homogeneously coloured structure (Fig. 4.a.II and 4.a.V). However the main part of visual information is often not given by surfaces overlapping in colour, which leads to high angular errors. In contrast, vertical wavelet coefficients represent an image as the magnitude of vertical edges (Fig. 4.b.I), which leads to a different effect. Instead of introducing an overrepresentation of pixels belonging to an object, an object in the wavelet domain results in a few more edges and possibly in the loss of some background edges due to occlusion (see Fig. 4.b.II). While some edges are not visible any more, tussocks in medium proximity dominate the difference image (Fig. 4.a.IV, tussock on the left) and thus the difference function due to their high spatial frequency. We believe this to be the explanation for the increased robustness of M_{wv}^1.

Angular Error Along Routes: In an attempt to connect our findings with regards to the RIDF to route following, we utilised 4 artificial routes. Each route is given by a main path, from which the snapshots are stored, and 4 lateral parallel paths on either side of the training route, spaced by 10 cm, which comprise the test locations. For each test location, we calculated the bearing that results from comparison with the route snapshots and determined the angular error between

$\hat{r}$ and r^* for different models. In addition to the pixel space based model M_{px} and the wavelet coefficients of level 1 one model M_{wv}^1, we also included 5 other models. We used two more wavelet models based on coefficients of level 2 (M_{wv}^2) and level 3 (M_{wv}^3), as well as a model M_g that performed a simple Gaussian low-pass filtering on images, to see how lower frequency components influence robustness. Furthermore, we used two different methods to extract the skyline height from images (scanning from top - M_{st} and scanning from bottom - M_{sb}) and calculated ξ_{st} and ξ_{sb} from this one-dimensional input, to see how much information is provided by the shape of objects in front of the sky and the horizon.

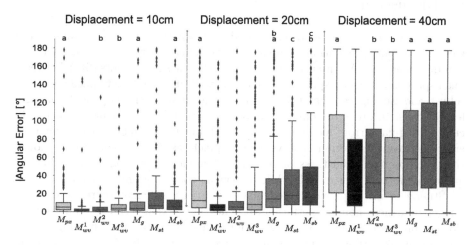

Fig. 5. Overall accuracy of heading recovery for different models. Angular error for different models (box labels) with increasing displacement (panels) from snapshot location as boxplots. Data is aggregated from 4 routes and displacements to either side of the route. In each panel, boxes sharing letters do not have significantly different medians. Boxes that do not share letters are significantly different (p-value < 0.05, Kruskal-Wallis test). n = 139 for each condition. (Color figure online)

For each channel and model, we collected the respective $\hat{r}$ and calculated the angular error at the 139 locations per channel. We then determined the median and the interquartile range (IQR) and visualised the distributions as boxplots (Fig. 5). While IQR and median absolute angular error increased for each model with increased displacement from the route, the wavelet based models consistently show a lower IQR and median when compared to other models (Fig. 5, red boxes). Indeed, with increased limitation to the lower frequency band of the signal (as given by M_{wv}^2, M_{wv}^3 and M_g) we observe increased angular errors, indicating that high frequencies may carry important information about the environment. It is noteworthy however, that M_{wv}^2 performed similar to M_{wv}^1, offering the possibility of a simpler (lower resolution) option to decrease angular errors. Across all experiments we observe that skyline height based models M_{st} and M_{sb}) are not robust when compared to raw pixel space. This is a strong indication that the skyline height without further processing is not a robust feature for orientation recovery at least in this simulated world.

All models show a noticeable amount of data points outside the 1.5 IQR interval. Upon closer inspection of our environment and routes we have been able to identify different types of locations responsible for this. Quiver plots (see e.g. Fig. 1) reveal that most of these are in regions where paths cross through virtual tussocks, leading to strong occlusion effects which impair the validity of image based comparison for all models.

4   Discussion

Here we investigate how a wavelet based representation might be suitable for view based route navigation with the goal of increasing robustness against lateral displacements. We first observed how RIDFs at single points differ between pixel space and wavelet space. We found that RIDFs in wavelet space are more robust and we suggest that this is mainly due to vertical components of high level details. In order to connect our results with route following we then calculated angular errors along routes with lateral displacements and compared errors between a selection of wavelet- and pixel-based models. We have shown that the observed robustness of the wavelet model extends to route following and outperforms other models while increasing computational efficiency.

Stuerzl et al. [31] investigated how a Fourier coefficient representation of images influences homing performance. They found that frequency representations of images can be used effectively for snapshot-based visual homing (using the difference between Fourier components as a proxy for image difference). These results support the idea of using frequency components for visual navigation. However, a drawback of Fourier analysis is the inability to localise frequencies in an image, which makes it difficult to localise salient image components. An alternative to Fourier coefficients was introduced in [14], who extracted localised Haar-like image descriptors at random points in a snapshot and used responses to these filters to determine familiarity and ultimately derive a homing direction. In contrast, we used filter responses of one level of detail throughout and applied them to the whole image. Furthermore, our environment, though virtual, was adopted from a real ant site and is notably different from the toy world used by [31] and the office environment used by [14,31]. Similar to [29], who observed an increased catchment area when using Zernike Moments, we observed increased robustness against displacement from the original route when using wavelet coefficients. The core difference between their work and ours is that they used summed Zernike Moments, leading to a rotation invariant representation of an image, which wavelets are not. Thus, when compared to the results reported by [14,29,31] for visual homing, our findings yield additional evidence that frequency based features are useful and in particular can be applied successfully to route following methods that rely on recovering headings.

In future work, we will optimise the wavelet approach for navigation in the real world. For instance, we intend to introduce a more elaborate mapping from wavelet coefficients to deriving a bearing and we will combine orientational features from different levels, which will add more energy from the lower frequencies which contain important information [31]. Finally, wavelets could be combined with an infomax learning rule [2] or a neural network (NN) trained to recall the route [23]. Alternatively, they could be used as the input to a biologically plausible network such as a mushroom body model [1]. As wavelets can be seen as analogous to the processing performed in the early stages of vision, optimising the wavelet coefficients or type for different NNs could not only improve navigation performance in robots but also shed light on aspects of the visual processing in insects.

References

1. Ardin, P., Peng, F., Mangan, M., Lagogiannis, K., Webb, B.: Using an insect mushroom body circuit to encode route memory in complex natural environments. PLOS Comput. Biol. **12**(2), 1–22 (2016)
2. Baddeley, B., Graham, P., Husbands, P., Philippides, A.: A model of ant route navigation driven by scene familiarity. PLOS Comput. Biol. **8**(1), 1–16 (2012)
3. Baddeley, B., Graham, P., Philippides, A., Husbands, P.: Holistic visual encoding of ant-like routes: navigation without waypoints. Adapt. Behav. **19**(1), 3–15 (2011)
4. Cartwright, B.A., Collett, T.S.: Landmark learning in bees. J. Comp. Physiol. **151**(4), 521–543 (1983)
5. Collett, T.S., Graham, P., Durier, V.: Route learning by insects. Curr. Opin. Neurobiol. **13**(6), 718–725 (2003)
6. Cooley, J.W., Tukey, J.W.: An algorithm for the machine calculation of complex Fourier series. Math. Comput. **19**(90), 297–301 (1965)
7. Differt, D., Möller, R.: Insect models of illumination-invariant skyline extraction from UV and green channels. J. Theor. Biol. **380**, 444–462 (2015)
8. Franz, M.O., Schölkopf, B., Mallot, H.A., Bülthoff, H.H.: Where did I take that snapshot? Scene-based homing by image matching. Biol. Cybern. **79**(3), 191–202 (1998)
9. Graham, P., Cheng, K.: Ants use the panoramic skyline as a visual cue during navigation. Curr. Biol. **19**(20), R935–R937 (2009)
10. Haar, A.: Zur Theorie der orthogonalen Funktionensysteme. Georg-August-Universitat, Gottingen (1909)
11. Harrison, J.F., Fewell, J.H., Stiller, T.M., Breed, M.D.: Effects of experience on use of orientation cues in the giant tropical ant. Anim. Behav. (1989)
12. Khotanzad, A., Hong, Y.H.: Invariant image recognition by Zernike moments. IEEE Trans. Pattern Anal. Mach. Intell. **12**(5), 489–497 (1990)
13. Klotz, J.: Topographic orientation in two species of ants (hymenoptera: Formicidae). Insectes Soc. **34**(4), 236–251 (1987)
14. Lee, C., Kim, D.: Visual homing navigation with Haar-like features in the snapshot. IEEE Access **6**, 33666–33681 (2018)
15. Lulham, A., Bogacz, R., Vogt, S., Brown, M.W.: An infomax algorithm can perform both familiarity discrimination and feature extraction in a single network. Neural Comput. **23**(4), 909–926 (2011)
16. Mallat, S.G.: A theory for multiresolution signal decomposition: the wavelet representation. IEEE Trans. Pattern Anal. Mach. Intell. **11**(7), 674–693 (1989)

17. Mangan, M., Webb, B.: Spontaneous formation of multiple routes in individual desert ants (cataglyphis velox). Behav. Ecol. **23**(5), 944–954 (2012)

18. Menegatti, E., Maeda, T., Ishiguro, H.: Image-based memory for robot navigation using properties of omnidirectional images. Robot. Auton. Syst. **47**(4), 251–267 (2004)

19. Möller, R.: Insects could exploit UV-green contrast for landmark navigation. J. Theor. Biol. **214**(4), 619–631 (2002)

20. Mote, M.I., Wehner, R.: Functional characteristics of photoreceptors in the compound eye and ocellus of the desert ant, cataglyphis bicolor. J. Comput. Physiol. **137**(1), 63–71 (1980)

21. Müller, M.M., Bertrand, O.J.N., Differt, D., Egelhaaf, M.: The problem of home choice in skyline-based homing. PLOS ONE **13**(3), 1–20 (2018)

22. Ogawa, Y., Falkowski, M., Narendra, A., Zeil, J., Hemmi, J.M.: Three spectrally distinct photoreceptors in diurnal and nocturnal Australian ants. Proc. R. Soc. B: Biol. Sci. **282**(1808), 20150673 (2015)

23. Philippides, A., Graham, P., Baddeley, B., Husbands, P.: Using neural networks to understand the information that guides behavior: a case study in visual navigation. In: Cartwright, H. (ed.) Artificial Neural Networks. MMB, vol. 1260, pp. 227–244. Springer, New York (2015). https://doi.org/10.1007/978-1-4939-2239-0_14

24. Roper, M., Fernando, C., Chittka, L.: Insect bio-inspired neural network provides new evidence on how simple feature detectors can enable complex visual generalization and stimulus location invariance in the miniature brain of honeybees. PLoS Comput. Biol. **13**(2), e1005333 (2017)

25. Seelig, J.D., Jayaraman, V.: Neural dynamics for landmark orientation and angular path integration. Nature **521**(7551), 186–191 (2015)

26. Shensa, M.J., et al.: The discrete wavelet transform: wedding the a trous and Mallat algorithms. IEEE Trans. Signal Process. **40**(10), 2464–2482 (1992)

27. Stone, T., Differt, D., Milford, M., Webb, B.: Skyline-based localisation for aggressively manoeuvring robots using UV sensors and spherical harmonics. In: 2016 IEEE International Conference on Robotics and Automation (ICRA), pp. 5615–5622 (2016)

28. Stone, T., Mangan, M., Ardin, P., Webb, B.: Sky segmentation with ultraviolet images can be used for navigation. In: Robotics: Science and Systems, Berkeley, USA (2014)

29. Stone, T., Mangan, M., Wystrach, A., Webb, B.: Rotation invariant visual processing for spatial memory in insects. Interface Focus **8**(4), 20180010 (2018)

30. Strother, J., Nern, A., Reiser, M.: Direct observation of on and off pathways in the drosophila visual system. Curr. Biol. **24**(9), 976–983 (2014)

31. Stuerzl, W., Mallot, H.: Efficient visual homing based on Fourier transformed panoramic images. Robot. Auton. Syst. **54**(4), 300–313 (2006)

32. Stuerzl, W., Zeil, J.: Depth, contrast and view-based homing in outdoor scenes. Biol. Cybern. **96**(5), 519–531 (2007)

33. Sun, X., Yue, S., Mangan, M.: A decentralised neural model explaining optimal integration of navigational strategies in insects. eLife **9**, e54026 (2020)

34. Vetterli, M., Kovacevic, J.: Wavelets and Subband Coding. Prentice-hall PTR (1995)

35. Wehner, R., Michel, B., Antonsen, P.: Visual navigation in insects: coupling of egocentric and geocentric information. J. Exp. Biol. **199**(1), 129–140 (1996)

36. Zeil, J., Hofmann, M.I., Chahl, J.S.: Catchment areas of panoramic snapshots in outdoor scenes. J. Opt. Soc. Am. A: **20**(3), 450–469 (2003)

Optimization of Artificial Muscle Placements for a Humanoid Bipedal Robot

Connor Morrow$^{(\boxtimes)}$ ⓘ, Benjamin Bolen ⓘ, and Alexander J. Hunt ⓘ

Department of Mechanical and Materials Engineering, Portland State University,
Portland, OR 97207, USA
comorrow@pdx.edu

Abstract. This work demonstrates an algorithm that is able to compute optimal placement for braided pneumatic actuators on a bipedal robot in order to emulate the biology of human legs. The algorithm calculates the torque that muscles are able to generate about a series of joints (back, hip, knee, ankle, subtalar, and metatarsophalangeal) in a human model. It then compares these torques to the torque that is achievable by a reduced number of pneumatic muscles actuating a bipedal robot model and optimizes the results to reduce the error between the robot and human model. The algorithm successfully finds new muscle placements that will be used in physical testing to verify that the torque output is correct and matches similarly to human capabilities. The algorithm was performed for three muscles about the back (lumbrosacral) joint: erector spinae, internal oblique, and external oblique. It generates placements capable of producing torque profiles that are more biologically realistic than the previously hand placed locations. Currently, the algorithm is not prevented from placing muscle paths that intersect the physical structure. This work will enable the development of controllable, physical models that more accurately capture force and torque capabilities of human muscles. Such physical models will enable more complete testing of how the nervous system performs effective control of over-actuated muscle systems, and if such systems have advantages for robotic applications.

Keywords: Biomimetic robotics · Optimization algorithm · Pneumatic artificial muscle · Braided pneumatic actuator · Opensim · Matlab

1 Introduction

Biomimetic robots are an important topic of research to the robotics community, due to their proposed ability to navigate through environments that are difficult for traditional robots. Robots have trouble navigating through spaces that contain uneven surfaces or stairs, as well as areas in which there is a transition

© Springer Nature Switzerland AG 2020
V. Vouloutsi et al. (Eds.): Living Machines 2020, LNAI 12413, pp. 257–269, 2020.
https://doi.org/10.1007/978-3-030-64313-3_25

between solid ground and something more unstable, such as concrete to sand [3]. Biomimetic robots hope to bridge the gap between what traditional robots are capable of and the adaptable nature that living organisms represent [1, 2, 11]. Biomimetic robots also serve a very important function in providing insight as to how biology works. By creating robotics that replicate animal physiology, we can test a variety of different hypotheses, such as how organic features help organisms navigate through their environment [8, 18], or how the nervous system controls rhythmic behavior [12, 16].

By developing a robot based on the human anatomy of the legs, pelvis, and back, we can begin to develop a robot that could easily navigate through a variety of different terrains and environments, while also learning about muscle coordination in humans that control smooth motions such as gait. This biomimetic robot will also allow us to investigate how central pattern generators (CPGs) produce and modulate gait [6, 13]. We can also produce results that will give more insight as to why organisms have biarticulate musculature [5]. In order to create this platform for testing these hypotheses, we must first work towards creating a physical structure with high fidelity to human anatomy that can closely mimic human movement patterns.

This work describes an iterative algorithm whose goal is to determine pneumatic artificial muscle (PAM) placement and orientation on a robot that result in torque profiles about lower body joints that closely match the torque profiles of a human. PAMs are a way of replicating muscle driven actuation that is seen in humans [14, 17]. The human model from which this work is based has 92 Hill-type muscle actuators controlling the lumbrosacral and leg joints [7]. The robot in development has reduced this to 54 muscle actuators [2]. However, even with the reduction in the number of planned muscles, it becomes a tedious and time consuming task to position PAM attachment locations by hand to find locations that best capture human torque capabilities and also represents a reasonably constructed robot model. This algorithm speeds up the development and construction of a biomimetic bipedal robot by determining the optimal placement of PAMs to best meet human capabilities.

2   Methods

The optimization algorithm was created in Matlab [15]. It begins with a calculation of the maximum torque that can be developed by human muscles about a each joint of the lower body: lumbrosacral, hip, knee, ankle, subtalar, and MTP. This torque calculation is determined by the muscle locations found in OpenSim model Gait2392 [4], through the methods described by Bolen and Hunt [2]. The algorithm then begins to systematically move muscle attachment points while minimizing a cost function. Figure 1 shows images of the robot in development as well as detailing the attachment points that are being optimized with this work.

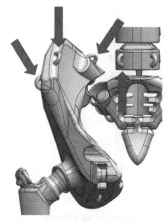

(a) Solidworks render of the bipedal robot.

(b) Zoom of the hip structure for the bipedal robot. The arrows indicate PAM attachment points.

Fig. 1. Solidworks models of the bipedal robot in development. The robot will replicate human features and will have attachment points for PAMs.

2.1 Human and Previous Robot Models

The optimization algorithm begins with calculating the maximum torque generated about each joint in a human model. The human model muscle locations come from the OpenSim model Gait2392 (Fig. 2a). The methods for calculating torque about a joint come from Hoy et al. [9]. To calculate the torque about each joint from a given muscle, a moment arm is calculated, originating from the center of rotation of the joint to the line of action of the muscle passing over it. The line of action of the muscle is calculated by creating a vector from the attachment point of the muscle prior to the joint to the attachment point after the joint. The moment arm is then calculated by taking the cross product of the unit vector of the muscle line of action and the axis of rotation of the joint. This moment arm is then multiplied by the maximum isometric force that the muscle can generate to calculate the torque. Because the moment arm changes as the joint moves through a rotation, the calculation has to be done for every orientation of the joint. This orientation is discretized in 100 joint positions for

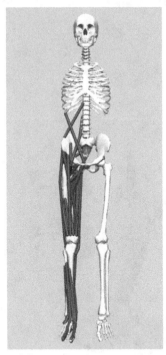

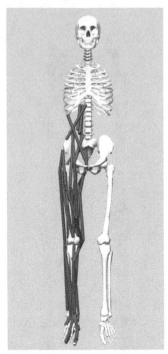

(a) Muscle placement on a
human model

(b) PAM placement on previous
robot model

Fig. 2. (a) The muscle placements on Gait2392 in OpenSim. (b) The muscle placements from Bolen and Hunt[2]. Both figures only show the muscles used for the right side of the body.

the purposes of the algorithm. For joints with more than one degree of freedom, the discretization is done for each degree of freedom.

The robot model that was developed by Bolen and Hunt reduced the number of muscles in Gait2392, going from 92 muscles to 54 (Fig. 2b). In their procedure, individual attachment points of each PAM were hand placed, with the goal of maintaining similar torque profiles about each joint in the robot model when compared to the human model. These muscle placements in OpenSim would then correlate with the placement of PAMs on a physical robot. The PAMs that will be used for the physical robot are Festo braided pneumatic actuators (BPAs). The BPAs have a range of diameters and the ones intended for use are 10 mm, 20 mm, and 40 mm. The maximum torque each PAM is able to provide is calculated similarly to the way the muscle torque was calculated. The force used in this calculation is calculated using the total length and diameter of the BPA [10]. The diameter of the BPA is chosen by determining which minimum diameter is needed in order to match or exceed a maximum isomeric force of the muscles that it is replacing from the human model.

2.2   Cost Function

Muscle attachment locations are optimized using an exhaustive search method according to the cost function in Eq. 1. The C values in the function are the constraints calculated during every iteration. The G values are the weights that assign relative importance of each cost component.

$$C_{Total} = G_1 * C_{Torque} + G_2 * C_{Length} + G_3 * C_{Distance} + C_{Diameter} \quad (1)$$

There are currently four constraints that contribute to the cost function. The first and most important constraint, by weight, is the difference in magnitude between the human generated torque (T_{Human}) and the PAM generated torque (T_{PAM}). This constraint is calculated by taking the difference between the torque generated at each discrete angle for the two degree of freedom joint (Θ and Φ).

$$C_{Torque} = \sum_{\Theta=1}^{100} \sum_{\Phi=1}^{100} ||T_{Human}(\Theta, \Phi) - T_{PAM}(\Theta, \Phi)|| \quad (2)$$

The second constraint pertains to the PAM length. The algorithm will often generate solutions with excessively large muscle lengths in order to match human generated torques. In order to dissuade the algorithm from choosing these solutions, as they would be impractical for physical construction, the length of each muscle (L_{Muscle}) contributes to the cost function.

$$C_{Length} = \sum_{Muscle=1}^{n} L_{Muscle} \quad (3)$$

The third constraint for the cost function is the distance from the solid body the points move. The physical robot can be constructed with attachment points not directly on the physical body, however the algorithm is discouraged from choosing points excessively far from the body. The constraint is calculated by summing the distances from the original points of each muscle on the human model ($p_{original,Muscle}$) to the new algorithmically generated points ($p_{new,Muscle}$).

$$C_{Distance} = \sum_{Muscle=1}^{n} \sqrt{p(x, y, z)_{original,Muscle} - p(x, y, z)_{new,Muscle}} \quad (4)$$

The final constraint is the diameter of the PAM that would be needed to generate that torque. For each PAM, the human muscle isometric force and the generated length of the muscle is used to calculate the size of a Festo BPA that will serve as the robot PAM. With shorter muscle lengths, BPAs need higher diameters to produce a given force. The larger the diameter of the muscle, the more difficult it will be to physically construct the robot. The algorithm tends to prefer larger muscle diameters, as the larger the diameter the shorter the muscle can be in order to achieve a specific torque. The cost function adds a constant value for each muscle depending on the diameter calculated. These constants appear as G_{40}, G_{20}, and G_{10} in Eq. 5. The value for these constants are larger for larger diameters and smaller for smaller diameters.

$$C_{Diameter} = \sum_{Muscle=1}^{n} \begin{cases} G_{40}, & \phi_{Muscle} = 40\,\text{mm} \\ G_{20}, & \phi_{Muscle} = 20\,\text{mm} \\ G_{10}, & \phi_{Muscle} = 10\,\text{mm} \end{cases} \tag{5}$$

The starting PAM locations for the muscle placements come from Bolen and Hunt [2]. The algorithm creates a starting cost value based on these previously determined positions. The algorithm then conducts an exhaustive search iteration for eight points around the starting locations. It chooses new locations for the muscle attachment points that are before a joint and after a joint. Eight new locations are created for each of these attachment points, by adding or subtracting a small distance, ϵ, to the original location in three directions. These points define a cube around the original point for the algorithm to conduct its search. Then the algorithm begins to calculate the updated cost function for each combination of these new points. Once all calculations have completed, the algorithm updates the new starting points with the points that correspond to the minimum cost value. The algorithm then repeats the generation of new points until it has found a local minima. Once this has occurred, the epsilon value used to determine new via point locations is decreased by multiplying it by a refinement rate term, γ. This tightens the range of analyzed points about the current minimum. When this process has been repeated and epsilon has been reduced to a negligible value, the algorithm ends.

3   Results

This section shows the results of the algorithm performing optimization about the set of muscles on the right side of the lumbrosacral joint. This joint was chosen as a test case for the algorithm, as it only includes three uniarticular muscles: the erector spinae, internal oblique, and external oblique. By focusing on this joint, the algorithm can be tuned to perform better for joints with larger sets of muscles. Only the muscles on the right side of the body are considered, as the left side of the body will mirror the results of the right side. The axes of interest that the torque acts about are the pelvis x and z axis, found in Fig. 3. Rotation about these axes are lateral bending of the back (x axis) and back flexion and extension (z axis). Figure 4 shows torque surfaces constructed from the human model and the generated model. Each point along the surface shows the combined torque of all muscles about the joint when the joint is rotated to the specified degrees. While the new model doesn't match the human model completely, it is an improvement over the previously hand placed model. This improvement can be seen in Fig. 5, which shows the absolute torque differences between the previous model and the human model as well as the absolute torque differences between the new model and the human model. In all models the x axis aligns with side to side bending of the back. The z axis aligns with back flexion and extension. We see that the results from the algorithm create a difference in torque that is closer to zero than the hand placed model. The previous robot model had a mean squared error of 22.9 kNm whereas the newly generated model has a mean squared error of 2.63 kNm.

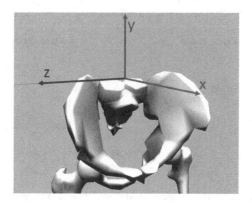

Fig. 3. Coordinate axes of the lumbrosacral joint.

Figure 6 shows the cost values from the functions described in Sect. 2. The algorithm performed 3073 iterations before it reached a minimum with ϵ less than 1 mm. The total cost value (Fig. 7) shows a consistent decline in magnitude. The starting cost value, which comes from hand placed locations, was 286, whereas the optimization process brought the value down to 171. The error component, representing the summed difference of torque between the human model and the algorithm generated model, was most prominent in the beginning of the iteration process. As the algorithm began to reach a minimum, the muscle length became equally important to the overall cost. The distance component played a negligible part in the algorithm and the diameter component did not change through all 3000 iterations. Table 1 shows what the final parameters were to obtain this solution. These parameters were arrived at by manually adjusting them over the course of multiple trial runs. $G1$ and $G2$ are much smaller than the other weights because the constraints that they modulate result in considerably larger values in the cost function than the other constraints.

Figure 8 shows what the placement of muscles and PAMs look like on the OpenSim model. The left set of images show muscle placement that contribute to bending about the lumbrosacral joint. The right set of images show what PAM placement and routing would look like within OpenSim.

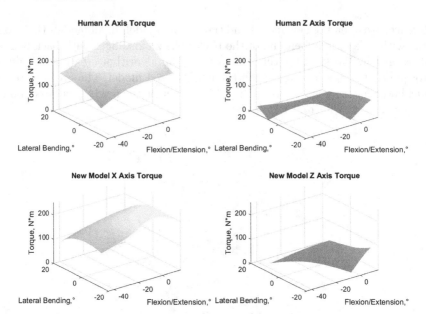

Fig. 4. Torque surfaces of the human model and the newly generated robot model. The top row shows the human torque capabilities about the lumbrosacral joint in the x and z axis. The bottom row shows the robot torque capabilities about the same joint and axes.

Table 1. Parameter values used in the optimization algorithm.

Parameter	Description	Value
G_1	Torque error weight	1e−4
G_2	Muscle length weight	1e−2
G_3	Distance weight	1
G_4	Diameter weight	1
G_{10}	10 mm diameter cost	1
G_{20}	20 mm diameter cost	5
G_{40}	40 mm diameter cost	15
ϵ	Distance from starting point	0.1 m
γ	Refinement rate	0.5

4   Discussion and Conclusion

Looking at the surface plots in Fig. 5, we see that torque difference between the human model and the algorithm model are closer to 0 than the previously hand placed model. The algorithm is able to achieve its intended goal of finding muscle attachment points that will closely match human torque capabilities in a manner that will allow construction of a bipedal robot. The mean squared

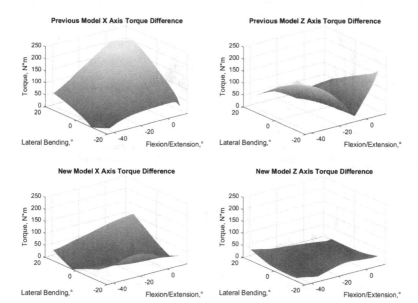

Fig. 5. Surface plots showing the absolute value of the difference between the PAM placement model and the human model. The top row shows the previous results from placing PAMs by hand. The bottom row shows the PAM placement results from the algorithm.

error was reduced by an order of magnitude between the hand placed model and the algorithmically generated attachment points. The new mean squared error of 2.63 kNm appears to be large, however it is the sum of the error about 1000 different positions. This averages to an error of 2.63 Nm per position. With continued refinement, this error can continue to go down.

The results from the optimization of lumbrosacral muscles are promising for future uses of this algorithm, but also point to deficiencies in the algorithm. First, looking at Fig. 7, we see that the distance component of the cost function is negligible to the other values. This shows that the algorithm was able to find a minimum that did not deviate too far from the starting point, without the need for this component. This result was surprising, as during the parameter tuning process of this work, often a solution would be found wherein the via point locations of the muscle were often very far from the robot body. While this component was negligible in this case, it will continue to be a valuable component, but will need to be further tuned when looking at other joints. In the same figure, we see that the diameter of the muscles remained constant. This was another surprising result and will likely be eliminated from the cost function in the future.

Finally, Fig. 8 shows odd or seemingly unwanted results in the PAM placement. Some of the PAMs do not have an insertion point directly on the physical structure of the model. That can be corrected for when developing the robot

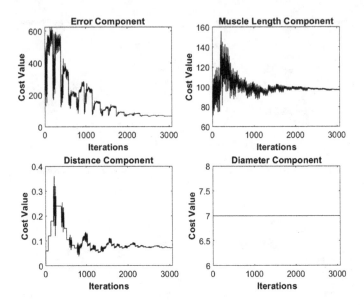

Fig. 6. Individual cost components contributing to the overall cost function.

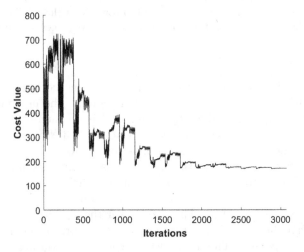

Fig. 7. Value of the cost function minimizes throughout iterations. There are large jumps at expected intervals as the algorithm tries to find the lowest cost value point out of 64 total combinations in an epoch.

through the use of cabling, by attaching an artificial ligament from the end of the muscle location to a colinear point on the robot body. There are also muscles that pass through the bones of the OpenSim model. This is not entirely a negative result of the algorithm, as the physical structure of the robot does not need to replicate the bone structure completely and can be developed with grooves or paths that allow the muscles to maintain their generated position.

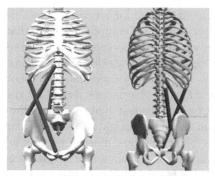
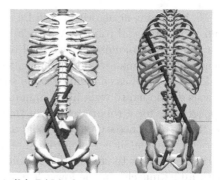

(a) Muscle placement on a human model

(b) PAM placement on a robot model

Fig. 8. Orientation of the erector spinae, internal oblique, and external oblique, on the human and robot model. A front view is on the left of each image and a rear view is on the right.

This can be changed, however, with the inclusion of a new cost component to the algorithm to penalize the cost function when it intersects areas known to contain a physical structure. Work has already been done to import the points that define the bone mesh from OpenSim into Matlab and this new constraint would use those points to determine when intersection are made of the muscle and the structure.

The work presented here describes an optimization algorithm that was created in Matlab that creates pneumatic artificial muscle placements on a bipedal robot that is meant to replicate the torques that are generated around human leg joints. The algorithm was successful in reducing the error between the human produced torque values and the PAM produced torque values. The algorithm requires further tuning and refinement, to place greater importance on components of the cost function that do not currently affect the cost value in the significant manner. The PAM attachment points that are generated do not create biomimetic paths for the PAMs. The routing could pose challenges when constructing a physical robot, as PAMs should not be bent or kinked. The current intended way of handling these routing issues on the physical structure will be to create a series of PAMs to represent longer muscles. This will allow the bending to be routed with a cable that then connects to the PAMs.

The next step for this specific project will be to continue to iterate on the types of constraints that are put in place for the robot. The current constraints include the error between the human calculated torque and the robot calculated torque, the length of the muscle, and the diameter of the muscle. Other constraints that were attempted but ultimately not implemented currently include penalizing the bending angle of the PAMs, penalizing distance from the attachment points to the physical structure, and penalizing PAMs when they intercept the physical structure. Along with this, the hyperparameter can also be tuned more finely to produce the results that we want.

This placement algorithm will be useful in the future for creating adaptable and robust bipedal robots. A bipedal robot created with compliant PAMs that are placed in a biomimetic way will have an easier time navigating an environment that humans are able to navigate through easily. Obstacles, such as steps or ledges, as well as changing ground surfaces, will be easily overcome by a robot that is developed to walk like a human. These muscle placements also afford the opportunity for a robotic platform that can be used to test biological hypotheses. Some hypotheses core to bipedal organism are the investigation of biarticular muscles, how balance is maintained and controlled, and how muscles coordinate with one another to create stable standing and gait. Creating a robotic platform with all 92 muscles in the lower legs with PAMs is infeasible currently, so steps have to be made to reduce the number of muscles while maintaining biomimetic properties. That is nearly achieved here. With continued improvement on the optimization algorithm, we can create those muscle placements to create a robot that will very closely match what a human is capable of with less complexity. The robotic model that we create here will represent a step forward towards capturing a greater amount of the complexity of the human musculoskeletal system, and enable more sophisticated investigations into how the complexity of the system affect control, both positively and negatively.

References

1. Asano, Y., Okada, K., Inaba, M.: Design principles of a human mimetic humanoid: humanoid platform to study human intelligence and internal body system. Sci. Robot. **2**(13), eaaq0899 (2017). http://robotics.sciencemag.org/lookup/doi/10.1126/scirobotics.aaq0899

2. Bolen, B.P., Hunt, A.J.: Determination of artificial muscle placement for biomimetic humanoid robot legs. In: Martinez-Hernandez, U., et al. (eds.) Living Machines 2019. LNCS (LNAI), vol. 11556, pp. 15–26. Springer, Cham (2019). https://doi.org/10.1007/978-3-030-24741-6_2

3. Buschmann, T., Ewald, A., Twickel, A.V., Büschges, A.: Controlling legs for locomotion-insights from robotics and neurobiology. Bioinspiration Biomimetics **10**(4), 041001 (2015). https://doi.org/10.1088%2F1748-3190%2F10%2F4%2F041001, publisher: IOP Publishing

4. Delp, S.L., et al.: OpenSim: open-source software to create and analyze dynamic simulations of movement. IEEE Trans. Biomed. Eng. **54**(11), 1940–1950 (2007). http://ieeexplore.ieee.org/document/4352056/

5. Deng, K., et al.: Neuromechanical model of rat hindlimb walking with two-layer CPGs. Biomimetics **4**(1), 21 (2019). https://www.mdpi.com/2313-7673/4/1/21

6. Grillner, S.: Biological pattern generation: the cellular and computational logic of networks in motion. Neuron **52**(5), 751–66 (2006). http://www.ncbi.nlm.nih.gov/pubmed/17145498

7. Hill, A.V.: The heat of shortening and the dynamic constants of muscle. Proc. Royal Soc. London B: Biol. Sci. **126**(843), 136–195 (1938). http://rspb.royalsocietypublishing.org/content/126/843/136

8. Hosoda, K., Sakaguchi, Y., Takayama, H., Takuma, T.: Pneumatic-driven jumping robot with anthropomorphic muscular skeleton structure. Autonomous Robots **28**(3), 307–316 (2010). http://link.springer.com/10.1007/s10514-009-9171-6

9. Hoy, M., Zajac, F., Gordon, M.: A musculoskeletal model of the human lower extremity: the effect of muscle, tendon, and moment arm on the moment-angle relationship of musculotendon actuators at the hip, knee, and ankle. J. Biomech. **23**(2), 157–169 (1990)

10. Hunt, A., Graber-Tilton, A., Quinn, R.: Modeling length effects of braided pneumatic actuators. In: IDETC/CIE 2017. ASME, Cleveland, OH, August 2017. https://asme.pinetec.com/detc2017/data/pdfs/trk-8/DETC2017-67458.pdf

11. Hunt, A., Schmidt, M., Fischer, M., Quinn, R.: A biologically based neural system coordinates the joints and legs of a tetrapod. Bioinspiration Biomimetics **10**(5), 055004 (2015). http://stacks.iop.org/1748-3190/10/i=5/a=055004

12. Hunt, A., Schmidt, M., Fischer, M., Quinn, R.D.: Neuromechanical simulation of an inter-leg controller for tetrapod coordination. In: Duff, A., Lepora, N.F., Mura, A., Prescott, T.J., Verschure, P.F.M.J. (eds.) Living Machines 2014. LNCS (LNAI), vol. 8608, pp. 142–153. Springer, Cham (2014). https://doi.org/10.1007/978-3-319-09435-9_13

13. Ijspeert, A.J.: Central pattern generators for locomotion control in animals and robots: a review. Neural Netw.: Official J. Int. Neural Netw. Soc. **21**(4), 642–653 (2008). http://www.ncbi.nlm.nih.gov/pubmed/18555958

14. Klute, G.K., Czerniecki, J.M., Hannaford, B.: McKibben artificial muscles: pneumatic actuators with biomechanical intelligence. In: Advanced Intelligent Mechatronics, pp. 221–226. IEEE (1999). http://ieeexplore.ieee.org/xpls/abs_all.jsp?arnumber=803170

15. MATLAB: version 9.7.0 (R2019b). The MathWorks Inc., Natick, Massachusetts (2019)

16. Scharzenberger, C., Mendoza, J., Hunt, A.: Design of a canine inspired quadruped robot as a platform for synthetic neural network control. In: Martinez-Hernandez, U., et al. (eds.) Living Machines 2019. LNCS (LNAI), vol. 11556, pp. 228–239. Springer, Cham (2019). https://doi.org/10.1007/978-3-030-24741-6_20

17. Tondu, B., Zagal, S.: McKibben artificial muscle can be in accordance with the Hill skeletal muscle model, pp. 714–720. IEEE (2006). http://ieeexplore.ieee.org/document/1639174/

18. Zang, X., Liu, Y., Liu, X., Zhao, J.: Design and control of a pneumatic musculoskeletal biped robot. Technol. Health Care **24**(s2), S443–S454 (2016). https://www.medra.org/servlet/aliasResolver?alias=iospress&doi=10.3233/THC-161167

Robofish as Social Partner for Live Guppies

Lea Musiolek[1]($\boxtimes$), Verena V. Hafner[1], Jens Krause[2], Tim Landgraf[3],
and David Bierbach[2]

[1] Department of Computer Science, Humboldt-Universität zu Berlin,
Berlin, Germany
lea.musiolek@hu-berlin.de
[2] Faculty of Life Sciences, Division of Biology and Ecology of Fishes,
Humboldt Universität zu Berlin, Berlin, Germany
[3] Dahlem Center for Machine Learning and Robotics, Freie Universität Berlin,
Berlin, Germany
https://adapt.informatik.hu-berlin.de/
https://www.agrar.hu-berlin.de/
http://berlinbiorobotics.blog/

Abstract. Biomimetic robots that are accepted as social partners by animals may help to gain insights into animals' social interaction skills. Here, we present an experiment using the biomimetic Robofish which resembles live guppies (*Poecilia reticulata*) - a small tropical freshwater fish. Guppy females were given the opportunity to interact with different open-loop controlled Robofish replicas. We show that guppies interacting with a lifelike Robofish replica scored higher on social interaction variables than did those faced with a simple white cuboid performing the same movements, although this effect weakened with time. Our study exemplifies the use of Robofish as a research tool, providing highly standardized social cues for the study of fish social skills such as imitation and following.

Keywords: Biorobotics · Fish · Social interaction.

1 Introduction

When equipping artificial agents with social interaction skills such as imitation, following and anticipation of others' movements [6], it makes sense to examine how animals implement and exploit such skills in their social interactions [4]. Some major issues when using live animals as social stimuli (social partners) are (I) consistent individual behavioural differences even between demonstrator animals, and (II) inevitable mutual influences between the focal and demonstrator animals. Here, the use of biomimetic robots is a promising solution. Biomimetic robots can be either interactive (closed-loop behaviour) or static

Supported by Germany's Excellence Strategy - EXC 2002/1 "Science of Intelligence".

(open-loop behaviour). In the current study, we outline how such a tool, the so-called Robofish [3,5], can be used to study social skills in live Trinidadian guppies (*Poecilia reticulata*), a small tropical freshwater fish. We compared live fish's responses towards a lifelike Robofish leading to a food source with those towards a simple cuboid object moving in a similar way. Trials were repeated on five consecutive days in order to enable social learning of the food source location. However, the fish did not eat the food reward and did not seem attracted to it, making this experiment unsuitable for addressing questions on goal-based learning. Instead, we focused on examining how live fish interacted with the replicas until the replicas reached the goal location. If lifelike replicas are accepted as social partners, we predicted that live fish should follow them more closely and should show higher movement synchrony with them than when faced with a cuboid replica.

2 Methods

2.1 Experimental Setup and Design

Our Robofish system essentially consists of a two-wheeled differential drive robot moving on a platform below a shallow square glass tank and moving a 3D-printed fish replica by way of a magnet [5]. The use of a semicircular barrier (see Fig. 1a) is due to our initial research question on goal learning as described above. In the *social* treatment, we tested live fish's reactions towards a guppy-like replica (Fig. 1b, right) that is accepted well by guppies [5]. In the *nonsocial* treatment, a simple white plastic cuboid replica (Fig. 1b, left) of similar length and breadth to the guppy-like replica was used instead.

(a)

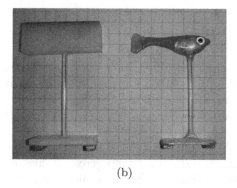
(b)

Fig. 1. a) Experimental setup overlaid with typical Robofish trajectories. b) Cuboid and lifelike Robofish replica.

2.2   Procedure of the Behavioural Experiment

Our sample consisted of 22 adult female Trinidadian guppies (*Poecilia reticulata*), marked individually with colour tags for better identification [1]. The Robofish trajectories were programmed open-loop as shown in Fig. 1a. After two minutes of acclimatization time inside the cylinder at one end of the test tank, its door was opened gently. As soon as the fish emerged by one body length, we started the Robofish on the trajectory to its goal. All trajectories (and thus all trials) took around 25 s to complete. All fish were tested on five consecutive days, making our basic design a mixed "two by five" one, with two treatments as between-subjects factor and five within-subject repetitions. The experiment complied with the current German law approved by LaGeSo (G0117/16 granted to D. Bierbach).

2.3   Analysis

All trials were video recorded with a Basler Ace 2K USB3 camera (50fps) and subsequently tracked with Ethovision XT 14 (same sample fps). From the tracks, we extracted the following response variables in order to describe social interactions among live fish and replicas: (I) Inter-individual distance (IID), the average distance between a fish and Robofish over all frames of a trial. (II) Normalized cross-correlations (Xcorr) between the frame-wise displacement vectors of the two subjects. Xcorr were computed for time lags of up to 10 s in either direction between the fish and robot displacement time series and the highest of these values was chosen. We fitted a linear mixed-effects model including treatment and experiment day as categorical fixed effects, their interaction, as well as random intercepts for the individual fish for both of our dependent variables [2]. Complete data and analyses are available upon request.

3   Results

A significant interaction between treatment and day for IID ($\chi^2(4, N = 22) = 12.11$, $p = 0.017$, Fig. 2a) prompted us to perform the same analysis also on a data subset containing only the first three days. Here, we found a significant main effect for treatment ($\chi^2(1, N = 22) = 8.38$, $p = 0.004$), with fish in the social treatment being on average 8.8 cm closer to the replica than those in the cuboid (nonsocial) treatment. Day had a significant effect on IID ($\chi^2(4, N = 22) = 17.05$, $p = 0.002$) across all five days, but not across only the first three days. While no significant effects were detectable for Xcorr across all five days, on the first three days fish tested with lifelike replicas tended to have higher Xcorr compared to those tested with cuboid replicas ($\beta = 0.09$, SE $= 0.09$, $\chi^2(1, N = 22) = 2.88$, $p = 0.09$, see Fig. 2b).

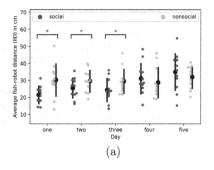
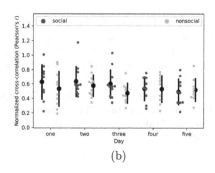

(a)   (b)

Fig. 2. Live guppies' responses to the different treatments. Means and SDs are shown in black, and significant differences marked with asterisks. a) Inter-individual distance (IID). b) Cross-correlation (Xcorr).

4 Discussion and Outlook

Taken together, our results add to the evidence that a moving lifelike Robofish elicits following behaviour more strongly than do similarly sized geometric objects. This is in line with findings showing that Robofish are better accepted when equipped with realistic eyes [5], probably because they are perceived as conspecifics. A possible explanation for the weakening effect of the lifelike Robofish after day 3 is the fish's increasing habituation to the test tank and a resulting eagerness to explore it independently [3]. Follow-up studies should address the problem of providing attractive rewards in order to more successfully examine social goal learning and anticipation.

References

1. Visible Implant Elastomer Tags. https://www.nmt.us/visible-implant-elastomer/. Library Catalog: www.nmt.us
2. Bates, D., Mächler, M., Bolker, B., Walker, S.: Fitting linear mixed-effects models using lme4. J. Stat. Softw. **67**(1), 1–48 (2015). https://doi.org/10.18637/jss.v067. i01
3. Bierbach, D., et al.: Using a robotic fish to investigate individual differences in social responsiveness in the guppy. Roy. Soc. Open Sci. **5**(8), 181026 (2018). https://doi. org/10.1098/rsos.181026. https://royalsocietypublishing.org/doi/full/10.1098/rsos. 181026
4. Brown, C., Laland, K.N.: Social learning in fishes: a review. Fish Fisher. **4**(3), 280–288 (2003). https://doi.org/10.1046/j.1467-2979.2003.00122.x. https:// onlinelibrary.wiley.com/doi/abs/10.1046/j.1467-2979.2003.00122.x

5. Landgraf, T., et al.: RoboFish: increased acceptance of interactive robotic fish with realistic eyes and natural motion patterns by live Trinidadian guppies. Bioinspir. Biomimet. **11**(1), 015001 (2016). https://doi.org/10.1088/1748-3190/11/1/015001. http://stacks.iop.org/1748-3190/11/i=1/a=015001?key=crossref.a6551d7466f00a0 21333beb71ff1a18b

6. Winfield, A.F.T., Hafner, V.V.: Anticipation in robotics. In: Poli, R. (ed.) Handbook of Anticipation: Theoretical and Applied Aspects of the Use of Future in Decision Making, pp. 1–30. Springer, Cham (2018). https://doi.org/10.1007/978-3-319-31737-3_73-1

Bioinspired Navigation Based on Distributed Sensing in the Leech

Sebastian T. Nichols[1], Catherine E. Kehl[1] (ID), Brian K. Taylor[1]([✉]) (ID),
and Cynthia Harley[2] (ID)

[1] The University of North Carolina at Chapel Hill, Chapel Hill, NC 27599, USA
brian.taylor@unc.edu
[2] Metropolitan State University, St. Paul, MN 55106, USA
cindy.harley@metrostate.edu

Abstract. Animals use sensors that are distributed along their body to process information from the environment, leading to behavioral actions that will prolong their survival. Although extensive research has been done in animal behavior and neurobiology, it is still unknown how these distributed sensors interact with each other to process sensory information. Several behavioral studies have used the leech as a navigation model system to understand how different stimulus modalities impact behavior. Neurophysiological studies examined the output of specific neurons in the leech when they were stimulated with electric pulses, and correlated the response of these neurons to observed behaviors. Our work uses existing data from animal experiments to construct a mathematical model that accurately replicates the behavior of a leech when it is given various forms of simulated stimuli. The distributed sensors in the leech were modeled by ellipses, allowing the neurons to detect stimuli in a two-dimensional environment and navigate towards a target location. The development and validation of this model offers a fast and low cost way to study leech behavior, complement animal experiments, and provide insights into the underlying mechanics of distributed sensing in animals. Additionally, the findings may provide insights into novel data-processing methods and architectures for man-made sensory systems that rely on multiple sensors.

Keywords: Distributed sensing · Multimodal sensing · Leech

1 Introduction

Distributed sensing refers to the spatial distribution of sensors in an organism, allowing it to detect stimuli from single or multiple sensory modalities (Fig. 1). Every animal with a nervous system uses an array of sensors (i.e., distributed sensing) to convert sensory stimuli to different behaviors. To successfully forage and survive, animals must be able to integrate and process distributed sensory information to direct action under a multitude of environmental conditions. In addition, distributed sensing and nervous-system-like computing offers several

© Springer Nature Switzerland AG 2020
V. Vouloutsi et al. (Eds.): Living Machines 2020, LNAI 12413, pp. 275–287, 2020.
https://doi.org/10.1007/978-3-030-64313-3_27

potential benefits for man-made systems, including 1) robustness where many sensors must fail before the entire system fails, 2) the use of less complex and/or resource-intensive sensors to obtain actionable information about the world [2], 3) the development of systems with lower size, weight, cost, and power requirements, 4) and improved adaptive navigation behavior [3].

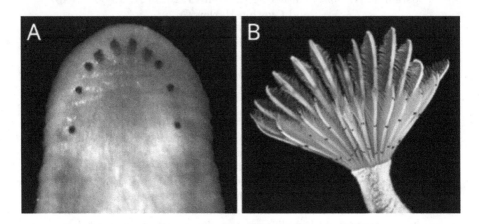

Fig. 1. From [1]. Two examples of distributed sensors arranged along an animal's body. Panel A shows visual sensors (black dots) located on the head of a leech (sensors continue along the rest of the body). Panel B shows eyes (black dots) dispersed along the tentacles of a fan-worm.

Leeches are a unique model organism for studying neurobiology and distributed sensing due to their arrangement of over 294 distributed visual and mechanoreceptors. Scientists have studied the Medicinal leech's nervous system to understand the relationship between individual neurons and certain behaviors [4–7]. However, it is still unknown how populations of neurons combine signals from different sensory modalities to generate the behaviors necessary for survival.

Previous experiments have studied multimodal sensing in the Medicinal leech, Hirudo verbana [8,9]. In these studies, leeches were exposed to different frequencies of water waves, which provided a variety of intensities of mechanical and visual stimuli in a laboratory-controlled environment. The physical motion of the water provides the mechanical stimulus, while the visual stimulus is generated by surface water waves creating a series of lenses that focus light at different spatial points (i.e., caustics). By measuring the percentage of leeches that successfully navigated to a target location (i.e., *find rate*), it was found that certain frequencies produced maximal find rates for both unimodal and multimodal stimuli. This led to experiments that measured the spike rate of leech neurons (specifically, so-called *S-cells*, which process multimodal sensory information) when stimulated by specific sensory frequencies and intensities both visually and mechanically [10]. The frequencies that generated the largest spike rates correlated with the frequencies that resulted in higher find rates, suggesting that the spike rates can be used as a behavioral predictor.

Various computational models have been implemented to simulate the neural response of neurons in animals [11–17]. The model proposed in [11] generates elliptical representations of spike rate distributions for two different populations of neurons: neurons that are sensitive to magnetic stimuli, and neurons that are sensitive to visual stimuli. The two representations are integrated to produce a resultant effective ellipse which computes the navigational behavior of the simulated agent. The results of this model matched the results of real-world animal behavior experiments where birds were given different visual and magnetic stimuli in a laboratory. The approach was later adapted by [13] to study magnetoreception and navigation.

In this study, the elliptical approach of [11] (referred to as the elliptical model) was adapted to model the leech's nervous system response to both mechanical and visual stimuli. Once the elliptical model was able to generate biologically relevant neural activity, a behavioral algorithm was used to transform the neural responses into behavioral actions. A computer simulated agent then used these actions to navigate towards the center of a given stimulus. We analyzed the trajectories of the agent to verify that the model exhibits similar behavior to that of a leech. From a biological standpoint, our model can serve as a complementary testing tool alongside real-world leech experiments to help discover the underlying mechanisms and principles of distributed sensing, sensor placement, and multimodal sensing. From an engineering standpoint, our model can be used in the development of man-made sensing, processing, and information systems and tools that are more precise, autonomous, and efficient.

2   Materials and Methods

This work uses an agent-based simulation in conjunction with the elliptical model to conduct all trials and experiments. Figure 2 illustrates a high-level overview of how our model and agent-based simulation works. Each section explains a piece of our system. Section 2.1 outlines how mechanical and visual stimuli are generated. Section 2.2 how spike rates are generated based on different stimuli. Sections 2.3 and 2.4 how the elliptical model is used to represent the leech's nervous system response. Sections 2.5 and 2.6 describe the navigational environment, and the parameters used in the experiments.

2.1   Stimuli Generation

In this study, the mechanical stimulus is simplified to be represented by a frequency and intensity value. Since the mechanical intensity of physical water waves decreases as they move across space, the intensities are modeled as a function of the displacement between the agent's location and the stimulus origin.

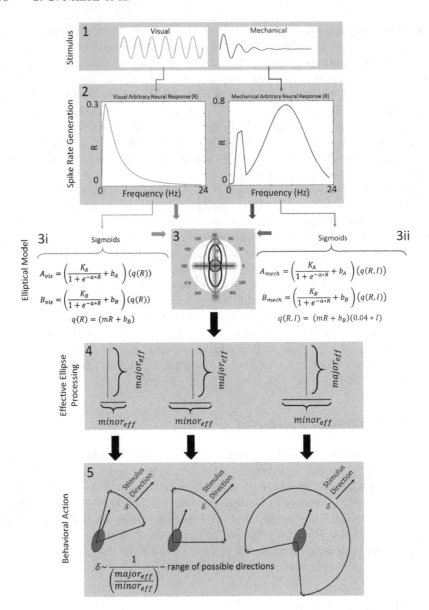

Fig. 2. continued

◀ **Fig 2.** Illustration of how raw sensory information is transformed into behavioral commands via the elliptical algorithm. Mechanical (blue) and/or visual (red) stimuli (Panel 1) generate an arbitrary spike rate R (Panel 2). This spike rate from each sensory modality is passed through sigmoidal curves that are used to compute the major (A_{vis} and A_{mech}) and minor axes (B_{vis} and B_{mech}) of ellipses due to the mechanical and visual stimuli (Panel 3). These ellipses, which represent the neural responses due to mechanical and visual receptors, are combined to form an integrated "effective ellipse" (black). The ratio of the effective ellipses' major ($major_{eff}$) and minor ($minor_{eff}$) axes is computed (Panel 4) and used to determine a motion direction that has a degree of variability (δ - Panel 5). Lower ratios lead to higher variability in motion direction (i.e., less certainty about the direction of the stimulus). In Panel 3, K_A and K_B are constants that determine the maximum size of the sigmoids used to compute the major and minor axes of the ellipses, while b_A and b_B determines the sigmoids' offset from zero. a is a rate parameter that defines the sigmoids' rate of change based on the spike rate R. The functions $q(R, I)$ alter the ellipses' major and minor axes based on both the arbitrary spike rate R, and the intensity I. (Color figure online)

$$g_{int} = \sqrt{(g_x - a_{sx})^2 + (g_y - a_{sy})^2} \tag{1a}$$

$$a_{dist} = \sqrt{(g_x - a_x)^2 + (g_y - a_y)^2} \tag{1b}$$

$$I = g_{int} - |a_{dist}| \tag{1c}$$

g_{int} is the initial intensity of the mechanical wave and is found computing the distance between the goal location (g_x, g_y) and the agent's starting position (a_{sx}, a_{sy}). a_{dist} is the distance between the goal location and the agent's current position (a_x, a_y). g_{int} and a_{dist} are used in Eq. 1c to find the intensity of the mechanical wave at the agent's current position. This allows the agent to follow intensity contours to determine if it is getting closer to the origin. We acknowledge that this model has several limitations, one being that the intensity can become negative when the agent is located further away from the starting location. However, because this is the first simulation we are aware of that seeks to translate leech sensing into navigation behavior, and because of the formulation of our navigation environment (see Sect. 2.5), it was felt that this was a simple approach that still retained the essence of the problem. We will incorporate a higher fidelity model that more accurately captures the physicality of the real-world in future studies.

For simplicity, the visual stimulus is represented by a frequency value and not an intensity value (see Sect. 4 for more details). Therefore, the spike rates that are generated only from visual stimuli do not depend on changes in intensity. The agent can still use changes in neural responses to navigate towards the target location when they are only given a visual stimulus.

2.2   Spike Rate Generation

The relative neural response in relation to different stimuli frequencies and intensities was mapped out using the data from [10], which showed that the spike rates generated from S-cells matched the behavioral responses from the leeches in [8]. Specifically, the frequencies eliciting higher spike rates were the same or close to the frequencies that lead to the highest find rates. A bi-modal distribution was fit to the mechanical data from [10] with peak neural responses at around 3 Hz and 14 Hz (Fig. 2). Since the neural response to mechanical stimuli increases with intensity, a linear scaling factor was included to model an increase in spike rate due to intensity. A skewed distribution was used to fit the neural behavior produced from visual stimuli with a peak around 1 Hz (Fig. 2).

2.3   Elliptical Model Construction

The spike rates are fed into sigmoid functions that output minimum and maximum spike rates for both the visual and mechanical stimuli. These minimum and maximum spike rates are used to calculate the major and minor axes of the elliptical model. Two sigmoid functions were used to take in relative neural responses and output minimum and maximum spike rates for both the visual and mechanical stimulus responses (Fig. 2 - panels 3i and 3ii). The maximum spike rate was set at 70 and the minimum spike rate was set at 30; each of which is an arbitrary value.

Per [11] and [13], and inspired by the anatomical structure of the leech, the following equation was used to generate ellipses to represent populations of spatially arranged neurons. This equation can be used for both visual and mechanical stimuli.

$$S_r(\theta_i) = \frac{A_r B_r}{A_r^2 cos^2(\theta_i - \phi) + B_r^2 sin^2(\theta_i - \phi)} \tag{2}$$

Subscript r refers to the mechanical response ($mech$), visual response (vis), or integrated/effective response (int). θ_i is the angular placement of the population of the ith population of neurons, and ϕ is the direction of the oncoming stimulus. For each θ_i, a population of neurons produces its own relative spike rates. A is the maximum spike rate, B is the minimum spike rate. $S_r(\theta_i)$ is a resultant vector of spike rates. By letting $x = cos(\theta_i - \phi)$ and $y = sin(\theta_i - \phi)$, one can verify that this equation has the form of an ellipse.

Once the ellipses for each sensory modality are computed, the integrated response is calculated by taking the absolute value of the difference between mechanical and visual responses [11].

$$S_{int} = |S_{mech} - S_{vis}| \tag{3}$$

This approach models lateral inhibition between populations of neurons [11], which has been observed in visual and tactile sensory processing, and results in higher contrast between sensory responses. Neurons with the strong activation inhibit the activity of neighboring neurons. In a leech that uses two types of stimuli to navigate, lateral inhibition ensures that the stimuli eliciting the strongest neural response will be used for the navigational decision making.

An example of the elliptical generation is displayed in Fig. 2 - panel 3. Note that because we are using the absolute value of the difference between two ellipses, the integrated/effective ellipse may have a shape that is not truly elliptical, as there can be multiple lobes in this distribution [11]. We use the term integrated/effective ellipse for simplicity.

Once the effective ellipse is created, the effective spike rates along its major and minor axes are computed, which are oriented with leech's body axes (Fig. 3). Using the example shown in Fig. 2 - panel 3, the black effective ellipse is split up into four equal sections. The sections at the top and bottom (along the bright pink major axis) represent the major axis neural response, and the sections at each lateral side (along the dark purple minor axis) represent the minor axis neural response. We sum each section to produce a gross neural response on each axis, then take the mean to compute a major effective spike rate ($major_{eff}$) and minor effective spike rate ($minor_{eff}$). A behavioral algorithm uses these effective spike rates to determine what action the agent should take.

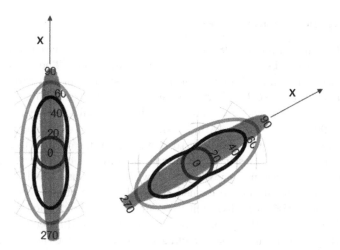

Fig. 3. Example of the a leech overlaid on the visual, mechanical, and integrated ellipses in two different orientations. The ellipses are oriented with the body axes.

2.4   Behavioral Algorithm

The behavioral algorithm in this model compares the change in the $major_{eff}$ and $minor_{eff}$ from the current time step to the previous time step. The first direction is chosen at random since the agent has no previous memory to compare its current neural response to. If the overall neural response decreases, then the agent knows it turned in the wrong direction in the previous time step and turns in the opposite direction at the current time step. This type of behavior has been verified experimentally [18].

If the neural response increases, then the agent continues to turn in that same direction. The agent's notion of where the stimulus is located depends on the ratio $\frac{major_{eff}}{minor_{eff}}$. The more aligned the agent's orientation is with the stimulus (i.e. heading straight towards the stimulus), the greater the ratio $\frac{major_{eff}}{minor_{eff}}$ (i.e., closer to an ellipse). The larger $\frac{major_{eff}}{minor_{eff}}$ is, the better the agent knows which direction the stimulus is coming from. In contrast, stimuli frequencies that generate lower values of $\frac{major_{eff}}{minor_{eff}}$ (i.e., closer to a circle) make it harder for the agent to determine the direction it should go to reach the goal.

Additionally, we use the ratio $\frac{major_{eff}}{minor_{eff}}$ to compute a variance that introduces error into the directed motion of the agent. The larger the ratio, the lower the variance, resulting in less motion error. The lower the ratio, the higher the variance, resulting in greater motion error (Fig. 2 - panels 4 and 5). The model uses a uniform distribution so there is an equal chance that the agent chooses any direction in this range of turn angles. Once the behavioral algorithm chooses a sign and direction, the agent turns accordingly and continues to move until it reaches the goal.

2.5   Navigational Environment

To match the environment of [8], the agent is modeled as a circle with a radius of 1.1 cm to match the average length of a leech, 2.2 cm. The target location is a circle with a radius of 7 cm. The agent must stay in the target location for at least 30 time-steps before it is counted as a successful find. The starting location is ($x = 13.00$ cm, $y = 13.00$ cm), and the goal location is ($x = 65.90$ cm, $y = 65.90$ cm) (see Figs. 4Aiii, 4Biii, and 5Aiii for example trajectories). Although the agent is currently able to move to any location in this study, we plot the agent's trajectories in a circle with a radius of 41.5 cm to match the arena setup of [8]. Preliminary studies in which we constrained the agent to only move within the arena (performed after submission of this work) 1) negate some of the potential non-physicality of our model, and 2) do not show any substantial performance degradation or qualitative result differences, and in fact show slightly improved find-rates, leading us to believe that the approach used in the present study is a valid starting point.

2.6   Experimental Setup

Simulations were performed to test the agent's ability to find a target location using the stimuli frequencies from [8]. The frequencies for mechanical and visual inputs were 2 Hz, 4 Hz, 8 Hz, 12 Hz, 20 Hz, and 24 Hz. Each experiment was performed using one hundred trials. For each frequency, the average find rate was computed over all the trials. Experiments were done using only mechanical stimulus, only visual stimulus, and combination of both stimuli (i.e., multimodal stimuli). For the multimodal experiment, both stimuli were generated from the same target location at the same exact frequencies.

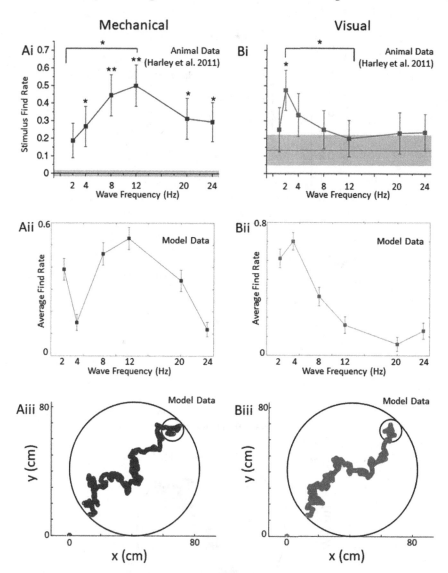

Fig. 4. Example results from the mechanical (A panels) and visual (B panels) stimulus experiments. The i panels show find rate data from [8] as a point of comparison. ii panels show find rate data from our experiments. iii panels shows example trajectories of the model.

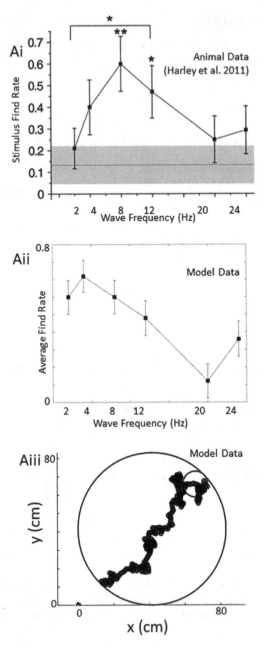

Fig. 5. Example results from the multimodal experiments. Ai shows find rate data from [8] as a point of comparison. Aii shows find rate data from our experiments. Aiii shows example trajectories of the model.

3   Results

Figure 4A shows the results of our model for the mechanical experiments, along with a comparison to data observed in real animals from [8], and an example trajectory. With the exception of 2 Hz, both the model and animal experiment data exhibit fairly good agreement, with a peak find rate of 0.5 at 12 Hz.

Figure 4B shows the results of our model for the visual experiments, along with a comparison to the data observed in real animals from [8], and an example trajectory. The find rates from model and the animal experiment data follow the same overall trends, with peak find rates occurring at 2 Hz, and find rates decreasing with increasing frequency. We note here that our model currently over-predicts the find rate (see Sect. 4 for details).

Figure 5A shows the results of our model for the multimodal experiments, along with a comparison to the data observed in [8], and an example trajectory. The find rates in the multimodal experiment are higher for all frequencies than for either of the visual or mechanical stimuli alone, demonstrating the elliptical model's ability to effectively combine multiple sensory inputs. However, the trends observed in our multimodal experiments reflect the trends in our visual experiments, suggesting that our model currently overly-weights the visual response (see Sect. 4).

4   Discussion and Conclusions

Overall, our model demonstrates fairly good agreement with the animal observations found in [8], though there are areas where it can be improved. In the mechanical experiments, an anomaly in the find rate trend occurred at 2 Hz where the modeled find rates came out to be substantially higher than the actual results. [10] showed a similar outlier in spike rate measurements, and stated that it did not correlate with the behavioral results found. Other differences in data occur at the higher end of the stimuli frequencies. The modeled find rates at 20 Hz and 24 Hz appeared lower than the actual data, suggesting that higher frequencies may elicit a different kind of motor behavior even if it does not create larger spike rates (Fig. 4Ai and Aii). For our visual experiments, while the trends between the modeled and observed data were the same, the peak find rates in the lower frequency range of the modeled data are higher than those of the animal experiment data. Better fits might be obtained by altering the model parameters of the visual part of the elliptical model, and modifying the variance rate. The higher frequencies elicited accurate find rates, although some of the trends do not line up with the animal experiment find rates. With additional tuning of our model, we believe that these discrepancies can be removed. Alternatively, this could be due to the fact that we only modeled the frequency, but not intensity of the visual stimulus for simplicity. In reality, the visual stimulus also depends on intensity. Including this effect would likely improve our results. Data from the multimodal experiments resemble the trends seen in the visual results, suggesting that our model currently over-weights the effects of visual stimuli. Preliminary efforts suggest that our model can be tuned to lessen impact of visual stimuli, and bring both the multimodal and visual experiments into better agreement with the observed animal data.

In summary, our findings indicate that there are similarities between the modeled behavior and actual behavior, demonstrating that the elliptical model can 1) be used to represent the distributed receptors along a leech's body, and 2) provide a neural representation that can perform similar behaviors. It also shows how neural activity can be linked to observed behaviors. It is especially encouraging that our model, an untuned and crudely simplified representation of a nervous-system response, is able to replicate actual animal behavior. This suggests that our model can be used as a complementary research tool alongside leech behavioral experiments. Combined with the results of [13], it also suggests that this approach might be leveraged to develop novel man-made navigation systems. A key feature of our model is that there is no explicit predefined map of the environment, yet with relatively simple processing, the agent is able to find the goal. Future experiments will vary the model's parameters in order to better validate the model against real-word behavioral data, particularly the visual and multimodal experiments. Additionally, other behavioral algorithms, and more realistic neural representations (e.g., conductance-based models [19], spiking neural networks [17], dynamic neural fields [16]) will be implemented, tested, and compared to both this simple model, and animal experimental data.

References

1. Harley, C.M., Asplen, M.K.: Annelid vision. Oxford Research Encyclopedias (2018)
2. Hochner, B.: An embodied view of octopus neurobiology. Curr. Biol. **22**(20), R887–R892 (2012)
3. McDonnell, M.D., et al.: Engineering intelligent electronic systems based on computational neuroscience [scanning the issue]. Proc. IEEE **102**(5), 646–651 (2014)
4. Lockery, S.R., Kristan, W.B.: Distributed processing of sensory information in the leech. I. Input- output relations of the local bending reflex. J. Neurosci. **10**(6), 1811–1815 (1990)
5. Kristan, W.B., Calabrese, R.L., Friesen, W.O.: Neural control of leech behavior. Prog. Neurobiol. **76**, 279–327 (2005)
6. Wagenaar, D.A.: A classic model animal in the 21st century: recent lessons from the leech nervous system. J. Exp. Biol. **218**, 3353–3359 (2015)
7. Moshtagh-Khorasani, M., Miller, E.W., Torre, V.: The spontaneous electrical activity of neurons in leech ganglia. Physiol. Rep. **1**, e00089 (2013)
8. Harley, C.M., Cienfuegos, J., Wagenaar, D.A.: Developmentally regulated multisensory integration for prey localization in the medicinal leech. J. Theor. Biol. **214**, 3801–3807 (2011)
9. Harley, C.M., Wagenaar, D.A.: Scanning behavior in the medicinal leech Hirudo verbana. PLoS One **9**(1), e86120 (2014)
10. Lehmkuhl, A.M., Muthusamy, A., Wagenaar, D.A.: Responses to mechanically and visually cued water waves in the nervous system of the medicinal leech. J. Exp. Biol. **221**(4), jeb17172 (2018)
11. Jensen, K.K.: Light-dependent orientation responses in animals can be explained by a model of compass cue integration. J. Theor. Biol. **262**, 129–141 (2010)

12. Taylor, B.K.: Validating a model for detecting magnetic field intensity using dynamic neural fields. J. Theor. Biol. **408**, 53–65 (2016)
13. Taylor, B.K.: Bioinspired magnetic reception and multimodal sensing. Biol. Cybern. **111**, 287–308 (2017). https://doi.org/10.1007/s00422-017-0720-3
14. Hunt, A., et al.: Development and training of a neural controller for hind leg walking in a dog robot. Front. Neurorobot. **11**(18) (2017)
15. Zhang, K.: Representation of spatial orientation by the intrinsic dynamics of the head-direction cell ensemble: a theory. J. Neurosci. **16**(6), 2112–2126 (1996)
16. Coombes, S., et al.: Neural Fields: Theory and Applications. Springer, Heidelberg (2014). https://doi.org/10.1007/978-3-642-54593-1
17. Kasabov, N.K.: Time-Space, Spiking Neural Networks and Brain-Inspired Artificial Intelligence. Springer, Berlin (2019). https://doi.org/10.1007/978-3-662-57715-8
18. Harley, C.M., Rossi, M., Cienfuegos, J., Wagenaar, D.: Discontinuous locomotion and prey sensing in the leech. J. Exp. Biol. **216**, 1890–1897 (2013)
19. Izhikevich, E.M.: Dynamical Systems in Neuroscience. MIT Press, Cambridge (2010)

A Plausible Mechanism for *Drosophila* Larva Intermittent Behavior

Panagiotis Sakagiannis[1]([✉]) [iD], Miguel Aguilera[2] [iD], and Martin Paul Nawrot[1] [iD]

[1] Computational Systems Neuroscience, Institute of Zoology, University of Cologne, Cologne, Germany
p.sakagiannis@uni-koeln.de
[2] IAS-Research Center for Life, Mind, and Society, University of the Basque Country, Donostia, Spain
http://computational-systems-neuroscience.de/

Abstract. The behavior of many living organisms is not continuous. Rather, activity emerges in bouts that are separated by epochs of rest, a phenomenon known as intermittent behavior. Although intermittency is ubiquitous across phyla, empirical studies are scarce and the underlying neural mechanisms remain unknown. Here we present the first empirical evidence of intermittency during *Drosophila* larva free exploration. We report power-law distributed rest-bout and log-normal distributed activity-bout durations. We show that a stochastic network model can transition between power-law and non-power-law distributed states and we suggest a plausible neural mechanism for the alternating rest and activity in the larva. Finally, we discuss possible implementations in behavioral simulations extending spatial Levy-walk or coupled-oscillator models with temporal intermittency.

Keywords: Larva crawling · Levy-walks · Neuronal avalanches

1 Introduction

The search for statistical regularities in animal movement is a predominant focus of motion ecology. Random walks form a broad range of models that assume discrete steps of displacement obeying defined statistical rules and acute reorientations. A Levy walk is a random walk where the displacement lengths and the respective displacement durations are drawn from a heavy-tailed, most often a power-law distribution. When considered in a 2D space reorientation angles are drawn from a uniform distribution. This initial basic Levy walk has

Supported by the Research Training Group 'Neural Circuit Analysis' (DFG-RTG 1960, grant no. 233886668) and the Research Unit 'Structure, Plasticity and Behavioral Function of the *Drosophila* mushroom body' (DFG-FOR 2705, grant no. 403329959), funded by the German Research Foundation. M.A. was funded by the UPV/EHU post-doctoral training program ESPDOC17/17 and H2020 Marie Skłodowska-Curie grant 892715, and supported in part by the Basque Government (IT1228-19).

© Springer Nature Switzerland AG 2020
V. Vouloutsi et al. (Eds.): Living Machines 2020, LNAI 12413, pp. 288–299, 2020.
https://doi.org/10.1007/978-3-030-64313-3_28

been extended to encompass distinct behavioral modes bearing different go/turn parameters, thus termed composite Levy walk. Levy walks have been extensively studied in the context of optimal foraging theory. A Levy walk with a power-law exponent between the limit of ballistic ($\alpha = 1$) and brownian motion ($\alpha = 3$) yields higher search efficiency for foragers with an optimum around $\alpha = 2$ when search targets are patchily or scarcely distributed and detection of a target halts displacement (truncated Levy walk) [5].

Nevertheless, the underlying assumption of non-intermittent flow of movement in Levy walk models complicates the identification of the underlying generative mechanisms as they focus predominantly on reproducing the observed spatial trajectories, neglecting the temporal dynamics of locomotory behavior. Therefore, Bartumeus (2009) stressing the need for a further extension coined the term intermittent random walk, emphasizing the integration of behavioral intermittency in the theoretical study of animal movement [2]. Here we aim to contribute to this goal by studying the temporal patterns of intermittency during *Drosophila* larva free exploration in experimental data and in a conceptual model, bearing in mind that power-law like phenomena can arise from a wide range of mechanisms, possibly involving processes of different timescales [5]. While our study remains agnostic towards whether foragers really perform Levy walks - a claim still disputed [5] - we suggest that intrinsic motion intermittency should be taken into account and the assumption of no pauses and acute reorientations should be dropped in favor of integrative models encompassing both activity and inactivity.

Drosophila larva is a suitable organism for the study of animal exploration patterns and the underlying neural mechanisms. A rich repertoire of available genetic tools allows acute activation, inhibition or even induced death of specific neural components. Crawling in 2D facilitates tracking of unconstrained behavior. Also, fruit flies during this life stage are nearly exclusively concerned with foraging. Therefore a food/odor-deprived environment can be largely considered stimulus-free, devoid of reorientation or pause sensory triggers, while target-detection on contact can be considered certain. Truncated spatial Levy-walk patterns of exploration with exponents ranging from 1.5 to near-optimal 1.96 that hold over at least two orders of magnitude have been previously reported for the *Drosophila* larva. The turning-angle distribution, however, was skewed in favor of small angles and a quasi-uniform distribution was observed only for reorientation events $\geq 50°$ [9]. Moreover, it has been shown that these patterns arise from low-level neural circuitry even in the absence of sensory input or brain-lobe function and have therefore been termed 'null movement patterns' [8,9].

Behavioral intermittency has not been described for the fruitfly larva. Previous empirical studies on adult *Drosophila* intermittent locomotory behavior have concluded that the distribution of durations of rest bouts is power-law while that of activity bouts has been reported to be exponential [12] or power-law [8]. Genetic intervention has revealed that dopamine neuron activation affects the activity/rest ratio via modulation of the power-law exponent of the rest bouts, while the distribution of activity bouts remains unaffected. This observation hints towards a neural mechanism that generates the alternating switches between activity and rest where tonic modulatory input from the brain regulates the activity/rest balance according to environmental conditions and possibly homeostatic state.

Here we analyze intermittency in a large experimental dataset and present a conceptual model that generates alternation between rest and activity, capturing empirically observed power-law and non-power-law distributions. We discuss a plausible neural mechanism for the alternation between rest and activity and the regulation of the animal's activity/rest ratio via modulation of the rest-bout power-law exponent by top-down modulatory input. Our approach seeks to elaborate on the currently prevailing view that these patterns result from intrinsic neural noise [8].

2   Materials and Methods

2.1   Experimental Dataset

We use a larva-tracking dataset available at the DRYAD repository, previously used for spatial Levy-walk pattern detection [9]. The dataset consists of up to one hour long recordings of freely moving larvae tracked as a single point (centroid) in 2D space. We consider three temperature-sensitive shibire^{ts} fly mutants allowing for inhibition of mushroom-body (MB247), brain-lobe/SOG (BL) or brain-lobe/SOG/somatosensory (BLsens) neurons and an rpr/hid mutant line inducing temperature-sensitive neuronal death of brain-lobe/SOG/somatosensory (BLsens) neurons. Each mutant expresses a different behavioral phenotype when activated by 32°–33° C temperature. We compare phenotypic behavior to control behavior in non-activated control groups. A reference control group has been formed consisting of all individuals of the four 32°–33° C control groups (Table 1).

Table 1. Dataset description and empirical results for rest/activity bout analyses.

T (°C)	treatment	larvae (#)	tracking time (h)	rest bouts (#)	activity bouts (#)	activity ratio (mu±sigma)
22	BLsens > rpr/hid$_{control}$	33	19.9	869	559	0.9 ± 0.21
32	BLsens > rpr/hid	21	17.16	2251	1504	0.6 ± 0.23
33	MB247/+	16	12.28	1067	666	0.72 ± 0.2
33	MB247 > shi^{ts}	16	13.43	1487	1021	0.64 ± 0.23
22	shi^{ts} /+	19	14.82	1370	861	0.77 ± 0.24
33	shi^{ts} /+	21	16.85	1191	768	0.75 ± 0.19
22	BL/+	17	12.5	570	387	0.87 ± 0.22
33	BL/+	17	10.81	391	286	0.87 ± 0.19
33	BL > shi^{ts}	14	12.78	879	629	0.82 ± 0.22
33	BLsens > shi^{ts}	10	10.53	1553	1007	0.44 ± 0.25
32-33	Reference control	87	59.84	3519	2279	0.83 ± 0.21

For the present study recordings longer than 1024 s have been selected. Instances where larvae contacted the arena borders were excluded. The raw time series of x, y coordinates have been forward-backward filtered with a first-order butterworth low-pass filter of cutoff frequency 0.1 Hz before computing the velocity. The cutoff frequency was selected as to preserve the plateaus of brief stationary periods while suppressing the signal oscillation due to peristaltic-stride cycles. Velocity values ≥ 2.5 mm/s have been discarded to account for observed jumps in single-larva trajectories that are probably due to technical issues during tracking. This arbitrary threshold was selected as an upper limit for larvae of length up to 5 mm, crawling at a speed of up to 2 strides/sec with a scaled displacement per stride of up to 0.25.

2.2   Bout Annotation and Distribution

In order to designate periods of rest and activity we need to define a suitable threshold V_θ in the velocity distribution as done for the adult fruitfly in [12]. We used the density estimation algorithm to locate the first minimum $V_\theta = 0.085$ mm/s in the velocity histogram of the reference control group. A rest bout is then defined as a period during which velocity does not exceed V_θ. Rest bouts necessarily alternate with periods termed activity bouts. The bout annotation method is exemplified for a single larva track in Fig. 2.

To quantify the duration distribution of the rest and activity bouts we used the maximum likelihood estimation (MLE) method to fit a power-law, an exponential and a log-normal distribution for each group as well as for the reference control group. Given the tracking framerate of 2 Hz and the minimal tracking time of 1024 s, we limited our analysis to bouts of duration 2^1 to 2^{10} s. The Kolmogorov-Smirnov distance D_{KS} for each candidate distribution was then computed over 64 logarithmic bins covering this range. Findings are summarized in Table 2 for the rest bouts and in Table 3 for the activity bouts.

3   Results

The results section is organized as follows. Initially we present a simple conceptual two-state model transitioning autonomously between power-law and non-power-law regimes. Next we analyse intermittency during larva free exploration in a freely available dataset [9]. Finally we compare mutant and control larva phenotypes in the context of intermittency.

3.1   Network Model of Binary Units Reproduces Larval Statistics of Intermittent Behavior

Previous work on *Drosophila* adult intermittent behavior reported that rest-bout durations are power-law distributed while activity-bout durations are exponentially distributed [12]. Our first contribution is to provide a simple model displaying how this dual regime might emerge.

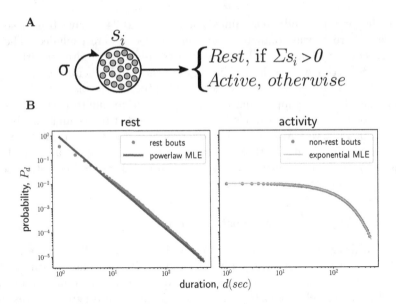

Fig. 1. Probability distribution of the duration d of rest and activity phases in a branching process model of $\sigma = 1$, simulated over 10^5 occurrences of each phase. Duration is measured as the number of updates until a phase is ended. Unit activation $s_i(t)$ propagates to neighbouring units creating self-limiting avalanches. In the rest phase, when $\sum_i s_i(t) > 0$, the system yields a power law distribution with exponent $\alpha \approx 2$. In the activity phase, when $\sum_i s_i(t) = 0$, one unit of the system is activated with probability $\mu = 0.01$, yielding an exponential distribution with coefficient $\lambda = 0.1$.

We define a kinetic Ising model with $N = 1000$ binary neurons, with homogeneous all-to-all connectivity (Fig. 1A). Each neuron i is a stochastic variable with value $s_i(t)$ at time t that can be either 1 or 0 (active or inactive). We assume that this neuron population inhibits locomotory behavior, so that when $\sum_i s_i(t) > 0$ the larva is in the rest phase, and otherwise the larva remains active.

At time $t + 1$, each neuron's activation rate is proportional to the sum of activities at time t, and will be activated with a linear probability function $p_i(t+1) = \frac{\sigma}{N}\sum_j s_j(t) + \frac{\mu}{N}$. Here, σ is the propagation rate, which indicates that when a node is active at time t, it propagates its activation at time $t + 1$ on average to σ other neurons. When one neuron is activated, this model behaves like a branching process [10], with σ as the branching parameter. If $\sigma < 1$, activity tends to decrease rapidly until all units are inactive while, if $\sigma > 1$, activity tends to be amplified until saturation. At the critical point, $\sigma = 1$, activity is propagated in scale-free avalanches, in which duration d of an avalanche once initiated follows a power-law distribution $P(d) \sim d^{-\alpha}$ (Fig. 1B, left), governed by a critical exponent ($\alpha = 2$ at the $N \to \infty$ limit) describing how avalanches at many different scales are generated.

When an avalanche is extinguished, the system returns to quiescence which is only broken by the initiation of a new avalanche. With a residual rate $\mu = 0.01$ the system becomes active by firing one unit and initiating a new avalanche. In this case the duration of quiescence bouts (the interval between two consecutive avalanches) follows an exponential distribution (Fig. 1B, right).

This simple conceptual model alternates autonomously between avalanches of power-law distributed durations and quiescence intervals of exponentially distributed durations. This alternation between power-law and non-power-law regimes can serve as a basic qualitative model of the transition between rest and activity bouts in the larva (cf. Discussion).

3.2 Parameterization of Larval Intermittent Behavior

We analyzed intermittent behavior during larval crawling in a stimulus-free environment (cf. Materials and Methods for dataset description). Each individual larva was video-tracked in space (Fig. 2A). From the time series of spatial coordinates we computed the instantaneous velocity and determined a threshold value (Fig. 2B) that separates plateaus of continued activity (activity bouts) from epochs of inactivity (rest bouts, Fig. 2C–D) following the analyses suggested in [12].

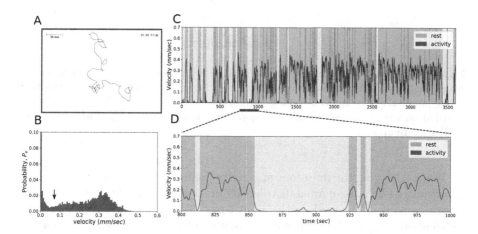

Fig. 2. Bout annotation methodology. A. Individual larva trajectory. Spatial scale and recording duration are noted. B. Velocity distribution for the single larva. The threshold obtained from the reference group, used for rest vs activity bout annotation is denoted by the arrow. C. The entire velocity time series of the larva. Rest and activity bouts are indicated by different background colors. D. Magnification of the velocity time series.

We start out with the analysis of experimental control groups that were not subjected to genetic intervention. As a first step we computed the number of occurrences of rest and activity bouts and the activity ratio, which quantifies the accumulated activity time as fraction of the total time (Table 1). For the reference control group we obtain an activity ratio of 0.83 albeit with a fairly large variance across individuals.

For the duration distribution of rest bouts we find that it is best approximated by a power-law distribution in all six control groups (Table 2) in line with previous results reported for the adult fruitfly [8,12]. The empirical duration distribution of rest-bouts across the reference control group is depicted in Fig. 3A (red dots). Again, the power law provides the best distribution fit. The exponent α of the power law ranges from 1.514 to 1.938 with $\alpha = 1.598$ for the reference control group.

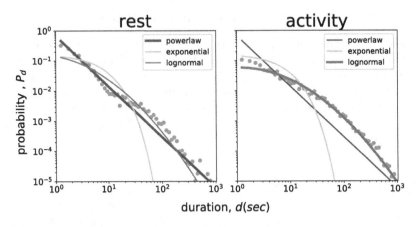

Fig. 3. Probability density of rest and activity bout durations for the reference control group. Dots stand for probability densities over logarithmic bins. Lines are the best fitting power-law, exponential and log-normal distributions. The thick line denotes the distribution having the minimum Kolmogorov-Smirnov distance D_{KS} (Tables 2 and 3). (COlor figure online)

When analyzing the durations of activity bouts we found that these are best approximated by a log-normal distribution in all groups (Table 3). This result is surprising as previous work in the adult suggested the mode of an exponential distribution [12]. For the reference control group Fig. 3B compares the empirical duration distribution of activity bouts with the fits of the three distribution functions.

3.3 Modification of Rest and Activity Bout Durations in Mutant Flies

Behavioral phenotypes in genetic mutants can help identify brain neuropiles in the nervous system of *Drosophila* larva that are involved in the generation of intermittent behavior, or that have an effect on its modulation. To this end we analyzed 4 experimental groups where genetic intervention was controlled by temperature either via the temperature-sensitive shibire protocol or via temperature-induced neuronal death (rpr/hid genotype). Each group is compared to a non-activated control group as shown in Fig. 4 and described in Table 1.

Interestingly, genetic intervention can have a large effect on the activity ratio. When inactivating sensory neurons and to a lesser extend the mushroom body the activity ratio is decreased (cf. BLsens > rpr/hid, MB247 > shi^{ts} and BLsens > shi^{ts} in Table 1). Inspection of the empirical duration distribution of rest bouts in Fig. 4 (first and third columns) shows that while the power-law fit is superior for all control groups, the log-normal fit approximates best the respective mutant distribution in 3 out of 4 cases (cf. MB247 > shi^{ts}, BL > shi^{ts} and BLsens > shi^{ts} in Table 2. This might hint impairment of the power-law generating processes due to neural dysfunction. In the fourth case of BLsens > rpr/hid the power-law is preserved but shifted to higher values. Regarding activity, the empirical distributions indicate that overall the activity epochs are severely shortened in time for both the BLsens > rpr/hid and the BLsens > shi^{ts} mutants in comparison to the respective control groups (second and fourth columns) hinting early termination of activity bouts by the intermittency mechanism.

Table 2. Distribution parameter fits of empirical rest bout duration. The relevant parameters for the best fitting distribution are indicated in bold text.

T (°C)	treatment	rest bouts						
		powerlaw		exponential		lognormal		
		alpha	KS D	lambda	KS D	mu	sigma	KS D
22	BLsens > rpr/hid$_{control}$	**1.938**	**0.089**	0.119	0.411	1.066	1.122	0.171
32	BLsens > rpr/hid	**1.6**	**0.094**	0.04	0.439	1.665	1.476	0.13
33	MB247/+	**1.58**	**0.06**	0.042	0.438	1.724	1.55	0.133
33	MB247 > shi^{ts}	1.41	0.167	0.029	0.246	**2.438**	**1.574**	**0.073**
22	shi^{ts}/+	**1.702**	**0.086**	0.049	0.494	1.425	1.369	0.149
33	shi^{ts}/+	**1.465**	**0.099**	0.027	0.384	2.151	1.699	0.103
22	BL/+	**1.783**	**0.046**	0.048	0.538	1.277	1.399	0.181
33	BL/+	**1.514**	**0.101**	0.039	0.406	1.944	1.623	0.127
33	BL > shi^{ts}	1.666	0.109	0.111	0.246	**1.502**	**1.189**	**0.103**
33	BLsens > shi^{ts}	1.483	0.125	0.033	0.387	**2.072**	**1.554**	**0.105**
32-33	Reference control	**1.598**	**0.061**	0.044	0.448	1.671	1.55	0.14

4 Discussion

As most neuroscientific research focuses either on static network connectivity or on neural activation/inhibition - behavior correlations, an integrative account of how temporal behavioral statistical patterns arise from unperturbed neural dynamics is still lacking. In this context, we hope to contribute to scientific discovery in a dual way. Firstly by extending existing mechanistic hypothesis for larva intermittent behavior and secondly by promoting the integration of intermittency in functional models of larval behavior. In what follows we elaborate on these goals and finally describe certain limitations of our study.

Table 3. Distribution parameter fits of empirical activity bout duration. The relevant parameters for the best fitting distribution are indicated in bold text.

T (°C)	treatment	activity bouts						
		powerlaw		exponential		lognormal		
		alpha	KS D	lambda	KS D	mu	sigma	KS D
22	BLsens > rpr/hid_control	1.351	0.177	0.017	0.249	**2.847**	**1.641**	**0.041**
32	BLsens > rpr/hid	1.591	0.196	0.096	0.189	**1.691**	**1.101**	**0.062**
33	MB247/+	1.428	0.149	0.032	0.248	**2.336**	**1.524**	**0.063**
33	MB247 > shi^ts	1.391	0.212	0.027	0.227	**2.557**	**1.412**	**0.035**
22	shi^ts /+	1.371	0.175	0.025	0.212	**2.699**	**1.528**	**0.066**
33	shi^ts /+	1.359	0.184	0.018	0.287	**2.786**	**1.634**	**0.044**
22	BL/+	1.335	0.191	0.018	0.214	**2.988**	**1.644**	**0.079**
33	BL/+	1.327	0.215	0.015	0.224	**3.058**	**1.566**	**0.042**
33	BL > shi^ts	1.483	0.179	0.045	0.252	**2.07**	**1.353**	**0.063**
33	BLsens > shi^ts	1.682	0.209	0.147	0.201	**1.466**	**1.011**	**0.096**
32-33	Reference control	1.366	0.173	0.019	0.26	**2.73**	**1.617**	**0.046**

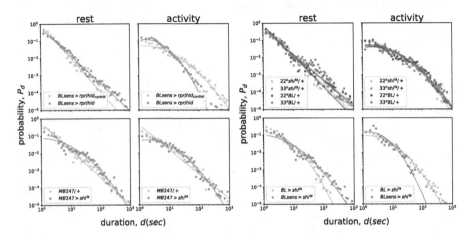

Fig. 4. Probability density of rest and activity bout durations for control and activated mutant genotypes. In the first two diagram pairs mutants are plotted against their single respective controls. In the fourth pair the rest two mutants are plotted with their 4 control groups shown in the third diagram pair. Dots stand for probability densities over logarithmic bins. Lines indicate the distribution with the lowest Kolmogorov-Smirnov distance D_{KS} among the best fitting power-law, exponential and log-normal distributions for each group (Tables 2 and 3).

4.1   Self-limiting Inhibitory Waves Might Underlie Intermittent Crawling and Its Modulation

The neural mechanisms underlying intermittency in larva behavior remain partly unknown. Displacement runs are intrinsically discretized, comprised of repetitive, stereotypical peristaltic strides. These stem from segmental central pattern generator circuits (CPG) located in the ventral nerve chord, involving both excitatory and inhibitory premotor neurons and oscillating independently of sensory feedback [7]. A 'visceral pistoning' mechanism involving head and tail-segment synchronous contraction underlies stride initiation [4]. Speed is mainly controlled via stride frequency [4]. Crawling is intermittently stopped during both stimulus-free exploratory behavior and chemotaxis, giving rise to non-stereotypical stationary bouts during which reorientation might occur. During the former they are intrinsically generated without need for sensory feedback or brain input [9], while during the latter an olfactory-driven sensorimotor pathway facilitates cessation of runs when navigating down-gradient. Specifically, inhibition of a posterior-segment premotor network by a sub-esophageal zone descending neuron deterministically terminates runs allowing easier reorientation [11].

It is reasonable to assume that this intermittent crawling inhibition is underlying both free exploration and chemotaxis, potentially in the form of transient inhibitory bursts. A neural network controlling the CPG through generation of self-limiting inhibitory waves is well suited for such a role. In the simplest case, during stimulus-free exploration, the durations of the generated inhibitory waves should follow a power-law distribution, behaviorally observed as rest bouts. In contrast, non-power-law distributed quiescent periods of the network would disinhibit locomotion allowing the CPG to generate repetitive peristaltic strides resulting in behaviorally observed runs.

The model we presented (cf. Sect. 3.1) alternates autonomously between avalanches of power-law distributed durations and quiescence intervals of exponentially distributed durations without need for external input. Therefore it can serve as a theoretical basis for the development of both generative models that reproduce the intermittent behavior of individual larvae and of the above mechanistic hypothesis for the initiation and cessation of peristaltic locomotion in the larva through disinhibition and inhibition of the crawling CPG respectively. To uncover the underlying neural mechanism and confirm/reject our hypothesis, inhibitory input to the crawling CPG should be sought, measured neurophysiologically and correlated to behaviorally observed stride and stride-free bouts during stimulus-free exploration.

Intermittent behavior in the *Drosophila* adult is subject to two modes of modulation, neither of which affects the distribution of the activity bouts. Firstly, high ambient temperature and daylight raise the activity ratio over long timescales by raising the number of activity bouts [12]. This is achieved by lowering the probability of the extremely long rest bouts, without affecting the power-law exponent of the distribution, which coincides with fewer sleep events (>5 min) observed during the day. This modulation is long-lasting and could result from a different constant tonic activation of the system. Secondly, dopamine neuron activation raises the activity ratio acutely by modulation of the power-law exponent upwards [12] skewing locomotion towards the brownian limit. This modulation could be transient in the context of salient phasic stimulation by the environment.

As mentioned above, during chemotaxis larvae perform more and sharpest reorientations, terminating runs when navigating down-gradient. In case the above hold for the larval nervous system as well, a hypothesis integrating both experimental findings could be that this behavior stems from transient olfactory-driven dopaminergically-modulated inhibition of the crawling CPG. Our conceptual model can be extended to address the above claims by adding tonic and/or phasic input.

4.2 Intermittency Can Extend Functional Models of Larva Locomotion

Traditional random walk models fail to capture the temporal dynamics of animal exploration [5]. Even when time is taken into account in terms of movement speed, reorientations are assumed to occur acutely. Integrating intermittency can address this limitation allowing for more accurate functional models of autonomous behaving agents. Such virtual agents can then be used in simulations of behavioral experiments promoting neuroscientifically informed hypothesis that advance over current knowledge and generate predictions that can stimulate further empirical work [1].

It is widely assumed that *Drosophila* larva exploration can be described as a random walk of discrete non-overlapping runs and reorientations/head-casts [9] or alternatively that it is generated by the concurrent combined activity of a crawler and a turner module generating repetitive oscillatory forward peristaltic strides and lateral bending motions respectively and possibly involving energy transfer between the two mechanical modes [3,6,13]. Both models can easily be upgraded by adding crawling intermittency which might or might not be independent of the lateral bending mechanism. In the discrete-mode case, intermittency can simply control the duration and transitions between runs and head-casts or introduce a third mode of immobile pauses resulting in a temporally unfolding random walk. In the overlapping-mode case the two modules are complemented by a controlling intermittency module forming an interacting triplet. Depending on the crawler-turner interaction and the effect of intermittency on the turner module, multiple locomotory patterns emerge including straight runs, curved runs, stationary head-casts and immobile pauses. This simple extension would allow temporal fitting of generative models to experimental observations in addition to the primarily pursued spatial-trajectory fitting, facilitating the use of calibrated virtual larvae in simulations of behavioral experiments.

4.3 Limitations

A limitation of our study is that due to the single-spinepoint tracking, it is impossible to determine whether micro-movements occur during the designated inactivity periods, an issue also unclear for adult fruitflies in [12]. It follows that in our analysed dataset and in [12], immobile pauses, feeding motions and stationary head casts are indistinguishable. Therefore, what we define as rest bouts should be considered as periods lacking at least peristaltic strides but not any locomotory activity whatsoever. Our relatively low velocity threshold $V_\theta = 0.085\,\text{mm/s}$ though allows stricter detection of rest bouts as it is evident from the higher activity ratio (higher than 0.7 in most control groups in comparison to lower than 0.25 in [12]). To tackle this, trackings of higher spatial resolution with more spinepoints tracked per larva are needed, despite the computational challenge of the essentially long recording duration.

Also, our results show that an exponential distribution of activity bouts [12] as reported for the adult fruitfly might not be the case for the larva, as we detected log-normal long-tails in all cases. Still, the exponential-power-law duality in our model illustrates switching between independent and coupled modes of neural activity. Substituting the exponential regime by other long-tailed distribution such as log-normal might require assuming more complex interactions between the switching regimes and will be pursued in the future so that generative models of the data can be fit.

References

1. Barandiaran, X.E., Chemero, A.: Animats in the modeling ecosystem. Adapt. Behav. **17**(4), 287–292 (2009). https://doi.org/10.1177/1059712309340847
2. Bartumeus, F.: Behavioral intermittence, Levy patterns, and randomness in animal movement. Oikos **118**, 488–494 (2009). https://doi.org/10.1111/j.1600-0706.2008. 17313.x
3. Davies, A., Louis, M., Webb, B.: A model of drosophila larva chemotaxis. PLoS Comput. Biol. **11**(11), 1–24 (2015). https://doi.org/10.1371/journal.pcbi.1004606
4. Heckscher, E.S., Lockery, S.R., Doe, C.Q.: Characterization of drosophila larval crawling at the level of organism, segment, and somatic body wall musculature. J. Neurosci. **32**(36), 12460–12471 (2012). https://doi.org/10.1523/jneurosci.0222-12. 2012
5. James, A., Plank, M.J., Edwards, A.M.: Assessing Lévy walks as models of animal foraging. J. R. Soc. Interface **8**(62), 1233–1247 (2011). https://doi.org/10.1098/ rsif.2011.0200
6. Loveless, J., Lagogiannis, K., Webb, B.: Modelling the neuromechanics of exploration and taxis in larval Drosophila. PLoS Comput. Biol. 1–33 (2019). https:// doi.org/10.5281/zenodo.1432637
7. Mantziaris, C., Bockemühl, T., Büschges, A.: Central pattern generating networks in insect locomotion. Dev. Neurobiol. (October 2019), 1–15 (2020). https://doi. org/10.1002/dneu.22738
8. Reynolds, A.M., et al.: Evidence for a pervasive 'idling-mode' activity template in flying and pedestrian insects. R. Soc. Open Sci. **2**, 150085 (2015). https://doi.org/ 10.1098/rsos.150085
9. Sims, D.W., Humphries, N.E., Hu, N., Medan, V., Berni, J.: Optimal searching behaviour generated intrinsically by the central pattern generator for locomotion. Elife **8**, 1–31 (2019). https://doi.org/10.7554/eLife.50316
10. Slade, G.: Probabilistic models of critical phenomena. The Princeton companion to mathematics pp. 343–346 (2008)
11. Tastekin, I., et al.: Sensorimotor pathway controlling stopping behavior during chemotaxis in the Drosophila melanogaster larva. Elife **7**, 1–38 (2018). https:// doi.org/10.7554/elife.38740
12. Ueno, T., Masuda, N., Kume, S., Kume, K.: Dopamine modulates the rest period length without perturbation of its power law distribution in Drosophila melanogaster. PLoS One **7**(2), e32007 (2012). https://doi.org/10.1371/journal. pone.0032007
13. Wystrach, A., Lagogiannis, K., Webb, B.: Continuous lateral oscillations as a core mechanism for taxis in Drosophila larvae. Elife **5**, e15504 (2016). https://doi.org/ 10.7554/elife.15504

Robophysical Modeling of Bilaterally Activated and Soft Limbless Locomotors

Perrin E. Schiebel, Marine C. Maisonneuve, Kelimar Diaz, Jennifer M. Rieser, and Daniel I. Goldman$^{(\boxtimes)}$

Georgia Institute of Technology, Atlanta, GA 30332, USA
daniel.goldman@physics.gatech.edu

Abstract. Animals like snakes use traveling waves of body bends to move in multi-component terrestrial terrain. Previously we studied [Schiebel et al., *PNAS*, 2019] a desert specialist, *Chionactis occipitalis*, traversing sparse rigid obstacles and discovered that passive body buckling, facilitated by unilateral muscle activation, allowed obstacle negotiation without additional control input. Most snake robots have one motor per joint whose positions are precisely controlled. In contrast, we introduce a robophysical model designed to capture muscle morphology and activation patterns in snakes; pairs of muscles, one on each side of the spine, create body bends by unilaterally contracting. The robot snake has 8 joints and 16 motors. The joint angle is set by activating the motor on one side, spooling a cable around a pulley to pull the joint that direction. Inspired by snake muscle activation patterns [Jayne, J. *Morph.*, 1988], we programmed the motors to be unilaterally active and propagate a sine wave down the body. When a motor is inactive, it is unspooled so that its wire cannot generate tension. Pairs of motors can thus resist forces which attempt to lengthen active wires but not those pushing them shorter, resulting in a kinematically soft robot that can be passively deformed by the surroundings. The robot can move on hard ground when drag anisotropy is large, achieved via wheels attached to the bottom of each segment, passively re-orient to track a wall upon a head-on collision, and traverse a multi-post array with open loop control facilitated by buckling and emergent reversal behaviors. In summary, we present a new approach to design limbless robots, offloading the control into the mechanics of the robot, a successful strategy in legged robots [Saranli et al., *IJRR*, 2001].

Keywords: Snake robot · Complex terrain · Passive dynamics

1 Introduction

The elongate, limbless body plan seen in organisms like snakes is versatile, facilitating locomotion in habitats ranging from aquatic to arboreal [5]. This adapt-

Supported by NSF PoLS PHY-1205878, PHY-1150760, and CMMI-1361778. ARO W911NF-11-1-0514, U.S. DoD, NDSEG 32 CFR 168a (P.E.S.), and the NSF Simons Southeast Center for Mathematics and Biology (SCMB).

P. E. Schiebel and M. C. Maisonneuve—These authors contributed equally to the work.

V. Vouloutsi et al. (Eds.): Living Machines 2020, LNAI 12413, pp. 300–311, 2020.
https://doi.org/10.1007/978-3-030-64313-3_29

ability makes limbless locomotion an attractive strategy for robots, especially those intended for tasks like search and rescue where the surroundings can be confined or unstable. However, this mode of locomotion requires coordinating a high degree-of-freedom body, a task which is further complicated by the addition of environmental heterogeneities.

There are two broad classes for the treatment of terrain heterogeneities in snake robots; obstacle avoidance [6] and obstacle-aided locomotion [28]. A challenge to both classes is obstacles that cause forces resisting forward motion. Traditional snake robots have one motor per joint ([7,16,20], Fig. 1A), and thus must use sensing and control strategies to avoid deleterious terrain interactions.

Ensuring useful robot coordination while bypassing obstacles generally requires sophisticated control. For example, Transeth et al. [28] developed a hybrid model to determine joint trajectories for obstacle aided locomotion. Computation can be simplified in some cases by using a lower-dimensional intermediary between motion planning and control such as shape functions [29] or virtual functional segments [21]. Decentralized control, inspired by biological central pattern generators [9], can further reduce central control complexity by offloading computation to local reflexes, whether to avoid obstacles [30], adapt to changes in the environment [10,24], or use obstacles for propulsion [13,14]. These strategies make use of knowledge of the terrain in a closed-loop control. Robots can collect this information using vision [18], contact sensing [2,27,30], contact force sensing [15], or joint-torque measurements [29].

In contrast to most limbless robots, snakes articulate their joints using bilateral musculature. The lateral body bends the animals use to generate propulsion during terrestrial locomotion are achieved by alternating unilateral activation of the epaxial muscles (Fig. 1B) [12].

We previously studied the desert-dwelling Shovel-nosed snake, *Chionactis occipitalis* (Fig. 1C), which uses a stereotyped serpenoid waveform (sinusoidally varying curvature) to move quickly (but non-inertially [25]) across its natural habitat consisting of a sandy substrate and sparse heterogeneities like rocks, twigs, and plants [17,25]. We found evidence that this snake used a control strategy in which it targeted the muscle activation pattern for a waveform that allowed fast motion on the granular substrate and did not change this pattern in response to collisions with the surroundings. Our study suggested that this "open-loop" movement was facilitated by unilaterally activated muscles which allowed the body to be passively deformed by the surroundings (Fig. 1D, [26]). This work indicated that a similar unilateral activation scheme could aid snake-like robots in navigating obstacles without the need for sensing or control which responds to the surroundings.

Addition of mechanical compliance can help prevent robots from becoming jammed in obstacles. This has typically been achieved by adding a torsional spring element to the actuators [20,22,24]. As these robots are still driven by a single actuator per joint, however, directional compliance such as observed in the animal can only be achieved using active feedback. Further, when deformed away

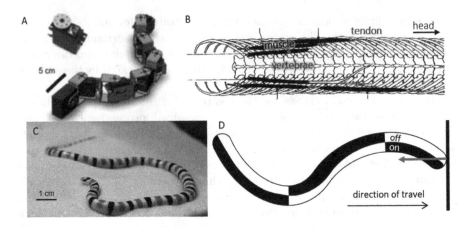

Fig. 1. Types of actuation in limbless locomotors. (A) CAD model of a limbless robot made of rigidly linked servomotors. Inset is a single motor used to bend the joints both left and right. (B) Simplified snake anatomy that illustrates musculoskeletal system used to create lateral body bends. From [5] (C) *C. occipitalis* on a model desert sand ($297 \pm 40\,\mu$m glass particles) in the laboratory. (D) Cartoon of muscle activation and asymmetric compliance. Black areas are active muscles, white are inactive. Muscle segments transition from "on" to "off" at the apexes of the waveform. When the animal experiences external forces, e.g. the gray arrow, the body buckles toward active muscles.

from its resting shape the compliant spring element will exert torque resisting the external force.

Our goal was to develop a robophysical model that captured the bilateral compliance of the snake. The design target was a robot that would be able to successfully execute snake-like waveforms and would offer very little resistance to forces acting to bend the joints toward active motor units. We began by simplifying to a pair of actuators per joint, one on either side, spanning a single joint (Fig. 2). Each individual actuator, like a muscle, can only act to close the joint in one direction. By working in tandem the actuator pairs bend the joint both directions.

We used our robophysical model to test the bilateral actuation scheme. The device was able to mimic the waveform of the biological snake to translate across a homogeneous substrate by using wheels to provide the necessary anisotropic forces [8,19]. The bilaterally-actuated robot passively re-orients its direction of motion when encountering a solid wall. Further, the robot is able to navigate a hexagonal lattice without feedback from the environment, by passively buckling and reversing. This indicates the utility of such a scheme in aiding limbless locomotion in complex terrains.

2   Materials and Methods

The robot consists of nine 3D printed segments attached by eight pin joints and 16 actuators, one on each side of every joint (Fig. 2A). The robot was modular such that segments could be added, subtracted, or replaced as needed. The bottom of each joint was designed to interface with LEGO blocks so that the robot-ground contact could be easily changed. For this experiment, we used LEGO wheels to create the anisotropic force needed for effective undulatory locomotion [8].

Each segment had a rigid midline and two curved side lobes that supported the motors, provided an attachment point for the Kevlar thread cables, and served to protect the cables from the surroundings. On the top of each side lobe there was a motor adapter. A joint consisted of two segments and two motor/pulley/thread assemblies, one on each side (Fig. 2). The joints could freely rotate in the horizontal plane but were designed to limit off-axis motion. Thus the robot's shape changes were largely constrained to two dimensions, although some vertical bending was observed, as further discussed below. Each segment had a holder for an IR reflective marker, and an OptiTrack motion capture system (Natural Point) tracked the position of the markers.

Inoue et al. [11] developed a biologically-inspired robot with bilateral actuation using McKibben-type actuators. The goal of the McKibben-actuated robot was to model the muscle morphology and dynamics of the animal as closely as possible. Our interest was to understand how the passive mechanical properties of the bilateral activation scheme facilitates navigating obstacles. For this purpose our robot has the advantage of an easily reconfigurable 3D printed design and the thread offers negligible resistance to compressive forces.

The target waveform for the robot's joint angles, ζ_i (Fig. 2C), was a *serpenoid curve* [6], $\zeta_i(t) = \zeta_{max} sin(ks_i + 2\pi ft)$. $k = 1$ is the spatial frequency, $f = 0.3$ Hz is the undulation frequency, and $\zeta_{max} = 0.87$ radians is the maximum joint angle. We chose to have one wave on the body, as this was few enough waves to be resolved with the number of joints but was also sufficient for forward motion without excessive slipping or over-torquing motors.

The motor-pulley-thread actuators had two states, actively shortening and passively lengthening, in which the motors were spooling and unspooling thread, respectively. On the active side the motor tracked the serpenoid joint angle positions, spooling the thread to reduce the gap between the pulley and adjacent segment's side lobe (Fig. 2C, red "on" cable). The change between active and passive occurred when the thread was maximally shortened, at peaks of the sinusoidal wave[1]. When a motor changed from active to passive, it would rapidly unspool to a set position where the joint could fully close without causing tension on the thread (Fig. 1C, black "off" cable). While the current study was focused on unilateral activation, this setup allowed for bilateral actuation as well and thus could be also used to explore co-contraction.

---

[1] The sign of the commanded joint angle velocity was used to determine state.

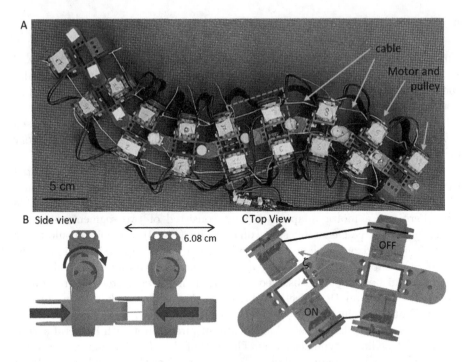

Fig. 2. Two-actuator-joint design for a biarticulated limbless robot. (A) Top down view of the robot on a rubber mat. Yellow dashed line encloses one joint unit. Note that the hemispherical head is seen in Fig. 4A. (B) Side view of the CAD model of a joint made of two segments. Cable path illustrated in yellow. The cable is affixed to the side lobe of one segment, passes through a hole in the lobe of the neighboring segment, and winds around the pulley. When the motor spools the cable in the direction indicated by the blue arrow, the cable generates force as shown by the green arrows. (C) Top view. The red and black lines are a cartoon of the cable on the actively spooling motor and inactive unspooled motor, respectively. Yellow arrows indicate the angle ζ between adjacent segments. (Color figure online)

We measured the relationship between commanded motor position and resulting joint angle (Fig. 3A). The relationship was predominantly linear, although there was some systematic deviation. For the current work we chose to use the linear relationship to control the robot.

It was necessary to empirically adjust the cable lengths so that each joint had the same range of motion. This was done by hand, such that there was some discrepancy between how well different joints tracked the commanded signal (Fig. 3B). Nevertheless, the current robot successfully tracked the commanded angles (Fig. 3D), leading to snake-like locomotion across a rubber mat substrate (Fig. 3C–F, forces generated by the wheels on this substrate are similar to those acting on a snake trunk segment moving through sand [19]). Importantly, like the sand-swimming snake studied in [25,26], the robot's dynamics were highly overdamped; if it stopped self-deforming, it rapidly stopped translating (see analysis of a similar propulsion scheme in [19]).

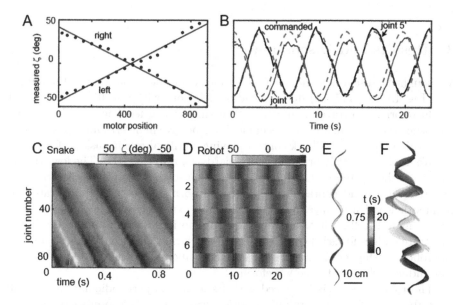

Fig. 3. Robot moves using lateral undulation (A) Robot joint ζ as a function of the commanded motor positions. Two motors are shown, one which bends its joint left (blue markers and line), and one which bends right (black markers and line). Lines are linear fits to the data. Slopes ± 0.1 and intercepts $+42.0$ and -43.9 for left and right motor, respectively ($R^2 = 0.98$ for both). (B) ζ as a function of time. Shown are joints 1 (light purple curve) and 5 (black curve). The commanded trajectory for each joint is a gray, dashed line. (C) Spacetime plot of ζ measured on the snake. We used a cubic-spline interpolant to upsample tracked points as in [25]. Note joint numbers are less than the number of snake vertebrae. (D) Spacetime plot of ζ measured on the robot. (E) Tracked snake midlines as the animal moves across the model desert sand, colored by time. (F) Tracked robot midlines on mat with wheels, colored by time. (Color figure online)

We next added a hemispherical head to the first joint so that the robot would not contact obstacles with a flat surface (see Fig. 4B). However, adding the head was unexpectedly detrimental to the robot's ability to remain coordinated and perform the serpenoid curve. Surprisingly, adding a 200 g weight between the head and the first joint resulted in coordination and effective locomotion. Observing the robot from the side, we noticed that when the robot was moving either without the head or with the head plus the additional mass, the segments at the curve apexes would slightly lift off the ground. This *sinus lifting* is observed in biological snakes [8,25] and serves to remove those segments which are not generating thrust from contact with the substrate. The robot with only the head and no added mass did not exhibit the lifting kinematics. Our hypothesis was that the mass of the head generated torque that prevented the motors from lifting segments, and torque from the added mass countered that of the head.

3   Results and Discussion

We sought to discover if the open-loop robot could body-buckle like the animal (e.g. Fig. 4A, t = 117 ms) during head-on collisions with a wall, and whether it would re-orient to travel along the wall without using feedback. Wall following has been studied from a neuromechanical perspective in invertebrate (cockroach) locomotion [4], with feedback control playing a critical role in task performance.

We used a vertically oriented whiteboard as a wall (Fig. 4B). The low-friction surface of the whiteboard simplified the system so that the robot was primarily experienced ground contact forces and wall normal forces. The substrate was a smooth wooden surface. While we initially explored robot locomotion on a rubber mat (Fig. 2A) that facilitated low-slip motion, we found impurities in the substrate (ridges for grip) could cause the waveform to deform. While slipping of the robot was higher on the wooden surface it allowed us to more easily observe wall-induced changes to the waveform.

The robot was initially placed with its long axis perpendicular to the wall (Fig. 4B, t = −2 s). The robot's position was randomly chosen between each trial to vary the phase of the wave and position of the head when it contacted the wall. In all cases the robot performed at least one full cycle of the waveform before contacting the wall. The experiment would stop when the long axis of the robot was fully parallel to the wall. The snake data was from [26]. In these experiments the animal moved freely across the model granular substrate into a vertical whiteboard wall.

The robot began by moving across the substrate using the serpenoid waveform (Fig. 4B, t = −2 s) similar to that used by the snake (Fig. 4A, t = −64 ms). The robot initially deformed under external forces from the wall, with large amplitude curves appearing on the body (Fig. 4B, t = 4.5 s). The animal also deformed, leading to areas of high curvature (Fig. 4A, t = 117 ms).

Unlike the snake, in some robot trials we initially observed a straightening behavior after impact (Fig. 4B, t = 0 s) and the increased amplitude became apparent after half a cycle (Fig. 4B, t = 1–4.5 s). After this initial interaction the front of the robot began to turn until the anterior segments were parallel to the wall (Fig. 4B, t = 8 s). If at this point the robot was not re-oriented sufficiently to continue along the wall, the same process would repeat one or more times (note head turning back into the wall at Fig. 4B, t = 10 s). Once the robot was rotated enough, it returned to its initial waveform and amplitude (Fig. 4B, t = 13 s).

While both the snake and robot turned to travel along the wall (Fig. 4C), this process required more gait cycles in the robot. We characterized the number of undulations the robot underwent before it successfully turned (defined as 70%

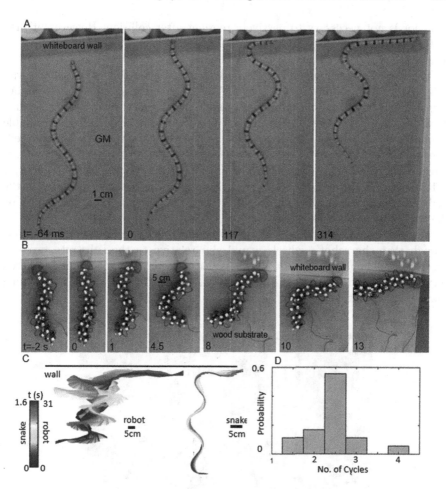

Fig. 4. Passive undulatory re-orientation during wall collisions. (A) The shovel-nosed snake *C. occipitalis* snake travels up the page on the model desert sand. The nose of the snake contacts the wall at t = 0 ms. Time relative to contact is shown above each frame. (B) Snake robot travels up the page on the wood substrate. Time is labelled above each from relative to the initial wall contact occurring at t = 0 s. (C) Tracked midlines of example robot (*left*) and snake (*right*) trials, colored by time. Wall location indicated by black line. (D) Probability for the number of cycles needed for the robot to execute a 90° turn after the wall collision (defined as 70% of the robot's long axis parallel to the wall). 18 trials included.

of the body parallel to the wall). The robot took on average 2.4 ± 0.6 undulation cycles to reorient (Fig. 4D). The animal never required more than one undulation, instead the body would buckle until the anterior end of the trunk was parallel to the wall (Fig. 4B, t = 314 ms) after which the snake would change behavior. The animals either explored the wall with the nose or vaulted the front of the body off the substrate to climb over it. The robot demonstrates that changing behavior is not necessary to passively reorient after collision. However, it may be that changing strategy after the initial buckling is desirable. For example, to reverse the direction change caused by the obstacle.

While both the robot and snake body buckled after collision with the wall (Fig. 4A, t = 4.5 s and Fig. 4B, t = 117 ms), the snake would bend to higher curvatures. The animal has more joints and a higher aspect ratio (length divided by width) than the robot. Increasing the number of joints increases the available resolution while increasing aspect ratio allows higher curvature bends before self-intersection of the body. The snake's morphology thus allowed it to use more waves along the body (average wavenumber on the surface of granular matter is 1.9 waves [25]). We hypothesize that this allows the posterior portions of the body to continue providing thrust while the front portion is being buckled by the environmental forces.

We note that, even in our setup where the robot-terrain friction was low-enough that the robot's wheels would slip relative to the substrate, we still observed buckling of the joints. This was because our mechanical design offered very little resistance, less than the other forces acting on the robot, to buckling toward active motors.

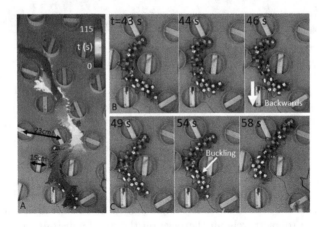

Fig. 5. Passive buckling and reversals facilitate open-loop traversal of a model cluttered terrain. (A) Tracked robot midlines as the robot moves up the page, colored by time. (B) Robot passive backing behavior in the lattice. Time is labelled above each frame. (C) Robot passive buckling behavior in the lattice. Time is labelled above each frame.

We next tested our robot in a simplified model for heterogeneous terrain, a regular array of posts rigidly affixed to a wood substrate (Fig. 5A). The robot was able to traverse the lattice with open-loop control, without any knowledge of its surroundings (Fig. 5A). The post diameter, 15 cm, was chosen to be large enough so that posts could not fit between the robot's joints and interfere with the thread. When the robot entered configurations where forces from the posts prevented forward motion (e.g. Fig. 5B, C), the passive mechanism helped resolve jams.

Buckling behavior, previously observed seen in the wall collision assay (Fig. 5C), was observed when the robot was jammed between posts. At t = 49 s in Fig. 5C the robot is jammed between four posts and the robot is unable to progress. At 54 s the force from the rightmost post buckles the body, allowing the robot to reposition itself and resume the nominal waveform, continuing past the top post by t = 58 s.

An emergent reversal behavior occurred when jamming deformed the waveform in a way that it did not provide sufficient propulsion. In Fig. 5C at t = 43–44 s the robot is stuck between several posts in a configuration that disallows the nominal waveform. At 46 s the front of the robot has moved slightly backward, allowing the head to progress around the post as seen at 49 s.

Unlike the control schemes used to prevent jamming in traditional snake robots [29], our robot was able to solve jams without sensing the obstacles or changing the motor activation pattern. However, this strategy did typically require multiple undulation cycles to become unstuck, and was not always successful. A trial was ended if for 10 undulations the robot was unable to progress. In 2/6 trials the robot did not progress.

Future work can characterize the genesis of the unsolvable jams. This can inform whether changes to the robot, such as increasing the number of joints and the maximum joint angles to give the robot greater flexibility more akin to that of the biological snake, will extend the situations where the purely passive mechanism can contend with adverse heterogeneities. Further study can also determine whether the robot without wheels can use the posts for propulsion as well as in which situations a more sophisticated sensing and control program is needed.

4 Conclusion

Here, we present a novel snake robot that relies on a two-actuator joint scheme to model bilateral muscle activation patterns seen in snakes [12]. Our robot is completely open loop, passively deforming and adapting to the environment without sensing or control. By offloading the control into the mechanics of the robot, a successful strategy in legged robots [23], our robot can capture snake-like behavior (e.g. buckling) and navigate complex terrain.

The two-actuator-joint scheme was able to mimic snake locomotion when freely moving while also allowing snake-like passive body buckling. We note the wall following scheme that emerges in our snake robot requires no feedback; in this way it complements the work of [4]. We posit that the wall following could be aided via addition of head contact sensing with a amplitude modulated turning scheme [1]. Further, our robot was able to traverse a multi-post array, resolving jams with passive body buckling and emergent backing behaviors.

While our work has drawn inspiration from snakes, many animals across different environments and length scales rely on undulatory locomotion, using bilateral activation of their muscles to generate and propagate waves along their body (e.g. *C. elegans* [3]). Therefore, we can use our robot (whose dynamics are highly damped [19]) to test the bilateral actuation scheme in undulators across different length scales and terrains. We expect that future limbless robots can take advantage of the principles discovered in our robophysical model.

References

1. Astley, H.C., et al.: Side-impact collision: mechanics of obstacle negotiation in sidewinding snakes. bioRxiv (2020)
2. Bayraktaroglu, Z.Y., Kilicarslan, A., Kuzucu, A., Hugel, V., Blazevic, P.: Design and control of biologically inspired wheel-less snake-like robot. In: The First IEEE/RAS-EMBS International Conference on Biomedical Robotics and Biomechatronics, 2006, BioRob 2006, pp. 1001–1006. IEEE (2006)
3. Butler, V.J., et al.: A consistent muscle activation strategy underlies crawling and swimming in caenorhabditis elegans. J. Roy. Soc. Interface **12**(102), 20140963 (2014)
4. Cowan, N.J., Lee, J., Full, R.J.: Task-level control of rapid wall following in the american cockroach. J. Exp. Bio. **209**(9), 1617–1629 (2006)
5. Gans, C.: Locomotion of limbless vertebrates: pattern and evolution. Herpetologica **42**(1), 33–46 (1986)
6. Hirose, S.: Biologically Inspired Robots: Snake-Like Locomotors and Manipulators. Oxford University Press, Oxford (1993)
7. Hopkins, J.K., Spranklin, B.W., Gupta, S.K.: A survey of snake-inspired robot designs. Bioinspir. Biomimet. **4**(2), 021001 (2009)
8. Hu, D.L., Nirody, J., Scott, T., Shelley, M.J.: The mechanics of slithering locomotion. Proc. Nat. Acad. Sci. USA **106**(25), 10081–10085 (2009)
9. Ijspeert, A.J.: Central pattern generators for locomotion control in animals and robots: a review. Neural Netw. **21**(4), 642–653 (2008)
10. Ijspeert, A.J., Crespi, A., Ryczko, D., Cabelguen, J.M.: From swimming to walking with a salamander robot driven by a spinal cord model. Science **315**(5817), 1416–1420 (2007)
11. Inoue, K., Nakamura, K., Suzuki, M., Mori, Y., Fukuoka, Y., Shiroma, N.: Biological system models reproducing snakes' musculoskeletal system. In: 2010 IEEE/RSJ International Conference on Intelligent Robots and Systems, pp. 2383–2388. IEEE (2010)
12. Jayne, B.C.: Muscular mechanisms of snake locomotion: an electromyographic study of lateral undulation of the florida banded water snake (nerodia fasciata) and the yellow rat snake (elaphe obsoleta). J. Morphol. **197**(2), 159–181 (1988)
13. Kano, T., Ishiguro, A.: Obstacles are beneficial to me! Scaffold-based locomotion of a snake-like robot using decentralized control. In: 2013 IEEE/RSJ International Conference on Intelligent Robots and Systems, pp. 3273–3278. IEEE (2013)
14. Kano, T., Yoshizawa, R., Ishiguro, A.: Tegotae-based decentralised control scheme for autonomous gait transition of snake-like robots. Bioinspir. Biomimet. **12**(4), 046009 (2017)
15. Liljeback, P., Pettersen, K.Y., Stavdahl, Ø., Gravdahl, J.T.: Experimental investigation of obstacle-aided locomotion with a snake robot. IEEE Trans. Rob. **27**(4), 792–800 (2011)

16. Liljebäck, P., Pettersen, K.Y., Stavdahl, Ø., Gravdahl, J.T.: A review on modelling, implementation, and control of snake robots. Robot. Auton. Syst. **60**(1), 29–40 (2012)
17. Mosauer, W.: Locomotion and diurnal range of sonora occipitalis, crotalus cerastes, and crotalus atrox as seen from their tracks. Copeia **1933**(1), 14–16 (1933)
18. Ponte, H., et al.: Visual sensing for developing autonomous behavior in snake robots. In: 2014 IEEE International Conference on Robotics and Automation (ICRA), pp. 2779–2784. IEEE (2014)
19. Rieser, J.M., et al.: Dynamics of scattering in undulatory active collisions. Phys. Rev. E **99**(2), 022606 (2019)
20. Rollinson, D., et al.: Design and architecture of a series elastic snake robot. In: 2014 IEEE/RSJ International Conference on Intelligent Robots and Systems, pp. 4630–4636. IEEE (2014)
21. Sanfilippo, F., Azpiazu, J., Marafioti, G., Transeth, A.A., Stavdahl, Ø., Liljebäck, P.: Perception-driven obstacle-aided locomotion for snake robots: the state of the art, challenges and possibilities. Appl. Sci. **7**(4), 336 (2017)
22. Sanfilippo, F., Helgerud, E., Stadheim, P.A., Aronsen, S.L.: Serpens: a highly compliant low-cost ros-based snake robot with series elastic actuators, stereoscopic vision and a screw-less assembly mechanism. Appl. Sci. **9**(3), 396 (2019)
23. Saranli, U., Buehler, M., Koditschek, D.E.: RHex: a simple and highly mobile hexapod robot. Int. J. Robot. Res. **20**(7), 616–631 (2001)
24. Sato, T., Kano, T., Ishiguro, A.: On the applicability of the decentralized control mechanism extracted from the true slime mold: a robotic case study with a serpentine robot. Bioinspir. Biomimet. **6**(2), 026006 (2011)
25. Schiebel, P.E., et al.: Mitigating memory effects during undulatory locomotion on hysteretic materials. Elife **9**, e51412 (2020)
26. Schiebel, P.E., Rieser, J.M., Hubbard, A.M., Chen, L., Rocklin, D.Z., Goldman, D.I.: Mechanical diffraction reveals the role of passive dynamics in a slithering snake. Proc. Nat. Acad. Sci. USA **116**(11), 4798–4803 (2019)
27. Tanaka, M., Kon, K., Tanaka, K.: Range-sensor-based semiautonomous whole-body collision avoidance of a snake robot. IEEE Trans. Control Syst. Technol. **23**(5), 1927–1934 (2015)
28. Transeth, A.A.: Snake robot obstacle-aided locomotion: modeling, simulations, and experiments. IEEE Trans. Rob. **24**(1), 88–104 (2008)
29. Travers, M.J., Whitman, J., Schiebel, P., Goldman, D., Choset, H.: Shape-based compliance in locomotion. In: Robotics: Science and Systems (2016)
30. Wu, X., Ma, S.: Neurally controlled steering for collision-free behavior of a snake robot. IEEE Trans. Control Syst. Technol. **21**(6), 2443–2449 (2013)

A Synthetic Nervous System Model of the Insect Optomotor Response

Anna Sedlackova, Nicholas S. Szczecinski$^{(\boxtimes)}$ ⓘ, and Roger D. Quinn ⓘ

Case Western Reserve University, Cleveland, OH 44106, USA
nss36@case.edu

Abstract. We seek to increase the sophistication of our insect-like hexapod robot MantisBot's visual system. We assembled and tested a benchtop robotic testbed with which to test our dynamical neural model of the insect visual system. Here we specifically model wide-field vision and the optomotor response. The system is composed of a Raspberry Pi with a camera outfitted with a 360° lens. The camera sits on a motorized turntable, which represents the "robot". Above the turntable sits another motorized system that rotates a drum with printed patterns around the camera, which represents the visual "background". The camera downsamples the visual scene and sends it to a synthetic nervous system (SNS) model of the insect optic lobe. The optic lobe is columnar. Each column detects changes in receptor intensity (retina), inhibits adjacent columns to increase dynamic range (lamina), compares time-delayed activities of adjacent columns to detect motion (medulla), then pools the motion of each column in a directionally-specific connectivity to compute the direction and speed of the wide-field scene (lobula plate). Our robotic model successfully encodes lateral wide-field visual speed into the activity of a pair of opposing Lobula Plate Tangential Cells (LPTCs). Furthermore, the optomotor response can be recreated by using the LPTCs to stimulate the neck motor neurons (MNs), producing a real-time, closed-loop dynamical model of the optomotor response.

Keywords: Synthetic nervous system · Optomotor response · Insect · Vision

1 Introduction

Despite their miniature brains of less than a million neurons, insects are able to solve complex vision tasks- locating prey, avoiding obstacles, tracking prey or mates - all with the use of environmental cues [1]. Insects can still outperform man-made robots and systems in visual tasks despite their limited metabolic and computational power [2]. The basis of this performance is the optic lobe of the insect brain, which uses a parallelized system of functionally-distinct layers to process visual input. Insects' ability to compute optic flow, also called "wide-field vision," has been thoroughly studied [3], but gaps in the knowledge remain. To test how well the current understanding of these networks can explain their function [4], we built an anatomically-constrained model of the optic lobe using our "synthetic nervous system" (SNS) approach, and use it as the basis of a robotic model of the insect optomotor response.

© Springer Nature Switzerland AG 2020
V. Vouloutsi et al. (Eds.): Living Machines 2020, LNAI 12413, pp. 312–324, 2020.
https://doi.org/10.1007/978-3-030-64313-3_30

What is known about the structure of the optic lobe? There are three separate neuropils contained within the optic lobe: the lamina, medulla, and lobula complex, which itself consists of the lobula and the lobula plate (for a review see [3]). Each of the neuropils contains organized columnar units corresponding to the ommatidial (i.e. lens) array in the retina and operates on neighboring columns in each successive layer. The lamina is stimulated by the retina and inhibits its neighboring columns to increase the contrast and dynamic range of incoming images. The medulla appears to correlate the activity of adjacent columns with a time delay in order to detect motion across the retina via "elementary motion detectors" (EMDs), the precise structure of which is not known. The lobula plate contains cells that run tangentially to the retinal columns and sum the motion responses of the medulla across the visual field. The output of these Lobula Plate Tangential Cells (LPTCs) encode the wide-field motion of the visual scene. Interneurons mediate these signals to the motor neurons in the thoracic ganglia, enabling motor centers to move the head or body in response to the wide-field motion [5].

Such interneurons that communicate wide-field visual cues with the motor networks are critical because such cues are primarily generated by the animal's own motion. Therefore, minimizing the optic flow is one way that insects may stabilize their gaze or posture. Simulating wide-field motion by displaying moving patterns that envelop the animal have been used to evoke the "optomotor response", wherein the animal turns its neck [6], adjusts its posture [7], or walks along a curve [8] in an attempt to cancel out this visual motion. Implementing such a system on board a robot may enable us to enhance the postural stability of the robot, while providing an opportunity to model how animals may use optic flow information to direct walking. Some robots have also used optic flow to avoid barriers while walking [9]. As a proof of concept, we model the robot as a single neck actuator that can rotate the "head".

In this manuscript, we describe the robotic hardware and our neural modeling approach. We summarize the structure of the insect lobe and explain the simplifications and assumptions we made while constructing our model. We show that the layers within our model perform the computations observed or hypothesized to occur in the animal. We show that the result of the visual processing is a rate-coded estimate of the speed and direction of the background's motion. We show that by using the output of the model to stimulate motor neurons that actuate the neck, our robot acts as a closed-loop dynamical neuromechanical model of the insect optomotor response. Finally, we discuss how this system will be expanded in the future in order to incorporate more features present in the insect optic lobe, while increasing its utility for robotic vision.

2 Methods

2.1 Robotic Hardware

Figure 1 presents the robotic hardware. The "head" consists of a Raspberry Pi with the Camera Module, equipped with a 360° lens (Fig. 1A). The head is rotated by one Dynamixel smart servo (Robotis, Seoul, South Korea). The "background" consists of a paper drum, the inside of which has a stripe pattern printed onto it. This is meant to mimic the experimental setup of studies of the insect optomotor response [8]. The head and background are connected to the same 3D printed chassis (Fig. 1B).

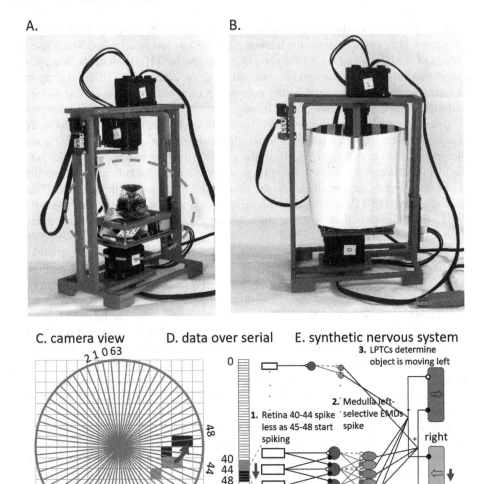

Fig. 1. Illustration of the robot hardware and SNS organization. A. The Raspberry Pi is equipped with the Camera Module. The blue dashed line encircles the Pi, camera, and 360° lens, which are assembled into a "head". B. The head rotates inside of a mobile background cylinder. C. The camera sees a radial image. The Pi sums the grayscale intensity of each bin and sends that value over a serial connection to the retina of the SNS. D. The retina transduces the intensity of the bins into the firing frequency of spiking neurons. E. The rest of the SNS performs lateral inhibition (lamina), generates direction-specific activity with EMDs (medulla), and then sums all EMD output to determine the motion of the background (LPTCs). (Color figure online)

The SNS model of the optic lobe runs on a laptop computer separate from the Raspberry Pi. The Pi processes and sends the data to the laptop over a serial connection by the following process. 64 × 64-pixel grayscale video is recorded and dissected for static images at about 25 Hz. Such low image resolution reduces serial traffic and is consistent with insects' comparatively low visual resolution [1]. This image is sorted into 64, 5.6 degree-wide angular "bins" along the azimuth, wherein each bin's intensity value is the average of all pixels it encapsulates (illustrated in Fig. 1C). Note that this system only "sees" along one axis, the azimuth; it cannot detect changes in the elevation direction. When a bin's intensity value changes in subsequent images, it is flagged for transmission over serial to the SNS in the next data sentence (Fig. 1D). Such a system reduces the length of sentences and thus increases the system's bandwidth.

Visual information from the camera is transduced into neural inputs at the retina layer of the optic lobe model (Fig. 1E). Each angular bin in the camera's field of view has a corresponding retinal cell. The average grayscale intensity of each bin is mapped to an applied current for the retinal cell with black mapping to a current of 0 nA, white mapping to a current of 20 nA, and intermediate values mapping in a graded way. Each retinal cell represents the first layer of a columnar network that enhances contrast, detects changes in pixels, and sums these changes over the field of view to compute wide-field visual velocity. This network is described in detail in Sect. 2.3.

The connection between the robot and the SNS is bidirectional. The SNS possesses motor neurons (MNs) for the "neck" of the robot to rotate the camera around the vertical axis. There are two MNs, each of which rotates the neck in the opposite direction. In our previous work, we found that the motor output of small animals can be approximated by using the sum of the MN voltages to set the servo's speed and using the difference of the MN voltages to set the servo's equilibrium angle [10]. If the commanded angle or speed of the servo changes, then a new command sentence is sent over serial from the SNS controller to the robot.

2.2 Synthetic Nervous System Organization and Design

The SNS model of the optic lobe is implemented with Animatlab [11] and its Robotics Toolkit [12]. Animatlab is an open-source 3D neuromechanical simulation software tool for simulating biologically-inspired organisms, robots, and neural networks. We wished to build a network that is biologically plausible but possible to run in real time. While the optic lobes of different insect species have behavior-specific visual processing networks, the overall structural organization is common for several kinds of arthropods including moths, flies, crabs, and mantises [13]. Since we are modeling a fundamental behavior observed in many species, we have combined information from multiple species. However, modeling more species-specific behaviors (e.g. mantis prey capture) would require modifying the network in species-specific ways.

Neural Modeling Techniques. Our network model is composed of integrate-and-fire neurons [14]. To simplify the description of the neurons, we write the equations in terms of U, the membrane voltage above the neuron's rest potential [15]. In addition, each neuron has a membrane conductance $G_m = 1$ and a constant spiking threshold $\theta = 1$.

The resulting dynamics of a neuron can be written as

$$\tau_m \cdot \frac{dU}{dt} = -U + I_{app} + I_{tonic} + \sum_{i=1}^{n} G_{s,i} \cdot \left(\Delta E_{s,i} - U \right) \tag{1}$$

$$\text{if } U \geq \theta, U(t) \leftarrow 0, \tag{2}$$

where τ_m is the membrane time constant, I_{app} is an applied current, I_{tonic} is a constant intrinsic current, n is the number of incoming synapses, $G_{s,i}$ is the instantaneous conductance of the ith synapse (computed below), and $\Delta E_{s,i}$ is the reversal potential of the ith incoming synapse relative to the postsynaptic neuron's resting potential. Each synapse's instantaneous conductance is reset to its maximum value $g_{s,i}$ when the presynaptic neuron spikes:

$$\tau_s \cdot \frac{dG}{dt} = -G \tag{3}$$

$$\text{if presynaptic neuron spikes, } G \leftarrow g. \tag{4}$$

In the following sections, we describe the desired function of connections within the network in terms of "gain" k, that is, the ratio between the postsynaptic and presynaptic neurons' spiking frequencies. Using our functional subnetwork approach for designing dynamical neural models, we can relate the gain to the neural and synaptic parameters, and directly tune their values [15].

2.3   Structure and Function of the Optic Lobe Model

Retina. The retina layer encodes visual information into the neural system. The retina cells respond to changes in light intensity in the visual field. The compound eye of the retina has a hexagonally-arranged structure of ommatidia, i.e. photoreceptors that lie below the lens. Insects have multiple retina cells per ommatidium [16]. However, to keep the model tractable, our model simply possesses one retina cell per ommatidium.

The retina layer in our network consists of 64 neurons that each take input from the corresponding angular bins described in Sect. 2.1 (Fig. 1E, white rectangles) Each neuron's applied current is a linear function of the average grayscale intensity of its corresponding optical bin. For simplicity, our retina only encodes *increases* in brightness, the so-called ON-ON pathways [3]. How this selection affects the performance of the motion detector is further explained in the medulla section. The retina neurons in our model have a time constant $\tau_m = 200$ ms and a tonic current $I_{tonic} = 0.5$ nA. These values ensure that the lamina neurons do not fire any spikes at the minimum input intensity and fire spikes at 100 Hz at the maximum input intensity.

Lamina. The lamina neurons function as a spatial filter, increasing the dynamic range of retina activity. Every neuron is excited by retina cells in its own column and inhibited by those from the adjacent columns, a connectivity pattern called lateral inhibition. This connectivity increases the contrast of the image.

In our model, the lamina layer consists of 64 neurons (Fig. 1E, violet circles). Every neuron in the lamina is excited by a corresponding neuron in the retina, and inhibited by the retina neurons of the neighboring columns (Fig. 1E). The lamina neurons have the same parameter values as the retina neurons. To cancel the lamina's response to a spatially uniform image, we wish for the gain of the incoming synapses to add to 0. Since each lamina cell receives excitation from one retina cell but inhibition from two, we designed the excitatory synapses to have a gain of 1.5 and the inhibitory synapses to have a gain of -0.25. For the excitatory synapses, $\Delta E_s = 160$ mV and $g_s = 1.064$ µS; for the inhibitory synapses, $\Delta E_s = -80$ mV and $g_s = 0.3072\mu$ S. Both synapse types have time constants $\tau_s = 2.17$ ms.

Medulla. The cells in the medulla respond to visual motion in a direction-dependent manner. The classical Reichardt detector structure computes the correlation of one column's activity with a time-delayed copy of a neighboring column's activity. This two-column comparison excites the medulla neuron in the "preferred direction". This model successfully predicts many gross features of motion vision in insects [3]. Recent neurophysiology suggests a new, "three-arm detector" model that combines preferred direction enhancement (the Reichardt detector) and null direction suppression (the Barlow-Lewick detector) [17]. Combining these mechanisms not only accurately replicates the response properties of the T4 and T5 cells in the medulla, but also accounts for the non-negative nature of signal transmission throughout the nervous system (i.e. neurons only spike when depolarized, not when hyperpolarized).

Our medulla model is based on the "three-arm detector" model [3]. Each layer possesses 126 neurons, half of which are excited by rightward visual motion, and half of which are excited by leftward motion. These correspond to the medulla's T4 neurons [3]. Figure 1E shows the medulla neurons (blue and orange circles), each of which receives an excitatory input from its corresponding lamina neuron, a delayed excitatory signal from its neighboring column's lamina neuron, and a delayed inhibitory signal from the contralateral lamina neuron. To perform the multiplication inherent to the Reichardt model, each medulla neuron operates as a logical AND gate. Specifically, it can only fire action potentials if is depolarized by both excitatory inputs simultaneously. The duration of its spiking encodes the speed of visual motion across those two columns of the optic lobe. To enforce AND gate functionality and prevent the medulla neurons from firing when only one excitatory input is present, each neuron's tonic stimulus $I_{tonic} = -19.5$ nA. Otherwise, all parameter values are the same as the other neurons. All excitatory synapses have $k = 1$ and all inhibitory synapses have $k = -1$. For the excitatory synapse, $\Delta E_s = 160$ and $g_s = 0.658\mu$ S. The neighboring column's excitatory synapse additionally has a delay $\Delta t = 100$ ms. For the inhibitory synapse, $\Delta E_s = -80$ mV and $g_s = 1.536\mu$ S.

Lobula Plate Tangential Cells. The lobula plate tangential cells (LPTCs) are large, motion-sensitive neurons that reside in the posterior lobula plate. They can be separated into four different layers, each activated by large-field motion in one of the four cardinal motion directions. They pool the output signals on their dendrites from many thousands of directionally-selective neurons [3]. The LPTCs depolarize in response to background motion in their preferred direction and hyperpolarize in response to motion in their null direction. The LPTCs, however, do not compute motion locally but rather integrate over a large part of the visual field. The lobula plate tangential cells inhibit each other such that right inhibits left and vice versa, and up inhibits down and vice versa [3]. These cells are commonly thought to detect optical flow that arises from self-motion.

In our model, the LPTCs sum the outputs of the T4 cells in the medulla in a directionally-selective way. We only model the right- and left-sensitive LPTCs. Figure 1E shows how the medulla neurons all feed into one of two LPTCs. These neurons have the same properties as the rest of the network. The synapses from the medulla to the LPTCs have the same properties as those from the lamina to the medulla. None of these synapses possess delays.

Motor Neurons. The motor centers receive input from the LPTCs via descending interneurons [5]. We modeled such connections by synapsing the LPTC neurons onto nonspiking neurons that represent the combined motor neuron (MN) and muscle membrane. These MNs function as leaky integrators, integrating incoming spikes over time but "leaking" to 0 activity when no spikes are incoming. These neurons have the same parameter values as the other neurons in the network, except that the spiking mechanism has been disabled. As described above, the MN voltages specify rotation and speed commands for the neck servomotor.

3 Results

LPTC Voltage Encodes Wide-Field Visual Motion. Figure 2 displays raster plots of retina, lamina, and medulla spiking activity in response to background motion. Each point represents one action potential. The retina encodes the stripe pattern of the background as it moves right for five seconds, and then left for five seconds. The lamina increases the contrast by amplifying range of firing frequencies seen in the retina (Fig. 3). The medulla neurons encode the direction of the background's velocity, with separate subpopulations encoding each direction. Each one of these layers encodes visual information as observed in animal systems.

LPTC Activity Reflects Wide-Field Pattern Velocity. Figure 4 shows how the LPTC neurons encode the velocity of the background. The LPTC spikes have been removed from the membrane voltage curves to more clearly show how the LPTC depolarization (solid lines) encodes the velocity of the background (dotted lines). However, when the background's speed becomes too high, the correlation operation performed by the medulla breaks down, and the LPTC voltage no longer reflects the background speed. This same phenomenon is observed in *Drosophila* [3].

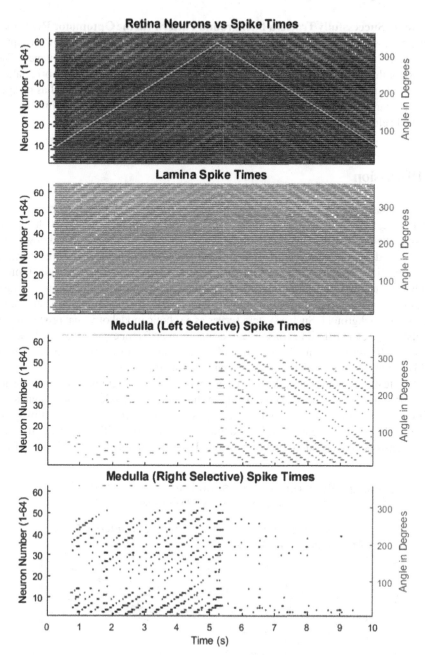

Fig. 2. Raster plots showing the spike times of each neuron (left axis) in each layer in response to background motion. The red line indicates the angle of the background (right axis). The retina encodes the motion, the lamina activity follows that of the retina, the left-selective medulla cells are active during leftward pattern motion, and the right-selective medulla cells are active during rightward motion. Colors match the anatomy in Fig. 1.

The Robot Successfully Tracks a Background Pattern via the Optomotor Response.
Figure 5 shows that the complete, closed-loop system can generate a functional optomotor response even as the movement of the background increases in frequency. The
velocity of the neck tracks that of the background, even though the absolute orientation
of the head and background are different. This is because the visual system has no specific landmarks to track. Because the system is closed-loop, neck rotation impacts the
observed velocity of the background.

4 Discussion

In this manuscript, we built a synthetic nervous system (SNS) model of parts of the
insect optic lobe, and used it to model the optomotor response observed in insects
[3, 6–8]. We applied the functional subnetwork approach [15] to tune the known and
hypothesized anatomical structure of the insect optic lobe without any machine learning
or optimization. The resulting network can process video data in real time (albeit more
slowly and at lower resolution than its biological counterparts), enhance its contrast,
compute its motion, and control the motion of a "head" as it attempts to stabilize its
gaze on the background. Such a system serves as a robotic model of visual processing in
insects, which can be used to consolidate results from different experiments and species
into one self-consistent model. Additionally, this system will form the basis of more
sophisticated visually-guided robotic behaviors in the future.

Despite the detail of our model, some known features of insect visual systems are not
yet incorporated. To reduce the complexity of the model, we modeled one-dimensional
(azimuthal, or left-right) vision only. Insects possess dedicated processing pathways to
see along the vertical axis as well [3], and thus our future work will expand the structure
of this network into an additional dimension. To further reduce the complexity of the

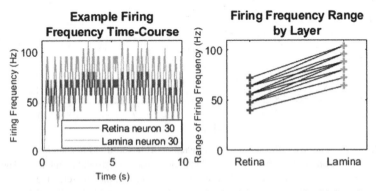

Fig. 3. (Left) The range of firing frequencies in the lamina appear to be higher than those in
the retina. (Right) Comparing each lamina neuron's range of firing frequencies to that of its
corresponding retina neuron confirm this.

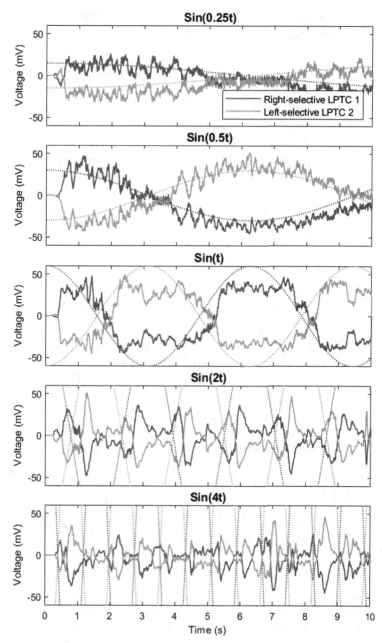

Fig. 4. At low frequencies, the LPTC voltage captures the actual background velocity (dotted lines). However, at high frequencies, the LPTC response amplitude decreases and its phase lags behind the actual velocity, meaning it cannot encode such rapid motions.

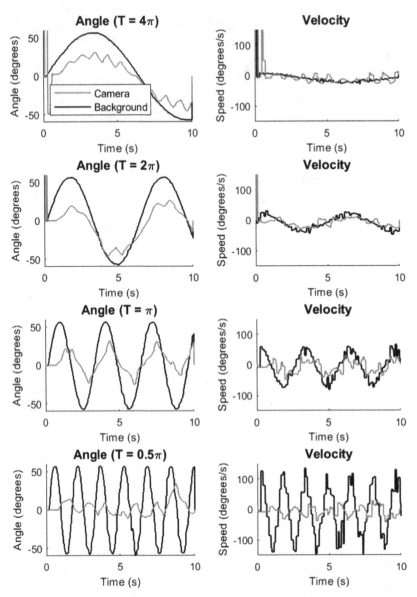

Fig. 5. The robot's optomotor response enables it to track wide-field visual motion. At low speeds (top), the camera's angle and velocity follow those of the background. However, when the background moves too rapidly (bottom), the response degrades, as expected.

model, we only modeled ON pathways, that is, pathways that respond to transitions from darkness to light, and omitted OFF pathways. However, both are known to play a role in the processing of motion vision [3]. In our future work, we will explore the impact of incorporating these additional (but seemingly redundant) pathways.

Our ultimate goal is to implement this model of insect vision onboard our insect-like hexapod robot, MantisBot [12]. In our past work, we have studied how descending commands from the brain may alter leg-local reflexes to direct walking behaviors [18]. We anticipate that descending pathways that mediate the optomotor response observed in walking insects will provide additional information with which MantisBot can stabilize its posture. We also anticipate that the gaze stabilization afforded by the optomotor response will make MantisBot more capable of identifying prey-like visual stimuli moving against the background. Such a system will enable us to generate and test hypothetical sensorimotor control networks both to consolidate results from neuroethology into one cohesive model, and to propose novel control algorithms for legged robots.

References

1. Egelhaaf, M., Boeddeker, N., Kern, R., Kurtz, R., Lindemann, J.P.: Spatial vision in insects is facilitated by shaping the dynamics of visual input through behavioural action. Front. Neural Circuits. **6**, 1–23 (2012)
2. Bagheri, Z.M., Wiederman, S.D., Cazzolato, B.S., Grainger, S., O'Carroll, D.C.: Performance of an insect-inspired target tracker in natural conditions. Bioinspir. Biomim. **12**, 025006 (2017)
3. Borst, Alexander., Haag, Jürgen, Mauss, Alex S.: How fly neurons compute the direction of visual motion. J. Comp. Physiol. A. **206**(2), 109–124 (2019). https://doi.org/10.1007/s00359-019-01375-9
4. Webb, B.: Robots with insect brains. Science. **368**, 244–245 (2020)
5. Suver, M.P., Huda, A., Iwasaki, N., Safarik, S., Dickinson, M.H.: An array of descending visual interneurons encoding self-motion in drosophila. J. Neurosci. **36**, 11768–11780 (2016)
6. Rossel, S.: Foveal fixation and tracking in the praying mantis. J. Comp. Physiol. A **139**, 307–331 (1980)
7. Nityananda, V., Tarawneh, G., Errington, S., Serrano-Pedraza, I., Read, J.: The optomotor response of the praying mantis is driven predominantly by the central visual field. J. Comp. Physiol. A. **203**(1), 77–87 (2016). https://doi.org/10.1007/s00359-016-1139-3
8. Dürr, V., Ebeling, W.: The behavioural transition from straight to curve walking: kinetics of leg movement parameters and the initiation of turning. J. Exp. Biol. **208**, 2237–2252 (2005)
9. Meyer, H.G., et al.: Resource-efficient bio-inspired visual processing on the hexapod walking robot HECTOR. PLoS ONE **15**, e0230620 (2020)
10. Szczecinski, N.S., Goldsmith, C.A., Young, F.R., Quinn, R.D.: Tuning a robot servomotor to exhibit muscle-like dynamics. In: Conference on Biomimetic and Biohybrid Systems. (2019)
11. Cofer, D.W., Cymbalyuk, G., Reid, J., Zhu, Y., Heitler, W.J., Edwards, D.H.: AnimatLab: a 3D graphics environment for neuromechanical simulations. J. Neurosci. Methods. **187**, 280–288 (2010)
12. Szczecinski, N.S., et al.: Introducing MantisBot: hexapod robot controlled by a high-fidelity, real-time neural simulation. In: IEEE International Conference on Intelligent Robots and Systems. pp. 3875–3881. Hamburg, DE (2015)
13. Joly, J.-S., Recher, G., Brombin, A., Ngo, K., Hartenstein, V.: A conserved developmental mechanism builds complex visual systems in insects and vertebrates. Curr. Biol. **26**, 1–9 (2016)
14. Mihalas, S., Niebur, E.: A generalized linear integrate-and-fire neural model produces diverse spiking behaviors. Neural Comput. **21**, 704–718 (2009)
15. Szczecinski, N.S., Hunt, A.J., Quinn, R.D.: A functional subnetwork approach to designing synthetic nervous systems that control legged robot locomotion. Front. Neurorobot. **11**, 37 (2017)

16. Borst, A.: Neural circuits for elementary motion detection. J. Neurogenet. **28**, 361–373 (2014)
17. Barlow, H.B., Levick, W.R.: The mechanism of directionally selective units in rabbit's retina. J. Physiol. **178**, 477–504 (1965)
18. Szczecinski, N.S., Getsy, A.P., Martin, J.P., Ritzmann, R.E., Quinn, R.D.: MantisBot is a Robotic Model of Visually Guided Motion in the Praying Mantis. Arth. Struct, Dev (2017)

Using the Neural Circuit of the Insect Central Complex for Path Integration on a Micro Aerial Vehicle

Jan Stankiewicz(✉) and Barbara Webb

Institute of Perception, Action and Behaviour, School of Informatics,
University of Edinburgh, Edinburgh EH8 9AB, UK
J.stankiewicz@ed.ac.uk

Abstract. We have deployed an anatomically constrained neural model for path integration on a real world, holonomic aerial platform. Based on the insect central complex, the model combines estimated heading and ground speed information to maintain a location estimate that can be used to steer the agent directly home after convoluted outward journeys. We implement a biologically plausible method to estimate ground speed using optical flow. We discover that a downward viewing, mechanically stabilised and height compensated vision system performs well in a range of natural environments, even when visual acuity is reduced to 3°/pixel. In a flat outdoor environment, the worst case final displacement error increases at a rate 1.5 m 100 m outbound travel. The field of view of the vision system has no impact on odometry performance.

Keywords: Central complex · Bio-mimetic · MAV · Computer vision

1 Introduction

Many species of flying insect routinely conduct long foraging journeys from which they can return directly to their starting location. We have recently developed an anatomically constrained model of how this behaviour can be accomplished by a path integration (PI) circuit located in the central complex (CX) of the archetypal insect brain [11]. Conceptually this circuit forms an allothetic navigation scheme that is globally anchored via a sky compass. It has been tested in simulation and over small distances on an indoor wheeled robot, but as yet has not been evaluated under the same natural conditions as a flying insect. Here, we present the results of deploying the CX model on an autonomous micro-aerial vehicle (MAV).

A key challenge was how to obtain biologically plausible ground speed estimates. Flying insects are thought to sense their egomotion primarily through

Supported by the Edinburgh Centre for Robotics and the Engineering and Physical Sciences Research Council. We thank Stanley Heinze who provided the neural data and the initial illustration for Fig. 3. Thanks also to Jiale Lu for his initial work.

V. Vouloutsi et al. (Eds.): Living Machines 2020, LNAI 12413, pp. 325–337, 2020.
https://doi.org/10.1007/978-3-030-64313-3_31

optical flow percepts which are computed with matched filters: *"ensembles of neurons which extract crucial components of stimuli while ignoring irrelevant information."* [6]. While neurons with receptive fields that resemble matched filters for rotational motion are well documented, circuits for inferring translational motion are less well understood. A problem with estimating translatory egomotion from optic flow is that flow magnitude is inversely proportional to the distance to the flow inducing surface (depth). In [2] the average horizontal flight depth value per photoreceptor is used to weight flow according to viewing direction. Here, we suggest that one reliable depth estimate can be used to adaptively tune all photoreceptor depth weights. We show that this approach can be successfully integrated to the CX circuit to produce effective PI behaviour for an MAV operating in real outdoor conditions.

2   Methods

2.1   Robotic Platform

The MAV (depicted in Fig. 1) was developed with an off-the-shelf airframe (Lumenier QAV400), avionics (flight controller, Pixhawk 2.1), differential GPS (Here+V2 RTK GNSS), range sensor (garmin lidar-litve v3), gimbal controller (Basecam simpleBGC 32-bit), RC receiver (FrySKY RX8R), singleboard PC (Odroid XU4)) and global shutter camera (Matrix vision Bluefox2, 200w). A custom top plate and the gimbal arms were fabricated from aluminium, the onboard GPS mast and RC receiver mounting brackets were 3D printed.

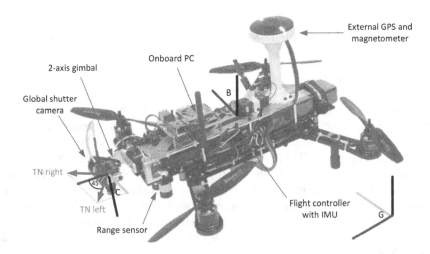

Fig. 1. Photograph of the MAV platform with annotation of key components and relevant (camera, C, global, G, and body, B) coordinate systems.

We made use of the PX4 flight stack on the pixhawk flight controller which was set to autonomous mode and communicated with via a UDP serial link handled using MAVROS. The CX module was wrapped in a ROS node and acted as a state in our generic behavioural state machine. A separate ROS node was developed to handle ground speed estimation. A major benefit of using the opensource PX4 ecosystem is that a customisable simulation model was available for use in the GAZEBO environment. This provided a realistic physical and graphical simulation setup, supporting rapid development and evaluation in otherwise untestable configurations. The PX4 flight stack features an extended Kalman filter software module (EKF2) which is used to provide *ground truth* location estimates. The differential GPS system that supports EKF2 in our setup has a reported horizontal accuracy of ± 6 cm, the heading error of the ground truth is unspecified.

The primary function of the camera in this system is to facilitate ground speed estimation. We therefore opted for a downward facing configuration on both the real and simulated MAVs. Insects are known to stabilise their head during flight [14] and because MAVs have a high degree of body vibration and the body necessarily pitches and rolls to generate translational thrust, we mimicked head stabilisation with a 2-axis gimbal and found this essential for good ground speed estimates (see Fig. 5).

2.2 Ground Speed Estimates from Optical Flow and Matched Filters

Flying insects have been shown to estimate distance travelled from optic flow [10]. Recent neural recordings in 2 species of bee have revealed two pairs of motion sensitive neurons that respond most strongly to flow-fields corresponding to animal head motion along orthogonal axes *left* $(-45°)$ and *right* $(45°)$ in azimuth with respect to the animal's anterior [11] (labelled TN left/right in Fig. 1). We mimic these neural properties, but rather than replicate the near-panoramic vision system of an insect, we used a conventional camera with a $42°$ field of view, pointing downward. One advantage of this configuration is that optical flow induced by pure yaw motion sums to zero when combined with translational matched filters with preferred directions that are parallel to the ground. However, as it is not apparent that the insect visual field actually includes the area directly below the animal [13], we also investigate the effect of raising the camera view angle in Sect. 3.

The processing pipeline for each speed cell is presented in Fig. 2a. The camera operates at 10 Hz. The preprocessing stage converts to grayscale and resizes to 150×235 pixels. A 2-frame Farnebäck dense optic flow algorithm [1] is used to compute the optical flow field. This is combined with matched filters for self-motion and weighted by a depth estimate for each pixel to obtain a ground speed estimate as follows:

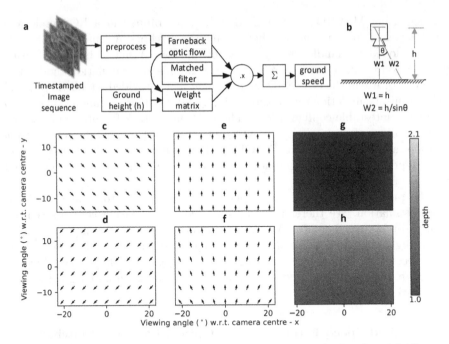

Fig. 2. a Pipeline for ground speed estimation. **b** Illustration of example weight factors, W1 and W2, based on pixel viewing image sensor height (h) and pixel viewing direction. **c&d** Matched filters for the left and right speed cells respectively when the camera is aligned with gravity and the camera x-axis is towards the front of the aircraft. **e&f** Matched filters for the dual camera setup (see Sect. 3) with the camera rotated ±45° about the body frame Z-axis, for **f** the camera is also pitched upwards +45°. **g** Depth weights for a downward facing camera. **h** Depth weights for a camera pitched up by 45°.

Matched Filters. We adapt the method in [2] to generate matched filters, i.e., neurons with a pattern of preferred motion across the visual field that corresponds to the predicted flow for self motion around or along a particular axis:

$$\mathbf{u}_{m,n}^i = d_{m,n} \times a^i \times d_{m,n}, \quad for \quad m \in \{1, w\} \quad n \in \{1, h\} \quad i \in \{Left, right\} \quad (1)$$

where $\mathbf{u}$ is a matched filter for the ith speed cell with pixel coordinates m, n. w and h denote the image width and height respectively. $d_{m,n}$ describes the viewing direction of camera pixel m, n and a_i is the vector of the axis that the neuron is tuned to (specified in the camera coordinate frame (c in Fig. 1)). Here, the left and right speed cell preferred directions are $-45°$ yaw $(-\frac{1}{\sqrt{2}}, \frac{1}{\sqrt{2}}, 0)$ and $+45°$ yaw $(\frac{1}{\sqrt{2}}, \frac{1}{\sqrt{2}}, 0)$. Quiver plots of example filters generated by this procedure are shown in Fig. 2c–f.

Weight Matrix for Depth. The world is modelled as a flat plane and the projected distance between a given pixel and the ground plane is calculated using the camera's commanded orientation and the aircraft's instantaneous height (see Fig. 2b):

$$\mu_{m,n} = \frac{height}{sin(\angle gravity, d_{m,n})} \quad for \quad m \in \{1, w\} \quad n \in \{1, h\} \tag{2}$$

Example depth maps according to the weight matrix are included in Fig. 2g&h. This matrix was also used to reject any flow outliers according to predefined maximum and minimum values (analogous to neural saturation). Any such pixels were labelled *noisy*, and the corresponding weight was set to 0.

Ground Speed Estimate. Egomotion (displacement) in the speed cell orthogonal basis can be estimated by summing the elementwise product of the flow field, matched filter and the weight matrix. This is functionally equivalent to the operations performed by wide-field tangential cells found in the lobular plate [2]. For best results this value is normalised by the number of non-*noisy* pixels. An absolute ground speed estimate can be found by multiplying the projected displacement with the image frame time interval:

$$speed\_cell^i = \frac{\sum_{m=1}^{w} \sum_{n=1}^{h} \left(F \cdot \mathbf{u}_{m,n}^i \cdot \mu_{m,n}^i\right)}{(w * h) - \sum (\text{noisy pixels})} \cdot \delta t \quad for \quad i \in \{Left, right\} \tag{3}$$

2.3   The Central Complex (CX) Circuit

The neural circuit for PI (see Fig. 3) was adopted from [11], and is an anatomically constrained model of the insect CX, that is, every neuron type and connection in this model has been mapped in the insect brain. The inputs to this system are the speed cells (TN) (described in Sect. 2.2) and the global heading, which is encoded by a set of 8 direction cells (TB1). The direction cells in insects receive input from their polarisation compass system [5], and exhibit a bump of activity that is correlated with the agent's current heading [8]. This activity can be modelled as a discretised (8 samples, 1 per cell) phase-shiftable cosine function $(-\pi, \pi)$, where the phase denotes the agent's azimuth in global coordinates.

The next layer consists of 16 memory cells (CPU4), split into left and right parts according to the input speed cell. Excitatory or inhibitory action is applied to each memory cell, at a rate proportional to the output of the relevant speed cell, according to the signed magnitude of the vertically aligned heading cell state (connectivity shown in Fig. 3). The activity of each cell thus reflects the total translation that has occurred up to that time, i.e., they collectively represent a constantly updated vector pointing back to the origin (a home vector). Specifically, the activity across the left and right sets of memory cells will also be a discretised cosine function where the phase represents the home direction, and the amplitude represents the range.

The third layer of 16 steering cells (CPU1) is also divided into left and right sets. These receive input from the memory cells, shifted by one column to the left or right respectively. They are also inhibited by the direction cells. Consequently,

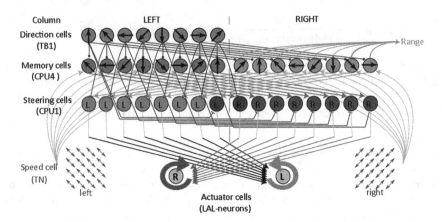

Fig. 3. CX model topology and key interfaces. Adapted from [11].

the relative activity of the left and right set of steering cells will reflect whether turning left or right would more closely align the two cosines: the current heading direction; and the home vector direction. Hence homing can be achieved by using their output to control steering.

This circuit is implemented as a firing rate neural model (see [11] for full details) on the MAV's onboard PC, using the magnetometer for the direction cell input, and mapping the steering cell output to the yaw rate. We additionally extract a range estimate from the current state of the memory cells, and attenuate both the steering command and translational speed $\propto 1/\text{range}$ when coming 10 m of the origin. This produces an effective 'stopping' behaviour at the estimated home location, preventing continuous search. However, as yet there is no direct neural evidence to support this hypothesised output from the memory cells.

2.4   Test Procedure

A schematic of the general test procedure is shown in Fig. 4, and the different test worlds (real and simulated) are depicted. The profile of the outbound route is designed to meet the following criteria: each flight path should be constrained in the overall direction to enable repeatability, but should not be identical; and the inbound route should cover different terrain to the outbound route. Consequently we model the outbound route as an L-shape with the major axis being twice as long as the minor axis. At 2 s intervals, a random sample from a Von Mises distribution ($\kappa = 10$) was added to the heading setpoint in order to give the outbound route a sinuous profile. Using this configuration, the impact of a particular parameter can be evaluated by repeating a given test several times with different preselected parameter values. Unless otherwise specified the test was repeated 10 times for each parameter with a default outbound duration of 100 s. The aircraft was commanded to fly 5 m above the ground using the range sensor. The trial is terminated when the memory cell range estimate falls below 1m, at which point the trial *final displacement error* is calculated as the horizontal euclidean distance between the EKF2 and CX model position estimates. The absolute *heading error* was also calculated throughout each trial as the minimum angle between the memory cell and EKF2 homeward bearings.

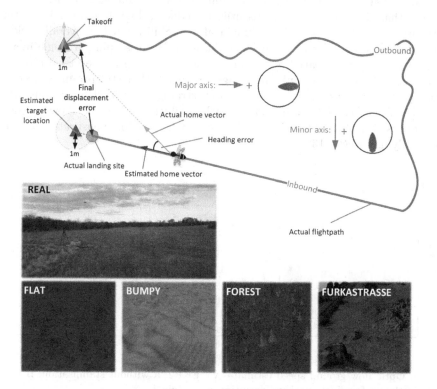

Fig. 4. Top: the general test procedure, and a photograph of the **REAL** test world (GPS:55.763377, −2.238153). Below: renderings of the simulated environments where **FLAT**: perfectly level, textured plane at $z = 0$ and normal to the XY plane in the world coordinate system. **BUMPY**: flat with a depth map in the interval $Z = 0 \rightarrow 2\,\mathrm{m}$ according to the depth profile inferred from a depth image of a natural scene. **FOREST**: flat but with 500 randomly placed oak and pine trees. **FURKASTRASSE**: repurposed mesh from https://wingtra.com/ of a natural scene containing asymmetrical ramping sections. Furkastrasse is also reskinned with a highly textured soil image to form **Furkastrasse retextured** (not shown).

A second mode of motion was used when testing the effect of camera pitch, because the optic flow induced by yaw rotations is no longer cancelled out if the view direction is not parallel to the ground plane. We hence separate translational and rotational optic flow by splitting the agent's motion into 4 s translations followed by rapid, saccadic rotations, during which optic flow is disregarded. This follows evidence of such motor patterns and visual suppression in flies [12].

3   Results

Accuracy of Ground Speed Estimation. The accuracy of the optic flow ground speed estimate (transformed to body frame coordinate system), compared to the EKF2 estimate, is shown for two flights, first without stabilisation by the gimbal (Fig. 5a) and then with gimbal stabilisation enabled (Fig. 5b). It is clear that the stabilisation is essential to reduce a high level of noise in the estimate. Some large deviations remain after stabilisation but overall a close estimate of the actual ground speed is obtained. By resampling a single image sequence at different spatial resolutions before processing in the visual pipeline of Fig. 2a we tested the minimum image resolution that still produces acceptable speed estimates. A brute force search strategy was used to optimise the Farnebäck *window size* parameter for each resolution. Figure 5c shows a good estimate is still obtained with only 3° acuity, which is commensurate with the eyes of flying insects [13].

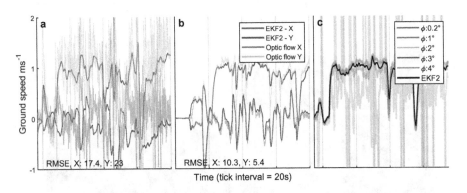

Fig. 5. Optic flow ground speed estimates vs. EKF2: **a** without stabilisation; **b** with stabilisation; **c** for different visual accuities, $\phi = °/$pixel

Effect of Terrain and Outbound Distance on Homing Performance. We evaluated the homing performance of the CX model for three different outbound distances (50,100,150 m) on the MAV in the real world, and in each of the simulated worlds described in Fig. 4. The results are summarised in Fig. 6a. For the real MAV and the flat simulated environment, the homing procedure always returned to 10 m of the starting point across all trials which is comparable to the accuracy of a GPS system. As expected, the final displacement error and its variance increase as a function of outbound distance. Note that even in the flat world there is a final displacement error bias suggesting that there is scope for improvement in the performance of the overall system. A linear interpolation of the real dataset yields the equation $y = 0.011x + 1.74$, indicating that the mean performance decreases 1.1 m per 100 m. An interpolation of the worst performing values produces a slope of 1.5 m/100 m.

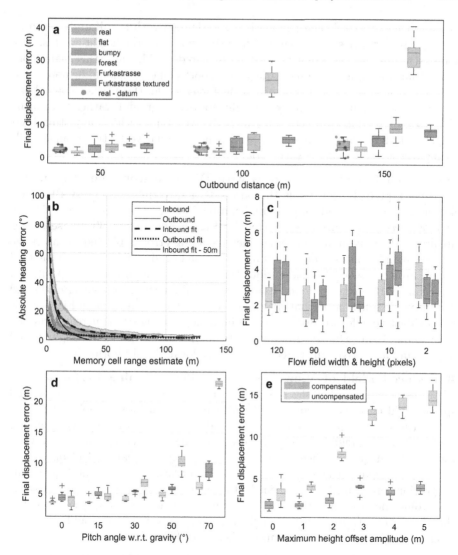

Fig. 6. Homing performance of the CX model. **a** For most test conditions, final displacement error is less that 10m, increasing gradually as outbound journey length increases. **b** Heading error decreases with distance. **c** Reducing the field of view of the camera does not affect homing performance. **d** Increasing camera pitch angle negatively affects homing performance, especially in uneven terrain. **e** Removing height compensation negatively affects homing performance.

There was a small performance decrease for the bumpy and forest environments, which feature smooth and discontinuous height variations respectively. The performance was severely impacted for the natural Furkastrasse environment, but this was found to be due to some featureless areas of the environmental mesh. When the mesh was reskinned with a uniformly textured pattern, performance is similar to the other non-uniform height worlds. The forested world was the worst performing textured world, suggesting high depth discontinuities are more problematic than smooth slopes. It should be noted that in order to achieve this performance in the forest world, the altitude control had to be adapted to maintain a fixed height above the ground, rather than using range sensor readings. Insects sometimes fly over gaps without adjusting their height but the ability to maintain a fixed height relative to the ground while flying over a tree canopy is speculation.

Directional Certainty Increases with Distance from the Origin. Previous work predicts that while the positional uncertainty of a noisy PI circuit increases with outbound foraging range, directional certainty increases [15] The first of these assertions is supported by Fig. 6a and in Fig. 6b the second is apparent. Here the moving average mean heading error is plotted for all range ordered samples of the *real* dataset as a function of radial distance from the trial origin. From geometric considerations the heading error should be $\propto$ positional error/range [15]; hence inbound heading error will be lower for shorter outbound distances when less positional error has accumulated (50 m curve in Fig. 6b) but it is evident that for all distances, the inbound heading error increases rapidly from under 10 m. This suggests accurate relocation of the exact origin would require an alternative "drift free" cue such as local visual information.

A Reduced Field of View Does Not Affect Homing Performance. We investigated whether the size of the field of view used to estimate ground speed would affect the accuracy of homing performance, by cropping the input before the final summing step in the visual pipeline. In Fig. 6c it can be seen that there is no tangible impact for any of the tested environments, even when the speed cell ground speed estimate is based on a visual field of only 2×2 pixels. An expanded field of view could potentially be detrimental given the proportional relationship between depth and optic flow, as in a natural scene this would increase the likelihood of encountering non-ground-plane objects in the visual field. Conversely, wider field of view measurements could provide a filtering and/or voting mechanism to reject flow field outliers.

Ventral Views Provide More Robust Optic Flow Information. In order to understand the practical implications of sampling optic flow from different view elevations, the view direction of the vision sensor was systematically raised. In simulation, the single downward facing camera was replaced with a pair of time synchronised cameras that were rotated $-45°$ and $45°$ in yaw respectively. These cameras were then pitched equally upwards by 0,15,30,50 or 70°. It was necessary to use saccade mode (see Sect. 2.4) for these trials to prevent a catastrophic reduction in homing performance in the Furkastrasse_retextured world. The results in Fig. 6d show that increasing the pitch angle reduces homing performance in all cases to some extent. This can be explained by the greater variance of μ weighting factors for higher pitch angles (see Fig. 2) resulting in those areas with higher weighting contributing more noise to the speed calculation. However, given the use of saccade mode, performance degradation due to pitch angle increase in the flat and bumpy worlds is modest in comparison to the natural scene which features large asymmetric ramping sections that cause large divergences between the assumed and actual depth values.

Height Compensation is Required for Successful Homing. Since neither the use of height estimation or maintenance of a constant ground height is a given for flying insects, we explored the impact of removing height input in the flat world, while introducing a randomly varying height profile along the outbound journey. Specifically, height profiles were generated by adding a random positive offset to 10 equally spaced points along the outbound journey (z_offset = U(0, maximum z offset)), and then making a linear interpolation along this height series according to the time into the outbound flight. The results, included in Fig. 6e, indicate that even with a modest maximum height offset of 2 m, homing performance is severely impacted if no height compensation is used in the visual processing pipeline.

4   Discussion

We have implemented the CX model presented in [11] on an autonomous MAV. This anatomically constrained neural circuit integrates ground speed in different compass directions to maintain an estimate of location with respect to an origin, providing a steering output to return home. Here we have introduced a biologically plausible matched filter to obtain ground speed from ventral optic flow. We show that in real world testing, which includes asymmetric inbound/outbound routes, random yaw saccades, and dynamic lighting and weather conditions, the worst case final displacement error increase 1.5 m 100 m of outbound distance. Thus this bio-mimetic system constitutes a medium range navigational aid with comparable accuracy to a GPS module over the range of 1 km.

This accuracy could bring a flying insect near enough to its goal to find it by search, but the decreased heading accuracy at short range (in Fig. 6b) suggests that efficient relocation of the nest requires alternative mechanisms. Moreover, some species of bee are known to commute several kilometers [3], so it seems likely that additional guidance cues such as odour and vision are used over longer ranges. In future work we will examine biologically plausible ways of extending the navigational range and improving close range homing capability of our biomimetic platform using *drift free* visual cues.

Our efforts primarily focused on developing a biologically plausible visual ground speed estimation system, consisting of a matched filter based optical flow subsystem. We have demonstrated that the acuity and frame rate of this system could be as coarse as $3°$/pixel 10 Hz respectively. Best results were achieved with 1) the camera directed towards the ground, 2) mechanical stabilisation against aircraft pitch and roll, and 3) height compensation. No discernible improvements in homing performance were observed in relation to an increasing field of view of the matched filter output, which could explain why neurons with a receptive field commensurate with a translatory optic flow matched filter have remained elusive in comparison to their rotational counterparts [7].

In future we aim to replace the magnetometer heading sensor with a biologically plausible sky compass [4]. We also need to consider a biologically plausible mechanism for height estimation as this appears to be necessary information for accurate PI. An alternative approach would be to implement an optic flow regulated autopilot [9], although this may not compensate for different visual terrain observed on the inbound route versus the outbound route. We suggest that further neurophysiological investigation of the CX speed cells (TN) using stimuli representing surfaces moving directly below the animal at different depths would also provide significant insight into this question.

References

1. Farnebäck, G.: Two-frame motion estimation based on polynomial expansion. In: Bigun, J., Gustavsson, T. (eds.) SCIA 2003. LNCS, vol. 2749, pp. 363–370. Springer, Heidelberg (2003). https://doi.org/10.1007/3-540-45103-X_50
2. Franz, M.O., Krapp, H.G.: Wide-field, motion-sensitive neurons and matched filters for optic flow fields. Biol. Cybern. **83**(3), 185–197 (2000). https://doi.org/10.1007/s004220000163
3. von Frish, K.: The Dance Language and Orientation of Bees. Oxford University Press, London (1967). https://doi.org/10.4159/harvard.9780674418776
4. Gkanias, E., Risse, B., Mangan, M., Webb, B.: From skylight input to behavioural output: a computational model of the insect polarised light compass. PLOS Comput. Biol. **15**(7), 1–30 (2019). https://doi.org/10.1371/journal.pcbi.1007123
5. Homberg, U., Heinze, S., Pfeiffer, K., Kinoshita, M., El Jundi, B.: Central neural coding of sky polarization in insects. Philos. Trans. R. Soc. B: Biol. Sci. **366**(1565), 680–687 (2011)
6. Kohn, J.R., Heath, S.L., Behnia, R.: Eyes matched to the prize: the state of matched filters in insect visual circuits. Front. Neural Circ. **12**, 26 (2018)
7. Longden, K.D., Wicklein, M., Hardcastle, B.J., Huston, S.J., Krapp, H.G.: Spike burst coding of translatory optic flow and depth from motion in the fly visual system. Curr. Biol. **27**(21), 3225–3236.e3 (2017). https://doi.org/10.1016/j.cub.2017.09.044
8. Seelig, J.D., Jayaraman, V.: Neural dynamics for landmark orientation and angular path integration. Nature **521**(7551), 186–191 (2015)
9. Serres, J.R., Ruffier, F.: Optic flow-based collision-free strategies: from insects to robots. Arthropod Struct. Dev. **46**(5), 703–717 (2017). https://doi.org/10.1016/j.asd.2017.06.003. http://www.sciencedirect.com/science/article/pii/S1467803917300066X
10. Srinivasan, M., Lehrer, M., Kirchner, W., Zhang, S.: Range perception through apparent image speed in freely flying honeybees. Vis. Neurosci. **6**, 519–535 (1991). https://doi.org/10.1017/S095252380000136X
11. Stone, T., et al.: An anatomically constrained model for path integration in the bee brain. Curr. Biol. **27**(20), 3069–3085.e11 (2017). https://doi.org/10.1016/j.cub.2017.08.052
12. Tammero, L.F., Dickinson, M.H.: The influence of visual landscape on the free flight behavior of the fruit fly drosophila melanogaster. J. Exp. Biol. **205**(3), 327–343 (2002). https://jeb.biologists.org/content/205/3/327

13. Taylor, G.J., Tichit, P., Schmidt, M.D., Bodey, A.J., Rau, C., Baird, E.: Bumble-bee visual allometry results in locally improved resolution and globally improved sensitivity. eLife **8**, e40613 (2019). https://doi.org/10.7554/eLife.40613
14. Viollet, S., Zeil, J.: Feed-forward and visual feedback control of head roll orientation in wasps (Polistes Humilis, Vespidae, Hymenoptera). J. Exp. Biol. **216**(7), 1280–1291 (2013). https://doi.org/10.1242/jeb.074773
15. Wystrach, A., Mangan, M., Webb, B.: Optimal cue integration in ants. Proc. Roy. Soc. B Biol. Sci. **282**(1816), 20151484 (2015). https://royalsocietypublishing.org/doi/10.1098/rspb.2015.1484

Can Small Scale Search Behaviours Enhance Large-Scale Navigation?

Fabian Steinbeck$^{(\boxtimes)}$ ⓘ, Paul Graham ⓘ, Thomas Nowotny ⓘ,
and Andrew Philippides ⓘ

University of Sussex, Brighton, UK
f.steinbeck@sussex.ac.uk

Abstract. We develop a spiking neural network model of an insect-inspired CPG which is used to underpin steering behaviour for a Braitenberg-like vehicle. We show that small scale search behaviour, produced by the CPG, improves navigation by recovering useful sensory signals.

Keywords: CPG · Braitenberg · Navigation

1 Introduction

Motor control is fundamental to the adaptive behaviour of natural and artificial systems, with one role being the production of active movement strategies to acquire and use key sensory information. A key neural component of motor systems are central pattern generators (CPGs) [1], for instance, those involved in the control of swimming movements of lamprey [2] or movement control in invertebrates [3]. CPGs have also been shown to be useful components for motor control in bio-inspired robots [4]. In insect brains, the Lateral Accessory Lobe is a key pre-motor area that has been shown to generate CPG like outputs in certain conditions. It is a conserved brain structure and is fundamental to a range of sensori-motor behaviours such as pheromone search in moths [5] and phonotaxis in crickets [6]. Computational models of the LAL have been developed to obtain a better understanding of how the LAL network can generate "flipflop" activity (Adden et al. (in prep.)) or how the LAL may contribute to pheromone plume tracking [7]. Here we develop a minimal spiking neural network model of the LAL, based on our previously developed general steering framework [8]. Our aim is to demonstrate that the model produces outputs that drive two distinct behavioural modes. Firstly, in the presence of sensory information it should output a steering signal that is proportional to that sensory information, so the location of a stimulus relative to the agent drives the steering. Secondly, in the absence of reliable sensory information, the network should produce a rhythmic output that can drive search patterns. We explore the adaptive properties of this network, by situating it in a simple Braitenberg-style animat (Fig. 1).

This work was funded by the EPSRC (grant EP/P006094/1).

V. Vouloutsi et al. (Eds.): Living Machines 2020, LNAI 12413, pp. 338–341, 2020.
https://doi.org/10.1007/978-3-030-64313-3_32

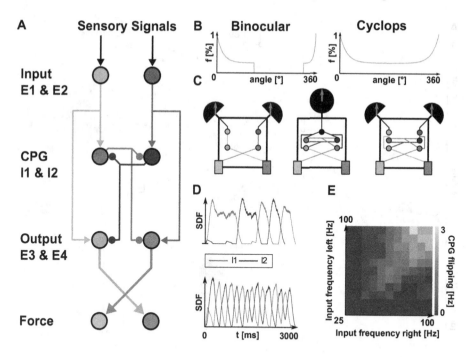

Fig. 1. A: SNN architecture, CPG-neurons correspond to Type III neurons in the LAL, Output-neurons to Type I neurons. B: spatial familiarity function, left: one eye of the pair, right: cyclops, C: Agent configurations. Gray arrows depict direction of maximum familiarity. Left = BB, Middle = Cyclops, Right = BBCPG. D: CPG output as Spike Density Function (SDF), top: low input (resulting in large zig-zag movements), bottom: high input (resulting in small zig-zag movements). E: CPG output space showing how unilateral input results in unilateral output and bilateral input results in flip-flopping.

2   Methods

In a 2D-simulation, we implement a Braitenberg-Agent approaching a beacon. A Braitenberg-vehicle is a simplistic model agent using primitive sensors which directly control actuators, making it an ideal platform to model taxis behaviours. The agent has one of two sensor types: 1. Braitenberg version: two sensors covering 180° each with an overlap of 90° (therefore a total coverage of 270°) and 2. Cyclops version: one sensor covering 360°. The spatial transfer function imitates a typical Rotational Image Difference Function (RIDF) [9]. 100 % familiarity is sensed if the beacon is straight ahead of the agent, approaching 25% (this is the typical approximate minimum value for a 360° rotary IDF) when the target is behind the agent (Cyclops), or 0% when outside the visual range (Braitenberg). The spatial resolution is restricted to 1°. The agent is controlled by a spiking neural network (SNN) that is based on the LAL architecture as described in Steinbeck et al. 2020 [7]. The input neurons (leaky integrate & fire [LIF]) are driven by the sensor signal and excite the ipsilateral CPG- and output-neurons.

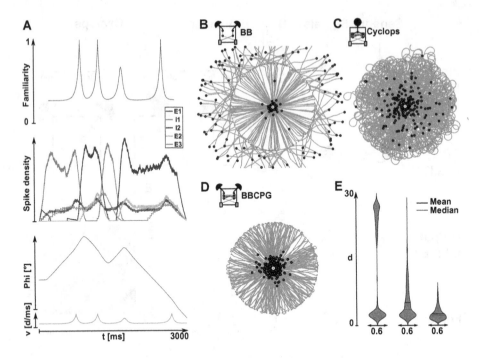

Fig. 2. A: one exemplary trial of Cyclops, top: familiarity, middle: Neuron spike density, bottom: heading and speed, B-D: paths and endpoints; B: Braitenberg, C: Cyclops, D: BBCPG, E: Endpoint distribution of left: BB, middle: Cyclops, right: BBCPG

The CPG neurons (adapting LIF) inhibit the contralateral CPG- and output-neurons. The output-neurons (LIF) excite the contralateral force neurons, which translate spikes into force (integration neurons, where activity represents acceleration). An imbalance of produced force leads to rotation. The SNN is tested in three versions: Braitenberg vehicle (BB), Cyclops and Braitenberg with CPG (BBCPG). The synaptic weights are the same for the same connections in all networks. The oscillation dynamics of the CPG are such that with low symmetric input the oscillation is slow and with strong symmetric input the oscillation is fast. Unilateral input results in no oscillation (Fig. 2).

3   Results

Each of 300 simulations was run for 3000 timesteps, and had a random initial starting position (15 units from the beacon) and heading. The trial was stopped if the agent reached the beacon. Each vehicle version was run 300 times. The BB vehicle converged towards the beacon if one sensor detected it at the beginning. If the beacon is in the agent's blind spot, it runs off into the approximate initial heading direction (which is due to spontaneous neuron activity). The distribution of endpoints is divided into two major clusters, one beyond the starting position, the other close to the beacon. The Cyclops converges towards the beacon in most trials, with only a low percentage running away. Due to the sinuous movements, a large area is covered. Almost all endpoints are located between the starting position and the beacon, therefore it is more successful than BB. The Braitenberg-CPG version converges towards the beacon in each trial. If it does not detect the beacon initially, the CPG driven small scale search steers the agent around (driven by Type III activity), until the stimulus becomes available and the proportional steering mode takes over (mediated by Type I neurons). The endpoints exhibit a smaller mean distance to the goal than in the other conditions.

4 Discussion

We have developed a spiking neural network model of an insect-inspired CPG which is used to underpin the steering behaviour of a Braitenberg-like vehicle. We show that a Braitenberg-only setup, or familiarity modulated CPG, have limited success navigating towards a beacon, while combining these approaches increases success. In future the system will be explored in terms of its biological plausibility to better understand the LAL network and it connection to other brain regions [10] and in more realistic scenarios we will investigate if this framework can improve navigation algorithms.

References

1. Wilson, D.: The central nervous control of locust flight. J. Exp. Biol. **38**(471–490), 8 (1961)
2. Ijspeert, A.J.: Central pattern generators for locomotion control in animals and robots: a review. Neural Netw. **21**, 642–653 (2008)
3. Grillner, S., Wallen, P., Brodin, L.: Neuronal network generating locomotor behaviour in lamprey: circuitry, transmitters, membrane properties and simulation. Ann. Rev. Neurosci. **14**, 169–99 (1991)
4. Selverston, A.I.: Invertebrate central pattern generator circuits. Philos. Trans. R. Soc. **365**, 2329–2349 (2010)
5. Kanzaki, R., Sugi, N., Shibuya, T.: Self-generated zigzag turning of Bombyx-Mori males during pheromone-mediated upwind walking. Zool. Sci. **9**, 515–527 (1992)
6. Zorovic, M., Hedwig, B.: Descending brain neurons in the cricket Gryllus bimaculatus (de Geer): auditory responses and impact on walking. J. Comp. Physiol. Neuroethol. Sens. Neural Behav. Physiol. **199**, 25–34 (2013)
7. Chiba, R., et al.: Neural network estimation of LAL/VPC resions of silkmoth using genetic algorithm. In: The 2010 IEEE/RSJ International Conference on Intelligent Robots and Systems (2010)
8. Steinbeck, F., Adden, A., Graham, P.: Connecting brain to behaviour: a role for general purpose steering circuits in insect orientation? J. Exp. Biol. 223 (2020)
9. Zeil, J., Hofmann, M.I., Chahl, J.S.: Catchment areas of panoramic snapshots in outdoor scenes. J. Opt. Soc. Am. A **20**(3), 450–469 (2003)
10. Sun, X., Yue, S., Mangan, M.: A decentralised neural model explaining optimal integration of navigational strategies in insects. eLife 2020;9:e54026 (2020). https://doi.org/10.7554/eLife.54026

Modeling the Dynamic Sensory Discharges of Insect Campaniform Sensilla

Nicholas S. Szczecinski[1]([✉]) [ID], Sasha N. Zill[2] [ID], Chris J. Dallmann[3] [ID],
and Roger D. Quinn[1] [ID]

[1] Case Western Reserve University, Cleveland, OH 44106, USA
nss36@case.edu
[2] Marshall University, Huntington, WV 25755, USA
[3] University of Washington, Seattle, WA 98195, USA

Abstract. Insects monitor the forces on their legs via sensory organs called campaniform sensilla (CS) that detect cuticular strain. The afferent signals from the CS produce highly dynamic, adaptive responses to even "simple" stimuli. To better understand the advantageous properties of the system, we constructed a dynamical model that describes some of these adaptive responses. We tuned the model parameters to reproduce the response time-courses from experimental data, and found that the model could describe a variety of additional responses with these same parameter values, suggesting that the model replicates the underlying dynamics of CS afferents without overfitting to the data. In addition, our model captures several gross characteristics of CS responses: 1) Responses encode the magnitude of the applied force; 2) The peak response reflects the rate at which the force is applied; 3) The response adapts to constant applied forces; and 4) The response shows hysteresis under cyclic loading. Improved replication of CS responses to applied forces will enable a more thorough understanding of how the nervous system detects forces and controls walking, and will lead to the development of more robust, self-calibrating strain sensors for robots.

Keywords: Insect · Campaniform sensilla · Robotics

1 Introduction

Campaniform sensilla (CS) are sensory organs embedded in the insect cuticle that measure strain [1]. Since stress and strain are related, CS effectively measure the forces acting on the leg. However, CS are not simple sensors. While the sensory discharge (i.e. total afferent nerve firing frequency) does reflect the static level of a constant applied force, the overall response is dominated by sensitivity to force dynamics (e.g. dF/dt) [2, 3]. CS might best be thought of as dynamic sensors whose discharges reflect both force and the rate of force [4] and exhibit hysteresis [2]. CS are also known to be sensitive to the orientation of forces applied to the leg [5, 6].

Supported by the National Science Foundation (Grant Number 1704436).

V. Vouloutsi et al. (Eds.): Living Machines 2020, LNAI 12413, pp. 342–353, 2020.
https://doi.org/10.1007/978-3-030-64313-3_33

Sense organs that detect forces are critical for animals to generate adaptive walking [7], and similar sensors may also help robots walk. One prominent role that such organs serve for insects is to indicate when a leg is in contact with the substrate by registering forces due to supporting and propelling the body (i.e. during the "stance phase"). This is particularly true for CS on the proximal leg segments [8, 9]. For this reason, we have assembled legged robots in the past that include strain sensors on proximal leg segments that return analog feedback regarding the forces acting on the leg [10, 11]. The robots' neural controllers incorporate this information to assist the transition between the stance phase and swing phase of stepping [12]. Related robots have similar sensor suites [13]. However, the performance of such a controller is sensitive to the precise tuning and calibration of the strain sensors, making them impractical for real-world robotic use. We believe that one reason insects are such adept walkers is that their CS are highly dynamic and adaptive, effectively comparing measurements to their "history" in order to accentuate their sensitivity to changing forces and cancel constant offsets. By more thoroughly understanding CS responses with a dynamic model, we anticipate that we can make our robot sensing more detailed and robust, which may lead to more effective walking control in the future.

The goal of this manuscript is to construct a dynamic model that captures the response of a group of CS when strained in its preferred direction [5, 6]. Previous experimental and modeling work has shown that the CS response is dominated by nonlinear effects, including a transient response that exhibits power law decay instead of exponential decay [14] and frequency-independent phase locking with periodic inputs [15]. These features preclude a linear systems description of CS responses, motivating the nonlinear systems description presented in this manuscript.

Our model's goal is to capture the following features of CS responses: Encode the amplitude of the applied force; reflect the rate of the applied force; adapt to constant applied forces; and exhibit hysteresis to cyclic applied forces. We hypothesize that such features will emerge from a simple dynamic model wherein the sensory response is the sum of three terms: One proportional to the instantaneous input; one that adapts to the current force level via a nonlinear low-pass filter; and a constant offset.

In this manuscript, we describe the collection of CS responses from animal experiments (i.e. "animal data") and the formulation and tuning of our dynamic model of CS responses. We use animal data to select values for our model parameters. We show that the model successfully describes animal data not used in the tuning process, supporting that our model is capturing the fundamental properties of the system. We show that the model can capture several gross features of CS responses, including responses that reflect both the level of force and the rate of force, as well as hysteresis in the response to cyclic loading. Finally, we discuss possible sources for these dynamics, possible implications for how the nervous system must process load, and what advantages these dynamics may offer robots in the future.

2 Methods

2.1 Animal Experimental Methods

Recordings were taken from the tibial CS of the American cockroach (*Periplaneta americana*). Activities of axons of the receptors were monitored extracellularly and identified by action potential amplitude and mechanical stimulation/ablation of the cuticular caps [2]. Force waveforms were generated by an analog to digital interface (Spike 2, Cambridge Electronics), applied to the tibia via a probe linked to a DC motor and monitored by strain gauges in the probe [4].

To aid in generating this model, we wished to test CS responses to ramp-and-hold stimuli with different ramp rates but the same hold amplitude. For all stimuli, the hold amplitude was 1.66 mN. The ramp durations tested were 0.125 s, 0.224 s, 0.456 s, and 0.915 s. Each ramp-and-hold stimulus was applied to the tibia 11 times. For each stimulus, the duration of the ramp phase was split into 20 bins. The number of spikes that occurred in each bin was counted and used to calculate the mean afferent firing frequency over that bin. Therefore, each "dataset" consisted of a single stimulus described by 20 time points and 20 frequency samples averaged from 11 repetitions of the stimulus. To test the model response to naturalistic stimuli like the animal might experience during walking, force waveforms obtained from freely walking insects were also applied [16].

2.2 Modeling Methods

Modeling Campaniform Sensilla Discharges. We wish to construct a dynamical model that predicts the discharge (i.e. instantaneous firing frequency) of an afferent nerve from a population of campaniform sensilla (CS) given a load stimulus applied in that population's preferred direction [5, 6]. The sensory discharge of such nerves is known to reflect both the amplitude and rate of a load stimulus [2]. In addition, the sensory discharge adapts as a constant force is applied. Therefore, we choose to model the sensory discharge as the sum of three terms: One proportional to the load stimulus; one that adapts to the load over time; and a constant offset. We expect that rate-sensitivity and hysteresis will emerge naturally from adaptation to stimuli.

We are not attempting to model the separate contribution of individual features in the system, for example, the mechanical response of the CS to limb bending, the intrinsic properties of the sensory or afferent neurons, or the processing performed by individual afferents in the nerve. At this stage, we wish to understand the phenomenological relationship between the force applied to an insect's leg and the rate-coded information carried by the afferent nerves from the CS to the rest of the nervous system. We will refer to these elements collectively as "the system." Possible contributions of each component of the system to the response are considered in the Discussion.

Conceptually, an adaptive response can be thought of as subtracting the long-term history of the input from the input value itself. Thus, the response will reflect the input's rapid changes relative to its history, but will eventually return to zero if the input stops changing and the history can "catch up". Under certain assumptions, it can be shown that such a system directly approximates the rate of change of the input [17]. But how should the long-term history of the input be calculated? In the following, we demonstrate how the properties of a low-pass filter inform the correlation between the total response and the rate of change of the input. Then, we show that a power law low-pass filter matches the response of CS.

Let the instantaneous firing frequency of a CS afferent, y, be the difference between the applied force, u, and a low-pass filtered version of the applied force, x, scaled by a constant, a:

$$y = a \cdot (u - x). \tag{1}$$

Let x be a low-pass filtered copy of u with time constant τ,

$$\tau \cdot \dot{x} = f(u - x), \tag{2}$$

where $f(z)$ is a function such that $f(0) = 0$ and $\frac{df}{dz} \geq 0 \, \forall z$. This implies that $f(z) < 0$ if $z < 0$, and that $f(z) > 0$ if $z > 0$. These conditions ensure that the only equilibrium state is $x = u$ and that the inverse function $f^{-1}(z)$ exists [18].

We seek to understand how y reflects $\dot{u}$, the time-rate of change of u. If $x(t) = u(t - \Delta t)$, then Eq. (1) would mimic a finite difference equation and y would be proportional to $\dot{u}$. How do we enforce that $x(t) = u(t - \Delta t)$, and how do we determine Δt? Let us consider the case where u is a ramp function of the form $u = \frac{A}{T} \cdot t$. We assume that the particular solution to Eq. (2) is the same as u, but delayed in time [17]. This implies that $\dot{x} = \dot{u} = \frac{A}{T}$. Plugging this assumption into Eq. (2),

$$\tau \cdot \frac{A}{T} = f\left(\frac{A}{T} \cdot t - x(t)\right). \tag{3}$$

We can solve Eq. (3) for the particular solution of x,

$$x(t) = \frac{A}{T} \cdot \left(t - \frac{T}{A} \cdot f^{-1}\left(\tau \cdot \frac{A}{T}\right)\right). \tag{4}$$

If we define

$$\Delta t = \frac{T}{A} \cdot f^{-1}\left(\tau \cdot \frac{A}{T}\right). \tag{5}$$

Then, x lags u by Δt, where

$$x(t) = u(t - \Delta t). \tag{6}$$

In the special case that $f(z) = z, f^{-1}(z) = z$ such that the solution to Eq. (4) becomes $\Delta t = \tau$ and $x = \frac{A}{T} \cdot (t - \tau)$, such that x lags u by a constant amount independent of the value of $\dot{u}$ [17]. However, we are not limited to this particular case. To understand how $f(z)$ impacts y, let us write the finite difference approximation of $\dot{u}$:

$$\Delta t \cdot \dot{u} \approx u(t) - u(t - \Delta t). \tag{7}$$

Substituting Eqs. (5) and (6) into Eq. (7),

$$\frac{T}{A} \cdot f^{-1}\left(\tau \cdot \frac{A}{T}\right) \cdot \dot{u} = u(t) - x(t). \tag{8}$$

Substituting Eq. (8) into (1), we find that y is proportional to $\dot{u}$ in steady state:

$$y = a \cdot (u - x) = a \cdot \frac{T}{A} \cdot f^{-1}\left(\tau \cdot \frac{A}{T}\right) \cdot \dot{u}. \tag{9}$$

Equation (9) simplifies when we recall that for this example, $\dot{u} = \frac{A}{T}$:

$$y = a \cdot f^{-1}(\tau \cdot \dot{u}). \tag{10}$$

Therefore, $\dot{u}$ maps to y according to the inverse function of the low-pass filter function, $f(z)$. For example, if a system's output follows a logarithmic encoding of the input's rate of change, then $f(z)$ should be an exponential function. The sensory discharge of CS reflect the rate of force according to a power law relationship [2, 3]. Therefore, our model's $f(z)$ should also be a power law with the reciprocal exponent of the power law correlation between $\dot{u}$ and y. However, if the response were modeled only by $f(z)$, then the model could not capture the observed component of the response that is proportional to and offset from the tonic applied force [2]. Thus, we add two such terms.

The model used in this manuscript is as follows:

$$y = \max(0, a \cdot (u - x) + b \cdot u + c), \tag{11}$$

$$\tau \cdot \dot{x} = sign(u - x) \cdot |u - x|^d, \tag{12}$$

where y is the instantaneous firing frequency (Hz) of afferent nerves from a population of CS; u is the instantaneous loading (mN) of the limb segment in the CS population's preferred orientation; x is a low-pass filtered copy of u; a scales the adaptation term $u - x$; b is the proportionality constant between u and y; c is a constant offset; d is the power law exponent that describes the low-pass filter function $f(z)$; and τ is a time scaling factor for $\dot{x}$. To avoid the introduction of imaginary numbers, Eq. (12) raises the absolute value of the argument, $u - x$, to the power of d, and then multiplies by the sign of the argument. In total, this model requires that five numerical parameters be tuned $(a, b, c, d,$ and $\tau)$.

Tuning Model Parameters. Model parameters were tuned via optimization. Gradient-based optimization (fmincon, Matlab, The Mathworks, Natick, MA) set the model parameter values to minimize the difference between the model's response time-course and the smoothed CS firing frequency response time-course given the same applied force. For each parameter value configuration tested, an applied force was specified and the model's response was simulated. The root-mean-squared error between the simulation output and the corresponding CS firing frequency response was returned as the objective to minimize. To test that the model could capture the underlying dynamics of the system and generalize to other cases, only two experimental time-courses (the fastest and the slowest) were used to tune the system. By selecting the most extreme stimuli, we test our model's ability to interpolate the dynamic response of the CS in response to intermediate stimuli.

3 Results

3.1 Model Tuning and Generalization

To avoid overfitting model parameters, we used two experimental datasets to tune model parameters, and then observed the goodness of fit to additional experimental datasets. Figure 1 shows four plots, each depicting the force input, the response from the corresponding animal dataset, and the response from the model. The two trials on the left were used to tune the parameter values, which are listed in Table 1. The two trials on the right show animal and model responses to additional stimuli, but these trials were not used to tune the parameters. Remarkably, the model responses on the right capture the dynamic nature of the animal responses despite not being tuned to do so. This suggests that the model captures the underlying dynamics of the system.

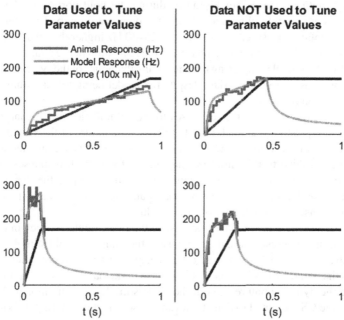

Fig. 1. Animal data were used to tune the constant parameters of the model. Left: Two datasets were used to select values for the parameters a, b, c, d, and τ that reduced the mean-squared-error between the animal response and the model response, given the same input force. Right: The model captures these other animal responses remarkably well, despite not explicitly being tuned to match.

Recent studies on stick insects have demonstrated that CS responses to force stimuli like those the animal would generate during locomotion are more dynamic and adapt less quickly than responses to conventional stimuli (i.e. ramp-and-hold stimuli) [4].

Table 1. Model parameter descriptions and values.

Parameter	Description	Value
a	Adaptation term scale	1088
b	Proportional term scale	40.45
c	Constant offset	−52.84
d	Exponent in low-pass filter function, i.e. $f(z) = z^d$	2.369
τ	Time constant for $\dot{x}$	2.668×10^3

We wished to see if the model could capture the same characteristics without retuning the model parameters. Figure 2 shows the model's response to both a ramp-and-hold stimulus and to a naturalistic stimulus. Figure 2A shows that the responses to the ramp-and-hold stimulus share several key characteristics: Both responses initially leap up to a high value; both responses then continue to grow, but at a reduced and apparently constant rate; both responses quickly adapt during the hold portion of the stimulus; both responses are quickly eliminated during the downward ramp. The peak response of the experimentally measured CS response is 25–30 Hz higher than that of the model. However, the shape of both the rising phase and the relaxation phase qualitatively match, suggesting that the model is capturing the underlying dynamics of the system. In addition, the adaptation phases largely overlap, despite the model being tuned without any data from the relaxation phase.

Figure 2B also shows that the responses to the naturalistic stimulus largely match between the model and the animal, despite the dynamic nature of the stimulus and not retuning the parameter values. The responses share several key characteristics: Both responses are sensitive to the initial increase in the force; both responses are largely constant between 10% and 40% of the stimulus duration, despite the dynamic nature of the force's rise; both responses slowly adapt, and then are silenced when the force noticeably decreases at around 80% of the stimulus.

Figure 2C compares the model's response to the two stimuli. As seen in the experimentally measured CS responses, the response to the ramp-and-hold stimulus increases more rapidly, reaches a higher response frequency, and adapts more quickly than the response to the naturalistic stimulus. The response to the naturalistic stimulus is persistent despite the dynamic nature of both the force stimulus and the model. These data suggest that the CS are tuned to detect relevant sensory features during walking [4].

3.2   Emergent Properties of the Model

Our model reproduces the linear encoding of tonic force levels as well as the power law reflection of the rate of force seen in insect CS [2]. Figure 3 shows data summarizing simulation experiments in which the model was subjected to a ramp-and-hold stimulus with a height A and a rise time T (i.e. $u(t) = \min(A \cdot t/T, A)$). Figure 3A shows that as in the animal, the sensory discharge long after the hold phase begins (in our experiments, 9.5 s in accordance with [2]) is linearly correlated with the amplitude of the force, A.

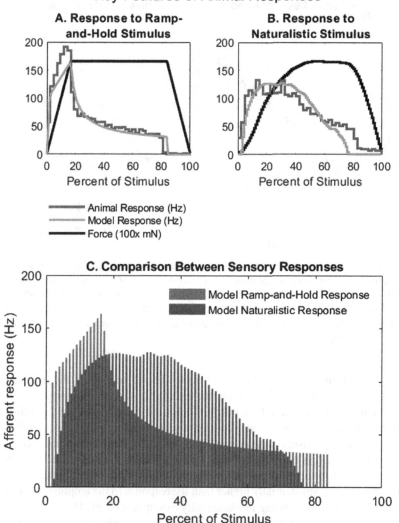

Fig. 2. The differences between the model's response to ramp-and-hold and naturalistic stimuli reflect those seen in the animal. A) Using the original model tuning, the model captures the animal response to both the ramp and hold portions of the stimulus. The model has not been tuned to capture the hold phase data. B) The model response to an animal-like force waveform resembles the animal response to the same stimulus, despite not being tuned to do so. C. As seen in the animal data, the model response to the ramp-and-hold stimulus peaks higher and adapts more quickly than the response to the naturalistic stimulus. This suggests a fundamental similarity between the model and the animal.

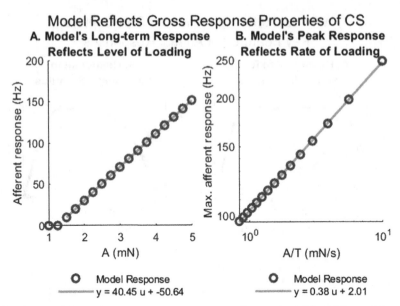

Model Reflects Gross Response Properties of CS

A. Model's Long-term Response Reflects Level of Loading

B. Model's Peak Response Reflects Rate of Loading

○ Model Response
····· y = 40.45 u + -50.64

○ Model Response
····· y = 0.38 u + 2.01

Fig. 3. The model shares the same gross response properties as animal CS. A) The model response linearly encodes the applied force amplitude A, 10 s after the stimulus is applied (ramp duration of 0.5 s). B) The model's peak response reflects the rate of loading $\frac{A}{T}$ via a power law relationship. Note the logarithmic axes. The slope of the line of best fit represents the exponent of the power law relationship. A value of 0.35 is consistent with previous characterizations of cockroach proximal tibial CS responses [2].

Our model response reflects the rate of force despite no explicit dependence on it. Figure 3B shows that as in the animal, the maximum sensory discharge reflects the rate of loading, A/T. Note that both the horizontal and vertical axes are logarithmically scaled, such that this apparently linear correlation is actually a power law correlation. The calculated slope is precisely in agreement with previous characterizations of cockroach proximal tibia CS, and is also roughly what would be expected based on our model tuning (i.e. $d^{-1} = 0.422$, compare to values in Table 1 in [2]). Also note that the response to the rate of loading is substantially higher than the response to the amplitude of the load. This is consistent with CS being fundamentally dynamic sensors [4].

Our model response exhibits hysteresis in response to loading and unloading as seen in insect CS [2]. Figure 4 shows data from a simulation experiment in which the model was subjected to a "staircase" stimulus, in which the applied force was stepped up and then stepped down at the same levels. The response in Fig. 4A shows large fluctuations due to adaptation, in which the response is strongly biased in the direction of the change in force. Figure 4B shows the form of the "staircase" stimulus. Figure 4C plots the mean sensory response during the tonic segments of the staircase. The color coding matches that in Fig. 4A, to impress a sense of time. The model's response to a given force depends on the history of the sensory input, that is, whether the force was increased or decreased to that level.

4 Discussion

In this manuscript, we assembled a dynamic model of the sensory discharges observed from afferent nerves from insect campaniform sensilla (CS). CS discharges are proportional to the bending forces applied to the leg, but also demonstrate strong adaptive responses and hysteresis. Additionally, such adaptation does not match the output of a linear model [14], so we derived a method for designing a nonlinear low-pass filter that can replicate the response properties of CS afferent nerves. We then subjected this model to stimuli like those applied to insect legs and used some experimental data to tune the constants in the model. Once complete, the model could capture the results of experiments whose data were not used to tune the model, including the response to highly dynamic inputs. In addition, the model exhibited the same gross responses seen in the animal: Linear encoding of the applied force level; power law reflection of the rate of the applied force; and hysteresis in response to cyclic loading.

The model we developed is only a phenomenological model, but may have benefits for experimental neuroscience and robotics. With a phenomenological description of CS response to a given force input, experimental stimuli can be derived that may produce more natural CS responses. For example, previous studies have shown that the history of

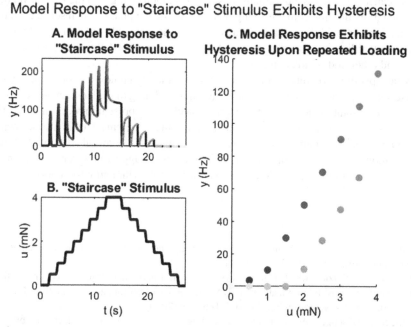

Fig. 4. As observed in the animal, the model response exhibits hysteresis. A) The response to a "staircase" stimulus shows the strong history dependence of the response; specifically, the response is biased in the direction of the rate of change of the force. B) The "staircase" stimulus. C) The mean model responses during the hold phases of the "staircase" reveal a clear hysteresis loop upon cyclic loading. The points are calculated as the mean response y while u is not changing. The color coding relates to the traces in A).

loading has discrete effects upon CS encoding, specifically, that pre-loading the leg resets the amplitude sensitivity, while dynamic properties (e.g. encoding the rate of change of force) are not altered by history [2]. Conversely, the model could be inverted to infer the instantaneous force acting on a leg given the CS recording during motion. Using animal kinematic and force measurements to build a model of insect walking has already led to a better understanding of the types of forces these sensors are subjected to as the animal walks freely [16]. Better understanding the responses to these forces will elucidate what information the nervous system has available to it regarding forces applied to its legs.

This model will also benefit robotics. To better understand how the insect nervous system uses CS feedback in the control of walking, we have built such strain sensors into the legs of our robots [10, 11]. Such sensors are particularly useful for detecting when a leg is in the "stance phase," during which it supports and propels the body, versus when it is in the "swing phase." In the past, these sensors have provided our stepping controllers with non-adapting feedback proportional to the force on the leg. However, calibrating such sensors to eliminate constant offsets while maintaining maximal sensitivity is critical for proper function; if the offset is too high, the sensors return false-positive information about leg loading; if the offset is too low, the sensors return false-negative information. We believe that our CS response model could be implemented to run in real-time onboard robots, enabling their sensors to self-calibrate. Such an algorithm would adapt to cancel out offsets, but remain sensitive to sudden changes in the force level (e.g. from a leg transitioning from the swing phase to the stance phase). Such self-calibration may increase the reliability of large arrays of analog sensors onboard robots that provide feedback regarding support and contact forces, environmental fluid currents (e.g. via hairs), and other body-wide conditions.

What specific structures might give rise to the dynamics we describe in this manuscript? Experimental data and computational modeling of spider mechanoreceptors suggest that adaptation arises due to adaptive ion channels present in receptor cells [19]. The viscoelastic hysteresis of the exoskeleton and the CS themselves is also known to contribute to sensory adaptation [20]. Future experiments may reveal additional sources of adaptation. Better understanding such sources may suggest new sensor designs or processing algorithms that would endow walking robots with animal-like mobility.

References

1. Zill, S.N., Schmitz, J., Büschges, A.: Load sensing and control of posture and locomotion. Arthropod Struct. Dev. **33**, 273–286 (2004)
2. Ridgel, A.L., Frazier, S.F., DiCaprio, R.A., Zill, S.N.: Encoding of forces by cockroach tibial campaniform sensilla: implications in dynamic control of posture and locomotion. J. Comp. Physiol. A Sens. Neural, Behav. Physiol. **186**, 359 (2000)
3. Zill, S.N., Büschges, A., Schmitz, J.: Encoding of force increases and decreases by tibial campaniform sensilla in the stick insect, Carausius morosus. J. Comp. Physiol. A Neuroethol. Sens. Neural, Behav. Physiol. **197**, 851–867 (2011)
4. Zill, S.N., Dallmann, C.J., Büschges, A., Chaudhry, S., Schmitz, J.: Force dynamics and synergist muscle activation in stick insects: the effects of using joint torques as mechanical stimuli. J. Neurophysiol. **120**, 1807–1823 (2018)

5. Zill, S.N., Moran, D.T.: The exoskeleton and insect proprioception. i. responses of tibial campaniform sensilla to external and muscle-generated forces in the American Cockroach, Periplaneta Americana. J. Exp. Biol. **91**, 1–24 (1981)
6. Zill, S.N., Schmitz, J., Chaudhry, S., Büschges, A.: Force encoding in stick insect legs delineates a reference frame for motor control. J. Neurophysiol. **108**, 1453–1472 (2012)
7. Ekeberg, Ö., Blümel, M., Büschges, A.: Dynamic simulation of insect walking. Arthropod Struct. Dev. **33**, 287–300 (2004)
8. Noah, J.A., Quimby, L., Frazier, S.F., Zill, S.N.: Walking on a "peg leg": Extensor muscle activities and sensory feedback after distal leg denervation in cockroaches. J. Comp. Physiol. A Neuroethol. Sens. Neural, Behav. Physiol. **190**, 217–231 (2004)
9. Akay, T., Bässler, U., Gerharz, P., Büschges, A.: The role of sensory signals from the insect coxa-trochanteral joint in controlling motor activity of the Femur-Tibia joint. J. Neurophysiol. **85**, 594–604 (2001)
10. Szczecinski, N.S., et al.: Introducing MantisBot: hexapod robot controlled by a high-fidelity, real-time neural simulation. In: IEEE International Conference on Intelligent Robots and Systems, Hamburg, DE, pp. 3875–3881 (2015)
11. Goldsmith, C., Szczecinski, N.S., Quinn, R.D.: Neurodynamic modeling of the Fruit Fly Drosophila melanogaster. Bioinspir., Biomim (2020)
12. Szczecinski, N.S., Getsy, A.P., Martin, J.P., Ritzmann, R.E., Quinn, R.D.: MantisBot is a robotic model of visually guided motion in the praying mantis. Arthropod. Struct. Dev. **46**(5), 736–751 (2017)
13. Schäffersmann, M., Schneider, A., Schmitz, J.: Self-adjustable transducer for bio-inspired strain detection in walking legs. In: Mobile Service Robotics. pp. 199–206. World Scientific (2014)
14. Chapman, K.M., Smith, R.S.: A linear transfer function underlying impulse frequency modulation in a cockroach mechanoreceptor. Nature **197**, 699–700 (1963)
15. French, A.S., Holden, A.V., Stein, R.B.: The estimation of the frequency response function of a mechanoreceptor. Kybernetik. **11**, 15–23 (1972)
16. Dallmann, C.J., Dürr, V., Schmitz, J.: Joint torques in a freely walking insect reveal distinct functions of leg joints in propulsion and posture control. Proc. Biol. Sci. **283**, 20151708 (2016)
17. Szczecinski, N.S., Hunt, A.J., Quinn, R.D.: A functional subnetwork approach to designing synthetic nervous systems that control legged robot locomotion. Front. Neurorobot. **11**, 37 (2017)
18. Khalil, H.K.: Nonlinear Systems. Prentice Hall, Upper Saddle River (2002)
19. French, A.S., Torkkeli, P.H.: The power law of sensory adaptation: Simulation by a model of excitability in spider mechanoreceptor neurons. Ann. Biomed. Eng. **36**, 153–161 (2008)
20. Chapman, K.M., Mosinger, J.L., Duckrow, R.B.: The role of distributed viscoelastic coupling in sensory adaptation in an insect mechanoreceptor. J. Comp. Physiol. A **131**, 1–12 (1979)

Evaluation of Possible Flight Strategies for Close Object Evasion from Bumblebee Experiments

Andreas Thoma[1,2](✉) ⓘ, Alex Fisher[2] ⓘ, Olivier Bertrand[3] ⓘ, and Carsten Braun[1] ⓘ

[1] FH Aachen, Hohenstaufenallee 6, 52064 Aachen, Germany
a.thoma@fh-aachen.de
[2] RMIT University, Bundoora, VIC 3083, Australia
[3] Universität Bielefeld, 33615 Bielefeld, Germany

Abstract. The need for robust and efficient obstacle avoidance algorithms for flying platforms increases at a fast pace. Strategies are required to maneuver around various obstacles. Since bumblebees are efficient fliers that need to navigate in cluttered environments, they are perfectly suitable test objects when seeking for avoidance strategies. In the present work, we study the maneuver of bumblebees confronted with a large rectangular obstacle lying on their direct path to the hive. The bumblebees could always evade the obstacle vertically or horizontally, e.g., fly over the obstacle or fly around the obstacle, respectively. The chosen evasion maneuver, i.e., the basic strategy employed by the bee, is considered the dependent variable. The influence of the distance to the obstacle, obstacle dimensions, acceleration, and flight speed were investigated and considered as independent variables. To evaluate the bumblebee behavior, linear regression, and the Horizontality Verticality Index (HV), an adaption of the Laterality Index, was used to estimate the preferred behavioral choice.

Examination of the bumblebee behavior revealed a strong tendency towards vertical evasion at higher distances to the obstacle, while the bumblebees evaded close obstacles horizontally. This is reasonable because climbing in flapping-wing flight is aerodynamically more efficient in forward movement than in hover flight. A linear function based on the HV Index was defined to estimate a relationship between distance to obstacle and evasion maneuver. Depending on the dimensions of the obstacle, alternative slopes of the HV function could be identified, indicating an additional dependency on the height-to-width ratio. However, taking the obstacle shape into account does not improve the predictability of an L1 LASSO regression model.

Finally, one possibility to include the HV index into a technical system as an element of an obstacle avoidance algorithm is discussed.

Keywords: Obstacle avoidance · Bumblebees · MAV · UAV · Flight control

1 Introduction

Autonomous vehicles are an overall increasing sector. Specifically, possible applications of unmanned aerial vehicles (UAV) are growing fast. The variety of applications ranges

© Springer Nature Switzerland AG 2020
V. Vouloutsi et al. (Eds.): Living Machines 2020, LNAI 12413, pp. 354–365, 2020.
https://doi.org/10.1007/978-3-030-64313-3_34

from drug delivery to inspection tasks. Stressful times with social distancing, like the pandemic spread of COVID-19, boost the necessity of autonomously flying delivery and surveillance drones. However, several challenges remain until an autonomously operating UAV service is established. One of these challenges is the development of a reliable obstacle avoidance system. Even though the field of bio-inspired flight control systems, especially the applied sensor technology, advanced recently [1].

We present possibilities and approaches to improve current obstacle avoidance algorithms, which are found by the analysis of obstacle avoidance strategies used in nature. More particularly, the flight behavior of bumblebees, *Bombus Terrestris*, is investigated, when encountering differently sized obstacles in different distances. The analysis aims at the derivation of fundamental strategies for improved obstacle avoidance. It is of particular interest, in which situations a vertical evasion is more desired than a horizontal evasion. The next section will present the theoretical background of this work, as well as the experimental set-up, which was used to extend the current body of knowledge. Section 3 will give an overview of the results from the conducted experiments, while Sect. 4 contains the conclusions drawn from the results. Finally, the last chapter will summarize the conclusions.

2 Background

Neuroethologists have studied the behavior of animals for decades. Their research revealed a variety of strategies on how animals navigate in different environments [2], avoid obstacles [3], optimize paths [4], and solve other problems [5, 6]. The study of insect behavior yield applications in technical systems such as network systems [7] and autonomous robots [8, 9]. Insects and, more precisely, bumblebees are astonishing foragers, which have been subject of investigation for decades.

2.1 Biological Findings and Their Possible Technical Application

Honeybees and bumblebees forage between rewarding food sources and their hive in often complex environments. They have to fly through clutter consisting of obstacles of different sizes, shapes, orientations, and textures. To avoid physical damage [10] and to perform the task of food collection as efficient as possible, insects need to go around objects obstructing their way [11]. Flying insects, in particular, can apply a variety of strategies and flight maneuvers to avoid objects and reach their goal efficient, fast, and safe [12–14]. Flying technical systems ("drones") have the same requirements and encounter the same challenges. When following a global path to a specific goal position, a flying platform will encounter different obstacles [15]. After obstacle detection, a local path, evading the obstacle, has to be determined. While several systems and methods for obstacle detection are known, e.g., LiDAR, radar, or camera with SLAM or SURF [16, 17], only a few strategies exist for the 3D obstacle avoidance maneuver. The p×4 avoid algorithm, which discretizes the world and evaluates different possibilities with a cost function, is one of the most sophisticated algorithms for obstacle avoidance [18]. However, this algorithm relies on one core function for all situations and does not adapt to different situations [19]. Another problem of optimization methods is the definition of what is optimal. While most ground-bound path planners define efficiency as the shortest possible path [20, 21], this is questionable for flying platforms, where a third dimension of movement has to be taken into account. Moving in the third dimension, e.g., up or downward, is energetically different from moving inplane. Because of this, 2D methods cannot easily be transferred to 3D. An understanding of the flight strategies of insects and the working principles behind their behavior might help to improve the current flight algorithm to a high degree [22].

Currently, much knowledge is available about the behavior of bumblebees in specific situations. Several research groups identified critical aspects of bee behavior when flying through tunnels. For example, bees maintain equidistance to both walls [23, 24], by maintaining equivalent optic flow on both eyes [25]. Additionally, by keeping optic flow constant, the flight speed is adapted to the width of the tunnel [25, 26]. Even though the behavior in an empty tunnel is understood quite well, none of the above gives information on obstacle encounters.

If challenged with a series of vertical or horizontal obstacles within a flight tunnel, bumblebees do not show any significant difference in the maneuver when avoiding the obstacles horizontally or vertically [27]. However, body size has a more significant influence on the flight behavior of bumblebees than the obstacle orientation. With increasing body size, flight performance is impaired [27]. However, this work investigates only one possibility to evade the obstacle in a very confined space such that the bee cannot decide between several alternatives.

When bumblebees have to decide to fly through two horizontally aligned gates, they tend to choose the wider gap [28]. However, this situation may change when gaps are not horizontally aligned, but the bees have to decide to avoid an object by moving upward or sideward.

Thus, we investigated the decision of bumblebees between vertical and horizontal avoidance in a tunnel.

2.2   Experimental Set-Up

Most research has focused on studying flight control inplane, either horizontal such as avoiding trees or vertical as in a 110 m hurdles. However, flying insects in nature can decide to fly above or around an obstacle. The goal of this work was to identify situations in which bumblebees prefer to fly over an obstacle instead of around. The experiments were conducted at the University Bielefeld. All experiments were performed with bumblebees, *Bombus Terrestris*, from two different colonies (Koppert, GmbH, Zeppelinstr. 32, Straelen, Germany). The hive was placed in a $0.5 \times 0.5 \times 0.3$ m^3 acrylic box, which was covered by a black cloth to mimic a natural situation. At arrival, the colonies consisted of less than 30 worker bees and one queen.

The hive enclosure was connected to a $1.5 \times 0.3 \times 0.3$ m^3 flight tunnel leading to a $1.0 \times 1.0 \times 0.75$ m^3 foraging chamber. A gravity feeder with a 30%/vol. Sucrose solution was placed on a podium in the center of the foraging chamber. Additionally, ground pollen was placed in the hive enclosure. Silicon tubes with an inner diameter of 25 mm connected hive, flight tunnel, and chamber. Closable gates, installed on both ends of the tunnel, were used to control in- and outflow of bumblebees. The bees had one week to habituate to the new environment before experiments started by flying at Libitum through the tunnel.

The walls of the tunnel were partly covered with a 1/f pink noise red pattern. The wall around the test area was transparent to allow filming the bumblebees. The floor was white, while the whole ceiling was transparent. The transparent tunnel wall was invisible for the bees, giving them the visual impression that no confinement is present to the side and the top. The bees collided multiple times during habituation with the transparent wall and ceiling.

To minimize the difference in the position before avoiding an obstacle, gates with one circular hole were used, forcing the bees to fly through specific waypoints. Before the experiments, the bees were trained to fly through the gates. The gate had a 3 cm radius circular hole in the center to allow the bumblebees to fly quickly through it. One gate was placed in front of the test track, one behind.

The general layout of the test section is presented in Fig. 1. To fly from the foraging chamber to the hive, bees had to fly from left to right. Before entering the test section, bumblebees had to pass a gate, defining the start position for this specific test flight. The obstacle with width w and height h was placed at a specific distance d to the entrance gate. Another gate was placed behind the obstacle to give the bumblebees a goal point. The entrance and exit gate were 90 cm apart. The entrance to the hive was located 30 cm behind the second gate. Three cameras, the Optronis CR3000×2 filming at a frame rate of 100 Hz, were used to record the movement of the bumblebees through the test section. Two cameras filmed the test section from above and a third camera filmed the test section horizontally from the side. We used a python tool to analyze the recordings based on OpenCV functions.

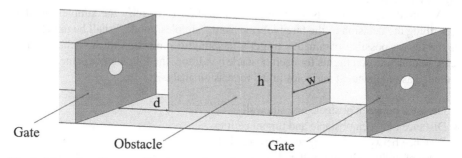

Fig. 1. The general layout of the test section. The tunnel walls between the two gates are transparent; otherwise, the walls are covered with a 1/f pink noise red pattern. The whole ceiling is transparent, while the whole floor is white; Gates and the obstacle are gray. (Color figure online)

Three different obstacles were used for the experiments presented in this work. All obstacles have the same length of 40 cm and varying height and width of 20×20 cm^2, 25×20 cm^2, or 25×25 cm^2. During all experiments, there was only one obstacle in the test tunnel at any time. The obstacle was placed at specific distances between 5 cm and 40 cm to the entrance gate. The following table shows the combination of obstacle and gate distance discussed in this work.

Table 1. Obstacle dimensions and Distances

No	Obstacle dimensions (w × h) [cm × cm]	Distance d [cm]
1	25 × 25	5.0
2	20 × 25	15.0
3	25 × 20	15.0
4	25 × 20	20.0
5	20 × 25	37.5
6	25 × 25	40.0

Only population-level behavior is investigated. Therefore, no bees were marked, and individual behavior or preferences are not considered. The obstacle situation was changed at least once a day such that it is doubtful that a single bee participated in one condition only. Additionally, in - and outbound flights were controlled to reduce the possibility that one bee is overrepresented in the test data. Before testing, the bees had several opportunities to fly through the test path, such that it is unlike that a naïve bee was recorded during the test runs. The experiments were designed to observe the phenomenology only. Any analysis to find out the reasons for the identified behavior is not the purpose of the presented work and will be investigated in later experiments.

From all flights investigated, only those flights directly leading from the entrance to the exit of the test section are considered for evaluation. Flights in which bees turn back and fly more than 3 cm in the wrong direction are not included. Out of 543 flights, 411 flights were thus analyzed.

We used logistic regression with L1 penalization to identify the simplest model, describing the decision of the bumblebees. Here, "simplest model" shall be understood as the fewest possible parameters to get a meaningful prediction of the behavior. For ten randomly chosen flights for each obstacle condition, the following parameters were included as independent variables in the regression analysis:

- Distance between obstacle and sidewall
- Distance between obstacle and tunnel ceiling
- Distance between the entrance gate and obstacle
- Ratio of width to height of the obstacle
- Ratio of distance to obstacle height
- Ratio of distance to obstacle width
- Average longitudinal speed of the bumblebee
- Average longitudinal acceleration of the bumblebee
- Average longitudinal speed in the first second after flying through the gate
- Average longitudinal acceleration in the first second after flying through the gate

We used the decision of the bumblebee to fly over or around an obstacle as the dependent variable. The recordings of the bumblebee flights were used to determine speed and acceleration for the chosen flights. The logistic regression with cross-validation was implemented in a python script based on Libsolver and Stratified K-Folds for model selection. To avoid the preference to one independent variable due to different scales, we normalized the independent variable such that their mean is zero, and their standard deviation is one. We used ten flights for each obstacle condition to avoid statistical bias.

3 Results

We wanted to investigate how the choice of bumblebees depends on the obstacle condition. However, the goal was not to investigate the actual sensory cues but to predict the bumblebee decision based on measurable quantities, which are transferable to autonomous flying platforms.

3.1 Influence of the Distance on the Decision

The distance between the entrance gate and obstacle is roughly the same distance between bee and obstacle when the bee sees the obstacle the first time. Any behavior might be depending on this initial contact. This distance is known for all 411 recorded flights, without further video evaluation. Therefore, the bees' preference for a specific evasion maneuver depending on the distance between gate and obstacle was investigated to get a first impression on the general behavior. Bumblebees tend to evade vertically for large distances between gate and obstacle, while they tend to evade horizontally otherwise (Table 1). In two cases, the bumblebees did both fly over and around the obstacle. Therefore, those two flights are not considered as vertical or horizontal evasion. Nonetheless, both flights are counted to the total number of flights, because the defined requirements were fulfilled.

Table 2. Summary of the choices made by bumblebees in different situations. The distance d between entrance gate and obstacle is given as well as the width w times height h of the obstacle in cm. Finally, the number (#) of horizontal evasions and vertical ones are depicted together with the total number (#) of flights. The proportional amount of choices is also presented

Distance D [cm]	Size W × h [cm × cm]	# Vert. Evasions [−]	# Hor. Evasions [−]	# Total [−]	Prop. Vert. Evasions [%]	Prop. Hor. Evasions [%]
5,0	25 × 25	14	71	85	16	84
15,0	20 × 25	2	60	62	3	97
15,0	25 × 20	23	76	99	23	77
20,0	25 × 20	26	24	50	52	48
37,5	20 × 25	79	3	84	94	4
40,0	25 × 25	31	0	31	100	0

3.2 Introducing the HV-Index

A mathematical function is required to implement a strategy in a technical system. To define such a function and for further investigation of the dependency on additional parameters, an adaption of the Laterality Index (LI) was developed. Usually, the Laterality Index is used as a measure of bias and gives the probability that a bee will fly left or right. However, this index is adapted such that differentiation between horizontal, e.g., flying around the obstacle, and vertical, e.g., flying over the obstacle, evasion is made. Therefore, this coefficient shall be called the Horizontality Verticality Index (HV). This index is defined analog to the LI index by:

$$HV = (V - H) / N \tag{1}$$

where H and V are the numbers of evasion routes, either horizontal or vertical, chosen by the bees. N = H + V is the number of flights. An HV index of 1 is associated with a bias for vertical evasion, while −1 is associated with a bias for horizontal evasion.

Figure 2 visualizes the HV Index for different distances between the obstacle and entrance gate. The results are grouped into three classes, depending on the obstacle dimensions. Additionally, a linear fit over all points is given.

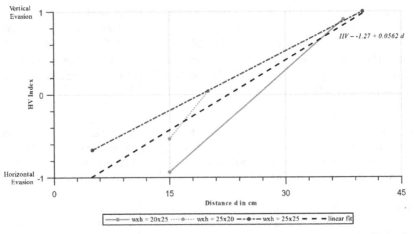

Fig. 2. Dependency of the HV-Index on the distance between entrance and obstacle. (Color figure online)

The linear fit has a positive slope of 0,056 per cm, indicating an increasing tendency to fly over an obstacle rather than around with increasing distance independent of the obstacle size. Additionally, the slope of the biggest and largest obstacle with a size of 25 × 25 cm is the smallest one (blue line). The slope of the wide but short obstacle (green line; 25 cm width and 20 cm height) is the steepest one.

3.3 Influence of Distances, Speed, Acceleration, Width-to-Distance, and Height-to-Distance on the Decision

The previous results do not show if the decision of the bumblebees depends on other parameters as well. It is also not clear if the distance itself or any parameter depending on the distance, as the height-to-distance ratio, leads to a specific choice. Therefore, a linear regression analysis of the ten parameters listed in Sect. 2.2 was conducted on ten randomly chosen flights per obstacle situation. The linear regression showed that the gate distance alone predicts whether the bee is flying over or around the obstacle with an accuracy of more than 80%. Figure 3 shows exemplarily three of the ten investigated parameters. Additionally, the coefficient is positive, indicating that the bee is more likely to fly over the obstacle with increasing distance.

4 Discussion

4.1 Discussion of Results

Table 2 shows an increasing proportion of vertical evasions with increasing distance; only the first line with a distance of 5 cm between the gate and obstacle misfits slightly.

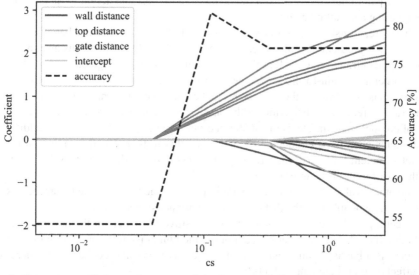

Fig. 3. Parameter coefficient and accuracy of the three most influencing independent parameters (wall distance, top distance, and gate distance) in logistic regression over the lasso penalty parameter cs (also commonly referred to as λ_1). To reduce diagram complexity, the parameters relevant for the highest accuracies are displayed. Where wall distance is the distance between sidewall and obstacle, top distance is the distance between the tunnel ceiling and obstacle, and gate distance is the distance between obstacle and entrance gate; intercept is the unpenalized intercept value of a LASSO regression. The highest prediction accuracy (82%) is reached at several gate distance regression coefficients between 0 and 1 while all other parameters are neglectable, i.e., coefficient = 0, at a penalty parameter cs $\approx$ 0.1. If wall and top distance are taken into account as well, i.e., coefficient $\neq$ 0, a prediction accuracy of more than 75% but less than 82% is reached

A reason for this might be that the bumblebee is not able to survey the entire situation because the obstacle is blocking the whole field of view. While reorienting and searching for a solution, the bee might see the upper corner of the obstacle first and choose to fly over the obstacle in some cases. An analysis of the recordings supports this statement. If the obstacle is very close to the gate, the bees show a searching behavior.

Investigation of the dependency of the behavior on the distance between gate and obstacle with the HV index (Fig. 2) indicates a positive, linear relationship between distance and decision. The optimal climb performance of bumblebees might be the controlling factor here. Analyses of flapping-wing aerodynamics indicate that forward flight is more efficient than hover flight [29]. Therefore, increasing altitude while flying forward is energetically more efficient than climbing vertically. This is the same for rotary wings, e.g., quadcopters or helicopters [30], leading to the conclusion that a UAV should evade a close obstacle horizontally to keep a certain minimal forward flight speed while an obstacle in greater distance should be overflown.

The slope of the three different obstacle types also indicates a dependency on the size of the obstacle. However, only two positions per obstacle were investigated. Nonetheless, these preliminary results show that an extended investigation on the dependency of the evasion maneuver on the obstacle dimensions is worth a more in-depth investigation. Additionally, the question arises, if the distance itself is the triggering parameter at all or if other parameters derived from the distance, e.g., obstacle height to distance ratio, are triggering a specific behavior.

Therefore, logistic regression was performed. It showed that the behavior of the bumblebees is predictable with an accuracy of more than 80% with the distance between obstacle and entrance gate itself as the sole parameter. The investigated ratio of obstacle width-to-height, height-to-distance, or width-to-distance does not influence the accuracy. However, it is possible that the differences in the ratios were not varied enough to show a measurable effect on the behavior. Additionally, the distance between gate and obstacle was often such that the decision of the bee was unambiguous. Therefore, additional experiments need to be conducted to investigate this further. The data points of Fig. 2 are not sufficient without further research for new findings derived from the slopes of the three different obstacle types, either.

The other evaluated parameters do not improve the accuracy of the linear regression at all. It is reasonable that the distance between tunnel sidewall and obstacle, as well as tunnel ceiling and obstacle, does not have a positive influence on the accuracy of the prediction model. The bumblebees cannot see the tunnel itself. Even though they know that there is a barrier from previous flights, there is no visual feedback, and therefore any effect on their behavior is doubtful.

Finally, the parameters speed and velocity do also not improve the predictability according to the logistic regression model. The confined space around the obstacle might explain this. The average flight speed in all recordings was relatively low, indicating that the bumblebees maneuvered carefully. The bees also had to fly through the gates, which the bees usually did with moderate velocity.

4.2 Technical Implementation

This section shall only discuss possible implementation methods. Nothing discussed in this work has been implemented yet. Cost functions are frequently used in technical applications to choose between several possibilities, also in some flight controllers. The obstacle independent linear regression curve of the format:

$$HV = 0.056\,d - 1.2732 \tag{2}$$

can serve as an element of a flight controller, in which the HV index can be understood as a bias or tendency to a specific avoidance direction of the flight control system. Equation (2) can either be used to define a corridor of possible evaluation points or to introduce a cost function penalty. In the first case, with increasing positive HV index, waypoints with decreasing horizontal distance from the current flight path are excluded from consideration; a negative HV index might lead to the exclusion of waypoints at specific vertical distances. The advantage of this approach is that the number of evaluated points is reduced before evaluation, which reduces the computational burden. In the second case, the HV index regression could serve as an additional penalty in a cost function. For example, the value a positive HV index can, obtained by Eq. (2), can be used as an additional penalty for horizontal deviation, while the absolute value of a negative HV index can be used as a penalty for vertical deviation. However, the specific values of the regression line need to be adjusted to the aerodynamic characteristics of the flying platform.

While the HV index might improve overall performance, it also bears two disadvantages. First of all, any HV index regression control is only as reliable as the distance measurement of the drone. Unfortunately, the accuracy of the distance measurement system often scales with its weight; high accuracy is often only available at the cost of relatively high weight. Secondly, the HV index regression cannot be used as some kind of gain. Otherwise, the evasion strategy would change with decreasing distance to the obstacle. Additional methods are required to ensure that the evasion strategy is fulfilled as intended. One possibility is to plan several waypoints ahead and only change the planning for safety-critical reasons.

5 Conclusion

This work analyses the behavior of bumblebees when evading obstacles in different distances and with different dimensions. It is observed that bumblebees, independent of the obstacle dimensions or their speed, tend to evade very close obstacles horizontally, e.g., fly around the obstacle, while they prefer to evade vertically, e.g., fly over the obstacle, if the obstacle is in greater distance. We found indications that the dimension of the obstacle might influence the decision of the bee as well. However, further research is required to give a qualitative statement.

Additional research on the specific reasons for the shown behavior is required to adequately define a function, which can be transferred in UAV control algorithms. However, one approach to transfer these methods to a technical application was presented. In this approach, the HV index regression curve can serve as a measure to exclude specific regions of the field of view for consideration of a cost function.

References

1. Han, J., Hui, Z., Tian, F., Cen, G.: Review on bio-inspired flight systems and bionic aerodynamics. Chin. J. Aeronaut. (in press, 2020)
2. Cheng, K., Middleton, E.J.T., Wehner, R.: Vector-based and landmark-guided navigation in desert ants of the same species inhabiting landmark-free and landmark-rich environments. J. Exp. Biol. **215**, 3169–3174 (2012)
3. Ravi, S., et al.: Gap perception in bumble bees. J. Exp. Biol. (2019). https://doi.org/10.1242/jeb.184135
4. Lihoreau, M., Chittka, L., Le Comber, S.C., Raine, N.E.: Bees do not use nearest-neighbour rules for optimization of multi-location routes. Biol. Let. **8**, 13–16 (2012)
5. Loukola, O.J., Perry, C.J., Coscos, L., Chittka, L.: Bumblebees show cognitive flexibility by improving on an observed complex behavior. Science (New York, NY) **355**, 833–836 (2017)
6. Howard, S., Avarguès-Weber, A., Garcia, J., Greentree, A., Dyer, A.: Numerical cognition in honeybees enables addition and subtraction. Sci. Adv. **5**, eaav0961 (2019)
7. Rathore, H.: Mapping Biological Systems to Network Systems. Springer, Cham (2016). https://doi.org/10.1007/978-3-319-29782-8
8. Bagheri, Z.M., Cazzolato, B.S., Grainger, S., O'Carroll, D.C., Wiederman, S.D.: An autonomous robot inspired by insect neurophysiology pursues moving features in natural environments. J. Neural Eng. **14**, 46030 (2017)
9. Philippides, A., Steadman, N., Dewar, A., Walker, C., Graham, P.: Insect-inspired visual navigation for flying robots. In: Lepora, N.F.F., Mura, A., Mangan, M., Verschure, P.F.F.M.J., Desmulliez, M., Prescott, T.J.J. (eds.) Living Machines 2016. LNCS (LNAI), vol. 9793, pp. 263–274. Springer, Cham (2016). https://doi.org/10.1007/978-3-319-42417-0_24
10. Mountcastle, A.M., Alexander, T.M., Switzer, C.M., Combes, S.A.: Wing wear reduces bumblebee flight performance in a dynamic obstacle course. Biol. Let. (2016). https://doi.org/10.1098/rsbl.2016.0294
11. Osborne, J.L., Smith, A., Clark, S.J., Reynolds, D.R., Barron, M.C., Lim, K.S., Reynolds, A.M.: The ontogeny of bumblebee flight trajectories: from naïve explorers to experienced foragers. PLoS One (2013). https://doi.org/10.1371/journal.pone.0078681
12. Zabala, F.A., Card, G.M., Fontaine, E.I., Dickinson, M.H., Murray, R.M.: Flight dynamics and control of evasive maneuvers: the fruit fly's takeoff. IEEE Trans. Bio-Med. Eng. **56**, 2295–2298 (2009)
13. Muijres, F.T., Elzinga, M.J., Melis, J.M., Dickinson, M.H.: Flies evade looming targets by executing rapid visually directed banked turns. Science **344**, 172 (2014)
14. Kern, R., Boeddeker, N., Dittmarand, L., Egelhaaf, M.: Blowfly flight characteristics are shaped by environmental features and controlled by optic flow information. J. Exp. Biol. **215**, 2501 (2012)
15. Pittner, M., Hiller, M., Particke, F., Patino-Studencki. L., Thielecke, J.: Systematic analysis of global and local planners for optimal trajectory planning. In: 50th International Symposium on Robotics, ISR 2018 (2018)
16. Kim, C.-H., Lee, T.-J., Cho, D.: An Application of stereo camera with two different FoVs for SLAM and obstacle detection. IFAC Pap. OnLine **51**, 148–153 (2018)
17. Aguilar, W.G., Casaliglla, V.P., Pólit, J.L.: Obstacle avoidance based-visual navigation for micro aerial vehicles. Electronics **6**, 10 (2017)
18. García, J., Molina, J.M.: Simulation in real conditions of navigation and obstacle avoidance with PX4/Gazebo platform. Pers. Ubiquit. Comput. (2020). https://doi.org/10.1007/s00779-019-01356-4
19. Baumann, T.: Obstacle Avoidance for Drones Using a 3DVFH Algorithm. Masters thesis (2018)

20. Gonzalez, J., Chavez, A., Paredes, J., Saito, C.: Obstacle detection and avoidance device for Multirotor UAVs through interface with Pixhawk flight controller. In: IEEE 14th International Conference on Automation Science and Engineering (CASE), pp. 110–115 (2018)

21. Alexopoulos, A., Kandil, A., Orzechowski, P., Badreddin, E.: A comparative study of collision avoidance techniques for unmanned aerial vehicles. In: IEEE International Conference on Systems, Man, and Cybernetics, pp. 1969–1974 (2013)

22. Sarmiento, T.A., Murphy, R.R.: Insights on obstacle avoidance for small unmanned aerial systems from a study of flying animal behavior. Robot. Auton. Syst. **99**, 17–29 (2018)

23. Serres, J., Masson, G.P., Ruffier, F., Franceschini, N.: A bee in the corridor: centering and wall-following. Sci. Nat. (Naturwissenschaften) **95**, 1181–1187 (2008)

24. Portelli, G., Serres, J.R., Ruffier, F.: Altitude control in honeybees: joint vision-based learning and guidance. Sci. Rep. **7**, 9231 (2017)

25. Srinivasan, M.V., Zhang, S.W., Lehrer, M., Collett, T.S.: Honeybee navigation en route to the goal - visual flight control and odometry. J. Exp. Biol. **199**, 237–244 (1996)

26. Srinivasan, M.V., Zhang, S.W., Chahl, J.S., Stange, G., Garratt, M.: An overview of insect-inspired guidance for application in ground and airborne platforms. Proc. Inst. Mech. Eng. Part G: J. Aerosp. Eng. (2004). https://doi.org/10.1243/0954410042794966

27. Crall, J.D., Ravi, S., Mountcastle, A.M., Combes, S.A.: Bumblebee flight performance in cluttered environments: effects of obstacle orientation, body size and acceleration. J. Exp. Biol. (2015). https://doi.org/10.1242/jeb.121293

28. Ong, M., Bulmer, M., Groening, J., Srinivasan, M.V.: Obstacle traversal and route choice in flying honeybees: evidence for individual handedness. PLoS One (2017). https://doi.org/10.1371/journal.pone.0184343

29. Sane, S.: The aerodynamics of insect flight. J. Exp. Biol. **206**, 4191–4208 (2003)

30. Zheng, L., Hedrick, T., Mittal, R.: A comparative study of the hovering efficiency of flapping and revolving wings. Bioinspir. Biomim. **8**, 36001 (2013)

Biomimetic Design of a Soft Robotic Fish for High Speed Locomotion

Sander C. van den Berg⬤, Rob B. N. Scharff⬤, Zoltán Rusák⬤, and Jun Wu$^{(\boxtimes)}$⬤

Department of Sustainable Design Engineering, Delft University of Technology, Landbergstraat 15, 2628 CE Delft, The Netherlands
j.wu-1@tudelft.nl

Abstract. We present a novel DC motor driven soft robotic fish which is optimized for speed and efficiency based on experimental, numerical and theoretical investigation into oscillating propulsion. Our system achieves speeds up to 0.85 m/s, outperforming the previously reported fastest free swimming soft robotic fish by a significant margin of 27%. A simple and effective wire-driven active body and passive compliant body are used to mimic highly efficient thunniform swimming. The efficient DC motor to drive the system decreases internal losses compared to other soft robotic oscillating propulsion systems which are driven by one or multiple servo motors. The DC motor driven design allows for swimming at higher frequencies. The current design has been tested up to a tailbeat frequency of 5.5 Hz, and can potentially reach much higher frequencies.

Keywords: Soft robotic fish · Oscillating propulsion · Marine robotics · Biomimetics

1 Introduction

Minimal disruption to the marine environment is an important requirement for the design of underwater vehicles for closeup observations of marine life, (deep) sea exploration, mining, and pipeline inspection. Robotic fish using oscillating soft tails have advantages compared to underwater vehicles that use rotary propulsion. Rotary propulsion typically operates at a relatively high frequency. This creates highly disturbing vibrations in the water and actively sucks in objects and wildlife into the propeller. In contrast, oscillating propulsion uses lower frequencies and a compliant tail that pushes obstacles away rather than entangling them. Moreover, oscillating propulsion has the potential to be more efficient than rotary propulsion. This is due to the harvesting of energy from the turbulence at the wake of the vessel's body and the absence of energy losses due to rotation of the water flow as seen in rotary propulsion. Small propellers used to drive underwater vehicles typically do not produce efficiencies above 40% [13], where oscillating motion has shown efficiencies of up to 87% in lab experiments [2]. The difference in efficiency becomes especially large at great depths,

© Springer Nature Switzerland AG 2020
V. Vouloutsi et al. (Eds.): Living Machines 2020, LNAI 12413, pp. 366–377, 2020.
https://doi.org/10.1007/978-3-030-64313-3_35

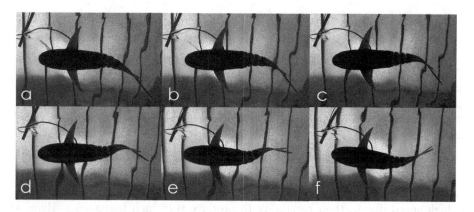

Fig. 1. Chronologically ordered snapshots of the soft robotic fish in action from a to f. A combination of an active and a passive tail segment is used to reproduce thunniform-like swimming.

where rotary propulsion systems have to exert large pressure on the rotary shaft to prevent water from seeping through, drastically reducing the efficiency of the system. In contrast, oscillating systems do not suffer from this problem as there are no rotating parts in contact with the water. However, the performance of the state-of-the-art soft robotic fish is still far from that of real fish and even from rotary propulsion in terms of both efficiency and speed. One of the reasons for this gap in performance is related to non-fluent motion of the tail of the robotic fish. In this work, we present a novel soft robotic fish design (see Fig. 1) by closely mimicking the fluent swimming motion seen in thunniform swimming.

Swimming speed of fishes depends on their propulsive mode. Accordingly, they are commonly classified according to their propulsive mode, which facilitates hydrodynamic analysis of swimming efficiency and performance. A commonly used classification by Lindsey [9] differentiates between twelve different swimming modes. Previous research has mostly focused on studying swimming modes that make use of the caudal fin and trunk to swim forward (i.e. anguilliform, subcarangiform, carangiform, and thunniform). Of these modes, thunniform swimming is known as the most efficient form of aquatic locomotion[11]. It uses the turbulence in the wake of the fish to create inwards turning vortexes on both sides. This produces a peak thrust in the middle behind the fish's tail, which is known as a reverse von Karman vortex street [3].

Different mechanisms for reproducing these fish-like oscillating motions have been proposed. A common approach is that of a multi-link system (see Fig. 2(a)). Here, the shape of the continuously curved tail is approximated by a series of rigid links that are controlled through internal or external motors. An example of a multi-link system is the RoboTuna [3]. An advantage of multi-link systems is the high degree of control on the oscillating motion due to the relatively high number of actuators. Therefore, multi-link systems are a popular choice for fish body kinematics studies [17].

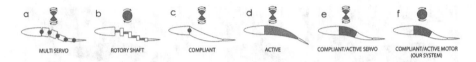

Fig. 2. Overview of robotic fish propulsion systems. The grey areas are actuated, whereas the white areas are passive. Grey dots are used to indicate actuated joints. The circle above each fish indicates whether the actuation is continuous or goes back-and-forth.

An effective propulsion mechanism is the use of a multi-link rotary shaft (see Fig. 2(b)). Generally speaking rotary shaft driven systems are able to reach a high speed due to their capability to produce very high frequencies. Here, a rotary shaft is led through hinging rigid links in the tail. Rotating the precisely curved shaft will create the oscillating motion. An advantage of this approach is that the motion of the robot stays the same for any tail beat frequency, allowing it to be tested at different frequencies without the need for modifications. However, its complex crankshaft design is prone to wear, and requires high precision fabrication. Moreover, the system does not allow for any easy steering mechanism. These limitations make it impractical to be used in practical applications. The Isplash fish makes use of this multi-link rotary shaft system [4]. A similar single rotary shaft mechanical solution with a single motor was presented by Yu et al. [18]. The recently reported Tunabot by Zhu et al. [20] also uses a single rotary shaft system resulting in record breaking speeds 1.02 m/s at 15 Hz, although it should be mentioned that these results were not achieved in free swimming but by fixing the head in a laminar flow tank. Both multi-servo and rotary shaft systems lack compliance when interacting with underwater flora and fauna.

Taking inspiration from soft robotics, recent research focused on using an active compliant tail driven by fluidic actuators [6] (see Fig. 2(c)). Although the introduction of the soft tail makes the fish safer and more adaptive, the fluidic actuators were not capable of reproducing the sigmoid-like tail movement seen in thunniform swimming. As a result, the fish has a relatively low speed and efficiency.

In an attempt to simplify the control and design of these fishes, a fish with a passive compliant tail was proposed [1,10] (see Fig. 2(d)). This solution has greatly reduced the complexity and costs of the system. However, this fish was not capable of accurately reproducing the sigmoid-like tail movement either. The free swimming fish presented in [10] reached a speed of 0.1 m/s, whereas the fish presented in [1] is slightly slower than that. This relatively low speed can be attributed to the sharp angle between the active and compliant part.

From there, an approach with a tail that contains both an active and a passive compliant part was proposed, enabling a smooth transition between the rigid head and compliant tail [19] (see Fig. 2(e)). This approach allowed for reproduction of reverse von karman vortices seen in thunniform swimming. Similarly to the passive compliant body design, this design only requires a single servo motor, greatly reducing the complexity and increasing the efficiency as compared to the multi-link design. Using this system, a speed of 0.67 m/s could be obtained [19]. Although this system was a major step towards a viable system, the system still had some limitations. The servo-driven system creates an almost triangular wave-form movement, whereas a more sinusoidal waveform would greatly improve the creation of reverse von Karman vortices [5]. Moreover, the maximum frequency of the servo-motor is limited. Therefore, the fish is unable to reach the tailbeat frequency needed to obtain a Strouhal number between 0.2 and 0.4, which is commonly found in nature and associated with energy efficient locomotion [12].

Our system (shown in Fig. 2(f)) solves the above mentioned challenges, result-ing in a higher speed and efficiency. A key innovation of our system is the use of the continuous rotation of a DC motor to pull the cables connected to both sides of the active tail segment, instead of the commonly used back-and-forth motion of a servo-motor. As a result, higher frequencies can be obtained with a more sinusoidal waveform. Our fish is able to reach speeds up to 0.85 m/s. Hereby, it outperforms the previously reported fast soft robotic fish by Zhong et al. [19] with a significant margin of 27%. This significant performance improvement is an important step towards real-world applications of soft robotic fishes.

This paper is organized as follows: Sect. 2 presents the design of our soft robotic fish, emphasizing how the various components of the design can be opti-mized for speed and efficiency. Section 3 focuses the methods and materials used to fabricate and test our design. The results will be discussed in Sect. 4. Finally, we conclude this work and discuss future work in Sect. 5.

2   Design

Our biomimetic design (Fig. 3) has a single-motor cable-driven oscillating sys-tem, in combination with a passive compliant tail segment to accurately repro-duce thunniform swimming. The continuous rotation of the DC motor effectively pulls the cables connected to both sides of the active tail segment. The use of a DC motor allows for achieving higher frequencies with a more sinusoidal wave-form, leading to improved speed and efficiency.

2.1   Motor

The soft robotic fish uses a DC-motor in combination with a gearbox system for propulsion, creating a motion as indicated in Fig. 2(f). Two gears on opposite sides of the motor shaft are rotated in opposite direction, pulling the left and right cable in a half cycle delay from each other, as illustrated in Fig. 4(a). As compared to the servo-motor driven system indicated in Fig. 4(b), a DC-motor driven active body allows for higher oscillation frequencies, and also creates a more cosine waveform of the active body and thus the caudal fin. In contrast, the rapid change in direction in servo-motors leads to a triangle-like heave motion. Hover et al. have shown that sawtooth and square angle of attack profiles are approximately 20% less efficient than a sine profile [5].

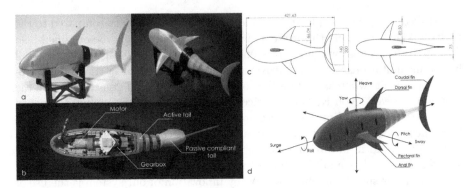

Fig. 3. (a) Design of the soft robotic fish, (b) internal view of the fish with the most important components indicated, (c) main dimensions of the soft robotic fish, and (d) terms for fish stability and fish anatomy.

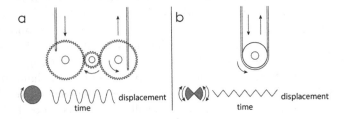

Fig. 4. On the left (a) the basic principle of our DC motor driven design. On the right (b), a servo-motor driven design. A graph of vertical displacement of the wires over time is depicted underneath both illustrations.

2.2   Active and Passive Tail

The active part of the tail is composed of four rigid elements connected by three compliant joints. The stiffness of the passive tail segment should be chosen such that an S-shaped tail (as shown in Fig. 1(a)) is realized. An S-shaped tail creates a more optimal angle of attack of the caudal fin for creating thrust. Anderson et al. performed experiments with pitching and heaving foils in which the highest efficiency was obtained with a maximum angle of attack of 20.2° with the direction of movement [2]. This is in line with previous research indicating an ideal maximum angle of attack of between 15° and 25° [13]. It should be noted that the stiffness that is required to obtain this ideal angle of attack is strongly dependent on the tailbeat frequency.

2.3   Body Length

To investigate the influence of the body length on the maneuverability and sway stability, the behavior of a fish with an active and passive compliant tail segment was modeled as a mass-spring-damper system in *Simulink*. The simulation consists of four main segments: the caudal fin, the passive compliant segment, the active segment and the passive head, as is shown in Fig. 5. Both the compliant and active segments consist of multiple sub-segments to achieve sufficiently fluent motion. The passive compliant segment and active segment consist of 4 and 5 sub-segments respectively, with a length of 30 mm each. The rotation of the active segment is modeled to be constant over all sub-segments and varies over time following a sinusoidal function with a frequency of 1.59 Hz and amplitude of 5.73° for each sub-segment.

The passive compliant segments were modeled having a consistent spring stiffness of 0.001 Nm/deg and a damping coefficient which was gradually reduced along the compliant segmentation from 0.005 Nm(deg/s) to 0.00075 Nm(deg/s) to simulate the decrease in surface area interacting with the surrounding water.

The body length was varied between 73.34 mm and 880 mm, corresponding to a ratio of head mass to total mass of 0.3 and 0.8 respectively. The distance between the centre of the caudal fin and the centre of rotation is used to express the maneuverability of the fish. The larger this distance is, the less maneuverable the fish is. The head sway stability is expressed as the angle between the passive head and the neutral line (indicated in blue in Fig. 5). A larger angle corresponds to a fish with lower sway stability. Lower sway stability leads to less efficient swimming, as energy is lost when the head is not aligned in the swimming direction. The results are shown in Fig. 6. A clear trade-off can be found between the maneuverability and sway stability. The tuna is an efficient long-distance swimmer with less need for quick maneuvers. Therefore, it has a relatively long body. We chose a similar length distribution for our robotic fish design (see Fig. 3(c)). At the same time, the relatively high length of the passive head provides space for the motor and gearbox.

2.4   Body Shape and Pectoral, Anal, and Dorsal Fins

The body shape and the pectoral, anal, and dorsal fins of the fish greatly influence its stability and sway (see Fig. 3(d)). The vertically compressed elliptical body shape is inspired by the tunafish, and can be found in a large portion of fish species. Although the shape is not intuitive from a hydrodynamical point of view as minimizing drag around a given volume would result in a body of revolution, the advantage of this adaptation is the damping of the larger side surface area minimizing swaying motion during sideways oscillation of the tail [8]. Moreover, the shape also reduces rolling and creates a larger distance between the center of rotation and dorsal and anal fins, preventing change in vertical angle [15]. In fast swimming fish e.g. marlin, sailfish and mahimahi a large side surface area at a distance as far as possible from the center line of yaw rotation (defined by the line between the center of mass and buoyancy) is also a common adaptation.

2.5   Caudal Fin Shape

The shape of caudal fin is critical for high-speed and efficient swimming. The caudal fin is illustrated in Fig. 3(d). When flapping the fin back and forth through the active and passive compliant tail, a pressure difference is generated between

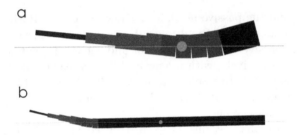

Fig. 5. *Simulink* model of the soft robotic fish. The different gray tones indicate the 4 main segments (from left to right: the tail, the passive compliant segment, the active segment and the passive head). The length of the passive head was varied between (a) 73.34 mm to (b) 880 mm. The centre of rotation is indicated in red. The neutral line is indicated in blue.(Color figure online)

both sides of the caudal fin. The pressure difference generates vortices at the tip of the fin. The energy put in creating these vortices dissipates and produces drag. The vortices at high fins (and long wings in flight) are smaller compared to the total length over which the pressure difference is maintained, resulting in a higher efficiency [14]. The chord ratio (in aeronautics generally referred to as aspect ratio) is defined as the ratio between the caudal fin height (wing length) to the mean caudal fin width (mean chord length). The thrust-to-drag ratio (lift in aeronautics) increases with chord ratio, meaning that the higher the tail is relative to its width, the more efficient it swims [2,7]. The caudal fin design has a backwards curving leading edge. Research has shown that a backwards curving leading edge was able to reduce drag by 8.8% as compared to a wing with the same chord ratio but a straight leading edge [16]. The caudal fins of highly efficient and fast long-distance swimming fish such as tuna closely match the design guidelines mentioned above. In contrast, fish that require high acceleration or maneuverability such as pikes have caudal fins with a much lower chord ratio. We perform experiments with a small caudal fin with a height of 140 mm and a larger caudal fin with a height of 200 mm (see Fig. 3(c)).

3   Fabrication and Experimental Setup

This section discusses the embodiment of the design and the setup that was used to evaluate its performance.

3.1   Materials and Fabrication

The body consists of four main components: the caudal fin, the passive tail, the active tail and the rigid body. The caudal fin is a lunate shape 3D-printed fin attached to the passive tail. The passive tail is a sheet which creates the desired bending at the desired tailbeat frequency and passive tail length. For this prototype, a 1 mm thick sheet of PETG of 74 mm length was used. The

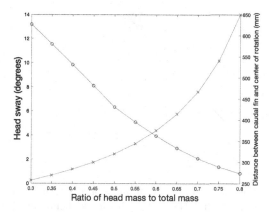

Fig. 6. Simulation results of the sway stability (circles) and maneuverability (crosses) versus the weight ratio of the head of the fish. The right axis indicates the distance between the caudal fin and the center of rotation, which is inversely related to the maneuverability.

sheet follows the contour of the passive tail with a minimum height of 17 mm. The active tail is swept from side to side by two cables attached on both sides of the active tail. The active tail is supported by a compliant backbone sheet that functions as a compliant joint. The sheet has a thickness of 1.2 mm, length of 66 mm and height of 20 mm. Four rigid 3D-printed ribs are attached to the backbone to support the hydrodynamic shape and cables. The active and passive tail are encapsulated by a waterproof silicone skin, created from a 3D-printed mold. The rigid body consists of two 3D-printed halves held together by bolts and nuts with a rubber sealing ring in between. The bottom half holds a gearbox, sinkers, and the DC-motor (see Fig. 3(b)), while the top half holds a connector to an external power supply for precise power control during testing.

3.2   Measurement Setup

A camera is placed parallel above the water. The camera (GoPro7) is set to linear settings to minimize deformation due to the lens, with a resolution of 1080 p, at 120 fps. As it is difficult to perfectly align the fish parallel to the water, calculations were performed to accurately determine the traveled distance speed. An example calculation is illustrated in Fig. 7. The speed of the robotic fish is measured by using the average length of a known segment of the fish to calculate the distance traveled divided by the time.

The speed is measured from the lowest voltage at which the motor starts turning, which is 5 V. The voltage is increased by increments of 0.5 V till failure of the prototype or the maximum specification of the motor are reached. At each voltage the experiment is repeated until at least three good straight swimming samples were captured. The tail sweep amplitude of the robotic fish is measured when the robotic fish is in the middle of the camera view in order to minimize any

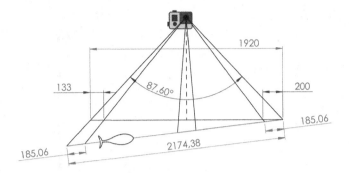

Fig. 7. The camera lens makes a horizontal angle of 87.6°. In this example a segment of the fish with a known length 0.2481 m is 133px at the beginning of the measurement and 200 px at the end of the measurement. Taking into account the projection the known segment of 0.2481 m is 185.06 px and has traveled a total of 2174.38 px within the frame.

field of view deformation. The length of the tail sweep amplitude is compared to the reference length onscreen of which the real length is known. The efficiency of the fish is measured through the Strouhal number, which can be calculated as:

$$St = \frac{f * A}{U} \tag{1}$$

where f is the tail beat frequency, A is the tail sweep amplitude and U is the speed. The Strouhal number is a dimensionless number, which is found to be between 0.2 and 0.4 for energy-efficient locomotion [12].

4   Results

The swimming performance of the biomimetic soft robotic fish is presented in this section. The supplementary video (https://www.youtube.com/watch? v=tvL4VXgySOI) demonstrates that our biomimetic robotic fish is capable of reproducing a thunniform-like swimming motion through the combination of an active and passive tail segment. Figure 8 shows the speed of the soft robotic fish for different tailbeat frequencies for the small caudal fin as well as the larger caudal fin. It can be seen that higher speeds could be obtained when using the larger caudal fin. A top speed of 0.85 m/s (2.02 BL/s) was achieved at a tailbeat frequency of 5.46 Hz.

Figure 9(a) shows the tail sweep length versus the tailbeat frequency. Note that the tailbeat frequencies between the experiments with the small and large caudal fin do not match, as applying a certain voltage will result in different tailbeat frequencies for the two designs. It can be seen that up to a tailbeat frequency of 2.2 Hz, the tail sweep length of the fish with the large caudal fin increases with an increase in tailbeat frequency. This can be explained by the tail moving in its eigenfrequency, causing it to overbend. At higher frequencies, the

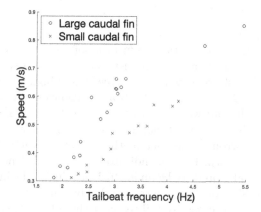

Fig. 8. Forward speed over tailbeat frequency for both the small as the large caudal fin.

tail sweep length starts to decrease due to deformation of the passive tail segment resulting in a more S-shaped tail (as shown in Fig. 1(a)). This is associated with higher efficiencies as the caudal fin has a more optimal angle of attack. This is confirmed by Fig. 9(b), where the Strouhal number approaches more optimal values (0.2–0.4) with an increase in tailbeat frequency. For the robotic fish with the large caudal fin, Strouhal numbers between 0.31 and 0.4 could be achieved at frequencies above 2.33 Hz. For reference, the servo-driven soft robotic fish by Zhong et al. [19] achieved Strouhal numbers between 0.36 and 0.6.

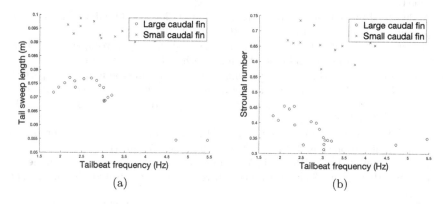

Fig. 9. (a) Tail sweep length over tailbeat frequency for both the small as the large caudal fin. (b) Strouhal number over tailbeat frequency for both the small as the large caudal fin.

5   Conclusion

This work presented a biomimetic design of a soft robotic fish for high-speed locomotion. During free swimming, the fish achieved a top speed of 0.85 m/s, outperforming previously reported fastest free swimming soft robotic fish by a significant margin of 27%. At higher tailbeat frequencies, the speed of the fish increased, whereas the tailsweep length decreased due to a more sigmoid-like tail shape resulting in a more optimal angle of attack. At a tailbeat frequency above 2.33 Hz, the Strouhal number of the prototype with the large caudal fin dropped below 0.4, which is an indicator of good efficiency. These results confirm the theoretically predicted gain in efficiency due to the increased tailbeat frequency and more sinusoidal waveform enabled by our novel propulsion system design. The stiffness of the passive tail segment should be tuned to the tailbeat frequency such that a sigmoid-like tail shape and optimal angle of attack is achieved. Future work will focus on controlling the stiffness of the passive tail segment dynamically in order to achieve efficient swimming at different speeds. Although our propulsion mechanisms allows for a relatively easy implementation of a steering mechanism, it has not been implemented in this prototype. This will be part of future work as well. The design of the soft robotic fish will be made available online.

References

1. y Alvarado, P.V., Youcef-Toumi, K.: Modeling and design methodology of an efficient underwater propulsion system. In: Robotics and Applications, pp. 161–166 (2003)
2. Anderson, J., Streitlien, K., Barrett, D., Triantafyllou, M.: Oscillating foils of high propulsive efficiency. J. Fluid Mech. **360**, 41–72 (1998)
3. Barrett, D., Triantafyllou, M., Yue, D., Grosenbaugh, M., Wolfgang, M.: Drag reduction in fish-like locomotion. J. Fluid Mech. **392**, 183–212 (1999)
4. Clapham, R.J., Hu, H.: *iSplash*: realizing fast carangiform swimming to outperform a real fish. In: Du, R., Li, Z., Youcef-Toumi, K., Valdivia y Alvarado, P. (eds.) Robot Fish. STME, pp. 193–218. Springer, Heidelberg (2015). https://doi.org/10.1007/978-3-662-46870-8_7
5. Hover, F., Haugsdal, Ø., Triantafyllou, M.: Effect of angle of attack profiles in flapping foil propulsion. J. Fluids Struct. **19**(1), 37–47 (2004)
6. Katzschmann, R.K., DelPreto, J., MacCurdy, R., Rus, D.: Exploration of underwater life with an acoustically controlled soft robotic fish. Sci. Robot. **3**(16), eaar3449 (2018)
7. Kermode, A.C.: Mechanics of Flight. Longman, London (1987)
8. Lighthill, M.J.: Aquatic animal propulsion of high hydromechanical efficiency. J. Fluid Mech. **44**(2), 265–301 (1970)
9. Lindsey, C.: 1 - form, function, and locomotory habits in fish. In: Hoar, W., Randall, D. (eds.) Locomotion, Fish Physiology, vol. 7, pp. 1–100. Academic Press (1978)
10. Mazumdar, A., Alvarado, P.V.Y., Youcef-Toumi, K.: Maneuverability of a robotic tuna with compliant body. In: 2008 IEEE International Conference on Robotics and Automation, pp. 683–688. IEEE (2008)

11. Sfakiotakis, M., Lane, D.M., Davies, J.B.C.: Review of fish swimming modes for aquatic locomotion. IEEE J. Oceanic Eng. **24**(2), 237–252 (1999)
12. Triantafyllou, G.S., Triantafyllou, M., Grosenbaugh, M.: Optimal thrust development in oscillating foils with application to fish propulsion. J. Fluids Struct. **7**(2), 205–224 (1993)
13. Triantafyllou, M.S., Triantafyllou, G.S.: An efficient swimming machine. Sci. Am. **272**(3), 64–70 (1995)
14. Videler, J.J.: Fish Swimming. Springer, Heidelberg (2012). https://doi.org/10.1007/978-94-011-1580-3
15. Weihs, D.: Stability versus maneuverability in aquatic locomotion. Integr. Comp. Biol. **42**(1), 127–134 (2002)
16. Westerhoff, H.V., Van Dam, K.: Thermodynamics and Control of Biological Free-energy Transduction. Elsevier, Amsterdam (1987)
17. Wu, Z., Yu, J., Tan, M., Zhang, J.: Kinematic comparison of forward and backward swimming and maneuvering in a self-propelled sub-carangiform robotic fish. J. Bionic Eng. **11**(2), 199–212 (2014)
18. Yu, J., Zhang, C., Liu, L.: Design and control of a single-motor-actuated robotic fish capable of fast swimming and maneuverability. IEEE/ASME Trans. Mechatron. **21**(3), 1711–1719 (2016). https://doi.org/10.1109/TMECH.2016.2517931
19. Zhong, Y., Li, Z., Du, R.: A novel robot fish with wire-driven active body and compliant tail. IEEE/ASME Trans. Mechatron. **22**(4), 1633–1643 (2017)
20. Zhu, J., White, C., Wainwright, D.K., Di Santo, V., Lauder, G.V., Bart-Smith, H.: Tuna robotics: a high-frequency experimental platform exploring the performance space of swimming fishes. Sci. Robot. 4(34) (2019). https://doi.org/10.1126/scirobotics.aax4615

The Use of Social Sensorimotor Contingencies in Humanoid Robots

Vasiliki Vouloutsi[1,2]([✉]), Anna Chesson[1], Maria Blancas[1,2], Oscar Guerrero[1,2], and Paul F. M. J. Verschure[1,2,3]

[1] The Synthetic Perceptive, Emotive and Cognitive Systems group SPECS, Institute for Bioengineering of Catalunya (IBEC), Barcelona, Spain
{vvouloutsi,pverschure}@ibecbarcelona.eu
[2] Barcelona Institute of Science and Technology (BIST), Barcelona, Spain
[3] Catalan Institute of Advanced Studies (ICREA),Barcelona, Spain
https://www.specs-lab.com

Abstract. This pilot study investigates the role of social sensorimotor contingencies as exhibited from a humanoid robot to allow mutual understanding and social entrainment in a group social activity. The goal is to evaluate whether sensorimotor contingencies can lead to transparent and understandable interactions while we explore the dimension of personality. We propose the task of taking a selfie with a robot and a group of humans as the benchmark to evaluate the social sensorimotor contingencies displayed. We have constructed two models of interaction with an introverted and extroverted robot. We also seek to address the gap in research in context and personality of social sensorimotor contingencies in HRI and contribute to the field of personality in social robotics by determining what type of behaviour of the robot attracts certain personalities in humans in group settings. Although the sample size was small, and there were no significant differences between conditions, results suggest that the expression of sensorimotor contingencies can lead to successful coupling and interactions.

Keywords: Human-robot interaction · Personality · Social robots · Social sensorimotor contingencies

1 Introduction

The application of robotics in social settings continue to present significant challenges despite the technological advances in the field. Social fluency cannot be achieved through simply following a fixed set of instructions, and goals within social interactions are not always clearly defined or broken down sequentially. For social interactions, and for meaningful long-term and repeated contact with humans, robots need to be equipped with a variety of capabilities including employing and understanding the same communication channels as those that humans employ as well as adapting to the dynamics of an ever-changing social environment [1].

© Springer Nature Switzerland AG 2020
V. Vouloutsi et al. (Eds.): Living Machines 2020, LNAI 12413, pp. 378–389, 2020.
https://doi.org/10.1007/978-3-030-64313-3_36

Social cognition is the ability to attribute meaning to the events that unfold during social interaction and engage meaningfully with appropriate social behaviour. Humans employ verbal and non-verbal communication channels (gaze, proximate distance, gesture and facial cues [2]) to determine the social meaning when interacting with another person. These sensorimotor channels of communication heavily rely on the context of social interaction, as the same non-verbal cues can have different meanings in different contexts. Humans can naturally understand these multimodal cues with a high level of precision and differentiation. Thus, one of the main challenges of Human-Robot Interaction (HRI) is to approximate or even resemble and contextually understand the richness of multimodal sensorimotor channel information.

The behaviour of social robots needs to be transparent and interpretable to be accepted by humans, and we can use recent theories on social cognition in humans as a framework from which to develop robots with interpretable and meaningful social behaviour. Theories suggest that social cognition is not representational, nor a symbolic process as previously accepted [3]. Instead, the ability to determine social meaning is developed through experience and shaping of social sensorimotor contingencies. Thus, social cognition and social skills are the mastery of sensorimotor information that has been learned in past experience in congruent social situations [4]. Sensorimotor contingencies represent action-motor loops that enable the categorisation of events, actions, objects and fluent interaction between an agent and its environment. This approach toward non-verbal interactions is supported by both psychology and neuroscience findings [5]. When applied in robotics, sensorimotor contingencies can be used, for example to study real-time collaboration and social entrainment in dyadic or multi-agent interactions when agents reciprocally and actively attend the actions of the partner [6]. Social behaviour and the communication channels employed are important factors that affect bonding, empathy and attributing mental states when interacting with a synthetic agent [7] and humans naturally tend to anthropomorphise non-human interactions. Thus, social salience can be utilised to modulate human expectations, and when expressed via social sensorimotor contingencies, it could be a way to improve the fluency and transparency of social interactions.

This work is grounded in the principles of sensorimotor contingencies and aims to investigate whether they can be a solid basis upon which to build a model for interactions with humans. We wish to extend dyadic interactions to group social activities, and study which sensorimotor contingencies are relevant and what type of behaviour (personality) displayed by a synthetic agent best takes advantage of humans' natural tendency to attribute social salience. The social activity we have chosen is that of taking a group "selfie". To be able to develop a synthetic agent that groups people together to take a selfie, we first need to answer the following questions: "How do humans perform this task using sensorimotor contingencies?", followed by "Are people capable of correctly reading the sensorimotor information displayed by a synthetic agent?", and finally, "Can the behaviour of a synthetic agent that relies only on sensorimotor information lead to a successful group selfie task?". To answer these questions, we performed three experiments. In doing so, we hope to further advance the field of social robotics by contributing to the research area of social sensorimotor contingencies and determining their effectiveness as an approach to design living machines with social and transparent capabilities from a human-focused perspective.

1.1 Social Sensorimotor Contingencies and Personality in Social Robotics

Social cognition can be considered as an experience generated by action, and context is paramount (the same actions can have different meanings and consequences in different contexts). While internal reflection about the mind-state of others occurs in several interactions, the meaning of many social interactions is the result of dynamic relationships formed by participatory sense-making, which allows two or more agents to generate the meaning of the social interaction together through dynamic coupling [5]. Many everyday social interactions (like handshakes, or hugs) provide examples of participatory sense-making. This enactive approach highlights the role of embodiment in sense-making without intermediary construction of internal representations. Indeed, interaction detection, in its basic sense can be depicted by reciprocal sensorimotor contingencies [8].

Sensorimotor contingencies in Human-Human Interaction (HHI) provide a working framework from which to model and analyse basic and higher-level behaviours (like personality) in social robotics. Personality is an important facilitator of HRI [9], and by definition, it characterises specific sets of stereotypical behaviours that help to predict an other's actions or make sense of their actions in a particular social context. In HRI settings, an individual's personality not only affects how the robot's personality is perceived but also the preferred personality of the robot in social interactions. Personality preferences are modulated by both task and group settings. In dyadic settings, extroverted robots are perceived as more intelligent, whereas introverted robots are perceived as more intelligent in group settings [10]. However, the evaluation of personality in social robots across various settings and groupings is highly fragmented [9]. A widely used metric to evaluate personality is the Big Five model [11], and extroversion/introversion is the most commonly assessed personality trait in HRI. As personality remains a major research area in HRI and is a known factor that affects social interaction, we included it as a factor to this work.

1.2 The Social Significance of Selfies

Most HRI research has focused on dyadic, one-to-one interactions, and few studies have focused on one-to-many group interaction settings. As the task domain affects the preferred and experienced personality of robots, we chose a social setting with an inherent group dynamic that is necessary to investigate the behaviours of the robot and their success in coordinating group interactions.

Given the ubiquity of selfies worldwide, we further expect that the general population will have sufficient experience with the task to make sense of the sensorimotor information displayed by the robot while taking a selfie. The rise of popularity of selfies is currently the subject of scholarly discussion and motivations for taking a selfie have been cited as multidimensional (as they are taken alone or in group settings) and a fun, creative outlet for self-fashioning and self-expression [12]. Taking a selfie with another person may seem like a form of enjoyable, shared self-expression, and as such, we want to investigate if this interaction can yield a similar result when performed with a synthetic agent. The task of taking a group selfie requires the social skills of recognising people who can be grouped, getting their attention, establishing a connection, conveying intention, gaining permission, maintaining connection and physical coordination by uniting participants for taking the photo. Here, we wish to ground these skills in sensorimotor contingencies while exploring the dimension of personality in the context of taking a selfie and how they affect the transparency and outcome of the interaction of taking a group selfie.

2   Methods

The main objective of this work is to make use of sensorimotor contingencies to allow for mutual understanding between humans and robots and present the system developed. We further seek to address the gap in research in context and personality of social sensorimotor contingencies (socSMCs) in HRI, by evaluating which higher-level behaviour as expressed through sensorimotor contingencies is interpretable and preferable to humans during the task of taking a "selfie". The personalities we evaluate are introvert and extrovert, as they are most commonly used in HRI, providing an easier comparison with other studies and are relevant to the task of taking a selfie. We make the assumption that a robot's use of socSMCs will allow for effective flow and coupling necessary to take group selfies regardless of the personality. We, therefore, hypothesise that humans will understand distinct combinations of contextually relevant sensorimotor cues in gesture, gaze and spatial relation leading to effective coupling. We further hypothesise that humans will prefer an extroverted robot due to the entrainment nature of the task and that extroverted behaviour will lead to a greater number of selfies taken and longer interactions.

To do so, we developed two models of interactions (introversion and extroversion) and analysed from a human-focused perspective, emphasising fluency and interpretability of the interaction. To focus on the effects of solely sensorimotor channels of communication, we removed verbal interaction. The robot relied solely on the use of sensorimotor information during interactions.

2.1   Setup

Drawing from literature in both HHI and HRI, the extroverted robot's behaviour as exhibited through social sensorimotor contingencies makes use of closer proximate distances, exhibits larger gestures, and acts as the "leader" (active) of the interaction while taking a selfie. In contrast, the introverted robot's behaviour results in larger proximate distances (by refraining from approaching others), exhibits smaller and less exaggerated gestures and acts as a "follower" (passive) during the task. To ensure that the personality models display sufficiently interpretable social sensorimotor contingencies, we conducted an observational study of selfie-taking in humans (experiment 1) along with a video pilot evaluating the robot's behaviour (experiment 2). The results of both informed the main experiment (experiment 3).

The Robot. To evaluate the robot's personality, we used the Pepper robot (SoftBank Mobile Corp.), which is an autonomous humanoid robot, 1,21m high that is equipped with speakers, microphones, cameras, and laser and bumper sensors. To take a selfie, the robot was equipped with a GoPro Hero7 camera mounted on the robot using a 3D printed "selfie stick" (Fig. 1, left). Experiments took place in a controlled environment, namely the eXperience Induction Machine (XIM), an immersive space constructed as an experimental platform to study human behaviour in complex but ecologically valid situations [13].

Robot Control. For the robot to successfully achieve the task of taking a selfie,a variety of capabilities, such as human recognition, navigation, obstacle and collision detection is necessary. The robot's control is based on the Distributed Adaptive Control (DAC) architecture [14], a biologically grounded cognitive architecture which characterises the link between mind, brain and behaviour. The robot's reactive behaviour is based on self-regulation system of homeostatic and allostatic control [15] and the personality of the robot arises from the interplay of these subsystems [16]. The control system has been tested in a variety of HRI scenarios [7] and provides autonomous behaviour in dynamic environments. Here, we focus on the robot's personality, as expressed by sensorimotor contingencies, using only the reactive layer of the DAC architecture. The robot randomly explores an area and looks for humans. Once humans are detected, the *get attention* behaviour is triggered followed by *communicate intention*. If amount of people is not sufficient (in the case the robot got the attention of only one person), then the *gather more people* behaviour is triggered. Once humans stand behind the robot to take the selfie (as detected by the robot's laser sensors), the *coordinate/take the selfie* behaviour is triggered for the taking of the selfie.

Experiment 1 - Selfie Taking in Humans. To create a baseline in the act of taking a selfie in group settings, we observed human behaviour in a task that emulated the final experiment. We asked participants ("selfie-takers") to approach a group of people to take a group selfie, using only sensorimotor information (gestures) without any verbalisation. First, participants completed a 10-item Big Five survey [11] to determine their personality and then performed the task of taking a selfie with a group. After the completion of the task, we asked the individuals who were approached for the selfie to complete the 10-item Big Five survey and evaluate which sensorimotor information allowed them to understand the request and agree to take the selfie. Finally, we asked the "selfie-takers" to report any actions they did to make the request clearer and result in taking a selfie. All interactions were filmed on an iPhone by the researcher, while participants took the selfies with their phones.

Experiment 2 - Evaluation of Robot Gestures. To assess the comprehension and perception of the information provided through socSMCs, we conducted an online study where participants rated the robot's behaviour based on the Godspeed questionnaire [17], and it's perceived personality. The Godspeed questionnaire is among the standard questionnaires used in HRI to evaluate the interaction and the human's perception of the robot in the following categories: perceived intelligence, animacy, anthropomorphism, likeability and perceived safety. The Godspeed items selected were Artificial – Lifelike (anthropomorphism), Inert – Interactive (Animacy), Unfriendly – Friendly (likeability), and Foolish – Sensible (perceived intelligence), based upon their relevance to the task of selfie-taking. Finally, we asked participants to provide a short response indicating what they believed the robot was trying to communicate based on the exhibited gestures alone. The only additional contextual information provided was that they could imagine the robot holding a camera in its right hand for the duration of the videos. Participants watched 8 videos in randomised order of the robotic gestures corresponding to the four defined selfie-taking behaviours: *get attention, communicate intention, gather more people,* and *coordinate/take the selfie* for both the introverted and extroverted interaction models. An snapshot of the videos provided can be seen in Fig. 1, right.

 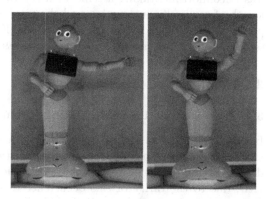

Fig. 1. Left: picture of the robot with the 3D printed bracelet and camera mounted on its arm. The robot is located in the XIM. Right: example of getting attention (extroverted and introverted robot).

Experiment 3 - The Selfie Task with the Robot. The final goal is to deploy this setup in public. In this pilot study, we conducted the experiments in a controlled environment (the XIM) to assess the interaction dynamics with the minimum amount of participants required to form a group (two individuals). The experiment began when participants entered the XIM where the robot was located in groups of two. We did not inform them about the robot's motivation for the interaction, nor we gave them specific instructions on how to interact with the robot, aside from informing them that the interaction would be non-verbal. Each pair was randomly assigned to either the extroverted or introverted robot.

We considered a successful selfie-taking when participants placed themselves behind the robot, in the camera's frame. The interaction was over after a successful selfie-taking followed by a salutation by the robot, or after 10 min had passed. Upon completion of the task, we asked participants to complete a survey on a tablet that contained the following information: demographics, the participant's personality and the robot's perceived personality (10-item Big Five questionnaire), the full Godspeed questionnaire, information about the participant's selfie-taking habits and preferences, and questions that evaluated the interaction and taking a selfie with the robot. Finally, participants were debriefed and also given the option to receive a copy of their selfie taken by the robot.

The selfie-taking habits were measured by "How often do you take selfies?" (Response: Never, Daily, Weekly, Monthly) and "I like taking selfies" on a 5-point Likert scale. To evaluate the interaction, participants also evaluated in a 5-point Likert scale the following statements: "Taking a selfie with the robot was fun", "Taking a selfie with the robot was engaging", "Taking a selfie with the robot was easy", "Taking a selfie with the robot was annoying", "Taking a selfie with the robot was natural", "I liked taking a selfie with the robot", "I was uncomfortable taking a selfie with the robot". Additionally, we logged the length of each selfie interaction and the total amount of successful selfie-taking per condition and recorded the interactions. Examples of individual and group selfies can be found in Fig. 2. The experiments were conducted in English.

3 Results

3.1 Experiment 1 - Selfie Taking in Humans

Initially, we asked random participants to take a selfie with a group of people that was unknown to them. From an early stage, it became apparent that the design of the experimental task created scepticism and distrust when applied to HHI, due to the rarity of this occurrence in actual social contexts. As it was difficult to find participants who would agree to take a selfie, we modulated the experiment to facilitate data collection by approaching a group of people and taking a member of the group aside to be the "selfie-taker". The task began when the "selfie-taker" returned to the group to take the selfie with the other members. In total, we conducted 6 selfie-taking interactions, two out of which were with a group of strangers and four with a group of friends (with a total of

Fig. 2. Examples of individual selfies of participants with the robot (left) and group selfies (right).

16 participants). In both scenarios, while participants were instructed to avoid speaking, some verbal communication was used as evident in the short responses which included the most important information in agreeing to take the selfie was "asking for the selfie".

Out of the six selfie-takers, 4 were determined to be extroverts and 2 introverts. These data are consistent with literature where there is a positive correlation between selfie-taking and extroversion [18]. Behavioural data showed little difference between the socSMCs observed during the interactions. Those who were approached to take the selfie were mostly evaluated as extroverted (only 1 out of the 16 people was evaluated as an introvert). This result could be explained by the nature of the task design, as possibly more extroverts could agree to participate. Given that the survey was done after taking the selfie, participants may have been influenced and reported higher scores on the extroversion items as a result of their recent social interaction. Furthermore, we observed closer proxemic behaviour in groups where participants knew each other. Finally, when participants evaluated the selfie-taking act, the most important cues were "facial expression" and "smiling" followed by eye contact, gestures and distance. The most important factors that led to the understanding of the request and agreeing to the selfie was "holding the phone in selfie position", "smiling", "being polite" and the verbal request for a selfie.

3.2   Experiment 2 - Evaluation of Robot Gestures

In total, 28 participants completed the online video pilot (13 females, mean age 37.6 y/o). For each robot personality, participants evaluated the following behaviours: *get attention, communicate intention, gather more people*, and *coordinate/take the selfie*. We found no significant differences across conditions in the Godspeed items. Furthermore, the answers varied when participants were asked to report the message the robot was trying to convey. For *get attention* in both extroverted and introverted robot behaviours, the gestured seemed clear, as it was reported as: "Hello", "Trying to get attention", "Over here!", but also as "goodbye". In the case of *communicate intention*, the gestures in both conditions were less clear as participants thought it was about already taken a photo or showing a photo already taken. Proxemics and participatory context could be important to attribute the correct meaning to the gestures. *Gather more people* gesture in the extroverted robot was understood as "gathering", "ushering", "move this way!", however also frequently attributed to directing traffic. As the robot in the video did not hold the camera, the context was missing, despite mentioning this in the introduction of the online experiment. In contrast, the introverted version caused confusion and was not properly understood. Here, in our effort to create some sense of animacy, we may have caused excessive movement of the torso, resulting participants to attribute this behaviour as dancing or being negative. Finally, *coordinate/take the selfie* for the extroverted robot was mostly clear and understood as "come here!" "inviting someone to join", as well as "move over". The introverted gesture had mixed responses: "saying no", "expressing negativity", "looking for something", "trying to find a spot for the picture", "saying: 'I can't see you'".

Taking this feedback, we improved the robot behaviour in the cases where the message was not clear. The overall results of the video pilot suggested that the potential differences in perception of the behaviour of the robot as exhibited by socSMCs may also lie in the context of the interaction and other sensorimotor cues like proxemics.

3.3   Experiment 3 - The Selfie Task with the Robot

In total, 20 individuals (6 females, mean age 33.0 STD 9.01) participated in groups of two in the selfie-taking task, resulting in 10 selfie interactions (5 for the extroverted and 5 for the introverted robot). We found no correlation between the perceived personality of the robot and the participant's own personality in both conditions. When looking at the average length of selfie interactions and the average number of group selfies, no significant differences were found in the average length of the interaction (average time for extroverted: 417 s, introverted: 356 s, $Z = 4.0$, $p = 0.345$), nor the average number of group selfies taken (extroverted: 2.4 ± 1.96 selfies, introverted: 1.2 ± 0.98 selfies, $Z = 4.0$, $p = 0.33$). The extroverted robot successfully concluded with group (and individual) selfies for 3 out of 5 interactions, whereas the introverted robot successfully concluded with group selfies for 3 out of 5 interactions and one interaction where participants took individual selfies but no group selfies. Trials with the extroverted robot tended to garner more group selfies while trials with the introverted robot tended to garner more individual selfies. The extroverted robot resulted in a total of 12 group selfies and 7 individual selfies while the introverted robot led to 6 group selfies and 12 individual selfies. We found no significant differences among conditions between the introverted and extroverted robot regarding the Godspeed questionnaire, however, the extroverted robot scored higher in animacy compared to the introverted one, while the introverted robot scored higher in agreeableness.

We further evaluated the enjoyment of the interaction. A Mann-Whitney test indicated no significant differences in the enjoyment of the interaction between the two conditions. Similarly, no differences we found in the following items: "Taking a selfie with the robot was engaging", "Taking a selfie with the robot was annoying", "Taking a selfie with the robot was natural", "I liked taking a selfie with the robot", "I was uncomfortable taking a selfie with the robot". Nonetheless, participants reported taking a selfie with the extroverted robot as easier than the introverted one ($U = 24$, $p = 0.0226$). Finally, the habit of taking selfies did not seem to affect the participant's enjoyment of the interaction, as there was no significant difference in the enjoyment of the interaction based on participants' normal selfie-taking behaviour. These results suggest that there was not enough evidence to support the hypothesis that participants would prefer the extroverted robot and that the extroverted robot would lead to a greater number of selfies and longer interactions compared to the introverted one. Nonetheless, participants were able to understand the behaviour of the robot as expressed by sensorimotor information and take a selfie with the robot.

4   Discussion and Conclusions

Due to a small sample size of this pilot study, the lack of significance amongst the two conditions is not surprising. While there is not enough evidence to support our hypotheses, the fact that both the introverted and extroverted conditions led to a successful coupling for a group selfie indicate that the expression of socSMCs is a viable method for coupling in Human-Robot Interaction scenarios. While this study provides a preliminary insight, several limitations need to be discussed.

The robot's behaviour was based explicitly on sensorimotor contingencies, and the resulting behaviours were based on animations conducted by the authors. Observational data from both the video and the debriefing session after the end of the main experiment suggest that further work needs to be conducted for the generation of fluent and transparent gestures. Other aspects of the experimental design may have affected the perception of the robot and task. For example, participants did not view the attached camera as serving an "entertainment" purpose as we would have expected. Instead, several participants perceived the camera as an inherent part of the robot (manufactured) that allowed the robot to see behind itself or as an additional method implemented to monitor the experiment. Participants reported that a cell phone combined with a selfie stick would make the task more transparent, as this is the traditional way of taking a selfie. However, due to the mechanics of the robot's hand and the maximum weight it can hold, such an approach is impossible. Some participants also mentioned that the experimental setting of the XIM led them to overthink the meaning of the gestures, and a more natural setting might have made it easier for them to understand the communicated message. This supports HRI research focusing on ecologically valid settings, as many social interactions (like taking a selfie) may be inhibited by the environmental and contextual expectations of the experimental settings.

The proposed experimental setup was conceptualised to resemble as much as possible a real-world scenario, where the robot would be placed in a public setting, navigate and look for people to take a selfie. A humanoid robot creates natural curiosity to participants who immediately approached the robot, and this prevented the robot from showing all the intended behaviours (like getting the attention of a participant) correctly. Additionally, all interactions were much closer than what we originally anticipated. Novelty and proxemics could have affected the way participants perceived the robot's behaviour.

Due to the small sample size, this study has just scratched the surface of what could be the relevant factors in HRI for group social settings, such as taking a selfie. Many improvements can be suggested for the interaction models of the selfie behaviour. We are currently working on incorporating a sophisticated cognitive architecture that can provide more robust interactions and improving the exhibited gestures.

Perhaps the most important reflection of the conclusion is that while HHI is a viable basis on which to base the design of HRI, HRI at this point in time is still fundamentally different than HHI. Studies such as this one help to fill the gap in research for some particular social contexts and can thus highlight what specific factors may influence HRI regarding a specific task. Ultimately the underlying basis and research question for this study, which sought to show that the same theories of social cognition in HHI can be applied to HRI, has been shown to be true. The robot's ability to successfully take a group selfie in the majority of cases displaying only social sensorimotor information, suggests that socSMCs are a powerful vehicle for conveying intention of a robotic agent in an interaction. However, the realities of the study have also shown that simply considering a social context in HHI and applying it directly to HRI cannot always be done. This is evident when considering the HHI selfie-taking observational pre-study, in which humans were shown to be incredibly shy and sceptical of strangers approaching them for any reason (especially for a selfie) contrasting with the final experiment where the humans exhibited no signs of scepticism towards the robot. This study contributes to the field by exploring the use of socSMCs and their link to personality in a social group setting and how they can be utilised to facilitate transparent interactions.

Acknowledgments. This work is supported by grants from the European Research Council under the European Union's Socialising Sensori-Motor Contingencies (soc-SMCs) grant agreement n. 641321.

References

1. Dautenhahn, K.: Socially intelligent robots: dimensions of human-robot interaction. Philos. Trans. R. Soc. B: Biol. Sci. **362**(1480), 679–704 (2007)
2. Knapp, M., Hall, J., Horgan, T.: Nonverbal Communication in Human Interaction. Cengage Learning, Boston (2013)
3. O'Regan, J.K., Noë, A.: A sensorimotor account of vision and visual consciousness. Behav. Brain Sci. **24**(5), 939–973 (2001)

4. Engel, A.K., Maye, A., Kurthen, M., König, P.: Where's the action? the pragmatic turn in cognitive science. Trends Cogn. Sci. **17**(5), 202–209 (2013)
5. Di Paolo, E.A., De Jaegher, H.: The interactive brain hypothesis. Front. Hum. Neurosci. **6**, 163 (2012)
6. Freire, I.T., Puigbò, J.-Y., Arsiwalla, X.D., Verschure, P.F.M.J.: Modeling the opponent's action using control-based reinforcement learning. In: Vouloutsi, V., et al. (eds.) Living Machines 2018. LNCS (LNAI), vol. 10928, pp. 179–186. Springer, Cham (2018). https://doi.org/10.1007/978-3-319-95972-6_19
7. Lallée, S., et al.: Towards the synthetic self: making others perceive me as an other. Paladyn, J. Behav. Robot. **1**, 136–164 (2015). Open-issue
8. Auvray, M., Lenay, C., Stewart, J.: Perceptual interactions in a minimalist virtual environment. New Ideas Psychol. **27**(1), 32–47 (2009)
9. Robert, L.: Personality in the human robot interaction literature: a review and brief critique. In: Robert, L.P. (ed.) Personality in the Human Robot Interaction Literature: A Review and Brief Critique, Proceedings of the 24th Americas Conference on Information Systems, August, pp. 16–18 (2018)
10. Leuwerink, K.: A robot with personality: interacting with a group of humans. In: Proceedings of the 16th Twente Student Conference on IT, vol. 4 (2012)
11. McCrae, R.R., John, O.P.: An introduction to the five-factor model and its applications. J. Pers. **60**(2), 175–215 (1992)
12. Dhir, A., Pallesen, S., Torsheim, T., Andreassen, C.S.: Do age and gender differences exist in selfie-related behaviours? Comput. Hum. Behav. **63**, 549–555 (2016)
13. Bernardet, U., Väljamäe, A., Inderbitzin, M., Wierenga, S., Mura, A., Verschure, P.F.: Quantifying human subjective experience and social interaction using the experience induction machine. Brain Res. Bull. **85**(5), 305–312 (2011)
14. Verschure, P.F.: Distributed adaptive control: a theory of the mind, brain, body nexus. Biol. Inspired Cogn. Archit. **1**, 55–72 (2012)
15. Vouloutsi, V., Lallée, S., Verschure, P.F.M.J.: Modulating behaviors using allostatic control. In: Lepora, N.F., Mura, A., Krapp, H.G., Verschure, P.F.M.J., Prescott, T.J. (eds.) Living Machines 2013. LNCS (LNAI), vol. 8064, pp. 287–298. Springer, Heidelberg (2013). https://doi.org/10.1007/978-3-642-39802-5_25
16. Vouloutsi, V., Verschure, P.: Emotions and self-regulation. In: Prescott, T.J., Lepora, N.F., Verschure, P.F. (eds.) Living Machines, a Handbook of Research in Biomimetic and Biohybrid Systems, chap. 34, pp. 327–337. Oxford University Press, Oxford (2018)
17. Bartneck, C., Kulić, D., Croft, E., Zoghbi, S.: Measurement instruments for the anthropomorphism, animacy, likeability, perceived intelligence, and perceived safety of robots. Int. J. Social Robot. **1**(1), 71–81 (2009)
18. Chaudhari, B.L., Patil, J.K., Kadiani, A., Chaudhury, S., Saldanha, D.: Correlation of motivations for selfie-posting behavior with personality traits. Ind. Psychiatry J. **28**(1), 123 (2019)

Fast Reverse Replays of Recent Spatiotemporal Trajectories in a Robotic Hippocampal Model

Matthew T. Whelan[1,2(✉)], Tony J. Prescott[1,2], and Eleni Vasilaki[1]

[1] Department of Computer Science, University of Sheffield, Sheffield S10 2TN, UK
{mwhelan3,t.j.prescott,e.vasilaki}@sheffield.ac.uk
[2] Sheffield Robotics, University of Sheffield, Sheffield S1 3JD, UK

Abstract. A number of computational models have recently emerged in an attempt to understand the dynamics of hippocampal replay, but there has been little progress in testing and implementing these models in real-world robotics settings. Presented here is a bioinspired hippocampal CA3 network model, that runs in real-time to produce reverse replays of recent spatiotemporal sequences in a robotic spatial navigation task. For the sake of computational efficiency, the model is composed of continuous-rate based neurons, but incorporates two biophysical properties that have recently been hypothesised to play an important role in the generation of reverse replays: intrinsic plasticity and short-term plasticity. As this model only replays recently active trajectories, it does not directly address the functional properties of reverse replay, for instance in robotic learning tasks, but it does support further investigations into how reverse replays could contribute to functional improvements.

Keywords: Robotics · Hippocampal replay · Computational modelling

1 Introduction

How the nervous system represents, stores and retrieves memories is an ongoing research problem, but an interesting hypothesis now gaining strong experimental support is that hippocampal replay plays an important role [6,7,10,13,18,29]. Place cell activities in the hippocampus, which are cells that respond preferentially when a rodent is positioned in the place cell's spatial receptive field [27,28], are often invoked during hippocampal replay events and are therefore a useful concept for understanding hippocampal replay. In its simplest form, hippocampal replay is the temporally preserved reactivation of recently active place cells during sleep [22,36,43] and during periods of awake immobility or quiescence [4,33], and have been shown to occur during brief periods of hippocampal sharp-wave ripple events [8]. Replays can reinstate the temporal ordering of the place cells in either the forward direction [22,36] or the reverse direction [11], termed *forward replay* and *reverse replay*, respectively.

© Springer Nature Switzerland AG 2020
V. Vouloutsi et al. (Eds.): Living Machines 2020, LNAI 12413, pp. 390–401, 2020.
https://doi.org/10.1007/978-3-030-64313-3_37

There are a number of important differences in both the behavioural and neural states between reverse replays and forward replays. For instance, whilst forward replays show to occur during both awake and sleep states, and can reinstate either remotely (i.e. reinstating experiences from locations that are spatially distant from the original experience) or locally [4], reverse replays tend to occur almost exclusively during awake replay events, reflecting the immediate local past experience [11]. And unlike awake forward replays, reverse replays are strongly modulated by rewards, such that the frequency of reverse replays initiating at reward sites increases in the presence of increased rewards and reduces in response to decreased rewards [1]. In addition, reverse replays are capable of emergence following only a single trial, and it has therefore been proposed that reverse replays may be a consequence of place cell excitability changes not relying on traditional synaptic plasticity, such as lingering place cell activities [8], or more recently long-term potentiation of intrinsic excitability [30]. Reverse replays may then induce synaptic changes that provide the mechanism for replays during states where the transient activity has faded, such as during sleep states [2]. These point towards an intricate interplay between transient excitability changes and synaptic plasticities in the emergence of the various forms of replay under different behavioural states.

Presented here is a biophysical, continuous rate-based network model of reverse replay implemented on a simulated version of the biomimetic robot MiRo [25], and is based on two recent models of hippocampal replay dynamics in recurrent CA3 networks [15,30]. Reverse replays in this model occur as a consequence of two modes of transient neural states. The first is due to the implementation of a time decaying model of *intrinsic plasticity*. Intrinsic plasticity is the ability of a cell to increase heterosynaptic long-term potentiation of post-synaptic potentials following recent activity [17,44], and has recently been proposed as a potential mechanism for the occurrence of reverse replays [30]. The second transient neural state implementation is in short-term plasticity, which acts to ensure unidirectional, stable replays [15]. This is due to short-term depression suppressing synaptic currents after a given amount of continuous firing, thus preventing unbounded synaptic transmissions.

2 Methods

2.1 Network Architecture

The network consists of 100 rate-based neurons representing place cells, arranged in a grid of size 10×10, each of which has its place fields spread evenly across an open circular environment. Each cell forms a bidirectional and symmetric synaptic connection to its 8 nearest neighbours, with all weights fixed at a value of 1. Figure 1 gives an example of the network architecture for a subset of cells.

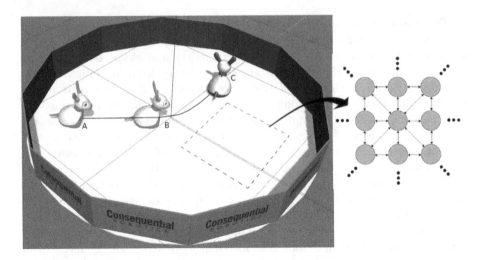

Fig. 1. The simulated environment used to test the model with the MiRo robot. The network architecture consists of a 10×10 array of place cells with place fields uniformly covering the environment. Bidirectional symmetric connections exist between each cell's eight nearest neighbours in space, as shown for a small patch of the environment here. An example trajectory is shown here, in which MiRo begins at the start position in A, passes through location B and ends in the goal location at C.

2.2   Network Dynamics

The activity of a single neuron, i, is described by a first-order decaying differential, with its activity increasing according to incoming recurrent synaptic inputs and place specific inputs, and reducing in response to a global inhibitory term

$$\tau_I \frac{d}{dt} I_i = -I_i + \sigma_i I_i^{syn} + I_i^{place} - I^{inh} \tag{1}$$

with $\tau_I = 0.05\,s$. σ_i represents the intrinsic plasticity, here acting to scale the incoming synaptic inputs (see below). The activity is passed through a linear rectifier with a lower and upper bound $0\,\text{Hz}$ $100\,\text{Hz}$ to give the final rate,

$$r_i' = \alpha \left(I_i - \epsilon \right)$$

$$r_i = \begin{cases} 0 & \text{if } r_i' < 0 \\ 100 & \text{if } r_i' > 100 \\ r_i' & \text{otherwise} \end{cases} \tag{2}$$

with $\alpha = 1$ and $\epsilon = 2$.

I_i^{place} is the place specific input, for which each neuron has associated with it a place field in the environment (in this instance a $2\,\text{m} \times 2\,\text{m}$ environment, Fig. 1). The place fields are spread uniformly across the environment, each having a centre point, (x_i, y_i). The place-specific input for neuron i is then given as an exponential of the distance the robot is from the place field's centre point,

$$I_i^{place} = I_{max}^p \exp\left[-\frac{(x-x_i)^2 + (y-y_i)^2}{2d^2}\right] \tag{3}$$

with $I_{max}^p = 50\,\text{Hz}$ and $d = 0.1\,\text{m}$.

I_i^{syn} represents the synaptic input and is given as the sum of the incoming synaptic connections from the cell's 8 nearest neighbours

$$I_i^{syn} = \lambda \sum_{j=1}^8 w_{ij} r_j D_j F_j \tag{4}$$

where w_{ij} represents the weight from neuron j onto neuron i. λ takes on a value of 0 or 1, depending on whether the robot is exploring or resting at the reward (see Sect. 2.3), respectively. D_j and F_j are short-term plasticity terms representing short-term depression and short-term facilitation, respectively, and are described by (as in [15], but see [9,37,41])

$$\frac{d}{dt}D_j = \frac{1-D_j}{\tau_{STD}} - r_j D_j F_j \tag{5}$$

$$\frac{d}{dt}F_j = \frac{U-F_j}{\tau_{STF}} + U(1-F_j)r_j \tag{6}$$

with $\tau_{STD} = 1.5\,\text{s}$, $\tau_{STF} = 1\,\text{s}$ and $U = 0.6$. If a cell fires continuously for a given amount of time, eventually D_j drops to 0 thus preventing that cell from any further synaptic transmissions.

The inhibitory input, I_i^{inh}, is a global term given as a summation of the whole network's activity

$$\frac{d}{dt}I^{inh} = -\frac{I^{inh}}{\tau^{inh}} + w_{inh}\sum_j r_j D_j F_j \tag{7}$$

with $\tau^{inh} = 0.05\,\text{s}$ and $w_{inh} = 0.1$, and acts to prevent too many cells being active at once.

The σ_i term in Eq. 1 is specific to each cell, representing the intrinsic plasticity for that cell. It acts to scale the incoming synaptic inputs and is described by

$$\frac{d}{dt}\sigma_i = \frac{\sigma_{ss} - \sigma_i}{\tau_\sigma} + \frac{\sigma_{max} - 1}{1 + \exp\left[-\beta(r_i - r_\sigma)\right]} \tag{8}$$

with $\tau_\sigma = 10\,\text{s}$, $\sigma_{ss} = 0.1$, $\sigma_{max} = 4$, $r_\sigma = 10\,\text{Hz}$ and $\beta = 1$. The second term is a sigmoid, and follows the modelling approach taken by Pang and Fairhall [30], but with the addition here of time decaying dynamics to model extinction effects. When the cell no longer fires, σ_i decays to a steady state value of σ_{ss}. If $\sigma_i > \sigma_{max}$, then σ_i is set to σ_{max}.

2.3 Two-Stage Dynamics

This model consists of two different behavioural states that define two different sets of network dynamics, similar to a previous two-stage modelling approach of CA3 replay dynamics [34]. The first behavioural state is defined as *active exploration*: the state in which MiRo is actively searching for the hidden reward. Under this state, it is assumed there is little to no synaptic transmission across the network due to the effects of high acetylcholine levels [21], which has been shown experimentally to inhibit the recurrent post-synaptic inputs in the hippocampal CA3 region [16]. To capture this effect, λ is set to 0 in Eq. 4 thus preventing post-synaptic transmission.

The second behavioural state is defined as *quiescent reward*, in which MiRo remains awake yet quiescent whilst it is at the reward point, and is the state under which reverse replays occur. It is assumed here that acetylcholine levels have dropped, similar to that found during slow-wave sleep states [21], thus permitting synaptic transmission in the CA3 network. To model this effect, λ is set to 1 in Eq. 4.

3 Results

3.1 Searching for a Hidden Reward

The model is run on the MiRo robot in a simulated open arena environment, having a diameter of 2 m (Fig. 1) and using simulation time steps of 10ms. Model equations are discretised using the Euler method with time steps of $\Delta t = 10$ ms to match the simulated time steps. [1] From a random start location, MiRo is left to freely explore its environment via a basic implementation of a random walk, with the goal of finding a hidden reward. This is the *active exploration* phase, and during this phase the network rates are driven solely by the place specific inputs with no recurrent synaptic transmissions. There is no synaptic plasticity implemented in this experiment, and so all weights, w_{ij}, are fixed at a value of 1. Figures 2A and 2B show the activity of the network during active exploration. Due to the distribution of the place-specific input, no more than 4 cells are active at any one time, though most often this amounts to no more than 2 or 3 cells being simultaneously active. This sparse representation during exploration provides a neural representation of space. Neurons that become active due to the place specific input then undergo increases in intrinsic plasticity, decaying exponentially (according to Eq. 8) when activity in the neuron drops.

Upon reaching the hidden reward location, MiRo pauses and enters the *quiescent reward* phase. Place specific inputs are computed using Eq. 3 and are input into the network via pulses of 0.1 s-ON and 1.9 s-OFF. Recall that during this phase, recurrent synaptic conductances are allowed. Due to the increase in synaptic recurrent conductance and post-synaptic activity being scaled by the

---

[1] Full code for the model (using Python 2.7) can be found at https://github.com/mattdoubleu/robotic_reverse_replay.

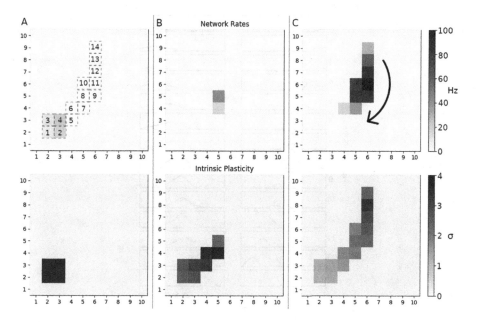

Fig. 2. Rates (top plots) and intrinsic plasticities (bottom plots) for the 10×10 network are shown here for the locations marked in the trajectory of Fig. 1. These are: A) MiRo is at the start location. The numbered boxes ranging from 1 to 14 here represent all cells that were active during the exploration phase and the temporal order in which they fired during exploration. B) MiRo is exploring the environment. C) MiRo has reached the reward and reverse replays are being initiated. The arrow indicates the temporal order of firing during this replay event.

intrinsic plasticity, activity propagates quickly through the network, reinstating the most recently active cells in a temporally reversed order to that seen during exploration. Figure 2C shows the activity of the network midway through a replay event. Notice the trace in the intrinsic plasticity plots, which transiently stores the most recent sequence of activity in the network and provides the mechanism for faithful replays of the recent trajectory. In this instance, many more cells are found to be simultaneously active, but their time points for peak activity retain the temporal ordering seen during exploration (Fig. 3).

For a more detailed comparison of the network's activity during the exploration and quiescent phases, Fig. 3 displays a time course plot of the rates for the 14 cells that were active during exploration in Fig. 2A. It is clear in Fig. 3 that the temporal ordering of cell firing during a reverse replay event is preserved in comparison to the ordering during exploration.

3.2   Removing Intrinsic Plasticity and Short-Term Plasticity

To show the effects of removing intrinsic plasticity from the model, σ_i is set to 1 for all cells and the model is run once more on a similar trajectory (Fig. 4).

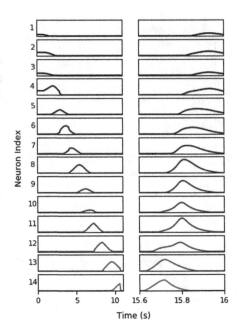

Fig. 3. A time course plot of the cell rates for the cells indexed in Fig. 2A. The lower and upper limits in each box plot is 0 Hz and 100 Hz. Plots on the left show the activities during exploration, occurring over a time period of approximately 12 s. The plots on the right show the activity during a reverse replay event. Note that Figs. 2A, B and C are snapshots of the network's activity at times 0 s, 5 s and 15.8 s, respectively.

In this instance, rather than a direct replay of the recent trajectory, the activity in the network displays a divergent replay event across the whole network from the point of initiation. This effect was similarly seen in the model of Haga and Fukai [15], who assumed a similar network architecture to this one but did not model intrinsic plasticity. This shows that the intrinsic plasticity is important for restricting the replay event to the previously experienced trajectory only. However, divergent replays could have potential benefits in the learning of goal-oriented paths (see Discussion).

When removing short-term plasticity whilst including intrinsic plasticity, activity propagates throughout the previous trajectory, but it does not dissipate (data not shown). Instead all the cells in the trajectory remain active indefinitely, since without the reduction of conductances due to short-term plasticity, they all continue to activate one another without end.

4   Discussion

We have presented here a biophysical model of a CA3 hippocampal network that produces fast reverse replays of recently active place cell trajectories. Whilst the network connectivity remains static and symmetric, the implementation of

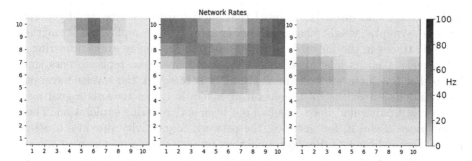

Fig. 4. Example of a replay event without intrinsic plasticity, where $\sigma_i = 1$ for all neurons. A similar trajectory as in Figs. 1/2 is taken here, with reverse replay events initiated at the same location. The heat maps, from left to right, show the temporal ordering of network activity during a replay event. As intrinsic plasticity is homogeneous across the network, there is no preferential trajectory for the sequence of cell activities to follow. As such a divergent wave propagates across the whole network from the point of initiation.

intrinsic plasticity produces asymmetries in the network that amplifies incoming synaptic currents, enabling activity to travel through the network along a trajectory determined by levels of intrinsic plasticity. Intrinsic plasticity was first introduced as a potential mechanism for hippocampal replays by Pang and Fairhall [30], but as we are running the model on the MiRo robot, for which it can very quickly cover a whole area, time decaying dynamics have had to be included so that the whole network does not become intrinsically potentiated. Given only a subset of the network becomes potentiated by intrinsic plasticity (i.e. those cells most recently active), this creates a certain level of sparsity in the network, and is interesting to compare with a previous computational model of replay dynamics by Chenkov et al. [5] who showed that sparsity in their network was important for generating effective and controlled replays. Yet, whilst they achieved sparsity by changing the number of synaptic connections, here it is achieved through intrinsic plasticity changes. These results nonetheless point towards a level of sparsity that is important for specific and controlled replays.

Another important component in this model for generating stable propagations of replay sequences is short-term plasticity effects. This mechanism was first shown by Haga and Fukai [15] in a reverse replay model. It is perhaps a useful analogy to consider short term plasticity in this instance having the effect of a 'refractory period' for activity propagation, in that it prevents further transmission of activity after a given amount of continuous activity. Refractory periods have been shown in previous models to ensure stable, unidirectional replays [19,30]. However, implementing refractory periods requires a model of spiking neurons, and so modelling short-term plasticity lends itself to rate-based implementations of replay. This is of course particularly useful in real-time robotic applications where spiking neuron models may be computationally inefficient. But short-term plasticity could have a more interesting property during reverse replays. Haga and Fukai [15] showed that short-term plasticity could generate reversed synaptic weight changes. This enables reverse replays to strengthen synaptic traces in the forwards direction, despite the replay event occurring in the reverse. Thus, whilst their model produced divergent replay events similar to that seen here when intrinsic plasticity is removed, the reversed synaptic potentiations proved useful in generating synaptic traces towards a goal location, even if particular place cells had not been active during exploration. These could prove useful if, for instance, the network connectivity provides a neural map of the environment. Replays could then provide a means to explore trajectories towards goal locations even for trajectories that have never been physically explored.

A third component of the model that was necessary for appropriately timed replays was the implementation of a two-stage dynamic, which prevented the network from transmitting recurrent synaptic currents during the *exploration phase*, but allowed synaptic transmission during the *quiescent reward* phase (where MiRo sat quietly at the reward location). This was based on findings that suggest different levels of acetylcholine during active exploration and sleep states [21], which alters CA3 synaptic conductances [16] – higher levels of acetylcholine inhibit synaptic conductance. However, what is not clear is that acetylcholine levels drop significantly enough during the quiescent reward state for which reverse replays occur, given it follows immediately after exploration [11]. Whilst levels of acetylcholine have been found to change quickly on the time scale of a few seconds, at least in the prefrontal cortex [31], it is unclear as to whether this occurs in the hippocampal CA3 region. What is perhaps interesting to note, however, is that cholinergic stimulation, which leads to an increase in acetylcholine, has been shown to suppress hippocampal sharp-wave ripples yet promote theta oscillations [38]. Given theta activity is found to co-occur with exploratory states [39], whilst replays occur usually during sharp-wave ripple events [8], this suggests that for reverse replays to arise, acetylcholine levels must phasically drop during a quiescent reward state to enable sharp-wave ripples.

4.1   Scope for Future Research

We argued previously that, though there are a number of computational models attempting to explain the dynamics of hippocampal replay, there had been little in terms of real-world robotic applications of these models [42]. And whilst there does exist reinforcement learning models that attempt to capture some of the functional properties of replay [3, 24, 26], they are not biophysical models, nor do they adopt continuous state-action spaces which are likely necessary for robotic applications. Thus, though these models may perhaps help answer the question of why replays are functionally useful, they do not answer how replays emerge. A complete model of hippocampal replay should ideally answer both these questions. This work attempts to understand the problem of how hippocampal replay emerges by utilising robotics to test the models in real-world settings, and in so doing, could help bridge the gap between those computational models that seek to understand how replays emerge with those that utilise replays for improving learning in artificial systems.

As noted, reverse replays are particularly thought to be involved in reinforcement learning, given their reward-modulated occurrences [1] and coordinated activity with neurons in the striatum [14,32]. As such, an investigation into whether reverse replays could improve learning in biophysical models of reinforcement learning, such as [40], should be conducted to further ground these hypotheses in theory. In particular, the model of Vasilaki et al. [40] belongs to a class of models termed three-factor learning rules [12], which predict that synaptic eligibility traces are necessary to support long-term synaptic modifications across behavioural timescales. The third factor, often a reward signal, dictates that synapses only undergo modifications in the presence of that third factor. Reverse replays however offer an alternative (though not mutually exclusive) mechanism to the synaptic eligibility trace hypothesis, since the replaying of cell trajectories could support the conditions necessary for synaptic modification under a third factor.

Finally, in order to generate cell activity that was place specific in this model, the global x-y coordinates for the robot had to be used which is a biologically unrealistic property of place cell emergence. Questions remain therefore around how other models of the hippocampus, ones attempting to understand the emergence of place cells, grid cells, head direction cells, etc. [20,35], could be consolidated with hippocampal replay models. In addition, there is the question of how hippocampal replay integrates with the rest of the brain. Interesting work at building a more complete cognitive architecture has been done by Maffei et al. [23], which includes a hippocampal model of place cell emergence. For path planning, shortest paths are found via a sweeping algorithm (Dijkstra's algorithm), but a more biologically plausible method might instead be through hippocampal replays.

Acknowledgements. This work has been in part funded by the Human Brain Project, under project number 785907 (SGA2).

References

1. Ambrose, R.E., Pfeiffer, B.E., Foster, D.J.: Reverse replay of hippocampal place cells is uniquely modulated by changing reward. Neuron **91**(5), 1124–1136 (2016)
2. Atherton, L.A., Dupret, D., Mellor, J.R.: Memory trace replay: the shaping of memory consolidation by neuromodulation. Trends Neurosci. **38**(9), 560–570 (2015)
3. Aubin, L., Khamassi, M., Girard, B.: Prioritized sweeping neural DynaQ with multiple predecessors, and hippocampal replays. In: Vouloutsi, V., et al. (eds.) Living Machines 2018. LNCS (LNAI), vol. 10928, pp. 16–27. Springer, Cham (2018). https://doi.org/10.1007/978-3-319-95972-6_4
4. Carr, M.F., Jadhav, S.P., Frank, L.M.: Hippocampal replay in the awake state: a potential substrate for memory consolidation and retrieval. Nat. Neurosci. **14**(2), 147 (2011)
5. Chenkov, N., Sprekeler, H., Kempter, R.: Memory replay in balanced recurrent networks. PLoS Comput. Biol. **13**(1), e1005359 (2017)

6. Cutsuridis, V., Cobb, S., Graham, B.P.: Encoding and retrieval in a model of the hippocampal CA1 microcircuit. Hippocampus **20**(3), 423–446 (2010)
7. Cutsuridis, V., Hasselmo, M.: Spatial memory sequence encoding and replay during modeled theta and ripple oscillations. Cogn. Comput. **3**(4), 554–574 (2011)
8. Diba, K., Buzsáki, G.: Forward and reverse hippocampal place-cell sequences during ripples. Nat. Neurosci. **10**(10), 1241 (2007)
9. Esposito, U., Giugliano, M., Vasilaki, E.: Adaptation of short-term plasticity parameters via error-driven learning may explain the correlation between activity-dependent synaptic properties, connectivity motifs and target specificity. Front. Comput. Neurosci. **8**, 175 (2015)
10. Foster, D.J.: Replay comes of age. Ann. Rev. Neurosci. **40**, 581–602 (2017)
11. Foster, D.J., Wilson, M.A.: Reverse replay of behavioural sequences in hippocampal place cells during the awake state. Nature **440**(7084), 680 (2006)
12. Gerstner, W., Lehmann, M., Liakoni, V., Corneil, D., Brea, J.: Eligibility traces and plasticity on behavioral time scales: experimental support of neoHebbian three-factor learning rules. Front. Neural Circuits **12**, 53 (2018)
13. Girardeau, G., Benchenane, K., Wiener, S.I., Buzsáki, G., Zugaro, M.B.: Selective suppression of hippocampal ripples impairs spatial memory. Nat. Neurosci **12**(10), 1222 (2009)
14. Gomperts, S.N., Kloosterman, F., Wilson, M.A.: VTA neurons coordinate with the hippocampal reactivation of spatial experience. Elife **4**, e05360 (2015)
15. Haga, T., Fukai, T.: Recurrent network model for learning goal-directed sequences through reverse replay. Elife **7**, e34171 (2018)
16. Hasselmo, M.E., Schnell, E., Barkai, E.: Dynamics of learning and recall at excitatory recurrent synapses and cholinergic modulation in rat hippocampal region CA3. J. Neurosci. **15**(7), 5249–5262 (1995)
17. Hyun, J.H., et al.: KV1. 2 mediates heterosynaptic modulation of direct cortical synaptic inputs in CA3 pyramidal cells. J. Physiol. **593**(16), 3617–3643 (2015)
18. Jadhav, S.P., Kemere, C., German, P.W., Frank, L.M.: Awake hippocampal sharp-wave ripples support spatial memory. Science **336**(6087), 1454–1458 (2012)
19. Jahnke, S., Timme, M., Memmesheimer, R.M.: A unified dynamic model for learning, replay, and sharp-wave/ripples. J. Neurosci. **35**(49), 16236–16258 (2015)
20. Jauffret, A., Cuperlier, N., Gaussier, P.: From grid cells and visual place cells to multimodal place cell: a new robotic architecture. Front. Neurorobot. **9**, 1 (2015)
21. Kametani, H., Kawamura, H.: Alterations in acetylcholine release in the rat hippocampus during sleep-wakefulness detected by intracerebral dialysis. Life Sci. **47**(5), 421–426 (1990)
22. Lee, A.K., Wilson, M.A.: Memory of sequential experience in the hippocampus during slow wave sleep. Neuron **36**(6), 1183–1194 (2002)
23. Maffei, G., Santos-Pata, D., Marcos, E., Sánchez-Fibla, M., Verschure, P.F.: An embodied biologically constrained model of foraging: from classical and operant conditioning to adaptive real-world behavior in dac-x. Neural Netw. **72**, 88–108 (2015)
24. Mattar, M.G., Daw, N.D.: Prioritized memory access explains planning and hippocampal replay. Nat. Neurosci. **21**(11), 1609 (2018)
25. Mitchinson, B., Prescott, T.J.: MIRO: a robot "Mammal" with a biomimetic brain-based control system. In: Lepora, N.F.F., Mura, A., Mangan, M., Verschure, P.F.M.J.F.M.J., Desmulliez, M., Prescott, T.J.J. (eds.) Living Machines 2016. LNCS (LNAI), vol. 9793, pp. 179–191. Springer, Cham (2016). https://doi.org/10.1007/978-3-319-42417-0_17

26. Mnih, V., et al.: Human-level control through deep reinforcement learning. Nature **518**(7540), 529 (2015)
27. O'Keefe, J.: Place units in the hippocampus of the freely moving rat. Exp. Neurol. **51**(1), 78–109 (1976)
28. O'Keefe, J., Dostrovsky, J.: The hippocampus as a spatial map: preliminary evidence from unit activity in the freely-moving rat. Brain Res. **34**, 171–175 (1971)
29. Ólafsdóttir, H.F., Bush, D., Barry, C.: The role of hippocampal replay in memory and planning. Curr. Biol. **28**(1), R37–R50 (2018)
30. Pang, R., Fairhall, A.L.: Fast and flexible sequence induction in spiking neural networks via rapid excitability changes. eLife **8**, e44324 (2019)
31. Parikh, V., Kozak, R., Martinez, V., Sarter, M.: Prefrontal acetylcholine release controls cue detection on multiple timescales. Neuron **56**(1), 141–154 (2007)
32. Pennartz, C., Lee, E., Verheul, J., Lipa, P., Barnes, C.A., McNaughton, B.: The ventral striatum in off-line processing: ensemble reactivation during sleep and modulation by hippocampal ripples. J. Neurosci. **24**(29), 6446–6456 (2004)
33. Pfeiffer, B.E., Foster, D.J.: Hippocampal place-cell sequences depict future paths to remembered goals. Nature **497**(7447), 74–79 (2013)
34. Saravanan, V., et al.: Transition between encoding and consolidation/replay dynamics via cholinergic modulation of can current: a modeling study. Hippocampus **25**(9), 1052–1070 (2015)
35. Sheynikhovich, D., Chavarriaga, R., Strösslin, T., Arleo, A., Gerstner, W.: Is there a geometric module for spatial orientation? insights from a rodent navigation model. Psychol. Rev. **116**(3), 540 (2009)
36. Skaggs, W.E., McNaughton, B.L.: Replay of neuronal firing sequences in rat hippocampus during sleep following spatial experience. Science **271**(5257), 1870–1873 (1996)
37. Tsodyks, M., Pawelzik, K., Markram, H.: Neural networks with dynamic synapses. Neural Comput. **10**(4), 821–835 (1998)
38. Vandecasteele, M., et al.: Optogenetic activation of septal cholinergic neurons suppresses sharp wave ripples and enhances theta oscillations in the hippocampus. Proc. Natl. Acad. Sci. **111**(37), 13535–13540 (2014)
39. Vanderwolf, C.H.: Hippocampal electrical activity and voluntary movement in the rat. Electroencephalogr. Clin. Neurophysiol. **26**(4), 407–418 (1969)
40. Vasilaki, E., Frémaux, N., Urbanczik, R., Senn, W., Gerstner, W.: Spike-based reinforcement learning in continuous state and action space: when policy gradient methods fail. PLoS Comput. Biol. **5**(12), e1000586 (2009)
41. Vasilaki, E., Giugliano, M.: Emergence of connectivity motifs in networks of model neurons with short-and long-term plastic synapses. PloS One **9**(1), e84626 (2014)
42. Whelan, M.T., Vasilaki, E., Prescott, T.J.: Robots that imagine – can hippocampal replay be utilized for robotic mnemonics? In: Martinez-Hernandez, U., et al. (eds.) Living Machines 2019. LNCS (LNAI), vol. 11556, pp. 277–286. Springer, Cham (2019). https://doi.org/10.1007/978-3-030-24741-6_24
43. Wilson, M.A., McNaughton, B.L.: Reactivation of hippocampal ensemble memories during sleep. Science **265**(5172), 676–679 (1994)
44. Zhang, W., Linden, D.J.: The other side of the engram: experience-driven changes in neuronal intrinsic excitability. Nat. Rev. Neurosci. **4**(11), 885–900 (2003)

Using Animatlab for Neuromechanical Analysis: Linear Hill Parameter Calculation

Fletcher Young[1]([✉]) [ID], Alexander J. Hunt[2] [ID], Hillel J. Chiel[1] [ID], and Roger D. Quinn[1]

[1] Case Western Reserve University, Cleveland, OH 44106, USA
fletcher.young@case.edu
[2] Portland State University, Portland, OR 97201, USA

Abstract. Modeling muscle-based locomotion in simulation requires reliable interactions between kinematic motion and kinetic forces. Simplifications made in simulation can sometimes obfuscate these interconnections and cause a system to operate in unexpected ways. We present a methodology for calculating muscle parameters that comprise a linear Hill muscle model in the neuromechanical software Animatlab. We examine two numerical issues in Animatlab that cause the muscle tension to become discontinuous, show how violating certain constraints can make the model inaccurate, and show how these issues can be avoided.

Keywords: Neuromechanics · Muscle model · Locomotion

1 Introduction

Animals are capable of adapting to their environment by adjusting their locomotion, and maintaining equilibrium in the face of uncertain surroundings. For example, mountain goats are able to scale sheer cliff faces in order to lick salt from a rock surface despite having hooves as end-effectors [1]. A better understanding of interconnected biological systems that allow animals to adapt to their environment would benefit numerous scientific disciplines including robotics, medicine, and neuroscience. Computer simulations of animal locomotion allow researchers to test biological mechanisms before undertaking time-consuming and expensive animal experiments and can help guide those experiments. New experiments then inform the simulation and the scientific cycle continues.

Simulations that include both the body and nervous system of an organism, known as neuromechanical models, provide insight into how biological systems coordinate locomotion [2]. Researchers have developed neuromechanical models of many animals, including cockroaches [3], rats [4, 5], and cats [6]. A predictable relationship between neural stimulation and kinetic output is critical for developing neuromechanical models that make useful predictions for experimental data. The utility of a computer simulation is largely dependent on the degree to which it accurately models neural, physical, and environmental systems, whose highly coupled nature determine the capabilities of the organism [7, 8].

© Springer Nature Switzerland AG 2020
V. Vouloutsi et al. (Eds.): Living Machines 2020, LNAI 12413, pp. 402–414, 2020.
https://doi.org/10.1007/978-3-030-64313-3_38

Animatlab, a simulator that couples a 3D physics environment with a neural control system, is one of the few simulation platforms that allows for neuromechanical modeling [9]. Animatlab has a neural editor that allows users to drag and drop components (neurons, sensors, etc.) and link them to muscle models in a physics environment. This process has been used to study the neural control of rats [10–12], cockroaches [13], dogs [14], and praying mantises [15, 16].

Simulating legged locomotion involves stimulating muscle models, which actuate articulated meshes of body segments. In Animatlab, muscles are connected to bodies by stationary attachment points and wrapped around body segments with via points. Motoneurons are then stimulated within the synthetic nervous system to generate motion that imitates hindlimb locomotion. Increasing the complexity of the neural system allows for more sophisticated locomotion features with the aid of compartmentalizing neural activity into hierarchical systems and the inclusion of sensory information.

We have developed a 3D rat hindlimb model with thirty-eight muscles in Animatlab, shown in Fig. 1 [17]. The inclusion of many muscles, including those that span more than one joint, allows us to explore the impact that complex muscle arrangements have on motoneuron firing patterns during locomotion. This is accomplished by decomposing joint kinematics into muscle activation patterns, which can be used to improve the predictive capability of the model when compared to experimental data. However, the accurate prediction of experimental results relies on formulations of muscle tension as dictated by active and passive parameters in the muscle model.

Currently, the process for calculating motoneuron activation for locomotion involves an optimization routine to distribute muscle tension using experimental joint torques and 3D moment arms. The resultant muscle profiles are continuous tension waveforms in the range of $[0, F_{max}]$. However, due to the mathematical representation of the muscle model in Animatlab, actual implementation of these activation profiles fails to replicate the predicted results. This is due to regions of the length-activation combination that introduce discontinuities in the tension profile in the simulated muscle. Understanding where these discontinuities arise is important for predicting the motoneuron activation necessary for coordinating locomotion.

This goal of this work is to articulate two different limitations for designing multi-muscle models in Animatlab. These limitations are in place globally in the physics simulator and locally when calculating individual muscle tension. In order to examine

Fig. 1. A neuromechanical model of the rat hindlimb developed in Animatlab with thirty-eight muscles. Colored lines represent muscle lines of action, muscle attachments are shown as small spheres that are stationary within individual bone reference frames. Colors denote general muscle grouping for visual clarity but do not have a functional significance. Muscle attachment points not directly on a bone surface represent soft tissue attachment (Color figure online).

these limitations, a method is first described for defining muscle parameters that allow us to then analyze the length-activation relationships for discontinuities. Understanding the limitations formalized in this work is important when developing a neuromechanical model in Animatlab.

2 Modeling Methods

2.1 The Linear Hill Muscle Model

Muscle models relate muscle length, velocity, stimulation, and tension with varying complexity [18–23]. The Animatlab linear Hill muscle, shown in Fig. 2, models the tendon as a series elastic spring connected to a muscle body comprised of a spring element, viscous damper, and active force generating component [24].

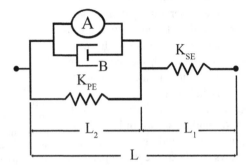

Fig. 2. The linear Hill muscle model implemented in Animatlab. The force generating component, A, is composed of a length-tension and stimulus-tension term. Circular ends represent muscle attachment points connected to bone meshes.

As derived by Shadmehr and Arbib [25], the time derivative of the internal tension for this model is:

$$\frac{dT}{dt} = \frac{K_{SE}}{B}\left(K_{PE}(L - L_{rest}) + B\frac{dL}{dt} - \left(1 + \frac{K_{PE}}{K_{SE}}\right)T + A_l A_m\right), \qquad (2.1.1)$$

where T is the muscle tension, K_{SE} is the series element stiffness, B is the damping coefficient, K_{PE} is the parallel element stiffness, L is the muscle length, and L_{rest} is the resting muscle length. The force generating component is composed of two terms: a parabolic length-tension factor, A_l, and a sigmoidal stimulus-tension term, A_m. The length-tension and stimulus-tension terms are calculated as

$$A_l(L) = 1 - \frac{(L - L_{rest})^2}{L_w^2} \quad \text{and} \quad A_m(V) = \frac{ST_{max}}{1 + exp(S(x_{offset} - V))} + y_{offset},$$

where L_w is the muscle width, ST_{max} is the maximum stimulus tension value, S is the steepness of the sigmoid curve, x_{offset} and y_{offset} are curve centering parameters, and V is the membrane voltage of the motoneuron. Graphical representations of these muscle relationships are shown in Fig. 3.

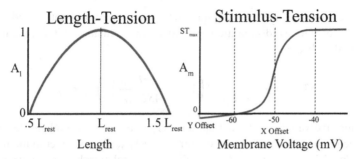

Fig. 3. The length-tension (left) and stimulus-tension (right) curves represent the capability of the muscle to generate forces as a result of motoneuron stimulation.

2.2 Formulation of Passive Muscle Parameters

We formulate passive muscle parameters (K_{SE}, K_{PE}, and ST_{max}) using maximum tension values from the literature [26] and muscle resting lengths from our 3D model. Muscle resting lengths are calculated as the muscle lengths when the leg is set to a neutral resting position (all joints at 90°).

It is our goal to use as much of the muscle force within the range of [0, F_{max}] such that the muscle tension does not saturate at the maximum force or bottom out unexpectedly at zero. Muscle parameters are selected as a set that, when maximally stimulated at steady state, generate submaximal muscle force. At steady state, the tension equation becomes

$$T^*(L, A_m) = \left(\frac{K_{SE}}{K_{SE} + K_{PE}} \right)(K_{PE}(L - L_{rest}) + A_l(L)A_m), \qquad (2.2.1)$$

where * denotes a variable at steady state. At steady state, the quantity on the right-hand side should never exceed the maximum tension. To determine the maximum value of the quantity on the right-hand side, we differentiate 2.2.1 with respect to muscle length, insert the expression above for A_l and simplify:

$$\frac{d}{dL}(K_{PE}(L - L_{rest}) + A_l A_m) = 0,$$

$$\frac{d}{dL}\left(K_{PE}(L - L_{rest}) + \left(1 - \frac{(L - L_{rest})^2}{L_w^2}\right)A_m \right) = 0,$$

$$K_{PE} - \frac{2A_m}{L_w^2}(L - L_{rest}) = 0. \qquad (2.2.2)$$

We choose the muscle width such that $L_w = .5L_{rest}$ [27] and rearrange 2.2.2 to find that the steady state tension is maximized when length and activation are related by

$$L = L_{rest} + \frac{K_{PE}L_{rest}^2}{8A_m} \qquad (2.2.3)$$

Plugging this relationship into Eq. (2.2.1), we can determine the steady state tension as a function of muscle activation,

$$T^*(A_m) = A_m \left(\frac{K_{SE}}{K_{SE} + K_{PE}} \right) \left(1 + \left(\frac{K_{PE}L_{rest}}{4A_m} \right)^2 \right). \qquad (2.2.4)$$

When the muscle is maximally stimulated, its tension should not exceed the maximum muscle force to avoid saturation. At maximum stimulation, ST_{max}, the necessary tension boundary becomes

$$ST_{max}\left(\frac{K_{SE}}{K_{SE} + K_{PE}}\right)\left(1 + \left(\frac{K_{PE}L_{rest}}{4ST_{max}}\right)^2\right) \leq F_{max}. \qquad (2.2.5)$$

We determine values for K_{SE}, K_{PE}, and ST_{max} by using a gradient descent optimization technique to minimize the cost function ST_{max}-F_{max} subject to the inequality constraint Eq. (2.2.5). This allows the stimulus-tension relationship to output any tension in the range $[0, F_{max}]$.

The relationship between steady state tension, length, and activation can be visualized as a surface, shown in Fig. 4, using passive parameters calculated for the biceps femoris posterior (BFP). The general shape of this surface is consistent for any combination of viable parameters (i.e., nonnegative spring elements).

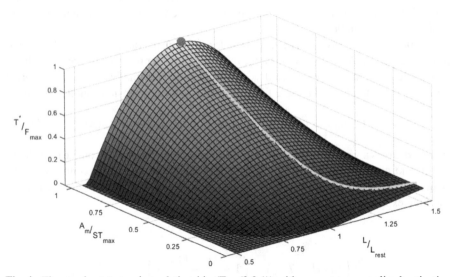

Fig. 4. The steady state tension relationship (Eq. (2.2.1)) with respect to normalized activation and length for the BFP. Any steady state configuration during locomotion will result in a position on the surface. The red surface indicates areas where the tension equation is set to zero to avoid outward compressive forces. The cyan line indicates the maximum tension value with respect to length (Eq. (2.2.4)). Muscle parameters are optimized so as to increase the maximum steady state tension (purple dot) without exceeding the maximum allowable muscle force (Eq. (2.2.5)) (Color figure online).

We seek to interface our model with neural systems designed using the functional subnetwork (FSN) approach developed by Szczecinski et al. [28]. In FSN design, neural activity is compartmentalized into functional groups whose interconnection simplifies neural activation into arithmetic relationships. FSN design in Animatlab utilizes non-spiking neurons with operating ranges of $[-60, -40]$ mV. We therefore define our motoneuron stimulus-tension relationship such that muscle activation operates within this range. When maximally stimulated, the activation term ST_{max} is attenuated to F_{max} due to the selection of K_{SE} and K_{PE}.

This introduces stimulus-tension bounds of

$$\frac{ST_{max}}{1 + exp(S(x_{offset} + .04))} + y_{offset} = ST_{max} \text{ and } \frac{ST_{max}}{1 + exp(S(x_{offset} + .06))} + y_{offset} = 0$$

with an x_{offset} of -50 mV. These equations can be solved simultaneously for S and y_{offset} values for each muscle.

2.3 Physics Timestep Limits for Calculating Tension

Animatlab utilizes the backward Euler method to represent the tension equation in Eq. (2.1.1) in a discrete form. At each timestep, the previous muscle state is used to determine values at the present state. The discrete form of the tension equation is

$$T_i = \left(1 - \frac{dtK_{SE}}{B}\left(1 + \frac{K_{PE}}{K_{SE}}\right)\right)T_{i-1} + \frac{dtK_{SE}}{B}\left(K_{PE}(L_i - L_{rest}) + B\frac{L_i - L_{i-1}}{dt} + A_{m,i}A_{l,i}\right). \quad (2.3.1)$$

Algorithmic discretization of differential equations can cause asymptotic instability depending on the selection of the timestep, dt [29]. To avoid asymptotic instability from developing in the muscle, the coefficient multiplied by the previous-state tension, T_{i-1}, should be bounded such that

$$\left|1 - \frac{dtK_{SE}}{B}\left(1 + \frac{K_{PE}}{K_{SE}}\right)\right| \leq 1. \quad (2.3.2)$$

This implies a trivial lower bound of

$$\frac{dtK_{SE}}{B}\left(1 + \frac{K_{PE}}{K_{SE}}\right) \geq 0, \quad (2.3.3)$$

which is always satisfied since all parameters are positive. Thus, a single upper bound is necessary for constraining the physics timestep,

$$dt \leq \frac{2B}{K_{SE} + K_{PE}}. \quad (2.3.4)$$

The physics timestep boundary condition for a system of muscles is the minimum value of Eq. (2.3.4) of any muscle in the system.

2.4 Steady State Length-Tension Stability Criteria

It is natural for muscle tension to settle to zero in instances where it is not activated and its length is less than or equal to its resting length. However, there are valid length-activation combinations that are incapable of producing force specifically caused by the way Animatlab calculates tension (red surface in Fig. 4). The inability to generate tension at seemingly valid length-activation combinations leads to errors when the force distribution optimization process attempts to utilize muscles that are within a tension deadzone. Avoiding the region in which valid length-activation combinations do not generate tension is important for determining locomotion-driving muscle tension.

Muscle is only capable of generating contractile tension, a quality that is not well reflected in spring-damper muscle models that are agnostic to force directionality. For this reason, Animatlab assigns negative muscle tension to zero in order to avoid generating outward compressive forces (red surface in Fig. 4). As a consequence, Animatlab represents tension as

$$T_i = \begin{cases} 0 \text{ if } T_i < 0 \\ T_i \text{ if } T_i \geq 0 \end{cases} \tag{2.4.1}$$

Assigning muscle tension to zero introduces discontinuities to the system, making it difficult to optimize a system of muscle tensions. Therefore, it is important to understand the interplay between length and activation that causes the muscle to enter a region of discontinuity. The steady state tension is continuous when

$$K_{PE}\left(L^* - L_{rest}\right) + A_l^* A_m^* \geq 0. \tag{2.4.2}$$

Rearranging this equation, we develop the length rule

$$L^* \geq L_{rest} - \frac{A_l^* A_m^*}{K_{PE}}, \tag{2.4.3}$$

which indicates that for a nonzero activation, there is a region on the length-tension curve below the resting length where tension is assigned to zero. Because A_l^* and L^* are coupled through the length-tension relationship with $L_w = .5 \, L_{rest}$, Eq. (2.4.3) can be expressed as

$$\frac{L^*}{L_{rest}} \geq 1 + \frac{1 - \sqrt{1 + 16a^2}}{8a}, \tag{2.4.4}$$

where

$$a = \frac{A_m^*}{L_{rest} K_{PE}}. \tag{2.4.5}$$

Discontinuous tension boundaries create regions of the length-tension and stimulus-tension curves that are not analyzable, represented by the shaded regions in Fig. 5.

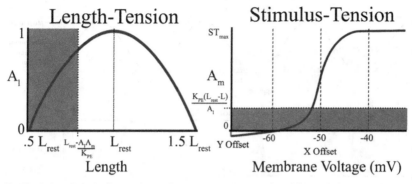

Fig. 5. Shaded regions indicate areas where curve values create a discontinuous tension profile. Depending on the length-activation combination, the discontinuous region has different bounds.

3 Application to a Rat Model

We apply these parameter calculations to a neuromechanical model in Animatlab. As discussed in Sect. 2.3, increasing the physics timestep beyond a critical threshold results in an asymptotically unstable tension calculation. To illustrate this effect, we hold the biceps femoris posterior (BFP) at a constant length and evaluate its internal tension while increasing the physics timestep. A parameter set was developed for the BFP using techniques described above (K_{SE} = 964.89 N/m, K_{PE} = 74.81 N/m, B = 10 Ns/m), which results in a maximum viable physics timestep of dt = 19.2363 ms (Eq. (2.3.4)). As shown in Fig. 6, increasing the physics timestep beyond that value results in a muscle tension with oscillations that grow with time.

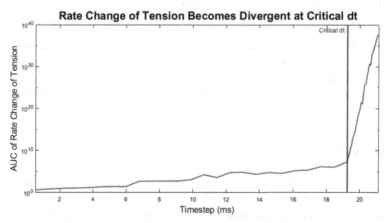

Fig. 6. The effect of increasing the physics timestep on an isometric muscle with no activation. Values are calculated as the area under the curve (AUC) of the rectified time variance of tension. When the physics timestep is below a critical value, oscillations in the rate change of tension do not grow over time. Once the timestep increases beyond the threshold value, the oscillations grow larger as the simulation time increases.

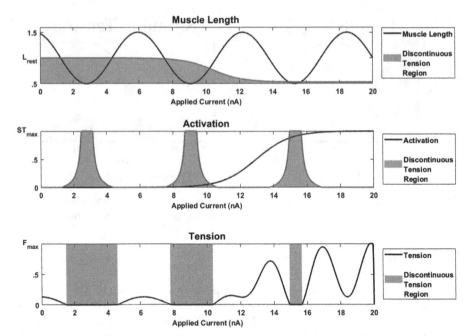

Fig. 7. The effect of muscle length and activation in determining the discontinuous region for tension. Although all length and activation values are within their respective bounds, the shaded areas indicate where the muscle is unable to generate tension. As stimulus is applied to the muscle, more of the sub-resting-length region of the length-tension curve is capable of generating a continuous tension profile. Increasing the stimulus on the muscle allows for greater deviation of the muscle length from its resting length without causing the tension to become discontinuous. For this reason, if one wants to generate a continuous tension profile, it may be necessary to stimulate the muscle if it is operating at lengths shorter than it resting length.

As formalized in Eq. (2.4.4), the discontinuous tension boundary is dependent on muscle length and activation. As shown in Fig. 7, muscle tension is set to zero in the shaded discontinuous regions. Understanding how the discontinuous tension region changes depending on the muscle properties is important for determining when muscles can be activated during locomotion.

4 Discussion

Models must be sufficiently complex to address biological theories while remaining computationally practical [30]. The nonlinear nature of biological systems, from the activity of individual neurons to the generation of tension in muscles, requires researchers to employ analytical methods that can obfuscate results if stability criteria are not considered. Although Animatlab is capable of modeling multiple subsystems of the locomotion control hierarchy, the computational methodology used by the system to develop kinetic relationships is susceptible to errors common in discrete numerical analysis.

Muscles are complex organs whose activity is varied over time and dependent largely on biological and situational context. Reducing a muscle to a spring-damper system disregards certain biological aspects of muscle, such as fatigue [31], the dynamic response to fast and slow contractions [32], and muscle energetics [33]. Additionally, a linear model does not include the asymmetric velocity profile in which the muscle activity differs while lengthening or contracting [19]. Understanding the limitations incurred by reduced models can help guide future implementations of neuromechanical models and contextualize analytical results when compared to experimental data.

When actual muscle is not activated and below its resting length, it, like the model, will not generate any tension. The model, though, treats tension like a switch and sets it to zero discontinuously when a critical combination of stimulation and length is crossed. Unlike real muscle, which generates a continuous tension profile while activation and deactivating. As a result, muscles in Animatlab are susceptible to oscillations in the tension profile when the muscle is resting near the discontinuous tension region.

For instance, while in a resting state and supported by a network of muscles, the weight of the leg itself can lengthen a muscle and pull it in to or out of a discontinuous tension region. In the case where the muscle is pulled out of a discontinuous tension region, the tension will suddenly be "switched on", causing the muscle to contract. When the length shortens, the tension turns off again. This leads to an oscillatory cycle in which the muscle is constantly moving in and out of the discontinuous tension region.

Abiding by the limitations described in this work, it is possible to mitigate many of the problems associated with modeling muscles in Animatlab. However, the non-biological aspects of a spring-damper system can still cause problems when trying to represent muscle. The inclusion of biological components may provide a solution for the limitations described.

Incorporating a series element damper in the model would be a way to represent energy loss in the tendon that may prevent the muscle from oscillating. The current series element is simply represented as an undamped spring, which could lead to oscillations. Minimizing the passive tension by reducing the magnitude of the parallel spring element could shrink the size of the discontinuous tension region. The parallel element stiffness is one of the only "free" muscle parameters that can be adjusted to change the discontinuous tension region but doing so would also change the tension output proposed by the optimization process. Modifying these elements would require changing how the program calculates muscle tension at a fundamental level that is beyond the scope of this work.

5 Conclusion

In this work, we have presented a methodology for formulating parameters for linear Hill muscles in Animatlab. We have shown the mathematical basis for the derivation of specific active and passive parameters, as well as the limitations for simulating muscles in a discrete form. Through this work, it is possible to create neuromechanical simulations that can be used to evaluate experimental data and develop our understanding of the underlying mechanisms that control locomotion.

Future implementations of Animatlab could enhance the existing linear Hill model through the inclusion of additional components in the spring-damper model, possibly through the addition of a series damper. Modifications to the model inherent to the program will necessitate an overhaul of the software itself, as Animatlab does not natively allow for different muscle models. However, the work presented here demonstrates the capability of the existing software to represent muscular activation so long as the simulation constraints are considered.

References

1. Lewinson, R.T., Stefanyshyn, D.J.: A descriptive analysis of the climbing mechanics of a mountain goat (Oreamnos americanus). Zoology **119**, 541–546 (2016). https://doi.org/10.1016/j.zool.2016.06.001
2. Nishikawa, K., Biewener, A.A., Aerts, P., et al.: Neuromechanics: an integrative approach for understanding motor control. Integr. Comp. Biol. **47**, 16–54 (2007). https://doi.org/10.1093/icb/icm024
3. Chiel, H.J., Beer, R.D., Sterling, L.S.: Heterogeneous neural networks for adaptive behavior in dynamic environments. In: Proceedings of the 1st International Conference on Neural Information Processing Systems, pp. 577–585. MIT Press, Cambridge, MA, USA (1988)
4. Aoi, S., Kondo, T., Hayashi, N., et al.: Contributions of phase resetting and interlimb coordination to the adaptive control of hindlimb obstacle avoidance during locomotion in rats: a simulation study. Biol. Cybern. **107**, 201–216 (2013). https://doi.org/10.1007/s00422-013-0546-6
5. Thota, A.K., Watson, S.C., Knapp, E., et al.: Neuromechanical control of locomotion in the rat. J. Neurotrauma **22**, 442–465 (2005). https://doi.org/10.1089/neu.2005.22.442
6. Ekeberg, Ö., Pearson, K.: Computer simulation of stepping in the hind legs of the cat: an examination of mechanisms regulating the stance-to-swing transition. J. Neurophysiol. **94**, 4256–4268 (2005). https://doi.org/10.1152/jn.00065.2005
7. Chiel, H.J., Beer, R.D.: The brain has a body: adaptive behavior emerges from interactions of nervous system, body and environment. Trends Neurosci. **20**, 553–557 (1997). https://doi.org/10.1016/S0166-2236(97)01149-1
8. Chiel, H.J., Ting, L.H., Ekeberg, Ö., Hartmann, M.J.Z.: The brain in its body: motor control and sensing in a biomechanical context. J. Neurosci. **29**, 12807–12814 (2009). https://doi.org/10.1523/JNEUROSCI.3338-09.2009
9. Cofer, D., Cymbalyuk, G., Reid, J., et al.: AnimatLab: a 3D graphics environment for neuromechanical simulations. J. Neurosci. Meth. **187**, 280–288 (2010). https://doi.org/10.1016/j.jneumeth.2010.01.005
10. Deng, K., Szczecinski, N.S., Arnold, D., et al.: Neuromechanical model of rat hindlimb walking with two-layer CPGs. Biomimetics **4**, 21 (2019). https://doi.org/10.3390/biomimetics4010021
11. Hunt, A.J., Szczecinski, N.S., Andrada, E., Fischer, M., Quinn, R.D.: Using animal data and neural dynamics to reverse engineer a neuromechanical rat model. In: Wilson, S.P., Verschure, P.F., Mura, A., Prescott, T.J. (eds.) LIVINGMACHINES 2015. LNCS (LNAI), vol. 9222, pp. 211–222. Springer, Cham (2015). https://doi.org/10.1007/978-3-319-22979-9_21
12. Young, F., Rode, C., Hunt, A., Quinn, R.: Analyzing moment arm profiles in a full-muscle rat hindlimb model. Biomimetics **4**, 10 (2019). https://doi.org/10.3390/biomimetics4010010
13. Szczecinski, N.S., Brown, A.E., Bender, J.A., Quinn, R.D., Ritzmann, R.E.: A neuromechanical simulation of insect walking and transition to turning of the cockroach *Blaberus discoidalis*. Biol. Cybern. **108**(1), 1–21 (2013). https://doi.org/10.1007/s00422-013-0573-3
14. Hunt, A., Szczecinski, N., Quinn, R.: Development and training of a neural controller for hind leg walking in a dog robot. Front. Neurorobot. **11** (2017). https://doi.org/10.3389/fnbot.2017.00018

15. Szczecinski, N.S., Martin, J.P., Ritzmann, R.E., Quinn, R.D.: Neuromechanical mantis model replicates animal postures via biological neural models. In: Duff, A., Lepora, N.F., Mura, A., Prescott, T.J., Verschure, P.F.M.J. (eds.) Living Machines 2014. LNCS (LNAI), vol. 8608, pp. 296–307. Springer, Cham (2014). https://doi.org/10.1007/978-3-319-09435-9_26

16. Szczecinski, N.S., Getsy, A.P., Martin, J.P., et al.: Mantisbot is a robotic model of visually guided motion in the praying mantis. Arthropod. Struct. Dev. **46**, 736–751 (2017). https://doi.org/10.1016/j.asd.2017.03.001

17. Young, F., Hunt, A.J., Quinn, R.D.: A neuromechanical rat model with a complete set of hind limb muscles. In: Vouloutsi, V., et al. (eds.) Living Machines 2018. LNCS (LNAI), vol. 10928, pp. 527–537. Springer, Cham (2018). https://doi.org/10.1007/978-3-319-95972-6_57

18. Thelen, D.G.: Adjustment of muscle mechanics model parameters to simulate dynamic contractions in older adults. J. Biomech. Eng. **125**, 70–77 (2003). https://doi.org/10.1115/1.1531112

19. Brown, I.E., Scott, S.H., Loeb, G.E.: Mechanics of feline soleus: II design and validation of a mathematical model. J. Muscle Res. Cell Motil. **17**, 221–233 (1996). https://doi.org/10.1007/BF00124244

20. Lloyd, D.G., Besier, T.F.: An EMG-driven musculoskeletal model to estimate muscle forces and knee joint moments in vivo. J. Biomech. **36**, 765–776 (2003). https://doi.org/10.1016/S0021-9290(03)00010-1

21. Buchanan, T.S., Lloyd, D.G., Manal, K., Besier, T.F.: Neuromusculoskeletal modeling: estimation of muscle forces and joint moments and movements from measurements of neural command. J. Appl. Biomech. **20**, 367–395 (2004)

22. Rode, C., Siebert, T., Herzog, W., Blickhan, R.: The effects of parallel and series elastic components on the active cat soleus force-length relationship. J. Mech. Med. Biol. **09**, 105–122 (2009). https://doi.org/10.1142/S0219519409002870

23. Hoy, M.G., Zajac, F.E., Gordon, M.E.: A musculoskeletal model of the human lower extremity: the effect of muscle, tendon, and moment arm on the moment-angle relationship of musculotendon actuators at the hip, knee, and ankle. J. Biomech. **23**, 157–169 (1990). https://doi.org/10.1016/0021-9290(90)90349-8

24. Hill, A.V.: The heat of shortening and the dynamic constants of muscle. Proc. R Soc. Lond. Ser. B – Biol. Sci. **126**, 136–195 (1938). https://doi.org/10.1098/rspb.1938.0050

25. Shadmehr, R., Arbib, M.A.: A mathematical analysis of the force-stiffness characteristics of muscles in control of a single joint system. Biol. Cybern. **66**, 463–477 (1992). https://doi.org/10.1007/BF00204111

26. Johnson, W.L., Jindrich, D.L., Zhong, H., et al.: Application of a rat hindlimb model: a prediction of force spaces reachable through stimulation of nerve fascicles. IEEE Trans. Biomed. Eng. **58**, 3328–3338 (2011). https://doi.org/10.1109/TBME.2011.2106784

27. Zajac, F.E.: Muscle and tendon: properties, models, scaling, and application to biomechanics and motor control. Crit. Rev. Biomed. Eng. **17**, 359–411 (1989)

28. Szczecinski, N.S., Hunt, A.J., Quinn, R.D.: A functional subnetwork approach to designing synthetic nervous systems that control legged robot locomotion. Front. Neurorobot. **11** (2017). https://doi.org/10.3389/fnbot.2017.00037

29. Torelli, L.: Stability of numerical methods for delay differential equations. J. Comput. Appl. Math. **25**, 15–26 (1989). https://doi.org/10.1016/0377-0427(89)90071-X

30. Winters, J.M., Stark, L.: Muscle models: what is gained and what is lost by varying model complexity. Biol. Cybern. **55**, 403–420 (1987). https://doi.org/10.1007/BF00318375

31. Tang, C.Y., Stojanovic, B., Tsui, C.P., Kojic, M.: Modeling of muscle fatigue using Hill's model. Biomed. Mater. Eng. **15**, 341–348 (2005)

32. Armstrong, R.B., Phelps, R.O.: Muscle fiber type composition of the rat hindlimb. Am. J. Anat. **171**, 259–272 (1984). https://doi.org/10.1002/aja.1001710303

33. Bhargava, L.J., Pandy, M.G., Anderson, F.C.: A phenomenological model for estimating metabolic energy consumption in muscle contraction. J. Biomech. **37**, 81–88 (2004). https://doi.org/10.1016/S0021-9290(03)00239-2

Spatio-Temporal Memory for Navigation in a Mushroom Body Model

Le Zhu[1]([✉]), Michael Mangan[2], and Barbara Webb[1]

[1] School of Informatics, University of Edinburgh, Edinburgh EH8 9AB, UK
Le.zhu@ed.ac.uk

[2] Sheffield Robotics, Department of Computer Science, University of Sheffield, Sheffield S1 4DP, UK

Abstract. Insects, despite relatively small brains, can perform complex navigation tasks such as memorising a visual route. The exact format of visual memory encoded by neural systems during route learning and following is still unclear. Here we propose that interconnections between Kenyon cells in the Mushroom Body (MB) could encode spatio-temporal memory of visual motion experienced when moving along a route. In our implementation, visual motion is sensed using an event-based camera mounted on a robot, and learned by a biologically constrained spiking neural network model, based on simplified MB architecture and using modified leaky integrate-and-fire neurons. In contrast to previous image-matching models where all memories are stored in parallel, the continuous visual flow is inherently sequential. Our results show that the model can distinguish learned from unlearned route segments, with some tolerance to internal and external noise, including small displacements. The neural response can also explain observed behaviour taken to support sequential memory in ant experiments. However, obtaining comparable robustness to insect navigation might require the addition of biomimetic pre-processing of the input stream, and determination of the appropriate motor strategy to exploit the memory output.

Keywords: Insect navigation · Mushroom body learning ·
Spatio-temporal memory · Sequence learning · Insect visual motion ·
Event-based camera

1 Introduction

In the task of finding food and going back home, visual memory is one of the key cues used by insects. Ants can use their previous visual experience of a route to follow it efficiently, even when other navigation cues such as path integration are unavailable. Moreover, ants can quickly recognise familiar surroundings after being blown off-course by a gust of wind or displaced by an experimenter [24].

Supported by China Scholarships Council (Grant No.201808060165).

V. Vouloutsi et al. (Eds.): Living Machines 2020, LNAI 12413, pp. 415–426, 2020.
https://doi.org/10.1007/978-3-030-64313-3_39

This capability, equivalent to solving the 'kidnapped robot' problem, is a recognised challenge for autonomous navigation systems, especially if only monocular visual information is available. Recognising a location from the current visual input can be difficult due to high variability across viewpoints, weather conditions, time of day, and seasons [13], yet insects provide an existence proof that it is possible using low-resolution vision and relatively limited neural processing.

Improved visual recognition has been achieved on robots by matching sequences of images [14,15] along a route. This reduces the impact of individual mismatches and demonstrates the benefit of incorporating the temporality of visual data in the learning regime. To date, bioinspired navigation models (with the possible exception of [5]) have largely overlooked the potential benefits of temporal cues for visual recognition, instead relying on repeated static view matching (see Fig. 1), with improvements sought through visual processing schema that remove input variability [21,23]. Yet it has been observed that the navigation behaviours of ants are not only affected by the current view, but also recent visual experiences [7]. We have recently found that altering the sequence of views experienced by ants on their homeward journey affects recall ability indicating a role for temporal cues [19]. Moreover, the peripheral processing in insect vision is highly sensitive to motion, i.e. they fundamentally experience a spatio-temporal input rather than static frames. There is an extensive literature on the use of motion cues by insects [20] for tasks from obstacle avoidance [3], to odometry [4], and identification of camouflaged landmarks [12] during navigation.

In this work, we investigate whether sensing and learning of motion flow patterns in a biologically-constrained associative network are sufficient for storage and recall of visual routes.

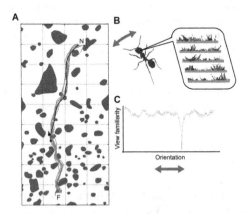

Fig. 1. Route following using an image-matching model, e.g. [2]. (A) The ant is assumed to store a set of view snapshots as it moves from the feeder (F) to the nest (N). (B) To follow the route, the ant scans left and right, comparing the current view to all stored views. (C) The view is most familiar (low value) when facing along on the route. Figure copied from [7], with permission.

2   Methods

2.1   Input: Bio-inspired Event-Based Camera

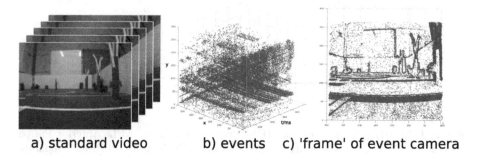

a) standard video   b) events   c) 'frame' of event camera

Fig. 2. Comparing standard video to an event-based camera view of the test arena in Fig. 4. Video (left) has static intensity frames at a fixed rate. 'Events' (centre) occur in continuous time whenever a pixel changes intensity; integrated over a period of forward motion, objects are visible in the movement 'frame' (right).

The input to our system is visual motion delivered in the form of spikes from an event-based camera DAVIS 346 (346×260 pixels). Event-based cameras (also called dynamic vision sensor (DVS)) output a spike when an individual pixel detects brightness change. While conventional cameras capture from the entire sensor at discrete time steps, event-based cameras only transmit pixel data when the intensity of a given pixel shifts up or down by a predetermined amount. This enables a time resolution of up to 1 ns (see Fig. 2). Event-based cameras are inspired by that of vertebrate retina [17], but the principle of function is also appropriate to represent motion perception in insect eyes. The asynchronous pixels resemble transient photoreceptor responses encoding intensity change; and neurons encoding either ON (dark to bright) or OFF (bright to dark) changes are found in the insect lamina (neurons L1, L2 and L3) [18]. However, the spatial acuity of insect eyes is usually between 2–5° of their visual field, which is lower than our camera resolution. Therefore, before feeding the camera output to the neural network, the event flow is re-sampled by 16 pixel $\times$ 10 pixel $\times$ 1 ms spatio-temporal windows, with a threshold for activation that also reduces noise. After re-sampling, the effective spatial acuity is 5 degrees and the temporal resolution is 1 ms. Note that there are additional processing steps in the insect visual motion pathway, but we have not included these steps in our modelling so far.

2.2   Mushroom Body Spiking Neural Network

Mushroom Body. The mushroom body (MB) is a multi-sensory processing and learning centre in the insect brain. We have previously implemented an

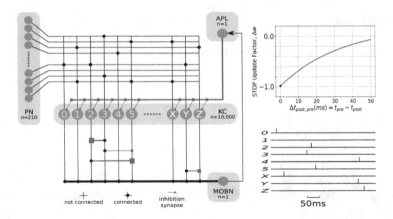

Fig. 3. Left: MB network structure (PN: Projection Neuron, APL: Anterior Paired Lateral, MBON: Mushroom Body Output Neuron, KC: Kenyon Cell (from 2 separate lobes, labelled by numbers and letters respectively). Right top: Modified STDP learning rule for KC-KC inhibition. Right bottom: Example of a KC spiking sequence. Here, 3 fires just before 2, followed by 5, so the weights between them change, shown by the varied width of synapses in the network picture. The nearer in time the KC pair fires together, the stronger their inhibitory connection will be.

image-matching model based on the MB circuit structure [1]. In that model, visual snapshots were used as input to projection neurons (PN) which fan-out to produce a sparse coding of the pattern by Kenyon Cell (KC) firing activity. Reward signals reduced the connection weights between KCs and an MB output neuron (MBON) for selected patterns corresponding to static images along a route. In the current model, the architecture (Fig. 3) is similar to [1], but we implement a different learning mechanism, inspired by the unexpected finding [6] that 60% of the input synapses of KCs are from other KCs, and 45% of the KCs output synapses connect to other KCs. Most of the KC-KC connections are axon-axon connections located in the peduncle and MB lobes. We also include the APL neuron which feeds back from the MBON to the KC and provides global inhibition that functions as a gain control. The other key difference is that the PN input is based on the continuous spiking signal from the event-based camera as it is moved along the route.

Neuron Model. The neuron models for PN, KC, MBON and APL are all modified from a standard Leaky-Integrated-Fire (LIF) neuron. Modifications are made to match each type of neuron to experimental recorded data as shown in Table 2.

The PN is modelled as:

$$\frac{\mathrm{d}v_{PN}}{\mathrm{d}t} = \frac{V_{rPN} - v_{PN}}{\tau_{PN}}, \frac{\mathrm{d}v_{thPN}}{\mathrm{d}t} = \frac{V_{rPN} - 1 - v_{thPN}}{\tau_{thPN}} \tag{1}$$

Table 1. Neuron model parameters. Values are collected from [11,22]

Parameters	PN	KC	MBON	APL
Resting Potential V_r (mV)	−55	−60	−55	−60
Threshold Voltage V_{th} (mV)	−40	−45	15	−45
Reset Potential V_{reset} (mV)	−45	−50	−50	−50
Time Constant τ (ms)	11.5	11.5	20	11.5

Table 2. Firing rate (Hz) for MB neuron in recording [9,16] and our model.

State	Neuron					
	PN		KC		MBON	
	Record	Model	Record	Model	Record	Model
Resting	3.87 ± 2.23	4	0.025	0.03	N\A	0
Before Learning	19.53 ± 10.67	20	2.32 ± 2.68	1.8	100–300	200–400
After Learning	19.53 ± 10.67	20	N\A	1.8	<100	<100

Values for the parameters in this equation can be found in Table 1. The two variables v_{PN} (PN membrane potential) and v_{thPN} (PN threshold voltage) are reset if the membrane potential exceeds threshold v_{thPN}:

$$v_{PN} = V_{resetPN}, \; v_{thPN} = v_{thPN} + 20 \tag{2}$$

The adaptive threshold voltage gives each PN 4 Hz baseline firing rate and limits the maximum activity when the input layer is too active. The KC layer has the largest number of neurons. To speed up the network, the model of KC has a constant threshold. Membrane potential of KC (same model for APL) is updated and reset by:

$$\frac{dv_{KC}}{dt} = \frac{V_{rKC} - v_{KC}}{\tau_{KC}}, \; v_{KC} = V_{resetKC} \tag{3}$$

Because the single MBON receives an excitation signal from all 10,000 KCs, the postsynaptic response is changed from membrane potential increase to a synaptic current increase. The membrane potential of MBON is updated by:

$$\frac{dv_{MBON}}{dt} = \frac{V_{rMBON} - v_{MBON}}{\tau_{MBON}} + i, \; \frac{di}{dt} = \frac{-i}{\tau_i} \tag{4}$$

and reset by:

$$v_{MBON} = V_{resetMBON}, \; i = 0 \tag{5}$$

Learning Rule. The network architecture and synaptic plasticity learning rule are illustrated in Fig. 3. The 210 PNs are one-to-one connected to re-sampled camera pixels. Each KC randomly connects to 5–10 PNs. All the parallel axons of KCs terminate at the dendrite of MBON. KCs are divided into two lobes. In each lobe, KCs are fully connected to each other by axon to axon connection. During learning, active KCs will strengthen inhibitory connections to KCs that fire shortly afterwards. Note this is an axon-axon inhibition, i.e., it inhibits the output of the downstream KC onto the MBON, rather than the KC's activation. The KC-KC synapse weights are all 0 before learning and are altered by STDP. Figure 3 visualises the learned KC-KC synapse based on a firing sequence example. After learning, when the same visual flow occurs, the KC firing sequence will be the same. Excitation from KCs to MBON will be weakened, due to the inhibition generated precisely for this sequence. The output can thus be interpreted as the (un)familiarity between current visual flow and stored memories.

3   Experiments and Results

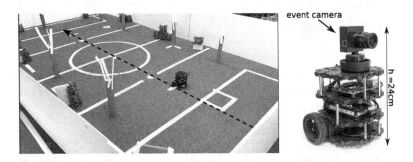

Fig. 4. Test arena and robot hardware. The test arena ($5\,\text{m} \times 3\,\text{m}$) consists of clean background and artificial vegetation randomly placed around robot pathways.

When testing in the indoor environment (shown in Fig. 4), the event-based camera is carried by a Turtlebot Burger3. The robot was commanded to move forwards at $0.2\,\text{m/s}$, commensurate with the speed of desert ants. In the test arena, visual motion was experienced as the robot followed a straight line from one end to the other.

Experiment 1: Learning Route Segments. We trained the network with segments of visual motion from 4 m route (black trajectory in Fig. 4), then tested the trained network for a replay of the whole route. The training segment varies in length (0.4 m to 2 m) and in location (taken from the start or middle of the route). The MBON membrane potential (input from KCs) and spiking rate during each test are plotted in Fig. 5.

Note that KC activity, and hence MBON output, is partly influenced by the density of visual cues, so will vary even in unlearnt segments. However, it is clear that for each learned segment, the MBON spiking rate drops dramatically, indicating this part of the route is recognised as familiar by the network.

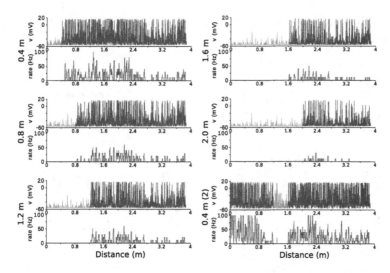

Fig. 5. MBON membrane potential and spiking rate plotted against travelled distance. Pink: learned route segment. Blue: unlearned segment (Color figure online).

After learning the visual flow over some travelled distance, the network memory capacity will be reached. This is because the longer the segment, the more KC-KC inhibition will be strengthened, and hence the MBON output will tend to reduce across all input patterns, trained or untrained. This can be seen in Fig. 5 '2.0 m', where the low rate of MBON spiking overall could make it difficult to distinguish learned (0–2 m) from novel (2–4 m) visual input. We return to this issue of memory capacity in the discussion. Also note that the drop in MBON input is less dramatic when the learned segment was taken from the middle of the route (Fig. 5 '0.4 m (2)'). This reflects the effect of 'internal noise' in the network dynamics: in the test, the network state at the start of the learned segment (1.2 m) depends on the preceding input, and hence differs from the initial (resting) state used when training with that segment. This affects the relative timing of the subsequent KC spikes, despite the same input during the segment, so the KC pattern is not identical. Nevertheless the segment that was learned can be easily distinguished.

Experiment 2: Adding Noise. Experiment 1 showed how the 'internal noise' can affect the familiarity. Here we explicitly test the effect of adding external noise to the input, by replacing some camera events with randomly generated events (i.e. in different pixels) at the original event time. We introduce a novelty index P ($P = \frac{MBON\ Spiking\ Rate_{after\ learning}}{MBON\ Spiking\ Rate_{before\ learning}} \times 100\%$) as a measure of the drop in MBON activity across a segment of the route. The results in Fig. 6 show that a noise level of 5% or more (equivalent to changing 1 input event every 1 ms) results in output for the learned segment that can no longer be distinguished from the unlearned segment, but for noise of 2% or less, the learned segment can be recognised.

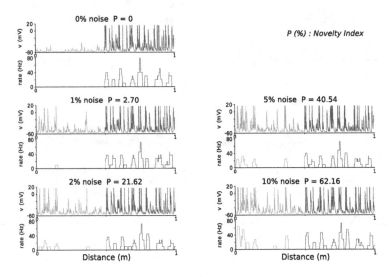

Fig. 6. MBON membrane potential and spiking rate plots in experiment 2 noise test. Visual motion flow on learned routes (pink) is tested with adding 1% to 10% noise.

Experiment 3: Off-route. A successful navigation model needs to not only recognise when it is on a familiar route, but also to be able to correct for deviations from the correct route. In previous image matching models, this is achieved by using gradient of familiarity around the positions where images are stored. Thus, ideally, the output of our network should remain low for small displacements (when the agent is almost but not quite on route) and increase as it is moved away from the route.

We firstly tested in a large arena (5 m × 3 m, Fig. 4) with relatively large displacements (10–50 cm or more parallel, or 40 cm at angles 5–60°, Fig. 7). Before learning, the MBON firing rate varies 200 Hz to 400 Hz. The variation is due to the unevenly distributed vegetation (see Fig. 2 and Fig. 4). After learning, testing the network with displacements parallel to the route, or at increasing angles to the route shows a 'valley' of novelty, dropping to 0 on the learned route.

We then tested smaller displacements in a 1.5 m × 1 m arena (Fig. 8, a). The results in Fig. 8 show a similar trend, with a low novelty index for the learned route (0,0), increasing with 2–12 cm parallel displacement (W) or 2–6 cm backwards displacement (S). The angular change has a stronger effect in increasing novelty even from 10°. Note that in most image-matching models, it is assumed that rotation on the spot will reveal the best matching direction. Here, it would not be practical for the robot to move along each angular segment to find which

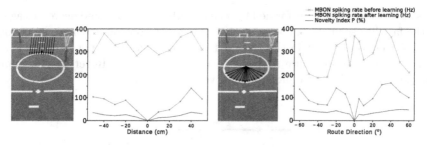

Fig. 7. Off-route tests. Averaged MBON spiking rate before (blue) and after (pink) learning are plotted, together with novelty index P (green) for different displacements parallel or at angle to the learned route segment (Color figure online).

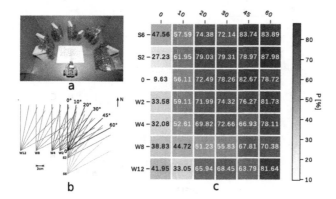

Fig. 8. Off-route test in a smaller arena with denser vegetation. Map in (b) shows the spatial distribution of learned and tested routes in (a) (W: west, S: south). (c): Novelty index P of all testing routes

best matches the visual flow experienced on the route. We return to this issue in the discussion.

Experiment 4: Sequence. Insects arriving a familiar location but in an unexpected order can trigger scanning and learning behaviour [7], suggesting sequence plays a role in visual memory. However, this could imply memory of ordered static images or of continuous motion flow; provided some temporal information about the input pattern is stored. Here we mimicked a recent experiment which tested sequence memory in ants by looking at the number of scans they made (indicative of unfamiliarity or confusion) when they experienced two familiar route segments in the correct order or in a novel order. After training the network 1.5 m of 2 m route (in Fig. 4 arena), the learned motion flow is: 1) chopped into 3 parts and the order rearranged; 2) reversed in direction, i.e. what would be experienced by the robot going backwards from the end to the start of the route, without changing heading direction. The result (Fig. 9) is that MBON activity rises at the novel junctions formed between familiar segments and decreases again as the familiar segment is traversed. If MB activity controls scanning behaviour in ants, this would explain the observed 'sequence' effects in ant behaviour, i.e. that they scan when route segments occur out of order. Reversing the input sequence causes dramatic increase of novelty.

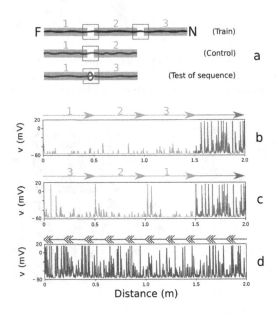

Fig. 9. Sequence test in ants (based on [19]) and results of experiment 4. a: Ants learned a route from F (feeder) to N (nest) which started with a distinctive channel (segment 1). Ants tested with the novel sequence [1, 3] stopped and scanned at the unexpected junction between two familiar segments, whereas control ants [1, 2] ran straight. b: the model produces a low output throught the correct sequence, c: the model spikes more at junctions when the sequence is reordered, d: a completely reversed input (running backward) is not recognised.

4   Discussion

We have presented a plausible neural mechanism by which route memory based on continuous visual motion can be stored. This is based on the insect MB connectome, and postulates a role for the recently observed, but functionally unexplained, KC-KC interconnections. In our spiking neural network model, the KC-KC interconnections can learn a spatio-temporal pattern using the STDP learning rule. Robot tests in two indoor environments have shown that this model can distinguish familiar from novel visual motion patterns, with some robustness to noise and small displacements. Route learning based on motion inherently encodes short sequences, and we show the model output is consistent with observed behaviour of ants when familiar segments of a route occur in a novel sequence. Our model has not yet been tested in more complex environments, but the next step will be to verify its robustness and generalisability in a natural environment.

The current model has a limited memory capacity (see experiment 1), but some simple modifications could increase the capacity: tuning the parameters to make KC firing sparser and thus slow the accumulation of inhibition; or simply increase the number of KCs. The size of MB in our model (only 10,000 KCs) is smaller than for insect navigators (e.g. the honeybee mushroom body has about 368,000 KCs [8]). Also, our model does lifetime learning of all incoming information, with no selection or forgetting. Learning in insect the MB is likely to be more sophisticated and efficient in dealing with redundancies in the sensory stream. This might also enhance robustness, as it seems likely that a repeated run on the same route in realistic conditions may easily exceed the 2% noise tolerance shown in Experiment 2. Introducing additional smoothing and motion processing layers between the event-based camera output and the MB input is also likely to be helpful. In the insect there are multiple neural layers of visual processing. Modelling these and other properties of the visual pathway is one of the obvious next steps for this work.

Another required step is to design a navigation strategy which can utilise the output of this model to generate proper route following patterns. Our model explains how an insect would know it is on route, but not how it would re-find the route. The novelty index results in Experiment 4 suggested that getting closer to the route should provide some drop in novelty, so an oscillation strategy as suggested in [10] could be effective, and will be explored in future work.

References

1. Ardin, P., Peng, F., Mangan, M., Lagogiannis, K., Webb, B.: Using an insect mushroom body circuit to encode route memory in complex natural environments. PLOS Comput. Biol. **12**(2), 1–22 (2016). https://doi.org/10.1371/journal.pcbi.1004683
2. Baddeley, B., Graham, P., Philippides, A., Husbands, P.: Holistic visual encoding of ant-like routes: Navigation without waypoints. Adapt. Behav. **19**(1), 3–15 (2011). https://doi.org/10.1177/1059712310395410
3. Blanchard, M., Rind, F.C., Verschure, P.F.: Collision avoidance using a model of the locust LGMD neuron. Robot. Auton. Syst. **30**(1–2), 17–38 (2000)
4. Cope, A.J., Sabo, C., Gurney, K., Vasilaki, E., Marshall, J.A.: A model for an angular velocity-tuned motion detector accounting for deviations in the corridor-centering response of the bee. PLoS Comput. Biol. **12**(5), e1004887 (2016)
5. Cope, A.J., Vasilaki, E., Minors, D., Sabo, C., Marshall, J.A., Barron, A.B.: Abstract concept learning in a simple neural network inspired by the insect brain. PLoS Comput. Biol. **14**(9), e1006435 (2018)
6. Eichler, K., et al.: The complete connectome of a learning and memory centre in an insect brain. Nature **548**(7666), 175 (2017)
7. Graham, P., Mangan, M.: Insect navigation: do ants live in the now? J. Exp. Biol. **218**(6), 819–823 (2015). https://doi.org/10.1242/jeb.065409. https://jeb.biologists.org/content/218/6/819

8. Groh, C., Rössler, W.: Analysis of synaptic microcircuits in the mushroom bodies of the honeybee. Insects **11**(1), 43 (2020)
9. Ito, I., Ong, R.C., Raman, B., Stopfer, M.: Sparse odor representation and olfactory learning. Nat. Neurosci. **11**(10), 1177 (2008)
10. Kodzhabashev, A., Mangan, M.: Route following without scanning. In: Wilson, S.P., Verschure, P.F.M.J., Mura, A., Prescott, T.J. (eds.) LIVINGMACHINES 2015. LNCS (LNAI), vol. 9222, pp. 199–210. Springer, Cham (2015). https://doi.org/10.1007/978-3-319-22979-9_20
11. Kropf, J., Rössler, W.: In-situ recording of ionic currents in projection neurons and kenyon cells in the olfactory pathway of the honeybee. PloS One **13**(1), e0191425 (2018)
12. Lehrer, M., Srinivasan, M.V., Zhang, S.W., Horridge, G.A.: Motion cues provide the bee's visual world with a third dimension. Nature **332**(6162), 356–357 (1988)
13. Lowry, S., et al.: Visual place recognition: a survey. IEEE Trans. Robot. **32**(1), 1–19 (2015)
14. Milford, M.: Vision-based place recognition: how low can you go? Int. J. Robot. Res. **32**(7), 766–789 (2013)
15. Milford, M.J., Wyeth, G.F.: SeqSLAM: visual route-based navigation for sunny summer days and stormy winter nights. In: 2012 IEEE International Conference on Robotics and Automation, pp. 1643–1649. IEEE (2012)
16. Perez-Orive, J., Mazor, O., Turner, G.C., Cassenaer, S., Wilson, R.I., Laurent, G.: Oscillations and sparsening of odor representations in the mushroom body. Science **297**(5580), 359–365 (2002)
17. Posch, C., Serrano-Gotarredona, T., Linares-Barranco, B., Delbruck, T.: Retinomorphic event-based vision sensors: bioinspired cameras with spiking output. Proc. IEEE **102**(10), 1470–1484 (2014). https://doi.org/10.1109/JPROC.2014.2346153
18. Ramos-Traslosheros, G., Henning, M., Silies, M.: Motion detection: cells, circuits and algorithms. Neuroforum **24**(2), A61–A72 (2018)
19. Schwarz, S., et al.: Route-following ants respond to alterations of the view sequence. https://jeb-biologists-org.ezproxy.is.ed.ac.uk/content/223/14/jeb218701
20. Srinivasan, M.V., Poteser, M., Kral, K.: Motion detection in insect orientation and navigation. Vis. Res. **39**(16), 2749–2766 (1999)
21. Stone, T., Mangan, M., Ardin, P., Webb, B., et al.: Sky segmentation with ultraviolet images can be used for navigation. In: Robotics: Science and Systems (2014)
22. Tabuchi, M., Inoue, S., Kanzaki, R., Nakatani, K.: Whole-cell recording from kenyon cells in silkmoths. Neurosci. Lett. **528**(1), 61–66 (2012)
23. Walker, C., Graham, P., Philippides, A.: Using deep autoencoders to investigate image matching in visual navigation. In: Mangan, M., Cutkosky, M., Mura, A., Verschure, P.F.M.J., Prescott, T., Lepora, N. (eds.) Living Machines 2017. LNCS (LNAI), vol. 10384, pp. 465–474. Springer, Cham (2017). https://doi.org/10.1007/978-3-319-63537-8_39
24. Wystrach, A., Schwarz, S.: Ants use a predictive mechanism to compensate for passive displacements by wind. Curr. Biol. **23**(24), R1083–R1085 (2013)

Author Index

Aguilera, Miguel 288
Amil, Adrián F. 92
Andreakos, Nikolaos 1
Angelini, Franco 12
Arsiwalla, Xerxes D. 116
Athanasiadis, Ioannis 17
Axenopoulos, Apostolos 17

Bertrand, Olivier 354
Bianchi, Matteo 12
Bicchi, Antonio 12
Bierbach, David 270
Blancas, Maria 378
Bolen, Benjamin 257
Boyer, Frederic 165
Braun, Carsten 354
Brossillon, Jonathan 165

Chatila, Raja 68
Chatzikonstantinou, Ioannis 23
Cheng, Tiffany 36
Chesson, Anna 378
Chiel, Hillel J. 55, 402
Clement, Étienne 165
Conrad, Stefan 46
Cutsuridis, Vassilis 1

Dallmann, Chris J. 342
Daras, Petros 17
Del Dottore, Emanuela 80
Deng, Kaiyu 55
Dewar, Alex 245
Diaz, Kelimar 300
Dromnelle, Rémi 68

Endo, Satoshi 128

Fan, Jie 80
Fiorello, Isabella 97
Fisher, Alex 354

Fitzpatrick, Marshaun N. 104
Freire, Ismael T. 116

Gabler, Volker 128
Garabini, Manolo 12
Giakoumis, Dimitrios 23
Girard, Benoît 68
Goldman, Daniel I. 300
Goldsmith, Clarissa 141
Graham, Paul 204, 245, 338
Guerrero, Oscar 378

Hafner, Verena V. 270
Harley, Cynthia 275
Herault, Johann 165
Hunt, Alexander J. 55, 257, 402

Iacob, Stefan 176

Jimenez-Rodriguez, Alejandro 192

Kagioulis, Efstathios 204
Kehl, Catherine E. 275
Khamassi, Mehdi 68
Kimura, Hiroshi 217
Knight, James C. 204
Kodono, Kodai 217
Kostavelis, Ioannis 23
Krause, Jens 270
Kwisthout, Johan 176

LaGrange, Seth 165
Landgraf, Tim 270
Lebastard, Vincent 165
Levy, Simon D. 230

Maier, Korbinian 128
Maisonneuve, Marine C. 300
Mangan, Michael 415
Mazzolai, Barbara 80, 97, 234

Meder, Fabian   234
Menges, Achim   36
Meyer, Stefan   245
Mondini, Alessio   97
Morrow, Connor   257
Musiolek, Lea   270

Naselli, Giovanna Adele   234
Nawrot, Martin Paul   288
Nichols, Sebastian T.   275
Nowotny, Thomas   204, 245, 338

Philippides, Andrew   204, 245, 338
Pourcel, Guillaume   68
Prescott, Tony J.   192, 390
Psaltis, Athanasios   17
Puigbò, Jordi-Ysard   92

Quinn, Roger D.   55, 104, 141, 312, 342,
    402

Renaudo, Erwan   68
Rieser, Jennifer M.   300
Rosado, Oscar Guerrero   153
Rusák, Zoltán   366

Sakagiannis, Panagiotis   288
Santina, Cosimo Della   12
Scharff, Rob B. N.   366
Schiebel, Perrin E.   300
Schmidt, Robert   192
Sedlackova, Anna   312
Speck, Thomas   46, 234
Stankiewicz, Jan   325
Steinbeck, Fabian   338
Szczecinski, Nicholas S.   55, 104, 141, 312,
    342

Taccola, Silvia   234
Tauber, Falk   46
Taylor, Brian K.   275
Thielen, Marc   234
Thill, Serge   176
Thoma, Andreas   354
Thomas, Peter J.   104
Tzovaras, Dimitrios   23

Urikh, Dina   116

van den Berg, Sander C.   366
Vasilaki, Eleni   390
Verschure, Paul F. M. J.   92, 116, 153, 378
Visentin, Francesco   80
Vouloutsi, Vasiliki   378

Wang, Xiang   36
Wang, Yangyang   104
Webb, Barbara   325, 415
Whelan, Matthew T.   390
Wilson, Stuart   192
Wollherr, Dirk   128
Wood, Dylan   36
Wu, Jun   366

Young, Fletcher   402
Yuan, Philip F.   36
Yue, Shigang   1

Zhu, Le   415
Zill, Sasha N.   342

Printed in the United States
By Bookmasters